To Robert H. Gundry

scholar, teacher, mentor, friend

CONTENTS

PREFACE

This is not quite the book I set out to write. My interest in hermeneutics initially arose out of my attempt as a theologian to clarify the role of Scripture in theology. What does it mean to be "biblical"? As a systematic theologian with a number of forthright exegete friends, I have long been aware of how easy it is to use Scripture to prove this or that doctrine, or to justify this or that practice, only to be accused of distorting the text. Of course, one does not have to be a scholar to misread the Bible; it can happen during daily devotions as well as during deconstruction. However, recent trends in hermeneutics may themselves be inadvertently aiding and abetting such misreading by propounding theories of interpretation that, in my opinion, drain the biblical witness of authority. I thus began writing this book with the aim of defending the Bible from its cultured hermeneutic despisers. If theology is largely biblical interpretation, then it is important to work with sound hermeneutic principles.

In the course of writing the book, several things happened. First, I came to appreciate certain aspects of deconstruction in a way that I had not anticipated. Second, I came to see that I was dealing with questions whose reach extends far beyond the realm of biblical interpretation alone. Insofar as postmodernity is a "culture of interpretation," I found myself dealing with issues at the very heart of the debate about the postmodern.[1] I have come to think that the way individuals and communities interpret the Bible is arguably the most important barometer of larger intellectual and cultural trends.[2] Third, and most important, I became increasingly convinced that many of the contentious issues at the heart of current debates about biblical interpretation, about interpretation in general, and about postmodern interpretation in particular, were really *theological* issues. I began to see meaning as a theological phenomenon, involving a kind of transcendence, and the theory of interpretation as a theological task. Instead of a book on biblical interpretation, therefore, I have written a theology of interpretation. To be precise, it is a systematic and trinitarian theology of interpretation that promotes the importance of Christian doctrine for the project of textual understanding. What started out as a work in hermeneutic theology has become a book on *theological hermeneutics*.

N. T. Wright, in his excellent work on interpreting the Gospels, is under no illusion about the scope of the task facing today's student of the Bible, whether academic exegete or preacher. Fully to account for how to read the Gospels as historical, literary, and sacred texts demands much more than looking words up in a dictionary. The serious student of Scripture needs to develop an epistemology (theory of knowledge) and hermeneutic (theory of interpretation): "Any philosophically minded literary critics looking for a worthwhile life's work might like to consider this as a possible project."[3] My own view of the project is even more ambitious than Wright's, involving not only epistemology, but the metaphysics and ethics of meaning as well. Such is the task I here undertake—to respond, from an explicitly Christian theological point of view, to the modern and postmodern challenges to biblical interpretation by marshaling a host of interdisciplinary resources and bringing them all to bear on the problems of textual meaning: Is there a meaning? Can we know it? What should we do about it?

I am aware that contemporary debates concerning theories of interpretation can be as intimidating to the lay reader as discussions of non-Euclidean geometry or quantum mechanics can be to the nonscientist. Nevertheless, meaning and interpretation are too important to be left to the specialists. Indeed, it follows from the Protestant emphasis on the priesthood of all believers that every Christian wrestle for himself or herself with the complexity of biblical interpretation. Reading Scripture is both privilege and responsibility.

The present work challenges what amounts to an emerging consensus that sees meaning as relative to the encounter of text and reader. The interpretation of Scripture, on this view, owes as much to community tradition as to the canonical text itself. The view here defended—that meaning is independent of our attempts to interpret it—is a minority opposition view in the parliament of contemporary literary theory.

Several groups have, at different times and places, read or heard portions of the following arguments. Students at various institutions endured the gestation of many of its arguments. I am grateful to those who participated in the "Biblical Interpretation" seminar at New College, Edinburgh, to my erstwhile doctoral students at Trinity Evangelical Divinity School who took part in my seminar on "Meaning, Truth, and Scripture," and to Tim Ward, one of my current doctoral students, who read most of the manuscript and offered helpful suggestions. Thanks also to those comparative literature students in Edinburgh University's "Literary Theory" course for allowing a theologian to pose awkward questions concerning the ethics of interpretation. A word of thanks is also due the Working Party on the Interpretation of Scripture of the Church of Scotland's Panel on Doctrine for their ecumenical toleration of my attempt to draw a distinction between right and wrong interpretation. I especially appreciated their alerting me to the dangers of abstruseness inherent in my project of reinvigorating author-oriented interpretation through a creative retrieval of Reformed theology and speech-act philosophy.

I wish to express my gratitude to Verlyn Verbrugge of Zondervan Publishing House for attending, both cheerfully and carefully, to the editorial details, as well as to the meaning, of my text. I owe a special thanks to Moisés Silva for soliciting, reading, and commenting on (and now marketing!) my manuscript. I must also thank my daughters, Mary and Emma, for their willingness to tell me what they thought the many books we have read together meant and for enduring, if not the "death" of the author, at least long periods of the author's absence. Special thanks go to my wife Sylvie for her shrewd reminders that there could be meaning in the text only if there *were* a text, and for her belief that this text would indeed one day appear.

I dedicate this book to Bob Gundry, who first suggested the topic to me and whose works illustrate the interpretive practice I attempt here to describe and theoretically defend. He has been all things—scholar, teacher, mentor, friend—to the author, and I offer this work as a partial repayment only of a great debt of gratitude for some thirty years of education and encouragement.

Kevin J. Vanhoozer
New College, Edinburgh
Easter 1997

NOTES

1. The term "interpretation" appears in the present work with two very different senses. The more positive sense (call it *realist*) treats interpretation as a mode of knowledge. The more negative sense (call it *nonrealist*) views interpretation as an exercise in human ingenuity and invention and fails to carry the connotation of knowledge.

2. This is so especially, but not exclusively, in Western societies. Had time and space permitted, I would have liked to have dealt more with the way emerging African and Asian theologies interpret the Bible and to explore how their approaches also reflect broader social and intellectual trends.

3. N. T. Wright, *The New Testament and the People of God* (London: SPCK, 1992), 61.

INTRODUCTION

Theology and
Literary Theory

CHAPTER ONE

Faith Seeking Textual Understanding

And then the interpretations—30,000 different interpretations!

S. Kierkegaard

What might "faith seeking understanding" mean when used to describe the task not of theology but of hermeneutics? Is understanding texts a matter of faith, or reason, or perhaps both? Is faith a necessary condition for understanding the Bible? Søren Kierkegaard tells three parables about hermeneutics in order to provoke his readers to self-examination. Do they have the kind of faith that seeks understanding, the faith that understanding apparently requires?[1]

THREE PARABLES ON READING AND REFLECTION

We begin with Kierkegaard's reading of James 1:22–27. One who hears the Word of God and does it is like a person who looks at oneself in the mirror and remembers what one sees therein. What kind of looking at oneself in the mirror of God's Word, he asks, is required in order to receive a true blessing? He replies that one benefits from looking at the Word only if one moves beyond inspecting the mirror to see oneself. James' parable thus "warns against the error of coming to inspect the mirror instead of to see oneself in the mirror."[2]

"To see oneself in the mirror." Kierkegaard's reading of this biblical image immediately presents us with a problem of and for interpretation. What does Kierkegaard mean by "to see oneself"? Is he suggesting that there is nothing in the text, so that a reader discovers only himself or herself in it, or is he saying that one sees oneself as one really is when one grasps the biblical meaning, say, about sin and salvation? To put it another way, do readers project themselves *onto* the text or discover themselves *in* the text? This "mirror image" raises what I believe to be the most important question for contemporary theories of interpretation, whether of the Bible or of any other book: Is there something in the text that reflects a reality independent of the reader's interpretive activity, or does the text only reflect the reality of the reader?

Kierkegaard's second parable, "the lover's letter," is about a man who receives a letter from his beloved written in a strange language. Desperate to read the letter, he takes a dictionary and begins to translate one word at a time. An acquaintance enters, interrupts his translating, and says: "Aha, you're reading a letter from your beloved."

The lover replies: "No, my friend, I sit here toiling and moiling with a dictionary. . . . If you call that reading, you mock me."[3] Kierkegaard's point is that linguistic and historical scholarship is not yet genuine reading. It is rather like examining and working on the mirror itself—looking *at* the mirror rather than *in* it. Such, he suggests, is the danger of modern biblical criticism.

In the parable of the "king's decree," Kierkegaard asks us to imagine a country in which a royal ordinance goes out. Instead of complying with the command, however, the king's subjects begin to *interpret*. Each new day sees new interpretations of the ordinance; soon the populace can hardly keep track of the various offerings: "Everything is interpretation—but no one reads the royal ordinance in such a way that he acts accordingly."[4]

Now, God's Word is both love letter and royal decree. Do we look at it or in it? Do we comply with or "interpret" it? Do we see ourselves in or project ourselves onto it? These parables should prompt readers to examine themselves to see if they are "in the faith" as they seek understanding. What was true in Kierkegaard's day is, I believe, even truer in ours. We need to examine the theory and practice of contemporary interpretation to see if it is "in the faith," for some readers contrive to deprive the Bible of its authority through interpretation. Kierkegaard laments: "'My house is a house of prayer, but you have changed it into a den of thieves.' And God's Word— what is it according to its purpose, and into what have we changed it?"[5]

The moral of Kierkegaard's parables is that readers have ceased to take the privilege and responsibility of interpretation seriously. The purpose of interpretation is no longer to recover and relate to a message from one who is other than ourselves, but precisely to evade such a confrontation. The business of interpretation is busyness: constantly to produce readings in order to avoid having to respond to the text. What is the purpose of such interpretation? Kierkegaard's answer is cynical yet insightful: "Look more closely, and you will see that it is to defend itself against God's Word."[6] In order to avoid seeing themselves in Scripture as they really are, some readers prefer either to look at the mirror or to project their own, more flattering, images.

PHILOSOPHY AND LITERARY THEORY: FROM PLATO TO POSTMODERNITY

We can sum up the so-called "postmodern" condition that is the context of contemporary discussions concerning the theory and practice of interpretation in a single phrase: "incredulity toward meaning."[7] Odd though it may sound, many interpreters today find it increasingly difficult, if not impossible, to believe in "meaning." Why has meaning become unbelievable? To answer this, we must ask the right preliminary question: What *is* meaning?

In their 1923 work *The Meaning of Meaning*, C. K. Ogden and I. A. Richards berated philosophers for their confusion about the meaning of "meaning."[8] They argued that much about language remains mysterious, most notably the relationships between words and what words refer to and between words and the way we think. They pleaded for an integrated, interdisciplinary approach to these fundamental questions. Twentieth-century philosophy has, by and large, responded to their call.

Indeed, it would be no exaggeration to say that language has become the preeminent problem of twentieth-century philosophy. Only recently, however, have philosophers begun to consider the problem of meaning in relation to literary texts as well as to language.

Plato, however, was there before (as usual): "Philosophy is but a series of footnotes to Plato." Plato turned his attention to the question of language and meaning in one of his lesser known dialogues, the *Cratylus*. The three participants—Hermogenes, Cratylus, and Socrates—each represent different positions that anticipate, often in extraordinary fashion, modern and postmodern theories.

The main issue at stake in the *Cratylus* is whether or not we can speak truly. Do words give us knowledge of the world or not? Hermogenes, a disciple of the Sophists, argues that words have only conventional meanings; like the names of slaves, they may be given or changed at the master's pleasure. Words are thus unreliable guides to the nature of things, for there is no necessary connection between a word and the thing it names. Hermogenes's picture of language as a system of arbitrary conventions is a precursor of sorts to Saussure's linguistics, a theory that has come to dominate a large part of the twentieth-century discussion.

Cratylus, the character after whom the dialogue takes its name, takes an all-or-nothing position. A name, he insists, is either the perfect expression of a thing or else it is a mere inarticulate sound, not a true name at all. Cratylus neatly encapsulates both the modern emphasis on meaning-as-reference and the postmodern emphasis on the indeterminacy of meaning. His thought is poised uneasily between two uncompromising metaphysical positions. On the one hand, he espouses, if only for the sake of argument, the belief that everything has a right name of its own, fixed (made determinate) by nature. This is the view we have come to associate with Plato: that the eternal Ideas are reflected by temporal things, and that words in turn are reflections of things. On the other hand, Cratylus does not really appear to believe what we might call the "imitation theory" of meaning. He follows Heraclitus's notion that "all is flux" and concludes that one ought not to say anything but only point with one's finger, since no true statement can be made about what is constantly changing. In other words, Cratylus ascribes the same transitoriness to *things* (the world) as to *signs* (words). Nothing true can be said, for both language and the world are in flux. Cratylus is a postmodernist before his time.

It is to counter Cratylus's skepticism that Socrates enters the discussion. He develops a mediating position that holds language to be *both* conventional *and* natural. It is the second part of his position that is problematic. What does it mean to speak of things "naturally"? Plato is inclined to say that when we name things, we are also defining their natures. The business of a name is to describe a thing's nature. One might cite 1 Samuel 25:25 as biblical support: "as his name is, so is he; Nabal [Fool] is his name, and folly is with him" (NRSV).

Plato devotes considerable space in his dialogue to exploring this "imitation theory" of meaning. But do words really imitate the world? Socrates appeals to etymologies or word origins. For example, the letter "r" naturally expresses (i.e., imitates) rapidity and motion, since "the tongue was most agitated and least at rest in the pronunciation of this letter."[9] The letter "l" expresses liquidity, because saying it requires the tongue to slip. So, in the English word "roll" we are to think of liquid motion or of rapid slipping (the "o" represents, of course, the circular nature of the rapid motion!). Socrates' serious linguistic point, and it is a brilliant one, is that language is *imitative* sound. Words *resemble* things.

Imitation, of course, runs into difficulty as a general theory of meaning. In what sense does "clown" resemble real clowns? Etymologies may be interesting, but they do not explain everything. In particular, one is hard pressed to see how such a theory could account for literary meaning (or, more particularly, for the differences among the four Gospels). Socrates himself confesses to some doubt about the correctness of his theory, but what are the alternatives? If one rejects the imitation theory, the only alternatives are to appeal to the "Deus ex machina" (e.g., the gods gave the first names) or to the "veil of antiquity" (i.e., we do not know how things got their names). Plato is unhappy with either alternative, for each would force him to acknowledge that he has no reason to believe that he can speak truly, that is, according to a thing's nature.

The present work continues the dialogue begun in the *Cratylus*. My conversation partners will include literary theorists and theologians as well as linguists and philosophers. While I agree with many contemporary thinkers that meaning is more than a matter of naming, I continue to share Plato's concern to defend the possibility of speaking truly. Whereas for Plato the divine origin of language was a hypothesis briefly considered and quickly disposed of, I will not be so hasty in dismissing the relevance of theology to the question of language and its interpretation.

Cratylus's skeptical position on language and interpretation is alive and well. Many postmodern thinkers believe (perhaps inconsistently) that the first truth about language and reality is that they are both in flux. Indeed, Joseph Margolis identifies the "master theme" of philosophy by a single question: "Does reality have an invariant structure or is it a flux?"[10] The issue is whether there is an abiding "truth" about things to which our interpretations might correspond. Margolis answers his question in the negative; neither the world nor human nature is invariant. Rather, everything is a human "construct"—an interpretation. What we take to be determinate reality, according to Margolis, is actually an effect of our linguistic practices. Something as basic as one's country, for instance, is less a physical given than a political construction: the product of consensual practices concerning geographical borders and social orders. Marriage, too, is a product of wedding ceremonies, an arrangement that reflects social conventions, not some eternal order. Even God, viewed by a present-day Cratylus such as Don Cupitt, is an effect of human practices, in this case, the practice of religion.

Interpretation, for Margolis, is likewise an activity that produces . . . what? Not commentaries, but the texts themselves. Interpretation is not merely a matter of putting a subjective gloss on an objective reality. No, his proposal is more radical. Through the activity of reading, interpreters *construct* the text, or rather, its meaning. This is a new role for interpretation, which, until fairly recently, say the mid-nineteenth century, had played a more modest, recuperative role: recovering verbal messages. Margolis denies that his is an anything-goes relativism; there are criteria for interpretation, but they are relative to a set of community practices. Practices, of course, change; they too are in flux—hence the postmodern "incredulity towards meaning."

The Literary Turn in Contemporary Philosophy

"Priest, teacher, artist—the classic degeneration"[11]

Traditionally, hermeneutics—the reflection on the principles that undergird correct textual interpretation—was a matter for exegetes and philologists. More recently, however, hermeneutics has become the concern of philosophers, who wish to know not what such and such a text means, but what it means to understand. "How is understanding possible?" has become the theme of much European philosophy.[12] This is not yet what I mean by the "literary turn" in contemporary philosophy, however. For it is one thing to say that philosophy reflects on principles that undergird literary interpretation, and quite another to suggest that philosophy itself is only a kind of interpretation. We owe the latter insight to Jacques Derrida, the father of "deconstruction" and an important voice in the present work. Deconstruction explores the "textuality" at work in all forms of discourse, thereby blurring what were once hard and fast lines between philosophy and literature.

Philosophy's "literary turn" has encouraged a spate of works in literary theory. The "theorist" of literature reflects on the principles and methods that govern interpretation and evaluation. The crucial task now is not the exegetical one of saying what a given text means, but the theoretical one of describing and explaining just what interpreters are after.[13] It follows that the literary theorist must be conscious of the broader social and cultural context of the interpreter. From the perspective of literary theory, we may no longer limit interpretation to the *practical* task of getting meaning out of texts, but must include the *political* task of situating the interpreter.

Behind the various theories and practices of textual interpretation lurk larger philosophical issues. Indeed, implicit in the question of meaning are questions about the nature of reality, the possibility of knowledge, and the criteria for morality. It may not be at all obvious that one is taking a position on these issues when one picks up a book and begins to read, but I will argue that that is indeed the case. Whether there is something really "there" in the text is a question of the "metaphysics" of meaning. Similarly, reading implies some beliefs about whether it is possible to understand a text, and if so, how. Whether there is something to be known in texts is a question of the "epistemology" of meaning. Lastly, reading raises questions about what obligations, if any, impinge on the reader of Scripture or any other text. What readers do with what is in the text gives rise to questions concerning the "ethics" of meaning. Together, these three issues give rise to a related question, "What is it to be human, an *agent* of meaning?"

Hermeneutics has of late exercised a certain hegemony over other disciplines. We now look at hermeneutics not only as a discipline in its own right but especially as an aspect of all intellectual endeavors. The rise of hermeneutics parallels the fall of epistemology. Instead of making robust claims to absolute knowledge, even natural scientists now view their theories as interpretations.

It was not always so. Hermeneutics was once upon a time the Cinderella of the academy. Philosophers such as Aristotle might pause to write one or two books on the art and science of interpretation, but they did not usually make of hermeneutics a full-time profession. This task fell to biblical scholars and theologians, whose livelihood and vocation depended on their being able to give an account of their exegesis. Cinderella was invited to the ball only in the nineteenth century, when hermeneutics branched out to become the study of human understanding per se. Wilhem Dilthey used the difference between "explaining" and "understanding" something as a means of distinguishing the natural from the human sciences. In the late twentieth century, hermeneutics grew even more ambitious, treating everything from Fords to fashions as "texts." With the waxing of texts came the waning of facts. Hermeneutic philosophers no longer consider knowledge as the result of a disinterested subject observing facts, but rather as an interpretive effort whereby a subject rooted in a particular history and tradition seeks to understand the strange by means of the familiar. Instead of "uninterpreted fact" serving as grist for the mill of "objective reason," both fact and reason alike are what they are because of their place in history and tradition. Hermeneutics is cousin to historical consciousness; the realization that we do not know things directly and immediately suggests that knowledge is the result of interpretation. Reality is a text to be interpreted, mediated by language, history, culture, and tradition.

The stroke of midnight, however, has now sounded. Hermeneutics no longer appears as attractive a philosophical method in the twilight of civilization that is "deconstruction." The notion that some interpretations may be correct—that they may correspond to something in the text not of our own making—has fallen into disrepute among the new breed of literary philosophers. The more radical antagonists of interpretation accuse philosophy itself of being only a work of literature, and philosophical justification only another piece of fiction. Behind the suggestion that philosophy is only a species of rhetoric lies more than a rhetorical point, namely, that neither philosophy nor hermeneutics enjoys a privileged perspective on the way things (e.g., reality, meaning) are. Hermeneutics is both disenchanted and disenfranchised by the suggestion that there are no principles for right and wrong interpretation, only preferences.

Jacques Derrida is the most prominent of the new "literary philosophers." Though he teaches philosophy in the French university system, he is hard to categorize. From one perspective his work appears to be a literary criticism of certain crucial philosophical texts, but from another it seems to represent a philosophical investigation of certain literary texts. The May 1992 decision to award him an honorary doctorate from Cambridge University met with unprecedented controversy, with the philosophers tending to oppose and the literary critics tending to support the move. Why are they saying such terrible things about Derrida and about "deconstruction," the shorthand term that has come to represent his thought?

Deconstruction, as its name implies, is a strategy for taking apart or *undoing*. It is about dismantling certain distinctions and oppositions that have traditionally guaranteed to philosophy its superior place among the humanities. It is, above all, *a strategy for putting philosophy in its place*. It also represents a sustained attempt to discern the limits of philosophy. Derrida claims that philosophers are never able, either by reflection or by self-reflection, to rise above their limited points of view to see the world, or even themselves, as God might. The mind may be a "mirror of nature," but what it reflects is ultimately not nature but its own capacities. Every attempt to "see" oneself thinking objectively is doomed to failure, for we are both part of the scene and outside it at once. Is philosophy only a "hall of mirrors" then? Some of Derrida's followers, and most of his detractors, interpret him in this way. Others suggest that Derrida's purpose is more subtle: he is trying not to crack the mirror but to point out the "tain" or back of the mirror, that is, the unreflected and unthought conditions for the very possibility of philosophical reflection.[14] In short, Derrida polices the limits of philosophy and arrests those foolish enough to transgress them. Philosophers typically distinguish their own talk about the world from other kinds: for instance, philosophy works with logic and seeks literal truth in the light of clear and distinct ideas, while literature plays with metaphors and other cloudy figures of speech under dark rhetorical skies. Derrida will have none of it. He believes that the history of Western philosophy is an elaborate bluff, that philosophers have no more access to truth than those who have not been initiated into its guild, and that the discourse of philosophy owes as much to rhetoric as other forms of speech.

To be sure, these ideas are not new. Nietzsche said something similar one hundred years ago. He was perhaps the first thinker seriously to imagine how philosophy might proceed after the death of God. If there is no absolute God's-eye-point-of-view, do life and history have meaning? And what is truth? Nietzsche held that, in the absence of a Creator, it was up to human beings to impose meaning and order on the world: "Ultimately, man finds in things nothing but what he himself has imported into them."[15] Truth is no longer the deliverance of the priest who handles revelation, nor of the teacher who has mastered reason; truth is rather the creation of the artist. The world is a picnic to which the interpreter brings the meaning. Language is the means humans use creatively to colonize a meaningless world. Words do not refer to the world so much as remake it, masking the absurdity of life with the rouge of rhetoric. What we call "truth" is really an illusion that we have come to believe. Accordingly, for Nietzsche, "he speaks most truthfully who recognizes the illusory nature of his speech." In other words, we are closest to the truth when we acknowledge our words, concepts, and theories as fictions. Whereas the philosopher creates without admitting it, the artist enhances life without forgetting that art is the result of his or her own creativity. Hence, art frees us from the illusion that there is one fixed and correct interpretation of the world.[16] The artist is, for Nietzsche, the best and most honest philosopher: a *creative* interpreter.

What art is to Nietzsche, literature is to Derrida. By reading the works of the philosophers in a literary fashion and exposing the rhetorical and literary strategies on which they rely for their effects, Derrida portrays philosophy as a species of human creativity. Philosophy, says Derrida, has long persuaded people of its authority by pretending to rely on logic and reason, but in fact the appeal to reason is really only a rhetorical ploy. Philosophy maintains its illusion of disciplinary grandeur only by systematically repressing the rhetorical and metaphorical aspects of its own discourse.

Authority and Ideology

The motive behind Derrida's strategy of undoing stems from his alarm over illegitimate appeals to authority and exercises of power. The belief that one has reached the single correct Meaning (or God, or "Truth") provides a wonderful excuse for damning those with whom one disagrees as either "fools" or "heretics." Derrida challenges the pretension of the philosopher and the exegete to have arrived at a fixed or correct view of things. This holds true whether the thing in question is a text, an event, or the world as a whole. Neither Priests, who supposedly speak for God, nor Philosophers, who supposedly speak for Reason, should be trusted; this "logocentric" claim to speak from a privileged perspective (e.g., Reason, the Word of God) is a bluff that must be called, or better, "deconstructed."

More is at stake in this debate than mere disciplinary one-upmanship. The question about authority in the humanities—how to interpret history and literature—relates to questions about humanity itself. Traditionally, one studied the humanities so that one's own humanity might flourish. The arts and letters cultivate properly human virtues. Yet who, asks Derrida, is in a position to know what humanity means or which human qualities should be cultivated? Why watch Shakespeare rather than TV sitcoms, or read Milton rather than Marvel comics? Why poetry rather than pornography? Why, indeed? Does it not have something to do with our ideas about the culture that we believe will best cultivate those "humane" and "humanitarian" virtues we most cherish? To this Derrida would doubtless reply: Who are "we"? Can "we" speak for others? Is it possible that the values that undergird the humanities are the values, ultimately arbitrary, of the socially, sexually, and intellectually prejudiced social power brokers?

Given the current crisis in the humanities and the related blurring of the lines between philosophy and literary criticism, it is both relevant and imperative that we approach the question of philosophy and literary criticism together. In light of these challenges, we must not abandon hermeneutical reflection but seek to do it better. "Is there a meaning in this text" is no idle query, especially if "text" now covers everything from written works to our individual histories to reality itself. Is there a meaning to life, or do we each have to invent one? Decisions about meaning, about how to interpret a text, are inextricable from questions about what it is to be human. The fate of hermeneutics and humanity alike stand or fall together. As the authors of *The Meaning of Meaning* put it, language is "the most important of all the instruments of civilization."[17] If there is nothing in what we say to one another, however, we lose the primary means for cultivating humanity. We are only now beginning to perceive the implications of this loss.

MEANING AND INTERPRETATION: THE MORALITY OF LITERARY KNOWLEDGE

Can we read in such a way as to avoid seeing ourselves—that is, those images that we project—in the mirror of the text? Can we by reading find out God? What exactly is reading? What is the point of this optical exercise of moving one's eyes from left to right down one page after another? How is it that black marks on white paper can inform us (e.g., make us more knowledgeable) and move us (e.g., to laugh, to cry, or to go and sell all our goods and give the proceeds to the poor)? Why is there something rather than nothing in texts? Is there a wrong way to read a book? Queries such as these give rise to hermeneutics. Hermeneutics is relevant not only to the interpretation of the Bible, but to all of life, insofar as everything from a Brahms symphony to a baby's cry is a "text," that is, an expression of human life that calls for interpretation.

Traditionally, interpretation referred to the procedure of getting "meaning" out of texts. However, several literary critics and philosophers have recently called for a moratorium on the term "meaning."[18] There are many things that readers do with texts, and to dignify only one of these by calling it "the meaning" is to choose arbitrarily to make one interpretive approach more important than the others. To define meaning too quickly is to launch a preemptive strike on reading strategies that may not be motivated by the same aims or interests. It is no longer self-evident, however, that all readers must read with the same aim in mind.

What, then, makes an interpretation count as more than mere opinion? Can we avoid reducing statements about meaning ("The meaning of x is y") to statements about personal preferences ("I like reading x as y")? As my title indicates, I have decided to employ the term "meaning" in order to stake the claim that literary knowledge—knowledge not only about the text but of what the text is about—is indeed possible.[19] At the same time, I sympathize with those who call for a moratorium on "meaning." A greater self-restraint with regard to that term would force all of us to clarify what we are really after as interpreters. Readers should be much more explicit as to their interpretive aims and objects, and they should be prepared to give a defense of them as well. If there is indeed a high moral ground of reading—a supreme interpretive good—it is best to stake it out carefully. Only after examining what readers actually do with texts will I suggest what meaning is and what ought to be done with it.

Back to the title. Perceptive readers will perhaps have noted allusions to two other books that, taken together, map out the territory that the present work seeks to traverse. The first allusion, in the subtitle, is to Van Harvey's *The Historian and the Believer: The Morality of Historical Knowledge and Christian Belief*.[20] Harvey's concern—the relation of faith and history in Christian theology—is, at first glance, unrelated to mine. What does historical knowledge have to do with hermeneutics? Harvey's work is relevant for the questions it raises concerning the "stance" of the historian, a stance that reflects a certain "morality of knowledge." He observes an apparent tension between the ethics of critical judgment (viz., knowledge) on the one hand, and the dynamics of belief (viz., faith) on the other. He thinks that belief has a distorting effect on historical inquiry. It is *immoral* for a historian to believe except on the basis of sufficient evidence. Moral historians are, methodologically speaking, from Missouri; they withhold belief until sufficient evidence enables them to see.

The values that undergird Harvey's morality of knowledge stem from the Enlightenment. The moral historian (read: literary critic) is autonomous, whereas the believer is submissive; a moral belief must undergo a process of rational assessment and justification; critically interpreted present experience is the norm for evaluating claims about the past. In the morality of knowledge, doubt is a virtue; credulity, a vice. To appeal to faith is to shatter the possibility of rational assessment. Harvey concludes that doubt is an intellectual virtue, more "moral" than belief. The present work takes up Harvey's challenge but applies it to the realm of hermeneutics: Can literary knowledge be both moral *and* faithful, critical *and* Christian?

The title also alludes to Stanley Fish's *Is There a Text in This Class?*[21] Fish is an influential literary critic whose career mirrors some of the decisive turns in contemporary hermeneutics. His 1967 *Surprised by Sin: The Reader in Paradise Lost* explores the possibility of a "Satanic reading" of Milton's epic poem.[22] Fish discovered that the reader, like Adam, makes the mistake of seeing Satan as the hero and so experiences the Fall in the reading. The meaning of Milton's work, Fish argues, is the reading *experience*. This theme later came to dominate Fish's work.[23]

According to Fish, there is no such thing as a meaning "in" the text "outside" the reader. Meaning is not prior to, but a product of, the reader's activity. Fish illustrates this point with an anecdote about a student who, on the first day of a new semester, enters a course on English literature and asks the professor, "Is there a text in this class?" The professor replies, "Yes, the *Norton Anthology of Literature*," but the student retorts: "No, I mean in this class do we *believe* in texts, or is it all the reader?" For Fish, this misunderstanding shows that there is no such thing as literal meaning.

Do we *believe* in texts? The morality of belief and the stance of the believer are issues not only for Harvey and Fish, but for anyone interested in biblical interpretation. With regard to biblical studies, exegetes now fight on at least two fronts. The paradigm shift from historical to literary studies (i.e., from Harvey to Fish) means that biblical scholars must now master two disciplines or risk not understanding what their colleagues say. It also creates a need to evaluate the morality of *literary* as well as historical knowledge claims. The phrase "literary knowledge" is ambiguous: it can refer both to knowledge *about* a text and to knowledge gained *from* a text. The urgent question is whether either kind of knowledge is even possible, much less moral.

Harvey's enthusiasm for Lord Acton's claim that "the beginning of wisdom in history is doubt"[24] finds its parallel in literary theories that encourage the reader's stance of suspicion and critique. Where modern historians treat the Bible's factual claims with skepticism, today's literary skeptics argue that the text has no stable or decidable meaning, or that what meaning is there is biased and ideologically distorted. The result is that the Bible is either not recognized as making claims or, if it is, that these claims are treated as ideologically suspect. Harvey's problem concerning the morality of knowledge has thus been transposed from history to literature: Can the responsible critic (in this case the reader) also be a believer?

Fish's approach to hermeneutics effectively removes authority from the Bible or, for that matter, from any text. Interpretation ultimately takes its cue not from the text, but from the reader's identity. It is not the canon but the community that governs the reader's interpretive experience. The contemporary literary critic increasingly tends not simply to describe the reader's response, but to *prescribe* it. The text, again, becomes only a mirror or an echo chamber in which we see ourselves and hear our own voices.

Taken together, Harvey and Fish define the project for the present work: to articulate and defend the possibility, in the vale of the shadow of Derrida, that readers can legitimately and responsibly attain literary knowledge of the Bible. The present work sets out to affirm that there *is* a meaning in the text, that it can be known, and that readers should strive to do so. Postmodern appearances to the contrary, we can continue to defend, and to promote, the possibility of understanding. I will, however, construct my case for meaning in dialogue with those who are its prosecutors.

For I concede that reading is never straightforward and that naive understanding is never adequate. The kind of literary knowledge that emerges at the end of this study, therefore, will be one that is chastened, not absolute.

THE THREE AGES OF CRITICISM: THE PLAN OF THE BOOK

The history of literary criticism is one of successive preoccupation with author, text, and reader, respectively. I adopt this threefold pattern of organization, corresponding to what has been called the "three ages of criticism," within both parts of the present work.[25] This threefold division parallels, in a certain fashion, the division in philosophy between metaphysics, epistemology, and ethics. I treat these problematics together, bringing philosophical questions to bear on the three ages of criticism. *This book treats the metaphysics, methodology, and morals of meaning*—twice. Part 1 sets out the major challenges to contemporary hermeneutics. As such, it represents my interpretation as a Christian theologian of the postmodern situation. Part 2 presents, at greater length, my own alternative constructive proposals for interpretation. I argue that literary theory relies not only on philosophical assumptions but on assumptions that are implicitly theological as well. Accordingly, I approach the metaphysics, epistemology, and ethics of meaning from an explicitly Christian perspective, that of trinitarian theology.

Part 1 is necessary for three reasons. First, because the challenges to traditional forms of exegesis and hermeneutics must be clearly understood and squarely faced. Second, to demonstrate my thesis that the crisis in contemporary interpretation theory is actually a theological crisis. Third, to ensure that I practice what I preach. It would be ironic indeed if a book about responsible interpretation mistreated the texts with which it disagreed. Good interpretation is hard work, and I will no doubt struggle at times with my own biases as I present and critique alternative positions. Yet charity must precede critique, even when the texts in question are those that argue for hermeneutic relativism and the instability of meaning.

The Age of the Author: Hermeneutic Realism and Non-realism

The first age of criticism, initiated with respect to biblical interpretation by the Reformers, is characterized by an interest in the author's (human or divine) intention. Friedrich Schleiermacher (1768–1834) gave what many believe to be the classic account of such author-oriented hermeneutics. However, Schleiermacher tends to equate meaning with psychology, a confusion that eventually brought author-centered interpretation into considerable disrepute. For Schleiermacher, a text is understood when we recover the author's consciousness. Language and literature express thought; grammar gives us access to psychology. The goal of interpretation is "to understand the text as well as or better than its author."[26]

Such an author-oriented view of interpretation carries with it philosophical implications and assumptions. The first, and most basic problem, concerns what I call the *metaphysics* of meaning. Metaphysical questions treat the nature of reality. For example, "What is an author?" is a metaphysical question. A surprising number of contemporary literary theorists find the concept of the author problematic, and a few deny the author's existence altogether. The intention of the author is an even more disputed concept: What is an intention? Are intentions in the head? Can an author's intentions be recovered? Why should a text's meaning be defined in terms of an author's intention?

The underlying issue concerns the objectivity of meaning and interpretation. Is meaning "fixed" by the author or by the text, or is it free-floating, varying from reader to reader (or does it arise from some combination of the above)? Those who invoke authorial intentions usually do so in order to provide a base for a stable, determinate, and decidable textual meaning. The "hermeneutic realist" holds that there is something prior to interpretation, something "there" in the text, which can be known and to which the interpreter is accountable.[27] By contrast, the hermeneutic nonrealist (e.g., Derrida, Fish) denies that meaning precedes interpretive activity; the truth of an interpretation depends on the response of the reader. The hermeneutic debate over meaning thus parallels its counterpart in metaphysics; the metaphysical nonrealist denies that there is a mind-independent reality to which our true descriptions must correspond. The nonrealist maintains that the world (or the meaning of a text) is a construct of the mind.

Chapter 2 presents the postmodern case against the author and against hermeneutic realism, focusing particularly on Derrida's poststructuralism and Fish's neo-pragmatism. Chapter 5, its constructive counterpart, makes the case for a realism of meaning by rethinking the role of the author. I employ a number of philosophical resources in this project, including the common-sense realism of Thomas Reid and the speech-act philosophy of J. L. Austin and John Searle, and offer a revised understanding of authorial intention based on the notion of the author as a communicative agent. Meaning, I will argue, is a form of *doing*. I also show how the concept of authorship is ultimately theological: both the "death" and the "resurrection" of the author depend on our ability to conceive of God as a communicative agent. The metaphysics of authorship is related, I submit, to the doctrine of creation and the *imago Dei*. Human authorship, that is, is grounded in God's ability to communicate himself through the acts of Incarnation and revelation.

The Age of the Text: Hermeneutic Rationality and Relativism

The second age of criticism raised the question of knowledge and the *epistemology* of meaning. What is the nature and method of literary knowledge? The so-called New Criticism of the 1940s lost interest in the author and instead focused on the text's formal features (i.e., the text, the whole text, and nothing but the text). In the 1960s critics turned their attention to certain deep structures that were thought to lay behind all forms of human life and thought. "Structuralist" critics study the integrity of the text's linguistic and literary conventions rather than the intentions of the historical author or the text's historical context. Text-oriented methods of interpretation aim at describing the immanent sense of the text. The goal here is to *explain* the text's form and structure (e.g., knowledge *about* the text) rather than to understand its reference (e.g., knowledge of what the text is *about*).

The critical focus shifts in the age of the text to the nature of interpretive rationality. What methods enable us to gain knowledge of the text? Is hermeneutics an art or science? Are those interpretations that survive the test of time objectively the "fittest," or are there also subjective factors at work? Are there criteria we can employ to eliminate false interpretations and to judge between better and worse interpretations, or is meaning relative to the individual or community that interprets it?

Hermeneutic relativism shadows the epistemological discussion like a parasite that lives off its host. Are there rational methods that we can use to arbitrate the conflict of interpretations about texts, or are all interpretations only arbitrary? Is there an alternative to hermeneutic anarchy, where everyone does what is right in his or her own eyes, and hermeneutic totalitarianism, where the individual's beliefs are governed by institutional powers? Can we make judgments about the probable meaning of a text, or is meaning strictly undecidable?

Chapter 3 examines arguments for hermeneutic relativism. For the sake of clarity, I prefer to describe positions that deny the possibility of interpretive knowledge as "hermetic" rather than hermeneutical. Hermes was the messenger of the gods, "hermeneutics" the study of interpreting messages. The hermetic writings of antiquity, on the other hand, derive from a confusion of Hermes with Thoth, the Egyptian god of wisdom whom the Greeks knew as "Hermes Trismegistus" ("thrice-great Hermes"). Thoth, however, far from being a trinitarian messenger god, was rather the fabled author of a number of mystical, philosophical, and alchemistic writings. "Hermetic," therefore, now refers to writings that are characterized by occultism and obscurity— features that are typical of certain contemporary literary theories as well. Deconstruction, insofar as it represents an alternative to hermeneutics, stands within the hermetic tradition.[28]

Chapter 6 responds constructively to Chapter 3 and offers a revised understanding of interpretation and literary knowledge, based on the notions of communicative rationality and of the text as a communicative act. The major philosophical resources that I employ in this project are the critical social theory of Jürgen Habermas and the new Reformed epistemology of Alvin Plantinga and Nicholas Wolterstorff. The major theological resource is Christology, which I relate to a new defense of the literal sense as the norm for interpretation (though I vigorously dispute the identification of *literal* interpretation with its *literalistic* counterpart). I argue that the process of interpretation is governed by certain rational procedures, though these must be modified to take account of the variety of literary genres. Finally, I claim that meaning can be adequately known through a process of "thick description" that views the text as a complex literary act and respects its various levels, including the canonical.

The Age of the Reader: Hermeneutic Responsibility or Freeplay?

Third, we face the problem of the reader and the *ethics* of meaning. In the 1970s and 1980s many critics rejected textual positivism (where the text is the object of scientific study) and instead began to examine the role of the reader. Indeed, some have even spoken of the Reader's Liberation Movement, the Reader's Revolt, and the Revenge of the Reader. This view of meaning as a function of reader response was a reaction to the structuralist idea that the text was an object independent of both author and reader. Reader response criticism stresses the incompleteness of the text until it is constructed (or deconstructed) by the reader. "Conservative" reader response critics note the way the text itself invites the reader to participate in the construal of its meaning; the text leaves blanks or indeterminacies for the reader to fill in, so that reading becomes a kind of dot-to-dot exercise. They also observe that we always read from within a tradition, that is, from within a clearly circumscribed set of social and cultural prejudices. Readers cannot help but read from this perspective or "horizon." On this view, meaning is the product of the interaction between text and reader (e.g., the "two horizons").[29] "Radical" reader response critics, on the other hand, tend to give the reader the initiative in putting questions to the text or simply in using the texts for their own aims and purposes; the text is simply an opportunity for the reader to pursue his or her own agenda. On this view, the text is inactive and the reader is the producer of meaning. What distinguishes the two schools of reader response criticism is that the radicals (usually hermeneutical nonrealists) deny that interpretations are constrained by the text.

How should one read? Though reading, like observation in the natural sciences, may be theory-laden, must we conclude that reading is hopelessly subjective (viz., arbitrary)? How, for instance, can we arbitrate the conflict of interpretations about biblical texts? If there is no "science of the text," how are we to judge between interpretations? Fish speaks for the pragmatists when he suggests that we simply stop worrying about interpreting texts and just *use* them. For Fish, there is no such thing as "the single correct interpretation," only different ways of using texts. Chapter 4 relates the ethics of interpretations to questions concerning human freedom and responsibility and to issues of politics and ideology.

Fish's pragmatism and Derrida's deconstruction agree this far: that there is no such thing as "disinterested," that is, innocent or objective, reading. All reading is ideological and guided by certain interests, for example, in the history of the text, in the way the text achieves its effects, in the attitude towards women exemplified in the text, in the conditions of the text's production, in the author's motive for writing, or in the way it has been received by different reading communities. Meaning becomes the correlate of a certain kind of inquiry, the product of a certain readerly activity. The text, with no aims nor interests of its own, is at the mercy of its reader. With only slight exaggeration, Mark Taylor characterizes interpretation as "a *hostile* act in which interpreter victimizes text."[30]

If readers are indeed active, what are their interpretive obligations? What should be the stance of the model—of the *moral*—reader? One's ethics have epistemological implications: "the relation between the knower and the known . . . tends to become the relation of the living person to the world itself."[31] One's stance towards the text, in other words, is indicative of one's style of being; one's morality dictates one's interpretation. Are there any constraints on the ways readers should "be" towards texts? Are there any limits on interpretive freedom? Fish says that a reading community's interest acts as a check on individual readers, but how do we decide which interpretive interests to adopt, which community to join? Are there any rational, or ethical, criteria to guide the wondering reader? Is there a *morality* of literary knowledge?

In response to the undoing of the reader in Chapter 4, Chapter 7 sets forth a theory of hermeneutic responsibility. To what interpretive ideals should the competent reader of Scripture, or of any other text, be committed in order to be a moral critic and a responsible person? I offer a revised version of reader response criticism based on the notions of communicative ethics and communicative efficacy. I argue that an interest in communication is both constitutive and regulative of the very activity of understanding. Again, I utilize a number of philosophical resources, but, in providing what is finally a sketch of what it is to be an understanding person, I move from philosophy to theology proper. What lies behind one's choice of interpretive principles is ultimately an understanding of oneself and, at least implicitly, an understanding of God. Moreover, the morality of literary knowledge is insufficient apart from the virtues of the interpreter. My thesis is that ethical interpretation is a spiritual exercise and that the spirit of understanding is not a spirit of power, nor of play, but the Holy Spirit. The theological doctrines that contribute to a discussion of the ethics of meaning, then, are pneumatology and sanctification.

"Is there a meaning in this text?" If I have here marshaled an interdisciplinary coalition, as well as the resources of systematic theology, to answer a simple question, it is because only such a cumulative force can respond effectively to the crisis in the humanities—a crisis that is slowly draining Western culture of its very humanity.

AUGUSTINIAN HERMENEUTICS

The present work thus tries to answer a single question: "Is there a meaning in this text?" The reader may be forgiven for thinking that the size of the answer is all out of proportion to the question. Nevertheless, philosophers, literary critics, and biblical exegetes are today finding it increasingly difficult to answer this question with a simple affirmative. For behind this hermeneutical question lurks philosophical and theological issues that are all too often overlooked. Why is meaning a theological question, and why should a theologian bother with it? My response is twofold: because theology has an interpretive dimension and because interpretation has a theological dimension. "Is there a meaning in this text?" is, as we will see, a thoroughly *theological* question.

The Interpretive Dimension of Theology

The first part of my response is the easier to demonstrate. Theology has been called a "text-centered science."[32] Doctrines are the result of a centuries' long process of interpreting Scripture. Biblical authority only becomes functional in one's theological method or in the life of the church as one begins to interpret the Bible. Indeed, the questions of biblical authority and biblical interpretation are practically inseparable.[33] Throughout its history, the church has been concerned with the interpretation of canonical texts, as well as with the classics written by the church fathers and Reformers. This concern is epitomized by *The Library of Christian Classics*, a compendium in twenty-six volumes of the most notable and representative theological authors and their works. In their preface to the series, reprinted in each volume, the general editors write as follows: "The Christian Church possesses in its literature an abundant and incomparable treasure."[34] To say that there is no meaning in texts is therefore to deprive the church of its accumulated wealth.

The Theological Dimension of Interpretation

It is more difficult to see the force of my suggestion that interpretation—not simply of Scripture but of texts in general—has a theological dimension. Indeed, the effect of the *death* of God on literary theory is easier to plot: "The death of God was the disappearance of the Author who had inscribed absolute truth and univocal meaning in world history and human experience."[35] The death of God is linked to the disappearance of the authority of the human author too: Roland Barthes writes that the refusal to assign a fixed meaning either to the world or to texts "liberates an activity we may call countertheological, properly revolutionary, *for to refuse to halt meaning is finally to refuse God.*"[36]

Similarly, Derrida's rejection of philosophy's traditional concern for rationality and truth is a theological move: "Deconstruction is the death of God put into writing."[37] Literary atheism is increasingly the order of the day; the postmodern reader no longer believes in God or in authors. Interestingly, one of the most powerful recent pleas on behalf of meaning comes from a literary critic, George Steiner, who states the fundamental issue in hermeneutics in explicitly theological terms: "[This essay] proposes that any coherent understanding of what language is and how language performs, that any coherent account of the capacity of human speech to communicate meaning and feeling is, in the final analysis, underwritten by the assumption of God's presence."[38] The present climate of hermeneutic agnosticism represents a theological challenge.

There is today more reason than ever for theologians to enter into dialogue with other students of contemporary culture. The issues with which philosophers and literary theorists are dealing are interdisciplinary and fundamental to our common humanity, for the question of meaning concerns not only texts, but human actions and history as well. Indeed, the question of meaning in texts is not far removed from the question of the meaning of life. Because the debates in the humanities concern the meaning *of* humanity, theologians neglect this conversation at their own peril.[39] The search for understanding is, I contend, inherently theological. Theology thus has something significant to contribute to discussions not only about biblical interpretation but about general hermeneutics as well: to debates about the respective rights of texts and readers, and about the values that drive culture and that culture cultivates. The present work is therefore a theological investigation into the roots of the current crisis in literary theory, namely, the deconstruction or "undoing" of author, text, and reader.[40]

"I Believe in Order to Understand"

Can the contemporary reader—the reader searching for a modern or postmodern moral stance—also be a believer? That is, can readers legitimately assume, or hope, that they will find something in the text that is not of their own making? Or do our interpretations tell us as much, if not more, about ourselves than they do about the text?

The present work takes an unabashedly Augustinian approach to these queries: "*credo ut intelligam*" ("I believe in order to understand"). This formula describes the critical stance of the believing reader as well as the proper epistemological stance for human beings in general. We are beings who believe, who seek to deepen and demonstrate our beliefs. To believe that there is meaning in texts is, as we shall see, an act of faith. However, one must not remain on the level of faith. Fideism is inappropriate in an age bedeviled by suspicion. Some of the most influential thinkers of the last century have been dubbed the "masters of suspicion," and they teach a systematic distrust of what appears to be the common sense account of things. The situation in postmodernity, however, is even more dire, involving not merely the so-called "hermeneutic of suspicion" but, more tellingly, *the suspicion of hermeneutics*.

My Augustinian apology for interpretation and for the reality of meaning contrasts sharply with two sets of opponents: the hermeticists, who claim to have discovered some key to the text other than the author's intention, and the cynics, who claim that meaning and understanding are no longer possible to achieve. I defend the belief that *we can come to know something other than ourselves when we peer into the mirror of the text*.

Paul Ricoeur strikes a distinctly Augustinian stance when he describes the hermeneutical circle: "You must understand in order to believe, but you must believe in order to understand."[41] Though Ricoeur acknowledges that criticism has an important role to play in understanding, the initial movement must be one of faith. We can formulate this faith in meaning in terms of the "interpreter's credo":

- I believe in hermeneutic realism
- I believe in hermeneutic rationality
- I believe in hermeneutic responsibility

The present work seeks a deepened understanding of these core beliefs by investigating and responding to the most compelling contemporary objections against them.

If faith is indeed related to literary understanding, it is only fitting that a theologian examine the assumptions and beliefs of philosophers and literary critics. Theology has a long history of involvement with hermeneutics. Augustine himself has much to say about reading, interpretation, and the relation of words to things. His writings provide considerable guidance in the endeavor to formulate the theology that funds a Christian morality of literary knowledge. Augustine believes, first, in the possibility of verbal communication: "When you are speaking with me I believe that you do not utter any merely empty sound, but that in everything that proceeds from your mouth you are giving me a sign by which I may understand something."[42] In the beginning, God created language; it is his good gift, designed to be enjoyed by his creatures. Moreover, it is the preeminent instrument for cultivating personal relationships, between one human and another and between humanity and God. As such, language is a kind of semantic sacrament, a means of communicating meaning through verbal signs.

Second, Augustine believes that the understanding we gain from communication is more important than the words themselves: "The knowledge is superior to the sign simply because it is the end towards which the latter is the means."[43] In what could be taken as a direct rebuke to the hermeneutic nonrealist, Augustine replies to the one who says, "I teach for the sake of talking," with the rejoinder, "Why don't you talk for the sake of teaching?"[44]

Third, in his treatise *On True Religion*, Augustine states that all heresy stems from the failure to distinguish Creator and creature. To be sure, Augustine has in mind theological heresies. The parallel failure to distinguish between text and commentary is, by analogy, perhaps the prime hermeneutical heresy. Readers who treat the text as a mirror onto which they project their own devices and desires fail to distinguish author from reader and so fall prey to interpretive idolatry.

Finally, with regard to the morality of literary understanding, Augustine advocates what is for him the prime hermeneutical virtue, namely, charity. This is a far cry from the typical modern approach that puts a premium on distrust and suspicion, a strategy best exemplified perhaps by an essay by W. K. Clifford entitled "The Ethics of Belief." Clifford argues that it is immoral to believe something unless you first have sufficient evidence or proof: "To sum up: it is wrong always, everywhere, and for anyone, to believe anything upon insufficient evidence."[45] In contrast, Augustine's treatise *On the Usefulness of Belief* states that "nothing would remain stable in human society if we determined to believe nothing that we could not scientifically establish."[46] With regard to reading, it "is most honorable to believe that an author was a good man, whose writings were intended to benefit the human race and posterity."[47] The first hermeneutic reflex, therefore, should be charity towards the author. If we come to a text believing that there is nothing in it, we are likely to go away as empty as we came. Augustine encourages readers to approach texts, particularly the classics and especially the Scriptures, in the expectation that they contain something valuable and true.

The text, then, is a treasure-trove of meaning. What if readers disagree about what riches these verbal vessels may contain? What happens when Christians hold conflicting interpretations of the Bible? Here again, Augustine commends charity. His chief hermeneutic maxim is to "choose the interpretation that most fosters the love of God and neighbor." Augustine's principle of charity offers a salient corrective to the present situation, in which the conflict of interpretations all too often disguises a conflict of interests and of powers. Readers who no longer believe in meaning are not able to find peaceful resolutions to interpretive disputes. The contemporary predicament pits reader against text, and reader against reader.

Lego ut intelligam ("I read in order to understand"). In an age that views interpretation in terms of violence and coercion, Augustine's call to faith and charity is needed more than ever. There is something in the text that is not of the reader's own making. The believing reader must not violate but venerate this "other." For readers come not only to knowledge but also to self-knowledge when they allow the text to have its say. The interpretive virtues that I will commend throughout this work also figure among the cardinal virtues of Christian theology: faith, hope, love, and humility. These are the same virtues that make society possible. Life together is largely interpretation; good hermeneutics makes good neighbors. The Golden Rule, for hermeneutics and ethics alike, is to treat significant others—texts, persons, God—with love and respect.

NOTES

1. Søren Kierkegaard, *For Self-Examination: Recommended for the Times*, tr. Edna and Howard Hong (Minneapolis: Augsburg, 1940).

2. Ibid., 23.

3. Ibid., 26.

4. Ibid., 36.

5. Ibid., 37.

6. Ibid.

7. I here amend Lyotard's famous definition of the postmodern condition as "incredulity towards metanarratives" (François Lyotard, *The Postmodern Condition* [Minneapolis: Univ. of Minnesota Press, 1984]).

8. London: Harcourt Brace Jovanovich, 1989 (repr.).

9. "Cratylus," from *The Dialogues of Plato*, tr. and intro. by B. Jowett (Oxford: Clarendon, 1892, 3d ed. in 5 vol.), 1:372.

10. Joseph Margolis, *Interpretation Radical but Not Unruly: The New Puzzle of the Arts and History* (Berkeley: Univ. of California Press, 1995).

11. John Updike, *The Centaur*, cited in Robert W. Funk, *Jesus As Precursor* (Philadelphia: Fortress, 1975), 33.

12. I am thinking particularly of the work of Martin Heidegger, Hans-Georg Gadamer, and Paul Ricoeur.

13. For an introduction to literary theory see Terry Eagleton, *Literary Theory: An Introduction* (Minneapolis: Univ. of Minnesota Press, 1983) and *The Johns Hopkins Guide to Literary Theory and Criticism*, eds. Michael Groden and Martin Kreiswirth (Baltimore: Johns Hopkins Univ. Press, 1994).

14. So Rodolphe Gasché, *The Tain of the Mirror: Derrida and the Philosophy of Reflection* (Cambridge, Mass.: Harvard Univ. Press, 1986).

15. Friedrich Nietzsche, *The Will to Power*, tr. Walter Kaufmann (New York: Vintage, 1967), 327.

16. For more on this "aesthetic turn" in philosophy, literary criticism, and theology, see my "A Lamp in the Labyrinth: The Hermeneutics of 'Aesthetic' Theology," *Trinity Journal* 8 (1987): 25–56, esp. 34–36.

17. Ogden and Richards, *The Meaning of Meaning*, xviii.

18. See Jeffrey Stout, "What Is the Meaning of a Text?" *New Literary History* 14 (1982): 1–12; Stephen Fowl, "The Ethics of Interpretation or What's Left Over After the Elimination of Meaning," *SBL 1988 Seminar Papers*, 69–81. Ogden and Richards give some twenty possibile definitions of "meaning" (*The Meaning of Meaning*, ch. ix).

19. A recent Pontifical Biblical Commission report begins by stating the modern exegete's claim to objective knowledge: "The historical-critical method is the indispensable method for the scientific study of the meaning of ancient texts" (J. L. Houlden, ed., *The Interpretation of the Bible in the Church* [London: SCM, 1995], 13).

20. New York: Macmillan, 1966.

21. Cambridge, Mass.: Harvard Univ. Press, 1980.

22. New York: Macmillan, 1967.

23. What shapes the reader's experience? Fish toyed for a time with the notion that the text is the cause of the reader's experience, but later came to reject it in favor of the idea that the reader's method of reading creates its object. For these two ways of viewing the meaning of "reader-response," see my "The Reader in NT Study," in Joel Green, ed., *Hearing the New Testament: Strategies for Interpretation* (Grand Rapids: Eerdmans, 1995), 301–28.

24. Cited in Harvey, *Historian and the Believer,* 111.

25. See Eagleton, *Literary Theory*, 74. It would also be appropriate to see the present work as an essay in "metacriticism," insofar as it studies the metaphysical, methodological, and moral assumptions that govern much literary (and biblical) criticism.

26. See Werner G. Jeanrond, *Theological Hermeneutics: Development and Significance* (London: Macmillan, 1991), 44–50.

27. Cf. the definition in Stephen Mailloux, "Rhetorical Hermeneutics," *Critical Inquiry* 11 (1985): 620–41: "Hermeneutic realism argues that meaning-full texts exist independent of interpretation. . . . The facts of the text exist objectively . . . and therefore correct interpretations are those corresponding to the autonomous facts of the text."

28. Wendell V. Harris organizes his entire book against deconstruction around this basic contrast (see his *Literary Meaning: Reclaiming the Study of Literature* [London: Macmillan, 1996]). Derrida's famous phrase, "There is nothing outside the text," shows that deconstruction may be hermetic in another sense as well.

29. See Anthony C. Thiselton, *The Two Horizons: New Testament Hermeneutics and Philosophical Description* (Grand Rapids: Eerdmans, 1980).

30. Mark C. Taylor, "Text As Victim," in Thomas Altizer et. al., *Deconstruction and Theology* (New York: Crossroad, 1982), 65.

31. Parker Palmer, "Community, Conflict, and Ways of Knowing," *Change* (Sept/Oct 1987), 22.

32. See, for example, Werner G. Jeanrond, *Text and Interpretation As Categories of Theological Thinking* (New York: Crossroad, 1988), xv–xix, 74–75.

33. Cardinal Ratzinger similarly links faith seeking understanding to biblical interpretation: "Theology is, and must remain, explication of the faith. If it ceases to expound, but, finding fault with the substance of the faith, changes it, giving itself a new text to comment, why, then it ceases to exist as theology" (cited in Aidan Nichols, *The Theology of Joseph Ratzinger: An Introductory Study* [Edinburgh: T. & T. Clark, 1988], 289).

34. See *Augustine: Earlier Writings*, ed. J. H. S. Burleigh (Philadelphia: Westminster, 1953), 9.

35. Mark C. Taylor, *Deconstructing Theology* (AAR Studies in Religion 28; Chico, Calif.: Scholars, 1982), 90.

36. Barthes, "Death of Author," in *The Rustle of Language*, tr. Richard Howard (New York: Hill and Wang, 1986), 54 (italics mine).

37. Carl A. Raschke, "The Deconstruction of God," in *Deconstruction and Theology*, 3. The current crisis of values in the Western world is ultimately theological. We could say, then, that "deconstruction is the death of God put into culture." For an anlysis of how theology interacts with both culture and hermeneutics, see my "The World Well Staged? Theology, Culture, and Hermeneutics," in D. A. Carson and John Woodbridge, eds., *God and Culture* (Grand Rapids: Eerdmans, 1993), 1–30.

38. George Steiner, *Real Presences* (Chicago: Univ. of Chicago Press, 1989), 3.

39. The present book is an attempt to respond to Patricia Ward's challenge: "If there is a conjunction among moral philosophy, ethics, and literary theory at the beginning of the 1990s, we should respond to that happy situation, enriching it with a theological dimension that transforms our teaching and our writing" ("'An Affair of the Heart': Ethics, Criticism, and the Teaching of Literature," *Christianity and Literature* 39 [1990]: 185).

40. In speaking of "literary theory" in this context, I mean to signal my intent to discuss the principles rather than the particulars of text interpretation. I will spend more time, that is, on the question, "What is meaning?" than on the question of the meaning of "atonement," of Rom 1:18, or of *The Lion, the Witch, and the Wardrobe*.

41. Paul Ricoeur, *The Conflict of Intepretations: Essays in Hermeneutics* (Evanston: Northwestern Univ. Press, 1974), 298. I present Ricoeur as a believing philosopher and offer a critical appreciation of the significance of his hermeneutics for Christian theology in my *Biblical Narrative in the Philosophy of Paul Ricoeur: A Study in Hermeneutics and Theology* (Cambridge: Cambridge Univ. Press, 1990).

42. *Augustine: Earlier Writings*, 71.

43. Ibid., 88.

44. Ibid., 89.

45. W. K. Clifford, *Lectures and Essays* (London: Macmillan, 1886), 346.

46. *Augustine: Earlier Writings*, 313. We will return to this theme of the indispensability of belief for practical purposes in Chapter 4, with our discussion of Thomas Reid and Alvin Plantinga.

47. Ibid., 300.

PART ONE

Undoing Interpretation:
Authority, Allegory, Anarchy

He is a slave to a sign who uses or worships a significant thing
without knowing what it signifies.

St. Augustine[1]

There is not a single signified that escapes, even if recaptured,
the play of signifying references that constitute language. . . .
This [play], strictly speaking, amounts to destroying
the concept of 'sign' and its entire logic.

Jacques Derrida[2]

Things fall apart; the centre cannot hold;
Mere anarchy is loosed upon the world.

W. B. Yeats[3]

The interpretation of texts lies at the center of Western history and culture, whether of the Academy, of the church, or of society in general. The very cradle of Western civilization was textual in nature. For centuries, the Hebrew and Christian Scriptures were the formative influences in Europe and in North America. The Bible remains an indispensable resource for understanding Western life and literature of the past. For members of the church, the Bible is an indispensable source for living wisely in the present as well.

In more recent times, the interpretation of texts has become a minority interest and, in the opinion of some, an impossible task. Today the sophisticated critic is as likely to inquire into the motives of the reader as the meaning of the text. Indeed, the very meaning of "interpretation" has shifted; instead of being a knowledge claim concerning some discovery one has made about the meaning of the text, interpretation has become a way of referring to what the reader *makes* of the text. The new-fashioned interpreter recognizes no reality principle (the way it is), only the pleasure principle (the way I want it to be). What is happening to meaning and interpretation, and what might be the consequences for Western civilization? What is happening in biblical interpretation, and what might be the consequences for the church?

Part 1 analyses the philosophical assumptions that lie behind contemporary attempts to "undo" the meaning of words, sentences, and texts. I offer an interpretation of the current crisis in the humanities by distinguishing two kinds of "postmodern" thinker: the deconstructor or *Undoer* and the pragmatist or *User*. These two philosophies lie behind much literary criticism and literary theory, as well as biblical interpretation. Though their ancestries may differ (Thiselton traces the neo-pragmatist back to C. S. Peirce and the deconstructor back to Saussure), they evince a common distrust of modernity's faith in scientific objectivity, reason, and morality.[4] They thus have common roots in the skepticism of Friedrich Nietzsche and the atheism of Ludwig Feuerbach. Users and Undoers are therefore best thought of as postmodern *unbelievers*.[5]

There have, of course, been earlier unbelievers—"the skeptic you always have with you"—though present-day suspicion is considerably more far-reaching. The contrast between modern and postmodern unbelievers may be illustrated by comparing Francis Bacon's "total reconstruction" of the sciences, arts, and all human knowledge with Derrida's total deconstruction.[6]

Bacon worked when the English Renaissance was at its peak. He was an apologist for science, and he believed that humanity was on the verge of a great epistemological leap forward with the discovery of the inductive method. Truth was to be had through careful observation of the facts of nature. Underlying this "total reconstruction" are two basic assumptions: first, that nearly everything that had hitherto passed for knowledge was mistaken, and second, that the mind is "like a mirror with a true and even surface fit to reflect the genuine way of things," hence an adequate instrument for obtaining knowledge. At first sight, Bacon's second assumption contradicts the first. In fact, Bacon claims that the mind (and here he is referring to the medieval mind) had fallen into bad habits.[7] It is Bacon's analysis of these "bad habits" that makes him a precursor of sorts to Derrida's "total deconstruction" of knowledge claims. The main difference, of course, is that Bacon believes that it is possible to polish the mirror of the mind so that it reflects reality, whereas Derrida rejects both the metaphor and the possibility that it implies.

Bacon thought that earlier scientists fell short of the inductive method out of a misplaced allegiance to four false notions or "idols" that encourage us to draw too-hasty generalizations. The "idols of the tribe" have their foundation in human nature itself and consist in a false trust in the reliability of our observations and sense experience. The "idols of the cave" refer to the prejudices of individuals and to the ways in which our particular situation colors our experience of the world. The "idols of the theater" are the dogmas, the "received systems," that are uncritically handed down through tradition. The "idols of the marketplace" have to do with the ambiguity of language; Bacon considers these "the most troublesome of all." It is all too easy, Bacon claims, to mistake one's own definition of a word for knowledge of the thing to which the word refers. The problem is that people often use words in different ways, so words alone cannot reveal the nature of things.[8] Language that is not disciplined by rigorous observation of the world therefore leads to mistaken thoughts. In this suspicion of language, Bacon is clearly a precursor of Derrida: "The ill and unfit choice of words wonderfully obstructs the understanding. . . . Words plainly force and over-rule the understanding, and throw all into confusion . . . for men believe that their reason governs words, but it is also true that words react on the understanding."[9]

Bacon's optimistic belief that adherence to the inductive method can overthrow these idols should not blind us to the severity of his critique. His analysis of the "idols" brilliantly depicts the ways in which the mind acts like a false mirror that distorts the way things are. He is particularly good at uncovering the *volitional* and *affective* aspects of prejudicial beliefs: "What a man had rather were true he more readily believes."[10] Similarly, what one already believes tends to make one disposed to accept what agrees with it or to reject what conflicts with it. Traditions thus enjoy an unwarranted authority, thanks to this "predetermination." Again, the way forward for Bacon is to repent of one's old nature and embrace the inductive method of natural science. As Roger Lundin points out, this is precisely what Charles Hodge recommends to exegetes and theologians: the Bible "is to the theologian what nature is to the man of science. It is his storehouse of facts."[11]

Derrida, like Bacon, is an iconoclastic thinker, though the idols that he seeks to overthrow concern meaning and interpretation. We might term these the *idols of the sign*: the idol of reliability (the sign corresponds to reality), the idol of determinacy (the sign has a single, fixed sense), and the idol of neutrality (the sign is a descriptive, not prescriptive or political, instrument). *Derrida is an unbeliever in the reliability, decidability, and neutrality of the sign.* He seeks to "undo" their privileged place in Western culture through another reflection on signs that focuses on their *instability, undecidability, and partiality*. Like Bacon, Derrida eschews generalities and prefers to attend to particulars. Yet deconstruction is not induction, for the particulars that Derrida collects have no conclusion. Indeed, Derrida studies the particulars with the express purpose of falsifying general rules, laws, and principles. Deconstruction is better viewed as *unduction*: as the negation, reversal, and contradiction of all methodological attempts to achieve knowledge or truth. "Unduction" is induction without end and without conclusion: the particulars swallow up any attempt to unify them or to domesticate their sheer plurality. Deconstruction offers a new criticism, though one without the common-sense realism and faith in scientific method that kept Bacon from becoming a skeptic.

Finally, Derrida presents his overthrow of the idols, as Bacon before him, in terms of liberation—from tradition, from truth, from authority, and as we shall see, from social oppression. His critics call such freedom "anarchy." Whether deconstruction is a genuine "renaissance" rather than a form of "nihilism" depends on whether it can make good its promise to liberate. To anticipate: Derrida claims that deconstruction liberates by undoing *reality*, or better, by undoing strong claims to have interpreted reality rightly. For "the real"—a true interpretation of the world and of human beings—acts like a straitjacket on human creativity. Derrida is thus an unbeliever in anything fixed that might constrain or coerce us—whether geography, genes, or genres—and so limit our freedom and creativity.

Ultimately, Derrida undoes philosophies and interpretations in order to keep things—the world, texts, human beings—*open*. Deconstruction is a strategy for resisting closure. Undoing is a half-serious, half-playful attempt to take things apart in order to show that there are different ways of putting them together. It would be wrong to mistake Derrida's play for mere foppery or amusing nonsense. As Montaigne noted in his *Essays*, "children at play are not playing about; their games should be seen as their most serious-minded activity." So it is with deconstructors: their games, when played in earnest to the end, undo commentaries, canons, and civilizations.

NOTES

1. St. Augustine, *On Interpretation*, 3.9.

2. Jacques Derrida, *Of Grammatology*, tr. Gayatri Chakravorty Spivak (Baltimore and London: Johns Hopkins Univ. Press, 1976), 7.

3. From W. B. Yeats, "The Second Coming."

4. Anthony C. Thiselton, *New Horizons in Hermeneutics: The Theory and Practice of Transforming Biblical Reading* (Grand Rapids: Zondervan, 1992), 83–84. According to Richard Rorty, "Pragmatists and Derrideans are, indeed, natural allies" (Rorty, "Philosophy Without Principles," in W. J. T. Mitchell, ed., *Against Theory: Literary Studies and the New Pragmatism* [Chicago: Univ. of Chicago Press. 1985], 135).

5. For a recent study of the commonalities of these two philosophical movements, the one Anglo-Saxon in provenance and the other Continental, see Chantal Mouffe, ed., *Deconstruction and Pragmatism* (London: Routledge, 1996). In his "Remarks on Deconstruction and Pragmatism," Derrida himself acknowledges that deconstruction "shares much . . . with certain motifs of pragmatism" (78). Most fundamental, perhaps, is their shared disbelief in metaphysical systems. Nature may abhor a vacuum, but not necessarily chaos. It is humanity that cannot stand to live in a world without structures. Both the Undoers and the Users insist on the non-naturalness of all systems, whether of science, politics, or theology.

6. Bacon called his new program for human knowledge the "great instauration [i.e., restoration]"

7. W. T. Jones compares Bacon's proposals for reform to those of Luther and refers to Bacon's position as "a kind of epistemological Protestantism" (*A History of Western Philosophy*, [New York: Harcourt Brace Jovanovich, 2d ed., 1969] 2.76).

8. Note that this is the same issue with which Plato dealt in the *Cratylus*.

9. Francis Bacon, *Novum Organum*, in *The Works of Francis Bacon*, eds. J. Spedding, R. L. Ellis, and D. D. Heath (London: Longman & Co., 1868), vol. 4, Part 1, secs. 41ff, cited in W. T. Jones, *History of Western Philosophy*, 2.78–79.

10. Ibid.

11. Charles Hodge, *Systematic Theology* (Grand Rapids: Eerdmans, 1979), 1.10. See Roger Lundin, Anthony C. Thiselton, and Clarence Walhout, *The Responsibility of Hermeneutics* (Grand Rapids: Eerdmans, 1985), 20–23.

CHAPTER TWO

Undoing the Author: Authority and Intentionality

The authority of the holy Scripture, for which it ought to be believed and obeyed, dependeth not upon the testimony of any man or church, but wholly upon God (who is truth itself), the author thereof.

Westminster Confession of Faith[1]

Why is there something rather than nothing? This is the age-old question of metaphysics, the study of what there is. "Is there a meaning in this text?" is a metaphysical question inasmuch as it interrogates the reality of meaning: Why is there meaning rather than nonsense? What kind of reality does meaning have? Why is there something rather than nothing *in a text*? The answer to this latter question has typically involved the notion of the author. Textual meaning, so the standard view goes, is the creation of an author. Specifically, meaning is located in the author's intention to convey a particular message through signs. According to Derrida, however, the notion of a mental intention is a metaphysical chimera that supports the further illusion that signs correspond to reality. The notion that signs represent the world in the mind or otherwise facilitate commerce between thought and reality is strongly contested by Derrida and corresponds to what I have called "the idol of reliability." *What postmodernity most puts into question is the notion that signs are reliable indicators of the way things really are.*

This chapter reviews the hitherto central role played by the author as ground of textual meaning and the reasons for the author's demise. Is there a voice in the text and, if so, is it the author's? Is the author the source of textual meaning? Can the author "control" the meaning of a text? And just what do these questions have to do with the philosopher's attempt to formulate theories about the nature of ultimate reality, with metaphysics, or for that matter, with theology? I shall argue that there is more than a coincidental relation between the so-called "death of God" in the nineteenth century and the death of the author in the twentieth.

AUTHORSHIP AND AUTHORITY: THE BIRTH OF THE "AUTHOR"

What is an author? Have texts always had authors, or is the author a relative novelty in the history of ideas? Must a text have an author? Is there anything particularly authoritative about authors' statements concerning the meaning of their own texts, and if there is, whence comes the author's authority? It will be helpful to review some salient facts about the life of the author before turning to examine the circumstances surrounding the author's untimely demise.

The connection between authors and authority is clearly seen in debates about the nature and interpretation of the Bible.[2] Most religious people are prepared to acknowledge God as the ultimate authority. There is no such consensus, however, when it comes to the locus of divine authority: Where is the voice of God to be heard? Who is in a position to speak for God? Jews and Christians traditionally acknowledge the right of the prophets and apostles to speak for God. They confess the Bible to be the supreme norm for faith and life because it claims to be, or to contain, the Word of God. Jesus himself could invoke no higher authority than to preface his remarks with the formula "it is written." Of course, one must go on to say what the word as written means. Authority without meaning is a merely formal and empty principle. Disputes about authority quickly turn into disputes about interpretation and about who determines which interpretation is correct. What exactly is the role of the author in such disputes?

Is There an Author Behind the Text?

In the beginning was the Word; yes, but what was the status of the Word before it was uttered? Do words really precede their speakers, or are words begotten from the mind of an author? In the case of the Logos in John's Prologue, we know that this Word was with God, *was* God. This Word was light and life, full of grace and truth. In this one case, at least, Word and Author fully coincide. Jesus is the sign of God, the incarnate token of God's presence, a fully reliable ("exact") representation of his being (Heb. 1:3).

Are all words as reliable as God's Word? Do human beings stand behind, or accompany, their speech the way God does his? Is there an *author* in this text? This is a question about the nature of authorship, not of the author's existence.[3] Do we believe in authors? On the one hand, the existence of authors is unproblematic. Indeed, it is often difficult to escape the presence of the author. The author is virtually omnipresent in contemporary society: signing lucrative publishing contracts, producing the books that fill our leisure hours, promoting their work on talk shows, autographing first editions. But what is the relation between authors and their works, apart from these economic, legal, and marketing connections? What, if any, connection is there between an author and the *meaning* of the text?

One way to conceive the author-text relation is to think in terms of cause and effect.[4] The author is the historical cause of a textual effect; his or her intention is the cause of the text being the way it is. No other explanation adequately accounts for the intelligibility of texts. The author, an intelligent cause, is the necessary and sufficient explanation of the text, an intelligible effect. The text thus serves as a kind of surrogate presence, a reliable expression and extension, of the author. As we shall see in due course, however, this modest picture of the historical author raises deeper, more metaphysical, questions. I turn first to examine the historical origins of the very idea of the author.

"Maker of Story and Verse": The Author As Origin of Meaning

Christians confess, in the words of the Apostles' Creed, their belief in God "the Father almighty, maker of heaven and earth." Is the author a God-like creator, an almighty maker of meaning? Recent studies of the rise of modernity suggest that the famous "turn to the subject," and the individualism that accompanied it, were actually theological, or counter-theological moves, in which powers and prerogatives formerly reserved to God were reassigned to human beings. As God stands behind the created order, its origin and source of stability, so the author stands behind the text. On this account, authorship is a distinctly modern development.

According to the so-called "secularization thesis," modernity is basically a transformed version of medieval Christianity.[5] The attributes of the medieval concept of God—a sovereign subject whose will is all-determining—gradually came to be transferred to the modern concept of the human self: "In the modern period the finite human thinker takes over some of God's functions as subject."[6] The modern self comes to resemble an absolute willing and thinking subject. This "turn to the subject" fueled an intellectual revolution that came to be known as the "Enlightenment." Modern philosophers such as Descartes and Kant were confident in the mind's ability to know the world and to make rational decisions. Knowing and willing subjects were free to think for themselves rather than to rely on tradition and authority.[7] The individual, as a free agent and free thinker, is autonomous—a law unto self. The modern subject, in short, has become an *author*: a creator of texts and a maker of meaning.

The modern self is, furthermore, the author of its own existence. According to Nietzsche, the individual self is the author of all value, meaning, and truth. Subjectivity is the "home" of meaning. It is in the individual's consciousness, then, that words and the world come together. The mind mirrors reality, and language mirrors thought. Thanks to the light of reason, the knowing subject, like Adam before the Fall, sees the world as it is and names it truly. Consequently, though there obviously were authors before the modern era, only modernity viewed the author as a sovereign subject of meaning. In the words of Roland Barthes: "The *author* is a modern character, no doubt produced by our society as it emerged from the Middle Ages, inflected by English empiricism, French rationalism, and the personal faith of the Reformation, thereby discovering the prestige of the individual."[8]

This parallel between God and the modern author also suggests a reason for recognizing the author's authority. The author is one who originates. The etymology of the term "authority" is "right, based on origin." Because the author originates meaning, "it is the author who has authority, author's rights."[9] That the author has proprietary rights over meaning is amusingly expressed by Humpty Dumpty in Lewis Carroll's fictional reflection on language and logic: "When *I* use a word . . . it means just what I choose it to mean neither more nor less."[10] Humpty Dumpty is a stand-in for the modern subject, for whom the mind is the dispatcher of meaning. There is no question as to who is the Master and what is the Slave. The subject alone is active; language is but the inert medium that the mind uses to express itself.

Traditional interpreters read for the author's voice. The text is a shell that contains a spark of the author's soul. The meaning is the message, which the reader extracts as from out of a bottle. Like Aladdin's lamp, a text might contain a genie, or a genius. To read is to fraternize with the great minds of the past. The goal of interpretation is to recover the original meaning of the text. Many methods have been proposed for recovering the original meaning of the biblical text: the grammatico-historical method, form criticism, and redaction criticism, to name but a few. Despite their differences, which stem from different views about how the text came to be and about its history, these approaches agree that recovery of original meaning alone makes for authentic interpretation. For if the author is the point of origin, then "original meaning" is identical with "author's meaning." The original meaning alone is the *authentic* meaning, the author's actual, authoritative meaning. Author, authority, authentic—all notions that, when bound together, reinforce the idea (or idol) of the sign's reliability.

There is a similar tendency towards origins among theorists and performers of early music. Several new classical groups stake their claim to fame on their use of "original instruments" or on the "authenticity" of their sound. The original intention of one composer after another is being recovered as conductors seek to replicate the conditions of the composer's time. Perhaps the outstanding example of the quest for authenticity is Gilbert Kaplan's recordings of Gustav Mahler.

Kaplan has pursued authenticity with a passion. A millionaire and self-taught conductor, Kaplan hired an orchestra in order to perform his own interpretation of Mahler's "Resurrection" Symphony. The concert was such a success that Kaplan was subsequently invited to conduct the symphony all over the world. He bought Mahler's autograph manuscript for $300,000 and, after careful study, reinstated a wrong-sounding F note that other conductors had emended to E-flat for the sake of greater harmony. Kaplan is explicit about his aims: "My goal was to come as close as possible to what Mahler had in mind."[11] Kaplan came to believe that Mahler's famous Adagietto from his Fifth Symphony (used as a theme for the film *Death in Venice*) was being misinterpreted. Instead of a dirge, Kaplan saw the piece as an expression of love. Where other conductors took twelve or thirteen minutes, Kaplan took just eight. He faulted other conductors for not making the requisite effort to achieve an authentic interpretation: "All I'm saying is that this piece has to be played in a way that is consistent with the composer's intention. It's not enough just to read the score."[12]

Many interpreters, lay readers and professional exegetes alike, pursue the original meaning of Scripture with a similar degree of passion and diligence. After all, the authentic interpretation of Mahler, while important, is not as religiously significant as that of Malachi, Matthew, or Mark. The performance of these latter texts is constitutive of one's identity not only as a critic but also as a Christian. Authentic Christianity thus depends on one's ability to recover the author's intention—say, the minds of Malachi, Matthew, or Mark—and perhaps through them, the mind of God.

The Father-Author and the Stable Home of Meaning

The author, as the one who originates and guarantees authenticity, also commands and controls meaning. Authorship implies ownership. The rise of authorship and the rise of capitalism in the modern world is no coincidence, for both are based on the concept of private property.[13]

The parallel between God and the author is again instructive. "The earth is the LORD's, and everything in it" (Ps. 24:1). God is the Author of being, of the book of nature. The meaning of the world has been inscribed by the hand of the Creator. It is God who originates the world, who upholds it, and who preserves the distinctions that give it meaning. God is the Author of authors, the Authority behind all authorities. Moreover, God's will is not an indefinite force but something definite. The author's will, similarly, though to a lesser extent, imposes itself on language and literature. Precisely because they have authors, texts don't mean just anything. The author's will acts as a control on interpretation. Thanks to an author's willing *this* rather than *that*, we can say that there is a definite meaning in texts prior to reading and interpretation. As God's will structures the universe, so the author's will structures the universe of discourse. The author is thus the ground of the "being" of meaning. E. D. Hirsch Jr., an outspoken advocate of the authority of the author, argues that without the author as an anchor of meaning, there would be no adequate principle for judging the validity of an interpretation. Kaplan could not claim to give authoritative and authentic performances of Mahler's symphonies if there were no norm to which these interpretations correspond. For Hirsch, the author's intention is the only practical norm, the sole criterion for genuine consensus, the sole guarantor of the objectivity of meaning. Strictly speaking, a sequence of words means nothing in particular until *somebody* means something by them. It is the author who determines verbal meaning.

Hirsch believes that interpretation only makes sense if one assumes that textual meaning is determinate, that is, if one holds that meaning is definite and unchanging. Determinacy implies "that a text's meaning is what it is and not a hundred other things ... it means what it means and nothing else."[14] Hirsch rests his case on the distinction between what a text *does* mean and what a text *might* mean. "The interpreter's job is to reconstruct a determinate actual meaning, not a mere system of possibilities."[15] Words alone don't mean; people do: "a word sequence means nothing in particular until somebody ... means something by it. There is no magic land of meanings outside human consciousness."[16] It is the author's exercise of his or her sovereign subjectivity that remains decisive for meaning. The stability of a text's meaning is therefore grounded in the will of its father-author.

The Author in Premodern and Modern Biblical Exegesis

By and large, biblical commentators since the Reformation sought the author's willed meaning too. Calvin's goal in interpretation, for instance, is clear: "It is the first business of an interpreter to let his author say what he does say, instead of attributing to him what we think he ought to say."[17] The more the interpreter wanders from the author's mind, the more he or she deviates from the author's purpose. Joseph Haroutunian says of Calvin's classroom practice that "the students were to know what the author of a given text meant by what he said, and any 'spiritual' meaning other than one derived from the author's intention was at once misleading and unedifying."[18] Calvin's concern for the literal sense was partly a product of his training as a Renaissance humanist. Fifteenth century humanists shared a passion for recovering the language and literature of Greece and Rome. The humanists worked to arrive at the original and genuine meaning of classical literature, which meant recovering the mind of the author. "The natural interpretation of a passage for them was one that did justice to the *intention* of the author."[19]

While modern historical critics may not view the authors of the Bible as inspired, the original meaning remains the object of interpretation for them as well. Benjamin Jowett, for instance, felt that the Bible should be read like any other book—for the message of its author. For James Barr, the virtue of historical critical exegesis is precisely that it acts as a check on the subsequent history of a text's interpretation by going back to the original sense. Both Barr and Jowett resist interpretations driven by dogmatic theology; it is important that the meanings of words as used in later theological debates are not being read back into the Bible as if they were the original meanings. The original sense is used as a check on such (mis)interpretations. In historical critical exegesis, then, the original sense is authoritative, not in the sense of being necessarily true, but insofar as it remains the norm for establishing the meaning of a passage (which may be true or false). We may conclude, therefore, that the concept of the author as the "home of meaning" lies at the center of premodern and modern interpretation alike.

UNDOING THE AUTHOR'S AUTHORITY

The author is the foundational principle in what we might call the traditional metaphysics of meaning. According to this standard picture, the author is the *sovereign subject of the sign*, the one who rules over meaning, assigning names to things, using words to express thoughts and represent the world. It is this picture of authorship, and of language, that Derrida, more than any other postmodern figure, sets out to dismantle by exposing the often-hidden philosophical (and theological) ideas that literary critics blithely presuppose. Behind the innocuous figure of the author as determiner of textual meaning, according to Derrida, lies the whole edifice of Western philosophy, together with its metaphysical scaffolding. In challenging the traditional picture of what an author is and does, Derrida attempts nothing less than an undoing of the central ideas of philosophy and theology alike. This is not surprising, for the crisis in contemporary philosophy and literary theory is fundamentally a theological crisis. Derrida's deconstruction of the author is a more or less direct consequence of Nietzsche's announcement of the death of God.

Hermeneutical Non-Realism: Undoers, Users, and Unbelievers

"Realism" is the metaphysical position which asserts that certain things are mind-independent.[20] *Hermeneutical realism* is the position that believes meaning to be prior to and independent of the process of interpretation.[21] For the "naive" realist, there is a perfect match between language and world; we speak truly when our language "corresponds" to what is there. Distinctions in language thus correspond to distinctions in reality. The naive realist follows Francis Bacon in giving pride of place to induction: it is enough to observe the phenomena and to describe them correctly. There is no gap between appearance and reality. The naive hermeneutical realist approaches texts with the same optimistic faith in the powers of observation. The good commentator, like the natural scientist, gives objective descriptions of textual phenomena. The true interpretation is the one that corresponds to what is really there, in the text.

For the non-realist, on the other hand, human language and thoughts do not correspond to objective realities or to stable meanings. What we cavalierly call "reality" is rather a human construction, at least in part. Kant exposed the lie of naive realism by demonstrating that the "world" is the product of human experience *as processed by conceptual categories*. The categories with which we think do not mirror the world but *mold* it; that is, *they impose distinctions on experience that may or may not be intrinsic to reality itself*. For Kant, we cannot know if certain features of the world are mind-independent or not, for human knowledge is limited to what we can experience, and experience is always already processed with categories imposed by the mind.[22]

The non-realist radicalizes Kant's point by claiming that the categories with which the mind processes experience are not necessary, as Kant thought, but arbitrary. It follows that there is no commonly agreed way of interpreting reality. The distinctions that make up the "natural order" are neither "natural" nor "given" but rather artificial and man-made. There is no such thing as an absolute, God's-eye point of view on reality, only a number of finite and fallible human perspectives. In short, there is no "authorized version" of reality. Non-realists contend that language and thought alike are always relative to some finite perspective or another. For the hermeneutical non-realist, then, meaning is not "there"; what one finds in a text depends on what aims, categories, and perspectives one brings to it. The contemporary malaise in postmodern literary theory ultimately stems, I believe, from this non-realist denial of the created order.

It is somewhat ironic that both naive hermeneutical realism and hermeneutical non-realism, in different ways, make interpretation redundant. In the one case, all that is needed is observation and description; interpretation is unnecessary. One either sees or does not see what is there. For the hermeneutical non-realist, on the other hand, interpretation is useless, for there is no "reality," no "meaning" to get right.[23]

The Undoers: Deconstruction

Jacques Derrida's appearance at a 1966 literary conference in Johns Hopkins University has been called "the single most radical development in hermeneutical theory" in the decade to follow.[24] Even Derrida's detractors acknowledge that his works "are among the most crucial documents of our period."[25] Nathan Scott sees deconstruction as a New Irrationalism, which threatens all the humanities, insofar as music, art, and literature are concerned to transmit and interpret classic texts that have been thought to illumine the human condition. Jürgen Habermas dismisses Derrida's ideas as a form of "militant latter-day unreason."[26] In the same vein, Hirsch describes Derrida as "currently the most fashionable of the theologians of cognitive atheism in the domain of literary theory."[27]

The furor over Cambridge University's decision to award an honorary doctorate is understandable; deconstruction seemingly betrays the very meanings and values that have undergirded Western culture since the beginning of the university. Indeed, in questioning the sanctity of reason and truth, Derrida's work seems to many to undermine the university itself. Worse, deconstruction appears to call into question the basic beliefs and ideas that legitimize traditional institutions and places of knowledge: church, university, state. Accordingly, it has been alternately "denounced as a terrorist weapon" and "dismissed as a harmless academic game."[28] At least one philosopher thinks that the major appeal of deconstruction is psychological; initiates have a sense of belonging to an intellectual elite with a kind of secret knowledge.[29] John Searle speaks for the majority of analytic philosophers when he denounces Derrida for neglecting recent work in the philosophy of language and for promoting misleading confusions: "As far as I can tell, Derrida knows next to nothing of the works of Frege, Russell, Wittgenstein, and so on."[30]

Though orthodox Christian theologians do not often discuss Derrida, those who do are also largely critical. Derrida's thought is perceived to be inimical to theology, not simply indifferent. Insofar as deconstruction casts down "the idols of the sign," then, it would appear to be against "God" too: "The sign and divinity have the same place and time of birth. The age of the sign is essentially theological."[31] Brian Ingraffia states that Derrida's thought "excludes God and anything that would take his place."[32] According to his detractors, then, Derrida is a nihilistic, anarchistic thinker who celebrates the arbitrariness of meaning and truth by dancing on the tomb of God.

This unflattering portrait of Derrida as a philosophical party-animal has been reinforced by a number of enthusiastic would-be American disciples. Literary critics at Yale and Johns Hopkins University found deconstruction's undoing of the distinction between "creative" and "critical" to be liberating. Indeed, some of Derrida's more avid disciples—Yale's erstwhile hermeneutical mafia—question the traditional privilege given to texts over commentaries, and with it the very distinction between text and interpretation: "We have entered an era that can challenge even the priority of literary to literary-critical texts."[33] These critics stopped worrying about "getting it right" as interpreters, preferring rather to celebrate their own interpretive creativity.[34] Deconstructive criticism represents nothing less than a total break with the traditional notions of objective observation and disciplined fidelity to the text. Such extreme appropriations of Derrida's thought are precisely what fuel the criticism that deconstruction, far from being a serious and respectable intellectual project, is instead a species of academic play, "textloose and fancy free."

Derrida also has his admirers. In the view of Richard Rorty, a former president of the American Philosophical Association, Derrida's principal contribution is to have demonstrated that philosophy is a kind of writing. Derrida undoes or collapses the distinction between literature and philosophy, and with it the myth that philosophy has privileged access to knowledge and truth. For Rorty, Western philosophy is only one story among many others that people tell to help them cope: epistemology is a way of getting through the night. What Rorty admires in Derrida is the latter's decisive break with the very question of truth. There is a kind of tragic courage in the admission that one can get neither the world nor the text "right."

Derrida has also found enthusiastic American followers among theologians and biblical scholars. Mark C. Taylor's books explore what he calls "a/theology."[35] His deconstructive theology represents an attempt to come to terms with the radical implications of the death of God. Indeed, one of Taylor's first forays into deconstructive theology was as a contributor to a book that included Thomas Altizer and William Hamilton, authors who were earlier involved in the "death of God" movement. In the field of biblical studies, Stephen D. Moore does for exegetes what Taylor has done for theologians, advocating deconstruction by expositing Derrida's texts and by giving deconstructive readings of biblical texts.[36]

Appropriately enough, Derrida's work has given rise to a sharp conflict between conservative and radical, right-wing and left-wing interpretations. The popular portrait of Derrida as the Mad Hatter of hermeneutics has recently been challenged by a number of studies that present Derrida as a serious philosopher. Deconstruction may involve play, but it is serious play. On his own account, Derrida wants to remain a philosopher, though one who takes language seriously.[37] According to Christopher Norris, Derrida is continuing the philosophical tradition of Kant, seeking out the conditions and the limits of reason.[38] Norris highlights the amount and the quality of rigorous analysis in Derrida's books. His work may have the effect of undermining certain received ideas, but his dismissal of them is certainly not cheap.[39] His deconstruction of certain classical oppositions—logic/rhetoric, speech/writing—is based on a rigorous reading of classic philosophical texts by Plato, Hegel, and Heidegger, among others.

Objections to the portrait of Derrida as a "death of God" theologian have become increasingly common. Louis Mackey counters the view that deconstruction is atheistic and nihilistic.[40] Kevin Hart contends that deconstruction's natural discussion partner is not atheism but rather negative theology, for what Derrida undoes is not theology as such but only metaphysical versions that seek to think God as supreme "Being."[41] Derrida has even been linked with Barth. Graham Ward argues that both thinkers are postmodern inasmuch as they share a similar problem—how to get beyond the language system in order to represent reality (Derrida); how to use words to speak of the Word (Barth)—and a similar response—we speak in awareness that our words are limited by otherness (Derrida) and by the Wholly Other (Barth).[42] Deconstruction here appears not as a statement of atheism or as a version of theism, but as a strategy for a postmodern, postmetaphysical theology.

Literary critics, philosophers, and theologians are thus divided as to the possibility of saving deconstruction from the excesses of its extreme practitioners. A similar confusion characterizes the discussion among committed Christians, as recent discussions in such journals as the *Christian Scholar's Review* and *Christianity and Literature* attest. For David Lyle Jeffrey, deconstruction is anti-Christian insofar as it refuses the possibility that language is a reliable medium of language and truth.[43] Similarly, Bruce Edwards and Branson Woodward contend that the Bible, not Derrida, should be the basis for a Christian understanding of linguistic and literary communication.[44] On the other hand, an increasing number of biblical scholars are adopting strategies for reading the Bible that, while they may not explicitly acknowledge Derrida by name, nevertheless show his influence.[45]

My purpose in examining Derrida is to explore further the connection between literary theory and theology. That the current crisis in hermeneutics is to a great extent a theological crisis is nowhere better demonstrated than in Derrida's work. I am not as concerned with defending either a right-wing or left-wing interpretation of Derrida; there are passages in his work that seem to support both sides in that debate. I have come neither to bury Derrida nor to praise him, but to understand him. Likewise, I am not interested in showing either that postmodernity is only a variant of modernity or that it is a significant new departure from it. My analysis will have succeeded if it yields a clearer understanding of the contemporary situation for hermeneutics and biblical interpretation, including an understanding of its *theological* dimension.

My own view of Derrida is neither conservative nor radical, but centrist: Derrida is a serious philosopher whose critique of philosophy shakes it to its very foundations and takes it to its breaking point. Like Kant, he correctly perceives, as a philosopher, the implications for knowledge and interpretation of the death of God; henceforth, we have "only human" (e.g., fallible) knowledge, "only human" (e.g., relative) truth. Yet he sees further than Kant in perceiving that the loss of God leads to the loss of the knowing subject (the hero of modernity) as well. Derrida has correctly analyzed the modern situation, or at least an aspect of it, *but he has done so by bracketing out orthodox Christian beliefs.* As Brian Ingraffia contends, the death of God that informs deconstruction is the death of the God of the philosophers, not of the God disclosed in Jesus Christ.[46] In my opinion, Derrida's starting point, though intelligible enough on its own terms, is not inevitable. While he needs to be heard, his is neither the last nor the only word on the subject. Nevertheless, Derrida's iconoclasm performs one positive function: that of cleansing the hermeneutical temple of the purveyors of cheap interpretations.

Undoing Structures. Deconstruction is not the same thing as destruction. It is not simply a matter of demolishing something through external force, but of disassembling it. Deconstruction is a painstaking taking-apart, a peeling away of the various layers—historical, rhetorical, ideological—of distinctions, concepts, texts, and whole philosophies, whose aim is to expose the arbitrary linguistic nature of their original construction.[47] Deconstruction is an intense analytical method, occasionally perversely so, that results in the collapse from within of all that it touches. It is an "analysis" in the etymological sense of the term (Greek: *analusis*): an "un-loosing" or "un-tying." Deconstruction is thus best understood as a kind of *undoing*, with all the attendant connotations that the term implies: untying, undermining, and ruining. In the words of one sympathizer, it is "a positive technique for making trouble; an affront to every normal and comfortable habit of thought."[48] The deconstructor is not so much interested in *what* the text says as in *how* it organizes its message. Like the psychoanalyst who listens to a husband and wife not for their ideas about relationships but in order to see how they relate, the deconstructor reads philosophical works not for their ideas about reality but with an eye on how they communicate, especially as this involves rhetorical procedures. Derrida wants deconstruction to function as a kind of intellectual therapy that helps philosophers, theologians, and literary critics confront their deep-seated fear of the messiness of language.

The emergence of deconstruction was itself a moment of undoing. Derrida had been invited to give a paper at Johns Hopkins University in 1966 on structuralism. Instead of building on the basic structuralist assumption—that language, and thought itself, depends on structures made up of binary oppositions (e.g., hot/cold, good/bad, light/dark)—Derrida surprised everyone by undermining or undoing the very idea of "structure."[49] Deconstruction is *poststructuralist* insofar as it denies the structuralist premises of an underlying system (e.g., of binary oppositions) that gives intelligibility to language and thought. For Derrida, structuralism is just another attempt, like that of Descartes, to stave off the threat of relativism by finding some stable ground for meaning. In the case of structuralism, however, it is not the sovereign subject but the language system itself that accounts for the stability of meaning by posit-ing distinctions (e.g., male/female; white/black; rational/irrational). Structures too—whether linguistic, familial, social, or philosophical—are ultimately arbitrary and artificial constructions. The point is that differences—even the distinction between truth and falsity—are not natural but man-made: "Identity (the archfoundation of all our philosophical and theological foundations) is constructed when people decide that certain distinctions make a difference, and others do not."[50]

Undoing Philosophy. As we saw in the Introduction, meaning for Plato concerns the relation between words and things. As things are pale reflections of eternal Ideas, so words are reflections of things; such is the gist of Plato's "imitation" theory of language. Augustine's "meaning as reference" view owes much to Plato and is typical of premodernity. In his *Confessions*, Augustine recalls how his parents taught him to speak: "When they named some object, and accordingly moved towards something, I saw this and I grasped that the thing was called by the sound they uttered."[51]

Modern philosophers of language pay more attention to the role of the mind but continue to stress the naming or representative function of language. Words are signs not only of things but also of *thoughts*. Language has an expressive as well as a referential function, twin aspects of the primary task of language: representation. The modern philosophical treatment of language culminated with the early work of Ludwig Wittgenstein, who, together with Bertrand Russell, argued that the purpose of language was to formulate true pictures of the world. According to this "picture theory" of language, the job of words is to name things, while statements or propositions picture facts: "A name means an object. The object is its meaning."[52]

For both the premodern Platonists and the modern propositionalists, then, meaning is a matter of naming, picturing, or referring to objects, facts, and the world. It is against this backdrop that Derrida appears as a "postmodern" thinker, an Undoer of modern (and premodern) theories of meaning and truth and of the belief that language and thought correspond to the world. In particular, Derrida directs his energies towards a sustained attack on "logocentrism," a catchall term for Western thinkers' preoccupation with meaning, rationality, and truth. Deconstruction is radical because it cuts at the root of traditional Western thought and theology: the *logos* ("speech," "word," "reason"). Logocentrism is the belief that there is some stable point *outside* language—reason, revelation, Platonic Ideas—from which one can ensure that one's words, as well as the whole system of distinctions that order our experience, correspond to the world. It is the desire for a center, for a point of reference, for an ultimate origin—anything on which we can non-arbitrarily hang our beliefs and values. In short, *logocentrism* stands for the fundamental presupposition that it is possible to speak truly: that our talk will be about reality, and not merely talk about talk.

The history of logocentrism, one might say, is a series of footnotes to Plato. Where then does Derrida think Plato, and Western philosophy after him, went wrong? Plato's great error, according to Derrida, was his notion that there is a realm of truths—the eternal Forms—to which reason has direct access without having to go through language. Signs are meaningful for Plato because they are related to reality, but only indirectly; they imitate, resemble, or represent either temporal things or human thoughts, which in turn represent eternal Ideas. The sign for Plato is thus a substitute presence for the thing itself. Language is not particularly problematic for Plato, just second best: not original, but derivative. It is a sign, though a step removed, of *presence*. This partly explains Plato's ambivalence towards literature. Literature is dangerous, often subversive, because it constructs a substitute world. Moreover, it is two steps removed from truth (the things themselves), being an imitation of the actual world, which in turn is but a shadow of the realm of Ideas. Philosophers must exercise a tremendous vigilance with regard to language, for it cannot only clarify but also cloud thinking. Indeed, Plato's dialogues are largely attempts to determine how words should be used so as not to mislead thought. Socrates' nemesis is the Sophist, who tries to persuade listeners not by argument but by a clever manipulation of language. Philosophical thought—logic, logocentrism—has nothing to do with rhetoric or sophistry, according to Plato. A clever use of language alone will not lead one to the truth.

Derrida spends roughly one hundred pages analyzing (undoing!) Plato's dialogue the *Phaedrus*.[53] This is the dialogue in which Plato extends his worry about literature to all forms of writing. Writing is one step further removed from thought than speech. To write down one's thought runs the risk of confusion and ambiguity. Language is closest to the mind, Plato apparently believed, when it remains speech. In speech, as opposed to writing, the speaker is "present" to ensure that the words will be related to the world as he or she intends.

Derrida locates the origin of logocentrism in Plato's preference for speech as the paradigm for the way language and thought are related to the world. The irony, as Derrida is quick to point out, is that though Socrates does not write, Plato does. Moreover, the way Plato chooses to warn others about the dangers of writing is to write about it. Derrida examines an ambiguous Greek term—*pharmakon*—that frequently recurs in the *Phaedrus* in connection with writing. Its two chief senses are "poison" and "cure." Derrida argues that both senses, though contradictory, coexist uneasily in the text. As Norris puts it: "Writing is both poison *and* cure, on the one hand a threat to the living presence of authentic (spoken) language, on the other an indispensable means for anyone who wants to record, transmit or somehow commemorate that presence."[54] In other words, a careful analysis of Plato's use of *pharmakon* undermines Plato's argument. What is true of this dialogue, moreover, is true of metaphysics in general. For Derrida, every system has stress points or fault lines that betray the fact of their construction—that is, their non-natural, and hence arbitrary, nature. Derrida thus shows how the arbitrary structures we construct (e.g., Plato's account of philosophy and literature, speech and writing) exclude things upon which they nevertheless rely: "To deconstruct is to identify points of failure in a system, points at which it is able to feign coherence only by excluding and forgetting that which it cannot assimilate, the absolute indigestible, that which is 'other' to it."[55]

Philosophers, says Derrida, have for the most part adopted Plato's derogatory attitude to literature and writing. They distinguish themselves from literary critics by virtue of their interest in being and rationality rather than the literary interests of fiction and imagination. Yet Derrida suggests that Socrates' apparent success in the dialogue may owe more to his effective rhetoric than to an alleged rational insight into the eternal order of things. What appears to be reasonable is actually only persuasive. The "voice" of reason, that is to say, is merely the voice that seems most persuasive to those who have the kind of values that philosophers have. With this insight, philosophy is undone, as is realism. For on Derrida's view, Plato's Ideas are neither necessary nor eternal, only an arbitrary and makeshift conceptual rigging. Neither language nor concepts latch onto the real; rather, philosophy itself is a species of writing, a kind of literature. Far from being a unique way of speaking about ultimate reality, then, metaphysics is rather the tribal language preferred by white European males, or as Derrida derisively calls it, a "white mythology."

The Users: Neo-pragmatism

The second influential version of hermeneutical non-realism—neo-pragmatism—has its roots in North American rather than Continental philosophy.[56] Rorty, an influential American philosopher and past president of the American Philosophical Association, has become, like Derrida, an ironic debunker of cherished philosophical myths, particularly the myth of "the real world." Rorty's first major work, *The Linguistic Turn*,[57] announced the displacement of the knowing subject by language; his second attacked the metaphor of the mind as a "mirror" that reflects or represents reality.[58] Like Derrida, Rorty (1) seeks to undo the exalted status of philosophy as the discipline that gives us privileged access to meaning and truth, suggesting instead that philosophy is more like literary or cultural criticism, and (2) espouses an anti-representationalist view of language, "which does not view knowledge as a matter of getting reality right, but rather as a matter of acquiring habits of action for coping with reality."[59]

Philosophy for Rorty is not an enquiry into "the way things really are," but simply one interpretation among others in a larger conversation about what interests us about our world. Concepts do not mirror nature or represent how the world really is; they are simply tools humans use for certain purposes. Our so-called "common sense" and our intuitions about reality are not, for Rorty, valid insights into the way things actually are so much as products of our social conventions and cultural practices. Not for Rorty the siren-call of absolute structures. He defines pragmatism as the view that "there are no constraints on inquiry save conversational ones."[60] We are free to approach the world with any number of "vocabularies" or ways of speaking and thinking. Rorty thus replaces the pursuit of knowledge with the art of conversation, that is to say, rhetoric.

Though there is no one authorized version of reality (or a text), Rorty recognizes a number of authorized versions. There is no one true philosophy, only diverse ways of talking about the world—varieties of philosophizing. We can never escape thinking in terms of some socially constructed and arbitrary "conversation." We can never escape language. Rorty asks: "Can the ubiquity of language ever really be taken seriously?"[61] Can we ever acknowledge that our truth claims reflect particular linguistic habits, habits that amount to arbitrary social conventions? Language is not a clear surface that reflects reality; it is rather the glass through which we see only darkly. Rorty here agrees with Derrida: *we can never break out of or rise above language to make sure that our words correspond to the world.*

If Rorty is a philosopher who sounds like a literary critic, Stanley Fish is a literary critic who sounds like a philosopher. Fish takes Rorty's pragmatism and applies it to the project of interpreting texts. Like Rorty, Fish eliminates the distinction between interpreting texts and using them. In particular, he rejects the notion that "getting it right" in interpretation means recòvering the author's mind or intention. The idea of the author is useful for some purposes, but we should not be fooled into thinking this concept corresponds to something in the text, nor should we think that everyone should use texts in order to find out something about their authors. We read books for many different purposes: for instruction, for entertainment, for encouragement, for escape.

Is there a meaning in this text? If one means, is there a stable meaning-conferring entity prior to the process of interpretation, a verbal vessel in which meaning is somehow "contained," Fish would answer in the negative: "The text as an entity independent of interpretation . . . drops out and is replaced by the texts that emerge as the consequence of our interpretive activities."[62] The text is not a spatial object to be filled with meaning so much as a temporal event in which meaning happens. That is, meaning is located not in some inert objective entity (the text), but in the dynamic experience of reading. Fish's point is the Kantian one. We can only know "phenomena," the things that appear in our experience, or more precisely, the things that our perceptual and conceptual apparatus let in. Things as they are in themselves—what Kant called the "noumena"—are simply unknowable and for all practical purposes become irrelevant. For Fish, the text-as-it-is-in-itself, an independent entity and noumenal reality, simply drops out of the picture. It is not a useful notion. The only text in the class, and the only meaning in this text, therefore, is the text and the meaning that readers produce through their interpretive practices. The significance of Fish's position must not be underestimated: on his view, it is not the author that is the historical cause of the text and creator of meaning, but the reader. In a real sense, for Fish, the commentary (viz., the work of interpretation) *precedes* the text.

Fish puts interpretation in its place, namely, in the reader's activity. The reader, moreover, is always situated in a particular interpretive community that dictates how texts will be read. The individual is not free to adopt another set of interpretive practices but is to a large extent conditioned, even socially and culturally determined, to act towards and respond to texts in certain ways rather than others. It should be obvious that Fish has moved considerably beyond modernity's notion of the sovereign knowing subject. Between the individual's mind and the world now stands a whole set of cultural practices: ways of experiencing, acting, and thinking. What constraints there are on interpretation stem not from the text (e.g., the given, the real, the world) but from the interpretive community. To put interpretation in its place means to call attention to the authority of interpretive communities.

Fish avoids a thoroughgoing solipsism by locating the "authorizing agency," the center of interpretive authority, not in the author, the text, or even the individual reader, but rather in the interpretive community. What were formerly considered "facts" about the text can now be seen to be the results of reading texts in ways that reflect those values that a particular interpretive community holds in high esteem. There is therefore no single correct interpretation, no "real meaning" in a text, only "ways of reading" that are extensions of a community's values and interests. With Rorty, Fish redefines truth in terms of "what seems good to us now." If interpreters would only come clean about the impossibility of literary knowledge, they would see that the only honorable course would be to admit that the truth is not out there, to be discovered eventually by reason, but is rather in the eye of the beholding community.

To say that we must read in order to recover the intention of the author is, for Fish, authoritarian. How dare you tell me what to be interested in or what to do with a text! Interpretive communities must be free to pursue their own interests. The neo-pragmatist is, hermeneutically speaking, pro-choice. Neither the author nor even the notion of truth has any authority for the user. Truth is demoted from its prior status as timeless and absolute to "what is good for us to believe here and now" or "what works for me in this situation." Truth—in metaphysics, morals, or meaning—is a label we assign beliefs that seem good to us, beliefs that perform some useful purpose.

The Unbelievers: Nihilism With a Human Face?

To understand the contemporary crisis in literary theory, we must look back to Nietzsche's attack on meaning and truth in the nineteenth century. Nietzsche, a non-realist, contends that meaning, truth, and the world itself are human constructions. Some find it easy to caricature Nietzsche, like Derrida, as a "silly relativist." This would be a perfunctory reading indeed. It is important not to confuse non-realism with the implausible position that everything exists only in the human mind; even non-realists believe that there is a physical reality "out there." The issue is rather whether language and thought about the world are primarily about ourselves: how *we* see, how *we* experience, how *we* talk, and therefore how *we* think, about the world. According to the non-realist, nothing is naturally given; everything is culturally "graven." All the meaningful distinctions that enable us to order our experience—for example, between trees and animals, between trees and other kinds of plants, between one tree and another, between one season and another—all these distinctions reflect not the "natural order of things" but a cultural-linguistic, man-made order. In short, *all the significant distinctions that make a meaningful world out of human experience are, in the final analysis, linguistic creations*. The non-realist is an unbeliever for whom words and concepts are nothing more than human contrivances.

The unbelievers—Derrida, Rorty, Nietzsche—are united in their opposition to Plato. It was Plato who founded the "literary genre" of philosophy, that is, the attempt to find language and concepts that approximate or correspond to truth, to the way things really are. Plato believes in transcendence, in a stable reality that stands over and above the play of language, that language and thought ought to represent. Nietzsche dismisses the Christian faith with his assertion that "Christianity is Platonism for the people." Rorty says that "pragmatists see the Platonic tradition as having outlived its usefulness"[63]—a polite way of saying that it is false! Speaking of his own brand of pragmatism, Rorty comments: "This post-positivistic kind of analytic philosophy thus comes to resemble the Nietzsche-Heidegger-Derrida tradition in beginning with criticism of Platonism and ending in criticism of Philosophy as such."[64] Similarly, Derrida decries Plato's attempt to attain, through reason, eternal truth. Deconstruction is the suspicion of metaphysics; it is the distrust of thinking about essences. Together, Derrida, Rorty, and Nietzsche reject the metaphysical impulse as misleadingly oriented to "transcendence," that is, to an extra-linguistic reality that can nevertheless be represented by language. For the hermeneutic unbeliever, any theory of meaning and truth that presupposes such a belief in transcendence is a form of "the idolatry of the sign."[65]

According to the unbelievers, logocentrism, in either its Platonic or Christian version, is a form of idolatry. The unbeliever refuses to countenance the possibility of transcendence—the possibility that there may be something beyond the sign. Nietzsche states: "No new idols are erected by me. . . . *Overthrowing idols* (my word for 'ideals')—that comes closer to being part of my craft."[66] As a non-realist, Nietzsche holds that there is nothing to interpret, no truth of the matter to which our readings must correspond or get right. "There are no facts, only interpretations."[67] Such is the credo of the hermeneutic non-realist.

Above all, hermeneutic unbelievers do not believe in authors: neither the Creator of heaven and earth nor the originator of meaning in texts. Again, it is not the author as a historical cause of the text that is in dispute. What the unbelievers dispute is the author as a metaphysical entity, as a ground or stable home of meaning. They object to the metaphysics of the author because they think it leads to a politics of authoritarianism that constrains readers and limits interpretation. Derrida is the captain of an intellectual *résistance* that is engaged for the sake of the liberation of the other in guerrilla warfare against the pretensions of metaphysics. The hierarchies that philosophy sets up—truth/falsity; philosophy/literature; straight/gay—are in fact power structures. Metaphysical attempts to suppress equivocation and ambiguity cleanse language the way that some megalomaniacs try to cleanse races. "Linguistic cleansing" is never a final solution, only an expression of the problem.

It is not difficult to see the ramifications of this critique of "true beliefs" on the history of theology. In Christian thought, the heretic was by definition one who held a position "other" than that of the church. "Orthodoxy" means having the right opinion. What is ultimately at stake in debates about the authority of the author is actually the question of who has the right to interpret and who interprets rightly.

To the non-realist, logocentric philosophy and interpretation alike are forms of systematic exclusion; anything that stops the play of meaning and truth is unduly repressive. Christians until recently have excluded Jewish interpretations of the Old Testament; the French until recently claimed authority over Algeria. Derrida, a French Jew born in Algeria, remembers his extreme isolation as a child. Derrida's philosophy as a whole can be seen as a reaction against the tendency of authorities to exclude "others." From his point of view, belief systems, whether of faith or reason, practice the systematic exclusion of voices other than their own. Athens and Jerusalem, each logocentric in its own way, use the notion of authority to justify what is in fact authoritarianism. In order to combat authoritarianism, then, the author's authority must be undone. Every voice, not only the author's, must be lifted up in interpretation.

Must hermeneutical non-realism lead to a relativistic nihilism? Not necessarily. While they may not believe in truth or in "the real world," Derrida, Rorty, and Nietzsche believe in humanity—in human creativity and in human rights. (Whether or not they also believe in human freedom is a question I discuss below). For the non-realist, there are no "givens": no eternal truths, no limits on what we can say or on how we can differentiate the world. On the one hand, then, the nihilist believes in nothing; on the other hand, he or she says that humans can invent value and truth. Call it *nihilism with a human face*: there is *nothing*—in the world, in the text—that is not the creation of some human individual or community. The question is: can such nihilism with a human face preserve humanity and human values? As G. K. Chesterton observed, those who stop believing in God do not then believe in nothing, they will believe in *anything*. And as Jesus observed, when one demon is cast out, one must beware that seven others do not take its place. It remains to be seen what demons, or monsters, will take the place of the author, once the latter is banished from the home of meaning.

A Gospel of Marks? The Voice of the Author

The Undoer has come to bury, not to praise the author. Derrida's claim that the fate of the author and the fate of Western metaphysics stand or fall together is both provocative and perplexing. Students of English literature know about the seventeenth-century Metaphysical Poets,[68] to be sure, but why must all poets and all authors be similarly metaphysical? The previous section began to answer that question by tracing the parallel careers of human authors and the concept of God. We now continue our investigation by examining other metaphysical issues presupposed by the phenomenon of writing and by the practice of exegesis.

While biblical exegetes try to resolve conflicts of interpretation about, say, the Gospel of Mark by determining which reading is most probably the author's intended message, the deconstructor proceeds quite differently. For Derrida, authorial intention is always frustrated by language rather than fulfilled by it. The language system is more fundamental than an author's use of it. Language is as deep, and as powerful, as an ocean; and the speaker, like a swimmer, finds himself or herself carried along by currents beneath the surface. Far from enjoying mastery over the sign, the author, at best, only copes with them, and is dragged under and engulfed by them at worst. How does Derrida view language and meaning? Why are "marks"—demythologized signs, signs that refer only to other signs, signs that do not point to something non-linguistic—more important than the author, than Mark?

Undoing Logocentrism: Speech Versus Writing

For Derrida, metaphysics is a three-stranded cord that has bound the imagination of Western thinkers tight. The three strands are language, mind, and world. "Logocentrism" is Derrida's term for the belief that the meaning of words and the truth of ideas is guaranteed by an authoritative source or center (e.g., Reason) that has direct access to the world. Thanks to the *logos*—the mind reasoning—the world is "present" to the mind as an idea. What the knowing subject knows in the first instance is his or her own mind, but the world is nevertheless "present," at least as a reflection. In undoing logocentrism, Derrida believes that he also demythologizes authorship, and hence the authority of the author's voice. Does Derrida kill the author ("we murder to dissect") or only speed the author's inevitable death in an act of hermeneutic euthanasia? An adequate answer must carefully examine the evidence. We turn, then, to an extended analysis of the death of the author in order to judge whether, and to what extent, deconstruction is a criminal philosophical act.

Voice: A Speaking Presence. Derrida defines metaphysics as the "science of presence," a science based on the logocentric assumption that there is a stable truth (the realm of being) "outside" or "above" language (the realm of the sign). Metaphysics apparently provides an independent criterion (viz., what there is) with which to assess our theories and interpretations about the world (viz., what we say there is). Derrida believes that this urge to metaphysics has led philosophers to privilege speech over writing, for the simple reason that speech is more intimately and immediately connected to the human subject than is writing. With the mind's eye we grasp the essence of things in ideas; with the mouth we express these ideas with words. Logocentrism stands for the harmonious alliance between reality, thought, and language. Logocentric hermeneutics is thus oriented towards voice, insofar as the latter is thought to be a substitute for the author's presence in the text. Derrida, however, rejects the notion that there is an "original" over against which our theories and interpretations may be measured. We have no direct access to anything real. On the contrary, all access to the world is mediated by the mind, which is in turn structured by some language system or other. Hence the "problem of presence": metaphysics is based on an illusion.

Speech, Derrida asserts, has always been the paradigm for presence in Western thought ("In the beginning was the Logos"). Descartes, the father of modern philosophy, believed in the ability of the human subject, through an act of self-reflection, to attain to clear and certain ideas (at least about the self). Meaning too originates in the speaker's consciousness inasmuch as meaning is a matter of words representing ideas. Consciousness is thus the anchor of meaning, and an interpretation is correct or incorrect if it corresponds or fails to correspond to what was in the author's mind. Authors, of course, have no need to interpret; they know immediately what they mean because they have direct and immediate access to their own thoughts. Cartesian subjects, we might say, invariably know their own minds. Meaning is immediately present to consciousness. That is why, in traditional interpretation, it is the author's say-so that determines what a text means. "Voice" is a speaking presence— presence speaking, a live report from an author's consciousness. Accordingly, "voice" becomes a metaphor for the event in which word, thought, and world come together, and hence for the author's authority or say-so. Logocentrism leads to the belief that the author's mind is a safe place in which to ground meaning and knowledge. Logocentrism is thus best understood as a "Platonism of meaning."[69]

For Derrida, the story of philosophy is "a white mythology which assumes and reflects Western culture: the white man takes his own mythology—his logos—that is, the *mythos* of his idiom, for the universal form of that which is still his inescapable desire to call Reason."[70] Logocentrism—the privileging of reason—is "nothing but the most original and powerful ethnocentrism."[71] The author, by extension, is also a mythological creature. To speak of the authoritative voice of the author is to fall prey to the illusion that the text represents the author's speech, and that speech in turn represents the author's mind.

What I wish to highlight in this account of deconstruction is the connection between the undoing of the author and the undoing of the metaphysical dimension of theology and philosophy. In both cases, what is undone is the claim that language corresponds to some non-linguistic presence. "Voice"—whether the voice of reason or of the author—combines the notion of speech and presence. Philosophy and theology each claim to speak with an authoritative "voice": God, Reason, Being, or some other principle that allows them to ground their language and beliefs in something that is not itself language. The voice of Reason, for instance, has functioned as the secular substitute for the voice of God for centuries. Literary critics and exegetes, similarly, claim to speak on behalf of the authoritative voice of the author. Why, asks Derrida, should speech be greater than writing?

Writing: A Silent Absence. Where Plato sees signs imitating things, Derrida sees only signs—signs that refer not to some higher realm, only sideways to other signs. Derrida follows the Swiss linguist Ferdinand de Saussure in claiming that meaning is a function of the difference between signs. For Saussure, a linguistic mark "is not a link between a thing and a name but between a concept [signified] and a sound pattern [signifier]."[72] A sign gains its sense not by referring to a thing but by differing from other signs (e.g., the word "hot" is not "cold," "warm," etc., nor is it "not," "lot," "dot," etc.). What gives a sign a specific meaning is its place in a system of signs from which it differs. Meaning for Saussure, as well as for Derrida, is always differential, never referential.

The meaning of a sign or "signifier" for Saussure is not some actual thing to which the sign refers, but rather a concept or "signified" that has come to be arbitrarily associated with it. It is only arbitrary convention that the letters G-o-d signify a divine rather than a canine entity. A word, after all, does not resemble anything but another word.[73] "Red" means what it means because it is *not* "bed," "fed," or "wed," and because it is not "blue," "green," "crimson," "maroon," or "pink." In other words, "red" is an arbitrary sign that takes its meaning from its place in a system of linguistic differences. And this is what language most essentially is for Derrida: a system of signs that mean what they mean by differing from one another.

Saussure distinguished the system of language (*langue*) from particular acts of saying or speaking (*parole*). Derrida observes that speech and thought are always secondary and derivative; the system of language is prior. Apart from language, thought is chaotic: "No ideas are established in advance, and nothing is distinct, before the introduction of linguistic structure."[74] For Saussure, the structure of *langue* is arbitrary; different languages employ different sets of contrasts. The boundaries between the colors green, blue, gray, and brown are, for instance, placed differently in Welsh than in English. In Welsh *glas* (blue) includes hues that English speakers would call green or gray. Color terms, like language in general, form a system of differences that speakers experience as "natural" but which are actually arbitrary and conventional. The world—the sum total of categories, distinctions, and connections—is not given, but written. The language learner, say, a child, learns a set of differentiating concepts "which identify not *given entities* but *socially constructed signifieds*."[75]

This analysis of language destroys the ideal of pure presence. If we grasp the implications of Derrida's concept of writing, we shall see that presence is only a mirage. Meaning is not the thing signified, but the endless displacement of one sign by another, a ceaseless play of signs that never come to rest on something in the world. Derrida claims to have discovered a systematic denunciation of writing in his analyses of texts by Plato, Rousseau, Hegel, and other philosophers. Whereas Heidegger accused philosophers of forgetting the question of Being, Derrida accuses them of forgetting, and repressing, the question of Writing.[76] Why have philosophers conspired against writing? Because writing is a threat to logocentrism, to the claim that philosophy and theology have access to something outside the system of language and the play of meaning, namely, "voice" or "presence." Writing is dangerous, for it substitutes arbitrary and lifeless signs for the authentic living presence of speech, thus making truth—the match of language and reality—impossible to achieve. *What really lies behind the authority of the author, then, are the biases of Western metaphysics.*

Meaning, then, is for Derrida a never-ending, differential play of signifiers. Signs acquire what sense they have from their contrast with other signs. The result is that meaning is horizontal, never vertical; immanent to language, not transcendent. In Derrida's terminology, there is no such thing as a "transcendental signified," an extra-linguistic referent that somehow escapes the endless play of language. In sum, Derrida undoes the basic metaphysical assumption—that there is access to an authoritative *logos* that guarantees the correspondence of language to reality—by arguing that writing is prior to speech. Just as *langue* is prior to *parole*, so the language system (writing) is prior to any attempt to say something (speech). Writing, moreover, is prior to thought. "Writing" is Derrida's general term for this all-too-human situation of having to make do with the mediation of signs (interpretation) rather than with immediate understanding (intuition). "Writing" stands for the deferral of presence: presence is "deferred" since we have access to it only through a system of signs. "Writing" is what we have *instead of* presence. In writing we live and move and have our being.

If writing is prior to speech, then there is no absolute origin of meaning—no authority. Writing is always already there; the speaking and thinking subject is always already preceded by cultural codes and systems of language. Because signs refer only to other signs, there is nothing to anchor meaning, nothing to stop the play of language. The meaning of a sign is a function of differences, a matter of what it is *not*. Absence is the first and last word; there never was and never will be a non-linguistic (and thus non-arbitrary) grasp of reality. Language is an endless ocean, bottomless and infinite, with neither anchor nor lodestar to guide its user to reality. Language swallows up both mind and world. To believe in transcendence—that marks stand in for, or refer to, a reality above the play of language—is to fall under the illusion of the reliability of the sign. Philosophers who perpetuate this illusion are only ventriloquists who project their own voices onto "Being" or "Reason." By contrast, Derrida's analysis overthrows this first "idol" of the sign.

Undoing the Subject: The Ghost in the Machine

The author turns out to be one more desperate attempt (the latest metaphysical ploy) to find an anchor outside the play of language with which to ground meaning. The non-realist need not adopt the counter-intuitive position that books write themselves, however. The deconstructor's point is more subtle than that. Derrida may not be aware of my existence, but if he were, he would not deny that I have written the present book. However, he would insist, first, that my intentions and efforts are not sufficient to ground its meaning or to control its interpretation, and second, that what I have written is not my own voice so much as the voice of all the teachers and texts that have had an impact on me. As an author, I am at best a weaver of a complex texture, not a sovereign subject lording it over my text.

"There Is Nothing Outside the Text". "There is nothing outside the text."[77] Perhaps no other statement of Derrida's has been more often quoted, and misinterpreted, than this one. Some commentators discredit Derrida by offering the perfunctory suggestion that he means that things such as oak trees or Ford Escorts do not exist. Such a reading is ludicrous. Derrida's point is rather that everything is part of a signifying system. Even natural objects are "written," that is, classified by some language system or other. A Douglas fir tree is what it is to me because of its place in a cultural practice, namely, by its being part of our family Christmas. It is difficult for me to think of a Douglas fir with a different set of connotations. Similarly, a Ford has its particular connotations because it is part of a signifying system that includes Yugos, Peugots, and Jaguars. The "meaning" of a Ford Escort is constituted by its differences from other cars (including other Fords). An Escort is a text in the context of other automobiles. There is no such thing as an "absolute Ford," whose meaning could be considered in a cultural vacuum. Rather, the particular value that we have come to associate with Fords depends as much on how the cars are marketed as how the cars are manufactured, and on how "Ford" is placed in the signifying system that includes "Jaguar," "Volkswagen," "Chevrolet," and "Toyota." What Derrida denies is that there is any presence, any kind of being or determinate reality outside the play of signs. There is no original ground or "home" of meaning, nothing beyond particular and contingent language systems, and therefore nothing to keep meaning centered, stable, and determinate.

We may recall the celebrated anecdote about the Indian philosopher who believed that the world rests on the back of a camel. When asked what the camel stood on, the philosopher replied, "It's camels all the way down." Derrida would doubtless have sympathy with such an answer. If a traditional exegete might say that his interpretation of Mark's Gospel rests on Mark, Derrida would doubtless reply, "No, it's *marks* all the way down." We never do reach the authorial presence of Mark, only marks that refer to other marks (or Marks that refer to Matthew and Luke). We can now see just how distant Derrida is from Descartes. Whereas modern philosophers root philosophy in consciousness ("I think, therefore I am"), Derrida sees consciousness itself as structured by language. For Derrida, however, the subject is never fully self-conscious. Neither Plato nor Mark ever manages to master his meanings or his message. All our concepts are contaminated by language; we never do have a point of view outside the play of language.

Différance and Dr. Johnson's Dictionary. *Différance* is Derrida's preferred term for the two ways in which the passage from sign to reality is blocked: it connotes both how signs *differ* from one another and how signs *defer* presence (e.g., a sign's reference to something other than a sign is endlessly postponed). As such, *différance* is also a fundamental category in Derrida's critique of reason, though in contrast with Kant's categories, it functions only negatively. For Kant, certain ideas have to be presupposed in order to account for how knowledge is possible in the first place. Derrida uses *différance* with the opposite intent—as the explanation for the *impossibility* of knowledge. What Derrida offers is a critique of *impure* reason.

Metaphysics, as we have seen, is the "science of presence." It is also the attempt to "decipher" reality, to arrive at the meaning of the Book of Nature and to reach some point that is "free from freeplay and from the order of the sign."[78] Metaphysics is the attempt to detextualize reality. In Derrida's opinion, however, writing is a virus or parasite that prevents metaphysics from ever functioning properly. "Writing" is the "freeplay" or dimension of instability that inhabits every attempt at communication. Kevin Hart well captures the intrinsic nature of this "tragic flaw" of the sign: "The sign's failure is structurally determined, and this is the starting-point for his [Derrida's] case against the metaphysics of presence."[79] The sign never really does re-present presence. "Presence" turns out to be an effect of differences, which is always deferred.

Philosophy may have begun when Thales said, "All is water," but Derrida's "All is writing" threatens philosophy's very existence insofar as it implies that meaning is never fixed, but rather always differing and deferring. Derrida's train of thought here is complex, but crucial. For Derrida, meaning is always absent from the sign itself, since meaning consists in the differences between signs. To deconstruct is to show that meaning is not really "there"; meaning is rather a function of *différance*—of signs differing from other signs and of endlessly deferred presence. "Meaning" is the pot of gold at the end of the rainbow of reading, which continually recedes as one approaches it. We never know what a sign is a sign of; when we go to the dictionary we only find other signs. Meaning is differential and hence never settles down in something non-linguistic or extra-linguistic. Meaning can only be stabilized by forcibly repressing its intrinsic *différance*: "Writing is the endless displacement of meaning which both governs language and places it forever beyond the reach of a stable, self-authenticating knowledge."[80]

Surely, one might object, Derrida is complicating matters unnecessarily. Some signs can be related to reality quite easily, by consulting a dictionary, for instance. Samuel Johnson's *Dictionary of the English Language* was published in 1755. He used quotations, mainly from the Elizabethan period, to illustrate usage and to justify his definitions. In his day, Johnson was labeled "the man who has conferred stability on the language of his country."

But when one does look up a word, one finds only other words. Take, for instance, Dr. Johnson's definition of "oats": "A grain, which in England is generally given to horses, but in Scotland supports the people." This definition tells us as much about Dr. Johnson and his times as it does the word in question. Wherein lies the authority behind dictionaries? In modern dictionaries, the goal is to describe the common usage of a term. However, common usage often changes, and with it the linguistic system of which the sign is a part.

In his Preface to the *Dictionary*, Dr. Johnson echoes Plato even as he anticipates the postmodern despair of the sign: "I am not yet so lost in lexicography, as to forget that words are the daughters of earth, and that things are the sons of heaven. Language is only the instrument of science, and words are but the signs of ideas: I wish, however, that the instrument might be less apt to decay, and that signs might be permanent, like the things which they denote."[81] This quote illustrates two key logocentric assumptions: that there is some guaranteed correspondence between thought and reality, and that words are the immediate expression of thoughts. But, almost as an afterthought, Johnson acknowledges the disruptive, indeterminate nature of language. The impulse to write a dictionary is linked to the logocentric desire to have stability in the realm of meaning.

For the hermeneutic non-realist, however, a dictionary does not tell us which words to stick onto things: "For the dictionary shows meanings to be relative and differential."[82] A dictionary does not allow us to follow meaning from sign to thing, but rather sideways from sign to sign. This is the metaphysical version of the proverbial "writer's block": between us and the world stands a language system. Indeed, there are many such language systems. And herein lies the trouble. *There is no one way to relate language to the world.* As Dr. Johnson knew all too well, the system of language is never closed and never comes to rest. Nothing, therefore, is ever fully self-present. Even the present moment—the presence of the present—is constituted by what it is not. The present can only be understood in terms of the past and the future, in terms of what is already passing away and in terms of what has not yet come.

Signatures and Signing Off: The Vanishing Subject. Of all words linked to the author, none is closer than the signature. In speech, one's voice is one's signature, a sure sign by which we recognize a speaker. In writing, however, our signature represents us. While the text is a substitute for the author's physical presence (cf. Paul's remark, "This is why I write these things when I am absent"—2 Cor. 13:10), the signature is the seal of the author's authority ("I, Paul, write this greeting in my own hand"—1 Cor. 16:21). Signatures specify the character of the relation between the author and the text in terms of ownership and responsibility. It should come as no surprise, therefore, that Derrida has discussed the signature in several of his works. Can the signature guarantee the author's authority in his or her absence?

Signatures are typically viewed as signs of an author's absent presence. One's signature may be a declaration of the author's legal right over a text or, in the case of a check, a promissory acknowledgment of one's financial obligation. The proper place for the signature seems to be outside the text; it is the site that signals the text's origin in the author's consciousness. By signing, the author confirms that a text is a legitimate expression of his or her will. The signature thus symbolizes the notion that the author is both the point of "origin" and of "control."

What traditional interpreters overlook, according to Derrida, is the fact that signatures are signs. As such, they belong to the economy of signs, which, as we have seen, forestalls transcendence. The author is part of "white mythology," another candidate for the stabilizing role of "transcendental signified." The very sense of an author's presence is, says Derrida, only an effect of writing. Moreover, just as a signifying system escapes the control of an individual presence or speech, so signatures, as signs, escape their original "owners." A signature functions in the absence of its author. As such, signatures have more to do with absence than with presence. Signatures too are signs that fail to signify something outside the text. Signatures too are marked by *différance*; like all signs, they fail to coincide with their origin.

Derrida argues that it is a trait of the sign that it can be repeated outside its original context: "This essential drift bearing on writing as an iterative structure, cut off from all absolute responsibility, from *consciousness* as the ultimate authority, orphaned and separated at birth from the assistance of its father, is precisely what Plato condemns in the *Phaedrus*."[83] Every sign, every mark, is thus constitutionally cut off from its putative origin. In affirming his unique presence, the author of the Gospel according to Mark must make use of marks that can be repeated, translated, even forged.

The conditions that enable the signature to work are also the conditions that make possible its undoing. Signatures cannot deliver on the presence that they promise. Or, as Derrida puts it: "La signature tombe" ("the signature fails"; "the signature encrypts"). The signature is only a futile attempt, a last rhetorical gasp, to invoke an authorial presence that would control the meaning of the text. In fact, there is nothing in a text that can stop readers from misunderstanding it. Simply adding a signature (one more sign) is insufficient to control a text's meaning: "Signatures do nothing to endure the passage of an author's 'true' intentions to those who read and set themselves up as authorized heirs and interpreters."[84]

To sign one's name with a flourish is the preeminent gesture of the self-centered modern subject, the same subject who aspires, perhaps unsuccessfully, to be the ground of rationality and truth. Even the signature cannot prevent this autonomous knowing subject from disappearing. For an increasing number of postmodern critics, the author is unavailable and largely irrelevant with regard to the processes of interpretation. *The author cannot fulfill the role of stabilizing signs that the metaphysics of meaning would seem to require.* Nevertheless, though deconstruction removes the author from the center stage of interpretation, the author does not entirely disappear. Derrida does not destroy authors, but puts them in their place. Where is this place? In the wings offstage, in the margins of discourse. As Burke puts it, "the author's determining will is inscribed as one factor amongst others."[85]

"The Death God Put Into Writing"

The author is a metaphysical construct, a figure linked to Western philosophy's and theology's logocentrism via the metaphors of "voice" and "presence." Deconstruction undoes these privileged notions by exposing the suppression of writing in Western intellectual history. To this point, I have presented deconstruction as a critique of metaphysics. In the next chapter we will examine deconstruction as a critique of reason. The two critiques converge in Derrida's critique of the sovereign subject. To the extent that the modern concept of the author accepts this picture of the autonomous self, it too is undone by Derrida's critique of the knowing subject. Modernity's turn *to* the subject is thus answered by postmodernity's turn *from* the subject. The death of the author follows from the death of the subject, and, as we will see, these two deaths are related to a third: the death of God. In Part 2 I will attempt to resuscitate the author; the present task, however, that of autopsy, is a necessary preliminary.

Authors Anonymous?

The Cartesian subject, the *cogito,* begat the autonomous author, one who speaks clearly in his or her own voice. Meaning is stable because the author is a stable subject. However, the mind/body contrast is another one of the hierarchical oppositions that Derrida sets out to undo. Cartesian mind/body dualism gives the false impression that the knowing subject's thoughts are immune from the earthly vicissitudes that affect the body. The notion that there is a spiritual realm—of meaning, rationality, truth—or a "true" world above the material, physical world is precisely one of the idols that Nietzsche sought to overturn. Consciousness—a given for Descartes—

is, for modern skeptics, an illusion. The Cartesian subject is too disembodied, too abstract to believe in any longer. The life of the mind is located not in some separate, spiritual realm of its own, as Descartes apparently believed, but is rather permeated by various material forces—biological, psychological, economic, political—that shape and condition it.

Masters of Suspicion: The Turn From the Subject. The so-called "masters of suspicion"—Freud, Marx, and Nietzsche—argue in different ways that the human subject is neither self-conscious nor self-present. Nor is the human subject a pure reason immune from the effects of history and culture. We are more mastered *by* than masters *of* our situation, more shaped by than shapers of our tradition, culture, and language. Because consciousness is subject to unconscious psychological, social, and historical forces, it is not the master of its own home. The modern home of meaning—sovereign authorial consciousness—was built on sand and has now spectacularly collapsed. To a great extent, it is this question as to which is prior—the human subject or the historical situation—that divides the moderns from the postmoderns. David Tracy writes of the moderns: "They were relatively confident about the power of reflection to eliminate and render consciousness translucent if not transparent."[86] It is the distinctive insight of postmoderns, however, that consciousness is not transparent, not even to itself. The only way to achieve self-knowledge is therefore through a critique of consciousness, through a hermeneutics of suspicion.

It was Freud who discovered the uncharted continent, deep and dark, of the unconscious. Freud exposed the rot in the Cartesian foundation, namely, the irrational substructures of human consciousness in the desires of the body. In his *The Interpretation of Dreams*, Freud argues that dreams mean something different from what they seem to say. Dreams speak the distorted language of repressed desires.[87] We may think we know why we made such and such a decision, for instance, but our conscious motive may not be the real motive. After Freud, consciousness is no longer the royal route to self-knowledge, but a problem for interpretation. If what we consciously say masks unconscious desires, then we must probe behind what we say to arrive at what we really mean.

Jacques Lacan, a psychoanalyst whose thought combines insights from Freud and from structuralist linguistics, has described language as the "structural unconscious." The self does not stand behind language but in the thick of it, caught in a swirling crosscurrent of competing discourses and vocabularies that determine the way one things and speaks. Now, if language is an arbitrary structure, and if the *logos* is shaped by language, then the *logos* itself is only an arbitrary way of apprehending the world. Against Kant, reason is never "pure." There is no such thing, then, as objective prelinguistic subject.[88]

Whereas Freud undermines consciousness by exposing the deep psychological drives that often hide behind the reasons we give others and ourselves, Marx undermines self-consciousness by exposing the socio-political factors that shape subjectivity: "It is not men's consciousness which determines their existence, but on the contrary their social existence which determines their consciousness."[89] Marx overturns the privilege of consciousness by situating the individual in a network of institutional forces and ideological relations. The author is not a poet—a creator of something new—but a pawn of political forces. What the masters of suspicion ultimately suspect is the subject's self-mastery. The human subject is not a rational but a political animal. It is not rationality but materiality—the condition of being an embodied animal—that gives the lie to the myth of sovereign consciousness.

Authors are, of course, no exception. What appears to be rational discourse may rather be a function of suppressed ideology, say, of repressed homosexuality. According to some critics, the apostle Paul may provide an example of both tendencies. The letter to the Romans has been psychoanalyzed, and the Pastoral Letters have been read as quasi-political documents that support a particular form of church government. The general point is that one can no longer ignore "the influence of the unconscious on the conscious, the role of the preconceptual and non-conceptual in the conceptual, the presence of the irrational—the economy of desire, the will to power—at the very core of the rational. . . . Nor is it possible to ignore the intrinsically social character of 'structures of consciousness.'"[90] The autonomous knowing subject has been decisively undone: "Once the conscious subject is deprived of its role as source of meaning—once meaning is explained in terms of conventional systems which may escape the grasp of the conscious subject—the self can no longer be identified with consciousness."[91] Consciousness has been displaced by the body. The secret of the autonomous knowing subject is that it was really the projection of a culturally and historically situated body and its desires.

Many are unwilling to let the subject pass quietly into the good night of deconstruction. Nathan Scott decries this dismissal of the subject, for the loss of authorship entails the loss of freedom and responsibility as well: "The doctrine lately imported from Paris would have it that persons are simply linguistically encoded machines and that, far from being the impresarios of language, they are its slaves."[92] Once again, we see how disputes in the humanities presuppose views about what it is to be human, a theme to which we will return in due course.

Implied Authors. Another argument against the author's authority comes from literary critics themselves, for whom the idea of authorial voice is evidence not of metaphysical but *rhetorical* presence. According to Wayne Booth, an influential literary critic at the University of Chicago, the main reason we cannot treat authors as authorities concerning their texts "is that we have many different conceptions of 'the author.'"[93] There is first the flesh-and-blood person who produced the text—the real, historical, "empirical author." Next there is the dramatized author, the "I" who narrates many stories and who speaks in many poems. This voice, like the voice who narrates David Copperfield ("I am born"), must not be confused with the empirical author; Charles Dickens is not David Copperfield.

In between the flesh-and-blood author and the narrator stands an intermediate figure: the implied author. The author is "implied" by the general ethos of a literary work: "We infer him as an ideal, literary, created version of the real man; he is the sum of his own choices."[94] Booth's thesis is that the implied author, no less than the characters in the text, is an implication, effect, or rhetorical "construct" of the text. That sense of authorial presence, of an ordering mind whose values and beliefs "control" the text, is a fiction and should not be confused with the actual historical person who produced the work. As Booth pointedly observes, "Heroic implied authors can be created by cowards, and generous, tender-spirited implied authors can be created by self-centered monsters."[95]

Umberto Eco's personal testimony illustrates the contrast between the empirical author and the implied author. The title of his second novel, *Foucault's Pendulum*, refers to the pendulum invented by Léon Foucault and not to the philosopher Michel Foucault, as many "smart" readers believed. Eco asks, "How can . . . the empirical author disprove certain free semantic associations that the words he used in some way authorize?"[96] Speaking for himself as an empirical author, Eco observes: "I was not responsible for this allusion. But what does 'I' mean? My conscious personality? My id? The play of language (of *la langue*) that was taking place in my mind when I was writing?"[97] His conclusion: the text and title are there; perhaps he *is* responsible for a superficial joke that he expressly wished to avoid. At any rate, "the whole affair is by now out of my control."[98] For Eco, we need to speak of the empirical author "only in order to stress his irrelevance and to reassert the rights of the text."[99] Enquiries about the empirical author may shed some light on how the text came to be, but not on what the text means.

The Death of the Author

By a strange reversal of fortunes, then, contemporary literary theory views the author as an effect of the text rather than its cause. The logocentric notion of a stable principle of meaning has been exposed as a metaphysical pretension. The notion of the author as lord of textual meaning was more than a metaphysical error, however. Some critics contend that the notion of the author is a repressive ideological construct that performs a political function. For such critics, the author must die if the text is to live and the reader is to be liberated.

Two French Epitaphs. Roland Barthes and Michel Foucault have each written epitaphs—words on the tomb—for the author. According to Roland Barthes, the author is a modern invention, the product of the individualism that accompanied Enlightenment rationalism and Reformation piety. Traditional interpretation, he complains, is captive to a personality cult: "The image of literature to be found in contemporary culture is tyrannically centered on the author, his person, his history, his tastes, his passions."[100] Barthes praises the French poet Mallarmé for being the first to see "the necessity to substitute language itself for the person who until then had been supposed to be its owner."[101] Mallarmé wants his writing to speak for itself; the author must die so that writing may live: "Writing is the destruction of every voice, of every point of origin."[102] Of course, Mallarmé knows that he is the historical cause of his poem, but in giving pride of place to writing he acknowledges that he is only weaving with words spun by others. Writing is the space where the individual subject slips away.

Once a piece of writing is distanced from the author, it is pointless to "decipher" a text: "To give a text an Author is to impose a limit on that text, to furnish it with a final signified, to close the writing."[103] A text is the crossroads where multiple writings, proceeding from different cultures and times, meet. Barthes here echoes the structuralist idea that the individual is merely the site where multiple languages and ideologies—nationalism, modernism, fundamentalism, feminism, etc.—intersect. The text, too, "is not a line of words releasing a single 'theological' meaning (the 'message' of the Author-God) but a multi-dimensional space in which a variety of writings, none of them original, blend and clash."[104]

What is particularly striking about Barthes's announcement of the death of the author is its connection to the death of God. Like Derrida, Barthes holds that the belief in meaning, in something that transcends the play of signs, is inherently theological. The author is God to his text: its creator, cause, and master. The reader is obliged to be the author's servant, passively collecting the meaning that, like manna, comes from the hand of the maker. Freed from the author, however, the text becomes a playground on which readers can exercise their own creativity. The death of the author becomes a necessary step in refusing to assign a "real" meaning to the text. Non-realism demands the death of the author in order to turn the traditional "Platonism of meaning" on its head. No longer reduced to a single message with a single correct interpretation, the text is opened to a pluralism of readings; meaning is effectively destabilized, and authority withers on the textual vine.

On a more traditional view of interpretation, the authenticity of a biblical book and its place in the canon are thought to be a function of who authored them. Apocryphal works of unknown or uncertain authorship were believed to possess inferior authority.[105] In the ancient church, the claim to authenticity was all-important, and disputes about who authored what were not so much academic debates as they were power struggles. The early church was aware of forgery and did not tolerate it.[106] Even today, many of the conservative-liberal debates are over the authorship of individual biblical books. As recently as the late nineteenth century, William Robertson Smith was tried for heresy for denying the Mosaic authorship of the Pentateuch and was removed from his professorial chair in Aberdeen. Those responsible for that decision perhaps glimpsed what is now all too apparent: without authors, texts have neither authority nor determinate sense.

What, asks Michel Foucault, *is* an author? Why assign a proper name to a given text? In addressing these questions, Foucault is interested primarily in how the concept of the author *functions*. The idea of the author functions as a unifying principle that allows one to group certain texts together and treat them as though they constituted a coherent group. For example, "Paul" functions as a device that enables us to smooth over awkward discrepancies between the letters to the Romans, Galatians, Corinthians, Ephesians, and so on. In addition to being the unifying principle of a single work, the author serves to neutralize the contradictions that might otherwise be found in a series of texts. The author saves us from hermeneutic relativism and from the indeterminacy of meaning. Interpreters may want to believe in a rational presence who controls textual meaning, but such a belief, according to Foucault, is dishonest if not idolatrous. The author is a stopgap figure invented by interpreters frightened by the prospect of endless meaning: "The author is the principle of thrift in the proliferation of meaning. . . . The author is therefore the ideological figure by which one masks the manner in which we fear the proliferation of meaning."[107]

With regard to the nature of historical authors, Foucault believes, like Barthes, that one's language and thought is always already structured by the dominant vocabularies of a given era and culture. For Foucault, "What is an author?" is no longer a metaphysical question. The author is not born a subject but only *becomes* one when he or she is "subjected" to a system of differences and distinctions—in short, when subjugated to a language. In yet another version of hermeneutical non-realism, Foucault examines the history of ideas and institutions and concludes that the "order of things" is neither given nor necessary. There is no such thing as universal truth about human beings. It may have seemed universally true to readers of *Pride and Prejudice* "that a single man in possession of a good fortune must be in want of a wife," but Foucault would contend that Jane Austen was only reflecting the "regime" of knowledge/truth/power that formed the mentality of the day. In our day, says Foucault, we have learned to replace the concept of "Man" with "Language." Indeed, Foucault announces the death of "Man": the autonomous subject whose speech is his own is no more. The author, similarly, is an idea whose use is no longer required. Instead of asking "Who is the real author?" or "What did he or she mean?" Foucault encourages us to raise new questions: "What is the ideology of this text; what is it trying to do; who controls it?" Behind these questions, however, lurks another, murmured with indifference: "What does it matter who's speaking?"

Between Atheism and Humanism. The fates of the author of traditional literary criticism and of the God of traditional theism stand or fall together. The death of the one has precipitated the death of the other. For the unbeliever, neither God nor meaning are mind-independent realities. What do unbelievers believe in? Is it possible to think, or act, at all without holding some metaphysical assumptions? Rowan Williams offers a helpful alternative definition of metaphysics as the attempt to clarify those basic insights into the nature of the real to which our practice commits us.[108] The point is that, in practice, *everyone* is committed to some kind of worldview. What, then, are the underlying commitments that fund the practice of deconstruction? Is it atheism? Is deconstruction "the death of God put into writing"?[109]

A number of theologians have struggled to articulate what theology might be like after deconstruction. For Carl Raschke, theology becomes "the composition of epitaphs."[110] The God that "dies" (i.e., the God that has become unbelievable to many inhabitants of late modernity and postmodernity) is the God of metaphysics and of theism—the Supreme Being, the Absolute, the all-knowing subject. Need the death of the metaphysical deity spell the end of theology? Could deconstruction perhaps be construed as "negative theology put into writing," where "negative" theology stands for the notion that God cannot be grasped by human categories? Several of Derrida's commentators have noted the similarity between *différance* and the God of negative theology.[111] Indeed, Derrida himself states: "Language has started without us, in us and before us. This is what theology calls God."[112]

It is too early to tell whether deconstruction and negative theology will prove to be allies. My own view is that Derrida would not be happy, having undone the God of metaphysics, to let him in through the back door of *différance*. The main point I wish to make, however, is that beliefs about human authors are tied to beliefs about God. The unbelievers find it impossible to accept either the traditional picture of God or that of the author, for both pictures assume a kind of agency and intelligence that stands outside language and controls it, making sure that words correspond to the world and guaranteeing the reliability and truth of speech. Ludwig Feuerbach, arguably the "grandmaster of suspicion," undid theological realism when he suggested that God was actually a projection of human values and beliefs. "God" is a construction, an objectification, by which human beings express their consciousness of the infinite. Consciousness of God is for Feuerbach indistinguishable from self-consciousness: "The divine being is nothing else than the human being, or rather, the human nature purified, freed from the limits of the individual man, made objective, i.e., contemplated and revered as another, a distinct being. All the attributes of the divine nature are, therefore, attributes of the human nature."[113] Feuerbach summarized his "deconstruction" of God with a short formula: atheism is the secret of religion.

According to postmodern unbelievers, the author is the projection of the reader in much the same way that God, for Feuerbach, is the projection of human being. As Feuerbach reveals atheism to be the secret of religion, so Derrida shows that absence is the secret of presence. All our habitual vocabularies and systems of thought conspire to hide a terrible truth: that there is no authoritative presence behind the text, nothing above or below what we say that "earths" it in reality.

This leads me to the final "master of suspicion": Charles Darwin. Both Rorty and Derrida, and perhaps Users and Undoers generally, see the world as a field of conflicting impersonal forces. Rorty acknowledges that "pragmatism starts out from Darwinian naturalism."[114] The way the world, including humans, is, is a result of chance happenings in the cosmos. Derrida is similarly Darwinian, though less explicitly so. The great systems or "stabilizations" that deconstruction sets out to undo are constructs—stabilizations "of something essentially unstable and chaotic."[115] Stability, in other words, is for Derrida always non-natural and man-made. Chaos and instability are the "first truths," as it were, of postmodernity. For if one accepts the Darwinian premise, then the distinction between an original goodness and a subsequent fallenness is simply unavailable. Hence, neither Rorty nor Derrida can acknowledge the possibility of a stable structure that would be part of a created order, and therefore good; rather, all structures are only futile attempts to create temporary stability out of an inherently unstable and recalcitrant world.

The question remains: To what vision of God, and of human beings, does the practice of deconstruction and the undoing of the author give rise? Hermeneutical non-realism seems to have begotten two contradictory pictures of interpretation after the death of the author, one characterized by an ineradicable sense of world-weariness, the other by an indefatigable sense of joy. In other words, is the loss of God, and hence of meaning, a cause for grief or for rejoicing?

The work of Mark C. Taylor and Don Cupitt, the leading American and English exponents of deconstructive theology respectively, is permeated with a manic-depressive tension between grief and relief at the deaths of God, the author, and meaning.[116] On the one hand, Taylor and Cupitt celebrate the end of authority: "God" constrains humanity as "meaning" constrains the reader. The age of the author is, for these thinkers, the age of oppression. The "real"—the stable order of things defined by words with stable meanings—hinders human freedom. With regard to language, Cupitt is a User: "Words are only the noises we happen to use to do purely human jobs. They don't *need* to have Meanings. . . ."[117] Like Nietzsche, Taylor and Cupitt try to turn the loss of meaning into a net gain for humanity. For it is only when we abandon the hope of a higher life and of recovering the hidden meaning of life that we can abandon ourselves to this life. We can frolic on the surface of the world, in the froth on which we impose our own distinctions. For Cupitt, the *summum bonum* is located not in another life, but in this one: "The happiness that comes when one realizes that one is completely immersed in and interwoven with the whole endless flux of things is *ecstatic immanence*."[118] In a startling reversal of Plato, the non-realist claims that the only distinctions in the world are the ones our words have invented; "for the anti-realist we are the only makers of meanings, truths and values, and our theoretical postulates, such as God, gravity and justice, have no being apart from the language in which we speak of them and the practical uses to which we put it."[119]

In his 1966 article, Derrida distinguished two ways of responding to the demise of logocentrism: one can mourn and write epitaphs, or one can celebrate and write eulogies. Nietzsche pursued the latter course, affirming the freeplay of the world "without truth, without origin, offered to an active interpretation."[120] Nihilism—the denial of meaning, authority, and truth—must not only be accepted, but *affirmed*. Only by affirming the death of the author can we be rid of the "Platonism of meaning" that prevents us from exploring our own creativity as readers.

Is the death of the author, or nihilism for that matter, truly liberating, or are the celebrations premature? Is there any place for joy and freedom in the wake of the death of God? Taylor and Cupitt, rather ironically, would have us believe that this is how things *really are*, and acknowledge the inconsistency of their making such a claim with blithe equanimity. Anything more than a shrug of the shoulders could, of course, suggest that they were trying to stake a truth claim. In fact, their position is parasitic on the deconstruction of metaphysics and on the undoing of the author.

A comprehensive response to the death of the author must await Part 2. One critical observation, however, would not be out of place. Seán Burke argues that those who wish to kill the author are responding to the excesses of those Romantic philosophers (e.g., Fichte, Schelling) who exaggerated the powers of the creative imagination in the first place. For poets such as Wordsworth, Nature "is no longer simply given but is in need of aesthetic completion."[121] The poet is no longer a privileged observer of God's handiwork but is now seen as imitating the divine act of creation itself. Johann Herder could thus remark: "The author is become a Creator-God."[122] Burke regrets the association between the concept of God and the concept of the author, for he believes that the Undoers are reacting against a false absolutist picture of the author as creative master of language. Models of the author are either too transcendent or too immanent: in the former case, the author is the master of language; in the latter, he or she is its slave. The author is either an autonomous agent or no agent at all. As I will argue in Part 2, human agency—in particular human freedom and responsibility—is indeed at stake, and what is needed is not a rejection of theological models but a more appropriate theological anthropology. For as Burke rightly comments, "the great crises of postmodernism are crises of authorship."[123]

UNDOING THE AUTHOR'S INTENTION

The death of the author, then, is much more than an item in current literary theory. It has to do with a radical critique of the task of interpretation and of the way Western culture has traditionally understood itself in relation to the classic texts of literature, philosophy, and the Christian faith. As we have seen, premodernity and modernity alike shared a similar aim in interpretation: to recover the meaning of the text, understood in terms of the intention of the author. Whether this was the intention of the human author (as in modernity) or of the divine author (as in much Medieval exegesis) was of secondary importance; up until fairly recently, there was a near consensus on the importance of the author's intention.[124] In short, the author's intention is the object of traditional interpretation, the longed-for "home of meaning" where the author's will, words, and world coincide.

What Derrida undoes is the possibility that the author's intention can serve as the ground and goal of interpretation. Are meanings voice-controlled? As we have seen, Derrida exposes an "ugly ditch" between conscious speech and "writing." Derrida contends that writing—the artificial and arbitrary system of differences and distinctions in terms of which an individual thinks and speaks—frustrates the conscious aims of the author. The author as sovereign subject has been undone, exposed as a metaphysical, rhetorical, and ideological construct. The author, like the signs he uses, is only a cipher that stands at a swirling crosscurrent of various competing forces and discourses that constitute him or her. Indeed, Harold Bloom portrays the author not as a master in command of his discourse, but as one who struggles to make one's voice heard over and distinct from those of previous texts. The case against the author seems so strong that we must ask whether an author can *ever* say what he or she means.

Meaning Defined: The Author's Intention as Ground, Goal, and Guide of Interpretation

In what follows I will develop the case for defining meaning and interpretation in terms of authorial intention by exploring E. D. Hirsch's magisterial defense of the position in *Validity in Interpretation*.[125] There are several reasons for choosing Hirsch as my point of departure. First, though he is a literary critic by profession, Hirsch has come to be regarded by many biblical exegetes as the preeminent champion of the author and of objectivity in interpretation. Second, he is one of the chief proponents of hermeneutical realism and valid interpretation on the contemporary scene; he believes that textual meaning is unchanging and determinate and that interpretations can be valid and correct. Third, Hirsch's work has attracted considerable attention; there are many chapter- and even book-length studies of his position. Fourth, Hirsch represents a good example of the particular version of author-oriented criticism to which the Undoers and Users have objected.[126]

Ground

Hirsch defines meaning as the message that the author intends to convey via the text. Interpretation is the quest for meaning, that is, the author's intended message. Everything depends for Hirsch on the objectivity and stability of the author's intention, which grounds and fixes meaning. It is thanks to the author's intention that the meaning of a text remains the same over time (and thus can be shared by many readers).

It is important to distinguish Hirsch's version of author's intention from other, more psychologistic accounts that owe more to a Romanticist desire for empathy and experience than to the quest for scientific knowledge. In German Romanticism in particular, works of genius and art were considered expressions of the self. Herder could write in 1778, for example, that *"living reading*, this divination into the soul of the author, is the *sole* mode of reading, and the most profound means of self-development."[127] Georges Poulet and the Geneva School of critics have more recently espoused this view of texts as the verbal embodiment of the author's consciousness. The goal of reading is to become so receptive as to reconstitute, perhaps even participate in, the author's own consciousness. Good interpretation, on this view, is a meeting of the minds of author and reader. As Poulet put it: "When I read as I ought . . . I am thinking the thoughts of another. . . . My consciousness behaves as though it were the consciousness of another."[128]

It is equally important to distinguish Hirsch's position from the one he attacks, namely, that a text has a meaning of its own. Texts do not have "careers," much less lives, of their own. They do not bring themselves into existence nor can they change what they are over the course of time. As far as Hirsch is concerned, "the meaning of the text" simply is "the meaning of the author." There is no significant or sustainable distinction between the two. In making this equivalence, Hirsch is claiming something about the nature of texts as well as about meaning, namely, that there can be no texts without authors. If, for instance, a wave arranges the pebbles on the shore into a pattern that resembles the phrase, "To be or not to be," Hirsch would deny that the arrangement of the pebbles was a text. Further, it would be a mistake to try and interpret the pebbles, for strictly speaking, they have no message.[129] For there to be meaning, there must be intention.

What are intentions? In ordinary usage, one's intention refers to what one plans to do. We speak of doing something intentionally as opposed to doing it accidentally. Even in this ordinary sense, intention is a mental phenomenon; molecules and machines have neither purposes nor intentions but are rather controlled by physical laws. Hirsch, however, uses "intention" in a more technical, philosophical sense, appealing in particular to the phenomenology of Edmund Husserl.[130] Intentionality means that human consciousness is always *about*, or *directed at*, something. Initially, Husserl directed his work against precisely the kind of Romantic psychologizing that focused on a person's experience rather than on the *object* of that experience.[131] It would therefore be a mistake to link Hirsch with Romanticist notions about recovering the author's *psyche*.

Husserl makes what for Hirsch is a critical distinction between an *act* of consciousness and an *object* of consciousness. It is of the essence of consciousness that it is always consciousness *of* something. One cannot simply be conscious. Even when we first awake in the morning, we are conscious *of* our being awake, *of* it being a new day. That consciousness is always *awareness of something* is, moreover, what separates mental from physical phenomena. Mental phenomena—the acts of consciousness— are always directed at something (e.g., a thought, a belief, a hope, a perception).[132] An "intention" is the act by which consciousness aims at something. Every intentional act of consciousness has an intentional object, that towards which consciousness aims. For example, the intentional object of believing is a proposition, while the intentional object of choosing is a possibility. Consciousness is intentional because it is always *about* something. Indeed, all acts of consciousness—perceiving, remembering, wishing, willing, believing, as well as meaning—are "intentional." For example, a belief can be about bananas (a banana, by contrast, is not "about" anything). Clearly, Hirsch has moved beyond the ordinary psychological understanding of intentionality (e.g., what an author was trying or planning to do).

By author's intention, then, Hirsch would have us understand the object (e.g., message) of which the author was conscious. The meaning of a text is not to be mistaken with a subjective mental act, either of the author or of the interpreter, but with the *object* of that act. There is meaning, says Hirsch, when someone wills to convey something by a particular sequence of signs. A spider's web, though it is a highly structured phenomenon, doesn't *mean* anything. Similarly, a random sequence of words generated by waves, or by a monkey, or by a computer doesn't mean anything either. Words alone do not mean, people do. Why? Because, says Hirsch, meaning is "an affair of consciousness, not of words."[133] Furthermore, a sequence of words means nothing in particular until someone actually wills to mean something by it: "The interpreter's job is to reconstruct a determinate actual meaning, not a mere system of possibilities."[134] Hirsch wants to recover not *langue* (the language system), but *parole* (the way that language was used on a particular occasion). Though the event of the author's intending cannot be reproduced, its object can be. Its reproducibility guarantees objectivity in meaning and in interpretation. The meaning of a text—what it says and what it is about—is stabilized by the author's intention.

Goal

Interpretation for Hirsch, therefore, is about recovering or reconstructing the author's intended meaning. The author's intention, he believes, provides a genuine norm for literary knowledge: "All valid interpretation, of every sort, is founded on the re-cognition of what an author meant."[135] Not just any recovery will do, however. Interpretation must be scientific, not a form of divination or spiritism. Interpretation must, therefore, have a method for gaining knowledge about its object: "What is at stake is the right of interpretation (and implicitly all humanistic disciplines) to claim as its object genuine knowledge."[136] Knowledge is objective only when it corresponds to a fixed object. The aim of the reader is to "think" the same "object" as the author. Hirsch thus believes that the goal of interpretation is *shared meaning*. His purpose in writing is "to give encouragement to those who are still willing to entertain the belief that knowledge is possible even in textual interpretation."[137]

Central to Hirsch's view about the goal of interpretation is the distinction between subject and object. Meaning must not be reduced, either to the intentional acts that produce it or to the intentional acts that seek to reproduce it. Different acts of consciousness may be directed at the *same* intentional object. My whole family can intend the same object—say, "next Christmas"—as the common object of our respective acts of "looking forward to." Meaning—the object of an author's intention—may similarly be shared by various readers. Hirsch defines verbal meaning as "the shareable content of the speaker's intentional object."[138] *An interpreter grasps the meaning of a text when he or she experiences sameness of content (or object) despite differentness of context.* On Hirschian terms, therefore, the meaning of the text can never simply be "what the text means *to me*." Valid interpretation is always a public affair. The goal of interpretation, then, is thus to reconstruct the single correct meaning of the text.

Guide

Hirsch has been widely criticized for his definition of meaning. The most frequent objection is that it is a stipulative definition that only has the force of a personal recommendation. Hirsch is doing a bit more than stating his personal preference, however. He is saying that unless you make the author's intended meaning the norm for interpretation, you will have no reliable means for discriminating between valid and invalid interpretations—between exegesis (what one gets out of texts) and eisegesis (what one puts into texts).

Hirsch also distinguishes "meaning" from "significance." Whereas the meaning is what the author intended, significance refers to the relation the author's meaning has to something else. "Meaning" is internal to the text-in-itself; "significance" describes the external relation a text's meaning has to something else: "Significance is always 'meaning-to,' never 'meaning-in.'"[139] On this view, the meaning of a text is unchanging, but its significance is inexhaustible, for the text, though "fixed" in itself, can enter new situations. Thus, while the "intentional object" (viz., the author's intended meaning) remains self-identical and unchanging, the various subsequent "intentional acts" that grasp it do not. Hirsch reserves the name "interpretation" for commentary on a text's meaning and calls discussion about a text's significance "criticism." To deny this crucial distinction entails a skepticism and relativism in interpretation insofar as it blurs the difference between what a text means in itself and what a text means to me. Yet it is precisely this distinction between meaning and significance, yet another binary opposition in which one term is subordinate to another, that postmoderns try to undo.

To sum up: for Hirsch, meaning is a matter of conscious acts and only incidentally of words: "A word sequence means nothing in particular until somebody means something by it. . . . There is no magic land of meanings outside human consciousness."[140] The author enjoys authority because conscious intention, not the range of possible dictionary definitions, is the source of stable meaning. The correct interpretation is the one that apprehends the author's intended meaning.

Has Hirsch grasped the true nature of interpretation, or is he guilty of the "metaphysical impulse," that is, of creating conceptual dichotomies (e.g., validity/invalidity; objective/subjective; meaning/significance) in order to impose his own will on other readers and to discipline literary criticism? Whatever we decide about Hirsch's "metaphysical impulse," it is clear that Derrida's "deconstructive impulse" is to undo distinctions that appear to be natural and necessary.

Interrogating Intention

Is it legitimate to appeal to what an author intended? The notion that the author's intention serves as ground, goal, and guide of interpretation prompts three fundamental questions: (1) the metaphysical question: What is the author's intention, and where is it located? (2) the epistemological question: Can we gain knowledge of an author's intention, and can we know when we have done so? (3) the ethical question: Why should we strive to recover the author's intention?

Whose Intention? Which Consciousness? What Context?

In Hirsch's account, "the author's meaning" assumes the role of the logocentric principle that stands above language and to which interpretation must correspond if it is to be "true" and "correct."[141] "What an author intended" becomes for Hirsch a transcendent, self-identical, stable, and unchanging object that grounds meaning because it somehow stands *outside* a system of signifiers. Meaning, it turns out, is a case of mind over linguistic matter.

Hirsch's belief in "the author's intention" puts him squarely on the side of what postmoderns dismiss as a "Platonism of meaning." According to his critics, Hirsch makes "the author's intention" into a thing-in-itself: "Hirsch endows meaning with all the properties of the classical notion of substantial reality (*res*), which is to say that he reifies it."[142] The Undoer claims that Hirsch seals off the home of meaning from the ill effects of writing. Does Hirsch effectively protect meaning from the instability and the freeplay of signs? If meaning is an affair of consciousness, are intentions in the author's head? Hirsch rejects the idea that readers can enter into some kind of mystical communion with the author. Authorial intent must rather be inferred from the text. But this means that intentionality is linguistically mediated: "Intentionality . . . is itself a text and must be subject to the fundamental condition of textuality that he [Hirsch] has announced: radical ambiguity. It is clear that he wishes to free intention from the contaminations of writing, but how this is to be done he never tells us."[143]

In his essay "Signature Event Context" Derrida opens up a conceptual gap—an "ugly ditch"—between verbal meaning and the author's intention. This "ugly ditch" also undoes the tie between a word sequence and any one specific context, for it is precisely the function of authorial intent to make a word sequence determinate by tying it to a particular context. For Derrida, the crucial point about signs is that they can be repeated in the absence of the one who produced them: "But the sign possesses the characteristic of being readable even if the moment of its production is irrevocably lost and even if I do not know what its alleged author-scriptor consciously intended to say at the moment he wrote it, i.e., abandoned it to its essential drift."[144]

Derrida does not deny the concept of intention, only that it is constitutive of a text's meaning. "'The question is,' said Alice, 'whether you *can* make words mean different things.'"[145] The point is that when one writes, one writes in a language to whose laws and logic one must submit. A critical reading must aim "at a certain relationship, unperceived by the writer, between what he commands and what he does not command of the patterns of the language he uses."[146] Subjectivity and intentionality are not prior to, but a function of, forms of life and systems of language. Hence, intention is never fully present to itself and is not transparent, even to the intender. In the words of Roland Barthes: "I am not an innocent subject, anterior to the text. . . . This 'me' which approaches a text is itself already a plurality of other texts."[147] In short: if the self is not a stable place outside the play of language, then intention cannot be so either.

Whereas for Hirsch language is essentially intentional, for Derrida language is essentially "iterable," that is, repeatable apart from an original intention (i.e., repeatable, but with a difference). Language both preexists and exceeds the author's intention. Language simply cannot be tied down to a single speaker, intention, or context. "One can always be quoted and therefore quoted out of context, against one's wishes. Iterability absents any intention."[148] A piece of language that could only be used once would not be language. Because a sign or a text can appear in new contexts, *iterability means non-identical repetition*. No authorial intention, no matter how intense, can prevent this contextual drift: "This essential drift bearing on writing as an iterative structure, cut off from all absolute responsibility, from *consciousness* as the ultimate authority, orphaned and separated at birth from the assistance of its father, is precisely what Plato condemns in the *Phaedrus*."[149] Derrida demonstrates how texts can drift away from their author's original intent in his essay "The Double Session." He there places texts by Plato and Mallarmé side by side, forcing the reader to make connections between these different works and to read each in light of the other. In order to undermine the privilege of speech by exposing the vicissitudes of writing, Derrida approaches every text with the aim of showing how its language frustrates the author's intention. The author's will cannot determine the meaning of the text. Indeed, Derrida even implies that with regard to language, the author lacks free will.[150]

Can Intentions Be Recovered?

What the traditional interpreter aims at is nothing less than the "imaginative reconstruction of the speaking subject."[151] How can we know what an author was intending? Hirsch admits that certainty is impossible and that the literary critic deals in likelihoods: "In hermeneutics, verification is a process of establishing relative probabilities."[152] Derrida, however, raises significant objections to reconstructing intention and, consequently, to verifying interpretation.

Against Reconstructing. For Derrida, interpretation—the task of reconstructing the author's intention—is undermined by the nature of the linguistic sign itself. As we have seen, the meaning of a sign is not the thing it represents but rather a function of its differences from other signs. Moreover, iterability is a permanent feature of a sign. Thus the fundamental problem arises: When a sign, or a text, is repeated (or read) in a new context, how can we decide which of its significations belong to the original context (viz., the authorial intention) and which belong to the new one? "A written sign carries with it a force that breaks with its context."[153] To repeat: iterability means *non-identical repetition*. What one hears in a different context may not be what the author intended to say. No amount of authorial intention can prevent this "contextual drift." Iterability undoes intentionality.

For many postmodern critics, then, "the author's intended meaning" is simply the name we give to the interpretations we like best. It would be preferable to speak not of "reconstructions" but simply of "constructions." After all, the only person who now speaks for the author is the interpreter. There is no author's intention to be found apart from the process of interpretation itself.

Against Verifying. Hirsch's hermeneutic optimism (some would say naiveté) partly accounts for his cool reception on the part of other literary critics. Hirsch maintains, against the unbelievers, that objective knowledge in interpretation is possible. To the postmodern ear, this sounds suspiciously like a hermeneutical version of naive realism, the view that we can obtain a direct view of the world (or meaning) as it really is, as though our minds (and their intentional acts) did not get in the way. Yet even natural scientists today acknowledge the theory-ladenness of our observations. How do we know when the fit between our theories and reality is true rather than merely likely or possible? The demand for verification is every bit as problematic in the case of authorial intention: How do we know when we've got it? On the other hand, if the author's intended meaning is only an ideal goal rather than a practical help, we are left with the question of criteria of verification: "If the notion of author's intended meaning is only regulative, the interpreter has nothing against which to criticize his own understanding."[154]

Surely the critic can check reconstructions of the author's intention against the past, as would historians? And surely the past is a stable ground of meaning too, is it not? As the Red Queen said to Alice when she reversed her answer as to the cause of lightning, "It's too late to correct it. When you've once said a thing, that fixes it, and you must take the consequences." The non-realist, however, insists that there is no past reality to be found. As A. K. M. Adam notes: "Once again, as with 'author's intentions,' so with 'the past': when a modern interpreter insists that the historical record of the past makes his interpretation of a text the best, he is always only talking about *his own interpretation* of that historical record."[155]

Against Totalizing. Deconstruction is best located, I have suggested, in the tradition of critiques of reason. Even more so than Kant's, Derrida's is a philosophy of limits. What Derrida ultimately undoes is our confidence that *just these concepts* must be the rational ones. Every set of categories, every set of distinctions, and every way of conceptualizing the world are all alike relative, situated, and contextual—never absolute, transcendent, or universal. When one fully accepts this insight, one can see that the very line between philosophy and poetry, which so worried Plato, appears somewhat artificial too. One can see why Nietzsche claimed that truths were only metaphors whose metaphorical status we have forgotten. One can see why some deconstructors can suggest that metaphysics is only a good story (a metanarrative), or why philosophy might be considered a species of epic poetry. For the power of philosophy, like all great literature, consists in the power of language to shape the way we see, speak, and think about the world.

What Derrida resists is any notion that encourages the metaphysical impulse to "totalize," that is, to achieve a unified perspective—to gain mastery over something by reducing it to the size of something one can grasp. While Derrida accepts Saussure's point that language is a system of differences, he rejects the idea that these differences can ever be contained in a system. *Différance* is ultimately non-systematic. Because all human thought is mediated by language, and because humans never attain a viewpoint above or outside of language, we simply do not possess the means for achieving a total perspective. To pretend otherwise is to use totalitarian methods—to *impose* or to force onto others a set of distinctions that one finds, for whatever reason, attractive. One can achieve that kind of order in the world, or in an interpretation, only by repressing (often violently) those elements that contradict our totalizing vision.

Deconstruction is thus a strategy for "de-totalizing." To deconstruct a text is to take issue with the text not as it is in itself (that is inaccessible to us) but rather with the text as it has been constructed as a purported totality with a single, coherent, and unified meaning. Kevin Hart describes deconstruction as "the demonstration that no text can be totalized without a supplement of signification."[156] It is not, then, that Derrida destroys the notion of authorial intention, but that he shows its inadequacy to the task (i.e., the task of serving as the ground, goal, and guide of meaning). Hart rightly sees the connection between what is totalizing, what is transcendent, and what is theological: "Any claim that a text is or can be totalized is theological."[157] "Theology" and "metaphysics" describe for Derrida the desire and the demand for totality. Derrida believes, with Nietzsche, that the desire for totalizing is in fact a covert desire for power. Deconstruction resists "the author" because it sees authorship ultimately as an authoritarian concept.

Should We Try to Recover the Author's Intention?

Is the author's intention a merely arbitrary norm for interpretation? Hirsch writes: "No one disputes that a reader can *try* to realize the author's intended meaning. The two important questions are: (1) whether he should try, and (2) whether he could succeed if he did try."[158] Hirsch answers with emphatic affirmatives. Meaning is something that the author *wills*. There is no criterion with which to distinguish valid from invalid interpretation other than that of the author's intention. Thus, while the author's intention is not the only possible norm, it is for Hirsch the only *practical* norm for an academic discipline of interpretation. One's decision how to read is not simply an academic matter, however; it also pertains to what I have called the *morality* of knowledge: "The choice of an interpretive norm is not regarded by the 'nature of the text,' but, being a choice, belongs to the domain of ethics rather than the domain of ontology."[159]

Even friendly critics, however, question Hirsch's argumentation. P. D. Juhl contends that Hirsch's book should be read not as an argument but rather as a pragmatic recommendation: if you want validity in interpretation, read for authorial intention.[160] In a later essay, Hirsch claims that the choice between his own realism and the idealism of Derrida and Rorty is ultimately a political, rather than an epistemological, issue. It is, he argues, a question of what kind of culture we wish to foster.[161]

Such an admission plays into the hands of the Oxford literary theorist Terry Eagleton, who feels that the kind of interpretive culture Hirsch fosters is a repressive authoritarianism: "Anything which cannot be herded inside the enclosure of 'probable authorial meaning' is brusquely expelled, and everything remaining within that enclosure is strictly subordinated to this single governing intention."[162] The aim of this policing is, apparently, the protection of private property: "For Hirsch an author's meaning is his own, and should not be stolen or trespassed upon by the reader."[163] What undergirds Hirsch's choice to read for authorial intent, Eagleton suggests, is capitalism. Why could one not appeal to other criteria, such as the formal structure of the work or the response of a community of readers? Why must the author be the authority in interpretation? "Like most authoritarian regimes . . . Hirschian theory is quite unable rationally to justify its own ruling values."[164]

If poststructuralists are correct, then what speakers say and what authors write is conditioned, perhaps even determined, by the signifying systems (viz., languages, vocabularies) that precede them and by the system of binary oppositions they must use even when they find it objectionable (e.g., Paul continues to think in terms of master/slave even as he asks Philemon to treat Onesimus as a fellow Christian). Stephen Moore states that readers sometimes have an ethical obligation "to read against the ideological grain of the biblical text at times, to set aside the traditional task of reconstructing the author's intention."[165] For Moore, unlike Hirsch, reading for the sole purpose of gaining knowledge of the author's intention may be an *immoral* interpretive act.

Intentional Fallacies

For a number of contemporary literary critics, to appeal to "what the author intended" in the course of one's interpretation is to make a category mistake: a serious error in reasoning based on the misleading belief that the author has something to do with meaning. This mistake was first pointed out in 1946 by two literary critics.[166] However, in the light of the undoing of the author, I believe we can discern four distinct "intentional fallacies." Any subsequent attempt to appeal to the author's intention (such as the one I make in Part 2) will henceforth have to show how it is not guilty of these errors.

1. The Fallacy of Relevancy

"New Criticism" was a mid-twentieth century American and English movement that privileged the autonomy and formal unity of the text rather than the personality or biography of the author. W. K. Wimsatt and Monroe Beardsley, in a celebrated 1946 essay entitled "The Intentional Fallacy," declared that the author's intentions were irrelevant for all interpretive purposes. To say otherwise is to confuse a psychological question with an interpretive one. I shall refer to their objection as the Fallacy of Relevance or, more specifically, as the Fallacy of Imported Biography.

Wimsatt and Beardsley believed that the text as a verbal entity functions nicely on its own. Extrinsic facts about the author's life have no intrinsic connection to the meaning of his or her text. Author-oriented critics habitually make the category mistake of confusing psychology with semantics. "What the author *wanted* to do is thus no help in our determining what he has done."[167] Whereas Hirsch proclaims meaning "an affair of consciousness," Wimsatt and Beardsley observe that "meaning could be established only by seeing how the words were actually used—not by discovering what the author would have liked the words to mean."[168] New Criticism is a type of literary formalism; formalists hold that meaning is a matter of linguistic convention rather than authorial intention.

We can surely agree that an author's announcements—both prospective and retrospective—of his intentions or plan of his work are irrelevant, for the simple reason that the author may fail in his intent.[169] But can we generalize from this statement of irrelevance to the conclusion that *everything* about the author is irrelevant?

While many of its admirers take "The Intentional Fallacy" as a blanket dismissal of the author's relevance, the New Critics themselves continued to take account of the author's general context (e.g., linguistic, historical, cultural). It would be extremely difficult, perhaps impossible, to make sense of a text without presuming something about its background. Christopher Tuckett, for instance, observes that we have at the very least to decide in which language a text is written. We must know whether the letters p-a-i-n were written—which is to say, *intended*—in English or French.[170] We must also know something about the time in which a language was written in order to determine whether a word such as "bad" meant bad (e.g., as in nineteenth-century Victorian England) or good (e.g., as in late twentieth-century American street culture). Identifying the author answers both questions; to name the author is to determine the language (culture) and time (history) in which a text was written.

2. Fallacy of Transparency

A second group of critics attack Hirsch's assumptions that meaning is an affair of consciousness and that an author knows his or her own mind. The author's intended meaning is, for Hirsch, the one that is "present" to consciousness. As we have seen, this notion comes loaded with metaphysical and logocentric assumptions about human subjectivity. Hirsch's notion that consciousness is transparent to itself is the basis of what Lentricchia calls his "hermeneutics of innocence."[171]

Meaning, say Hirsch's opponents, is a matter not of consciousness, but of the subconscious, the unconscious, or the collective consciousness. Freud says that our conscious intentions are masks that hide our unconscious fears, drives, and desires. Lacan says that language is itself structured like the unconscious. Feminists point out, for instance, that the traditional Western language systems are prejudicial against women. Foucault generalizes the point even further: the system of signifiers we learn as children has the effect of fostering a particular kind of social order. The native speaker is not aware of the "deep structure" of the binary oppositions; the differences and distinctions it generates appear natural. Behind every "natural" language, however, is an arbitrary set of cultural values.

David Bordwell, in his classic study of film theory, speaks of "symptomatic" meanings. Unlike an author's explicit or intentional meaning, a "symptomatic" meaning is one that the work divulges "involuntarily."[172] Hitchcock's film *Psycho*, for example, is on one level about a crazed murderer, but Bordwell suggests that its symptomatic meaning may concern the male fear of female sexuality. (Something similar has been suggested by interpreters of Paul, Augustine, and Luther!) The point about symptomatic meanings is that they reflect subconscious or supraconscious (e.g., cultural) forces that lie outside the conscious intention and control of the author. The Fallacy of Transparency is cured by the "hermeneutics of suspicion" and its distrust of surface appearances. A text reveals less about an author's consciousness than about the cultural forces that shape his or her thinking. Behind the intended message of the author lie unintended messages about the history and society in which the author lived.

3. Fallacy of Identity

A third mistake—the Fallacy of Identity—collapses the distinction between the author's intention and what is said in the text by treating them as one and the same. Whereas the first fallacy makes an epistemological mistake by using what the author wanted to say as *evidence* for what he or she did say, this fallacy commits the *ontological* error of identifying meaning with a mental phenomenon. Paul Ricoeur argues that such an identification overlooks what happens when the author commits his or her thoughts to writing: "The author's intention and the meaning of the text cease to coincide."[173] Writing marks what Ricoeur calls the "semantic autonomy" of the text. Whereas the mental intention of the author is a short-lived event, the text launches out on a career of its own. The author's intention, as a moment in one's psychical life, is a transient event and can neither be reproduced nor shared. Like the New Critics, then, Ricoeur advocates a "de-psychologizing" of interpretation.[174]

For his part, Derrida argues that a text must necessarily differ from the author's intention, insofar as signs are, by their very nature, repeatable. Derrida does not imagine, however, that one can simply abandon the notion of authorial intention. What he puts into question is whether it can act as a logocentric principle and thus serve as the ground of meaning. Again, Derrida's purpose is not to destroy intention but to put it in its place: to situate, perhaps to insinuate it, in writing. Derrida's verdict on Rousseau can stand for his view of intentions in general: "His declared intention is . . . *inscribed* within a system which it no longer dominates."[175] In short, it is a mistake to confuse verbal meaning with a mental phenomenon.

4. Fallacy of Objectivity

Every version of hermeneutic realism demands some such distinction as that which Hirsch draws between meaning and significance—between a stable object and the series of attempts to perceive it. The realist insists that the interpretive object has a real independence, that it stands over against the interpretive acts. "Once it is admitted that a meaning can change its characteristics, then there is no way of finding the true Cinderella among the contenders. There is no dependable glass slipper we can use as a test. . . ."[176] Hermeneutic non-realists, on the other hand, hold that meaning is objectively undecidable. There is no glass slipper, only a slippery slope on which meaning slides uncontrollably into significance, so that the meaning of the text is in no way separable from its meaning for us.

Hirsch labels those who insist on the artificiality of the distinction between meaning and significance "dogmatic relativists" or "cognitive atheists."[177] He makes this judgment thanks to an outdated binary opposition (viz., objective/subjective) and a similarly outdated positivistic concept of science.[178] Philosophers of science such as Thomas Kuhn argue that scientific knowledge is not a copying of reality but a construction of it. The theories and assumptions we bring to the world—what Rorty calls our "vocabulary"—determine what we find there. It is not so much Hirsch's definition of meaning that needs redoing, according to this objection, so much as his outdated conception of scientific knowledge.

For the non-realist, the object of consciousness does not exist apart from the subjective acts of consciousness that constitute it. The later Husserl, flirting with idealism, seemed to think that the object of consciousness has neither being nor meaning apart from consciousness. He only kept himself from sliding into subjectivism by saying that no one subject's consciousness constitutes reality; reality is rather "the ideal object of all possible conscious acts."[179] This is not subjectivism, but something more akin to inter-subjectivism and to the authority of Fish's interpretive communities: "Reality is independent, not necessarily of thought in general, but only of what you or I or any finite number of men may think about it."[180]

If the distinction between a stable, unchanging meaning and a dynamic, changing significance cannot be maintained, then Hirsch's project of objectivist interpretation collapses. That the distinction does fail is, of course, the non-realist's thesis. For the non-realist, objects are really "projects"—products of our attempts to know them.

It should be evident that Hirsch's distinction between meaning (the stable selfsame message of the text itself) and significance (the changing message of the text for us) can no longer be maintained on these terms. The implications for meaning and for biblical authority of such a collapse are far-reaching: "What a text really means is . . . inseparable from the history of the interpretations it engenders."[181]

In the next two chapters, we will examine what sense, if any, can be made of the notions of the "meaning of the text" and "the meaning of the text for us" as opposed to "the meaning of the author." Does a text, cut off from its author, have any meaning, much less a career?

HAS THE BIBLE LOST ITS VOICE?

Why should biblical exegetes and theologians pay attention to postmodernity? What has "writing" to do with Holy Writ? We can point, in answer to the first question, to the growing influence not only of deconstruction but of a number of other post-structuralist approaches to exegesis. Moreover, a number of critical approaches that apparently little or nothing to do with deconstruction nevertheless share Derrida's suspicion of logocentric interpretation. With regard to the second question, perhaps it is sufficient to point out that the Bible, while in some ways a special case, is in many respects like any other text. If signs in general are unreliable guides to reality, why should the Bible be any different?

Norman Petersen notes that biblical critics are often "victims of an academic cultural lag."[182] Stephen Moore comments that, while biblical scholars have engaged in the debate about authorial intent, they have "tended to gloss over its complexities."[183] What are the consequences for biblical interpretation of the death of the author? There seems to be a connection of sorts between the breakup of the author's monopoly on meaning, on the one hand, and the proliferation of approaches to interpretation on the other. If there is no stable ground of meaning (no hermeneutical realism), then there is ultimately nothing that stands over against our interpretations to challenge and correct them. If the distinction between text and commentary is undone, then the image in the mirror of the text becomes blurry indeed. In that case, it is impossible to say whether we are seeing an author's intended message, an objective meaning, or merely our own reflections.

Biblical Interpretation and Authority

Historically, the authority of the biblical texts was closely related to the question of authorship. It was commonly held that prophetic or apostolic authority was the most important criterion for including a text in the canon. Furthermore, commentators since the Renaissance and Reformation have made the author's intended meaning their exegetical goal. Significantly, the first works of biblical criticism in this era questioned claims to prophetic or apostolic authorship. In the seventeenth century, for example, Thomas Hobbes claimed that Moses could not have written the whole Pentateuch. About the same time, Spinoza suggested that all twelve books from Genesis to 2 Kings were probably written by Ezra. Yet even the most radical historical critics, who denied that Moses, Paul, or the Evangelists wrote the books that bear their names, still believed that the meaning of a text is the author's intended meaning (whoever that may be), which can be inferred from a study of the text and its original situation. The idea of the author was essential to textual meaning, even though his identity might be contested. For the postmodern literary critic, however, the author's voice is undecidable and indecipherable; there is no presence that can "fix" or halt the play of possible textual meanings.

How does such authorial laryngitis affect biblical authority? The answer is brief but massive in its implications: *biblical authority is undone*. The Undoers effectively strip the Bible of any stable meaning so that it cannot state a fact, issue a command, or make a promise. Furthermore, without the author to serve as touchstone of the distinction between meaning and significance, every interpretation becomes just as authorized a version as another. A text that cannot be set over against its commentary is no authority at all. Finally, biblical authority is undermined by the instability of meaning because, if nothing specific is said, the text cannot call for any specific response. Interpreters can give neither obedience nor belief to texts that lack specificity. If there is no meaning in the text, then there is nothing to which the reader can be held accountable.

Jesus As Author of Faith: Is Christology Logocentric?

"There is nothing outside the text." This would probably have come as a surprise to the authors of the New Testament, for whom their documents were testimonies of a reality they believed to be more than the product of the play of signifiers.

According to the Prologue of the Fourth Gospel, Jesus is the "Word of God," the Word (*logos*) who was (and is) with God and who is God. Jesus, one might say, is both signifier and signified; he does not only represent God but is himself God's presence. His name—Immanuel—describes his nature: "God with us." Jesus Christ is God's tabernacle on earth (John 1:14), the body in whom "God was pleased to have all his fullness dwell" (Col. 1:19), in whose face is reflected the knowledge and glory of God (2 Cor. 4:6). The New Testament presents Jesus not as the "trace" of God but as God's "image," reflecting the glory of God and bearing "the exact representation of his being" (Heb. 1:3). The belief in Jesus as the Logos, therefore, seems to be a prime instance of what Derrida attacks as "logocentrism." Jesus Christ is the referent of the biblical texts, as Jesus himself explained to his disciples at Emmaus: "Then beginning with Moses and all the prophets, he interpreted to them the things about himself in all the scriptures" (Luke 24:27, NRSV). What the deconstructor finds objectionable about Christology is the claim *that Jesus is a reliable sign of God's own being and presence*. "Christian theology, with its doctrinal emphasis upon purity of origins—*creatio ex nihilo*, Mary's immaculate conception and Jesus' virginal conception—stands as a paradigm for the metaphysics of presence. Derrida can therefore speak, in one breath, of 'the philosophical or Christian idea of pure origin.'"[184]

As we will see below, deconstruction is more like the Jewish tradition, in which the commentaries on biblical books became sacred texts in their own right and generated further commentary.[185] The implication is that Christianity privileges speech—the living word—in a way that Judaism does not. Yet it would be an exaggeration to say that "Christianity engendered an attitude of principled mistrust toward the written word."[186] Derrida's association of Christianity with the biases of logocentrism is not wholly justified. Certainly origins are important. Both the Gospels of Mark and John begin with the Greek word for "beginning" (*archē*). Similarly, Hebrews 12:2 calls Jesus the "author" (*archēgos*) of our faith. Earlier in the same letter he is called the "author of . . . salvation" (Heb. 2:10). Colossians identifies him as the one "by whom all things were created" (Col. 1:16). Not only is Jesus the sign of the presence of God, but he is the originator of creation and salvation. Jesus' supreme authority follows from his authorship. Moreover, the Bible virtually defines life and death, heaven and hell, in terms of God's presence and absence. The story of salvation is the story of how humanity regains the presence of God through God's gracious gift of Christ.[187]

The Johannine letters describe the knowledge of God in terms of a relationship: life in the transforming presence of the Logos. We also find in these letters a vigorous defense of the principle of bivalence. John speaks of beliefs that must be either true or false. Either Christ is the "home" or locus of God's presence, truth, light, and the fullness of being and grace, or he is not. Jesus himself certainly appeared to have a logocentric understanding: "I am the light of the world"; "I am the way and the truth and the life" (John 8:12; 14:6). Christology here appears wholly logos-centric: Jesus Christ is the source and center, not only of meaning and truth, but of joy, freedom, and abundant life as well. Much of the Johannine letters is given over to warning about antichrists. These texts give us not merely rhetorical, but pragmatic criteria—two "vital" signs—for discerning God's "real presence": one's confession of Jesus as the Christ come in the flesh, and one's living a life of love. According to John, only the Spirit's vivifying presence can enable one to make such a confession and live such a life.

There is some warrant, therefore, in calling Christianity logocentric. Against Derrida, however, this emphasis on God's presence in Christ does not lead to a diminished regard for the written word.[188] That divine revelation is mediated through Word and Spirit—that is, through Scripture read in faith—was a constant theme of the Reformers, for instance. And, precisely because the written word is accompanied by the Spirit, the Christian need not choose between logocentrism and writing (as defined by Derrida). On the contrary, the authenticity of the written text is guaranteed by a "real presence."[189] In the Christian tradition, then, written words may mediate personal presence, just as Christ mediates the presence of God.

After Authorship: Whither "the Meaning of the Text"?

Recovering the author's intent remains the goal of much modern exegesis, even if the author is demythologized, that is, stripped of his supposed inspiration and apostolicity. Even many literary critics continue to hold the view "that the gospel text has a primary, recoverable meaning: what its author intended."[190]

Postmodern Biblical Criticism

More radical literary critics—the "postmoderns"—no longer assume that the individual Gospels are shaped by a single author or even that they display a unified single purpose. The postmodern reader has awakened from the dream of stable meanings. James Dawsey's *The Lukan Voice: Confusion and Irony in the Gospel of Luke*, for instance, is a painstaking analysis of the contradictory voices and points of view that inhabit Luke's Gospel. Dawsey suggests, using statistical analyses among other techniques, that the point of view of the narrator of Luke's Gospel differs from that of Jesus, and from the "real" author's too. The narrator is unreliable and writes from a theological perspective that the author does not endorse: "In a sense, the author sided with Jesus against his own narrator."[191] Moore poses a difficult question: "Having loosed a cacophony of voices and viewpoints, can Dawsey instigate closure by subjugating this cacophony to a controlling authorial voice and viewpoint?"[192] Echoing the suspicion that the author is really an ideological construct, Moore asks: "If he is not simply to be regarded as a historical figure inefficiently managing our scholarly discourse in absentia, from some remote point antecedent and external to it, who or what is he in addition?"[193] Who, or what, is "Luke"? The postmodern reply is uncompromising: "Luke" is the name we give to our best interpretation; "Luke" is a projection of our desire for a unifying center and ground to textual meaning; "Luke" is an expression of the reader's will; *I* am "Luke."

Deconstruction lifts up every voice so that no one voice—not the narrator's, or the author's, or the reader's—dominates. This desire to life up every voice explains why the Undoers pay special attention to what seems out of place or ancillary in a given text. Moore believes that conservative biblical criticism conveniently overlooks contradictions and difficulties in the text, as these would upset the unity formed by a "totalizing authorial intention."[194] Because the author can no longer be considered a unified controlling presence, interpreters can no longer appeal to "the author" as the guarantor of correct interpretation.

The various critical approaches to biblical interpretation gathered together in *The Postmodern Bible*, for all their differences, "share a suspicion of the claim to mastery that characterizes traditional readings of texts."[195] Their task is to examine the move that establishes *authority* in interpretation. Whose reading counts, and why? This is an excellent query. For the loss of the author does not abolish the question of authority, but only resituates it.

Unless an Author Dies . . .

Just how new and how significant is the notion of the death of the author? Biblical critics have long believed that large portions of Scripture were anonymous anyway and that they were not really written by the men whose names they bear. "The anonymity of the biblical writers chimes in nicely with the 'death of the author.' . . . The historicist mode of identifying biblical authors is but the last spasm of a moribund dinosaur."[196] For some commentators, this discovery has been liberating: "For if a work is pseudonymous, then it is free to be interpreted on its own terms and independently of other writings of its alleged author."[197] Do we therefore have to say of the author what Jesus said of himself: that it is better that he go away? According to J. Severino Croatto, a liberation theologian, "this physical absence . . . is semantic wealth. The closure of meaning imposed by the speaker is now transformed into an openness of meaning."[198] Absence can, of course, be disheartening. When told by the angel in the tomb that Jesus was not there, the women were afraid (Mark 16:6–8). Is the death of the author a liberating or a debilitating hermeneutical event?

No one disputes the obvious fact that the biblical authors are gone and cannot be interviewed. Disagreements only arise over the questions of whether the author's intention is accessible and relevant to the work of the interpreter. Croatto believes that the Bible, if linked to the original authors, becomes a "closed deposit" of meaning, a relic of distant times and people. He wants the text to speak today, to the present situation, and believes that meaning must be produced by contemporary readings: "We read a *text*, not an author."[199] And again: "Authors . . . 'die' in the very act of coding their message. The inscription of meaning in any account or text is a creative act in which one lays down one's life, figuratively speaking."[200] Unless an author dies, "the meaning of the text" cannot live.

Many postmodern readers therefore waste no time writing epitaphs for the author, but rather celebrate by feasting at his or her wake. "Feasting" here means producing new and imaginative interpretations, no longer constrained by the requirement to reproduce approximations of the author's intention. Interpretation is a moveable feast lost in the labyrinth of language, in the constantly shifting patterns formed by the play of signifiers that destabilizes every effort to arrest the movement from sign to thing. "Meaning is always in the process of forming, deforming, and reforming."[201] From this perspective, the death of the author is the Magna Carta of creative interpretation. Dostoyevsky's adage on the death of God is easily adapted to the current situation in literary theory: "If there is no Author, then everything is permitted." Is this announcement, however, a reason to dance or to despair? I can think of three reasons to do both: to dance, yes, but to do so anxiously, aware that one is quickstepping on the edge of an abyss.

(1) *If "the author" dies, so too does human agency.* The burden of the Undoers' analysis of texts is to uncover the various socio-political and linguistic forces that shape an author's discourse. From a poststructuralist perspective, it is difficult to believe that what we say or do is really an action we have initiated, rather than an event that happens to us for reasons beyond our conscious control. The author, we may recall, is only one factor in a larger system of signifiers, ideas, and forces that can never be mastered and over which we have no control. How free (and responsible) are speakers and interpreters? If authors cannot author, can *any* agent act? This is an urgent question, and not for hermeneutics only; for it is by no means clear that the freedom to undo texts leads to the liberation of the self rather than to the self's undoing.

(2) *If "the author" dies, so too does the possibility of speaking truly about texts.* We are left with Derrida's choice between two interpretations of interpretation: either to read *for* the truth or to read *freed from* the urge to truth. Should we abandon the quest for truth (as Rorty and other poststructuralist prophets have already exhorted) and commit (or resign?) ourselves to exposing false claims to truth or totalization? If the first problem leads to a despair about human agency, the second leads to a despair about biblical commentaries. What are commentaries doing if they are not trying to grasp the author's intended message? *The postmodern situation generates nothing less than a legitimization crisis in biblical studies.* Richard Coggins is therefore right to ask: "Can the commentary be kept distinct from the propaganda weapon?"[202]

(3) *If "the author" dies, so too does the possibility of meaning in texts.* This third inference may not be readily obvious. I will return to it in the following chapter, where

we explore at greater length attempts to interpret the text without the author. To anticipate: what is "the meaning of the text" if it is *not* the author's intended message? The short answer—to be developed in chapter 4—is that the author is never really absent. The reader has simply taken his or her place.

NOTES

1. Westminster Confession of Faith, ch. 1, art. IV.

2. See, for instance, Bernard Ramm's *The Pattern of Religious Authority* (Grand Rapids: Eerdmans, 1957); G. R. Evans, *Problems of Authority in the Reformation Debates* (Cambridge: Cambridge Univ. Press, 1992).

3. For an excellent and wide-ranging survey of the issues, see Seán Burke, ed., *Authorship From Plato to Postmodernity: A Reader* (Edinburgh: Edinburgh Univ. Press, 1995).

4. Jorge J. E. Garcia defines "author" as "the person who is responsible for the production of a text" ("Can There Be Texts Without Historical Authors," *American Philosophical Quarterly* 31 [1994]: 245).

5. For an attempted refutation of this thesis, see Hans Blumenberg, *The Legitimacy of the Modern Age* (Cambridge, Mass.: MIT Press, 1983).

6. Frank B. Farrell, *Subjectivity, Realism, and Postmodernism—The Recovery of the World* (Cambridge: Cambridge Univ. Press, 1994), 2.

7. John E. Thiel argues that theologians only became "authors" in the sense of creative thinkers with the dawning of modernity. See his *Imagination & Authority: Theological Authorship in the Modern Tradition* (Minneapolis: Fortress, 1991), ch. 1, esp. 19.

8. Roland Barthes, "The Death of the Author," in Burke, ed., *Authorship*, 125.

9. Peter Kreeft, *Between Heaven and Hell*, 30. Mark C. Taylor acidly comments: "Since He enjoys the privilege of origin (*which is the origin of privilege*), the author is authoritative" (*Erring: A Postmodern A/theology* [Chicago: Univ. of Chicago Press, 1984], 80, emphasis mine).

10. Lewis Carroll, "Through the Looking-Glass," in *The Philosopher's Alice*, ed. Peter Heath (New York: St. Martin's, 1974), 193.

11. *The Independent Magazine*, June 20, 1992, 41.

12. Ibid., 42.

13. The book contract is a case in point. Under a clause entitled "Moral Rights," a contract I recently signed invokes the Copyright Design and Patents Act of 1988 (U.K.), which guarantees my right to be identified as the author, noting that this is called "the right of paternity."

14. E. D. Hirsch Jr., *Validity in Interpretation* (New Haven: Yale Univ. Press, 1967), 230.

15. Ibid., 47.

16. Ibid., 4.

17. Preface to Calvin's *Commentary on Romans*.

18. Joseph Haroutunian, ed., *Calvin: Commentaries* (Philadelphia: Westminster, 1958), 21.

19. Ibid., 28.

20. See Timothy Williams, "Realism and Anti-realism," Ted Honderich, ed., *The Oxford Companion to Philosophy* (Oxford: Oxford Univ. Press, 1995), 746–48.

21. The hermeneutical version of realism requires a slight qualification of this definition: while meaning may be dependent on the author's mind, it is certainly not dependent on that of the reader.

22. Kant develops this argument in his justly famous *Critique of Pure Reason*, tr. Norman Kemp Smith (London: Macmillan, 1933).

23. In Part 2 I argue, on the basis of Christian theology, for a critical realism in hermeneutics. Meaning is really there, independent of the interpretive process, yet it is inaccessible apart

from human constructions. This more moderate realist claims neither that interpretations are absolutely true, nor that interpretations are only useful fictions, but rather that interpretations yield true, though partial, knowledge of textual meaning.

24. Richard Palmer, "Hermeneutics," in Flôistad, *Contemporary Philosophy*, 2:470.

25. Nathan A. Scott Jr., "The New *Trahison des Clercs*: Reflections on the Present Crisis in Humanistic Studies," *The Virginia Quarterly Review* 62 (1986): 412.

26. Cited in Christopher Norris, *What's Wrong With Postmodernism? Critical Theory and the Ends of Philosophy* (London: Harvester Wheatsheaf, 1990), 50.

27. E. D. Hirsch Jr., *The Aims of Interpretation* (Chicago: Univ. of Chicago Press, 1976), 13.

28. Opinion cited by Christopher Norris, *Deconstruction: Theory and Practice* (London: Methuen, 1982), xii.

29. John M. Ellis, *Against Deconstruction* (Princeton: Princeton Univ. Press, 1989), 151.

30. John R. Searle, "Literary Theory and Its Discontents," *New Literary History* 25 (1994): 637.

31. Jacques Derrida, *Of Grammatology*, tr. Gayatri Spivak (Baltimore: Johns Hopkins Univ. Press, 1976), 14.

32. Brian D. Ingraffia, *Postmodern Theory and Biblical Theology* (Cambridge: Cambridge Univ. Press, 1995), 224.

33. Geoffrey Hartman, "The Interpreter: A Self-Analysis," in *The Fate of Reading and Other Essays* (Chicago: Univ. of Chicago Press, 1975), 18. Other Yale literary critics whose works have been influenced by deconstruction include Paul de Man and Harold Bloom.

34. Norris describes Hartman as deconstruction "on the wild side" and suggests that he follows Derrida's example "but rarely seeks to emulate his rigor of argument" (*Deconstruction: Theory and Practice*, 98).

35. See his *Erring: A Postmodern A/theology*, where he states: "*Deconstruction is the hermeneutic of the 'death of God' *" (6).

36. See, for instance, Moore, *Poststructuralism and the New Testament: Derrida and Foucault at the Foot of the Cross* (Minneapolis: Fortress, 1994). I find it slightly ironic that Moore's exegesis of Derrida's texts are much more conventional than his readings of the New Testament.

37. Derrida, "Remarks on Deconstruction and Pragmatism," in Chantal Mouffe, ed., *Deconstruction and Pragmatism* (London: Routledge, 1996), 77, 81.

38. See Christopher Norris, *Derrida* (London: Fontana, 1987).

39. Other works that commend Derrida as a serious philosopher include Rodolphe Gasché, *The Tain of the Mirror: Derrida and the Philosophy of Reflection*, and Henry Staten, *Wittgenstein and Derrida* (Lincoln: Univ. of Nebraska Press, 1984).

40. Louis Mackey, "Slouching Towards Bethlehem: Deconstructive Strategies in Theology," *Anglican Theological Review* 65 (1983): 255–72.

41. See Kevin Hart, *The Trespass of the Sign: Deconstruction, Theology and Philosophy* (Cambridge: Cambridge Univ. Press, 1989).

42. Graham Ward, *Barth, Derrida and the Language of Theology* (Cambridge: Cambridge Univ. Press, 1995).

43. David Lyle Jeffrey, "*Caveat Lector*: Structuralism, Deconstruction, and Ideology," *Christian Scholar's Review* 17 (1988): 436–48.

44. Bruce Edwards and Branson Woodward, "Wise As Serpents, Harmless As Doves: Christians and Contemporary Critical Theory," *Christianity and Literature* 39 (1990): 303–15.

45. I am thinking not only of the explicit examples mentioned in the chapter on Derrida in Elizabeth A. Castelli et al., eds., *The Postmodern Bible* (New Haven: Yale Univ. Press, 1995), but also of approaches such as feminist criticism, which shares with deconstruction a desire to undo privileged oppositions such as rational/irrational, spiritual/physical, and of course

male/female. On the connection between feminist criticism and deconstruction, see David Rutledge, *Reading Marginally: Feminism, Deconstruction and the Bible*, Biblical Interpretation 21 (Leiden: E. J. Brill, 1996).

46. Ingraffia, *Postmodern Theory and Biblical Theology*.

47. In this respect, there is a close tie to Nietzsche's genealogical analysis. Both Derrida and Nietzsche attempt to demystify truths that appear absolute by showing that they are, far from being "given," actually the products of a historical process that has constructed and legitimized them.

48. Norris, *Derrida*, xi.

49. Published as "Structure, Sign, and Play in the Discourse of the Human Sciences," in Richard Macksey and Eugene Donato, eds., *The Languages of Criticism and the Sciences of Man* (Baltimore: Johns Hopkins Univ. Press, 1970).

50. A. K. M. Adam, *What Is Postmodern Biblical Criticism?* (Minneapolis: Fortress, 1995), 29.

51. Augustine, *Confessions*, 1.8.

52. Wittgenstein, *Tractatus Logico-Philosophicus* (London: Routledge and Kegan Paul, 1961), 3.203.

53. In Derrida, *Dissemination*, tr. Barbara Johnson (London: Athlone, 1981), 61–171.

54. Norris, *Derrida*, 37–8.

55. *The Postmodern Bible*, 120.

56. Richard Rorty, for instance, stands in the tradition of John Dewey (though without the latter's faith in progress) and C. S. Peirce.

57. Chicago: Univ. of Chicago Press, 1967.

58. Richard Rorty, *Philosophy and the Mirror of Nature* (Princeton: Princeton Univ. Press, 1979).

59. Rorty, *Objectivity, Relativism, and Truth*, Philosophical Papers, vol. 1 (Cambridge: Cambridge Univ. Press, 1991), 1.

60. Rorty, *Consequences of Pragmatism* (Minneapolis: Univ. of Minnesota Press, 1982), 165.

61. Rorty, "Pragmatism and Philosophy," in Baynes (ed.), *After Philosophy*, 57.

62. Fish, *Is There a Text?* 13.

63. Rorty, "Pragmatism and Philosophy," 27.

64. Ibid., 36.

65. I will argue in Part 2 that the real scandal of transcendence is not Plato's so much as that of Jesus Christ. What we have in the Unbelievers is not an ascetic form of thought so much as another kind of theology.

66. Friedrich Nietzsche, *Ecco Homo*, in *On the Genealogy of Morals and Ecco Homo*, tr. and ed. Walter Kaufmann (New York: Vintage, 1989), 218.

67. Nietzsche, *Will to Power*, par. 481.

68. A group of seventeenth-century poets influenced by John Donne's concern with first causes and last things and by the stylized wit with which he wrote about these themes.

69. I borrow this phrase from Habermas, who uses it to describe Descartes's view of the knowing subject. See Jürgen Habermas, *Philosophical Discourses of Modernity*, tr. Frederick G. Lawrence (Cambridge: Polity Press, 1987), 171.

70. Derrida, "White Mythology," *New Literary History* 5 (1974): 9–11.

71. Derrida, *Of Grammatology*, 3.

72. Saussure, *Course in General Linguistics* (New York: McGraw-Hill, 1959), 66.

73. The few exceptions, usually instances of onomatopoeia, prove the general rule.

74. Saussure, *Course in General Linguistics*, 110. It should be stated that Derrida applies Saussure's linguistics to philosophy in general in a manner that Saussure never envisioned. Thiselton points out that Derrida has turned Saussure's concept of "difference" into a virtual

worldview (*New Horizons in Hermeneutics*, ch. 3). See also Martin Krampen, "Ferdinand de Saussure and the Development of Semiology," in M. Krampen, ed., *Classics of Semiotics* (New York: Plenum, 1987), 59–88, esp. 78–83.

75. Catherine Belsey, *Critical Practice* (London: Routledge, 1980), 44.

76. Kevin Hart, commenting on Milton's *Paradise Lost*, suggests that the original sin of Adam was precisely this desire for unmediated knowledge. Only God knows without signs, that is, without having to interpret (Hart, *The Trespass of the Sign*, 3–4).

77. Derrida, *Of Grammatology*, 158.

78. Derrida, "Structure, Sign, Play," 264.

79. Hart, *Trespass of the Sign*, 12.

80. Norris, *Deconstruction: Theory and Practice*, 29.

81. Johnson, "Preface" to *Dictionary of the English Language*, 1755.

82. Don Cupitt, *The Long-Legged Fly: A Theology of Language and Desire* (London: SCM, 1987), 21.

83. Derrida, "Signature Event Context," *Glyph* 1 (1977): 181.

84. Norris, *Derrida*, 199.

85. Seán Burke, *The Death and Return of the Author: Criticism and Subjectivity in Barthes, Foucault and Derrida* (Edinburgh: Edinburgh Univ. Press, 1992), 143.

86. David Tracy, *Plurality and Ambiguity: Hermeneutics, Religion, Hope* (San Francisco: Harper & Row, 1987), 77.

87. See Paul Ricoeur, *Freud and Philosophy: An Essay on Interpretation* (New Haven: Yale Univ. Press, 1970). For Ricoeur the moral is that consciousness is not a given but a hermeneutic task; who we are is only grasped by means of interpreting what we do.

88. See Jacques Lacan, *Ecrits: A Selection*, tr. Alan Sheridan (New York: W. W. Norton, 1977).

89. Cited in Thiselton, *New Horizons*, 382.

90. Thomas McCarthy, "Introduction," in Habermas, *Philosophical Discourse of Modernity*, ix.

91. Jonathan Culler, *Structuralist Poetics: Structuralism, Linguistics, and the Study of Literature* (London: Routledge, 1975), 28.

92. Scott, "The New *Trahison des Clercs*," 417.

93. Wayne C. Booth, *Critical Understanding: The Powers and Limits of Pluralism* (Chicago: Univ. of Chicago Press, 1979), 268. Booth here distinguishes five different senses in which one may be said to be an "author."

94. Wayne C. Booth, *The Rhetoric of Fiction* (Chicago: Univ. of Chicago Press, 1961), 74–75.

95. Booth, *Critical Understanding*, 269.

96. Umberto Eco, *Interpretation and Overinterpretation* (Cambridge: Cambridge Univ. Press, 1992), 80.

97. Ibid., 81.

98. Ibid., 83.

99. Ibid., 84.

100. Roland Barthes, "The Death of the Author," in Burke, ed., *Authorship*, 126.

101. Ibid.

102. Ibid., 125.

103. Ibid., 129.

104. Ibid., 128.

105. See Robert Carroll, "Authorship," in *A Dictionary of Biblical Interpretation*, eds. R. J. Coggins and J. L. Houlden (Philadelphia: Trinity Press International, 1990), 73.

106. See Margaret Barker, "Pseudonymity," in *A Dictionary of Biblical Interpretation*, 568–71.

107. Michel Foucault, "What Is an Author?" in *Textual Strategies*, ed. Josué V. Harari (London: Methuen, 1979), 159.

108. Rowan Williams, "Between Politics and Metaphysics," *Modern Theology* 11 (1995): 3–22.

109. This phrase is taken from Carl A. Raschke, "The Deconstruction of God," 3.

110. Ibid.

111. The God of negative theology is the God of whom nothing can be affirmed except that he is a mystery, beyond the reach of human language and concepts.

112. Derrida, "How to Avoid Speaking: Denials," in Harold Coward and Toby Foshay, eds., *Derrida and Negative Theology* (Albany: SUNY Press, 1992), 99.

113. Ludwig Feuerbach, *The Essence of Christianity* (Buffalo: Prometheus Books, 1989), 14.

114. Rorty, "Remarks on Deconstruction and Pragmatism," in Mouffe, ed., *Deconstruction and Pragmatism*, 15.

115. Ibid., 83.

116. See Mark C. Taylor, *Erring: A Postmodern A/Theology*, and Don Cupitt, *The Long-Legged Fly*, esp. chs. 15, 16 "The Mourning is Over" and "On the Level," and Don Cupitt, *The Last Philosophy* (London: SCM, 1995), for an account of his non-realism.

117. Cupitt, *The Last Philosophy*, 33.

118. Ibid., 119.

119. Ibid., 148.

120. Derrida, "Structure, Sign, Play," 164.

121. Burke, *Authorship*, xx.

122. Cited in Burke, *Authorship*, xxii.

123. Ibid., xxix.

124. The situation in Jewish thought is different. See ch. 3 for a discussion of rabbinic interpretation and theories of textuality.

125. A work that was published, coincidentally, in 1967—the same year as Derrida's *Speech and Phenomena*, a deconstruction of Husserl's theory of signs.

126. In putting the fourth point in this way, I am, of course, holding open the possibility that there is another version of author-oriented criticism, and of authorial intention, that escapes the criticisms levelled against Hirsch. This other version is presented in detail in ch. 5.

127. Cited in M. H. Abrams, *A Glossary of Literary Terms*, 4th ed. (New York: Holt, Rinehart and Winston, 1981), 134.

128. Poulet, "Phenomenology of Reading," *New Literary History* 1 (1969–70), cited in Abrams, *A Glossary of Literary Terms*, 134–35. Significantly, Poulet made generous use of all an author's writings (e.g., correspondence, journals) in order to reconstruct a more complete picture of an author's sense of self.

129. Unless, of course, we had reason to assume that they were arranged by an invisible or divine author. This example of pebbles on the seashore has been widely discussed in the literature. See especially Steven Knapp and Walter Benn Michaels, "Against Theory," *Critical Inquiry* 8 (1982): 723–42; John R. Searle, "Literary Theory and Its Discontents," 649–56; Jorge J. E. Garcia, "Can There Be Texts Without Historical Authors," 245–53.

130. Hirsch maintains that Edmund Husserl's theory of meaning is the most detailed, penetrating, and convincing account of meaning with which he is acquainted (Hirsch, *Validity*, 58). Franz Brentano, an important precursor to phenomenology, believed intentionality to be the defining characteristic of mental as opposed to physical phenomena. Husserl studied with Brentano and used his insights to revise Descartes's theory of the human subject. See W. T. Jones, *A History of Western Philosophy*, 2d ed. rev. (New York: Harcourt Brace Jovanovich, 1975), 5:106–7, 250–75.

131. It should be noted that Hirsch's use of Husserl is confined to citing only the latter's early work, *Logical Investigations*. Husserl later espoused "transcendental idealism," a position

to which Hirsch would probably be diametrically opposed. For a fuller account of the relation of Hirsch and Husserl, see G. B. Madison, *Hermeneutics of Postmodernity: Figures and Themes* (Bloomington: Indiana Univ. Press, 1988), 7–12.

132. Husserl's philosophy is called "phenomenology" because of its focus on phenomena, that is, on the objects that appear *in* consciousness as a result of the acts *of* consciousness.

133. Hirsch, *Validity*, 4.

134. Ibid., 231.

135. Ibid., 126.

136. Ibid., 205.

137. Hirsch, *Aims in Interpretation*, 12.

138. Hirsch, *Validity*, 219.

139. Ibid., 63.

140. Ibid., 4.

141. The author's intention is thus the "ontological" ground of meaning; that is, if it were not for author's intentions, meaning simply wouldn't *be*.

142. G. B. Madison, *Hermeneutics of Postmodernity*, 6.

143. Frank Lentricchia, *After the New Criticism* (London: Methuen, 1980), 279.

144. Derrida, "Signature Event Context," 182.

145. Lewis Carroll, "Through the Looking-Glass," in *The Philosopher's Alice*, ed. Peter Heath (New York: St. Martin's, 1974), 193.

146. Derrida, *Of Grammatology*, 158.

147. Cited in Hoy, "Must We Mean What We Say?" in Brice R. Wacterhauser, ed., *Hermeneutics and Modern Philosophy* (Albany, N.Y.: SUNY Press, 1986), 408 (translation mine).

148. Leonard Lawlor, "Dialectic and Iterability: The Confrontation Between Paul Ricoeur and Jacques Derrida," *Philosophy Today* 32 (1988): 189.

149. Derrida, "Signature Event Context," 181.

150. It may well be that, as Seán Burke and Christopher Norris have argued, Derrida is wrongly associated with the "death of the author" movement (Burke, *Death and Return of the Author*, 140ff.; Norris, *Derrida*, 112–13). It is nevertheless clear that Derrida, while he has not killed the author, has at the very least left him mortally wounded.

151. Hirsch, *Validity*, 242.

152. Ibid., 236.

153. Derrida, "Signature Event Context," 182.

154. David C. Hoy, *The Critical Circle: Literature, History and Philosophical Hermeneutics* (Berkeley: Univ. of California Press, 1978), 33.

155. A. K. M. Adam, *What Is Postmodern Biblical Criticism?* 21.

156. Hart, *Trespass of the Sign*, ix.

157. Ibid., 32.

158. Hirsch, *Aims*, 8.

159. Ibid., 7

160. P. D. Juhl, *Interpretation: An Essay in the Philosophy of Literary Criticism* (Princeton: Princeton Univ. Press, 1980), 12.

161. Hirsch, "The Politics of Theories of Interpretation," in *The Politics of Interpretation*, ed. W. J. T. Mitchell (Chicago: Univ. of Chicago Press, 1983), 329–30.

162. Eagleton, *Literary Theory*, 68.

163. Ibid.

164. Ibid., 69.

165. Moore, *Poststructuralism and the New Testament,* 116.

166. W. K. Wimsatt Jr. and M. Beardsley, "The Intentional Fallacy," in *The Verbal Icon: Studies in the Meaning of Poetry* (Lexington: Univ. of Kentucky Press, 1954).

167. This particular formulation of the fallacy is, I believe, sound; it is fallacious to mistake the meaning of a text for what the author was planning to say. It is important to note that Wimsatt and Beardsley understand "intention" in its ordinary sense, that is, as the "design or plan in the author's mind," not in the technical sense that characterizes Hirsch's treatment ("Intentional Fallacy," 4). Wimsatt repeated his objection twenty years later in "Genesis: A Fallacy Revisited," in Molina, ed., *On Literary Intention*, 137–38.

168. As cited by John Barton in his *Reading the Old Testament: Method in Biblical Study* (London: Darton, Longman & Todd, 1984), 150.

169. See Steven Knapp on Milton's failure in *Literary Interest: The Limits of Anti-Formalism* (Cambridge, Mass.: Harvard Univ. Press, 1993), ch. 1.

170. Christopher Tuckett, *Reading the New Testament: Methods of Interpretation* (Philadelphia: Fortress, 1987), 160. Tuckett makes a similar point about the necessity of "what the author intended" for determining a text's genre, a suggestion I will develop considerably in Part 2.

171. Lentricchia, *After the New Criticism*, ch. 7.

172. David Bordwell, *Making Meaning: Inference and Rhetoric in the Interpretation of Cinema* (Cambridge, Mass.: Harvard Univ. Press, 1989), 9.

173. Paul Ricoeur, *Interpretation Theory: Discourse and the Surplus of Meaning* (Fort Worth: Texas Christian Univ. Press, 1976), 29. Note that Ricoeur is using "writing" in its ordinary sense, not in the Derridean sense of "the impersonal system of language that precedes spoken and written discourse."

174. Ricoeur also cautions against viewing the text as an authorless entity, though this theme is not as pronounced as that of the semantic autonomy of the text in his subsequent work (cf. his *Interpretation Theory*, 30).

175. Derrida, *Of Grammatology*, 243. From this quote, it appears as if Derrida is confusing "intention" with "what an author planned or tried to say."

176. Hirsch, *Validity*, 46.

177. Hirsch, *Aims*, 3.

178. Madison, *Hermeneutics of Postmodernity*, 13–22.

179. Ibid., 11.

180. C. S. Peirce, "How to Make Our Ideas Clear," in *The Collected Papers of Charles Sanders Peirce*, ed. Hartshorne and Weiss (Cambridge, Mass.: Harvard Univ. Press, 1931–35, 1958), 5:408.

181. Madison, *Hermeneutics of Postmodernity*, 13–22.

182. Norman Petersen, *Literary Criticism for New Testament Critics* (Philadelphia: Fortress, 1978), 24–25.

183. Stephen D. Moore, *Literary Criticism and the Gospels: The Theoretical Challenge* (New Haven: Yale Univ. Press, 1989), 54n.12.

184. Hart, *Trespass of the Sign*, 36.

185. I will explore this connection more fully in the following chapter. See Susan Handelmann, *The Slayers of Moses: The Emergence of Rabbinic Interpretation in Modern Literary Theory* (Albany: SUNY Press, 1982).

186. Norris, *Derrida*, 229.

187. Cf. Acts 3:15: "You killed the author of life, but God raised him from the dead."

188. It should be noted, of course, that "writing" for Derrida is a metaphor for the endless freeplay of signifiers that never come to settle on reality. In this sense, there is a clear bias in Christian faith against writing, if taken in this latter sense only.

189. I discuss the role of the Spirit in ascertaining the meaning of the text in ch. 7 below. I also suggest that trinitarian theology escapes the deconstructive undoing of the "science of presence." God's trinitarian presence should not be confused with the way beings appear in space and time.

190. Moore, *Literary Criticism and the Gospels*, 12. Moore assumes throughout *Literary Criticism and the Gospels* that most attempts by biblical scholars to use literary-critical techniques continue to operate with a metaphysics of the author.

191. James Dawsey, *The Lukan Voice: Confusion and Irony in the Gospel of Luke* (Macon, Ga.: Mercer Univ. Press, 1986), 110.

192. Moore, *Literary Criticism and the Gospels*, 32.

193. Ibid., 38.

194. Ibid., 34.

195. *The Postmodern Bible*, 2. It is interesting to note that the collective way in which *The Postmodern Bible* was written "is itself part of our implicit critique of prevailing understandings of authorship" (16).

196. Robert Carroll, "Authorship," in *A Dictionary of Biblical Interpretation*, 74.

197. Tuckett, *Reading the New Testament*, 58.

198. J. Severino Croatto, *Biblical Hermeneutics: Toward a Theory of Reading As the Production of Meaning*, tr. Robert R. Barr (Maryknoll, N.Y.: Orbis, 1987), 17.

199. Ibid., 46.

200. Ibid., 16–17.

201. Taylor, *Erring*, 179.

202. Richard Coggins, "A Future for the Commentary?" in Francis Watson, ed., *The Open Text: New Directions for Biblical Studies?* (London: SCM, 1993), 174.

CHAPTER THREE

Undoing the Book: Textuality and Indeterminacy

The previous chapter noted the passing of the author, the source or origin of meaning as a metaphysical concept. Authors, according to the Undoer, are rhetorical constructs, not a part of the natural order of things. Lest it be forgotten, however, Derrida's early undoings were directed not at the notion of the author but against the notions of structure and stability.

"Writing" not only renders the author superfluous, but it also upsets the stability of linguistic and literary structures. Writing is therefore a condition of the *impossibility* of literary knowledge. The differential play of language prevents thought from ever coming to rest in a justified belief about "the way things are." Different vocabularies represent different ways of constructing or carving up the world by means of distinctions that are imposed on, rather than derived from, experience. The Book of Nature contains sheaves of empty pages. If there is no Author, then every interpretation is permitted.

Hermeneutic non-realism leads inexorably to hermeneutic relativism (or, less polemically, hermeneutic indeterminacy). *Différance* denies the possibility of knowledge by undoing determinate meaning—Hirsch's stable object of literary knowledge. "Determinate" meaning is meaning that is definite, meaning that can be defined and specified. The word "determinate" carries the connotations of "determine," "definite," and "terminate." When Hirsch speaks of determinate meaning, he has in mind a meaning that has been *determined* by its author (ground), a meaning made *definite* by the words chosen and their context, and a meaning that *terminates* the activity of the interpreter once it has been recovered (goal and guide).[1] "Indeterminate" meaning, on the other hand, is meaning that is not fixed, but "loose"—indefinite, vague, open.

If all determinate order is a result of creative interpretation, it becomes difficult to believe in any one conceptual framework or interpretive scheme. Once one accepts the lack of a ground for determinate meaning, it is impossible to believe in definitions or in final interpretations. How then can we distinguish a scholarly commentary from uninformed opinion? If there is to be a morality of literary knowledge, there must be some criteria to distinguish a false (e.g., bad, invalid, incorrect) interpretation from one that is true (e.g., good, valid, correct).

After the author, what controls on meaning and interpretation are left? Many twentieth-century literary critics believe that the text can stand—and mean—on its own. Some have even redefined interpretation theory as a science of the text. Not authorial intentions, but literary conventions, such as the text's organization, style, and codes, determine meaning. As we will see, however, neither text nor author is capable of surviving deconstruction. The autonomous text offers no more resources for limiting the play of meaning than does the strangulated voice of the anonymous author. *Textuality* overthrows the Idol of Determinacy, and with it, the very possibility of literary knowledge.

DEMEANING MEANING?

The critique of the author is only one aspect of the non-realist offensive in philosophy and literary theory. The larger target, of Undoers and Users alike, is the idea of meaning itself, together with the quest for knowledge in interpretation that it encourages. The postmodern rejection of epistemology (viz., the attempt to specify the nature and norms of knowledge) casts the practice of interpretation in a radically different light. The collapse of the metaphysics of meaning provokes a crisis in the methods of interpretation.

Demeaning Metaphysics

Traditional readers quickly fall under the spell of the "authority of meaning." As we have seen, Derrida undoes this authority by exposing the metaphysics on which it rests as "white mythology." The non-realist maintains that the very question of a correspondence between our words and the way things are degenerates into nonsense. If we have no independent, non-linguistic access to reality—or to the text-as-it-is-in-itself—it makes no sense to ask if our language corresponds to the world.

Demeaning Aristotle

The connection between the metaphysics of meaning and the epistemology of interpretation is best observed not in Plato but in Aristotle, thanks to the latter's treatises on language, logic, and scientific method. It is particularly instructive to consider his *Metaphysics* and his *On Interpretation* together. For Aristotle, metaphysics is the science of "first things," of origins, of Being. We form a true idea of a thing when its form (*eidos* = image, idea) is present to the mind's eye. Words are signs that point beyond themselves, making possible a "vision" of the thing itself. Thought represents reality, spoken words represent thought, and written words represent spoken words.[2] Interpretation and metaphysics converge in Aristotle's definition of truth: "To say of what is that it is or of what is not that it is not, is true."[3]

Nouns alone are neither true nor false. Only propositions—sentences in which something is predicated of a subject—can be true or false, and only true propositions can tell us something about the world. Other uses of language are neither true nor false. "A prayer is, for instance, a sentence but has neither truth nor falsity. Let us pass over all such, as their study more properly belongs to the province of rhetoric or poetry."[4] With this criterion, Aristotle is able to distinguish philosophy, with its concern for truth, from literature. Philosophy is about predication: knowing what to say of something. The mind apprehends the true nature of things through predication. By and large, Aristotle's categories have shaped Western philosophy, literary criticism, and biblical interpretation alike.[5]

According to Derrida, Aristotle could only privilege the philosophical over the literary by forgetting or repressing philosophy's "poetic" origin. The concept of an idea (*eidos*), for instance, is itself a metaphor. After all, the mind doesn't literally "see" the form or essence of a thing. Furthermore, words cannot point beyond themselves; they are incapable of making a thing "visible" because signs refer only to other signs.

In Derrida's view, Aristotle commits the original philosophical sin by mistaking his discourse (viz., metaphysics) for the language of heaven. He succumbs to "a white mythology which assumes and reflects Western culture: the white man takes his own mythology (Indo-European mythology), his logos—that is, the mythos of his idiom, for the universal form of that which is still his inescapable desire to call Reason."[6]

Derrida objects to Aristotle's notion that there is a "proper" way to speak, namely, the way of predication, in which words are "fixed" to things like so many labels. There is no non-metaphorical realm in which we can speak and think. As we have seen, Derrida denies that we ever get outside texts or language. This does not mean that "all is language," only that we never have non-linguistic access to the world. We never have metaphysics, that is, without metaphor. With this insight, Derrida undoes Aristotle's quest for determinate meaning and proper predication. Specifically, he undoes the binary opposition that privileges "proper" meaning (predication) over figurative meaning (rhetoric): "Derrida's critique of philosophy is an indictment of the idolatry of literalized metaphors, of a thought process that mistook signs for things, reifying them into spurious abstract meanings which were then posited as the 'proper' sense."[7]

The World Well Lost?

Rorty agrees with Derrida that philosophy errs in its preoccupation with "theory," that is, with ways of seeing ultimate reality (Gk. *theoria* = "sight"). As Derrida disavows fixed points outside writing, so Rorty rejects fixed points of view outside history or culture. Instead of trying to know or to determine the essence of something, the pragmatist inquires about its usefulness in particular situations. One can look at the world—or a text—in a number of different contexts, with a number of different questions. Even the physical world lacks a univocal nature; who is to say whether Newton's picture is truer (e.g., less metaphorical) than Monet's?

Rorty judges the entire history of philosophy from Plato onwards to have outlived its usefulness. Despite centuries of debate over truth as the correspondence of words to the world, we still are unclear as to the precise nature of the relation. For the pragmatist, sentences are true not because they correspond to reality, but because they work—because they perform some useful service. Rorty's skepticism about Truth (with a capital T to signify its absoluteness) is similar to Derrida's: there just is no way "of breaking out of language in order to compare it with something else."[8] Attempts to get "behind" language to something that legitimates it do not work. Rorty can find no starting points prior to and independent of particular cultures. He acknowledges that Western thinkers have found the notion of a "transcendental signified" intoxicating. Yet our concepts are not magical keys that unlock the "way things are," only tools we use for this or that specific purpose.

What, then, is the use of philosophy? Rorty wonders "whether philosophy should try to find natural starting points that are distinct from cultural traditions, or whether all philosophy should do is compare and contrast cultural traditions."[9] In other words, rather than trying to convince others that we have got it absolutely right (e.g., gained knowledge, meaning, truth), Rorty encourages us to exchange strategies for solving concrete problems. Instead of worrying about whether we are using the right language, we should rather appreciate the plurality of human vocabularies and the different purposes to which they can be put.

Rorty has not been slow in applying his philosophical pragmatism to literary criticism. He recommends abandoning the notion of "the" meaning of the text. With both metaphysics and meaning safely out of the way, we may collapse the distinction between "interpreting" and "using." We can stop worrying about "knowing" and begin to enjoy "interpreting." We can call off the search for Truth, in order to do something useful.

Demeaning Method

Francis Bacon believed that science has two goals: "light" (i.e., an insight into the true structure of the world) and "fruit" (i.e., an ability to make the world of benefit to humanity). Postmodern science is content with fruit: instrumental success, the ability to use the world in ways that serve human interests. Postmodern thinkers have sidestepped the law of photosynthesis, at least with regard to epistemology; the light of reason is no longer needed for the growth of knowledge.

Demeaning Objectivity: Discovery or Invention?

If one is to succeed, one must ask the "right" preliminary questions. So says Aristotle. But who is to say which preliminary questions are the right ones? Aristotle, as we have seen, wanted to know what could be predicated of what is. The ideal of knowledge, according to classic and modern philosophy, demands a privileged standpoint and a perceptual paradigm (e.g., *eidos, theoria*). Undoers and Users insist that no human individual or group enjoys a privileged standpoint (not even the philosopher) because no one can see the world as it "really" is (i.e., apart from the mediation of some linguistic scheme). Consequently, how one sees the world or textual meaning is a function of one's interpretive method. Epistemology—especially the ideal of objective knowledge—turns out to be "white mythology" too.

To some extent, recent developments in philosophy of science corroborate this point. Many philosophers of science today would demur at the suggestion that scientific theories allow us to see the world as it is in itself, or that they yield the "single correct interpretation" of physical reality. Instead, theories are complex models or conceptual frameworks that often emerge from a root metaphor (e.g., the world as machine or as organism).[10] Scientists always approach the world with some conceptual framework already in place, at least provisionally; whatever else it means, "objectivity" cannot mean "seeing things as they really are," apart from a particular point of view.

In his *Against Method*, Paul Feyerabend, perhaps the closest thing to a deconstructor among the philosophers of science, draws the following moral from the context-bound nature of scientific thought: if correspondence to the real is neither necessary nor possible for science, then there is no one set of rules—no one theory of interpretation—that the scientist must follow.[11] The way one sees the world—the "Book" of

Nature—depends on the interpretive strategy with which one approaches it. Knowledge for Feyerabend is "an ever-increasing ocean of mutually incompatible (and perhaps even incommensurable) alternatives."[12] Critics of Feyerabend suggest his position degenerates into subjectivism: "Perhaps his point is that science is 'more fun' if done this way."[13] In any case, science fails to yield objectivity: the coveted God's-eye point of view.

Knowledge is always relative to a theoretical or interpretive framework. On this point, many contemporary philosophers, scientists, and literary critics seem to have agreed. Hence the epistemological question, for scientist and literary critic alike: If interpretation is no longer a matter of "getting it right," then what is it? Vincent Leitch supplies one possible answer: "Literary criticism, we know, is more creation than discovery, and we know that criticism is less demonstration and proof than individual insight and construction."[14] Even this remark concedes too much to the ideal of scientific objectivity for postmodern tastes. As we have just seen, scientific theories are creative and beholden to metaphorical imagination too.[15] What are knowers and interpreters doing if not making discoveries? According to Nelson Goodman, they are making worlds.[16] There is not one world but many—worlds without end. Knowledge in the postmodern world is always contextual, always perspectival, always relative to some point of view or other. Obviously, there can be no "God's-eye point of view" after the death of God. There can be no authorized version of reality, only a plurality of alternative, sometimes competing, versions. It follows for Goodman that the concept "world" is only meaningful *inside* a version. All would-be interpreters of the world see the world only from within a vocabulary, only from inside a version. The alternative is to say that the "world" is that which lies beyond our versions and our vocabularies, but an unspeakable, unknowable world is of no use to anyone.[17]

Demeaning Interpretation

If interpretation cannot discover the structure of reality or the meaning of the text, does it then degenerate into relativism? The pragmatists have a ready answer: it's not that there are no constraints on interpretation, but that these constraints vary from one interpretive community to another, depending on their purposes and interests.

In a highly regarded article, "What Is the Meaning of a Text?" Jeffrey Stout argues that attempts to define meaning should be regarded as ways of *doing* certain things with texts, not as capturing the "essence" of meaning.[18] Stout calls for a moratorium on the term "meaning"; instead, we should describe what our actual interests in texts are. We would then know what our debates and disagreements were really about. For Stout, the goodness of an interpretation is relative to the interpreter's goal. He does not expect us to find a hermeneutic equivalent of Kant's categorical imperative, that is, a single duty or rule that regulates all reading. If there is no hermeneutic imperative to which all interpretive acts are responsible, it follows that "getting it right" need not be the overarching purpose of interpretation. The goodness of an interpretation is not necessarily a function of its "rightness." Neither rationality nor "method" leads us to the way texts really are. There is no privileged view—not even Reason—that allows us to sift through theories in order to find those that correspond to the real. Must the alternative be some sort of hermeneutic subjectivism, where every reader does what is right in his or her own eyes?

Stout, Rorty, and Fish, all pragmatists, subscribe to something like the following credo: "We believe in using texts for our own purposes, not in discovering their 'true' nature (they have none)." Meaning is not contained in a text like a nut in its shell; meaning is whatever it is that interests us about a text. Methods (theories) of interpretation are simply ways of dignifying and developing our interests. By realizing that there is no meaning "there" in texts to "get right," we can learn, as Fish did, to stop worrying and to love interpretation.

If metaphysics is a myth, what is left of philosophy? of literary criticism? Certainly, grand claims to have attained "the meaning" of the world, or of texts, are no longer allowed. *What is left over after the elimination of metaphysics, I suggest, is "comparative hermeneutics": the analysis and criticism of the way various cultures see and interpret.* Argumentation gives way to conversation and story-telling, and philosophy becomes an "edifying discourse" that no longer makes knowledge claims.[19] Recall the non-realist point: there is no vision of the true—beatific or otherwise—only versions.

It is simply not helpful, on the pragmatist account, to ask which description is the true one. There simply are no criteria that transcend culture and cultural practices. A criterion only functions in a given social practice, because a group of people need "to get something done."[20] Does it follow, then, that there is no limit to what interpreters can get out of texts, or do with them? Who, if anyone, can say whether a particular interpretive interest or method is legitimate or not? Indeed, who is in a position to limit the proliferation of interpretations? "The attempt to limit the range of relevant meaning-conferring contexts or to halt the endlessly self-dissolving instabilities of writing has been stigmatized as 'authoritarian.'"[21] It is not yet clear how the Users and the Undoers navigate the narrow waters between the Scylla of interpretive authoritarianism and the Charybdis of interpretive anarchy.

WHAT IS A TEXT?

The most radical question of all in hermeneutics concerns the nature of texts.[22]

I know well enough what it is, provided that nobody asks me; but if I am asked what it is and try to explain, I am baffled.[23]

"Meaning," like time, is an abstract notion. We can no doubt sympathize with Augustine's ability to tell the time while being wholly unable to say "what it is." "Meaning," similarly, is an everyday notion that we employ without hesitation; yet, if we are asked, "What is meaning?" we may find ourselves thoroughly perplexed. Let us therefore heed Stout's call for a moratorium on the term "meaning," at least temporarily, and focus our attention on the nature of the text. What is a text? Werner Jeanrond rightly states: "Every theory of interpretation postulates a theory of text."[24] Similarly, every theory of text postulates a theory of the author and the reader.[25]

The Book of Books

The autonomous text was the primary focus of scholarly activity during the "second age of criticism."[26] While many theorists observed a moratorium on the concept of meaning, there was no such circumspection with regard to the notion of the text.

Indeed, literary critics offered up whole theories of "textuality." What unites the various approaches in the second age of criticism is their attempt to place literary criticism on a scientific footing by defining its object—the autonomous text—and establishing its own methods and procedures.[27] One of the first casualties resulting from this renewed attention to the text, interestingly enough, was the concept of the "book."

What is behind the contemporary tendency to draw a sharp distinction between "book" and "text"? The dictionary definition of "book" gives some clue: "a written or printed work consisting of pages glued or sewn together along one side and bound in covers."[28] This brief definition, with its allusions to the author, to unity, and to "closure," encapsulates all that the literary theorist finds objectionable in the concept of the book. Derrida, for instance, opens *Of Grammatology* with a chapter entitled "The End of the Book and the Beginning of Writing." What we find is that *"the book" symbolizes the "idol of determinacy," the illusion that texts have fixed meanings.*

A book is more than the sum total of its words and sentences. It is a totality, a structured whole with thematic coherence—ideological "glue." Books are "closed," or rather enclosed, by the author's will, symbolized by a book's binding. Derrida comments:

> The idea of the book is the idea of a totality, finite or infinite, of the signifier. . . . The idea of the book, which always refers to a natural totality, is profoundly alien to the sense of writing. It is the encyclopedic protection of theology and of logocentrism against the disruption of writing . . . against difference in general.[29]

Because the idea of the book suggests totality, Derrida finds it inherently theological. Books stabilize, control, and close down the play of meaning.

The concept of the book as an intelligible unity requires the concept of the author as its controlling presence, the one who intends a discourse as a meaningful whole; a book is the author's *work*.[30] Books are writings "held within bounds by the author's sovereign presence."[31] Indeed, what else could confer identity on a text "if not the fact of having been produced by a particular author on a particular occasion"?[32] According to the Undoers, then, to believe in books is to be taken in by the illusion of metaphysics—by the idea that a voice from outside the play of language can rise above the endless ambiguities of writing in order to produce a self-contained work.

The image of the "book of nature" suggests that physical reality itself is a meaningful whole. Medieval theologians argued from the order in nature to the existence of God, whose "signature" the book of nature indelibly bears. The metaphor of the book implies that everything fits together. The encyclopedias of the eighteenth and nineteenth centuries were perhaps the most ambitious attempt to state the overall coherence of things. The Bible is perhaps the paradigmatic book inasmuch as it strives for comprehensiveness by recounting the story of God's relation with the world and with humanity. The Bible is the Book of books, which reveals the end of all endings: the meaning of history. The concept of the Bible as the Book of books makes sense, of course, only if its author is the Author of the universe.

Those features that characterize the book—unity, a controlling authorial presence, closure—become most pronounced in the case of the Bible: "Christianity is a religion of the book, and the West is a book culture. . . . The notion of the book is,

in an important sense, theological."[33] Northrop Frye sees the whole realm of literature as a self-contained verbal universe, with the Bible as the "great code" that provides the key to its deciphering. The Bible is thus a "closed" book with eternally fixed
meanings, and its imaginative framework generates the much wider (logocentric)
unity in European literature.[34] Francis Watson mentions a second, very different, way
in which the Bible may be considered a "closed book." If we assume that the Bible is
a book with an authorially authorized determinate meaning, we will read it "enclosed
in an academic institution which licenses a single, restricted interpretative paradigm."[35] On this second view, the Bible does not close itself but *has been closed* by the
assumption that there is a single correct interpretation.

The "book" is therefore a theological idea, insofar as it implies that there is a single unified meaning and a comprehensive order. Any claim that a text can be totalized
(e.g., interpreted as a unified whole) is thus a "theological" claim: "The word 'theological' pertains, then, to the use of any vocabulary in which meaning or being is said
to be wholly resolved by reference to an origin, end, center or ground."[36] Conversely,
Derrida's claim that "there is nothing outside the text" is profoundly anti-theological.

From "Closed Book" to "Open Text"

If the Book of Books has lost its status as divine, the notion of the "Text" . . .
has taken its place. Literary criticism has become a kind of substitute theology.[37]

What is a text? For Roland Barthes, "the Text . . . is read without the Father's
inscription."[38] A text is not the work of a personal agent, but a *network* of diverse cultural codes. Barthes, along with other literary critics who have sacrificed the author
(e.g., structuralists, conservative reader-response, canon critics, etc.), nevertheless
cling to the notion of determinate meaning by assigning a certain priority to the text
itself. Umberto Eco, for instance, likens a text to a "machine conceived in order to
elicit interpretations."[39] While acknowledging the role of the reader in producing or
realizing meaning, these critics insist that the text—by virtue of its autonomy and
integrity—continues to exert some influence over its interpretation.

In both deconstruction and pragmatism, "the text is denied a substantial presence."[40] The text is merely the adventure playground of interpretation, the site of verbal slides, swings, and sandboxes that afford the reader the means to exercise his or
her imagination. The text is a possiblity that can be taken up in different ways. Indeed,
because the text can never be received in its integrity but only be used, *using* the text
is indistinguishable from *abusing* it: "Interpretation is a *hostile* act in which interpreter
victimizes text."[41]

To speak of texts rather than books is to effect more than a change in terminology. It is to change paradigms. It is to participate in an epistemological shift as radical as the change from Newtonian to Einsteinian science. Whereas the book
resembled an unchanging substance, the text is more like a field of shifting forces.
Whereas the book can be studied as though it were a discrete object at some distance
from the interpreting subject, the text only comes to light as it is observed from different points of view. With this insight we have the seeds of a "special relativity" the-

ory of interpretation. In contrasting the book as a metaphysical entity with the text as a methodological field, Barthes writes: "*The Text is experienced only in an activity, in a production.*"[42] What this means is that the text depends on the process of interpretation for its very being in a way that the book does not. Such a change is consonant with the general shift from realism to non-realism in recent literary theory. The question I wish to pursue as we turn now to consider three recent theories of textuality is whether, in light of this epistemological shift, it is still possible to speak of "the meaning of the text."

The Horizon of the Text: Gadamer and Ricoeur

Perhaps no twentieth-century philosophers have done more on behalf of hermeneutics than Hans-Georg Gadamer and Paul Ricoeur. In similar ways, Gadamer and Ricoeur have tried to explain how interpretation is possible after the metaphysical shift away from the author and after the epistemological shift away from Newtonian objectivity. Despite other differences, Gadamer and Ricoeur are agreed in privileging the "horizon" or "intention" of the text rather than the author, and in viewing the text as a well of *possible* meaning from which diverse readers draw different interpretations. In short, the text has a sense potential, but actual meaning is the result of an encounter with the reader.

Explanation or Understanding? Fusing Horizons. Does the text shape interpretation or does interpretation shape the text? Gadamer and Ricoeur reject this either-or and take a both-and approach instead. Meaning is the result of a two-way encounter between text and reader. Understanding texts is not like knowing objects, as Cartesian epistemology would have it, where the object is mirrored in the subject's mind. The reader is not simply a detached, neutral observer of texts; meaning is not something that can be "explained." On the contrary, understanding is something that happens when the interpreter "participates" in the text. The celebrated image of the "hermeneutical circle" suggests that the subject is always already involved in the object that is to be understood.[43]

The reader, far from being a detached observer, occupies a standpoint that limits and conditions what can be known, not outside history, but within a history that is itself the result of previous interpretations. Gadamer calls such a cultural-historical standpoint a "horizon." One's horizon defines the limits beyond which one cannot see. One's horizon is linked to one's prejudices, to one's habits of looking at the world in particular ways. Readers, in other words, always come to texts with a certain "preunderstanding." At the same time, the text also has a horizon, for it too reflects the prejudices of its historical situation. Interpretation, then, is like a dialogue in which the reader exposes himself or herself to the effects of the text, while the text is exposed to the reader's interests and prejudices. Understanding is a matter of "fusing" the horizons of the text and reader.

If understanding is a fusion of horizons, it follows that a text does not have a single correct interpretation, for each reader brings a different horizon to the text. Because of this variable, there can be no one formula for hermeneutic fusion. Whereas for Hirsch the object of understanding is always the same (viz., the author's intended message), understanding for Gadamer is an iterable event: "To understand a text always means to apply it to ourselves and to know that, even if it must be understood in different ways, it is still the same text presenting itself to us in different ways."[44] Meaning is not, therefore, "in" the text; it is rather "in" the act of reading. Meaning is the result of interpretive fusion.

Though Hirsch judges Gadamer's view to be too subjective, it is actually quite conservative when placed on the spectrum of contemporary positions. Gadamer still believes that there is something in the text that is one of the determining factors in interpretation. By stressing the horizon of the text, Gadamer insists that the act of reading is not a *creatio ex nihilo* but a co-creation; for the text, through its verbal sense, gives something to the reader. Though the author's intention is unavailable, reading should be guided by the intention of the text.[45]

The World and Work of the Text. Ricoeur defines "text" as a "discourse fixed by writing."[46] Like spoken discourse, a text says something about something. It has a sense (what it says) and a reference (what it is about). Writing, however, is more than a new medium of discourse; writing has a profound effect on the message of discourse too. Ricoeur states: "The dialogical situation has been exploded. The relation writing-reading is no longer a particular case of the relation speaking-hearing."[47] According to Ricoeur, the separation of a text from its author is not a loss to be mourned but a gain to be celebrated. The autonomy of the text is the condition of its "surplus" of meaning, that is, of its transcending its original situation and having something to say to readers in the present: "What the text signifies no longer coincides with what the author meant; henceforth, textual meaning and psychological meaning have different destinies."[48] The text enjoys a threefold semantic autonomy: it is independent of its author, of its original audience, and of its original referent. Thanks to writing, "The text's career escapes the finite horizon lived by its author."[49]

Ricoeur's account of the work and world of the text amplifies and clarifies Gadamer's image of the horizon of the text. The horizon of the text includes both sense and reference. In the first place, the text has autonomy and enjoys its own *sense*. A text is not simply a sequence of words and sentences but a "composition," a work with a particular genre and style, a verbal work. Most importantly, for Ricoeur, a text's *structure* imposes certain limits on interpretation. The hermeneutical circle is not a vicious one, for the reader's presuppositions can be "checked" against the text's formal features (e.g., style, syntax, structure). Among the formal methods that can be used to study the text's structure, Ricoeur appeals primarily to structuralist techniques. However, he believes that structuralists err by staying too long on the level of text-internal analysis. It is one thing to dissect a text as though it were an inert object, scientifically exposing its grammatical parts and explaining its literary codes, and quite another to treat the text as a dynamic object that actually reaches out and transforms the world of the reader.

By virtue of its autonomy from the author, then, a text has a verbal and structural integrity of its own. By virtue of its autonomy from its original context, the text also has a reference of its own. In oral discourse, reference is determined by the ability of the speakers to point to or otherwise specify what they are talking about. With writing, however, there is no longer a common situation. The original context of the text may be quite distant from the contemporary context of the reader.[50] Yet it is precisely the abolition of ostensive reference (i.e., pointing and saying "this here") that is the condition of a second-order reference. A text's inability to show us what it is speaking *about* turns out to be the condition for its ability to project a "world."

With his revised account of sense and reference, Ricoeur gives a precision to Gadamer's notion of the fusion of horizons. As interpreters, Ricoeur believes, we do not meet a mind *behind* the text; rather, we encounter a possible way of looking at things, a possible world, *in front of* the text. Texts for Ricoeur do refer to the world, but not in the mode of empirical description. Instead of describing actual situations, texts display possible ways of viewing or living in the world.[51] The fusion of horizons is a matter of decoding the sense of the text and of unfolding its referent.

The Role of Reader. It should now be clear why Barthes likens the shift from book to text to the Einsteinian revolution in science. The position of the observer (or the reader) partly determines what will be seen (or understood). What one sees is relative to one's "position"—a viewpoint that includes one's history, prejudices, and values. On this view, a text has only *potential* meaning until a reader "awakens" and makes sense of it: "Texts come to life only when people become involved in them."[52] Yet the question remains: Can we speak intelligibly about "the sense of the text" or of "textual intention" after the disappearance of the author?

Interpretation on Ricoeur's view corresponds to the two aspects of the text: one explains the text's structure as a written work and responds to the world that the work mediates and unfolds. A text, then, is like a musical score; it can be analyzed (e.g., in terms of its theme and developments, its harmony and melody, its overall form, etc.) or it can be performed. Simply to analyze the score, however, is not yet to interpret it: "Reading is like the execution of a musical score; it marks the realization, the enactment, of the semantic possibilities of the text."[53] This analogy with musical performance illustrates the fusion of horizons: the text presents something determinate to be enacted, while at the same time leaving certain choices to the performer.[54]

Most appropriations to date of literary methods by biblical scholars correspond to this conservative version of "reader-response" criticism. The text has certain indeterminacies or gaps that the reader needs to fill in, but the text itself provides some guidance as to how to do so. Wolfgang Iser likens the reader's situation to that of stargazers who see different images in the same constellation: "The 'stars' in a literary text are fixed; the lines that join them are variable."[55] Iser and Ricoeur stress the reader's involvement in the "making of meaning," but the reader on their view does not create *ex nihilo* but rather follows the indications of the text. There is some indeterminacy in interpretation (not all performers need play a Beethoven sonata in exactly the same way), but it is always an indeterminacy within textual boundaries. The text both constrains and frees the reader; it invites but also limits interpretation. Ricoeur sums up his position as follows: "Perhaps we should say that a text is a finite space of interpretations: there is not just one interpretation, but, on the other hand, there is not an infinite number of them. A text is a space of variations that has its own constraints. . . ."[56] The notion that the text has a horizon of its own that meets the horizon of the reader introduces into biblical interpretation "just enough of the reader but not too much."[57] Or does it? Once a text is cut off from its author, what kind of integrity does it have, and does the reader respect it?

Let us return to the seashore and to the pebbles that appear to spell out a line from *Hamlet*: "to be or not to be." Would we say that the pebbles form a text, with its own "intention" and sense potential? One option would be to determine whether or not its cause was an author, that is, an intelligent entity that intended to convey some sort of message. Would the pebbles be a text if their arrangement was known to be the result of the waves? (I am here assuming that the interpreter is a naturalist and would not appeal to divine intervention.) Jorge Garcia helpfully distinguishes between the entities out of which a text is made (e.g., black marks on white paper, seaweed) and the text itself (a verbal message) and points out that "the causes that account for them need not be the same."[58] The waves alone may be the cause of the pebbles lying as they do, but the waves cannot produce a text because they do not intend to convey any message. In this case, therefore, the "author" of the text is the first person to see a message in the pebbles.

The point of this example is that "the sense of the text" is logically inseparable from "the intention of the author." Unless we are able to relate a set of signs to someone who intends to convey meaning through them, we are not even able to determine whether they have sense potential. For the range of possible meanings of a word depends, minimally, on what language is being used, and when. In other words, the meaning of a word sequence depends on our ability to relate it to a historical author. Garcia's conclusion is worth quoting in full:

> Texts outside history are silent. The point I am making is metaphysical, for it concerns the fact that in order for entities to acquire meaning and become signs and for signs to compose texts, they must be picked and endowed with meaning in certain arrangements at some point in history. Otherwise they are no more than the entities they are. Texts outside history are not texts.[59]

Nicholas Wolterstorff agrees that Ricoeur's notion of the autonomy of the text is flawed: "There is no such thing as the sense of a text."[60] Wolterstorff makes the point that, in imagining what sense a text may convey, we are actually imagining what someone might say with just these words. Referring to Ricoeur's analogy of the interpreter executing a musical score, Wolterstorff observes that what actually happens in "performance interpretation" is that we ask ourselves, "What might someone who shared my convictions have meant by these words?" In short, far from being autonomous, "the sense of the text" turns out to be the sense the words would bear had *we* been their author.

Gadamer, Ricoeur, and like-minded hermeneutical philosophers believe that autonomous texts can structure the act of reading. What, however, is to stop readers from reading their own meaning and agendas into texts? What is to stop readers from taking "every text captive" to their egotistical imaginations? What is to stop readers from using the text as a mirror in which they not only see, but project, themselves? According to Stephen Moore: "Reader theory in literary studies is a Pandora's box into which we, infant literary critics of the Bible, have barely begun to peer."[61]

Empty Text Syndrome

Authorless texts, then, may aspire to autonomy but ultimately succumb to the arbitrary, to the whims of the reader. Pragmatist interpretation is a case in point:

"Either literary texts are self-subsistent repositories of meaning responsible for the experience readers have of them . . . or literary texts are the end-products of reading experiences, objects themselves constituted by such experiences and not antecedent to them."[62] In their book *Biblical Interpretation*, Robert Morgan and John Barton reflect a pragmatist view of texts: "Texts, like dead men and women, have no rights, no aims, no interests. They can be used in whatever way readers or interpreters choose."[63] With Fish, they contend that a text is not a stable entity with fixed properties. Texts are not as "solid" as that. What properties a work comes to have depends on a reader's experience of it. What a text becomes is an index of what people use it for.

Against the hermeneutic philosophers we considered above, pragmatists deny that the text has "intentions." The text does not "aim" to "do" anything. Such anthropomorphizing, they believe, hearkens back to discredited author-oriented ideas. Fish turns Ricoeur's picture of interpretation on its head: the reader's interpretation does not conform to textual intentions, but rather textual intentions conform to the reader's interpretation. "I 'saw' what my interpretive principles permitted or directed me to see, and I turned around and attributed what I had 'seen' to a text and an intention."[64] This is Fish's "Copernican Revolution" in interpretation theory: *interpretation does not conform to the text, but the text conforms to the interpretation*. With this revolutionary move, the vaunted semantic autonomy of the text effectively disappears: "The entities that were once seen as competing for the right to constrain interpretation (text, reader, author) are now all seen to be the *products* of interpretation."[65]

We must take care to avoid caricaturing hermeneutic non-realism. Fish is not saying that there is nothing in bookshops but what customers imagine they see. Of course books exist. Fish's point is rather that *what* we see in texts—the structured patterns, the sense—is an effect of our interpretive acts. Far from being autonomous, then, the text is at least partially *constituted* (not simply actualized) by our interpretations. All our descriptions of the text are conditioned by our questions and context. The determinate sense of the text is a function of the determinate situation of its interpreters. Is Fish a hermeneutic solipsist? Do the readers see only themselves at the bottom of a text rather than another world, a different horizon, in which case there can be no hope of *shared* meaning?

Rorty shrugs off the charge that a pragmatic rather than an ontological view of the text leads to a "silly relativism," that is, a relativism where anything goes.[66] Pragmatists insist that readers are not free to say just anything, for they are members of an interpretive community with specific purposes, interests, and authority. For example, the question "Is there a text in this class?" has a determinate meaning within particular contexts. In Hirsch's classroom, the question concerns which textbooks will be used. In Fish's classroom, the question means, "Do we believe that texts have a nature independent of the activity of the reader?" The User's point is that communication always take place within situations where a set of assumptions and practices (e.g., an interpretive scheme) is already in place.

Interpretation or Grammatology?

Theories of interpretation focus on how texts convey messages. After all, Hermes is the "messenger" god. Theories of textuality, however, might be better termed "hermetic" insofar as they view the text as (1) hermetically sealed from outside influences (e.g., the author, the original context), (2) indeterminate and disconnected from external reality, and (3) repositories of multiple, sometimes hidden, meanings.[67] Whereas the "book" functions like a sign directed to its destination by an author, the text is a free-floating system of signifiers that never comes to rest in any one context. The book—a product of the author's voice and breath—is thus a pneumatological, not a grammatological, entity.[68] In Derrida's view, then, Ricoeur's call for a new concept of interpretation that affirms the autonomy of the text does not do full justice to the phenomenon of writing. Derrida calls for a way of dealing with texts beyond hermeneutics and interpretation: grammatology.

Textuality. Derrida coins the term "grammatology" as the name for a study of "writing" no longer governed by logocentrism. In grammatology, the ink is just about the only thing that does not disappear; author, meaning, reference, even context—all vanish. In contrast to the bound book, a structured and determinate whole, the text is a network of signs and of other texts, radically open and indeterminate. The text is not a lamp unto our feet that lights our path, but an unending labyrinth that leads everywhere and nowhere at once. Whereas the goal of hermeneutics is to "understand" a text by determining its meaning, grammatology insists that the meaning of texts is undecidable: there is more than one way to skin a text.

Grammatology studies writing, not as a medium for a message but as the site of *différance*. The Latin verb *textere* means "to weave." For Derrida, a text is a tissue of signs that is itself enmeshed in a fabric of other tissues, other texts. Grammatology is the systematic attempt to "undo" these tissues and threads from one another. "There is nothing outside the text" means that all language and all thought, every word and every concept, is part of a worldwide web of signifiers. Every text is actually an "intertext," for every text is related to other texts. *Textuality means that there is no knowledge that is not mediated by some signifying system or other.* At no point can the interpreter grab onto something that is not itself open to multiple interpretations. Again, Derrida is not saying that everything is only texts; he is not transforming the world into a library. Rather, as Hart reminds us, "[Derrida] does not say that everything is *only* a text but that everything is *also* a text."[69] If everything is also a text, then we never get to the bottom of things; we never reach a non-textual, self-evident reality that allows interpretive activity to come to rest. Deconstruction undoes logocentrism by unraveling the texture of every *logos* (e.g., consciousness, authorial intention, ideas, revelation). To affirm textuality, then, is to affirm a plurality and undecidability of meaning. There is simply nothing non-textual to which one can appeal to halt the inexorable march of indeterminacy.

Far from establishing the autonomy of the text, then, textuality undermines it. *To affirm textuality is to affirm the text as incomplete in and of itself.* The text is not a totality. Indeed, deconstruction is the attempt to find those points in the text where the text fails to cohere. Even the most carefully constructed text will betray its incompleteness; as a system of differences, every text eventually comes apart. Derrida discovers a tension between what a text apparently wants to say and what it is systematically constrained to mean: "To deconstruct is to identify points of failure in a system, points at which it is able to feign coherence only by excluding and forgetting that which it cannot assimilate, that which is 'other' to it."[70] Why is incoherence inevitable? Not because authors cannot think logically, but rather because they must think within signifying systems—vocabularies—that are constructed on a set of binary oppositions whose arbitrary structure cannot ultimately be justified. Hermeneutics seeks to cut off the loose threads in order to preserve the meaning of the whole, but Derrida claims that such repression only masks the play of differences. Grammatology is the undoing of any interpretation that treats its text as a seamless garment. The grammatologist teases out the loose threads, the opposing forces that crisscross within the text itself.

Contextuality. The prime rule for hermeneutics, as in real estate, is "location, location, location." In the case of determining meaning, "location" means context. It is the context that helps us determine whether "He's hot" refers to someone's temperature, angry disposition, marketability, or tennis game. Context refers both to a text's historical place (e.g., Who produced it? For what purpose? When? Why?) and to its literary place (e.g., Is it in the Bible? Is it a novel? Is it in English?). The reader similarly has a context that includes both a historical situation and a place in an interpretive community.

For Derrida, texts are independent not only of their authors and their original contexts, but also of any single determining context, including that of their readers: "A written sign carries with it a force that breaks with its context, that is, with the collectivity of presences organizing the moment of its inscription."[71] The possibility that a text may drift away from its origin and original context is not a possibility outside language but rather the condition for the very possibility of language. Indeed, it is for this reason that textual meaning is undecidable: because texts are not anchored to a stabilizing context. On the one hand, we are able to read texts even when we don't know where they come from. On the other hand, our reading is contextual, only one possible reading among many others. For instance, the word *hypostasis* floats between various differential systems; it appears in 2 Corinthians 9:4, in Origen, and in the Council of Chalcedon in 451. What does it really mean? The very question is misguided. There is no "real" meaning in the sense of an absolute meaning, unconnected to any particular context. "Iterability," we may recall, means that signs are repeated in a non-identical way. What holds for the single sign holds also for texts. Exodus may have one meaning, for instance, when read by Jews, another by seventeenth-century Puritans, and still another in the base communities of the poor in Latin America.[72]

Hirsch bases objectivity in interpretation on the possibility of shared meaning. Does sharing meaning require sharing a context? How can contexts be shared? Jonathan Culler comments: "Some texts are more orphaned than others."[73] Derrida disagrees. *All* texts are cut off from their fathers, from their originating presences. No one person or situation "owns" a text. Even physical proximity to a speaker need not necessarily entail a shared context; presence is always mediated, by our bodies, our clothes, our actions, as well as our speech. Sharing a context is never simple nor straightforward. Throughout the history of its interpretation, the Bible has been read within many different contexts: Greek-speaking and Latin-speaking, Latin American and South African, Protestant and Roman Catholic, feminist and psychoanalytic, and so forth. Are some of these contexts more fruitful for interpretation than others? Do some contexts blind rather than illumine their readers to textual meaning? To Undo-ers and Users, such questions about proper context are as undecidable as questions about the single correct interpretation of a text.

Despite their differences, both hermeneutical (e.g., Gadamerian, Ricoeurian) and grammatological (e.g., Derridean, Fishian) approaches abandon the ideal of objective literary knowledge by acknowledging that meaning is largely the product of historically situated ways of reading or decoding. Thiselton summarizes the problem: "Hermeneutics reveals that all *claims* to knowledge, indeed what is deemed to *count* as knowledge, arises only from within some given social tradition, in which the context of *convention* determines what is acceptable or 'rational.'"[74] We might call this the "general relativity thesis" of literary theory: what interpreters observe in a text is wholly dependent on the interpreter's "trajectory" (e.g., prejudices, aims, interests) and "position" (e.g., gender, race, class).

MEANING IN ANTIOCH AND ALEXANDRIA

> For the letter kills, but the Spirit gives life. (2 Cor. 3:6)

> What constitutes a text is a slippery thing to define.[75]

If there is meaning in this text, is it single or plural, plain or secret? The debate about whether texts are determinate and subject to one "literal" interpretation or indeterminate and subject to multiple "spiritual" interpretations is hardly new. Indeed, in Jewish and early Christian exegesis, most interpreters took for granted that a biblical text had more than one sense. What is more, early Jewish and Christian thinkers, far from worrying about multiple meanings, actually seemed to revel in them. The ability to ascribe some meaning other than the obvious one was considered a necessary condition of the Bible's relevance.[76] The Bible itself reworks earlier texts in order to make them applicable to later situations: "As the rabbis, Augustine, and Luther knew, the Bible, despite its textual heterogeneity, can be read as a self-glossing book."[77]

There is a world of difference, however, between the older Christian allegorists and their newer, post-Christian counterparts. For while the early Christians did indeed find meanings beyond the letter, these meanings were usually limited in number and always subject to theological constraints. To speak of meaning in Antioch and Alexandria is ultimately to be reminded that the way one views the literal and spiritual senses of a text is related to the way one envisages the incarnation of the Word of God; one's commentary is connected to one's Christology.

Letter and Spirit

The history of biblical interpretation makes for a complex but fascinating story.[78] I wish here to follow only one of its subplots, namely, the conflict between literal interpretation on the one hand, and midrashic and allegorical interpretation on the other. It is vital that, at the outset, we distinguish between allegory as a kind of text and allegory as a principle of interpretation. An allegorical text is one that intentionally makes sense on at least two distinct levels (cf. Gal 4). An allegorical interpretation is one that treats a text as meaning something *other* (from Gk. *allos*, other, another) than what it apparently says.[79]

Alexandria: Looking Beyond the Letter

Allegorical interpretation makes sense of texts that have been resituated within alien cultures and conceptual frameworks. Reading the Bible allegorically was a liberating experience for both Jews and Christians who wished to commend the Scriptures to the sophisticated Greek intellectuals in ancient Alexandria.[80] Philo, a first-century Jewish philosopher, claimed that one could find Greek philosophy in the wisdom of Moses, if one knew how to look and looked hard enough. By allegorizing, Philo perceived the spirit through the letter of the Jewish law and so revealed the presence of Plato in Moses: "Essentially, Philo's commentaries on the Scriptures try to explain how to translate biblical language into the language of moral philosophy."[81] With regard to biblical names, for instance, Alexandrian allegorists worked with equivalencies such as Adam = Natural Reason, Eve = the Senses, Egypt = the Body, Israel = the Soul, and so on.

In similar fashion, Christians argued that one could find Christ in the Old Testament. By and large, allegorical interpretation represented a powerful means of bringing ancient texts to bear on contemporary problems. It represented an interpretive strategy for declaring "this means *that*." As such, it was a vital means for gaining knowledge of the hidden meaning of the text for the express purpose of rendering the text relevant.[82]

For Origen, a third-century Christian philosopher, the literal sense of the text is often inferior to the spiritual meaning, just as for Plato earthly things are shadows of heavenly Forms and just as the human body is inferior to the spirit: "The spiritually minded commentator will accept the letter, but treat it ascetically, as the good religious treats his flesh, in order to devote himself to the spirit."[83] As divinely inspired, Scripture has a unified deeper meaning as well as a "surface" meaning. On its "carnal" (e.g., literal, historical) level, the Bible is not altogether edifying or consistent. Furthermore, in the early church, the literal approach was associated with the failure of the Jews to see Christ in the Old Testament. Paul spoke of a "veil" over Jewish hearts, which prevented them from understanding the true meaning of the law. "Literalists" were therefore outsiders, readers who could not see that to which the letter pointed. Moreover, the literal sense sometimes led to theological absurdities. For instance, Origen could not conceive how three "days" could have passed before the creation of the sun and moon. Nor could he see the point in recounting Noah's drunken antics. For Origen, the literal meaning is often commonplace; it is the meaning that only the simplest of readers sees in the text. He compares reading the text literally to eating the Paschal lamb raw. One derives more spiritual nourishment from the biblical stories when read allegorically. For example, the story of Rebecca drawing water from the well and meeting the servant of Abraham points to the deeper truth that we must come daily to the wells of Scripture in order to meet Christ.

Coming to meet Christ, coming to meet God—such was the ultimate aim of allegorical reading for the Alexandrians. The early church fathers sought the moral and spiritual meaning, not merely knowledge about what mortals said and did but rather knowledge about the nature and will of the immortal God.

Antioch: Looking Through the Letter

At first glance, it would seem that Christian theology itself provides the major warrant for allegorical interpretation. Is not Jesus Christ the true reference of Old Testament prophecy? Is it not right to read the whole Old Testament as saying one thing (e.g., about Israel) and meaning another (e.g., the fulfillment in Christ and in the church)? If so, then the whole Bible—or at least the Old Testament—contains an allegorical sense and should therefore be read allegorically. On the other hand, if a text says something other than the sense of its letter, why can it not mean just anything? In the early church, heretics were adept at using the Bible to support their own points of view. One group, the Gnostics, cited Jesus' own words in Matthew 7:7 in their defense: "Seek and you will find." Consequently, some defenders of the faith formulated an opposing maxim: "we prefer to find less meaning in the Bible, if possible, rather than the opposite."[84]

The "school of Antioch" flourished in Syria in the late fourth and early fifth centuries. According to its leading exponent, Theodore of Mopsuestia, the task of the biblical commentator is to offer explanations of difficult words and passages in terms of their original historical situation. The Antiochenes claimed that no text means "other" than what it clearly says.[85] The Antiochenes insisted that God's revelation was in history and that this history was the referent of the biblical text when interpreted literally. The literal meaning—the letter—directs the reader's attention to God's action in the actual world of historical truths, not to an ideal world of symbolic truths. The unity of the Bible consisted in its being a history of salvation, not a system of intellectual truths. Antiochene interpretation was, by and large, firmly rooted in history rather than philosophy.

The Rabbis: Living in the Letter

Jewish interpretation represents yet a third attitude towards the letter. For the rabbis, the Torah is God's own Word and contains the sum total of God's wisdom for his people. Because it is a divine product, even the very letters of Scripture are filled with profound meaning. The Torah does not refer to one thing so much as to *all* things. Interpretation is the means by which the Torah speaks to subsequent generations in different situations.[86] The rabbis also believed that the Scripture is intentionally incomplete, requiring supplementation by the oral Torah, that is, by the authoritative interpretation of the written law that God also gave to Moses and that has been handed down from Moses to the rabbinic schools. The Torah is thus both perfect *and* incomplete. Everything is contained therein, but it only comes to light through the process of continual interpretation or *midrash* (from the root *darash*—to seek, inquire into, investigate). Midrash is concerned with "what it means," with overcoming the distance between the text and the situation of the interpreter.

Like allegorical interpretation, midrash often goes beyond what the surface meaning of the text seems to warrant.[87] Rabbinic commentary is frequently creative rather than descriptive, such that an outsider typically sees it as eisegesis—a reading into Scripture of ideas that were not in the mind of the historical author. From the rabbis' perspective, however, midrash simply draws out the divine meaning latent in Scripture. Interpretation, in other words, represents a further unfolding of divine revelation.

It is no surprise, therefore, that the rabbinic commentaries themselves became author-itative: "The elevation of later commentary to the status of earlier primary text is one of the extraordinary characteristics of Rabbinic interpretation."[88] Though the rabbis' inter-pretations often conflicted with one another, there is no conflict of authority, because it is the whole dialogue—as part of the oral Torah revealed to Moses—that is authori-tative. The "text" is now not so much an autonomous object that precedes tradition as a dimension of an interpretive tradition. It goes without saying that the goal of literary knowledge—to apprehend determinate meaning—is hardly possible in a hermeneu-tics where interpretation is an aspect of the text and text is an aspect of interpretation.

In his important study of deconstruction and theology, Kevin Hart notes the affinities that Derrida has with Jewish rather than Greek thought. Derrida, for instance, defines Judaism as "the birth and passion of *écriture* [writing]."[89] It is Chris-tian theology, we may recall, that is born with the genesis of the sign. Unlike Chris-tian exegesis, then, which comes to rest when the letter points to the Spirit or to Christ, Jewish exegetes enjoy no such interpretive Sabbath: "The Rabbinic tradition . . . based itself on the principle of multiple meanings and endless interpretability, maintaining that interpretation and text were not only inseparable, but that inter-pretation—as opposed to incarnation—was the central divine act."[90] That is, only by going further into the letter can one find a relevant meaning. Rabbinic exegesis puts a different twist on Derrida's observation that "there is nothing outside the text."

The Literal and the Figural

Just what is the sense of the letter? Does the letter have a single determinate sense, or does it contain the wisdom of the whole universe in latent form, as the rab-bis thought? For almost a thousand years, Christian readers focused on the divinely intended, spiritual sense of the Bible. "Any interpretation which could be put upon the text and was in keeping with the faith and edifying, had the warrant of God him-self."[91] In the twelfth century, however, the literal sense came to be seen as the most important, due largely to developments in the study of language and logic. By the sixteenth century, the Reformers considered the literal sense to be the only "proper" sense. But what is the literal sense, and does literal interpretation imply that Jesus Christ is *not* the proper reference of the Old Testament? What is at stake in these questions is ultimately the possibility of literary knowledge. Does the text afford enough light with which to identify a determinate meaning, or does it ultimately need to be read in the light of something else that illumines it?

The Literal Sense

Most dictionary definitions describe the literal sense as the primary meaning of a term, as the meaning established by common usage. The literal meaning is the "plain and ordinary" meaning. For Aristotle, the "proper" meaning of a noun is the object with which it is normally associated. Metaphors, by contrast, are a form of "deviant" naming, and for which reason Aristotle relegates figurative language to the realm of rhetoric as opposed to philosophy. Figurative language is "a deviation from what speakers of a language apprehend as the ordinary, or standard, significance or sequence of words, in order to achieve some special meaning or effect."[92] Metaphors, similes, synecdoches are all "tropes," that is, deviations or "turns" from the ordinary or "proper" course of language.

It is most important in what follows to distinguish the literal sense of Scripture from *literalistic* interpretation. A literalistic reading might be one that insisted on staying on the level of ordinary usage, even when another level is intended. A moment's reflection should suffice to expose the problems with such a literalistic reading: no one really thinks that Jesus has hinges and a knob when he says, "I am the door." A literal interpretation, however, can include figurative senses, if they are intended. Many church fathers maintained a healthy respect for the literal sense, even while chastising the Jews for the literalism that led them to miss the references to Christ in the Old Testament.

To confuse the Antiochene emphasis on the literal sense with a simple-minded literalism is a most regrettable mistake. John Chrysostom, another Antiochene exegete, wrote: "We must not examine the words as bare words, else many absurdities will follow, but we must mark the mind of the writer."[93] For the Antiochenes, the literal sense "covered the whole meaning of the writer, including his metaphors and figures."[94] Indeed, Beryl Smalley describes Theodore as "the first and very likely the only commentator of antiquity to introduce literary criticism into the study of the text."[95]

Literal Versus Figural Interpretation

What is a literal interpretation? Can we through literal interpretation find Christ in the Old Testament? While figurative reading seems to open the text up to multiple interpretations and to wholesale allegorizing, the reality is more complex. For the biblical text, literally interpreted, may itself point to a figural sense.

Augustine. The best place to begin studying the relation between the literal and the figural is with Augustine, whose *On Christian Doctrine* places his discussion of biblical interpretation within a larger theory of signs and the Christian faith. For Augustine, all knowledge concerns either things or signs. Signs are either proper or figurative. They are "proper" when they signify some thing (e.g., "Babylon" signifies the capital city of the Babylonian empire); they are figurative or allegorical when by indicating one thing they actually signify another (e.g., the city Babylon signifies an oppressive power that opposes the people of God). The literal reading determines to what things the signs refer.

Augustine offers a simple rule for deciding when to interpret allegorically: if a biblical text seems neither to teach a truth of the faith nor to illustrate love of God or neighbor, take it as figurative. "What is read should be subjected to diligent scrutiny until an interpretation contributing to the reign of charity is produced. If this result appears literally in the text, the expression being considered is not figurative."[96] When confronted with a range of interpretive options, then, Augustine's advice is to choose the one that best fosters love of God and neighbor. He is aware that this will lead to a text having multiple meanings, but here too he offers a limiting criterion: "When from a single passage not one but two or more meanings are elicited, even if what he who wrote the passage intended remains hidden, there is no danger if any of the meanings may be seen to be congruous with the truth taught in other passages of the Holy Scripture."[97]

While this may not be literal interpretation, it is certainly not arbitrary nor indeterminate. The literal sense determines that to which the *signs* refer; the rule of faith and the principle of charity determine that to which the *things* refer. On Augustine's view, *both* sign and thing have determinate and proper reference. Moreover, Augustine advocates a thorough analysis of the literal sense as a control on arbitrary reading.[98] As such, Augustine represents a synthesis of the Alexandrian and Antiochene approaches.

Aquinas. Figurative interpretation becomes more problematic with the rise of theology as a university subject. In the opening pages of his *Summa Theologica*, Aquinas considers possible objections to the multiple meanings of Scripture. Multiple meanings are (1) inappropriate for a science such as theology, (2) inappropriate if the creation of the interpreter, and (3) improper if not intended by the author. God, of course, can use the referents of literal discourse to signify something else. "The literal sense is the whole meaning of the inspired writer, and the spiritual the significance which God has given to sacred history."[99] This distinction is important. For Aquinas it is not the signs that are equivocal but the things signified by the signs: "The point of separation between the literal and spiritual senses now lay between meanings consciously put there by human authors, and meanings unknown to the human authors and of eternal validity put there by God, who had guided their conscious and unconscious work."[100] Aquinas is a good representative of twelfth-century interpreters, with their developing sense of language and logic and their tendency to analyze and clarify puzzling literal statements in Scripture instead of allegorizing them away.

The Reformers. With the Renaissance came a new concern for a grammatical and historical study of texts in the original languages. The Reformers too were concerned to recover the original sense, which they felt had been buried under centuries of spiritual interpretation. Luther in particular lost patience with the allegorical method; in the hands of allegorizers, the Bible was like a nose of wax that could be turned this way or that. In Luther's words: "I consider the ascription of several senses to Scripture to be not merely dangerous and useless for teaching but even to cancel the authority of Scripture whose meaning ought always to be one and the same."[101] For Luther, the authoritative sense of Scripture was not secret or hidden, but clear: "The Holy Ghost is the all-simplest writer that is in heaven or earth; therefore his words can have no more than one simplest sense, which we call the scriptural or literal meaning."[102]

At the same time, Luther acknowledged, with the Antiochenes, that the "literal" could include the spiritual sense if the author intended it.[103] With this insight, we arrive at an important hermeneutic principle, namely, that allegorical interpretation—reading for a sense other than the obvious one—is appropriate only if the text *is* an allegory.

Is it allegorical interpretation to find Christ in the Old Testament? Is the Old Testament an allegory? The Reformers, though insisting that Christ was the proper referent of many Old Testament passages, were unwilling to call their interpretation allegorical or to view the Bible as replete with allegory. They viewed key persons, actions, and events in the Old Testament as "figures" or "types" that, while historically real themselves, nevertheless prefigured later persons, actions, and events in the New

Testament. The crucial difference between figural or typological interpretation and its allegorical counterpart is that the former relates two items that stand in a historical relation of anticipation and fulfillment, whereas no such relation regulates the connection between the literal and spiritual senses in allegory. Hans Frei makes the important point that, though the Reformers set the literal sense in opposition to allegory, it was not opposed to figural interpretation: "Far from being in conflict with the literal sense of biblical stories, figuration or typology was a natural extension of literal interpretation. It was literalism at the level of the whole biblical story and thus of the depiction of the whole of historical reality."[104] For the Reformers, *history* itself has a determinate meaning—imposed not by the reader but intended by God—that culminates in God's self-revelation in Christ. The Reformers' typological interpretation followed from their Christology: the wisdom of God is not hidden on some higher conceptual level above the literal sense, but manifest in the literal meaning of the story of Jesus Christ.[105]

Is Meaning Ever "Proper"?

Distinguishing the "proper" or literal meaning from its improper or figurative counterpart has been a long-established practice in Christian interpretation of the Bible. Derrida and Fish, however, object to the very idea that meaning can ever be "proper," and in so doing they undercut the very distinctions between literal and figurative interpretation. In the allegorical tradition, the spiritual sense often corresponded to the philosophical sense—to the concept signified by a word. In locating meaning in an intelligible conceptual realm, allegorical interpretation gives stability to the "spiritual sense": "*This* (word) means *that* (concept)." Allegorical interpretation sees the meaning of a text as constituted outside the text in another framework: the conceptual. However, Derrida, Fish, and the newer postmodern allegorists use the figurative power of words to unsettle fixed concepts. The Undoer resists the allegorist's confident identification of the hidden meaning: "No text, [Derrida] argues, can be translated into philosophical language without remainder; there will always be a supplement which resists formalisation."[106] Indeed, from Derrida's perspective, meaning itself becomes "the allegory of a text."[107] Fish agrees: "There is no such thing as literal meaning if by literal meaning one means a meaning that is perspicuous no matter what the context and no matter what is in the speaker's or hearer's mind, a meaning that because it is prior to interpretation can act as a constraint on interpretation."[108]

"Proper" meaning—whether literal or allegorical—is part and parcel of the metaphysics of presence. How can a term or a text have a proper meaning if it does not even have a proper context? The problem with speaking about a proper sense is that it prematurely closes this play of signs. In the opinion of many postmodern interpreters, any appeal to some natural or higher order, prior to language and interpretation, is logocentric and ethnocentric.

For Derrida, proper meaning (*le sens propre*) connotes both propriety and property. Disputes about literal meaning are disputes over who "owns" meaning. Interpretive disputes are really power struggles. To ask a reader to conform to the "proper" meaning of the text is, in Derrida's opinion, a form of oppression, the same kind of oppression that pretends there is a "proper" way to dress or a "proper" way to paint.

It is the oppression that inevitably follows the claim that one possesses truth. Derrida states that this oppression of "the proper interpretation" is actually the source of all oppression in the world.[109]

Allegorisms Old and New

In Derrida's view, allegorizing is preeminently the philosopher's way of dealing with ancient texts. After all, the primary thrust of the logocentric thinker is to say, "This means that." What of the contemporary penchant for seeing multiple meanings in texts? Is this not a new form of allegorizing? Indeed, does not Derrida's own emphasis on indeterminacy foster the notion that a text has several senses? While there are indeed historical precedents for deconstruction, I believe they are to be found in the rabbinic and gnostic traditions of biblical exegesis, not in Christian allegorizing, much less in figural interpretation. Furthermore, the similarities between contemporary literary theory and rabbinic and gnostic interpretation are not coincidental: a similar theology funds their respective literary practices. The new element in modern and postmodern allegorizing is, above all, the a/theology that governs its practice. When Derrida reads for senses other than what the text seems to say, he is aiming not to arrive at a spiritual sense, but rather to multiply the carnal senses of the text.[110] The new allegorism locates textual meaning not in a system of higher truths, but in a sea of indeterminacy.

Augustine and Premodernity

Christian allegorism, let loose by Augustine and domesticated by Aquinas, has nothing to do with arbitrary or anarchic interpretation. Augustine's biblical interpretation, though it often appears fanciful, was actually governed by his christianized Neo-Platonic view of the world, which saw all things as summed up and fulfilled in Christ. Both the words of Scripture and the things of which Scripture speaks point, therefore, to something else. For the Christian, the end to which everything is referred, the true object of enjoyment, is God the Father, Son, and Holy Spirit.[111] Far from having multiple indeterminate senses, then, the Bible, together with the whole world, has for Augustine a single determinate sense. *It is the Trinity that ultimately functions as Augustine's criterion for allegorical interpretation.* Allegorical interpretation is the attempt to find the three-in-one in a multitude of signs and forms. Exegetical decisions ("this means that") ultimately are made within the interpretive framework of trinitarian theology. As Francis Watson correctly notes, *"Christian doctrine ... has a hermeneutical function."*[112] Here we simply note the role of Christian doctrine in passing. In Part 2, however, I will return at much greater length to trinitarian theology for the sake of developing a contemporary theological hermeneutics.

Kant and Modernity

The hermeneutical function of doctrine continues into the modern era, as a brief examination of Immanuel Kant's reading of Scripture demonstrates. Kant's problem was similar to that of the Alexandrian philosophers, namely, how to make an ancient text intelligible and plausible in a new context. Specifically, Kant's challenge was to extract a meaning from Scripture that would be useful in the Age of Enlightenment to readers who could not perhaps accept a supernaturalist worldview. What drives Kant's interpretation is his belief that the purpose of religion is to assist humanity in its moral striving. Morality is to Kant what charity was to Augustine.

Kant's *Religion Within the Limits of Reason Alone* is an extended allegorical interpretation, primarily of Genesis and the Gospels. The book represents "a thoroughgoing interpretation of [Scripture] in a sense agreeing with the universal practical rules of a religion of pure reason."[113] Kant is clear that we must prefer a morally useful interpretation to a literal interpretation that contains nothing at all helpful to morality. This is clearly an example of allegorical interpretation, except that the philosophical system that Kant coordinates with Scripture is moral rather than metaphysical. Though Kant was himself a great believer in duty, he thought nothing of providing interpretations that were "very forced" so long as they served the purposes of morality. According to Kant, the final purpose of reading holy Scripture "is to make men better; the historical element, which contributes nothing to this end, is something which is in itself quite indifferent, and we can do with it what we like."[114] Moral usefulness, he asserts, is "the highest principle of all Scriptural exegesis."[115] The "spirit" hidden in the letter of the text is for Kant the spirit of morality. It is hardly coincidental that Kant viewed Jesus Christ as a moral exemplar rather than as God Incarnate. Once again, one's Christology regulates what "other" meanings, beyond the literal, one finds in the Bible.

Gnosticism and Postmodernity

The New Testament encourages us to "test the spirits" (1 John 4:1), and we would do well to extend this maxim to the spiritual senses of Scripture. "My name is Legion, for we are many" (Mark 5:9). While there may not be anything particularly demonic about the multiplicity of allegorical senses, we may at least question their alleged spirituality.

What kind of spirit animates intertextual freeplay? To label postmodern thinkers "gnostic" appears at first sight to be both anachronistic and inaccurate. Were not the Gnostics an ancient, premodern movement? Is not their stress on knowledge (Gk. *gnosis* = knowledge) something that sets them apart from most postmoderns, whom I have earlier labelled unbelievers? Despite these apparent differences, I believe there are at least three important parallels between the two movements. First, and most fundamental, is a shared dualism. Postmoderns develop the gnostic dichotomy body and spirit into a dualism of language and the world.[116] For Derrida, all we have is carnality—the play of signs—never spirit (e.g., the world, reality, truth). Ronald Hall puts it well: "The spirit of writing is, by definition for Derrida, a perpetual breaking, a perpetual *sundering*, a perpetual hovering, a perpetual play of signs. The spirit of writing is essentially disembodied, essentially a break with the world."[117] Gnostics and Undoers deny Incarnation—the preeminent Christian premise that Word has become flesh.

Second, Gnostics and deconstructors emphasize salvation through right knowledge. Of course, Derrida does not put it quite that way. The knowledge he finds liberating is not the same as that of the Gnostics. Yet the thrust of deconstruction, like Gnosticism, is that a certain kind of knowledge—the knowledge of *différance* and its effects—liberates us from false totalizations and oppressive systems. With the realization that there is no fixed order to things comes the freedom to associate things at will. Release comes about not by denying, but rather by acknowledging *différance*.

Finally, this knowledge of the secret workings of language is won not through rational explanations so much as means that are more mysterious than methodical. *Gnosis* is attained not by the light of reason, but through the murkier means of a quasi-mystic intuition.

The contemporary emphasis on "freeplay" in interpretation bears a superficial resemblance to earlier allegorical interpretation insofar as both approaches encourage multiple meanings. As we have seen, however, early Christian allegorizing was neither unprincipled nor unfounded. The church fathers' allegorical interpretation was regulated by Neo-Platonist philosophy and trinitarian theology. By contrast, deconstruction celebrates its deregulation: the freeplay of signs is endless. There is no Neo-Platonic "One," no Christian three-in-one, that fulfills the sign and stops the play of meaning. Both Derrida and the pragmatists reject the metaphysics of presence. But is metaphysics so easily dispatched? Can either Undoer or User do without certain assumptions about the nature of reality? Could we perhaps be seeing in contemporary literary theory a return of the repressed, namely, a return of pre-Christian visions of the real?

The Reemergence of Hermetic and Rabbinic Interpretation in Postmodernity. The idea of "secret" meanings in texts, hidden in language to all but the initiate few, has a long history. "Hermetic literature" designates a body of writings associated with Hermes Trismegistos, a man of vast learning acquainted with both Greek philosophy and Egyptian magic. His writings dealt with the knowledge of things divine. Hermetic thinkers suggested that the order of the universe described by Greek mathematics and rationalism could be subverted "and that it was possible to discover new connections and new relationships in the universe."[118] Hermetic thinkers explored the secret connections between things, connections based not on rational categories such as cause and effect but rather on perceived similarities. In Christian Neo-Platonism, as we have seen, truth coheres. God may be beyond human language, but reality is ultimately non-contradictory. Hermetic thinkers, however, believed that "language, the more ambiguous and multivalent it is, and the more it uses symbols and metaphors, the more it is particularly appropriate for naming a Oneness in which the coincidence of opposites occurs."[119] The ultimate secret of Hermetic wisdom is another secret: that reality at its core is contradictory and incoherent.[120]

Umberto Eco observes a persistent influence of Hermetic thinking throughout Western history—on second-century Gnosticism, on twentieth-century existentialism, and perhaps on deconstruction. What these diverse movements share is a certain contempt for the "plain" meaning. Eco sees a number of parallels between ancient Hermeticism and the postmodern emphasis on "textuality": (1) A text is open-ended, capable of infinite interconnections; (2) to redeem the text one must destroy its pretense of meaning and suspect "that every line of it conceals another secret meaning; words, instead of saying, hide the untold";[121] (3) the real reader is the one who understands "that the secret of a text is its emptiness";[122] (4) truth encompasses opposites.[123]

Eco's second novel, *Foucault's Pendulum*, is both parable about postmodernity and a fable about the dangers of gnostic overinterpretation: "If you look at the world in a certain way, everything is connected to everything else."[124] The secret is beyond the capacity of discursive knowledge. "Electricity, radioactivity, atomic energy—the true initiate knows that these are metaphors, masks, conventional lies, or, at most, pathetic surrogates, for an ancestral, forgotten force, a force the initiate seeks and one day will know."[125] The hero of *Foucault's Pendulum* gets caught up in the quest for secret knowledge: "I began to question everything around me: the houses, the shop signs, the clouds in the sky, and the engravings in the library, asking them to tell me not their superficial story but another, deeper story, which they surely were hiding— but finally would reveal thanks to the principle of mystic resemblances."[126] Connecting things in this way, the narrator opines, "leads you to think that every detail of the world, every voice, every word written or spoken has more than its literal meaning, that it tells us of a Secret. The rule is simple: Suspect, only suspect. You can read sub-texts even in a traffic sign that says 'No littering.'"[127]

The new allegorism of deconstruction, which sees multiple levels of hidden meanings, is the inverse of its Christian predecessor. In Christian allegorization, signs and things speak "the rational and univocal discourse of God"; in Hermeticism texts speak "the irrational and ambiguous discourse of Hermes."[128] We are now in a position to formulate a general rule describing the relation between meaning and metaphysics: *textual meaning will only be as determinate and decidable as the conception of reality that it ultimately presupposes.*

From a slightly different perspective, Susan Handelman states that "there are striking and profound *structural* affinities between the work of our most recent and influential (Jewish) thinkers like Freud, Derrida, and Bloom, and Rabbinic models of interpretation."[129] Where Freud explores the details of dreams for signs of repressed unconscious desires, the rabbis studied the details of the Torah for signs of God's infinite wisdom. For both Freud and the rabbis, the surface meaning contains a hidden meaning. Freudian psychoanalysis and Jewish midrash thus represent similar interpretive strategies; each discovers in its respective text—the Torah, the dream—layer upon layer of hidden meaning.

Freud, like the rabbis and like Derrida, looks for knowledge in secret places, on the margins of consciousness. Dreams in particular were the "royal road to the unconscious," precisely because they eluded a person's conscious control and censure. Freud interprets dreams, and he interprets them meticulously: "We treated as Holy Writ what previous writers have regarded as an arbitrary improvisation."[130] Freud believes that dreams have a logic of their own: *not the logic of a syllogism but the logic of juxtaposition.* The unconscious is structured like a language, like a grand intertext that juxtaposes ideas, feelings, and things through free association. If one just looks hard enough, one will discover surprising connections and convergences between things that appear to have no logical or rational connection. For instance, an object or color might have a special significance to a person because of a previous traumatic experience (a device that Alfred Hitchcock exploited more than once in his films to great effect).

Handelman highlights the phenomenon of "displacement," a prominent theme in Freud and the rabbis alike. Displacement pertains to identifying with and then substituting one thing for another. For example, Freud believed that every child secretly identifies with its father and wants to take the father's place. Handelman suggests that Freud's work displaces the authority of Gentile culture (viz., the conscious thinking ego associated with Greek thought) with psychoanalysis (viz., the unconscious manifestation of latent meaning associated with Jewish interpretation). The Undoer too seeks to "kill" the father-author and to displace logocentrism. We can recognize in deconstruction a rebellion against the "paternal authority" of the text. Freedom comes through interpretation, for deconstructionist interpretation *is* displacement, as Handelman rightly observes: "Derrida's reality is not being, but absence; not the one, but the other; not unity but plurality, dissemination, writing, and difference . . . he is the new high priest of the religion of absence."[131] Whereas Philo discovered Plato in Moses, *Derrida has discovered Moses—the inexhaustible significance of the rabbinic letter—in Plato.*

Body, Spirit, Text.

> The world was full of marvelous correspondences, subtle resemblances; the only way to penetrate them—and to be penetrated by them—was through dreams . . . .[132]

Handelman argues that the rabbinic understanding of creation is the theological key to their handling of the text. God created freely and from nothing. At the heart of creation, then, is neither reason nor necessity (characteristic of Greek thinking about the cosmos), only will and contingency. Moreover, everything in creation is on a par; no part of the world is closer to God than another. Handelman makes the following inference: "The absence of hierarchical interpretation in Rabbinic thought may be connected to the absence of the concept of the hierarchy of being."[133] In other words, the rabbis drew connections between things not on the basis of a created order where everything has a determinate place, but rather on the basis of juxtaposition—free association. These connections destabilize logic and thereby deny the possibility of a straightforward or literal interpretation. In the beginning, one might say, was textuality. . . .

If Eco and Handelman are right, contemporary literary theory, philosophy, and theology are even more tightly interwoven than we might have expected. If God is dead or inaccessible, there can be no "proper" association of sign with thing or between things, but only "free associations," the freeplay of sign with sign, of sign with thing. Freud's "free association," rabbinic correspondences, Derrida's "freeplay of signs"—all are types of gnostic play in which concepts are connected not logically but haphazardly. Contemporary literary theory thus inadvertently confirms Chesterton's remark that when people stop believing in God, they don't then believe in nothing; they believe in *everything*.

Two literary critics, each associated with Yale, illustrate what I have termed the new gnostic allegorism. The literary theories of Harold Bloom and Paul de Man presuppose, each in its own way, a type of body-spirit dichotomy with regard to meaning, if only to deny that language ever corresponds to the world or that interpretations ever capture the literal meaning of texts. Bloom and de Man thus represent, from the standpoint of Christian theology, what one critic calls the "anti-incarnational extremes of hyperspiritualism and hypertextuality."[134]

In his *The Anxiety of Influence*, Bloom (a self-professed Jewish gnostic) compares the figure of the author to Milton's Satan. Like Satan, the author is not content with playing second fiddle to previous creator-authors. Authors are reluctant to admit that their texts are derivative rather than original, that they cannot say anything without invoking a host of literary and conceptual allusions. In order to assert his identity, therefore, the author must deny his paternity and write Satanic verses: "The modern poet is heroic because like Satan he refuses the 'incarnation of God's son', refuses the creation as ordered by God."[135] One must either rebel or renounce one's creativity, one's God-like originating power. The lie of Milton's Satan is, in Bloom's view, a heroic assertion of originality.

Readers, no less than poets, are in similar danger of losing themselves unless they too exert their creativity through *misreading*, which for Bloom is just another name for interpretation.[136] Traditional literary critics are less than pleased with this portrayal of their discipline: "Bloom's idea that criticism is poetry invites an interpretive anarchy."[137] The best criticism or commentary is for Bloom a kind of poetic reenactment, a form of authoring. We may here recall the rabbinic belief that their commentaries on the Torah were also part of the text. Appropriately enough, in *Kabbala and Criticism* Bloom invokes a comparison between the rabbis' esoteric commentaries and the critic's creative misreading.[138]

In a later book, *Poetry and Repression*, Bloom describes Romanticism as the search for a gnostic freedom from the anxiety of being influenced by law or nature: "Gnosticism is the fulfillment of Bloom's search for a mode of poetic experience and for a critical stance discontinuous with all that we know as father-haunted and community-bound."[139] On the one hand, Bloom grants the premise of intertextuality—that all writing and interpretation is a network of interconnected texts; yet, at the same time, he affirms his belief that the "strong" interpreter can rise above the encounter of text with text in order to make a genuinely creative association of his own: "The imagination is freed from reduction to textuality only by becoming a radically disincarnate spirit."[140] Bloom leaves us with a disembodied creative spirit hovering above the sea of intertextuality.

Paul de Man, Yale literary critic, friend and follower of Derrida, contrasts symbol and allegory as rival modes of understanding. Whereas symbol stands for the belief that language can attain reality, allegory acts as the reminder that there always exists a gap between signs and the reality they seek to render. Allegory is superior to symbol because it calls attention to its own arbitrary character. De Man thus denies what Bloom asserts, namely, the priority of the creative imagination over textuality and intertextuality. De Man deploys his allegorical interpretation with the intention "of undoing that assurance of intelligible sense and logic which governs most interpretive styles."[141] The literary critic who believes he or she has mastered the play of textual figuration and arrived at a stable, determinate sense is sorely deluded, for language is essentially figurative and not referential.

De Man is another example, then, of what I am calling the "new allegorism." His is an allegorism that seeks not to arrive at a higher meaning but rather to show why one never can arrive. His is an allegorism without a determinate "other" meaning.[142] *The new allegorist differs from the old, in other words, in acknowledging the undecidability of the other meaning.* It is the intertextual nature of the texts themselves that resists allegorical closure. The only "truth" of allegorizing is its disclosure of *différance.* De Man points out that allegory and irony share an identical structure, since "in both cases, the relationship between sign and meaning is discontinuous."[143] Unlike classical allegory, which sought to fix the meaning of the text in a stable system of truths, irony is "the systematic undoing . . . of understanding."[144]

For the new allegorists, the text is a patchwork of previous texts, a manifestation of unconscious forces, and is ultimately as opaque as the world itself. All claims to the contrary are dismissed as paternalistic. "Fathers"—church fathers, biological fathers, author-fathers—exert a certain claim and extort a certain guilt from their children, who desire to be free from the burden of obedient conformity and logical association. According to the new allegorists, texts and commentaries alike betray the tell-tale signs of their construction out of other texts. Textuality thus resists authority; and because it does so, the text is condemned to be forever orphaned.

One's interpretation, I have argued, will only be as determinate as one's overall worldview. The worldview of many postmoderns, I have further suggested, is characterized by the lack of a concept of a created or logical order. The postmodern worldview is rather a mishmash of arbitrary connections, of a system of differences that cannot be contained in any one structure—of *différance.*

The literary theories that make up the new allegorism are, to use Dawson's fine phrase, "surrogate theologies."[145] To be precise, they are anti-incarnational theologies. Bloom's gnostic hyperspiritualism denies that meaning is really in the text. His is a hermeneutic Docetism that recalls the heresy that Christ only seemed (Gk. *dokeō,* to seem) to have a real body. Bloom locates meaning in another realm—the realm of the spirit—which he associates with the imagination and distinguishes from the language of the text. De Man is just as anti-incarnational, but for the opposite reason. He is a hypertextualist who reduces meaning to intertextuality and the endless play of signs: "De Man offers a hyperkenosis (or complete emptying out) of self and meaning into letter."[146]

A view of the world thus undergirds the postmodern view of the language-world relation. From a Christian perspective, Christology is the key to understanding both the true nature of the world and the errors of the new allegorism. To quote Dawson once again: "The Christian account of incarnation insists that ultimate meaning has become mysteriously but deeply integrated with all the material stuff of life. . . . In contrast, Bloom insists that meaning is to be found elsewhere, while de Man insists that meaning is simply not to be found."[147] The question "Is there a meaning in this text?" is, in the final analysis, linked to another: "What think ye of Christ?"

TEXTUAL INDETERMINACY: THE RULE OF METAPHOR

A noun is proper when it has but a single sense. . . . No philosophy, as such, has ever renounced this Aristotelian ideal. This ideal is philosophy.[148]

The "turn to the text" is a turn away from the ancient Greek paradigm of language that has dominated Western philosophy. According to this standard view, language is an instrument of thought. Meaning lies in individual words and is a matter of naming things. Meaning, moreover, is primarily literal or univocal; figurative language therefore has to be "translated" or reduced into literal language in order to be understood and in order to be clear enough to be useful to the philosopher.

As we have seen, the logocentric alliance between reality, thought, and language is precisely what the Users and Undoers call into question. The new paradigm of "textuality" reconceives the word-concept-world relation quite differently. Textuality calls attention to the instability of words and texts and gives rise to what Eco has termed the "Hermetic drift" in contemporary interpretation. Of all words that impede the philosopher's progress, metaphors have traditionally been thought to be the worst. Metaphors are equivocal; they do not have one clear sense, so that they cannot give rise to clear and distinct knowledge. Metaphor thus represents the epitome of textuality; in metaphor, meanings refuse to stand still.

"Interpretation is the work of concepts. It cannot help but be a work of elucidation . . . and consequently a struggle for univocity."[149] Concepts strive for univocity, for clear and distinct ideas—the very opposite of metaphors. The aim of interpretation, then, like philosophy, would seem to be univocal knowledge. Is literary knowledge, not necessarily an exhaustive but at least a partial knowledge, within the reader's grasp? Interpretation may be the work of concepts, but deconstruction challenges every claim to conceptual stability and totality. Derrida is out to deconstruct the very idea "that meaning can always be grasped in the form of some proper, self-identical concept."[150]

Derrida accuses philosophy of forgetting its roots in writing. Two traits of writing in particular—metaphoricity and intertextuality—frustrate the thinker who wants language to "stand still" so that it can be interpreted. Metaphoricity undermines the stability of concepts; intertextuality undermines the stability of context. Whereas in the preceding chapter deconstruction undid being, it here appears as the undoing of knowledge. Concepts are undone when they are unmasked as metaphors, as figures of speech masquerading as privileged keys that unlock reality. If interpretation is the work of concepts, and if concepts are metaphors, and metaphors "writing," then truly there is nothing outside the text. *Textuality, we might say, is interpretation's undoing.* What Derrida ultimately challenges is the philosopher's prejudice that reason can somehow dispense with metaphor.

Why Metaphors Are User-Friendly

Aristotle, we saw earlier, pictured the "proper" relation of language to the world in terms of predication. Language is meaningful and true when what is said corresponds to the way things are: S is P (subject-predicate). Aristotelian logic deals with the relations between proper statements of this kind. "If one were to say that the word has an infinite number of meanings, obviously reasoning would be impossible; for not to have one meaning is to have no meaning."[151] Figurative speech, on the other hand, plays havoc with the laws of logic. For example, is the statement, "The Lord is my shepherd," true or not? That depends on whether metaphors have determinate meaning. It is Derrida's contention that concepts and texts alike are radically metaphorical and are thus irreducible to literal language. The question arises, therefore, whether metaphors (and texts insofar as they partake in metaphoricity) can be interpreted (e.g., assigned stable meaning). Must we extend Heisenberg's "uncertainty principle" from physics to literary criticism too?[152] Is undecidability the last thing to be said about the conflict of interpretations?

Deviant Behavior?

Aristotle's famous definition of metaphor consigned it to the margins of philosophy for centuries: "Metaphor consists in giving the thing a name that belongs to something else."[153] On this standard account, metaphor is a deviant naming, a swerve from literal meaning. In metaphor, a name is transferred from its proper place and assigned to a context where it does not belong. Metaphor is a matter of words playing truant. More negatively, Thomas Hobbes describes metaphor as an abuse of speech; it lies somewhere in between self-deception and lying. In metaphor, words are used "in other sense than they are ordained for—and thereby deceive others."[154] Metaphor takes connotations that belong with one kind of thing and smuggles them into another.

Aristotle presents the so-called "substitution theory" of metaphor: one name (the figurative) takes the place of another (the literal) on the basis of a supposed resemblance. The implication here is that metaphor does not discover or express something new, but only states more decorously what could be said literally. On this view—one to which most philosophers have until recently subscribed—metaphor is merely a linguistic decoration. With regard to the question, "Can metaphors be interpreted?" the standard answer is yes. A metaphor is successfully interpreted when it is unpacked, translated into literal speech, and hence reduced to its underlying literal resemblance.

What does Aristotle's analysis of metaphor have to do with literary interpretation? Just this: the same dynamic by which metaphors are reduced to literal speech could be said to characterize the work of interpretation in general. The attempt to state "the meaning" of the text exemplifies, on this analogy, what we might call the *substitution theory of interpretation*. Commentary is to text what metaphor is to literal speech. On this view, commentaries and metaphors are merely decorative glosses that can be stripped back to a plainer, proper sense. This, at least, is Derrida's critique of philosophy and interpretation alike.

Many contemporary thinkers believe this account of metaphor to be inadequate.[155] They challenge the idea that a metaphor can be translated into literal speech, much less into clear and distinct concepts. On the contrary, metaphors say something new, something that cannot be reduced to a literal paraphrase. For metaphor is not about how things are classified and labelled, but about how things relate. Metaphor is the linguistic process by which certain resemblances are not restated, but invented and discovered.

Begetters of Meaning

Metaphor, the erstwhile whipping boy of the philosophers, has recently come into its own. Metaphors are now seen to be a matter not only of words, but of sentences. Indeed, Ricoeur has shown metaphors to be "texts in miniature."[156] He argues that metaphors create a "surplus of meaning" that cannot simply be reduced to some literal paraphrase. It follows that metaphors exercise a cognitive, as opposed to a merely aesthetic or decorative, function. To be precise, metaphors are indispensable cognitive instruments that enable thought to perceive resemblances between things that would not otherwise be observable.[157]

Metaphor is the imagination making creative connections, thinking laterally, talking out loud. Metaphors work by "confusing the established logical boundaries for the sake of detecting new similarities which previous categorization prevented our noticing."[158] Unlike symbols, which are tied to things, metaphors are the free creations of discourse. The tension in metaphor is not something that occurs between two terms (e.g., "God," "rock") but rather the tension that accompanies two opposed interpretations of an utterance ("God is a rock"). The literal interpretation is absurd, and its very absurdity calls for a metaphorical interpretation. The association of ideas in a metaphorical statement is the result neither of induction nor deduction; neither scientific observation nor logical reasoning create metaphors. Indeed, metaphor subverts logic; it has been called an "intentional category mistake."

This is not to suggest that metaphors are irrational. On the contrary, many scientific discoveries are results of a new "seeing as" (e.g., Newton's seeing the world as a "mechanical universe"). Philosophers of science are happy to view scientific models as large-scale metaphors. Mary Hesse states that rationality consists in nothing less than the continuous adaptation of our language to our expanding world, "and metaphor is one of the chief means by which this is accomplished."[159] Thanks to metaphor, we can set the unfamiliar in the context of the familiar in order to understand it in new ways (e.g., light as a wave or as a stream of particles). Metaphor may perhaps be as powerful an instrument for exploring the world as the microscope. For by reworking language, metaphors enable us to see things differently.

According to Ricoeur, metaphors do not merely repackage meaning; they create it. They thus open up new possibilities for seeing, and categorizing, the real. Ricoeur draws an important conclusion from metaphor's creative power: "Real metaphors are not translatable."[160] Metaphor, in other words, is much more than a secondary substitute for literal speech. It is therefore Ricoeur's contention that metaphor has a surplus of meaning that exceeds the literal, and thus performs a cognitive function that can only be approximated, not exhausted, by the univocal discourse of the concept. Indeed, Ricoeur suggests that metaphors not only disrupt old ways of seeing things, but are perhaps responsible for begetting such ways in the first place: "The 'metaphoric' that transgresses the categorial order also begets it."[161] In other words, resemblances between things, resemblances that give birth to concepts and universals, are a product of the metaphoric imagination. Today's dictionary meaning was yesterday's metaphor.

Metaphorical Interpretation

Ricoeur's emphasis on the inexhaustibility of metaphors is well-taken. Yet Ricoeur is able to coordinate metaphors and concepts in a way that Derrida is not. For Ricoeur, as we have seen, interpretation—even of metaphor—is the work of concepts. The one discourse does not simply dissolve into the other. If it did, we would not be able to draw the line between text and commentary. From the discussion thus far, it is clear that we need to respect the *irreducibility* of metaphor. Yet it is also important to preserve the interpreter's ability to *say something* about the meaning of metaphor. In what follows I defend the position that *metaphors, like texts, are determinate enough to convey stable meaning without being exhaustively specifiable*. Metaphors, perhaps like much literal language itself, are neither wholly univocal nor wholly equivocal.

It is one thing to interpret metaphors, however, and quite another to interpret metaphorically. To interpret metaphorically is to see resemblances between texts and other texts or contexts where none were intended. Whereas metaphor, in the hands of an author, is an indispensable cognitive instrument for formulating new insights, metaphorical interpretation is a method employed by the reader to undo the notion that a text has literal meaning.

In Western philosophy, truth has traditionally been associated with literal speech, with speech about being, with describing "what is." Metaphors, on the other hand, speak about beings in the mode of "is and is not" (e.g., God is and is not a rock). Derrida reads the history of Western philosophy as the systematic repression of metaphor; metaphysics, in particular, represses the "is not." Where metaphor "transfers" meaning from one domain to another, so metaphysics transfers a concrete image to the realm of abstract truth. "Meta" is that movement that carries words "beyond."[162] For Derrida, such "transgression" is the original philosophical sin: the metaphorical "as" is mistaken for the metaphysical "is."[163] In short: *metaphysics is the attempt to give a literal interpretation of "what is."* The problem, as Derrida sees it, is that all language—indeed, all reality—is, so to speak, metaphorical in nature; "is and is not" is thus truer to the *différance* behind things. Instead of being one figure of speech among others, then, metaphor is for Derrida the clue to language and reality in general. Deconstruction exposes the metaphorical "is and is not" at the bottom of metaphysical "is."[164]

It was Nietzsche's madman who first informed modern Europeans that God was dead. Metaphysics—the project of describing ultimate reality—had already received a mortal wound from Kant. It only remained for Nietzsche to work out the implications of God's demise for language and interpretation. One consequence was immediately apparent: without God, the world has no ultimate meaning. Whatever meaning we find in the world is meaning we have created. In Nietzsche's view, metaphor is the instrument whereby humans create meaning in the world. We do not discover so much as create relations between things. What, then, is truth? Truth, says Nietzsche, is a mobile army of metaphors; truths are illusions of which one has forgotten that they *are* illusions. What we take as literal or proper speech—for example, "the leg of a chair"—is really metaphor that has either died or been forgotten.

Philosophers prefer to believe their illusory interpretation of reality; they choose to exchange the truth for a lie. For Nietzsche, however, it is essential that we acknowledge our philosophies as fictions. If we do not, they will return to oppress us. For once established as truth, a theory is difficult to dislodge. "Truth" for Nietzsche discourages further exploration; it stifles creativity, not to mention humanity itself. Metaphors, on the other hand, are user-friendly; they make possible and encourage creative readings of the world.

Language—and thought—is essentially metaphorical, characterized more by free and creative association (a horizontal relation between words) rather than by a natural or logical association (a vertical relation between words and the world). As

Don Cupitt puts it: "The meaning of signs is always 'sideways' and differential, not referential."[165] It is only the handiwork of metaphor that divides "animals" from "plants" by inventing perceived similarities. Whether humans are to be classified with "animals" (as in Aristotle's definition of man as "the rational animal") or not is a matter not of metaphysics, of some ultimate natural scheme of things, but of metaphor. Epistemology ultimately rests on a figure of speech. This, at least, is the postmodern hypothesis: that reality is ultimately a construction of linguistic usage, where pride of place for world-making goes to metaphor. On this view, metaphysics is merely the result of a highly persuasive media campaign.

Derrida's rule of metaphor is perhaps best stated in terms of "taking every thought captive." No thought, no idea, no concept is allowed to break free from writing and establish a non-linguistic beachhead from whence it can make superior truth claims. If there is nothing beyond (*meta-*) language, then metaphysics is at bottom metaphorical. The tension between the "is and is not" subverts the clean crispness of Aristotelian logic. Philosophical concepts strive to eliminate ambiguity, but they can only do so at the cost of repressing the play of identity and difference that lies at the heart of metaphor. Derrida is explicit about the consequences of the metaphorical "is and is not" for syllogistic reasoning: "Metaphoricity is the logic of contamination and the contamination of logic."[166] *Metaphor thus stands for the inescapable captivity of thought to language.*

Derrida's maxim—"there is nothing outside the text"—means here that there is no non-metaphorical way of speaking about the world. For Derrida, it is only prejudice that privileges philosophical as opposed to poetic language. Philosophers refuse to read their own texts as a species of literature. Philosophy covers its tracks, keeping its origins in metaphor and myth in the shadows of its prehistory. Philosophy cannot, therefore, be strictly separated from literature; concepts are merely the rebellious progeny of metaphors.

From the premise that all language and thought is metaphorical, Derrida concludes that all interpretation should be metaphorical—creative, marked by free association, irreducible to literal paraphrase, equivocal. Clearly, if interpretation is metaphorical, it is difficult to speak of determinate meaning in texts or of commentaries as yielding knowledge of a text's determinate meaning.

Metaphors of a Higher Order

Texts appear to be closed and self-contained. There are a finite number of pages bound together in an enclosed space. It would seem to follow that there are a finite number of ways to interpret texts as well. Both appearances, according to the Undoers, are deceptive. The text, like the sign itself, is constituted more by differences— by what it is not—than by a stable presence or meaning. Metaphoricity is simply the phenomenon of *différance,* now repeated on the level of the sentence and the text, rather than the sign.

Metaphoric Narratives

Is it legitimate to interpret texts metaphorically, as though they were metaphors? Both Ricoeur and Derrida agree that what is true of metaphor applies also to texts.

There are at least three ways in which texts resemble metaphors: (1) Like metaphor, the text deviates from its literal sense by virtue of being written and so freed from its author and original situation. Like the metaphor, in other words, the text is "transferred" into a new semantic domain. The text is thus free to enter into creative association with and to address new contexts. (2) Thanks to this transfer, textual reference becomes indeterminate. What texts are about becomes a function of how readers make sense of them in new contexts. Like the metaphor, then, the text has multiple meanings. (3) Just as one cannot substitute a literal paraphrase for metaphor, so one cannot simply substitute an interpretation (e.g., the work of concepts) for the text. There is a surplus of meaning in both that resists the interpreter's attempt to reduce them to a literal or univocal meaning.

C. H. Dodd called Jesus' parables "extended metaphors." Ricoeur goes further. He cites parables as a paradigmatic example of metaphoric narrative. Indeed, Jesus calls attention to their metaphoric nature by prefacing them with the formula "the kingdom of God is like." The parable as a whole is not only about "a certain man" but rather about how God's reign transforms ordinary reality. The metaphoric tension is thus between the plot of the parable and everyday life. Thanks to the parable, in other words, we are able to gain a new insight into the world that would not be possible without the story. The parable cannot be paraphrased in literal speech; without the story we lose the insight.

The Intertext

Though each parable can stand on its own, they are grouped together and make sense together. Moreover, they are embedded in a Gospel—another text. Ricoeur claims that this "intertextual" structure, whereby one reads a text in the light of another text (e.g., parables in the light of the passion narrative, and vice versa), is the key to metaphorical interpretation. The Gospel, in turn, is what it is because of its location with regard to other texts (e.g., the Law and the Prophets). The story of Jesus makes sense in light of the stories Jesus tells as well as in light of earlier stories about Israel. It is intertextuality, similarly, that enables us to relate the Old to the New Testament, to say that "*this* (Israel's history) means *that* (Jesus' history)." Like the two terms in a metaphor, the two Testaments are brought near to one another thanks to the creative imagination. Next, on an even higher level, the Bible as a whole, taken as a text, interacts with the reader. Finally, the reader's life too is a kind of text, constituted in turn by various forms of contemporary discourse (e.g., religious, social, political, familial, etc.).[167]

Ricoeur therefore views intertextuality as a species of the genus metaphor. Two texts that have no literal or logical connection are nevertheless seen together, and as a result of this dynamic interaction new meaning is produced—"resemblance" is created. Whereas metaphor associates two semantic fields (e.g., "God" and "rock"), intertextuality associates two or more textual fields, effectively creating a new context in which to read a text.[168] Intertextuality means that texts are open—open to the effects of past texts and to the contexts of present readers.

Intertextuality is thus another way of restating Derrida's maxim that "there is nothing outside texts." There is no such thing, that is, as a text-in-itself. Strictly speaking, a text is not itself; texts become themselves only as they differ and relate to other specific texts. A text "is a relational event, not a substance to be analyzed."[169] A text is part of a network of texts that has no center, no beginning, and no end. Some critics have used intertextuality as an excuse for textual "freeplay." If there is no constraining context, why not spin off Freudian, Marxist, feminist, structuralist, etc., interpretations of, say, *Winnie the Pooh*, or of the Gospel of Mark, for that matter?[170] This is precisely the Undoer's goal: systematically to peel away the various layers of textual construction. Deconstruction functions as a kind of conceptual "source criticism" that traces the history of various textual traditions that are enfolded in a given text. Every text is an intertext; it is and is not itself.

Biblical Indeterminacy

How metaphorical is the biblical text? Have biblical interpreters and theologians, in their zeal for conceptual clarity, similarly forgotten that Scripture and theology are forms of writing? How far should the biblical commentator be concerned to provide a literal paraphrase of the biblical text? How far should the theologian go in demetaphorizing Scripture? The aim of many theologians is to reproduce the full measure of biblical truth in a coherent conceptual system. Theology aspires to the absolute clarity of the concept; metaphors are conceptually unclean. For others, however, such as Ricoeur, such an enterprise is misguided. Metaphors nourish thought; thought would atrophy without metaphor. No paraphrase, neither commentary nor systematic theology, can ever exhaust the riches of the metaphor. Still other theologians seize the metaphorical nature of religious language as an opportunity to celebrate human creativity. When one discovers that metaphors undergird metaphysics, one realizes that "the world, knowledge and the human condition do not *have* to be constituted in any one particular way, however basic."[171] Apparently, neither God nor the world has a fixed shape; views of God and world alike are shaped by language.

Metaphorical Theology: Theological Indeterminacy

Sallie McFague's *Models of God* wrestles with this fundamental problem of indeterminate meaning and undecidability. For McFague, the Bible, like all writing, speaks "sideways," in metaphors. Neither reason nor revelation escapes the web of writing. She takes for granted that the biblical ways of speaking about God, because they are metaphors, do not actually correspond to God's nature or his relation to the world. Rather, the metaphors create a model, a way for us to view God. Some biblical metaphors, however, are "outmoded or oppressive."[172] We are therefore free to associate God with new semantic fields and thus to create new models or imaginative pictures. Though theology is "*mostly* fiction," McFague contends that some fictions are better than others. But what does "better" mean in this context? It certainly cannot mean "more accurate representation."

McFague's main criterion about the worth of a metaphor is its "appropriateness for our time."[173] She makes the pragmatist gambit: *choose the metaphors for God and God's relation to the world that most enhance the kind of life you prefer.*[174] She believes that such metaphors as "mother" or "lover" more accurately convey the loving relation of God to humanity than the traditional metaphors of father and king. Similarly, she suggests that we view the world as God's "body" rather than "God's realm." Such a model is more conducive to a greener theology and thus more appropriate (viz., useful) for our ecological age.

McFague's view of biblical metaphor coincides nicely with Rorty's pragmatic stance towards language in general. Language is considered true when words are useful for a certain practice. Rorty claims that metaphors survive by good luck, by being useful. Metaphors that prove extremely useful may be promoted to the rank of concepts. Rorty espouses a kind of Darwinian perspective with regard to the growth of language: every so often, a chance linguistic mutation just happens to serve humanity's purposes better. Good metaphors are sheer contingencies of linguistic behavior:

> For all we know or should care, Aristotle's metaphorical use of *ousia*, St Paul's metaphorical use of *agape*, and Newton's metaphorical use of *gravitas*, were the results of cosmic rays scrambling the fine structure of some crucial neurons in their respective brains. . . . It hardly matters how the trick was done. The results were marvelous. There had never been such things before.[175]

It's metaphors all the way down. There is no non-metaphorical word that can be said of God. The pragmatists' "God" is indeterminate: "The innovative power of human linguistic behavior, in causal interaction with the environment, is all that is left of God."[176] Metaphor is a strategy for expanding language, but language remains differential, not referential, and truth remains a matter of utility.

Intertextual Theology: Canonical Indeterminacy

Intertextuality both confirms and challenges the traditional idea of canon. "Canon" (Gk. *kanōn*, measuring rod) refers to a list of recommended or authoritative books.[177] The canon of the Old and New Testaments, as well as that of the Bible as a whole, encloses a space within which texts deemed authoritative can interact and inform one another. Brevard Childs believes that the "canonical context" of the biblical books—by which he means not only the final form of the biblical books but their positions in relation to one another in Scripture—is the most important index of their meaning: "The ordering of the tradition for this new [canonical] function involved a profoundly hermeneutical activity, the effects of which are now built into the structure of the canonical text."[178]

Canon confirms intertextuality by showing it at work. New Testament texts refer directly and indirectly to certain Old Testament texts; the meaning of the Synoptic Gospels is in part a function of their differences from one another; later texts are shot through and through with the vocabulary and themes of earlier texts. In short, the books within the biblical canon form a "separate cognitive zone" and are "interrelated like the parts of a single book."[179] The canon encourages a play of meaning, as it were, but only within carefully prescribed boundaries.

Intertextuality has the last word, however, ultimately challenging and then exploding the idea of canon as a fixed text. It does so in two ways. First, intertextuality challenges the idea that a text has a self-same meaning: "A canonical approach depends on the possibility . . . that a text is capable of being *not synonymous with itself*—in other words, that the very same sequence of words can mean different things in different contexts."[180] For example, Psalm 22 means one thing by itself, another taken with the Psalms as a whole, and still another when cited by Jesus. Consequently, "the meaning of a text . . . is never fully present. Meaning is always in the process of forming, deforming, and reforming."[181]

Second, intertextuality challenges the idea that Scripture interprets Scripture, that is, the notion that the biblical texts should ultimately be read in light of one another. Modern biblical criticism has suggested that the canon is a late and arbitrary imposition on the books contained within it. The canon, in other words, is an illegitimate fence around the Scriptures, while *sola scriptura* is the attempt (again illegitimate) to create an interpreter-free zone. The Undoer dismantles the fence and opens the texts to associations with other texts and contexts. We have already noted the resemblance between deconstruction and rabbinic interpretation. A typical page of the Talmud combines voices from different times and countries: "Texts echo, interact, and interpenetrate."[182] Intertextuality is the free association of diverse voices, the centrifugal force that explodes the centripetal constraint of canon. Meaning is not something located in texts so much as something that happens between them. *It is precisely because this "between" cannot be stabilized that intertextuality undermines determinacy of meaning.* With the notion of intertextuality, the line between text and commentary is blurred to the point of almost disappearing. If there is no such thing as a text in itself, then interpretation "is actually intrinsic to the text's own becoming."[183]

The related concepts of "book" and "canon" represent parallel attempts to close textual ranks and to limit the play of meaning. Just as "text" explodes the idea of book, so too "intertextuality" explodes the idea of canon. Just as there is no one text that can be regarded as the absolute origin of another text, so there is no stable context from which to determine the fixed meaning of a text. Mark Taylor draws the inevitable conclusion:

> The codependence of texts precludes both the mastery of one text by another and the subservience of one text to another. Scriptural relativity breaks the rule of canon and disperses authoritative tradition. . . . With the unravelling of book, canon, and tradition, scripture becomes free to drift endlessly.[184]

INTERPRETIVE AGNOSTICISM?

Are there any criteria that enable us to distinguish better from worse interpretations? Is knowledge in interpretation possible? Can interpreters make truth claims about the meaning of texts? Or are we living in a time of metaphor and intertextuality, a time without absolutes or judges, when every reader may do what is right in his or her own eyes?

Two contrasting interpretations of interpretation now compete for the soul of Western culture. One seeks to decipher and to locate a stable determinate meaning; the other affirms the freeplay of signs and gives up the search for some vantage point outside language. The one seeks understanding; the other tries to avoid being taken in. According to the first view, readers must stop the Hermetic drift and try to swim ashore. According to the second, Derridean view, readers must accept, and perhaps enjoy, the free-floating play of meaning. From this vantage point, those who make knowledge claims are the ones who are immoral and irresponsible. In the new morality of literary knowledge, honesty means confessing the artificiality of one's interpretations.

"Absolute" Interpretation

In the traditional view of interpretation, hermeneutics resembles epistemology in that both disciplines aim at objective knowledge. The philosopher makes theories that accurately represent the world, the Book of Nature; the interpreter writes commentaries that represent the meaning of the text. In both cases, thinking is accountable to something outside it (e.g., the world, the text). There is an absolute standard by which to measure our truth claims and our interpretations alike. Traditional interpretation is "absolute" in a second sense as well: it resists the notion that our standpoints interfere with our knowing. As we have seen, the modern subject is a miniature version of the deity of medieval theology. Reason aims at absolute knowledge: a God's-eye point of view—knowledge that is true not just for me here and now, but true for all at all times and places.

"Anarchic" Interpretation

Postmodern thinkers fear that realism, whether metaphysical or hermeneutical, is always authoritarian. If meaning is independent of the interpreter's attempt to know it, then the interpreter is accountable to something prior to oneself. Neither the Undoer nor the User mourns the loss of such a concept of meaning and the concomitant notion of the authority of the text. Derrida rather celebrates "the joyous affirmation of the play of the world and of the innocence of becoming, the affirmation of a world of signs without fault, without truth, and without origin which is offered to an active interpretation."[185] The burden of the Real is lifted; instead of having slavishly to imitate, humans are free to create, to become "like gods." Interpretation as *poiesis* (making, producing) replaces interpretation as *mimesis* (copying, imitating).

"There are no facts, only interpretations."[186] For Nietzsche, only those who are too weak to create the world for themselves believe in truth: "That the value of the world lies in our interpretations . . . this idea permeates my writings."[187] What counts as a "fact" is relative to an interpretation. Bultmann makes a similar point with regard to Gospel interpretation: what the facts are depends on the presuppositions we bring to the text. If there is no uninterpreted bedrock of fact, then our interpretations—our alleged discoveries of textual facts—are in reality fictions we create. Interpretation is no longer a matter of knowing, but of inventing. The demise of hermeneutics—of theories of understanding and literary knowledge—gives rise to the endless play of meaning.

Antinomian Play

If there are no literary facts, then literary criticism becomes a mode of play. The sole responsibility of the critic is to guard against totalizing interpretation that pretends to have discerned the meaning of a text. The critic does this by undoing the text, exposing its contradictory logics, and releasing the freeplay of signs. "Play" becomes the rule of metaphoric intertextuality. The game of interpretation has many players but no winners. The hard saying of deconstruction and pragmatism alike is that "there is nothing deep down inside us except what we have put there ourselves, no criterion that we have not created in the course of creating a practice."[188]

The Undoer exposes the play of differential relations between sign and sign, text and text, and text and context. "'Play' is itself a technical term for the absence of a transcendental signified—the goal of traditional interpretive searches for 'the meaning' of the work."[189] For example, Derrida interprets a Platonic dialogue about *mimesis* in light of Mallarmé's short prose-poem about a mime whose gestures imitate no model. There is no logical or historical association between these texts, only a linguistic similarity based on the term "mimetic." Whereas philosophy tries to disambiguate concepts, literature "operates in a realm that undermines alternatives and the logic of identity."[190] Derrida's reading "embodies the lawless amorality of nonexclusive relativity."[191]

In the absence of authors and authority, interpreters no longer need to conform. Against Augustine and the older allegorists, who believed that signs referred to truths, Derrida maintains that the play of signs is purely horizontal. Yet paradise lost is also paradise regained; the loss of transcendence is only the negative condition for a new liberation. *The loss of transcendence (the belief that signs and texts have fixed meanings) opens up every horizontal possibility.* We are freed to play, limitlessly and endlessly, at non-conformity. The grounds for Western culture and philosophy—God, substance, self—are in the final analysis only *playgrounds*. Deconstruction loosens rigid structures and sets the carousel of meaning in perpetual motion. The metaphor of carnival, often invoked to describe deconstruction, is apt; after all, nothing liberates from authority as much as laughter.[192]

Power Play

What is left of literary criticism if there are no facts, only playful interpretations? Whereas mimetic criticism serves the epistemological mandate to gain knowledge about texts, poetic criticism serves the political mandate of putting forward an individual's or a community's point of view. Knowledge (*mimesis*) has been eclipsed by "make-believe" (*poiesis*). "To say that we must have respect for facts is just to say that we must, if we are to play a certain language game, play by the rules."[193] As Fish puts it, literary criticism becomes "an attempt on the part of one party to alter the beliefs of another so that the evidence cited by the first will be seen *as* evidence by the second."[194] For the postmodernist, "the only justification that truth-claims can have is their persuasive efficacy, their power to convince in the context of existing belief-systems."[195]

For Nietzsche and Derrida, reason is an authoritarian force of repression; for Foucault, knowledge is a form of power. From the Undoer's perspective, any claim to have attained objectivity in interpretation is suspected of being mere political posturing. It is all too easy to confuse good reasons with *my* reasons, objectivity with how *I* see things. It is also easy (and, as we will see, convenient) to find the will to power (individual or corporate) behind claims to have determined the meaning of a text.

Cupitt agrees with Derrida about the political dimension of knowledge claims. Church and society alike seek political power by appealing to something higher than discourse. Augustine called this higher something the "City of God"; Plato called it the "Republic." For some this something higher is made manifest through revelation; for others, it is discovered with reason. In any case, since there is something to which life and language should conform, we may say that there is an order and constraint on human freedom. Cupitt calls this system of constraints "Culture."

Cupitt supplies a postmodern theological basis for anarchic interpretation. He contrasts Culture (the authority of an established order of meanings) with Desire (the autonomy of the individual seeking innovative self-expression).[196] Culture relies on the notion of determinate meaning and gives rise to authoritative interpretation because it believes there is something to which our interpretations, and our lives, should conform. Knowledge in interpretation is tied up with cultural conformity—with obedience and with a hermeneutics of duty. The hermeneutics of Desire, by contrast, is anarchic. It resists the order and constraints that Culture slaps on freedom. Culture, insofar as it stifles creativity, represses humanity. Cupitt connects Culture to Law, Desire to Life.[197]

The Ends of Interpretation

The undoing of the epistemology of meaning is related to the changing paradigm of what it is to interpret a text. Proponents of the new allegorism, of metaphorical interpretation, and of the hermeneutics of desire no longer recognize a reality principle (the way the text is), only the pleasure principle (the way I want the text to be for me, for us). I have attempted to show how the end of interpretation as a means for acquiring knowledge about textual meaning has not spelled the end of interpretation so much as the beginning of a new end or purpose for interpretation: self-realization through creative play.

What is the aim of deconstruction? What is deconstruction for, if it is not for making some kind of truth claim about something? Norris, we may recall, sees Derrida as a continuation of Kant's agenda of inquiring into the nature and limits of Reason. Derrida's critique of Reason is more radical than Kant's, for Derrida holds that Reason is what serves our ethico-political interests.[198] Behind rationality lies value (ethics) and power (politics). Deconstruction is a kind of "sophistic acid" that strips away the layers of rhetoric that disguise values as truths. The end of deconstruction is to destabilize any interpretation of the text that pretends to have got it right.

Deconstructive literary criticism is anarchic: without origin, without control. Yet this "anarchy is not a nihilistic destruction of all authority, but a belief in a plurality of authorities."[199] The Undoer plays one authoritative voice off another in order to resist totalization and totalitarianism. The conflict of interpretations—that is, the conflict between the two interpretations of interpretation (Culture/law/duty vs. Desire/freedom/play)—is related to a more basic conflict of values. Behind these debates about the nature of interpretation lie conflicting visions of what it is to be authentically human. Whether there is determinate meaning in texts is ultimately linked with the question of whether there is determinate meaning to human life. At the root of current disputes over hermeneutics, then, we find not only an epistemological dispute about the aims of interpretation but an ethical dispute over the aims of life.

Desire yearns to be free of hermeneutical, epistemological, and ethical constraints. Interpretation has become, for Nietzsche, "a means of winning mastery over that which calls into question one's own autonomy."[200] For postmoderns, interpretation is not about gaining knowledge—doing one's epistemic duty towards texts—as much as it is about fulfilling desire. Accordingly, neither Nietzsche nor Cupitt mourn God's passing, nor that of the Book: the author's meaning must die so that the interpreter might live.

"Adequate" Interpretation

Is there no alternative between absolute and anarchic interpretation, or between a gnostic appeal to hidden meanings and an agnostic abandonment of the quest for meaning? We have seen that the notion of the absolute text finally dissolves into a sea of relativity. Far from securing determinate meaning, the authorless text gives rise to multiple meanings (allegorical, metaphorical, intertextual). And just as indeterminacy is constitutive of the text, so undecidability seems to be constitutive of the process of interpretation. The net result of the undoing of the epistemology of meaning seems to be that authority is reassigned once more, away from the text and onto the reader.

There is a third possibility, an alternative between absolute and anarchic interpretation, that I will explore further in Part 2. It is a kind of interpretation, neither absolute nor arbitrary, that yields *adequate* knowledge—adequate for the purpose of understanding. Interpreters may not know everything but they often know *enough*—enough to understand a text and to respond to it appropriately. Only the premise of adequate literary knowledge can ensure that interpretation will be *responsible*. In contrast to the skepticism of the Undoers, I argue that interpretation is not an all-or-nothing affair. We need not choose between a meaning that is wholly determinate and a meaning that is wholly indeterminate. Neither need we choose between a meaning that is fully present and a meaning that is forever deferred. It may well be that the deferral of meaning is not a permanent state, only temporary. One day we may be able to understand as we have been understood. As we will see in Part 2, even eschatology has a role to play in a theological hermeneutics. For now, however, we see through the text, darkly.

But we *do* see. There is something in the text that can be known, though perhaps not exhaustively. We must therefore distinguish between the *inexhaustibility* of meaning and its *indeterminacy*. The former need not imply the latter; it is one thing not to know everything, quite another to know nothing. Take, for instance, the dominical metaphor: "Our Father which art in heaven. . . ." According to Ricoeur, "real metaphors are not translatable. . . . This is not to say that they cannot be paraphrased, just that such a paraphrase is infinite and incapable of exhausting the innovative meaning."[201] Well and good. Yet it does not follow that metaphors are wholly indeterminate or undecidable in their reference. Metaphors may have a relatively determinate meaning without being exhaustively specifiable. Janet Martin Soskice notes that understanding God as Father may not yield a single correct sense, and it surely does not yield a literalistic sense, but it does give rise to a relatively stable model that exercises a "regulative" function for subsequent language and thought about God.[202] In certain respects (e.g., in terms of origin or creation, care, and providence), God is our Father.

Interpretation is not a matter of translating all figurative language into clear and distinct propositions. Our interpretations may adequately, though not exhaustively, grasp the metaphorical and textual meaning. This is simply to acknowledge that our interpretations, while not arbitrary, are revisable and incomplete. Wittgenstein pointed out that words have "rough edges"; even "literal" language is rarely clear and precise.[203] We might say the same of texts. For there are many different kinds of texts, just as there are many uses of language, and each of these kinds and uses enjoys its own type (and degree) of precision. Philosophers are being unrealistic in expecting language to be consistently univocal. And commentators are being unrealistic when they seek to reduce biblical narrative either to "what it teaches" or to "what actually happened." A concept has one kind of precision, a metaphor has another, and a narrative has yet another.

Texts may be determinate enough to convey meaning without being specifiable enough to overcome all ambiguity. Texts may be rough, but they do have edges. Literary knowledge, like its scientific counterpart, is both adequate (i.e., sufficient for the purpose of understanding and appropriating) and provisional (i.e., open to correction in the light of further enquiry). As we will see in Part 2, texts do not convey meaning in one way only, so that they can simply be reduced to a single (e.g., literal, univocal) level. On the contrary, texts are communicative acts that can be described on several levels. However, interpreters do not have to reduce texts to univocal language in order to understand them. The Undoers rightly register a critique of such hermeneutical positivism. No, what interpreters need is competence: a feel for what kind of meaning is being communicated and with what degree of clarity and distinctness. The interpreter must seek not only knowledge but wisdom: a profound acquaintance with and appreciation of the diversity of language and literature. Hermeneutics involves more than a wooden application of methodological principles; hermeneutics requires good judgment. My question about the presence of meaning in texts cannot finally be answered until we consider whether the reader has the eyes and ears—the moral and aesthetic sensibilities, the wisdom and judgment—to perceive it.

NOTES

1. While the prefix "de-" in "deconstruction" has the force of undoing, the "de-" in "determinate" derives from the Latin preposition for "down to the bottom of, thoroughly" and has the effect of strengthening the verb: "to terminate completely." "Determinate" thus carries the connotation of finality and closure.

2. Aristotle, *On Interpretation*, 1.16a 3.

3. Aristotle, *Metaphysics*, Bk. 4, 7.1 1011b.

4. Aristotle, *De interpretatione*, 1.17a 4.

5. Moore comments: "With little exaggeration it can be said that the modus operandi of the biblical guild has generally consisted of an *adequatio intellectus et rei*, the aim of interpretation being one of correspondence to the essential semantic properties of the biblical texts, properties contained within the texts, awaiting discovery" (Moore, *Literary Criticism and the Gospels*, 121).

6. Derrida, "White Mythology," 9–11.

7. Susan A. Handelman, *Slayers of Moses: The Emergence of Rabbinic Interpretation in Modern Literary Theory*, 118

8. Rorty, "Pragmatism and Philosophy," 32–33.

9. Ibid., 54.

10. See Stephen Pepper, *World Hypotheses: A Study in Evidence* (Los Angeles: Univ. of California Press, 1970).

11. Feyerabend, *Against Method: Outline of an Anarchistic Theory of Knowledge* (London: New Left Books, 1975). On the mutual influence between science and hermeneutics, see Vern S. Poythress, *Science and Hermeneutics* (Grand Rapids: Zondervan, 1988).

12. Feyerabend, *Against Method*, 30.

13. Frederick Suppe, "Afterword," to *The Structure of Scientific Theories* (Urbana-Champaign: Univ. of Illinois Press, 1977), 641.

14. Vincent B. Leitch, *Deconstructive Criticism: An Advanced Introduction* (London: Hutchinson, 1983), 264.

15. For more on the role of the metaphorical imagination in science, see Mary Hesse, *Revolutions and Reconstructions in the Philosophy of Science* (Bloomington: Indiana Univ. Press, 1980).

16. Nelson Goodman, *Ways of Worldmaking* (Indianapolis: Hackett, 1978).

17. For an impressive attempt to preserve rationality and truth without metaphysical realism, see Hilary Putnam, *Reason, Truth , and History* (Cambridge: Cambridge Univ. Press, 1981), and *Realism With a Human Face* (Cambridge, Mass.: Harvard Univ. Press, 1990).

18. Jeffrey Stout, "What Is the Meaning of a Text?" *New Literary History* 14 (1982): 1–12.

19. Rorty, *Philosophy and the Mirror of Nature*, 372.

20. Rorty, "Pragmatism and Philosophy," 59.

21. Stefan Collini, "Introduction: Interpretation Terminable and Interminable," in Eco, *Interpretation and Overinterpretation*, 7.

22. Anthony Thiselton, *New Horizons in Hermeneutics*, 49.

23. Augustine, *Confessions*, 2.14.

24. G. Jeanrond, *Text and Interpretation As Categories of Theological Thinking*, 73.

25. For a fuller survey of some of the issues treated in this section, see Thiselton, *New Horizons in Hermeneutics*, chs. 2–3 (55–141). Robert Detweiler sees "a powerful link . . . between theories of the self and theories of the text" (Robert Detweiler, *Breaking the Fall: Religious Readings of Contemporary Fiction* [New York: Harper & Row, 1989], 12). To the indeterminate text corresponds the fragmented self of postmodernism.

26. Much twentieth-century criticism, from the Russian formalists to the Anglo-American new critics and the French structuralists, falls into this period. The focus of each of these movements is the text itself, rather than its author, historical context, or contemporary readers.

27. A classic statement of this aim is Northrop Frye, *Anatomy of Criticism* (Princeton: Princeton Univ. Press, 1957).

28. "Book," in *The Concise Oxford Dictionary of Current English*, 8th ed.

29. Derrida, *Of Grammatology*, 18.

30. In Part 2, I return to the notion of the text as work, that is, as the result of an author's action.

31. Norris, *Derrida*, 63.

32. Knapp and Michaels, "Reply to Rorty," in *Against Theory*, 141.

33. Taylor, *Erring*, 76. Cf. George Steiner's eloquent plea for a return to literacy and a book-based culture, "After the Book," in *On Difficulty and Other Essays* (Oxford: Oxford Univ. Press, 1978), 186–203.

34. See Northrop Frye, *The Great Code: The Bible and Literature* (London: Routledge and Kegan Paul, 1982); *Words With Power, Being a Second Study of the Bible and Literature* (New York: Harcourt Brace Jovanovich, 1990).

35. Watson, *The Open Text*, 3.

36. Hart, *Trespass of the Sign*, 32.

37. Handelman, *Slayers of Moses*, xiii.

38. Barthes, "From Work to Text," in *The Rustle of Language*, 61.

39. Eco, *Interpretation and Overinterpretation*, 85.

40. See Moore, *Literary Criticism and the Gospels*, 133.

41. Taylor, "Text As Victim," in *Deconstruction and Theology*, 65.

42. Barthes, "From Work to Text," 58.

43. For extended treatments of Gadamer's theory of interpretation, see David Hoy, *The Critical Circle: Literature and History in Contemporary Hermeneutics*; Anthony C. Thiselton, *The Two Horizons: New Testament Hermeneutics and Philosophical Description* (Grand Rapids: Eerdmans, 1980), ch. 11; Joel C. Weinsheimer, *Gadamer's Hermeneutics, Tradition and Reason* (Palo Alto, Calif: Stanford Univ. Press, 1987).

44. Hans-Georg Gadamer, *Truth and Method* (New York: Seabury, 1975), 359.

45. In Part 2 I will argue, contra Gadamer, that one cannot successfully separate the intention of the text from the intention of the author.

46. Ricoeur sees both speech and writing to be modes of "discourse." He therefore objects to Derrida's notion that writing has a root distinct from speech; see Ricoeur, *Interpretation Theory*, 26.

47. Ricoeur, *Interpretation Theory*, 29.

48. Ricoeur, *Hermeneutics and the Human Sciences* (Cambridge: Cambridge Univ. Press, 1985), 139.

49. Ricoeur, *Interpretation Theory*, 30.

50. Ricoeur writes: "In spoken discourse the ultimate criterion for the referential scope of what we say is the possibility of showing the thing referred to as a member of the situation common to both speaker and hearer" (*Interpretation Theory*, 34).

51. See my *Biblical Narrative in the Philosophy of Paul Ricoeur: A Study in Hermeneutics and Theology* for a fuller examination of the way in which Ricoeur applies this understanding of texts to Scripture.

52. Jeanrond, *Theological Hermeneutics*, 78.

53. Ricoeur, "What Is a Text?" in *Hermeneutics and the Human Sciences*, 159.

54. Frances Young explores the analogy between texts and musical score in relation to Scripture in her *The Art of Performance: Towards a Theology of Holy Scripture* (London: Darton, Longman & Todd, 1990).

55. Wolfgang Iser, *The Implied Reader* (Baltimore: Johns Hopkins Univ. Press, 1974), 282.

56. Ricoeur, "World of the Text, World of the Reader," in *A Ricoeur Reader: Reflection and Imagination*, ed. Mario J. Valdés (London: Harvester Wheatsheaf, 1991), 496.

57. The phrase is borrowed from Stephen Mailloux, cited in Moore, *Literary Criticism and the Gospels*, 106.

58. Garcia, "Can There Be Texts Without Historical Authors?" 247.

59. Ibid., 252.

60. Nicholas Wolterstorff, *Divine Discourse: Philosophical Reflections on the Claim That God Speaks* (Cambridge: Cambridge Univ. Press, 1995), 172.

61. Moore, *Literary Criticism and the Gospels*, 107. I treat reader-oriented criticism in more detail in the next chapter.

62. Annette Barnes, *On Interpretation: A Critical Analysis* (Oxford: Basil Blackwell, 1988), 86–87.

63. Robert Morgan and John Barton, *Biblical Interpretation* (Oxford: Oxford Univ. Press, 1988), 7.

64. Fish, "Interpreting the *Variorum*," in *Is There a Text?* 163.

65. Fish, *Is There a Text?*, 16–17.

66. Rorty, "Texts and Lumps," *New Literary History* 17 (1985): 12.

67. See Harris, *Literary Meaning*, chs. 1–4.

68. Derrida, *Of Grammatology*, 17.

69. Hart, *Trespass of the Sign*, 165.

70. *The Postmodern Bible*, 120.

71. Derrida, "Signature Event Context," 182.

72. A. Dranti and Charles Goodwin, in *Rethinking Context* (Cambridge: Cambridge Univ. Press, 1992), argue that contexts must themselves be seen as something dynamic rather than static. Contexts are not only constraints on but products of language. Derrida goes even further: we should not think of contexts as something in the world that can be observed; rather, contexts are themselves interpretive constructs. Thus Derrida's challenge: Can we rigorously determine what we mean by "context"?

73. Jonathan Culler, *Structuralist Poetics*, 133.

74. Thiselton, *New Horizons*, 395.

75. Geoffrey Hartman, *The Fate of Reading and Other Essays*, 13.

76. Moisés Silva comments perceptively: "Allegorical interpretations are very difficult to avoid for a believer who wishes to apply the truth of Scripture to his or her life" (*Has the Church Misread the Bible? The History of Interpretation in the Light of Current Issues* [Grand Rapids: Zondervan, 1987], 63).

77. Gerald L. Bruns, "Midrash and Allegory: The Beginnings of Scriptural Interpretation," in Robert Alter and Frank Kermode, eds. *The Literary Guide to the Bible* (Cambridge, Mass: Harvard Univ. Press, 1987), 626.

78. See Robert Grant and David Tracy, *A Short History of Biblical Interpretation* (Philadelphia: Fortress, 1984); Moisés Silva, *Has the Church Misread the Gospel?* G. R. Evans, *The Language and Logic of the Bible: The Earlier Middle Ages* (Cambridge: Cambridge Univ. Press, 1984); Beryl Smalley, *The Study of the Bible in the Middle Ages* (Oxford: Basil Blackwell, 1983, 3d ed.).

79. Heraclitus, one of the earliest theorists of allegory, defined it in the first century B.C. as "speaking one thing and signifying something other than what is said" (*Homeric Questions*, 5.2).

80. See Frances Young, "Alexandrian Interpretation," in *Dictionary of Biblical Interpretation*, 10–12.

81. Bruns, "Midrash and Allegory," 638.

82. Hart finds the same totalizing aim in the allegorical hermeneutic of Alexandria as in Western philosophy as a whole, *Trespass of the Sign*, 57–59.

83. Beryl Smalley, *Study of the Bible in the Middle Ages*, 2. Origen's view is frequently misunderstood as having no place for the literal or historical sense. For an atttempt to qualify the sense that Origen is an allegorizer, see Silva, *Has the Church Misread the Bible?* ch. 3.

84. Tertullian, *De Pudicitia*, 9.22.

85. Cf. Theodore's treatise *On Allegory and History*, which was directed against Origen.

86. Jeanrond lists four interpretive methods in Jewish exegesis, *Theological Hermeneutics*, 16–18.

87. Jacob Neusner distinguishes three types of midrash and describes what he calls "midrash as parable" as an allegorical approach. See his *What is Midrash?* (Philadelphia: Fortress, 1987), 7–12, 80–101.

88. Susan Handelman, *Slayers of Moses*, 41.

89. Cited in Hart, *Trespass of the Sign*, 50.

90. Handelman, *Slayers of Moses*, xiv.

91. Evans, *Language and Logic of the Bible: The Road to Reformation* (Cambridge: Cambridge Univ. Press, 1985), 42.

92. M. H. Abrams, *Glossary of Literary Terms*, 63.

93. Cited in Regina Schwartz, ed., *The Book and the Text: The Bible and Literary Theory* (Oxford: Basil Blackwell, 1990), 4.

94. Smalley, *Study of the Bible in the Middle Ages,* 14.

95. Ibid., 15.

96. Augustine, *On Christian Doctrine*, 3.15.

97. Ibid., 3.27.

98. Indeed, much of Book 3 in *On Christian Doctrine* concerns strategies for disambiguating a text by, for instance, looking at the context or by choosing the meaning that accords with the rule of faith. Again, Alexandrian interpretation may not have been as arbitrary as was once thought. Whereas Augustine stressed divine charity as an interpretive norm, Origen stressed wisdom. Though von Harnack dismissed Origen's hermeneutics as a form of "biblical alchemy," recent studies suggest that allegorical interpretation was systematic after its own fashion. See Frances Young, "Alexandrian Interpretation," 10–12.

99. Smalley, *Study of the Bible in the Middle Ages*, 41. For a comprehensive study of the fourfold sense of Scripture that prevailed in the Middle Ages, see Henri de Lubac, *Exegèse médiévale: les quatre sens de l'écriture* (Paris: Aubier, 1959).

100. G. R. Evans, *The Language and Logic of the Bible: The Road to Reformation*, 43.

101. Luther, *WA*, 42.657–58.

102. Cited in Farrar, *History of Interpretation* (Grand Rapids: Baker, 1961), 329.

103. See, for instance, Luther's comments on Gen. 2:7 in his *Commentary on Genesis*.

104. Frei, *Eclipse of Biblical Narrative* (New Haven: Yale Univ. Press, 1974), 2.

105. For a more extended study of the differences between typology and allegory and the relation of each to literal interpretation, see Paul Noble, *The Canonical Approach: A Critical Reconstruction of the Hermeneutics of Brevard S. Childs* (Leiden: E. J. Brill, 1995), 306–13; Hans Frei, *Eclipse of Biblical Narrative*, 2–7, 25–34.

106. Hart, *Trespass of the Sign*, 154.

107. Ibid., 155.

108. Fish, *Doing What Comes Naturally: Change, Rhetoric, and the Practice of Theory in Literary and Legal Studies* (Oxford: Clarendon, 1989), 4. Fish's definition of literal meaning is unnecessarily restrictive (see Gregory Currie, "Text Without Context: Some Errors of Stanley Fish," *Philosophy and Literature* 15 [1991]: 212–28). I will put forward an alternative view in Part 2 that relies on John Searle's "Literal Meaning," in his *Expression and Meaning* (Cambridge: Cambridge Univ. Press, 1979).

109. See his "Violence and Metaphysics: An Essay on the Thought of Emmanuel Levinas, in *Writing and Difference*, tr. Alan Bass (London: Routledge & Kegan Paul, 1978), 79–153.

110. For additional documentation of this point, see Edgar McKnight, *Post-Modern Use of the Bible: The Emergence of Reader-Oriented Criticism* (Nashville: Abingdon, 1988), 27–65.

111. Augustine, *On Christian Doctrine*, 1.5.5.

112. Watson, *Text, Church and World: Biblical Interpretation in Theological Perspective* (Grand Rapids: Eerdmans, 1994), 241 (emphasis his).

113. Kant, *Religion Within the Limits of Reason Alone*, tr. T. N. Greene and H. H. Hudson (New York: Harper & Row, 1960), 100.

114. Ibid., 102.

115. Ibid.

116. It is possible that some NT texts attempt to rebut the gnostic dualism between body and spirit. Gnostics denied the Incarnation because they believed that physical matter was inherently evil. See Stuart George Hall, "Gnosticism," in *A Dictionary of Biblical Interpretation*, 264–66.

117. Ronald Hall, *Word and Spirit: A Kierkegaardian Critique of the Modern Age* (Bloomington: Indiana Univ. Press, 1993), 178.

118. Eco, *Interpretation and Overinterpretation*, 34.

119. Ibid., 32.

120. This is similar to the skepticism of Cratylus, who argued that nothing meaningful or true could be said since everything is in flux.

121. Eco, *Interpretation and Overinterpretation*, 39.

122. Ibid., 40.

123. Ibid., 18–20.

124. Eco, *Foucault's Pendulum* (London: Picador, 1990), 315.

125. Ibid., 289–90.

126. Ibid., 361.

127. Ibid., 377–78.

128. Eco, *Limits of Interpretation* (Bloomington: Indiana Univ. Press, 1990), 20.

129. Handelman, *Slayers of Moses*, xv. See also the discussion of Derrida's Jewishness in Christopher Norris, *Derrida*, 228–30.

130. Sigmund Freud, *Interpretation of Dreams* (New York: Avon, 1965), 552.

131. Handelman, *Slayers of Moses*, 172.

132. Eco, *Foucault's Pendulum*, 184–85.

133. Handelman, *Slayers of Moses*, 103

134. David Dawson, *Literary Theory* (Minneapolis: Fortress, 1995), 12. Raman Selden comments that Bloom's combination of allegory, Freudian psychology, and kabbalistic mysticism "is a daring one" (*A Reader's Guide to Contemporary Literary Theory*, 2d ed. [London: Harvester Wheatsheaf, 1989], 95).

135. Handelman, *Slayers of Moses*, 182.

136. See Bloom, *A Map of Misreading* (Oxford: Oxford Univ. Press, 1975).

137. Lentricchia, *After the New Criticism*, 339.

138. Bloom, *Kabbala and Criticism* (New York: Continuum, 1975).

139. Lentricchia, *After the New Criticism*, 341.

140. Dawson, *Literary Theory*, 44.

141. Norris, *The Contest of the Faculties: Philosophy and Theory After Deconstruction* (London: Methuen, 1985), 41.

142. The explicitly theological nature of de Man's position is clearest in his essay "The Rhetoric of Temporality."

143. Paul de Man, *Blindness and Insight*, 2d ed. (London: Methuen, 1983), 209.

144. De Man, *Allegories of Reading: Figural Language in Rousseau, Nietzsche, Rilke and Proust* (New Haven: Yale Univ. Press, 1979), 301.

145. Dawson, *Literary Theory*, 118.

146. Ibid., 12.

147. Ibid., 120.

148. Derrida, *Margins of Philosophy*, tr. Alan Bass (Chicago: Univ. of Chicago Press, 1982), 247.

149. Ricoeur, *Rule of Metaphor: Multi-Disciplinary Studies of the Creation of Meaning in Language* (London: Routledge & Kegan Paul, 1978), 302.

150. Norris, *Derrida*, 19.

151. Aristotle, *Metaphysics*, Bk 4.1006a 34-b13.

152. Werner Heisenberg's "uncertainty principle," formulated in 1927, states that while we can determine either the position of a subatomic particle or its momentum, we cannot determine both these characteristics at the same time.

153. Aristotle, *Poetics*, 1457b 7–8.

154. Thomas Hobbes, *Leviathan* (New York: Liberal Arts, 1958), ch. 4 (39).

155. See esp. Max Black, *Models and Metaphors* (Ithaca, N.Y.: Cornell Univ. Press, 1962), and Paul Ricoeur, *The Rule of Metaphor*.

156. "Hence the relation between the literal meaning and the figurative meaning in a metaphor is like an abridged version within a single sentence of the complex interplay of significations that characterize the literary work as a whole" (Ricoeur, *Interpretation Theory*, 46).

157. See Ricoeur, *Rule of Metaphor* and *Interpretation Theory*, 46–53.

158. Ricoeur, "Creativity in Language: Word, Polysemy, Metaphor," in *The Philosophy of Paul Ricoeur* (Boston: Beacon, 1978), 131.

159. Mary Hesse, *Models and Analogies in Science* (Notre Dame: Univ. of Notre Dame Press, 1966), 259.

160. Ricoeur, *Interpretation Theory*, 52

161. Ricoeur, *Rule of Metaphor*, 24

162. Ibid., 288.

163. This is the transgression alluded to in the title of Kevin Hart, *The Trespass of the Sign*.

164. For a fuller discussion of this point, see Handelman, *Slayers of Moses*, 16–25. For a comparative study of Ricoeur and Derrida on metaphor, see S. H. Clark, *Paul Ricoeur* (London: Routledge, 1990), 137–47; Mario Valdés, "Introduction," *A Ricoeur Reader* (London: Harvester Wheatsheaf, 1991), 21–25. For a fuller account of Ricoeur's own theory of metaphor, see Vanhoozer, *Biblical Narrative in the Philosophy of Paul Ricoeur*, 56–85. Ricoeur's own treatment of Derrida may be found in *The Rule of Metaphor*, 284–95.

165. Cupitt, *The Long-Legged Fly*, 100.

166. Derrida, *La Dissémination* (Paris: Seuil, 1992), 149.

167. For more on Ricoeur's notion of intertextuality as "biblical imagination," see my *Biblical Narrative in the Philosophy of Paul Ricoeur*, 199–204.

168. Bultmann's theology, for example, can be viewed as a product of his reading Paul, Luther, and Heidegger in light of one another.

169. Bloom, *Kaballa and Criticism*, 106.

170. Frederick C. Crews, in his *The Pooh Perplex* (London: Robin Clark, 1979), offers a witty send-up of these and other interpretive approaches by showing how they can be imposed on A. A. Milne's stories.

171. Cupitt, *The Long-Legged Fly*, 29.

172. Sallie McFague, *Models of God: Theology for an Ecological, Nuclear Age* (Philadelphia: Fortress, 1987), xi.

173. Ibid., 13.

174. Ibid., 192n37 and 196n13.

175. Richard Rorty, *Contingency, Irony, and Solidarity* (Cambridge: Cambridge Univ. Press, 1989), 16.

176. J. Wesley Robbins, "'You Will Be Like God': Richard Rorty and Mark C. Taylor on the Theological Significance of Human Language Use," *Journal of Religion* 72 (1992): 389.

177. Kermode states that *kanōn* came to signify other things as well, including "an ethical norm or a rule or criterion" (Kermode, "The Canon," in Alter and Kermode, eds. *The Literary Guide to the Bible*, 604).

178. Childs, *Introduction to the Old Testament As Scripture* (Philadelphia: Fortress, 1979), 60.

179. Kermode, "The Canon," 605–6.

180. Barton, *Reading the Old Testament*, 172.

181. Taylor, *Erring*, 179.

182. Handelman, *Slayers of Moses*, 47.

183. Taylor, *Erring*, 180.

184. Ibid., 179.

185. Derrida, "Structure, Sign, Play," 264.

186. Nietzsche, cited in Taylor, *Deconstructing Theology*, 90.

187. Nietzsche, *The Will to Power*, 330.

188. Rorty, "Pragmatism and Philosophy," 60.

189. Hoy, "Must We Mean What We Say?" 410.

190. Derek Attridge, in Derrida, *Acts of Literature* (London: Routledge, 1992), 128.

191. Taylor, *Erring*, 166.

192. Cf. Mikhail Bakhtin, *Rabelais and His World*, tr. H. Iswolsky (Cambridge: M.I.T. Press, 1968), 123.

193. Rorty, "Texts and Lumps," 4.

194. Fish, *Is There a Text?* 365.

195. Norris, *Derrida*, 155.

196. See Cupitt, *The Long-Legged Fly*, 8.

197. Ibid., 112–13. The next chapter treats the politics of interpretation in more detail.

198. See Derrida's "The Principle of Reason: The University in the Eyes of Its Pupils" *Diacritics*, 29 (1983): 3–20.

199. Handelman, *Slayers of Moses*, 204.

200. Cited in Scott, "New Trahison," 410.

201. Ricoeur, *Interpretation Theory*, 52.

202. Janet Martin Soskice, *Metaphor and Religious Language* (Oxford: Clarendon, 1985).

203. See Dan Stiver, *The Philosophy of Religious Language: Sign, Symbol, and Story* (Cambridge: Cambridge Univ. Press, 1996), 59–67.

CHAPTER FOUR

Undoing the Reader:
Contextuality and Ideology

Since the death of the godlike author, any number of idols have
been erected in his place under the names of our diverse theoretical schools. . . . Each of these schools promises its own version
of salvation through correct interpretation in a grounded, and by
that token valid, reading of texts.

Howard Felerpin[1]

The birth of the reader must be requited by the death of the Author.

Roland Barthes[2]

This new reader sounds very much like the old Author whose
death he is announcing, his authoritarian tone itself symptomatic
of the authority vacuum left by the demise of the Author and the
communal sanctions that authorized Him.

Howard Felerpin[3]

We come now to the third age of criticism, an age in which the privilege, and the
burden, of meaning fall on the reader. For if the author is not the origin of meaning and if there is no such thing as "the sense of the text," then meaning must be the
creation *ex libris* of the reader. Jane Tomkins, introducing a highly regarded volume
on reader-oriented criticism, signals the turn towards hermeneutic non-realism this
way: "Meaning has no effective existence outside of its realization in the mind of a
reader."[4] Interpretation thus becomes "more creation than discovery . . . less demonstration and proof than individual insight and construction."[5] Meaning in the age of
the reader is located neither behind nor in the text, but rather *in front of* it.

One of the first things small children learn in school is how to read. Reading
appears to be a simple enough activity, until we begin to analyze it. What is a reader?
And what is reading if not an activity oriented towards something other than one's
own thoughts? What is reading if it is not faith seeking understanding? These queries
about the reader and reading are as controversial as our earlier questions about the
author and the text. Every literary theory is ultimately a theory about reading. Moreover, to say whose reading counts is ultimately to invoke an ethics, perhaps even a
theology, of interpretation.

On the traditional account, the reader is a detached observer of authorial intention or of verbal sense. Readers are both active and passive: by scanning the page and deciphering marks, they receive something not of their own making. F. R. Leavis, for instance, believed the critic's task was to extract universal moral truths from literary classics for the benefit of the "common reader." Even on this traditional view, however, reading can be dangerous: "It can change our perspective, stir our emotions, and provoke us to action."[6] Recent literary theory, however, throws into question the alleged impartiality of the reader as well as the objectivity of his or her observations. The reader is no *tabula rasa* or blank slate; on the contrary, what the reader finds in a text is largely a function of what one brings to it. The reader's observations are not objective but "theory-laden." Indeed, Users such as Fish claim that we can know only what our methods of reading allow us to know. The last idol to be overthrown by postmodern theory is therefore the "idol of neutrality."

It is not surprising that the focus in contemporary literary theory should come to rest on the reader. The turn to the reader follows logically from hermeneutic non-realism. If there is no meaning in the text-in-itself, it stands to reason that what meaning readers find has been put there. Meaning in this third age of criticism is the reader's projection, interpretation a means not of reproducing but of *producing* meaning. It is only appropriate, therefore, that postmodern theorists subject what Marx calls the "modes of production" to searching criticism.[7] Whether there is meaning in texts now turns into the question of who controls interpretive procedures. When it comes to making meaning, who is in charge?

Interpretation in our time is less a matter of what a text says than of what the reader does with it, or rather, of who the reader *is*. A person's identity affects, and possibly determines, the way that person reads. Tell me who you are and I'll tell you how you read. Meaning is located neither in authorial consciousness nor in the structure of the text, but is rather a function of the reader's location. The third age of criticism brings *contextuality* rather than textuality to the fore.

Undoers and Users alike attack the myth of the objective reader. Reading is not about accumulating knowledge but about transmitting culture and satisfying desire. The key question in the third age of criticism is: *Whose reading of the Bible counts most, and why?* One's answer invariably betrays one's politics. If, as Foucault maintains, knowledge claims are really exercises in power, then deciding whose interpretation counts ultimately becomes a political issue. To the contextualist, of course, all things are political: "For whatever the text's apparent politics, it can always be made over . . . into the mouthpiece of the reader's own politics. . . . The process is one of systematic misconstruction, a kind of textual harassment."[8]

THE BIRTH OF THE READER

To publishers and booksellers, readers are primarily consumers; "voracious" readers "devour" books. Barthes objects to the consumer mentality of interpretation that regards a text "like a cupboard where meanings are shelved, stacked, safeguarded."[9] For Barthes, the reader is not only a consumer but a *producer* of meaning. In the traditional picture of interpretation, however, the reader was not free to make meaning.

Terry Eagleton accordingly describes the third age of criticism as a "Reader's Liberation Movement." Reader-oriented literary theory works on behalf of oppressed readers, "brutally proletarianized as they have been by the authorial class."[10]

It was not always so. As recently as the 1960s, structuralists treated the reader as a passive observer of textual codes and conventions. A code is, of course, inert and meaningless until someone makes sense of it. Since the late 1960s, however, attention has turned to the reader's activity in decoding and recoding.[11] A text is incomplete until it elicits a response from the reader.

Poststructuralists—those who believe in the essentially unstable nature of sign systems—study the effect of the reader's location (e.g., social, historical, theological) on the act of interpretation.[12] The poststructuralist is thus in a better position to account for the fact that one text may provoke a host of different readings. Behind the veil of objectivity lie certain vested interests. Reading, to restate a now familiar refrain, is a theory-laden form of observation. What are the norms that govern the reader's production of meaning, and where do they come from? These questions will lead us to discuss not only the morality, but also the politics, of literary knowledge. The traditional reader is ultimately undone by the postmodern suspicion that interpretation is merely a sophisticated cover for an individual's or a community's will to power.

What Is a Reader?

According to Eco, the text is a machine designed for eliciting responses from ideal readers. Rhetorical criticism analyzes the techniques that dictate the responses of the compliant reader. By studying how the text achieves its effects, such criticism brings the reader into the field to be described. Strictly speaking, however, the ideal reader does not exist; he or she is a textual construct, an implication of the text. This ghostly, insubstantial reader is simply an effect of textual rhetoric.

Viewing texts as rhetoric—that is, in terms of strategies and techniques of persuasion—leads eventually to a consideration of the real readers' responses. We need to distinguish ideal readers, who are internal to the text, from their real (e.g., historical, actual, empirical) extra-textual counterparts. "The empirical reader is only an actor who makes conjectures about the kind of Model Reader postulated by the text."[13] Yet another interpretive approach—reception criticism—studies the history of how texts have actually been read by real readers, past and present.[14] *To shift critical attention from rhetoric to reception is to move from the paradigm of textuality to that of contextuality:* "Readers who were not original recipients made sense in their context with their needs."[15] It is likely that the needs of twentieth-century Baptists in Georgia differ from the first-century Galatians who first received Paul's letter. Yet Galatians continues to be read and appropriated in Atlanta, and indeed, all across the globe. Can contemporary Southern Baptists, or members of some other denomination for that matter, play the role of Paul's ideal reader? Or does one's location—one's gender, race, and class—disqualify real readers from ever attaining the ideal?

The Place of the Reader

As Einstein has taught us, what we see is relative to our position and speed. So it is with the location of the reader. Educated monks of the twelfth century read the Bible differently from today's seminary graduates. Every reader is situated in a particular culture, time, and tradition. No reading is objective; all reading is theory-laden. There is no innocent eye; there is no innocent "I." Consider, for instance, the following, far from neutral, description of the socio-political position of postmodern readers in America:

> Most of the important literature departments in America are dominated by a flagitious anti-establishmentarian and Marxist united front of feminists, reader-response theorists, semioticians, and deconstructionists commonly motivated, as the Left always is, by a political hatred of democratic capitalism and a metaphysical hatred of the permanent things of human existence as expressed and represented in literature.[16]

The claim to see texts as they are is illusory. Every reader sees what one can see from one's position in society, space, and time. Reading is a dialogue between text and reader, between the discursive strategies inscribed in the text and those that shape the culture of the reader. Reading, then, is no exception to relativity theory. Like it or not, what we find in texts is a function of who, and where, we are. This may not be at all obvious. We tend to believe that the way we see things reflects truly the way things are. But who is "we"? The reading self is not a detached knowing subject, but is always in the grip of some vocabulary, some value system. "We are never not in a situation. . . . A set of interpretive assumptions is always in force."[17] Reading is never disinterested. Of course, this admission is threatening to any exegete whose lifetime efforts have been directed at getting the objective meaning out of texts. Such heroic attempts to retrieve textual meaning prompts one postmodern exegete to offer the following proposal: "Today, it is not our biblical texts that need demythologizing so much as our ways of reading them."[18]

Is There a Reader in the Text?

Early reader-response critics were "conservative" with regard to the role they assigned real readers. They confined their attention to the implied reader, that is, to the reader in the text. Textual meaning is encoded, but it exists in a state of suspended animation until it is read. Reading awakens, as it were, the sleeping message. The differences between actual readers is unimportant; the meaning is frozen in the code. The code, in turn, is a script or role for the reader to follow. Meaning requires the participation of the reader, but this reading is textually pre-programmed. In the words of one cynic, this view gives the literary critic "just enough of the reader but not too much."[19]

"Radical" reader-response critics object, however, that this view puts the reader in thrall to the text, if not to the author. The wardens may have changed, but the reader is still in chains. The reader is both "in" and "of" the text, bereft of any independent voice. Though the reader's role appears to have been elevated, in fact the only reader that counts is the implied reader—"an unchanging property of the text."[20] Eco distinguishes between "closed" texts that call for a prescripted response, and "open" texts that solicit the reader's participation in the creation of new meaning. However, according to the Undoer, *all* texts are open, for no texts contain a meaning that is independent of the way readers approach them. How then should we read: according to the text or against it, obediently or independently?

A recent commentary on Romans well illustrates the conservative reader-response approach:

Our method treats Romans as a literary communication employing rhetorical devices and means of argumentation intended to persuade its recipients to feel, think or act in certain ways. . . . By mentally placing ourselves in the position of the implied reader(s) of the text and making the responses that the process of reading or listening to it demands or requires, we hope to experience more precisely and fully what this epistle is meant to communicate.[21]

In other words, if the actual reader plays the role of the ideal reader, he or she will actualize or decode the text as the author intended. The reader's response is still a way of conforming to the text.

Is the Reader a Writer?

In contrast to the preceding position, radical reader-response critics direct their attention to the real reader outside the text. They complain that conservative reader-response approaches "invariably disempower the reader. They circumscribe and limit. . . . They lead to the idea that *the* reader is *in* the text, that there is an inside and outside the text and that we can always know which side we are on."[22] What distinguishes radical readers from their more conservative counterparts is that the former no longer believe that certain responses fit the text better than others.

Both Undoers and Users, insofar as they affirm the indeterminacy of meaning and the partiality of interpretation, are types of radical reader-response critics. As I have already suggested, the turn to the reader follows logically from the rejection of hermeneutic realism. Radical reader-response theory simply extends Kant's critique of the concept of the thing-in-itself to the text. Transposed to literary theory, Kant's Copernican Revolution inverts the traditional picture of interpretation: *instead of reading conforming to text, the text conforms to reading.* The meaning in the text is, at least in part, the construction of the reader.[23] Unlike Kant, however, the radical reader-response critics deny that all rational readers process the world (or the text) in the same way.

How, then, do readers move from text to interpretation? The process by which meaning was obtained by the ancient hermeticists, as we have seen, was too haphazard: a matter of intuitive, non-cognitive, and unsystematic procedures hidden in the depths of the soul. The new allegorists, no less than the old, continue to divine meaning rather than to deduce it from the text. Already in the 1950s, Northrop Frye was comparing text-oriented approaches to interpretation to "a mystery religion without a gospel, or to chemistry in its alchemical stage."[24]

The analogy with chemistry is apt. But the composition that counts most is that of the reader—the character, history, and hopes that distinguish one person from another. One reason, then, that the same text yields different interpretations is because different readers react differently. The periodic table of the hermeneutical elements includes contextual factors as well as textual ones. Poststructuralists no longer believe in alchemy; the chemistry of interpretation can be explained by analyzing the ingredients (viz., socio-political, religious, ideological) that readers bring to the experience of reading in which the fusion of horizons takes place. If the reader is as unstable an element as the text, then surely there is little hope that the interpreter can "get it right."

Barthes suggests that the reader should be more concerned with "writing" the text than with getting the text "right." To continue the chemistry analogy, we might say that Barthes encourages the reader to experiment with the text, in order to produce as many meanings as possible. On this view, the author supplies only the raw materials of meaning; the laboratory of interpretation belongs to the reader. What has come to birth in the third age of criticism is the notion that the reader, in producing meaning, is ultimately a writer.

The Work of the Reader

What ought the newborn reader do? Edgar McKnight speaks for a growing number of biblical exegetes who have turned to literary rather than historical methods: "*The thesis of this book is that readers make sense.*"[25] Both conservative and radical reader-response critics agree that the reader, to varying degrees, "completes" the text. The two approaches diverge, however, over the nature of the reader's action: Is it primarily obedient or essentially free? At the heart of the contemporary debate in the age of the reader is the question of interpretive norms. Are there norms for reading, or are readers free to write?

Determinate Reading

Wolfgang Iser, a conservative reader-response critic, argues that the meaning of a text depends on the reader's creativity in filling in the "gaps," the areas of indeterminacy.[26] The text is not meaningful (i.e., full of meaning), but contains only a dynamic potential for sense. Without the participation of the reader, the text is only a virtual message—a *could* be. These gaps can be completed in various ways. But there are limits. The text provides hints and opportunities. In Iser's view, the author intends the reader to experience the pleasure of co-creation. Though active, the reader's work is clearly derivative, not original: the text gives to the reader a set of instructions and a set of tasks. The reader must participate, but the nature of this participation is governed by the text. Reading is a process whereby the reader gradually creates a coherent interpretation as the various parts and clues are put together.[27]

Indeterminate Reading

While Iser's implied reader may be an interesting theoretical notion, the fact of the matter is that real readers inevitably do more than follow the text's guidelines: "The actual readings of actual readers determine the fate of the text. They say how the text fares in the world and in history. In this sense, the reader is indeed king."[28] Iser does not explain why readers so often follow some other set of instructions than that of the text. According to his critics, Iser's prescriptions ultimately amount to nothing more than a description of how *he*, and perhaps his colleagues, read. The radical reader-response critic wants to know why the practice of a few should be normative for everyone.

By contrast, Frank Kermode, commenting on his own interpretation of the parable of the Good Samaritan, declares: "My way of reading . . . seems to me natural; but that is only my way of authenticating, or claiming as universal, a habit of thought that is cultural and arbitrary. My reading would certainly not have seemed 'natural' to the church Fathers, for instance."[29] Kermode thus acknowledges the poststructuralist point about the contextuality of the reader and its contribution to the process of interpretation.

The reader, like the text, is the product of various cultural codes. This is Fish's version of the reader's Copernican Revolution: "The text as an entity independent of interpretation and (ideally) responsible for its career drops out and is replaced by the texts that emerge as the consequence of our interpretive activities."[30] With this revolution, we have come full circle: *a text is now not the cause of a reading, but its effect*. For Fish, a text is only in the eye of the beholding reader. Only the reader can breathe life into the inert body of the text: "The unity of a text is not in its origin but in its destination."[31] By deciphering and rendering the text coherent, the reader brings it into being. In an ironic role-reversal with far-reaching consequences, the newborn reader lays claim to authorial rights.

Centrifugal Reading

Robert Scholes distinguishes centripetal reading, which grasps the text on its own terms, from centrifugal reading, which relates the text to the reader's world.[32] To this point, we have examined the reader's role in making sense of the text by decoding or explaining its structures. But a text's sense—the "what" of discourse—is incomplete without a reference, an "about what." The reader, in other words, must decide how to respond to the "world" of the text, to what the text is about. For example, in reading the Pentateuch, the reader of Scripture must decide how to respond to the Law. What does the world of the biblical text have to do with my world, with ancient Jerusalem, or with present-day Athens, Georgia?

The reader's response is not limited to "making sense" of the text; it includes the reader's response to the sense eventually made. Ricoeur charges structuralist readings of short-circuiting the process of interpretation by remaining on the level of explanation rather than pressing on to understanding. They explain the text's formal features but fail to engage with the text's subject matter. An interpretation of, say, a Bach concerto is incomplete until the piece is performed.

For Ricoeur, the reader's work ends not with application but with appropriation. The change in terminology is significant. The reader is not in control of meaning as though interpretation were some kind of technology of the text. Rather, the text proposes and projects a world, that is, a possible way of seeing the nature and value of human beings. When the world of the text rebounds upon the world of the reader, interpretation transforms the reader's world by offering a person a new way of understanding oneself (e.g., as under grace not law). The truly responsive reader lets the text "read" him or her. Good readers view themselves in light of the text and thus come to understand themselves in a new way. "It is by an understanding of the worlds, actual and possible, opened by language that we may arrive at a better understanding of ourselves."[33] Texts can therefore collide with the world of the reader and transform it; they have real centrifugal force. Reading thus begins to take on the appearance of a struggle between the aims of the text and the aims of the reader.

THE AIMS OF READING: LITERARY KNOWLEDGE
AND HUMAN INTERESTS

Today, it is not our biblical texts that need demythologizing so much as our ways of reading them.[34]

Reading, like observation, is theory-laden. What readers find to be "there" in the text is partly a matter of what they bring to it: their aims and agendas. To speak of the reader's birth is to acknowledge that it is the reader who "makes sense." Deconstruction undoes the reader to the extent that it exposes the hidden forces not only in the text but in reading as well. Deconstruction both demystifies and complicates the process of reading by showing that our natural habits of reading are in fact institutionalized, historically conditioned cultural products. Reading is not impartial but *interested*.

On one level, there is nothing wrong with a reader having a certain interest. Indeed, why would one even want to read in the first place unless one is motivated by some purpose? The kind of "interest" in view here, however, is something different from mere curiosity. It is more a matter of having certain concrete goals. Science, for example, proceeds from an *instrumental* interest, an interest in explaining and controlling nature. Without this interest, science would not even be possible. What, then, are the interests that motivate reading and interpretation?

This is not a new question. Rudolf Bultmann argued in the 1950s that all readers approach the biblical text with certain presuppositions already in mind. Bultmann acknowledges that one can read the Bible with various interests—psychological, historical, cultural, etc.—that are usually related to one's situation in life. One can read Plato with a historian's interest in ancient Athens or with a philosopher's interest in truth. Bultmann was especially concerned to clarify one's interest in reading the Bible. For him, the religious quest is motivated by an interest in the meaning of human existence. We read the Bible to learn what possibilities are open to us as human beings. Bultmann's interest in the range of human possibilities eventually gave rise to his theory of existentialist interpretation, which led, in turn, to his reading the Bible as a collection of myths whose real message pertained to human existence, not to God conceived as some supernatural being.[35]

Bultmann's approach illustrates how an interpretive interest may blossom into a full-fledged interpretive theory. Yet even something as fundamental as human existence does not exhaust the range of interests with which readers approach texts: "A text may even be read by unintended readers for unintended purposes. A literary text may be read to pinpoint a geographical site, a biblical text may be scrutinized for examples of certain grammatical constructions."[36] However, these interests are often not those of the text. We may recall in this context Morgan's chilling remark: "Texts, like dead men and women, have no rights, no aims, no interests."[37] It is the reader, that is, who decides to approach the text with a certain set of questions, problems, and expectations. The interests that control one's reading—be it an interest in the history behind the text, the grammar of the text, or one's existence in front of the text—is a function of the reader's choice.[38]

What are some typical interests? Here is a brief list of aims (call them "ruling interests") that have generated whole schools of interpretation:

1. the author's intention (grammatical-historical criticism)
2. the history of a text's composition (source, form, redaction, tradition criticism)
3. the literary or structural features of a text (structuralist criticism)
4. the way a text works and achieves its effects (rhetorical criticism)
5. the possible ways of being in the world that a text displays (existentialist criticism)
6. the way a text depicts women (feminist criticism)
7. the way a text aids or hinders social transformation (liberationist criticism)
8. the way a text resists unified interpretation (deconstructive criticism)

This list is not exhaustive, only illustrative.

What about the meaning of a text? May one be interested in that too? The problem with this question is that each of the interests mentioned above may lay claim to the term *meaning*. That is, each could claim that it was after the text's meaning (or, in the case of deconstruction, in showing why the quest for meaning is impossible). We are now in a better position to appreciate the sting in the Undoer's critique: *all claims about reading for "the meaning" are actually covert strategies for pursuing one interest to the exclusion of others*. To talk of meaning, then, is to mask one's true interpretive interest.[39] Interpreters pursue their own agendas with impunity by pretending that they are simply uncovering the "natural" meaning. But what appears to be a "natural" interest is, in fact, the product of a particular socio-political practice. One person's "common sense" is another person's prejudice.

The Aims and Ethics of Interpretation

Behind every interpretive method is an interpretive aim, and behind every interpretive aim is a conception of an interpretive good. To speak of the ethics of interpretation is thus to raise the question of whether there are any universal goods toward which all interpreters should aim.

The "Critical" Aim: Description

Legal philosopher John Finnis believes that there are certain basic goods that are good for everyone. One of these goods is knowledge, of interest to all who aim for truth. All human societies display a concern for and interest in truth, Finnis argues, regardless of their specific location or particular interests.[40] What if one's explicit aim is to gain literary knowledge—knowledge about the origin, nature, and content of a text? Traditional literary criticism was, after all, considered a form of knowledge, as the following remarks attest. Alexander Pope, for instance, expected the critic to know practically everything about a text:

> You then whose judgment the right course would steer,
> Know well each ancient's proper character;
> His fable, subject, scope in every page;
> Religion, country, genius of his age:
> Without all these at once before your eyes,
> Cavil you may, but never criticize.[41]

Matthew Arnold, over a century later, had similarly exacting standards: "I am bound by my own definition of criticism: a disinterested endeavor to learn and propagate that best that is known and thought in the world."[42] T. S. Eliot, speaking in the twentieth century, agrees: "The critic, one would suppose, if he is to justify his existence, should endeavor to discipline his personal prejudices and cranks . . . and compose his differences with as many of his fellows as possible, in the common pursuit of true judgment."[43]

The above statements are representative of a certain "traditionalist" criticism that assumes historical and philological methods can yield knowledge of texts. The kind of knowledge at which the traditionalists aim turns out to be largely about the author's intention.[44] Those who approach the biblical text with historical-critical methods have similar aims. In each case, it is assumed that the critic may attain determinate knowledge, at least approximately.

After knowledge comes application. The traditionalists assigns a twofold role to the critic: to become clear about the meaning of the text, then to assess its continuing significance for persons today. Textualists such as the New Critics, on the other hand, are content to fulfill only the first part of this mandate. They see no need to justify the study of literature in terms of something else; they wish to make the study of literature into an academic discipline—indeed, a science—in its own right. For the New Critics, literature and literary criticism alike are autonomous: literature is a unique form of language, and the categories of literary criticism are intrinsic to literature. The world of the literary text is hermetically sealed off from other concerns, such as psychology, morality, or religion.

As E. D. Hirsch Jr. points out, however, not all texts aim to be "literary." To focus on a text's formal features runs the risk of missing the main point. C. S. Lewis makes a similar observation: "Those who talk of reading the Bible 'as literature' sometimes mean, I think, reading it without attending to the main thing it is about; like reading Burke with no interest in politics, or reading the Aeneid with no interest in Rome."[45] Karl Barth makes much the same point about historical critics who do not read the Bible critically enough, insofar as they miss the theological by concentrating on the process of a text's composition.

It is precisely this critical description of a text's form and matter, together with the ambition to attain knowledge rather than merely to express opinion, that the poststructuralists put into question. We may recall the conclusion of the previous section, namely, that what readers see largely depends on where they stand and on who they are. Can the reader ever be a dispassionate observer?

The "Ethical" Aim: Evaluation

The activity of the literary critic does not come to an end with describing the text. The critic also offers moral judgments about the worth of a text. Indeed, ethics relates to literary knowledge in two ways. First, there is the question of which aim we should choose or to what critical school one should belong. "At the heart of the current debate over literary theory is the question of which normative aims one ought to have in studying literature."[46] Second, ethics has to do with the evaluation of texts. How are we to evaluate texts once we have described them? Should we adopt an extrinsic criterion, as did Plato, who judged whether a work was good or bad by inquiring whether it was good or bad for the state? Or should we use an intrinsic criterion, as did Aristotle, for whom a work is good or bad to the extent that it succeeds in fulfilling its own aims?

Traditionalists hold that the literary critic should illumine textual meaning and indicate its value for humanity. For Matthew Arnold, literature itself is the "criticism of life." Human well-being is thus the interest that ultimately governs literary criticism. What, however, is "good" for human beings? Once again, we see that strategies of interpretation are related to broader ethical questions. If one's evaluation of the text finally depends on one's basic values, then we seem to be further than ever from achieving literary knowledge in the pluralistic public square.

The Utilitarian Aim: Using Texts

From Rorty's perspective, the distinction between describing and evaluating texts is a non-starter. There is no such thing as "description" if by this we mean the kind of critical insight that discerns a text's true nature. There is, for Rorty, no text-in-itself prior to and independent of the text-as-read-by-me. Everyone's a critic; both our descriptions and evaluations of texts are governed by certain interests. And there are as many descriptions of texts as there uses to which they may be put.

Rorty, Fish, and Derrida all agree that "meaning" refers not to something "in" texts but rather to what happens in the experience of reading. Meaning is less about some fixed nature of the text-in-itself as it is about the function of the text-for-me. In other words, meaning is not an ontological property, but a function, of texts. Strictly speaking, there is no meaning in the text to respect. The User thus urges the interpreter to come clean: abandon talk about "textual meaning" and speak instead of "reader interests."[47] As far as the User is concerned, description and evaluation are merely functions of the uses to which texts are put. Once again, it is the reader's context that determines what one finds in the text. The User's point is simply this: no single interest should be equated with the meaning of the text.

In opposition to Rorty, Eco believes that in recent years, the rights of the User have been overstressed.[48] While not at all ruling out the activity of the reader, Eco argues that interpreters should be interested in something more than their own agendas. Critically to interpret a text "means to read it in order to discover, along with our reactions to it, something about its nature."[49] In using a text, critics trample on its rights: "To use a text means to start from it in order to get something else, even accepting the risk of misinterpreting it."[50] The debate between Rorty and Eco about whether texts should be "used" or "interpreted" is symptomatic of the confusion over the aims and ethics of contemporary interpretation.

Towards Which Criticism?

Some are bewilder'd in the maze of schools,
And some made coxcombs nature meant but fools.[51]

Learning to read is a never-ending challenge. Word recognition—making sense of bundles of letters—is only the beginning. After spelling and phonics comes grammar and eventually criticism, with its myriad ways of describing and evaluating texts in light of specific interpretive questions and interests. Finally, literary theories emerge when an initial approach, now hardened into a shared strategy of reading, becomes the basis for a full-blown explanation of what meaning is.[52]

How then should we read? To what critical school, if any, should we subscribe, and why? This is the practical question. According to Hirsch, it is a question answered by an ethical choice, based "upon a value-preference, and not on theoretical necessity."[53] But how can we defend our choice of values? A second, more theoretical query necessarily follows from our having to choose at all, namely, if all literary judgments are interested, is all literary criticism relative? If one's values ultimately shape one's interpretations, then must we not abandon hope of a "morality" of literary knowledge that would be comparable to what, in Van Harvey's[54] eyes at least, gives dignity and objectivity to the study of history?

Whose Interest, Which Partiality?

Are all interests in texts equally valid? Is any one interest more ethical, or less ethical, than another? Is there something that all readers should be observing or doing as they undertake an analysis or evaluation of, say, *Gulliver's Travels* or the Gospel of Mark? Do we ever have the right, or responsibility, to challenge a reading, and perhaps to declare it false? Is there such a thing as a "bad" interpretation? Pragmatists such as Jeffrey Stout deny that there is a hermeneutical equivalent of the moral imperative.[55] Take, for instance, the following principle: "Thou shalt not neglect the author's intention." To what authority could one possibly appeal as the basis for this hermeneutical commandment?

Biblical interpreters struggle with the same questions. Stephen Fowl, in a 1988 address to the Society for Biblical Literature, observed that most interpretive interests are imperialistic—dismissive of other interests. Fowl sees three options for the present-day biblical exegete. First, we could simply celebrate the plurality of interpretive interests. In order to eliminate silly or perverse interests, we could agree that "the only criterion for pursuing an interpretive interest is that it is interesting to sufficient numbers of interpreters to enable a conversation to take place."[57] This criterion, however, raises problems of its own, as Fowl makes clear. For instance, who determines whose interests are sufficiently interesting? "The one question that the pluralist community could never answer, on other than practical grounds, is whether its members should pursue one interest over another."[58]

Second, we could use the reading strategy that will best foster peace, freedom, and justice for society. Elisabeth Schüssler Fiorenza, for example, says that readers of the Bible have a responsibility to their context to choose interpretive models that will yield readings that have ethical consequences. Biblical exegesis, she argues, is a socially conditioned activity that has ethical and political consequences, and thus social and political responsibilities. The biblical scholar is particularly responsible for "the elucidation of the ethical consequences and political functions of biblical texts in their historical as well as in their contemporary sociopolitical contexts."[59] Readers have a responsibility, in other words, to evaluate the impact of a text on the contemporary context. On this view, the morality of literary knowledge means choosing the reading that is most likely to foster social justice.

Third, Fowl says we could abandon the quest for moral universals in favor of the interpretive interests of a particular community. Within a specific community, there is a prioritization of interpretive interests, but outside that community no criteria are available to arbitrate the conflict of interpretive approaches.[60] Instead of aspiring to universals, readers should be content to belong to their own hermeneutic tribes.

How Readers Respond to Interpretive Pluralism

Whatever option we choose, we must still acknowledge that ours is only one of many methods for interpreting the Bible. How should such an acknowledgment affect one's stance towards one's own reading? How can we seriously maintain that one reading is better, or more interesting, or more adequate than another? Fowl wonders whether "meaning" should perhaps refer to "that reading which synthesizes all or most of these interests into some sort of macro reading."[61] The obvious problem with such an interpretive ecumenism, however, is that many readings are mutually exclusive. Furthermore, the ecumenically minded reader must be able to state certain non-arbitrary limits as to what would be considered an acceptable reading. Otherwise, it would be impossible to identify misinterpretations. The question therefore remains: *What is the status of one's own interpretation when confronted with the plethora of alternatives?* Can readers continue to believe in a meaning that transcends the Babel of interpretations?

I will now propose an alternative typology to set alongside Fowl's list of possible responses to interpretive pluralism. The following four positions represent quasi-theological stances towards the possibility of literary knowledge in a pluralistic situation.[62]

Interpretive Dogmatism. Interpretive dogmatists hold that there is one and only one correct approach to textual meaning: theirs. Interpretive dogmatists believe absolutely in their own interpretations. There is one true meaning on this view: a "God's-eye point of view." Interpretive dogmatism results in a critical monism; only one set of categories correctly describes the text. Dogmatists are not surprised when others do not see things similarly; it's just that they have yet to be enlightened.

Interpretive Atheism. At the opposite end of the spectrum are interpretive atheists, who do not believe in meaning. There is nothing "there" in a text to get right. Interpretive atheists do not, therefore, really "believe" in their interpretations; they are critical nihilists. There is nothing that transcends the play of signs or the uses to which they are put. The purpose of interpretation is either to be interesting or to oppose and irritate the interpretive dogmatist.

Interpretive Polytheism. Interpretive polytheists, a rapidly increasing critical tribe, believe that there are many legitimate aims of interpretation and many legitimate points of view. One's description of a text is relative to the set of concerns and expectations that precede and accompany the reading process. A text may, therefore, mean many, perhaps even contradictory, things. My interpretation has a right to exist, but so do those of other critical schools. Such interpretive inter-faith dialogue abounds at present. Interpretive polytheists do not believe, however, in a "super-theory" that will eventually allow believers in different approaches to compare and correlate results. Interpretive polytheists will never speak the same language or worship at the same shrine.

Interpretive Trinitarianism. The doctrine of the Trinity may at first seem to have little to do with the rarefied disagreements of literary theorists. I can here only hint at an approach that will be more fully developed in Part 2. First, and most important: *Christian orthodoxy believes that God is essentially the one who communicates himself to others in trinitarian fashion.* A trinitarian theology of the Word of God conceives God as author, as message, and as power of reception: "In the beginning was the communicative act."[63] *The God of Jesus Christ is the self-interpreting God.* The Incarnation, wherein God goes out of himself for the sake of communicating himself to another, grounds the possibility of human communication by demonstrating that it is indeed possible to enter into the life of another so as to achieve understanding.

Second, there is a certain methodological analogy between theology and literary theory, based on their shared concern to speak of transcendence: of that which transcends the world (God) and of that which transcends language (meaning).

Third, with regard specifically to pluralism, we must note the following parallel. As each person of the Trinity offers a different perspective on the one true God, so there may be a limited plurality of perspectives on meaning.[64] While exhaustive knowledge of God is beyond our grasp, our limitations do not prevent us from saying, on the basis of God's self-communication, certain concrete things (e.g., "God is love," "Jesus Christ is the only begotten Son of God") or from ruling other things out (e.g., "Love is God," "Jesus Christ was merely a human"). The possibility of mediate or revealed knowledge stands in marked contrast to the sterile dichotomy of either absolute knowledge (interpretive dogmatism) or absolute skepticism (interpretive atheism). This attitude may be termed "critical fideism." It is consonant with the Augustinian hermeneutics referred to in the Introduction: "We believe in order to understand." To be precise, we may believe in the possibility of right interpretations; yet at the same time we must subject them to criticism, realizing that no one set of descriptive categories can render the complex reality of meaning (or God) with other than relative adequacy.

In short, by specifying the ground and goal of interpretation, trinitarian theology offers to biblical interpreters a paradigm for general as well as biblical hermeneutics.[65] To show just how this is so is the burden of Part 2. For present purposes, it suffices to point out that trinitarian theology enables us to conceive of interpretive plurality in terms of harmony (three-in-one; one-in-three) rather than conflict. Christians believe that reality is ultimately a matter of interpersonal communication and communion, not of an impersonal (and conflictual) *différance*.[66]

INTERPRETIVE VIOLENCE

Karl Barth once remarked, after reading a review of one of his books, that he felt as though he had been cannibalized.[67] Being misunderstood is one thing, being willfully misunderstood quite another. Is it possible that some interpretive methods legitimate misunderstanding? Are some interpretive approaches inherently violent? In an age dominated by the reader, can the text be anything other than a passive victim? Mark C. Taylor apparently thinks not: "If the text is not to lie fallow but is to be impregnated, it must be penetrated, ruptured, victimized."[68] The scene Taylor describes is not the bliss of the wedding bed—there is no marriage of two minds in deconstructive criticism—but rather the pain of interpretive rape.

Historical criticism was supposed to free readers from the tyranny of interpretive traditions and the violence of partisan exegesis. The modern biblical scholar approached the text in a neutral and disinterested manner, with a method and set of critical tools that could in principle be used by anyone, regardless of race, creed, or color. Modern philosophers, at about the same time, were seeking universal criteria for rationality. Universal criteria, in the philosophy of religion and exegesis alike, were thought to be the only practical way forward after a century of religious wars between people of the same faith who interpreted the Bible along denominational lines. From the late eigtheenth century until about the mid-twentieth century, biblical criticism was considered a bona fide science. Modern readers made a fateful inference: to read critically meant negating one's own particularity and context.[69] Interpretation was about discovering a meaning for all times and cultures.

In an era committed to objectivity, "eisegesis"—reading something into the text that was not there—was the cardinal hermeneutic sin.[70] Calvin had earlier encouraged readers to respect the text: "It is an audacity akin to sacrilege to use the Scripture at our own pleasure and to play with them as with a tennis ball, which many before us have done."[71] According to contemporary postmodern critics, however, eisegesis is virtually synonymous with interpretation, because all reading is contextual—"interested"—and meaning is not objectively "there." In the age of the reader, eisegesis, like the notion of heresy, is an endangered conceptual species.

Postmodern critics have been quick to point out the naiveté of modern biblical criticism's alleged impartiality. While supposedly providing a ground on which people of different backgrounds and religious persuasions could meet and discuss on equal footing, historical criticism is in fact imperialistic and sexist: "The model clearly emerged not only out of a European setting but also out of a male European setting."[72] Under the guise of neutrality, the historical-critical model in fact *dehumanized* the reader, requiring that all contextual factors and commitments be put off before the task of biblical interpretation could begin. Just as historical critics accused their premodern predecessors of imprisoning the text in the ecclesiastical straitjacket of dogmatic systems, so postmoderns accuse historical critics of imprisoning the text in the academic straitjacket of liberal-democratic European values.

The postmodern critique of modernity raises an important question regarding the ethics of interpretation: Is there any interpretive approach that does not sanction some form of institutional violence? Interestingly enough, both moderns and postmoderns claim the high moral ground of justice and liberation.

Liberation Hermeneutics: Between Freedom and Force

Which type of criticism—historical-critical or poststructural—has a better claim to the title of "liberation hermeneutics"? This is a most important question, but I do not intend to answer it just yet. I do wish to make one preliminary observation: whereas the historical critic seeks to free the reader from *tradition*, the Undoer seeks to free the reader from the *text*. Feminist and other ideological critics contend that readers have for too long been slaves of oppressive ideologies inscribed in the biblical texts. Derrida speaks disparagingly of "interpretive slaves who faithfully execute the providential designs of the 'master.'"[73]

In the opinion of the Undoers and Users, the real perpetrators of interpretive violence are those who maintain that there is a right (and thus a wrong) way to read. What is deemed oppressive in the context of postmodern hermeneutics is the claim that there is such a thing as a morality of interpretation and universal norms, rather than a plurality of ethical aims. The claim that there is a right way to read is, furthermore, tied up in complicated ways with the concepts of God and meaning—with the notion that there is something transcendent, something independent of the process of interpretation, to which the reader is accountable. Does the postmodern denial of transcendence lead to more freedom or less? Does the reader's liberation from tyrannical traditions and determinate texts lead to a genuine freedom or to a new form of slavery (and to an older form of interpretive violence, namely, eisegesis)?

Undoing the Ties That Bind

Derrida, we may recall, undoes the traditional concept of meaning as authorial intention by severing the tie between a text and its original context. The original context no longer defines the *circumstantia litterarum*, "the way the words go." By reading texts in light of other texts and contexts, the reader forces the words to go *another* way. Derrida, we may recall, affirms a joyful, life-affirming style of interpretation that celebrates its freedom from closed orders and totalizing systems. Texts and humans alike are thus radically open—"free."

Or are they? The original context may no longer dominate one's reading, but some context or other remains a determinative factor. The *Postmodern Bible* collective states that "reading and interpretive strategies are socially, politically, and institutionally situated and . . . draw their energy and force from the subject positions of readers and interpreters."[74] Is the "force" attributed to the context of the reader liberating or oppressive? Is it indeed the case that the freeplay of the text leads to the freedom of the reader? Just what does liberation mean in the context of hermeneutics?

Deconstruction may be said to be liberationist in two senses. Undoing is liberating, first, in the sense of freedom *from*, insofar as it resists the imposition of textual (and cultural) frameworks. Freed from the largely hidden textual strategies of ideological repression, the reader is free *for*, well, more interpretation. Totalizing, absolutist interpretations are undone in order to release an endless plurality of readings. "Deconstruction perhaps has the effect, if not the mission, of liberating forbidden *jouissance*. . . . It is perhaps this *jouissance* which most irritates the all-out adversaries of 'deconstruction.'"[75] Derrida claims the ethical high ground with respect to interpretation: the Undoer is a freedom fighter, the quintessential *contra*.

Ventriloquism as Victimization

Certainly texts have limited power. They must wait patiently on a shelf until a reader takes, opens, and begins to read them. Even then, as we have just seen, the text is at the mercy of the reader's whims. A page might be memorized and taken to heart, or it might be used to paper the bottom of the bird cage. Unlike living dialogue partners, the text cannot talk back, protest, or defend itself. Readers always seem to have the last word. They can ignore, skip over, read into, and at the limit, close texts. Texts may look intelligent, says Socrates, but when you ask them a question, they either preserve a solemn silence or else "always say only one and the same thing."[77] The text is hapless and helpless, inert and mute, until taken up by a reader. But what is to stop the reader from projecting his or her own voice into the mute text? Can the text ever have an independent say?

The text in the age of the reader resembles a ventriloquist's dummy: it serves as an opportunity for projecting one's own voice. In the words of Moore: "The text for me is encrusted reading: a totalizable sum of prior and potential readings, an unconscious reservoir."[78] To be a text, we might say, is to be perceived. Strictly speaking there are no "texts-in-themselves," only "readings." The text here becomes an occasion for readers to realize themselves. "A book is a mirror. If an ass peers into it, you can't expect an apostle to look out"[79] Is this right? Do we see only ourselves—our own concerns and those of our interpretive community, in the mirror? We are back to our opening parable and to Kierkegaard's question as to how to read the Bible in order to receive a blessing.

Humpty Dumpty, in response to Alice's question whether he can make words means different things, replies that it is a matter of "which is to be the master," words or readers. The postmodern critic concurs with the hermeneutics of Wonderland: dictionaries carry no sacred or metaphysical authority, only that of majority rule. Texts mean what interpretive communities take them to mean. So, which is to be the master? More pointedly, who changes whom? This is perhaps the basic issue: Can a text transform its reader, or is transformative power the exclusive prerogative of the interpreter?

The "dialogue" between text and reader in the third age of criticism "is egotistically shifted toward the present: criticism is not an homage to the truth of the past or to the truth of 'others'—it is a construction of the intelligibility of our own time."[80] According to Eagleton, "there is no reading of a work which is not also a 're-writing.'"[81] George Steiner laments the postmodern loss of the traditional distinction between authors and readers: "The evacuation of intentionality from the original text, the denial of a stable core of signification, is not only an epistemological game. It entails a premise of equality as between 'constructor' and deconstructor, as between text and the gloss."[82]

The problem, briefly, is that deconstructors can no longer draw a consistent distinction between literature and criticism. If there is no autonomous text to "get right," if everything we see in texts is a function of our readerly interests, then there is no difference between the text and our interpretation of it. If the text has no integrity of its own, then readers can have their own way with it. They can disregard what it says and say what it means to them. Such interpretive freedom, however, comes at the expense of the text itself. Interpretation in the age of the reader has become "the substitution . . . by a kind of hermeneutical violence, of one chain of signifiers for another."[83] Taylor admits that, on his view, "Interpretation is a *hostile* act in which interpreter victimizes text."[84] It follows that a text only takes on meaning insofar as it submits to interpretive violence: "There is no text-in-itself which subsists apart from interpretation."[85] With this violence, the Reader's Liberation Movement reaches fruition, reaches for the fruit, that is, that makes interpreters like gods, creators rather than recipients of meaning.

If meaning is not really "there" before the reader makes it, then it is difficult to see how texts can ever challenge or transform their readers? Textual impotence is a high price to pay for the liberation of the reader. Bereft of authors or authority, texts become entirely subject to the play of interpretive interests and lose the possibility of substantially modifying or directing those interests. Can readers be protected from oppressive interpretive communities that permit some ways of reading but prohibit others, and if so, how? It is important to pursue the response of the Undoers and the Users to this query, for it would be wrong to construe them as hermeneutic hedonists, who read for their own personal pleasure only. Enjoyment is only one aspect of the Undoers' liberationist ethics; alongside *jouissance* is a concern for justice. Indeed, postmodern theories about interpretive play could not be more serious; for the contest is ultimately over politics, and the prize is social power.

POWER READING AND THE POLITICS OF CANON

Should freshmen at Stanford University have to read Shakespeare? Can the situation of a white Elizabethan male be relevant to modern Californians? What does sixteenth-century Stratford have to do with twentieth-century Stanford? These questions are not obviously political.[86] Nevertheless, Shakespearian texts have become a battleground for the so-called "culture wars," in which the combatants fight not over land but rather over the territory of the human spirit.[87] The argument over whether Shakespeare should be required reading is not about Shakespeare so much as it is about the idea of a common core of values. To ask whether one believes in a "canon" of English literature—a list of classic books—is to raise a question about the possibility of transcontextual, permanent goods. The very idea of a text having a "permanent value" is anathema to those who wish, in the name of freedom, to rebel against authority and to accord to the reader the privilege of "making sense." The idea of "prescribed" texts that must be read in "prescribed" ways restricts the freedom of the interpreter playfully to invent meaning and pursue self-realization.[88] Moreover, the notion of a canon implies that these prescribed texts also prescribe ways of living insofar as they identify what is of permanent value to human beings. In short, the existence of a literary canon implies something about human existence. Traditional literary critics cherish the canon as the set of books that contain a wealth of moral knowledge about the nature and meaning of the human condition.

Those who resist the idea of canon, on the other hand, do so as much for moral and political as for literary reasons. They refuse to recognize permanent values that transcend the concrete situations of texts and readers. Neither readers nor texts are ever "neutral"; they are rather historically and culturally "situated." To pretend otherwise, to speak of "transcontextual values," is yet another strategem for those with power to mask their interest behind the guise of "truth." It is to mistake *our* interests and values for universal interests and values. The Reader's Liberation Movement is aptly named, for it is driven by political motives, namely, the desire to unmask texts and interpretations alike as effects of socio-political power. The hermeneutics of suspicion must be applied to the practice of criticism itself, especially to the concept of a literary canon.[89] The culture wars in the humanities constitute nothing less than a pitched battle for the human spirit itself. Debates about meaning are ultimately political struggles about the meaning of freedom and the shape of the good life. *Indeed, it may well be that such ethical and political considerations provide the main motivation for hermeneutic non-realism.*

Whether one believes in a literary canon or not, then, may be a reflection of one's politics (and of one's theology). This connection is an important part of my thesis: the postmodern attack on hermeneutics is a crisis not only in the humanities but a crisis in the very notion of humanity itself. At the heart of the debate about meaning is a dispute about the nature and meaning of human freedom and the good life, as the following quote by Eagleton attests: "Any method or theory which will contribute to the strategic goal of human emancipation, the production of 'better people' through the socialist transformation of society, is acceptable."[90] Eagleton's own neo-Marxist vision is clear, but in the end he begs the vital question of who gets to define "better people" and how to do so.[91] The question underlying the age of the reader and the hermeneutics of liberation is simply this: What does it mean to be human?

Ideology and Interpretation

Ideology is partially constitutive of what, in our societies, "is real."[92]

The "best" reading is the one that produces "better people." While this may be true (recall Augustine's belief that the best reading was the one that fostered love of God and neighbor), "better" and "best" cannot function as helpful criteria until they are defined. It is far from self-evident that the reason why one community values a text will be valid for other interpretive communities too. Matthew Arnold's celebrated definition of criticism—the effort to learn and transmit the "best" that has been said and thought—aspires to universality but in fact begs the question, "Best *for whom?*"[93]

The Political Situation of Ideas

Undoers and Users are united in their insistence that ideas and values are always situated in specific social contexts. Ideas are produced and used for particular purposes, which is another way of saying that ideas have "material" conditions. According to the so-called cultural materialists, the values that inform a culture are always related to what is at bottom a political purpose: the exercise of power in society. Any answer to the questions about the best books to read (e.g., canon) and the best way to read them (e.g., criticism) will therefore be related to the corporate will to power and to some ideological interest. Eagleton remarks that "ideology" refers to "the ways in which what we say and believe connects with the power-structure and power-relations of the society we live in."[94] An even briefer though sobering definition of ideology is "meaning in the service of power."[95]

There is no innocent reading; it is impossible to read anything through eyes other than one's own. For Eagleton, interpretation is inescapably ideological. To interpret—to produce meaning—is to serve someone's interest: "To study ideology . . . is to study the ways in which meaning (or signification) serves to sustain relations of domination."[96] Indeed, the struggles over the "means of production" of meaning are among the most violent a society can experience (e.g., the feminist revolution). The value judgments one makes about what to read and how to read it reflect a concern not for objective knowledge but for power over the minds, and perhaps the bodies, of others.

Ideological criticism diminishes the importance of the author's intention. Why? Because for postmoderns the author too is largely a product of ideology. In addition, cultural materialists insist that the deepest sources of meaning lie outside the control and the consciousness of the speaking subject. Just as the psychoanalyst perceives deeper meanings in Freudian slips, so the political critic listens for hidden political assumptions (Marxist slips?). Indeed, one way to view ideology criticism is as a kind of psychoanalysis of society's unquestioned beliefs and values—of the cultural Id, as it were.[97] Ideological criticism is thus a species of the hermeneutics of suspicion. It falls to the critic of ideology to distinguish the "real" (e.g., the covert material and political forces) from the "ideal" (e.g., the overt meaning and message of the text).

For Undoers, the "best" reading is the one that challenges and overturns the dominant ideology by exposing and dismantling it, even if that means reading against the apparent sense of the text: "Ideological reading . . . is a deliberate effort to read against the grain—of texts, of disciplinary norms, of traditions, of cultures. It is a disturbing way to read because ideological criticism demands a high level of self-consciousness and makes an explicit, unbiased appeal to justice."[98] Ideological critics feel no need to apologize for importing their concerns into the process of interpretation. What counts ethically is whether one's interpretation has a liberating effect on the reader's present context. In a relativistic age, "best" means "best 'for us today' according to some standard that is compelling in our present historical circumstances."[99]

Feminist Criticism and Ideology Critique

Feminist criticism has displayed greater sensitivity to the political implications of language and interpretation than perhaps any other contemporary approach. It represents yet another variation on the hermeneutics of suspicion. What has come to be called "feminist interpretation" does not name a specific method for reading, but rather a set of approaches to texts that resists patriarchy—the ideology that legitimates social structures that privilege men and disempower women—and foster women's liberation.[100] Behind the varieties of feminist criticism lies an overriding interest in justice for women (and to some extent, other marginalized groups). The act of reading is fundamentally ethical: interpret in the way that is *best for women today*.

Ideological critics are aware that texts not only represent a system of human relations in the world but also tend to reproduce it. This is the ideological function of literature: to preserve the power relations that structure society. In shaping the way we see the world and ourselves, stories sustain and enact social power. Those who control how language is used control the most powerful instrument for shaping human consciousness. For the feminist critic, texts—whether novels or advertisements (or, as we will see, Scripture)—do not mirror the real world (e.g., who women really are) but rather "construct" it by representing a particular cultural understanding of the place and role of women as though it were "natural." Patriarchy, by legitimating the domination of women by men, tries "to disguise the fact of reality as a social and historical production and to return it to the world of nature."[101] Gender is less a biological constant than a social construct, a product of language and texts. "He"—the third person singular masculine pronoun—is much more than a part of speech; its systematic use to refer to both men and women is a political instrument for the oppression of women and, indeed, their negation.

Feminist and deconstructive criticism, both arising out of the 1960s, share a number of overlapping concerns.[102] Most important for our purposes, they share a common aim: the undoing of the privileged hierarchies that dominate both society and language itself. These privileged hierarchies are upheld both by politics and by rhetoric.[103] Eagleton comments: "For of all the binary oppositions which post-structuralism sought to undo, the hierarchical opposition between men and women was perhaps the most virulent."[104] Feminist readers are ideology critics who undo textual hierarchies by reading against the grain, that is, by exposing the world of the text as an effect of rhetoric rather than as a picture of reality.

Reading "From Below": The Authority of Interpretive Communities

It would be misleading to imply that the Reader's Liberation Movement has resulted in interpretive anarchy. Even readers liberated from determinate meaning are not entirely free. For although texts are no longer able to constrain interpretation, interpretive communities can (and do). Though the reader produces meaning, the modes of production are not haphazard. On the contrary, they are regulated by interpretive communities. Every reader is either born into or joins a community with shared convictions about the best procedures for producing interpretations and about the goods that form the goal of a particular interpretive practice. Meaning for Fish is determinate only in the sense that readers always read within particular contexts with specific interpretive rules. In short, while texts may be indeterminate, social contexts are surely not.

If postmodernity stands for anything, it is for the demise of a universal standpoint and the subsequent celebration of the diverse particular perspectives from which we view the world, each other, and our texts. Understanding for postmoderns is always contextual, never universal. Postmodernity does not mean the end of all authority, however, only of universal norms; local norms remain in force. Interpretation is always "from below," shaped by the reader's contextually conditioned context and regulated by the authority of community-based norms. Hence, if interpretation is indeed a form of power reading, it remains to be seen *whose* power it is and whether its force is liberating. For while truth has been described as a force that sets one free (John 8:32), postmoderns see truth as a rhetorical device used by the strong to justify their power over the weak. This leads us to a crucial problem for the postmodern critic: *To what do we appeal when the context rather than the text is the oppressor?* Have the postmodern prophets led us out of the captivity to canon only to enslave us to the dominant interests of the interpretive community? The question remains: Is the exodus from modernity, and from meaning, a deliverance or a new bondage?

The Social Construction of Textual Meaning

Other disciplines, including the natural and human sciences, now regularly appeal to the authority of the interpreting community as a mediating alternative to an objectivist realism on the one hand and a subjectivist relativism on the other. This is only to be expected: I have argued that contemporary developments in hermeneutics are but a microcosm of larger intellectual and cultural trends. To speak of the birth of the reader as an inter-disciplinary event is to admit that knowledge is always context-relative. As we have seen, Users contend that literary and scientific knowledge alike is ultimately a function of community interests. Physics is no more privileged than poetry when it comes to representing the "real"; rather, both are seen as products of social practices that in turn are generated by different interests. For the User, "facts" are the results of an interpretive practice, not its foundation.[105]

We can never read a text as it is in itself, but only as we have been taught by our community. Fish argues that we can never get outside the prevailing norms of our community; there is no theoretical high ground to occupy. "Theory" is simply the description of an already existing practice that one wishes to justify rhetorically.[106] What really governs our intellectual practices is not "theory" but ideology: a jumble of prejudices, interests, and values that we may be able to rationalize but never rationally justify.

The Sociology of Literary Knowledge. What saves Fish's reader-based hermeneutics from relativism is his insistence that readers make sense *together*. The facts are facts by virtue of institutional agreement. Fish is not making a ridiculous assertion, such as, "The world's not out there, you're making it all up as you go along," but rather, "What you see is always shaped and colored by the interpretive practices of your base community." He thus neatly reverses Calvin's dictum concerning Scripture as the spectacles of faith; according to Fish, one views the text through the spectacles of the faith community.

Can Fish successfully escape subjectivism by appealing to inter-subjectivity? "Silly relativism" may be avoided, but cultural relativism—where standards for knowledge, truth, and goodness are community-dependent—is not so easily shaken. Meaning is not objectively "there" (in the text) but relative to interpretive communities and their interests. "What I finally came to see was that the identification of what was real and normative occurred within interpretive communities."[107] Fish thus opts, if not for relativism, then for a hermeneutic variation on the special relativity thesis: what an interpreter sees in a text is relative to one's place and time, one's interpretive community. "The text as an entity independent of interpretation . . . is replaced by the texts that emerge as the consequence of our interpretive activities."[108] Literary knowledge is a matter not of interpretations conforming to texts, but of texts conforming to communal interpretations.[109]

The business of literary criticism is not to determine a correct way of reading or to achieve literary knowledge, but rather "to establish by political and persuasive means (they are the same thing) the set of interpretive assumptions from the vantage of which the evidence (and the facts and the intentions and everything else) will hereafter be specifiable."[110] Context, again, is everything. What we find in a text is a function of who and where we are.

Is There a Self-Critical Principle in Fish's Text? Where readers reign, reality recedes. Fish's pragmatist creed is briefly stated: "I now believe that interpretation is the source of texts, facts, authors, and intentions."[111] Literary knowledge is for Fish a kind of self-fulfilling prophecy: readers will see what they are encouraged and taught to see.[112] The literal meaning is the one the institution permits; the "natural" sense is the one *nurtured* by the community.

Does Fish's account of interpretation adequately describe the reader's experience? Can he explain how texts can transform readers, or how texts can be read critically *against* the reading commmunity? Fish cannot say. There is nothing outside our context that could be used to challenge it, because everything that we see (the facts) is already a product of our interpretive conventions. Thus, we have to conclude that there is no text in Fish's class—no text, that is, strong enough to resist interpretation.[113]

What is lacking in Fish's account of the interpretive process is how texts may challenge, and perhaps transform, the reader and the interpretive community. It is difficult to see how, on Fish's account, the text could ever be used to criticize a dominant ideology, or how any interpretive community could be challenged as to its particular reading aim and method. It is the User's account of literary knowledge that is the main stumbling block. If all appeals to the text-in-itself are ruled out, and if all argumentation is relative to the norms of each interpretive community, then the only way to resolve interpretive differences is through majority rule. Fish is aware of the problem: "Does might make right? In a sense the answer I must give is yes, since in the absence of a perspective independent of interpretation some interpretive perspective will always rule by virtue of having won out over its competitors."[114] It is difficult to see how Fish could account for, say, Luther's experience of reading Scripture—for the joy of discovering something new, for the challenge to his community's hermeneutical conventions.

Can texts "kick back," resist misreadings, challenge our practices and beliefs, or overturn our literary theories? Consider the story of Augustine's conversion, a life-transforming experience occasioned by the children's song that prompted Augustine to "take up and read." How could reading one verse from the Bible have played so great a part in shaping Augustine's life? Why is reading a dangerous, world-shattering prospect? Why do certain societies have an Index, a list not of prescribed but proscribed books? Ray Bradbury imagined in *Fahrenheit 451* a future totalitarian society where the firemen's job is to *burn* "dangerous" books. The weapons of the underground resistance movement consisted simply in classic works of literature (the canon) that its members had committed to memory. How can we account, on Fish's view, for the strange power of books to transform us? Fish does not say.

Finally, we may ask of Fish whether his scheme constrains or encourages interpretive violence. True, there is no room for the vigilante or terrorist interpreter on Fish's account; individuals work within institutions. On the other hand, as Niebuhr points out, institutional pride is more powerful and more sinister than that of an individual. Fish and Rorty are consistent pragmatists when they define knowledge in terms of persuasion rather than foundations. But in the absence of ideology-free facts about texts, how does the process of persuasion work? How, for instance, would they respond to Foucault's contention that "knowledge" is in fact the power of discourse (rhetoric) and the discourse of the powerful (politics)? According to Foucault, those within a given community of discourse are considered "normal" while the outsiders are labeled "abnormal"—mad, marginalized, perhaps monsters. Institutions can be cruel and unforgiving to those who fail to conform. Indeed, one might say that Fish, by according a relatively absolute authority to interpretive communities, has created an environment that is potentially User-*unfriendly*. The situation is even worse for texts: they exist as hostages to fortune in communities that legitimate gang violence by calling it interpretation.

The Social Construction of Biblical Meaning

Interpretive traffic, *pace* Fish, is rarely one way. Biblical interpretation is pulled between two opposing forces: the sense potential of the text and the interests of the reader. But the text, according to Jeanrond, "is a somewhat weaker partner which, for instance, is unable to defend itself against violations of its integrity by ideological readers."[115] This raises crucial problems for biblical authority. Can the canon (and here I mean the Christian Scriptures) be taken captive by an ideological community? How does our discussion concerning the politics of reading relate to the ecclesiastical debate concerning the relative authority of Scripture and tradition?

The conflict of interpretive communities is not, of course, new. The first Christians claimed to have found in Christ the interpretive key to the Hebrew Scriptures: "It was not a different canon but a distinctive method of reading which differentiated the church from the synagogue."[116] In the early church, the authoritative interpretation of the newly formed New Testament was that of the "authorized" community. Precisely because readers can do violence to texts, Irenaeus denied the right of heretics to interpret the Scriptures. There was only one "canonical" context in which the Bible could be read and interpreted, namely, the apostolic church. For the church fathers, right reading occurs only as an authentic Christian community.

By the sixteenth century, however, there were a number of communities that had laid claim to the title "Christian." In 1546, at the Council of Trent, the Roman Catholic Church declared that, with regard to matters of faith and morality, no one should dare challenge the interpretation of the institutional church, "whose task it is to determine the true sense and interpretation of Holy Scriptures."[117] This interpretive privilege for the ecclesiastical hierarchy is precisely what Martin Luther had challenged. Luther claimed that any Christian had the right to interpret the Bible. He also affirmed the "perspicuity" or clarity of the Bible, claiming that its meaning was clear for those who attended to the grammar of the text and to the leading of the Spirit. Calvin, similarly, argued that the meaning and authority of Scripture did not depend on the church. Rather, Scripture legitimates its own authority: "Scripture interprets Scripture."[118] By this latter phrase the Reformers indicated that obscure passages should be read in light of clearer ones. In so doing, they claimed to have a criterion with which to distinguish a true reading of Scripture from its official, ecclesiastically sanctioned, interpretation.

The interpretive freedom of the Protestants was quickly limited, however, by the Lutheran and Reformed confessions, which set the parameters for what would be considered acceptable readings in their respective communities. By the seventeenth century, the conflict of interpretations between rival confessional communities resulted in all-out religious wars. According to Lindbeck, these religious conflicts paved the way for modernity and the Enlightenment: "Communal certainties were undermined by Christian fratricide (much more unsettling than ever before in the West because it was between established churches), and many turned for firm foundations to individual reason and experience."[119] Enlightened critics in the eighteenth century concluded as often as not that biblical proof texts did not support the doctrinal use to which they were being put in a confessional community. Modernity thus replaced the authority of the priest with that of the scholar. In the academy, the scholar's interest in the history of the Bible's composition replaced the believer's interest in its religious use.[120]

And so we come to our present postmodern situation, in which the search for a fixed point outside language has been abandoned. Rorty calls it a "post-philosophical" situation—one in which "neither the priests nor the physicists nor the poets nor the Party were thought of as more 'rational' or more 'scientific' or 'deeper' than one another."[121] In the postmodern world, "common sense" suggests not universal standards but rather a particular *community* sense. As in the early church, so authority today attaches to communities, though it is considerably more difficult now to demonstrate apostolic lineage.

Significantly, a number of recent works by Christian theologians endorse Fish's concept of the authority of interpretive communities. I shall here consider only two.[122] The first, *Text and Experience: Towards a Cultural Exegesis of the Bible*, calls readers to interpret Scripture in ways that draw on their unique cultural identities. "Cultural exegesis" studies how different people groups read Scripture differently. In a multicultural world, it is only to be expected that there will be a variety of different readings. While the fact of multiculturalism is indisputable, there is a difference of opinion with regard to its significance. Some, for instance, would contend that the readings of certain groups—the poor, women, African-Americans, etc.—should have more authority than others. Latin American liberation theologians, for instance, privilege the reading perspective of the poor. Though not an apostolic community, the poor are nevertheless considered to be the authorized interpreters because their context is similar to those for whom the Bible was written and because their position enables them to read in an anti-ideological fashion.

By and large, however, the contributors to *Text and Experience*, while granting an important role to one's cultural context, do not go as far as Fish and suggest that meaning is created by interpretive communities. The authority of interpretive communities is not absolute, but secondary to that of the text. What they suggest instead is that the variety of perspectives, taken together, give us a fuller insight into the *historical* meaning of biblical texts:

> Thus, what we would like to know from the liberation theologians is whether the poor Brazilian peasants who read the Bible can give any insights into what the text means *for others besides themselves*. . . . *That* is the question of cultural exegesis of the Bible. Can the native American elder, the Indian or African student or scholar, give all of us new ideas about what the text *historically meant?*[123]

This is an important strategy for reading in a multicultural age without abandoning the morality of literary knowledge, and I will return to it in due course.

Stanley Hauerwas's *Unleashing the Scripture: Freeing the Bible From Captivity to America* represents a more consistent version of Fish's ideas. According to Hauerwas, it is dangerous to think that individual readers can come to "the meaning" of the Bible on their own. Common sense is not sufficient for understanding the Bible. On the contrary, readers need to be trained by the church—the authorized interpretive community—in order to read the Bible correctly. It is only biblical critics—and fundamentalists—who think that Scripture has an objective meaning. Hauerwas aptly entitles his second chapter "Stanley Fish, the Pope, and the Bible." He agrees with Fish that texts are products of interpretation: "There simply is no 'real meaning' of Paul's letters to the Corinthians once we understand that they are no longer Paul's letters but rather the Church's Scripture."[124] The crucial question for Hauerwas, as for Fish, is that of interpretive norms: What are we reading for? This, says Hauerwas, is a political question that concerns the value of interpretation. When it comes to the politics of interpretation, Fish and the Pope are on the same side; the church as an interpretive community alone has the authority to decide on values.[125]

There is a world of difference, of course, between saying that we need a number of different perspectives to discover independent textual meaning and saying that each perspective constructs a different text, each with its own meaning. Hauerwas could be read in either way. On the one hand, he could be saying that unless readers are also committed Christians, they will not understand the biblical message. On the other hand, he could be saying that the text only becomes Scripture when read in a certain way. The latter possibility raises questions about divine authority and the locus of the Word of God. Is the church under the Word, or is the Word under the church? If the latter, what is to stop the interpretive communities from becoming authoritarian? What, specifically, does it mean to read in the church? Most important, in *which* church should we read in order to interpret correctly? Fish's proposals ultimately fit a Roman Catholic context much better than that of churches shaped by the Reformation, which assign supreme authority to the text rather than to an interpretive tradition.

At least Christian communities have a privileged text. There is controversy in postmodernity, as in the early church, over whether there should be a "canon" of works that enshrines our most important values, and if so, over which texts should be included. There is confusion in postmodernity, as there was in the early church, about who has the right to specify what the crucial questions are and over "who is empowered to speak truthfully about them."[126] Who today is in a position to speak for the text? One community? One denomination? Or perhaps an ecumenical interpretive community that would be marked by hermeneutic power-sharing? It may be that consensus will only be won when each community engages in a certain measure of self-criticism. To paraphrase Eco, one has the impression that, of late, the rights of interpretive communities have eclipsed the rights of the text.

Lindbeck pleads for a return to the Christ-centered way of reading the Old Testament that generated both the New Testament canon and constituted a unified Christian community. This "classic" hermeneutic, which read the Bible with a Trinitarian rule of faith, was marked by its ability to build both consensus and community:

It was Scripture—initially Hebrew Scripture read Christologically—which had the consensus, community, and institution-building power to make of these communities the overwhelmingly dominant and therefore Catholic church. It does not even seem farfetched to say that it was the Bible which conquered the empire in defiance of the normal laws of sociological gravity: non-violently, despite persecution, and without special economic, social, cultural, or ethnic support.[127]

Insofar as Lindbeck successfully reverses Fish—in contending that the text is what constructs social reality rather than vice versa—he may have found a way to escape the relativity of interpretive communities.[128]

UNDOING BIBLICAL IDEOLOGY

Undoing is both demanding as a procedure and unsettling in its results. Do Christian ministers, teachers, and other students of the Bible really need to make the effort to understand deconstruction and other types of postmodern interpretation? I believe they do. Christians need to make the effort to engage the new masters of suspicion for three reasons. (1) We have an obligation to be intellectually honest, even charitable. Too many critics have written off deconstruction without taking it seriously, that is to say, without taking the time to understand it. Nothing is to be gained by burning straw men. (2) Postmodernity is an interdisciplinary phenomenon that has occasioned a crisis in culture and Christianity alike. It is difficult to minister the Word if one has little understanding of one's cultural context. (3) Deconstruction and other types of postmodern interpretation have become more and more prevalent in the academy and, increasingly, the church. In a 1982 issue of *Semeia* devoted to "Derrida and Biblical Studies," Robert Detweiler wrote that Derrida "poses perhaps the greatest contemporary threat to traditional biblical scholarship."[129] Interpreters of the Bible have responded to this threat in different ways, however. Some exegetes see deconstruction as a threat not only to one's profession but also to one's profession of faith. Others welcome Derrida's demythologizing of the myth of objective scholarship. For this latter group, deconstruction is liberating in its critique of totalitarian systems of interpretation. This brings me to a fourth possible reason for confronting deconstruction: it may have something to teach us.[130]

Using, by contrast, is easy. It is relatively straightforward to read the Bible from the perspective of one's own experience, to declare "what the Bible means to me." The Bible can be used either to support a way of life or to condemn it. Users wish to enlist the text on the side of whatever is in their community's interest; Undoers, by contrast, show why the text resists being co-opted by any one system of ideas and values, by any one context of experience. Both Undoers and Users agree, however, that their respective approaches to interpretation contribute to the project of human liberation.

Protestant interpreters should have no compunction in undoing ideologically motivated interpretations of the Bible. Most agree with the principle that it is wrong to use the Bible as a prop to support some prior interest. The third article of the Barmen Declaration (1934) states: "We reject the false doctrine that the church could have permission to hand over the form of its message and of its order to whatever it itself might wish or to the vicissitudes of the prevailing ideological and political convictions of the day."[131] In practice, the distinction between using and interpreting the Bible is often hard to draw. Nevertheless, the distinction remains vital.

The matter is slightly more complicated, however, if what is thought to be ideological is not one's interpretation but the biblical text itself. On the one hand, to say that the Bible is ideological literature is not necessarily pejorative. Defined neutrally, ideology denotes "the systems of assumptions and conviction against which everything in the story . . . is evaluated."[132] For Meir Sternberg, the ideology of a text has to do with the worldview it presents to its reader: "It remains a universal of writing that representation is never dissociated from evaluation."[133] Texts are ideological insofar as they reflect certain attitudes, values, and assumptions. Ideology is thus a synonym for worldview.

Ideology, like rhetoric, may therefore be used for good purposes as well as evil. A given story, for instance, can be told to illustrate a moral truth, or it can be told to legitimate, say, the divine right of earthly kings.[134] The Bible is ideological literature insofar as it seeks, through its rhetoric, to shape readers' minds and hearts in order to brings their attitude into alignment with its own.[135] According to Sternberg, the worldview of the Bible is unique: "If the Bible is ideologically singular—and I believe so—then its singularity lies in the world view projected, together with the rhetoric devised to bring it home."[136] One aspect of the Bible's ideology is its view that God and humans are distinct with regard to knowledge. God is omniscient; human knowledge has limits.[137] The rhetoric of the Bible aims to persuade readers of their need to receive the Word of God. If, as Catherine Belsey maintains, it is "the role of ideology to *construct people as subjects*,"[138] then we may say that one purpose of biblical narrative is to constitute people as *covenantal* subjects under God. Surely, if the Bible represents the *divine* ideology, it need not be considered oppressive and unethical.

On the other hand, many critics continue to associate ideology with the illegitimate use of power. Marxists, cultural materialists, and new historicists alike emphasize the rootedness of ideas (and hence ideologies) in concrete socio-political contexts. These ideology critics are just as keen to expose the interests of contemporary readers (e.g., in economic systems that are based on distinctions of gender, race, and class) as they are to expose texts as social products.[139] Its critics define ideology as "the confusion of linguistic with natural reality."[140] Such confusion is not innocent, for it is the means that the powerful use to impose their value system on others: "Ideology legitimates ruling-class domination by making its ideas and norms appear natural, just and universal."[141] Ideology on this view is a willful distortion that conceals the real (i.e., arbitrary) nature of social relations in order to justify a social order wherein one class of people dominates another. To speak of the ideology rather than the theology of the Bible "draws attention to the social and political aspects of biblical thought."[142] One way of undoing the Bible, then, is to expose its ideas as historically conditioned by the socio-political struggles of the past.[143]

Politics and the Law: Deconstructing Deuteronomy

In order both to draw together the arguments of the preceding sections and to illustrate deconstruction at work, I propose to look at how two biblical critics, Robert Polzin and John Barton, "undo" the worldview of Deuteronomy.[144] Deuteronomy is particularly susceptible to deconstructive analysis, insofar as it projects a value system and a vision of authority that depends on arguments about (divine) "origins" and (divine) "speech."[145] Deuteronomy "lays down the law" and enforces its stipulations with a theology of retributive justice.

To undo this text is to reveal the political and religious interests behind the Deuteronomic discourse. Possible candidates for interested parties include the Levitical priests who were entrusted with the book of the law, the prophets of religious reform, or the community of scribes and lawmakers.[146] Both the Torah (the five books of Moses) and the Deuteronomic history (Joshua–2 Kings) are political documents that, through the skillful use of rhetoric, suggest that the law and the prophetic interpretation of Israel's history have their origins, and thus their authority, in the very word of God. "The central ideology of Deuteronomism concerns the divine word, often as mediated by prophets."[147]

The Rhetoric of Authority

Speech and writing are prominent themes in Derrida and Deuteronomy alike. In Deuteronomy 31 Moses ends his sermon, fixes it in written form (31:9), commissions Joshua as his successor, and deposits the law in the ark. The written law, moreover, was to be read at regular intervals so that future generations could "hear" the voice of God (31:10–11). The law becomes a substitute for God's presence. Now Derrida's major aim, as we have seen, is to undermine the hierarchy that privileges speech over writing. "The Bible is no exception to this privileging, since it is constituted as the *word* of God dictated and written down by God's agents."[148] To undo this privilege, the would-be deconstructor subjects the text of Deuteronomy to a searching analysis. The very name "Deuteronomy," for instance, means "second law," and suggests distance from God's original speech. Deuteronomy is an "iteration" of the Decalogue, first given on Sinai, to a new situation, in a new context.

Robert Polzin dismantles Deuteronomy through a careful dissection of its rhetoric of authority. Like Derrida, he multiplies his interpretive loaves by feasting on marginal details. On the surface, Deuteronomy is a story in which, for the most part, there are only two speaking parts: Moses and God. The emphasis is squarely on the law of God, laid down in Moses' speech. Yet Polzin detects a subtle attempt to blur the distinction between Moses' voice and that of God. Moses' first discourse to the people (1:6–4:40) explains how Moses speaks for God. Half of the address contains a report of direct divine discourse; there is a clear distinction between Moses' voice and God's voice. In his second address (5:1–28:68), however, Moses reports God's speech in indirect discourse. Polzin sees great ideological significance in this minor stylistic difference: it is the rhetorical means of identifying Moses' own interpretation with the very words of God. "This contrast between the subordinate style of Moses' first address and the supremely authoritative promulgation of the law code in the second address is the main compositional means by which the Deuteronomist exalts Moses' teaching authority."[149] Whatever else Moses or the narrator may say about the uniqueness of the Word of God, the text makes the authoritative status of the voice of Moses "*almost* indistinguishable from that of the voice of God."[150] Deuteronomy appears simultaneously to establish and to undermine the law as *God's* Word. In sum, Deuteronomy's rhetorical practice undermines its theological theory.

Polzin next argues for a second displacement. The narrator of the book is anonymous, though sometimes his voice merges with that of Moses: "Such artful contaminations are the basis for the deep-seated, as well as superficial, 'double-voiced' nature of Deuteronomy."[151] At several points the narrator's voice "interrupts" that of Moses (e.g., 2:10–12; 3:11; 31:1). Polzin detects in these parenthetical comments a "subtle but effective" strategy to "blur or soften" Moses' status: "The narrator's utterances are spoken in two ideological voices which interfere with one another: an overt, obvious voice that exalts Moses as it plays down its own role, and a still, soft voice that nevertheless succeeds in drawing attention to itself at the expense of Moses' uniqueness."[152] In other words, the narrator, in identifying his voice with that of Moses (and God), tacitly claims authority for his own understanding of the law and its application. Polzin undoes the authority of Deuteronomy by showing how Moses takes the place of God, only to be replaced in turn by the rhetorical strategies of an anonymous narrator.

Polzin's account fails to answer one important question, however: Just who benefits from an ideology that stresses the authority of God's laws (Deut. 4:1–40) as well as a regard for the poor (15:7–11)? In whose interest are the Ten Commandments (5:6–21)? Here the ideology critics seem to be on weak ground. For the Ten Commandments, it could be argued, are in *everybody's* interest.[153]

The Rhetoric of Retribution

Another characteristic theological theme in Deuteronomy is that of retribution: blessings for obedience, punishment for moral and spiritual failure. According to John Barton, the ideology of divine retribution for sin is undermined in, of all places, the prophets. The prophets' theological interpretation of Israel's history, largely based on the "whole package of ideas" from Deuteronomy, makes use of the idea of divine retribution to explain Israel's and Judah's calamity. Yet Barton suggests that this theory was made to fit the facts through skillful use of rhetoric: "Prophetic rhetoric is designed . . . to make the contingencies of human history look like divine necessities."[154] The prophets' purpose is not only to warn the people of imminent disaster (this could be determined by observing the political situation), but to provide a theological justification for Israel's exile. Their genius is to retell history in such a way that the downfall of Israel appears inevitable, given the character of God and the spiritual corruption of Israel. In Barton's words: "We should not be taken in too much by the force of their rhetoric. It was not really obvious that God was bound to punish Israel. The fact that even modern readers of the Bible are inclined to speak as if it was is a tribute to the rhetorical skill of the classical prophets."[155] What is left of the biblical text after its undoing by deconstruction? Its rhetoric—its power to persuade "beyond the bounds of pure reason, its ability to provoke its readers into willing its success even beyond its deserts."[156]

Politics and the Land

Perhaps the most explicit example of how the Bible has an ideological bearing on political questions concerns its use in debates about land. Colonizers have, throughout history, appealed to the Bible to justify territorial annexation.[157] It has often proved all too easy for political leaders—in South Africa, in South America, etc.—to justify conquest by appealing to the example of Israel's conquest of Canaan. On the other hand, the dispossessed have identified with another moment in Israel's history: the exodus from Egypt. These voices from the margin protest when the Bible is used to rationalize their non-identity as a people. David Jobling sees a connection between deconstruction and liberation theology: both movements criticize any theology that pretends to be universally applicable, forgetting that ideas emerge out of a particular socio-historical context. Jobling states: "I believe that this conjunction of radical literary method with radical political commitment will be of incalculable importance in biblical studies."[158]

Reading With the Dispossessed

Liberation theologians read Scripture not to interpret the world differently, but to change it. Their starting point for biblical interpretation is the situation of the poor and oppressed. What the Bible means seems different when read from the context of the ghetto rather than the university.[159] Reading the Bible from the perspective of the poor "favours application rather than explanation."[160] The poor in Latin America, for instance, sees texts that speak of liberation as having direct application to their situation. For these readers, meaning is not a theoretical matter but an eminently practical one.[161]

The experience of poverty, says Carlos Mesters, "is for the liberation exegete as important a 'text' as the text of scripture itself."[162] It is hard to say whether this experience represents an epistemological or an ethical prerequisite for biblical interpretation; perhaps it represents both. If the text is always read in social contexts that are dominated by certain interests, then the perspective of the poor may uniquely qualify them to find a message that eludes the affluent. Mesters acknowledges that in interpreting "from below" the emphasis "is not placed on the text's meaning in itself but rather on the meaning the text has for the people reading it."[163] The *primary* text, for Mesters, is the community's experience of life (i.e., the contemporary context). It is precisely this emphasis on the socio-political location of the reader that prompts Thiselton to ask some hard questions of the hermeneutics of liberation: "Do they merely reflect back the horizons of the community of protest in self-affirmation, or do they offer a social critique under which all (or many) communities may experience correction, transformation, and enlargement of horizons?"[164]

Reading Scripture from the perspective of a black South African has made Itumeleng J. Mosala sensitive to an ideological struggle within the Bible itself, namely, between the God of the landless peasants (e.g., Israelites before and just after the Exodus) and the God of the Israelite royal and landlord classes (e.g., during the period of the monarchy, after the conquest of the Promised Land). Mosala believes that both the biblical text and the process of reading the Bible are the site of "class conflict." He accounts for the different biblical ideologies by relating the text to its original class context. Before the monarchy, the people lived in agricultural, egalitarian societies. David's conquest of the land resulted in a system of land tenure and taxation. The book of Micah contains, according to Mosala, both ideologies, but the monarchical ideology (chs. 4–7) is dominant: "The central themes of this monarchy ideology are stability, grace, restoration, creation, universal peace, compassion, salvation. They contrast radically with the ideology of premonarchic Israel which has themes like justice, solidarity, struggle, vigilance."[165] Though Micah is a ruling class document, Mosala believes there is another voice "in the margins" that supports the oppressed, "premonarchical" blacks in South Africa today. Mosala argues that Black Theology has helped to explode "the myth of rational objectivity in theology."[166] White theology (a cousin of Derrida's white mythology?) is bound to white values.

The View From Canaan

To take another example: the book of Exodus is often used by liberation theologians in Latin America as an inspiration in their struggle for social justice. However, to other, differently situated readers, the Exodus account and its aftermath is anything but liberating. Palestinian Christians are shocked when the Bible is used— by Jews and Christians—to justify the Israeli occupation of their homeland. Since the restoration of the state of Israel in 1948, the Exodus and Conquest narratives have worked against Palestinian liberation.[167] Palestinian Christians believe that "for many Zionist Jews and Christians, and for the State of Israel, the land has become an idol."[168] They recall the story of Naboth's vineyard (2 Kings 21), which is concerned not merely with land but with God's concern for justice. Naim Ateek argues that God's covenant with Israel at Sinai must be viewed in light of the new covenant in Christ with the whole of humanity.

The biblical stories of the Exodus and Conquest are felt to be singularly inappropriate by Native American Indians as well. Robert Allen Warrior, in "A Native American Perspective: Canaanites, Cowboys, and Indians," notes that the experience of Native Americans leads them to identify with the Canaanites, "the people who already lived in the promised land."[169] On the other hand, early Puritan and later European settlers in North America saw the United States as the new "people of God." It was America's "manifest destiny" "to overspread the continent allotted by Providence for the free development of our yearly multiplying millions."[170] The westward expansion was justified by an analogy between Israel and North America. The comparison was so closely drawn that some Puritan preachers were evidently "fond of referring to Native Americans as Amalekites and Canaanites—in other words, people who, if they would not be converted, were worthy of annihilation."[171] Warrior makes the hermeneutical point that the Conquest narrative of the book of Joshua provided white settlers with an ideology that justified destroying indigenous peoples. The Bible's political interpretation contributed not merely to colonization, but to genocide.

It is indisputable that the Bible has been used in ways that oppress certain persons or peoples. But is this the fault of biblical ideology or of the way the Bible has been interpreted? Reading, as I will argue in chapter 7, does not escape the effects of original sin. The reader's spiritual condition, as well as his or her social location, will have an impact on the process of interpretation—all the more reason for preserving an independent "meaning in the text" over against the interpreter's interests. One does not need to have read Marx to criticize how the Old Testament has been used by, say, European colonizers. For the text itself contains sufficient resources with which to provide adequate checks and balances on attempts to appropriate it for alien political purposes.[172]

I have already said that the Ten Commandments are in everyone's interest. Other Old Testament texts too propound what we might call an ideology of holiness and social justice. Leviticus 19, for example, grounds its prescriptions for holy living in the holiness of God: "Be holy because I, the LORD your God, am holy" (Lev. 19:2). The entire chapter represents a fine blending of cultic requirements and ethical obligations, culminating in what Jesus later calls the "second commandment" (Mark 12:31): "Love your neighbor as yourself" (Lev. 19:18). Of particular significance is the extension of this command to foreigners: "The alien living with you must be treated as one of your native-born. Love him as yourself, for you were aliens in Egypt" (Lev. 19:34). Finally, Leviticus 19 expresses a concern for the well-being of the poor and foreigner alike: "Do not go over your vineyard a second time or pick up the grapes that have fallen. Leave them for the poor and the alien" (19:10). Significantly, these same themes are also to be found in the book of Deuteronomy.[173]

Politics and the Body

We turn now from the politics of the land to the politics of the body. The representation of women in the Old Testament is, according to Francis Watson, "one of the central theological-ethical issues of our current hermeneutical situation."[174] The issue in feminist interpretation of the Bible is not genocide but gender. "Gender" is not a biological but a cultural and ideological category; it refers to the meaning that a sociopolitical framework ascribes to one's biological sex. It is a way of "writing" the body, of inscribing women into the structure of socio-political relations. The meaning of the body, in other words, is a construct of language—and the flesh became word. Foucault states that "the body is also directly involved in a political field. . . . Power relations have an immediate hold upon it; they invest it, mark it, train it, torture it, force it to carry out tasks, to perform ceremonies, to emit signs."[175] Some feminists argue that the Bible is sexist, representing women as property, docile servants, or subservient to men. The Canadian novelist Margaret Atwood has recently exploited fears about fundamentalist interpretation in her novel *The Handmaid's Tale*. What would happen if Christian fundamentalists achieved political control of the United States? Atwood's answer: they would bring back the institution of the handmaid and use women's bodies to produce children.

Feminist theology stands for a number of disparate movements. "The agenda is to get everyone to see what has passed as 'universal' theology has been partial in its exclusion of women and their insights."[176] What they have in common is the critique of ideology—in this case, patriarchy (i.e., the rule of males)—and the privileging of women's experience and interests. Feminist hermeneutics also share with deconstruction a suspicion of fixed meaning and the concomitant notion of correct interpretation.[177]

A Feminist Biblical Hermeneutics

According to Elisabeth Schüssler Fiorenza, "feminist theory insists that all texts are products of an androcentric patriarchal culture and history."[178] The challenge for the feminist reader is to interpret the Bible in such a way that its oppressive potential is neutralized while its liberating power is released. This may involve interpreting the Bible in such a way that what the text means (in the contemporary context) will not be limited by what the text explicitly says (in its own compositional context). *Feminist interpretation seeks to liberate the text from its own ideological limitations.* Schüssler Fiorenza states that the "revelatory canon" for theological evaluation "cannot be derived from the Bible itself but can only be formulated in and through women's struggle for liberation from all patriarchal oppression."[179] In other words, interpretive authority lies outside the text, in those social practices that encourage the liberation of women.

Schüssler Fiorenza is explicit about her "canon outside the canon." As a norm, the liberation of women "places biblical texts under the authority of feminist experience insofar as it maintains that revelation is ongoing and takes place 'for the sake of our salvation.'"[180] Sheila Briggs aptly describes the significance of this decision to make the contemporary context the arbiter of textual interpretation: "One has moved from the authority of the text to the authority of social practices, from orthodoxy to orthopraxis. . . . A transmutation and transvaluation of hermeneutical categories has taken place which places normative value in the kind of social practices which aim at liberation of the oppressed."[181]

Writing the Body

Cupitt likens the body to the text: the body "belongs to culture which is a system of signs; and therefore it is legible."[182] Foucault agrees: just as in Saussure's linguistic theory, where a sign comes to have a meaning by virtue of its place in a system of differences, so the human individual comes to have an identity in a system of *social*, rather than linguistic, relations. The Bible and Western culture "write" a social programming for the body that effectively controls one's sense of bodily identity as well as one's relations with other bodies. The Old Testament law, for example, constructs gender and sexuality by its prohibitions and by its hierarchical oppositions (e.g., man-woman, clean-unclean, virgin-harlot, heterosexual-homosexual). As we have seen, postmoderns hold all such binary thinking to be necessarily oppressive: "We are not dealing with the peaceful coexistence of a vis-à-vis but rather with a violent hierarchy. One of the two terms governs the other."[183] Feminists complain that, in the cultural system of Christian patriarchy, the "body" (associated with women largely because of Christian interpretation of the figure of Eve in Genesis) has always been considered lower than the "mind" or "spirit." These and other linguistic differences "map" the body and colonize sexuality.

Patriarchy inscribes the body in yet another of those culturally constructed, culturally privileged hierarchical oppositions: "man-mind-speech" dominates "woman-body-writing." Indeed, some feminists have argued that the gender difference is *the* crucial hierarchical opposition: the sexual difference, in other words, together with its implied male dominance, is the basic model for all other oppressive oppositions.[184] Derrida coins the term "phallogocentrism" to signal the complicity of Western metaphysics (logocentrism) with the notion of male firstness (phallocentrism).[185] Julia Kristeva, following Freud and Jacques Lacan, suggests that the phallus is the transcendental signifier of modern Western patriarchy; patriarchy is dominated by the rule of law, a rule summed up in the symbol "father."[186] With a little help from

Freud and Derrida, then, feminist readers seek to undo both patriarchy and the "paternal authority" of the biblical text.[187]

Feminist interpreters of the Bible wish to read in a way "that will enable them to appropriate its message for themselves as women."[188] They are not particularly interested in the historical author's intention: "Discussions of intention are paternity tests . . . they are concerned with the patriarchal need to establish principles to determine which ideas are the author's true progeny and which are illegitimate."[189] For feminist readers, biblical interpretation is authoritative only when it releases the oppressed and engenders human freedom. However, for some the struggle for liberation has turned violent. Mary Daly, a radical feminist theologian, believes that the language of the Bible contributes to patriarchy and calls for a "castration of language and images that perpetuate the structures of a sexist world."[190] Castration is only the last of a series of violent acts to which ideological critics subject the text—all in the name of reader liberation. Of course, the castrated text cannot help but speak falsetto.

There is no question that the Bible *can* be read from a variety of perspectives, some of which are no doubt foreign to their original authors. Not all interpretive possibilities are expedient, however, nor are all ethical. Feminists appeal to the idea of liberation as their rationale for reading against the grain of the text; but if all reading is contextual and theory-laden, is not feminist interpretation merely a matter of substituting one ideology for another? Ideological interpretation in this sense resembles the logical fallacy of begging the question: the interpretive result (i.e., the "conclusion" of the process of reading—liberation for women) is already contained in the interpretive interest (i.e., the "premise" with which one begins—the normativeness of women's experience). Thiselton rightly describes the consequences of using the biblical texts to support some prior interest: "Predominately pragmatic uses of biblical texts have the status of exercises in self-justification and potential manipulation."[191] If the community's interest and experience—the present context—provide the framework for interpreting Scripture, what happens when the framework itself is corrupt? To assign priority to the reader's context and interest is to immunize one's interpretive community from the very possibility of criticism *by the text*. Reading the text on these terms is like projecting one's image onto the mirror of the text, a hermeneutic strategy that sentences the interpretive community to stare at its own reflection. Such a narcissistic hermeneutics stands little chance of expanding one's self-knowledge, or for that matter, of achieving genuine liberation.

THE ETHICS OF UNDOING: THE "NEW MORALITY" OF KNOWLEDGE

Readers of the present work may at this point be tempted to dismiss postmodern criticism as either nihilistic or trivial, as either ungodly blasphemy or intellectual gamesmanship. Derrida's insistence on the freeplay of signs, his dismantling of theories and theologies, his playful interpretations—all seem to justify the criticism that deconstruction is "not serious," or worse, that it is actually "immoral."[192] This is a severe accusation. Before Christian readers pass judgment we must interpret Derrida as charitably as possible. To do so is risky; we may find our cherished beliefs challenged, perhaps overturned. But not to risk oneself in an attempt to understand the other is even more dangerous; to refuse to be honest is to risk losing one's integrity and hence to damage oneself.

I have argued in this chapter that postmodern critical "play" has a liberating purpose. All readers are subject to institutional forces, to ideological peer pressure as it were: "Each society has its regime of truth, its 'general politics' of truth: that is, the types of discourse which it accepts and makes function as true."[193] It is against this backdrop that we must discuss the ethics of undoing. Derrida subverts institutional attempts to "control" textual meaning by showing how the text ultimately escapes any one system of interpretive constraints. Texts can always be read in new contexts, with different interests. From the perspective of deconstruction, the critique of the ideology of the "one true meaning" gives rise to a new morality of literary knowledge. The moral reader is the one who *refuses* to believe in fixed meanings and final solutions.

Van Harvey, representing the modern morality of knowledge, claims that persons are not entitled to hold a belief in the absence of sufficient justification. Tradition is initially suspect; beliefs are guilty until proven innocent. The modern knowers have an ethical responsibility (1) to assume a critical posture toward belief, (2) to be objective, (3) to take responsibility for their own critical judgments, and (4) to base their judgments on evidence alone. The newer, postmodern morality of knowledge goes much further. If the structure and determinations of the text (and of the world) are imposed rather than discovered by language, *then the moral stance towards knowledge is to suspend belief indefinitely—I disbelieve* in order to *withstand*. In the absence of the possibility of an authorized version, the only moral thing to do is to resist any one version's attempt to become authoritative. Plantinga rightly unfolds the logic of this position: "Thus does anti-realism breed relativism and nihilism."[194] For once one sees Derrida's point, one *sees through* every claim to knowledge and truth. In Plantinga's words: "But once you 'see' . . . that there isn't any such thing as truth as such, then you may also see . . . the futility, the foolishness, the pitiable self-deluded nature of intellectual commitment."[195]

Deconstructing Dogma: Undoing the Idolatry of Knowledge

What follows from this "new morality" of knowledge for biblical interpretation? The implications are immense and far-reaching. It is not only this or that knowledge claim, this or that interpretation, that becomes suspect; it is rather that the idea (and ideal) of knowledge has become problematic. Indeed, the very idea of interpretation and the very ideal of understanding have become almost unbelievable. This loss of belief on the part of postmodern critics and theorists ultimately stems, I have argued, from a prior theological event: the "death" of God.

The so-called "death of God" theologians of the 1960s viewed the demise of God as the passing away of an idol, the deconstruction of a philosophical construct—the supreme being of classical theism.[196] In announcing the two deaths—of God, of the author—deconstruction also declares the death of meaning (viz., determinate textual sense) and interpretation (viz., correct understanding). The death of God also marks the birth of the reader and of what Plantinga calls "creative anti-realism": the celebration of humanity's power to structure and differentiate the world. The "death of God put into writing" gives rise to a state of permanent interpretive jubilee; once one acknowledges the artificial nature of the world and of interpretation, one is free to read endlessly. The new morality of literary knowledge, insofar as it concerns the refusal of understanding, has one overriding maxim: "You shall not believe in absolutes." John Caputo confesses his unbelief in no uncertain terms: "I reject all forms of privileged positions above the flux. . . . I write . . . from below, and I ask all who do otherwise how they acquired their elevated position. . . . The aim is always to avoid the illusion that our institutions and practices, that our reason and our faith have dropped from the sky."[197]

Is is idolatrous to believe in a single correct interpretation? Interpretations are hardly "graven images" that call forth worship. On the other hand, an "image" is a likeness of something. As an image mirrors the original, so an interpretation mirrors the text. Yet Scripture insists that the transcendent God can be neither named nor imaged. "To be able to name and image something is to have power over it, to be able to control and manipulate it."[198] Is it possible that, in the name of interpretation, some might seek to "control," if not God himself, then God's *Word*? Is there not a real danger of mistaking one's interpretation, which is always secondary, contextual, and never ultimate, for the text itself—a danger we might call *the idolatry of literary knowledge*? If so, then it is important to add that *what is idolatrous is not the belief in a single correct interpretation but rather the conviction that it is our exclusive possession*.

The book of Isaiah presents idolatry as a dimension of the sin of pride.[199] To believe in the absoluteness of our interpretations is like worshiping our own creations; it is like thinking one reads with the eyes of God. Derrida's notion of *différance* casts down ideological interpretations that pretend to represent the text without remainder: "As critique, deconstruction asserts nothing; it show how any text resists complete formalization by producing a supplement."[200] *I wish at this point to commend deconstruction as a standing challenge to interpretive pride.*

The virtue of deconstruction, according to David Clines, is that it undoes dogma: "The deconstructive strategy eliminates dogma as dogma, and in recognizing that multiple philosophies are being affirmed in the deconstructible text loosens our attachment to any one of them *as dogma*."[201] The human heart craves dogma, together with the sense of security that comes with knowing that one is absolutely right. The problem with dogmas is that they can be used in support of fascism as well as faith: absolute knowledge corrupts absolutely. Perhaps we can say that deconstruction, like Deuteronomy itself, has a pedagogical function. Like the law, which reminds us of the inadequacy of our sanctification, deconstruction reminds us of the inadequacy of our interpretation. Where, however, does deconstruction get us? After casting down the graven images, the Idols of the Sign, what does deconstruction put in their place? Nothing but empty spaces. Having cleansed the home of meaning of its author, the Undoer may find that seven other worse spirits return to take possession of the text (cf. Matt. 12:45). Of course, readers always occupy particular places; interpretation is never context-less. Yet it is easy to forget one's place, and even easier to forget that one's particular point of view is only partial. This applies to Undoers as well. Like idolaters who worship their own creations, deconstructors may be tempted to think too highly of their own *negations*. It is an open question, therefore, as to which is the greater arrogance: believing that one has correctly understood, or believing that one has refuted the very possibility of understanding.[202]

Doing Justice to the Other

Stated negatively, deconstructive ethics is a matter of resisting interpretive totalization and closure. But what is to be *done* after this undoing? Stated positively, the ethics of deconstruction is a matter of respecting "otherness," of refusing to absorb the other—whatever is not myself—into my way of thinking and doing. One biblical critic whose sympathies lie with Derrida writes

> that deconstruction means guarding the heterogeneity of the text, remaining vigilant against closure, adhering to a critical stance which respects complexity, difficulty, obscurity; deconstructive readings do not seek to transcend the text and achieve a totalizing operation on it; deconstructive readings must always be critical, above all self-critical.[203]

The theme of the "other" is central to the work of Emmanuel Lévinas, who sees ethics as primarily concerned with what happens when the self encounters another.[204] The first responsibility of thought is not to grasp the other but to let it be. Ethics in a postmodern key questions the knower's attempt to subdue or master the other by forcing it into a system of ideas. Indeed, ethics questions philosophy, insofar as philosophy is itself the attempt to reduce all forms of otherness "by transmuting their alterity [otherness] into the Same."[205] Modern philosophy in particular, insofar as it has made epistemology primary, reduces what is other into a totalizing conceptual scheme. As such, philosophy becomes a form of intellectual imperialism: "You will submit to my categories." For postmodern thinkers inspired by Lévinas and Derrida, however, "the realm of ethical discourse is that which exceeds all given conceptual structures, but exceeds them through a patient interrogation of their limits."[206]

What, finally, Derrida seeks to undo is any reading that represses otherness—of the text, of different contexts—for the sake of a totalizing interpretation. An interpretation is "totalizing" insofar as it claims to be both exhaustive and comprehensive. Deconstructive analysis exposes the bits of the text that can be read either against the text itself or against its reader's interpretation. Deconstruction also exposes the extent to which all interpretations are conditioned by their historical and socio-political contexts. The deconstructor questions the legitimacy of determining textual meaning by making any one of these possible contexts decisive, as well as the legitimacy of trying to rise above all limited and particular contexts. Because readers are not allowed to privilege any one context, however, meaning remains forever undecidable.[207] *Doing justice to the text as other, then, means undoing every attempt to understand it.* To comprehend is to "take to oneself"—the classic selfish, not ethical, gesture. For Derrida, therefore, the ethics of deconstruction is a matter of affirming the inescapable otherness of the text and the inescapable undecidability of its proper interpretive context.

Transcendence and Immanence

What does the deconstructor do after casting down authoritative interpretations? Is undoing a form of doing or not? Does the end (being undone, loosed, liberated) justify the deconstructive means (undoing)? As we have seen, undoing authors, texts, and readers often involves a certain amount of interpretive violence. And using texts to propound one's own ideology transforms the reader into a usurper—a pretender to the power and the rights of the author. In the light of deconstructive undoing and pragmatist using, the following question takes on no little urgency: Is it really the case that postmodern criticism champions the other?

Deconstructive ethics amounts to an iconoclastic gesture followed by a shrug of the shoulders: first resistance, then undecidability. There is no escape from context, no escape from a plurality of possible meanings. Yet, at the end of the day, must we not say, decide, *do* something? Or is undoing ultimately a matter of *not* doing? If the responsibilities of the reader are merely negative—"Thou shalt not impose coherence and finality"—then is it ever possible to move beyond the ethics of prohibition to an ethic of love? Simon Critchley suggests, on behalf of deconstruction, that its role is to ensure that the interpreting community "remains an open community, at the service of ethical difference."[208] The just society is the one that allows itself constantly to be criticized; the Undoer serves the community by being a critical gadfly. The philosopher's most difficult task has always been that of thinking the limits of reason itself. "For it may be in the questioning of reason itself—a questioning nonetheless patient and meticulously argued—that philosophy can best live up to its present responsibilities."[209]

Where does this postmodern vision of interpretive responsibility come from? What are the underlying beliefs that support the practice of respecting the other? Why should we accept this version of responsibility? Derrida never explicitly addresses these questions. The ethics of deconstruction follows, I believe, from its tacit theology: to be exact, from its understanding of transcendence and immanence. On the one hand, the otherness of the text transcends all attempts to know it; on the other hand, all attempts at knowledge are immanent, "from below," driven by local interests and entangled in political struggles. Transcendence for Derrida entails unknowablity. What is known, on the other hand, is always immanent, always relative—relative, that is, to this or that context. Immanence thus implies undecidability.[210]

To pose questions about interpretive responsibility—about the goods of interpretation—is to pass not only from the ethical to the theological, but also from the critical to the *metacritical*.[211] Metacriticism examines principles of criticism and proposed criteria for successful readings. It asks less about the how than the why; specifically, *why should readers adopt one set of interpretive aims and interests rather than another?*[212] Or simply: why read at all? This is no idle query in a postmodern context where many readers are skeptical about the very possibility of understanding. Henceforth, contemporary hermeneutic theories must be prepared to give a rational, ethical, and ultimately *theological* account of the hope of interpretation that is implicit within them.[213]

Meanwhile, it would appear that postmodern readers are condemned to disbelief. The new morality of literary knowledge resists believing *in* anything, even in one's own interpretations. I have argued that deconstruction is neither a "silly relativism" nor a kind of nihilistic play. What relativistic and nihilistic moments there are in deconstruction serve a fundamentally ethical purpose: to prevent the knower-interpreter from forcing what is other into the straitjacket of "grand theory." Despite their alleged concern for the other, however, I have suggested that Undoers in fact have difficulty *encountering* the other. How can the postmodern critic really be said to respect the other if the other's presence is always deferred, if what the other says is always undecidable? Does the postmodern reader do anything for the victimized text besides pass by? Might it be that, despite the rhetoric about ethics, postmodern critics actually are afraid to meet the other? And what else is the fear of encountering the other—whether a person or text—but the fear that the encounter may change us, the fear that *we* may be "undone"?

To forestall this threat, ever present in reading, it is tempting to claim absolute knowledge—a God's-eye point of view. I have acknowledged deconstruction's help in blocking this unethical move. Interpreters must resist the temptation "to be like God." Yet deconstruction poses an equally tempting possibility—that there is no determinate word for which the reader is accountable ("Did God say?"). The postmodern temptation, in other words, is to claim *to know nothing at all*. If meaning is undecidable—if nothing concrete, determinate, or specific has been said—then to what can we be held responsible? Bereft of the authority of author and text, the postmodern reader inhabits an ethical situation similar to that of the Israelites in the time of the Judges when there was no king, and "everyone did as he saw fit" (Judg. 21:25).

In the final analysis, we must reject the postmodern contention that suspicion—the critical moment—is all there is to the ethics of interpretation. While absolute knowledge may indeed suppress the other, it is my thesis that postmodern skepticism too represents an inadequate response to the demands of the other. Fortunately, there is an alternative between the absolutely knowable and the absolutely undecidable.[214] A proper fear of the other, of the *author*, is the real beginning of literary knowledge.

NOTES

1. Howard Felerpin, *Beyond Deconstruction: The Uses and Abuses of Literary Theory* (Oxford: Clarendon, 1985), 204.

2. Barthes, "Death of the Author," 55.

3. Felerpin, *Beyond Deconstruction*, 203.

4. Jane P. Tomkins, "An Introduction to Reader-Response Criticism," in *Reader-Response Criticism: From Formalism to Post-structuralism* (Baltimore: Johns Hopkins Univ. Press, 1980), ix.

5. Vincent B. Leitch, *Deconstructive Criticism*, 264.

6. Margaret Davies, "Reader-Response Criticism," *A Dictionary of Biblical Interpretation*, 578.

7. Marx believed that material (e.g., economic, social) conditions determine a society's way of thinking and its system of values. He also believed that it is the mode of production that determines a society's ideology. As we will see, the third age of criticism similarly turns to material conditions (viz., politics) in order to explain the conflict of interpretations.

8. Felerpin, *Beyond Deconstruction*, 33.

9. Barthes, *S/Z* (New York: Hill and Wang, 1974), 200–201.

10. Eagleton, *Against the Grain: Essays 1975–85* (London: Verso, 1986), esp. ch. 13: "The Revolt of the Reader," 181.

11. John Barton suggests that structuralism was already a theory about reading insofar as it attempts "to prescribe 'correct' methods, not for reconstructing what the author . . . meant, but for producing a contemporary reading of what he actually wrote" (*Reading the Old Testament*, 126).

12. Poststructuralism tries to deflate the scientific pretensions of structuralism to literary knowledge. Raman Selden aptly comments: "If structuralism was heroic in its desire to mas-

ter the world of man-made signs, poststructuralism is comic and anti-heroic in its refusal to take such claims seriously" (*A Reader's Guide to Contemporary Literary Theory*, 70).

13. Umberto Eco, *Limits of Interpretation*, 59.

14. For more on reception theory, see Hans Robert Jauss, *Toward an Aesthetic of Reception Theory* (Minneapolis: Univ. of Minnesota Press, 1982), and Robert C. Holub, *Reception Theory: A Critical Introduction* (London: Methuen, 1984).

15. McKnight, *Postmodern Use of the Bible*, 174.

16. D. D. Todd, in a review of Robert Alter's *The Pleasure of Reading in an Ideological Age*, *Philosophy and Literature* 14 (1990): 421.

17. Fish, *Is There a Text?* 284.

18. Moore, *Literary Criticism and the Gospels*, 66.

19. Stephen Mailloux, quoted in ibid., 106.

20. Ibid., 99.

21. John Paul Heil, *Paul's Letter to the Romans: A Reader-Response Commentary* (New York: Paulist, 1987), 1.

22. Temma F. Berg, "Reading In/to Mark," *Semeia* 48 (1989): 197.

23. Cf. Hilary Putnam's revised Kantianism: "The mind and the world together make up the mind and the world" (*Reason, Truth, and History*, xi).

24. Felerpin, *Beyond Deconstruction*, 27.

25. *The Bible and the Reader* (Philadelphia: Fortress, 1985), 12.

26. See Wolfgang Iser, *The Implied Reader: Patterns of Communication in Prose Fiction From Bunyan to Beckett* (Baltimore: Johns Hopkins Univ. Press, 1978).

27. Jeanrond complains that on Iser's view the reader is not merely obedient, but a virtual slave of the text (*Text and Interpretation*, 110).

28. Ben F. Meyer, "The Challenge of Text and Reader to the Historical-Critical Method," in Wim Beuken, Sean Freyne, and Anton Weiler, eds., *The Bible and Its Readers*, Concilium 1991/1 (London: SCM, 1991), 10.

29. Kermode, *Genesis of Secrecy* (Cambridge: Harvard Univ. Press, 1979), 35.

30. Fish, *Is There a Text?* 13.

31. Barthes, "Death of the Author," 129.

32. Scholes, *Protocols of Reading* (New Haven: Yale Univ. Press, 1989).

33. Ricoeur, "Myth As the Bearer of Possible Worlds," in Richard Kearney, ed., *Dialogues With Contemporary Continental Thinkers* (Manchester: Manchester Univ. Press, 1984), 45.

34. Moore, *Literary Criticism and the Gospels*, 66.

35. See Bultmann, "The New Testament and Mythology," in Hans Werner Bartsch, ed., *Kerygma and Myth: A Theological Debate*, 2d. ed. (London: SPCK, 1964), 1:1–44.

36. Bernard C. Lategan, "Introduction: Coming to Grips With the Reader," *Semeia* 48 (1989): 8.

37. Barton and Morgan, *Biblical Interpretation*, 7.

38. Insofar as they are not derived from the text itself, the reader's interests may be said to be "extra-textual." For a critique of extra-textual theology (i.e., one that interprets the Bible from some framework other than that derived from the text), see George Lindbeck, *The Nature of Doctrine: Religion and Theology in a Postliberal Age* (Philadelphia: Westminster, 1984).

39. I return to this point in Part 2, where I explicitly refute the suggestion that, because readers find only themselves and their own opinions, texts are unable to challenge or address us.

40. John Finnis, *Natural Law and Natural Rights* (Oxford: Clarendon, 1980), 81–85. To be sure, the Undoer would be quick to attack Finnis's claim that the concern for truth is "natural" rather than "political."

41. Alexander Pope, *An Essay on Criticism*, 1.118–23.

42. Matthew Arnold, "The Function of Criticism at the Present Time," in *Essays in Criticism* (London: Macmillan, 1865).

43. T. S. Eliot, "The Function of Criticism," in *Selected Essays* (London: Faber & Faber, 1932), i.

44. See M. H. Abrams, "The Limits of Pluralism: The Deconstructive Angel," *Critical Inquiry* 3 (1977): 426, and Lentricchia, *After the New Criticism*, 178.

45. C. S. Lewis, *Reflections on the Psalms* (London: Geoffrey Bles, 1958), 2–3.

46. Stout, "Relativity in Interpretation," 112.

47. See Rorty, "Texts and Lumps," *Objectivity, Relativism, and Truth: Philosophical Papers*, 1:78–92; Stout, "What is Meaning?" and Fowl, "The Ethics of Interpretation or What's Left Over After the Elimination of Meaning," *SBL 1988 Seminar Papers*, 70.

48. Eco, *Interpretation and Overinterpretation*, 23.

49. Eco, *Limits of Interpretation*, 57.

50. Ibid.

51. Pope, *An Essay on Criticism*, 1.15.

52. Felerpin trenchantly notes that each of the theoretical schools requires a communal faith to sustain its dogmatism (*Beyond Deconstruction*, 207).

53. Hirsch, *Aims of Interpretation*, 77.

54. See the discussion of Van Harvey in chapter 1 (p. 23).

55. Stout, "Relativity of Interpretation," 104.

57. Fowl, "The Ethics of Interpretation," 75. This is the neo-pragmatist's preferred response: "Let us then celebrate the diversity of interpretations as a sign that our texts are interesting in more ways than one" (ibid., 8).

58. Ibid., 76.

59. Schüssler Fiorenza, "The Ethics of Interpretation: Decentering Biblical Scholarship," *Journal of Biblical Literature* 107 (1988): 15.

60. Fowl associates this third position with the moral philosophy of Alistair MacIntyre, developed in his *After Virtue*.

61. Fowl, "Ethics of Interpretation," 71.

62. I am indebted in what follows to Wayne Booth's discussion of pluralisms in his *Critical Understanding*, ch. 1.

63. Cf. Karl Barth's trinitarian exposition of the doctrine of revelation in his *Church Dogmatics* I/1.

64. In Part 2 I will explore the parallels between three sets of triads: Father, Son, and Spirit; author, text, and reader; metaphysics, epistemology, and ethics.

65. Cf. Hirsch's attempt to specify the ground and goal of hermeneutics in terms of the author's intention in ch. 2 above.

66. I owe the insight that the Trinity enables Christians to construe reality in terms of harmony rather than anarchy and violence to John Milbank, *Theology and Social Theory: Beyond Secular Reason* (Oxford: Blackwell, 1990), esp. ch. 12.

67. See Karl Barth, *Letters 1961–1968*, ed. Geoffrey W. Bromiley (Grand Rapids: Eerdmans, 1981), 8.

68. Mark Taylor, "Text As Victim," 66.

69. See Fernando F. Segovia's analysis of modern biblical interpretation in his "The Text As Other: Towards a Hispanic American Hermeneutic," in Daniel Smith-Christopher, *Text and Experience: Towards a Cultural Exegesis of the Bible* (Sheffield: Sheffield Academic Press, 1995), 277–85.

70. See Margaret Davies, "Exegesis," in *A Dictionary of Biblical Interpretation*, 220.

71. Cited in Bernard Ramm, *Protestant Biblical Interpretation: A Textbook of Hermeneutics*, 3d ed. (Grand Rapids: Baker, 1970) , 58.

72. Segovia, "Text As Other," 283.

73. Cited in Taylor, "Text As Victim," 58.

74. *Postmodern Bible*, 267.

75. Derrida, *Acts of Literature*, 56.

77. Plato, *Phaedrus*, 275D.

78. Stephen D. Moore, *Mark and Luke in Poststructuralist Perspective* (New Haven: Yale Univ. Press, 1992), xviii.

79. Attributed to G. C. Lichtenberg.

80. Barthes, *Critical Essays*, tr. Richard Howard (Evanston: Northwestern Univ. Press, 1972), 260.

81. Eagleton, *Literary Theory*, 12.

82. George Steiner, "Narcissus and Echo: A Note on Current Arts of Reading," *American Journal of Semiotics* 1 (1981): 8.

83. Lentricchia, *After the New Criticism*, 169.

84. Taylor, "Text As Victim," 65.

85. Ibid., 67.

86. Shakespeare's politics—specifically, whether he was a royalist or an anarchist—is currently one of the most bitterly contested issues in Shakespeare criticism. See Brian Vickers, *Appropriating Shakespeare* (New Haven: Yale Univ. Press, 1993) for a critique of ideological interpretations of Shakespeare.

87. For a critique of the "culture of hermeneutics," see my "The World Well Staged?" esp. 25–30.

88. The Stanford students protested against the idea of a canon and staked their claim to interpretive freedom by shouting ,"Hey, Hey, Ho, Ho! Western culture's got to go!"

89. This is the secular equivalent of Moore's call to biblical scholars to demythologize their processes of reading (*Literary Criticism*, 172).

90. Eagleton, *Literary Theory*, 211.

91. I shall argue in Part 2 that non-realism is not in fact conducive to human freedom.

92. Thompson, *Studies in the Theory of Ideology* (Cambridge: Polity, 1984), 5.

93. See the preface to the 1883 edition of Matthew Arnold, *Literature and Dogma*.

94. Eagleton, *Literary Theory*, 14.

95. John B. Thompson, *Ideology and Modern Culture: Critical Social Theory in the Era of Mass Communication* (Palo Alto, Calif.: Stanford Univ. Press, 1990), 7.

96. John B. Thompson, *Studies in the Theory of Ideology*, 4.

97. See Terry Eagleton, *Ideology: An Introduction* (London: Verso, 1991).

98. *The Postmodern Bible*, 275.

99. Hirsch, *Aims*, 78. Hirsch is referring to critics who have abandoned the author's intended meaning as a norm for valid interpretation.

100. See "Feminist Criticism" in Irena R. Makaryk, *Encyclopedia of Contemporary Literary Theory: Approaches, Scholars, Terms* (Toronto: Univ. of Toronto Press, 1993), 39–52.

101. Christine Gledhill, "Recent Developments in Feminist Criticism," in *Film Theory and Criticism: Introductory Readings*, 4th ed., ed. Gerald Mast, Mashall Cohen, and Leo Braudy (Oxford: Oxford Univ. Press, 1992), 99.

102. Eagleton notes that deconstruction got under way after the student revolutions of 1968: "Unable to break the structures of state power, post-structuralism found it possible instead to subvert the structures of language" (Eagleton, *Literary Theory*, 142). For a comprehensive analysis of the relation between deconstruction and feminist criticism, see David Rutledge, *Reading Marginally: Feminism, Deconstruction, and the Bible* (Leiden: E. J. Brill, 1996).

103. The skillful use of language to achieve one's ends—rhetoric—may be employed by sincere critics for the sake of truth rather than deception. As we will see, biblical discourse is

rhetorical too. See Martin Warner, *The Bible As Rhetoric: Studies in Biblical Persuasion and Credibility* (London: Routledge, 1990), esp. "Introduction" and ch. 8.

104. Eagleton, *Literary Theory*, 149.

105. Cf. Hilary Putnam: "The only criterion for what is a fact is what it is rational to accept" (*Reason, Truth, and History*, x).

106. Fish, *Doing What Comes Naturally*, 380.

107. Fish, *Is There a Text?* 15.

108. Ibid., 13.

109. Contemporary film criticism and theory provides an excellent example of the interdisciplinary nature of interpretation theories. The same hermeneutics of suspicion and the same ideology critics (Marxists, feminists, deconstructionists, etc.) can be found in film theory and criticism. David Bordwell describes "how an institution constructs and constrains what is thought and said by its members" (*Making Meaning*, xii).

110. Fish, *Is There a Text?* 16.

111. Ibid.

112. Gregory Currie calls Fish's thesis "internalism" ("Text Without Context," 213).

113. It is not clear what interpretation is interpretation *of* for Fish.

114. Fish, *Doing What Comes Naturally*, 10.

115. Jeanrond, *Theological Hermeneutics*, 7.

116. Lindbeck, "Scripture, Consensus, and Community," in Richard John Neuhaus, ed., *Biblical Interpretation in Crisis* (Grand Rapids: Eerdmans, 1989), 76.

117. Cited in Jeanrond, *Theological Hermeneutics*, 170. Bernard Ramm helpfully suggests that this constitutes the Roman Catholic "formal theory" of the clarity of Scripture (*Evangelical Heritage: A Study in Historical Theology* [Grand Rapids: Baker, 1981], 32).

118. See Calvin, *Institutes*, 1.7.

119. Lindbeck, "Scripture, Consensus, and Community," 84.

120. For much of the twentieth century, biblical critics have sought ways to enable these two interpretive frameworks—the religious and the critical—to live harmoniously together. See Barton and Morgan, *Biblical Interpretation*, esp. chs. 1, 6, and 8.

121. Rorty, "Pragmatism and Philosophy," 56.

122. Other works that could be mentioned include R. Sugitharajah, ed., *Voices From the Margin: Interpreting the Bible in the Third World* (Maryknoll, N.Y.: Orbis, 1991), and Cain Hope Felder, ed., *Stony the Road We Trod: African-American Biblical Interpretation* (Minneapolis: Fortress, 1991).

123. Daniel Smith-Christopher, *Text and Experience: Towards a Cultural Exegesis of the Bible* (Sheffield: Sheffield Academic Press, 1995), 16.

124. Stanley Hauerwas, *Unleashing the Scripture: Freeing the Bible From Captivity to America* (Nashville: Abingdon, 1993), 20.

125. The decision about the values or norms that guide interpretation is a "metacritical" decision. My problem with Fish and Hauerwas is that they do not provide sufficient reasons for choosing one set of norms over another, and that the norm they do choose does not easily admit of self-correction. Scott C. Saye claims that Karl Barth also acknowledges the authority of interpretive communities and thus shares some important themes with Fish ("The Wild and Crooked Tree: Barth, Fish, and Interpretive Communities," *Modern Theology* 12 [1996]: 435–58).

126. Gary A. Phillips, "Exegesis As Critical Praxis: Reclaiming History and Text from a Postmodern Perspective," *Semeia* 51 (1990): 14.

127. Lindbeck, "Scripture, Consensus, Community," 78.

128. We will return to this theme in Part 2.

129. Detweiler, "Introduction," *Semeia* 23 (1982): 2.

130. I explore this possibility in Part 2, where I suggest that a little bit of deconstruction may be a beneficial thing. Taken in small doses, deconstruction drives us not to despair but to greater humility.

131. "The Barmen Declaration," in Clifford Green, ed., *Karl Barth: Theologian of Freedom* (London: Collins, 1989), 149. The text of the Barmen Declaration was largely the work of Karl Barth.

132. Moore, *Literary Criticism and the Gospels*, 56.

133. Meir Sternberg, *The Poetics of Biblical Narrative: Ideological Literature and the Drama of Reading* (Bloomington: Indiana Univ. Press, 1985), 37. Sternberg believes that it is important not to confuse the ideology of the text with the ideology of the reader, poetics with politics.

134. Along these lines, I find it interesting that the Bible's account of the institution of the Israelite monarchy is far from positive. See, for example, 1 Sam. 12.

135. Sternberg, *Poetics of Biblical Narrative*, 482; cf. Auerbach: "We are to fit our own life into its world, feel ourselves to be elements in its structure of universal history" (*Mimesis: The Representation of Reality in Western Literature* [Princeton: Princeton Univ. Press, 1953], 15).

136. Sternberg, *Poetics of Biblical Interpretation*, 37.

137. Sternberg argues that this cognitive antithesis is built into the very structure of biblical narrative and so shapes the experience of reading.

138. Belsey, *Critical Practice*, 58.

139. Cf. the article by Christopher Rowland, "Materialist Interpretation," in *A Dictionary of Biblical Interpretation*, 430–32.

140. Paul de Man, *The Resistance to Theory* (Minneapolis: Univ. of Minnesota Press, 1989), 11.

141. Douglas Kellner, "Marxist Criticism," in *Encyclopedia of Contemporary Literary Theory*, 96. This sense of ideology is the one that dominates Marxist social theory. See Sam Solecki, "Ideology," in *Encyclopedia of Contemporary Literary Theory*, 559.

142. Carroll, "Ideology," in *Dictionary of Biblical Interpretation*, 309 (see esp. N. K. Gottwald, *The Tribes of Yahweh* [1979]).

143. The theological question raised by ideology criticism is how the Bible, if it is a human as well as divine product, can communicate God's revealed Word without ideological (and cultural) contamination.

144. Biblical scholars speak of the "Deuteronomic history" to refer to all the biblical books from Deuteronomy up to and including 2 Kings (excluding Ruth). The idea is that the theology, or ideology, of Deuteronomy permeates the telling of Israel's history from the time of Moses to the Babylonian exile. The major theme of this history is that the possession of the land is conditional on obedience to the law. Martin Noth, the scholar who first propounded the theory, believed that the books were the work of a single author, though for my purposes I need only assume a "singular ideology," not a single author or editor. See A. D. H. Mayes, "Deuteronomistic History," in *A Dictionary of Biblical Interpretation*, 174–76.

145. The Hebrew title for the book, *debarîm*, means "words."

146. The latter suggestion assumes a late date for the composition of the book, namely, during the early reign of King Josiah, just prior to the "rediscovery" of the Book of the Law recounted in 2 Kings 22:8–20. For an example of this critical approach to the book, see Ronald E. Clements, "Deuteronomy, the Book of," in Bruce M. Metzger and Michael D. Coogan, eds., *The Oxford Companion to the Bible* (Oxford: Oxford Univ. Press, 1993), 164–68.

147. Carroll, "Ideology," 310.

148. Kerry McKeever, "How to Avoid Speaking of God: Poststructuralist Philosophies and Biblical Hermeneutics," *Journal of Literature and Theology* 6 (1992): 233.

149. Polzin, "Deuteronomy," in *The Literary Guide to the Bible*, 95. See also Robert Polzin, *Moses and the Deuteronomist. A Literary Study of the Deuteronomic History* (New York: Seabury, 1980).

150. Ibid., 96.

151. Ibid., 93.

152. Ibid., 94.

153. I shall return to the possiblity of universal interests in interpretation in ch. 7 below.

154. David J. A. Barton, "History and Rhetoric in the Prophets," in Warner, ed., *The Bible As Rhetoric*, 52.

155. Ibid., 63–64.

156. Clines, "Deconstructing the Book of Job," in Warner, ed., *The Bible As Rhetoric*, 78.

157. Examples include the Conquistadors in Peru, the Puritans in New England, and the Boers in South Africa.

158. David Jobling, "Writing the Wrongs of the World: The Deconstruction of the Biblical Text in the Context of Liberation Theologies," *Semeia* 51 (1990): 81.

159. According to Christopher Rowland, European and American biblical scholars who believe that the "normal" interpretation is the one that seeks what the text originally meant also represent "a powerful interest group which . . . regulate[s] the canons of the production of meaning" ("Materialist Interpretation," 431).

160. Dan Cohn-Sherbok, "Liberation Theology," *Dictionary of Biblical Interpretation*, 397.

161. I agree. In Part 2 I liken the interpreter to a disciple, though I insist that the text, rather than the contemporary context, should take the lead in determining how to apply meaning.

162. See Christopher Rowland, "Materialist Interpretation," 430.

163. Cited in ibid.

164. Thiselton, *New Horizons*, 410.

165. Itumeleng J. Mosala, "Biblical Hermeneutics of Liberation: The Case of Micah," in R. S. Sugirtharajah, ed., *Voices From the Margin: Interpreting the Bible in the Third World* (London: S.P.C.K., 1991), 114.

166. Itumeleng J. Mosala, "The Use of the Bible in Black Theology," in Sugirtharajah, ed., *Voices from the Margin*, 50.

167. See Naim Stifan Ateek, "A Palestinian Perspective: The Bible and Liberation," *Voices From the Margin*, 280–86.

168. Tim Blewett, "Bible, Land, Justice—The Challenge of Na'im Ateek and Palestinian Liberation Theology," *Theology* (May/June 1993): 212.

169. Robert Allen Warrior, "A Native American Perspective: Canaanites, Cowboys, and Indians," *Voices From the Margin*, 289.

170. John L. O'Sullivan, cited in J. E. Johnson, "Manifest Destiny," in *Dictionary of Christianity in America*, ed. Daniel G. Reid, et al. (Downers Grove, Ill.: InterVarsity, 1990), 703.

171. Ibid., 293.

172. What about the Conquest narrative? Can Christians apply the book of Joshua to new situations (e.g., the Crusaders, the Conquistadors)? My strategy, were I to construct an adequate response, would be to appeal to the fuller canonical context of the biblical text itself. In the immediate literary context, it is clear that the taking of Canaan was to be a once-for-all event. It had to do with the fulfilling of a specific divine promise to Abraham and cannot, therefore, be made into a general principle. Moreover, the land was not simply a possession, but "the vehicle of a benefit, the promised rest" (Brevard Childs, *Biblical Theology of the Old and New Testaments* [London: SCM, 1992], 146). Finally, in the context of the canon as a whole, it is Jesus, not Joshua, who leads his people into a new, eschatological rest (Heb 4:1–11).

173. For instance: "[The LORD your God] defends the cause of the fatherless and the widow, and loves the alien, giving him food and clothing. And you are to love those who are aliens, for you yourselves were aliens in Egypt" (Deut. 10:18–19).

174. Watson, *Text, Church and World*, 201.

175. Michel Foucault, *Discipline and Punish: The Birth of the Prison,* tr. Alan Sheridan (New York: Vintage/Random House, 1979), 25.

176. Ann Loades, "Feminist Theology," in David F. Ford, ed., *The Modern Theologians: An Introduction to Christian Theology in the Twentieth Century* (Oxford: Blackwell, 1989), 2:250.

177. See Toril Moi, *Sexual/Textual Politics: Feminist Literary Theory* (London: Methuen, 1985).

178. Elisabeth Schüssler Fiorenza, *In Memory of Her: A Feminist Theological Reconstruction of Christian Origins* (New York: Crossroad, 1983), xv.

179. Ibid., 32; cf. Ellen K. Wondra, "By Whose Authority? The Status of Scripture in Contemporary Feminist Theologies," *Anglican Theological Journal* 75 (1993): 83–101.

180. Schüssler Fiorenza, *Bread Not Stone: The Challenge of Feminist Biblical Interpretation* (Boston: Beacon Press, 1984), 14. Anne E. Carr raises two problems about using women's experience as a hermeneutical principle: First, what exactly is "women's experience"? Second, whatever it is, it cannot serve as a norm for interpretation, for if it did it would yield only more of the same and thus fail to provide for self-criticism ("The New Vision of Feminist Theology," in Catherine Mowry LaCugna, ed., *Freeing Theology: The Essentials of Theology in Feminist Perspective* [San Francisco: HarperCollins, 1993], esp. 21–25).

181. Sheila Briggs, "'Buried with Christ,'" 277.

182. Cupitt, *Long-Legged Fly*, 137.

183. Derrida, *Positions,* tr. Alan Bass (Chicago: Univ. of Chicago Press, 1981), 41. Against Derrida, I would argue that recognizing some hierarchical oppositions may well be the condition of human liberation. A person who refuses to acknowledge the binary opposition of Creator-creature, for instance, will never be correctly attuned to the structure of reality.

184. See, for example, Gerda Lerner, *The Creation of Patriarchy* (Oxford: Oxford Univ. Press, 1986).

185. See "Choreographies" in Derrida, *The Ear of the Other*, esp. 171, 179, 184, and Derrida, *Acts of Literature*, 57–60.

186. See Eagleton, *Literary Theory*, 187–88.

187. Handelman, *Slayers of Moses*, ch. 7.

188. See Susan Lochrie Graham, "Silent Voices: Women in the Gospel of Mark" *Semeia* 54 (1991): 146.

189. Ibid., 147.

190. Cited in Deborah F. Middleton, "Feminist Interpretation," in *Dictionary of Biblical Interpretation*, 232.

191. Thiselton, *New Horizons*, 452. If we are to read the Bible from the perspective of "our" experience, how specific must we be if we are to avoid marginalizing someone? So-called womanist interpreters of the Bible feel that the experience of black women is significantly different from that of white women. But what makes that difference of more significance than, say, whether one is in one's twenties or forties, whether one comes from the North or the South, whether one is blond or brunette?

192. So Gadamer, as cited in Simon Critchley, *The Ethics of Deconstruction: Derrida and Lévinas* (Oxford: Blackwell, 1992), 3n.6.

193. Foucault, *Power/Knowledge: Selected Interviews and Other Writings, 1972-1977*, ed. Colin Gordon (New York: Pantheon, 1980), 132.

194. Alvin Plantinga, "Augustinian Christian Philosophy," *Monist* 75 (1992): 303. Plantinga's term for non-realism is "creative anti-realism."

195. Ibid., 304.

196. Carl A. Raschke, "The Deconstruction of God," 3. The quote is worth citing in full: "Deconstruction, which must be considered the interior drive of twentieth-century theology

rather than an alien agenda, is in the final analysis the death of God put into writing, the subsumption of the 'Word' by the 'flesh,' the deluge of immanence."

197. Caputo, *Radical Hermeneutics: Repetition, Deconstruction, and the Hermeneutic Project* (Bloomington: Indiana Univ. Press, 1987), 279, 272.

198. Darrell J. Fasching, "Idolatry," in Donald W. Musser and Joseph L. Price, ed., *A New Handbook of Christian Theology* (Nashville: Abingdon, 1992), 246.

199. See Barton, "History and Rhetoric in the Prophets," in *Bible As Rhetoric*, 62.

200. Hart, *Trespass of the Sign*, 144–45.

201. Clines, "Deconstructing the Book of Job," 79.

202. Vern S. Poythress applies a creation-fall-redemption schema to hermeneutics and refers explicitly to "interpretive sins." He also recognizes an essential connection between theology and hermeneutics; every act of interpretation is simultaneously an interpretation of oneself, an interpretation of God's Word, and an interpretation of the world ("Christ the Only Savior of Interpretation," *Westminster Theological Journal* 50 [1988]: 305–21). I return to the theme of theological hermeneutics in Part 2.

203. Berg, "Reading In/to Mark," 191. As I have argued throughout this chapter, however, it is not clear to me how Undoers and Users can be sufficiently self-critical.

204. Lévinas is primarily concerned with other human persons. The other is not an object that can be summarily classified, but a singularity that demands our infinite attention. For an introduction to Lévinas, see his *Ethics and Infinity*, tr. R. A. Cohen (Pittsburgh: Duquesne Univ. Press, 1985).

205. Critchley, *Ethics of Deconstruction*, 6. Lévinas defines philosophy as "the alchemy whereby alterity is transmuted into sameness" (6) and ethics as "respect for alterity" (12).

206. Norris, *Derrida*, 224.

207. Critchley calls deconstruction "a philosophy of hesitation" to bring out this aspect of undecidability (*Ethics of Deconstruction*, 42). For a defense of the centrality of "undecidability" in Derrida, see Gary A. Phillips, "'You Are Either Here, Here, Here, or Here': Deconstruction's Troublesome Interplay," *Semeia* 71 (1995): 207–8.

208. Critchley, *Ethics of Deconstruction*, 238.

209. Norris, *Derrida*, 237.

210. It should be noted, however, that Derrida's version of the distinction between transcendence and immanence is not a particularly Christian one. Though some have tried to associate Derrida with the project of negative theology, where God is above human language and concepts, Derrida has to date politely refused the compliment. For a thorough discussion of the relation of Derrida to negative theology, see Kevin Hart, *The Trespass of the Sign*, 184–86, and Coward, ed., *Derrida and Negative Theology*.

211. See Barrie A. Wilson, "Metacriticism," in *Encyclopedia of Contemporary Literary Theory*, 102–10.

212. Thiselton rightly points out that the nature of the texts themselves ought to have some bearing on the formulation of one's interpretive purposes, a suggestion I will explore at greater length in ch. 6 (see Thiselton, *New Horizons*, 316–18).

213. This is the project of Part 2. Another such attempt is that of Wolfhart Pannenberg, who notes that meaning pertains to the interrelation of parts and wholes, and develops a theological account in which the future of the God-world relation, anticipated in Jesus Christ, is the ultimate interpretive context. See Thiselton, *New Horizons*, 331–38.

214. The alternative, first sketched at the end of ch. 3 and to be explored more fully in Part 2, is adequate knowledge—adequate, that is, for the purposes of communication between human persons who, by virtue of their being created in the image of God, are communicative agents.

PART TWO

Redoing Interpretation:
Agency, Action, Affect

Any coherent account of the capacity of human speech
to communicate meaning and feeling is, in the final analysis,
underwritten by the assumption of God's presence.

George Steiner[1]

An agent's action is like a statement in a dialogue. . . .
Responsibility lies in the agent who stays with his action, who
accepts the consequences in the form of reactions and looks
forward in a present deed to the continued interaction.

H. Richard Niebuhr[2]

He that owneth his words and actions, is the Author.

Thomas Hobbes[3]

Books are not absolutely dead things, but do contain a potency of
life in them to be as active as that soul whose progeny they are. . . .
As good kill a man as kill a good book: who kills a man kills a reasonable creature, God's image; but he who destroys a good book,
kills reason itself, kills the image of God, as it were in the eye.

John Milton[4]

Can we continue to speak, in the wake of deconstruction, of a morality of literary knowledge? Van Harvey insists that the modern theologian must abide by the same standards of rationality that prevail in other academic disciplines. David Tracy agrees, noting of the theologian that "his ethical commitment to the morality of scientific knowledge forces him to assume a critical posture towards his own and his tradition's beliefs."[5] But it is precisely this assumed superiority of "scientific knowledge" that deconstruction, and postmodernity in general, calls into question. Just as modern biblical critics, in the name of secular reason, felt a moral obligation to question traditional biblical interpretation, so many postmodern critics today, in the name of multicultural difference, question whether modernity offers anything more than the pretense of objectivity. Difference and otherness have replaced rationality and universality in the postmodern pantheon.

The "morality" of literary knowledge. This phrase, after sustained deconstruction, may now stick in our throat. As we have seen, Derrida undoes the presumption that there is some "natural" order, "natural" sense, or "natural" law by deconstructing the category "natural" into its arbitrary historical and cultural constructions. There are no natural givens, no universal essences, no plain meanings; like language, everything is always and only a social construction. The postmodern critic sees through knowledge claims that are in fact only camouflage for institutional power, symptoms of political struggle. What, then, should readers do with Scripture in the postmodern world?

Though no friend to deconstruction, George Steiner, the celebrated literary critic and "veritable priest of reading,"[6] nevertheless acknowledges that deconstruction is, on its own terms, irrefutable: "The break with the postulate of the sacred is the break with any stable, potentially ascertainable meaning of meaning."[7] For Steiner, the idea of a "secular poetics"—of an encounter with language and literature that remains only on the level of language and literature—while not necessarily self-contradictory, nonetheless fails to explain how and why words can inform and transform us. We read, listen to music, and appreciate art in order to encounter something more than signs, sounds, and shapes. We wait on "spirit"—a "real presence," mediated to us *through* signs, sounds, and shapes. Many postmodern critics accept Derrida's premise that "the age of the sign is essentially theological," then proceed to dismiss both meaning and God. The postmodern world lacks height and depth. To say "there is nothing outside textuality" is to make meaning a surface phenomenon of language only, wholly immanent. Steiner, by contrast, urges readers to make the wager on the meaningfulness of meaning, a wager on transcendence.[8] Steiner sees "with absolute clarity that the most essential repudiation lying at the heart of the whole deconstructive enterprise is a theological repudiation, and thus, as he feels, the one kind of faith (in unfaith) may be countered only by another kind of faith."[9] Consequently, Derrida's announcement of the death of meaning alerts us to the indispensable tie between literary theory and theology. *Deconstruction, wholly inadvertently and with some irony, proves that God is the condition for the possibility of meaning and interpretation.*[10]

My task in Part 2 is thus to explore the theology that undergirds this "other faith," the wager on transcendence, and to do so from an explicitly Christian perspective. I will therefore present a constructive alternative to Derrida's version of responsible reading, an alternative that takes its basic orientation from the Christian belief that God communicates with others ("In the beginning was the Word") and that humans, created in God's image, are likewise communicative agents. I conduct my critique of deconstruction more by indirect dialogue than by direct debate. For whereas debate assumes a good deal of common ground, dialogue need not. In dialogue, we might not even agree about what the crucial questions or issues are. It is because I start somewhere else, with a different set of concerns, that I must dialogue rather than debate with Derrida. Even a point by point rebuttal of deconstruction would still let deconstruction set the agenda, just as modernity sets the agenda for its deconstruction by postmodernity. I wish instead to make a fresh start on the question of textual meaning, inspired by a Christian understanding of God, language, and transcendence.[11]

Part 2 has a tripartite, indeed trinitarian, structure. I appeal to the Trinity not to justify a particular critical approach, as in Origen's distinction between the body, soul, and spirit of a text, but rather because any account of meaning and interpretation is already theological. In light of the Christian confession of God as creator, redeemer, and sanctifier, we may say that God is the one who communicates himself—Father, Son, and Spirit—to others. God's self-communicative activity results in creation, Christ, and church. *The triune God is communicative agent (Father/author), action (Word/text), and result (Spirit/power of reception).* I propose that we take God's trinitarian self-communication as the paradigm of what is involved in all true communication. Scripture certainly portrays God, in contrast to the dumb idols, as a speaking God. And according to Hebrews 1:1 and the Nicene Creed, God is the one who "spoke through the prophets" (*est locutus per prophetas*). A Christian theological account of hermeneutics, as of anything else, must discipline notions of meaning and interpretation achieved in abstraction from distinctly Christian beliefs. In the following chapters, therefore, I draw on the resources of various doctrines—creation, Incarnation, and sanctification—in order to bring Christian faith to bear on such hermeneutical topics as the author, the text, and the reader.

It is partly in response to a postmodern demand—namely, respect for the other—that I develop a Christian approach to the question of meaning. In the first place, it is important to appreciate the "otherness" of Christian faith. Alvin Plantinga disagrees with Harvey's understanding of the morality of knowledge and advises Christian philosophers to get on with their own agendas, to pursue their own research programs. What is needed is "less accommodation to current fashion and more Christian self-confidence."[12] Since philosophy is a clarification and deepening of prephilosophical beliefs, Plantinga believes that we as Christians have both a right and a responsibility to begin our reflection about God, the world, and ourselves from Christian premises. To this list I now want to add *meaning*. My contention, briefly stated, is that because the undoing of interpretation rests on a theological mistake, we need theology to correct it. Second, I will argue that Christian theology, not deconstruction, is the better response to the ethical challenge of the "other." The Christian story is itself powerful testimony to God's respect and love for the other. The gospel is the story of God's going out of himself for the sake of the human other. Can readers do something similar for the sake of the author?

Part 2 thus responds to Plantinga's call to develop a positive Christian philosophy. How shall we think about meaning and interpretation from the perspective of trinitarian theology? What, for instance, shall we say of the metaphysics, methods, and morals of interpretation in light of the doctrines of creation, Incarnation, and redemption? This positive project of exploring how Christian theology bears on the question of meaning is similar to John Milbank's recent attempt to rethink social theory in light of Christian doctrine. Milbank argues that theology should not conform to social theory, for social theory is born and bred of "secular reason," that is, of the modification or rejection of orthodox Christian beliefs. I wish to apply a similar argument to the relation between theology and literary theory. So-called secular literary theories are anti-theologies in disguise. As we have seen, Derrida's notion that *différance* is the ground of our being inscribes conflict—binary oppositions—into the very fabric of human reality and is a rejection of the doctrine of creation. Christian theology, as Milbank observes, recognizes no such original violence. Christianity exposes the non-necessity of supposing "that difference, non-totalization and indeterminacy of meaning necessarily imply arbitrariness and violence."[13] The created order is neither chaotic nor conflictual, but covenantal—intended and destined for joy and peace.

Thus inspired by Plantinga's advice and Milbank's example, the chapters in Part 2 develop the potential of theology to dialogue with deconstruction and to develop an alternative literary theory. What happens if we begin with explicitly Christian assumptions about reality, knowledge, and ethics? We will have to retrace our steps, but this time from a different theological starting point and with different philosophical resources. Yet from time to time our path will cross with that of other postmodern pilgrims, and we will have to negotiate our way carefully between the delirium of the arbitrary and the despair of the abyss.

NOTES

1. George Steiner, *Real Presences*.
2. H. Richard Niebuhr, *The Responsible Self*.
3. Thomas Hobbes, *Leviathan*.
4. Milton, *Areopagitica*.
5. Tracy, *Blessed Rage for Order* (New York: Seabury, 1978), 7.
6. The phrase is from Nathan A. Scott Jr. and Roland A. Sharp's "Preface" to their *Reading George Steiner* (Baltimore: Johns Hopkins Univ. Press, 1994), ix.
7. Steiner, *Real Presences*, 132.
8. Ibid., 4.
9. Nathan A. Scott, Jr., "Steiner on Interpretation," in *Reading George Steiner*, 4.
10. I take this to be Steiner's point when he writes: "It is a theology, explicit or suppressed . . . which underwrites the presumption of creativity, of signification in our encounters with text, with music, with art. The meaning of meaning is a transcendent postulate" (*Real Presences*, 216).
11. For all his insight into the theological presuppositions of literary theory, Steiner does not really articulate anything like a doctrine of God.
12. From his inaugural lecture to the John A. O'Brien Chair of Philosophy at the University of Notre Dame on November 4, 1983, "Advice to Christian Philosophers," 10. See also Plantinga, "Augustinian Christian Philosophy," esp. 308–17.
13. Milbank, *Theology and Social Theory*, 5.

CHAPTER FIVE

Resurrecting the Author: Meaning As Communicative Action

Conventional signs are those which living creatures show to one another for the purpose of conveying, in so far as they are able, the motion of their spirits or something which they have sensed or understood. Nor is there any other reason for signifying, or for giving signs, except for bringing forth and transferring to another mind the action of the mind in the person who makes the sign.[1]

Augustine

The interpretive question about the author is one of a set of related metaphysical, aesthetic, and ethical questions about the philosophical subject.

H,. L. Hix[2]

Structural and deconstructive theory's 'final no' to meaning is not a denial of meaning, but a denial that people can control it; it is a loss of faith in human action.

John K. Sheriff[3]

The fear of the author is the beginning of literary knowledge." We have seen that there is good reason to be anxious for the safety of the author; with so many critics proclaiming the author's death, it is only natural to fear for one's lives. But can we also fear authors in the sense of respect them? Can we, for example, continue to make sense of the phrase that now commonly follows the copyright symbol in newly published books: "The moral right of the author has been asserted"?

To inquire after the nature of the author is also to ask what it is to be human. Human beings are *homo loquens* (the speaking animal), but what precisely is our relation to language and how central is it? For Derrida, the human speaker is more a slave than a master of language. Indeed, it is precisely because language cannot be mastered or stabilized that postmodern critics go on to speak of the death of the author and the death of the subject. For postmodern critics, the language system structures speech and thought alike.

Fortunately, the categories "master" and "slave" do not exhaust the options for describing the relation of human beings to language. In this chapter I will explore the

201

image of the author as *citizen* of language, with all the rights and responsibilities attaching thereto. Language is indeed our environment, but it is neither open field nor prison house. Language is like a city in which there is both overall structure and diverse neighborhoods, a city in which speakers have freedom of movement within (city) limits.

For Augustine, the purpose of the city of language is to lead one to the city of God. Language exists for the sake of communication, and signs are to be used for this purpose. In his *On Christian Doctrine*, Augustine draws a distinction between the useful (*uti*) and the enjoyable (*frui*). The highest end of human beings is enjoying God. Language, when rightly used, is one of the chief means that lead to this joy. Derrida, on the other hand, dismisses this aspect of utility and focuses on the pleasure, on the *jouissance*, of language: "The advent of writing is the advent of this play."[4] There is perhaps no better contrast of the two theories of language than that signaled by the difference between Christian "joy" and postmodern "play."

This contrast also leads to one of the central theses in this chapter. To begin thinking about language and human beings from the perspective of Christian belief is to recognize the centrality and interrelatedness of *communication* and *communion*. To respect the moral rights of the author is essentially to receive his or her communication, not to revise it. This reception, in turn, is the basis for a literary knowledge that can perhaps become the basis for personal knowledge, for communion over space and time. In the final analysis, a secular picture of language holds Derrida captive. The following pages fill out what I hope will be another, less misleading, picture of language and of those who write and read it.[5]

THE PHYSICS OF PROMISING: FROM CODES TO COMMUNION

For the philosopher John Searle, the problem of meaning is the problem of how we get "from the physics to the semantics."[6] How do physical sounds and visible marks become a verbal message, for example, a promise? How can we move from molecules (or morphemes) in motion to meaning? How can we account for a poem moving us to tears, a promise that evokes a firm hope, or a parable that prompts us to sell all our goods and give the profits to the poor? How can we account for the hundreds of daily transactions, punctuated by simple phrases ("Come in"; "Please be quiet"; "That will be $4.99, please"; "I love you"), that shape our lives? Does deconstruction adequately account for what is, after all, an everyday occurrence, namely, communication? We are back to questions concerning the metaphysics of meaning, but metaphysics here pertains to those commitments about the way things are that are implied by our most important communicative practices. If we ask why practices such as promising are more than arbitrary, we must engage in metaphysics.

Let us henceforth think of meaning not as something that words and texts have (*meaning* as noun) but rather as something people do (*meaning* as verb). Better said: a word or text only has meaning (noun) if some person means (verb) something by it. "Meaning," like the word "act," refers not only to *what* is done but to the *process* of doing it. We can then say of meaning what has been said of guns: words don't kill (or state, or question, or promise, etc.); *people* do. Meaning, therefore, is not an indeterminate thing, much less the intermediate state of a sleeping text that must be wakened to life, but a determinate action. What characterizes ordinary language is less the "freeplay" of a sign system than a "rule-governed form of behavior."[7] Both linguistic signs and human selves look different than their deconstructed counterparts from the perspective of this new model of language and meaning. *For, with the notion of meaning as a form of action, the author returns, not in his or her Cartesian guise as an all-determining self-conscious subject, but as a communicative agent.* Meaning, I contend, has less to do with the play of linguistic elements in an impersonal sign system than with the responsibility of communicative agents in inter-subjective social situations.

The Self and the Sign: *Langue*

As we saw in Part 1, poststructuralists believe that meaning is hermetically sealed in systems of language. Signs have meaning only as elements in linguistic codes. *Langue* (language as formal code) is prior to *parole* (language in actual use). These language codes determine the way we speak, think, and act; *langue* thus refers to the broader cultural-political systems in which we find ourselves enmeshed as well. Derrida points out that *langue* as a whole is arbitrary; the elements can always be arranged differently. A language code is not related to the world, but only to itself ("there is nothing outside the text"). What were formerly considered "natural" phenomena (e.g., Lévi-Strauss on kinship structures) are now seen as arbitrary social conventions. In learning a language, a speaker learns a system of differences and distinctions (e.g., "Incest is bad grammar").

What then becomes of the speaking subject in postmodern accounts of language? The answer is complex and perhaps contradictory. On the one hand, the subject has lost the power of free speech, able only to say what the language system allows. *Langue* "takes every thought captive." On such a deterministic view, speakers may be inclined to renounce responsibility for their speech, thus falling prey to the temptation of communicative sloth. Lévi-Strauss formulated the slogan of the decade for the French intellectuals of the 1960s: "The goal of the human sciences is not to constitute man, but to dissolve him."[8]

On the other hand, some postmoderns follow Nietzsche in his insistence that strong speakers—poets—are free to rewrite the world, to invent new distinctions and new systems of differentiation. Postmodern philosophy and literary theory in their assertive mood recognize no reality principle, only a pleasure principle: the pleasure of creating new patterns and configurations. Language here becomes a means for imposing our will on the world; the speaker is not a captive to language but a co-creator. The temptation in this extreme is not sloth but pride. Note, however, that on both extremes there is little place for speaking subjects to take responsibility for their words. These postmodern views undo the connection between words, speakers, and world. There is therefore nothing to hold the play of language in check nor anything to give it purpose. Postmodern language, like postmodern life, becomes tragic, signifying nothing.

The Self and the Sentence: *Parole*

One's view of language and literary theory rebounds upon one's view of human beings. The modern view pictures the subject in conscious control; the postmodern picture shows the subject in a textually induced coma. The alternate picture defended in the present work portrays the subject as communicative agent, neither sovereign nor slave, but rather citizen of language. To repeat: A picture of language as an arbitrary system of differential signs holds deconstruction captive. Postmodern views of language are concerned more with semiotics (the science of signs) than with semantics (the science of sentences).[9] In what follows, I will contrast the system of language with its actual use, the impersonal language code with the "covenant of discourse."

A Sign of a Higher Order?

Ricoeur takes an important first step towards an alternative picture, I believe, by insisting that a sentence is not merely a sign of a higher order, but a new entity altogether: "The *logos* of language requires at least a name and a verb, and it is the intertwining of these two words which constitutes the first unit of language and thought."[10] Plato long ago concluded that words by themselves are neither true nor false; but sentences—language as used, language as discourse—connect words "in a synthesis which goes beyond the words."[11] The sentence, in other words, is more than the sum of its parts and introduces a level of complexity and uniqueness that cannot be described by semiotics. Ricoeur sees semiotics and semantics "as the two sciences which correspond to the two kinds of units characteristic of language, the sign and the sentence."[12] Ricoeur here expresses the fundamental difference between semiotics and semantics: "For me, the distinction between semantics and semiotics is the key to the whole problem of language."[13] In short, semantics is the study of sentences, that is, of language used in particular situations.

What has this view of sentences to do with the nature of the self? Just this: both the sentence and the self are what the philosopher P. F. Strawson calls "basic particulars."[14] The human person is a "basic particular"—a primitive concept that cannot be explained by something more basic. Strawson rejects attempts to explain persons in terms of something else, be it kinship structures or chemicals, cultural codes or genetic codes. The sentence is a "basic particular" in much the same way (and for similar reasons). *Just as we can apply two sets of predicates (physical and mental) to persons, so we can apply two kinds of description (semiotic and semantic) to sentences.* This claim is, I believe, of the utmost importance, for sentences and persons alike. Postmodern critics tend to reduce the study of sentences (and persons) to categories appropriate to *langue* only. Sentences are not simply products of a language system, however, mere blips of an impersonal code, but rather meaningful personal actions. We can therefore say of a given sentence that it is a promise (or a command or an assertion), not only that it is in English, that it has nouns and a verb, or that it manifests a patriarchal ideology. A promise is a basic particular—a speech act of a responsible communicative agent—that resists all attempts to reduce it to causal laws, either of physics or of socio-linguistics. In short, the fate of the sentence and the fate of human freedom and responsibility stand or fall together.

The Design Plan of Language: Covenantal Communication

How, then, do we get from the physics to the semantics? My Augustinian strategy—faith seeking textual understanding—begins with a biblical theme and develops it philosophically. Language, I submit, is a gift of God, to be used gratefully and responsibly as we communicate with others. In order to highlight the gift-like nature of language, I will contrast what I call the "evangelical" view of language with a secular "evolutionary" point of view.

Language is a God-given capacity that enables human beings to relate to God, the world, and to one another. Specifically, language involves a kind of relating with God, the world, and others that yields personal knowledge. Language, that is, should be seen as the most important means and medium of communication and communion. In Genesis 2, for example, God and Adam relate by means of language. Adam also relates to his world by using language to name the animals (Gen. 2:19–20), an extraordinary scene that shows how humans make the distinctions and connections that both invent and discover the world.[15] Given the centrality in Scripture not only of naming, but of other uses of language (e.g., praising, prophesying, promising, preaching, etc.), and given the many biblical passages on the correct use of the tongue (e.g., James 3), it is clear that God holds speakers accountable for what they say. More importantly, the Bible represents God as the preeminent speaker. Much of what he does takes the form of speech: promising, forgiving, commanding, and so on. The God of the Christian Scriptures is a God who relates to human beings largely through verbal communication. Of course, God can embody his Word with a completeness that humans cannot: God's Word was made flesh. *God's Word is thus something that God says, something that God does, and something that God is.*

As beings created in God's image, humans too have the capacity to communicate and to understand, though as with all our other human capacities, communication too has been affected by the Fall.[16] Nevertheless, it is correct to assert that humans have not only the "dignity of causality" (Pascal) but also the *dignity of communicative agency*. With this privilege of language comes responsibility. The Old Testament shows how the fate of individuals and nations depends on the way in which persons respond to God's message that comes through the Law and the Prophets. The underlying presupposition of the story of Israel, and the story of humanity as a whole, is that humans are able to understand the Word of God and words in general. The New Testament goes further: it pictures language (e.g., parables, preaching) as having the power to transform people's lives.

My argument, then, is that there is a "design plan" for language.[17] Language, like the mind, another divine endowment, was designed by God to be used in certain ways. The design plan specifies when our communicative faculties are functioning properly. Proper function is a matter of accomplishing the purpose for which one's faculties were designed. The proper function of our cognitive faculties, for instance, is to produce true belief. The proper function of our communicative faculties, I contend, is to produce true interpretation—understanding. Of course, our faculties will only produce understanding when they are (1) working properly (2) in a communicative environment that is appropriate to them. These are important conditions. With regard to the first, we have seen that readers often have biases and interests that impede the proper functioning of their interpretive capacities. Second, as the Christian doctrine of the Fall implies, neither our faculties nor our environment is in perfect working order. The communicative environment is corrupt, riddled with people

using language as an instrument of coercion rather than conversation and communion. Nevertheless, our design plan leads us still to believe that when we encounter
a sentence, someone is trying to communicate with us.

Plantinga argues, with regard to epistemology, that there appears to be "no successful naturalistic account of the notion of proper function."[18] This may be true of
language and interpretation too. As we have seen, the death of God leads postmodern
literary theorists to announce the death of the author and the undecidability of meaning. If there is no God, how can we speak of the "proper function" of language? We
seem to be faced with two rival hypotheses: either evolutionary psychology or evangelical theology. According to the former, language is the chance product of nature.[19]
From the perspective of evolutionary psychology, the primary purposes of language,
as of all other human capacities, are survival and reproduction. Language is useful for
getting along with others, and getting along with others is useful in surviving (and in
reproducing). Yet evolution need not underwrite language as anything more than a
useful tool for coping with the world—a tool for manipulation, not communication,
much less a medium of meaning and truth. Indeed, an evolutionary account is unable
to provide an account of language as anything other than instrumental.

The real question, says Plantinga, "is whether there is a satisfactory *naturalistic*
explanation or analysis of the notion of proper function."[20] He observes that naturalistic evolution does not provide sufficient reason to believe that human cognitive faculties produce for the most part true beliefs. This is "Darwin's Doubt": Darwin
doubted whether the operation of the human mind, developed from the mind of
lower animals, is trustworthy. My concern is with what we may call "Derrida's Doubt"
about the reliability of language to communicate with others and to mediate knowledge of the world.[21] Evolutionary psychology, then, fails to sustain the belief that the
purpose of our linguistic faculties is to communicate with and understand others.

If we begin not from Derrida's Doubt but from Christian doctrine, we can formulate the following thesis: *the design plan of language is to serve as the medium of
covenantal relations with God, with others, with the world.* There are two dimensions to
this covenant of discourse: the inter-subjective bond between speakers and the objective bond between language and reality. First, language is the medium in which we
relate to others.[22] Speakers have a responsibility for their linguistic actions, for example, to be true to their word, as in a promise. Language is not a code that bespeaks
the subject, but a covenant that bestows dignity and responsibility on the agent of language. Far from relieving speakers from responsibility, then, the institution of language actually grounds and enables it. Second, language is the medium in which we
relate to and seek to understand the world.[23] Scientists use language not only to name
and classify the world, but to form models (via metaphors) for understanding the
world in its more complex dimensions as well. It is precisely this bond between our
words and the world that the Undoers have called into question, as George Steiner
rightly notes: "*It is this break of the covenant between word and world which constitutes one
of the very few genuine revolutions of spirit in Western history and which defines modernity
itself.*[24] Compared with the rupture of this covenant, he continues, "even the political revolutions and great wars in modern European history are, I would venture, of
the surface."[25]

Can we still believe that some of our sentences are meaningful and true? Can we continue, in the face of deconstruction, to believe in the bond between our words and our world? Can we regain this covenantal trust? I believe we can. I believe we must. And I see no reason why we cannot begin thinking about language and literature from explicitly Christian assumptions, according to which the design plan of language is to facilitate human interaction with the world and with one another. These two covenantal dimensions are, in fact, connected. The notion that words may mediate the world (the "reality principle") is the condition for their serving as a means of social interaction (the "responsibility principle"). The promise, for instance, makes possible a three-way bond between the speaker, the world in which something is to be done, and the hearer. If, on the other hand, there is nothing in what we say, then there can be neither response nor responsibility in interpretation. For the Undoer, as we have seen, responsible interpretation consists in *resisting* the attempt to link our words to the world, to the way things are. For these postmodern unbelievers, the ideas of truth and reality are coercive: only *undoing* truth claims makes one free. For the Christian believer, however, the ideas of truth and reality are freedom enabling; we are not liberated from, but *by* the truth.

And yet—there is no question that the bond between word and world has become problematic. On the one hand, in a fallen world language no longer infallibly does what it was designed for. There is no question of returning to the innocence of Eden. Cartesian certainty, an absolute knowledge grounded in the knowing subject, is neither possible nor Christian. A little lower than the angels, we humans know only in part, through the glass of language, darkly—not because of some defect in language but because of our unseeing eyes and unclean lips. One should never be too casual, therefore, in claiming understanding. When it comes to interpreting texts, honesty forbids certainty. Human knowing, of books and of the Book of Nature, is mediate and approximate. Here Christians can agree with chastened postmoderns. On the other hand, we must not forget that humans were created with the ability to communicate and to understand by means of language. *It is therefore no little part of our Christian vocation to bear witness to the trustworthiness of the institution of language by being responsible authors and responsible readers.*

DISSENTING VOICES: SPEECH REHABILITATION

There are significant philosophical resources available to the theologian who wishes to seek a fuller understanding of language as a covenantal medium of interpersonal communication. Here I introduce three of the most important: Searle's speech acts, Ricoeur's hermeneutics, and Habermas's social theory. The burden of this chapter will be to integrate all three into a comprehensive theory of literary meaning as communicative action. Significantly, each of these three philosophers also happens to be a prominent and effective critic of deconstruction.[26]

John Searle: Ordinary Language Philosophy

Perhaps the most direct counterarguments to deconstruction have come from devotees of the philosophy of "ordinary language," an approach that had its roots in

Cambridge and Oxford during the 1940s and 1950s.[27] Ordinary language philosophers are united in their belief that language can only be understood in the situation and circumstances of its *use*. Their motto, in direct opposition to Derrida's, might well have been: "There is nothing (e.g., no utterance, no text) outside a context." To philosophers of ordinary language, the so-called "linguistic turn" is not an insoluble complication but rather a solution to certain long-standing philosophical problems. Common language, like common sense, is to be trusted as the repository of human wisdom, the accumulation of all the distinctions and connections humans have found worth making.

Steiner represents what we could call a common sense hermeneutical realism: "I take it to be a moral and pragmatic fact that the poem, the painting, the sonata, are prior to the act of reception, of commentary, of valuation."[28] It is sometimes necessary to restate "banalities," such as "the world is more than my consciousness of it."[29] What follows is a philosophical defense of several hermeneutical distinctions whose truth even postmoderns take for granted, at least in practice. The metaphysical question about the nature of meaning only arises when we ask what makes the commitments that undergird our ordinary conversations more than arbitrary personal preferences.

Ludwig Wittgenstein: Ordinary Language at Cambridge

According to Ludwig Wittgenstein (1889–1951), skeptical philosophies of language rest upon a false picture of how language relates to the world. Wittgenstein was himself once captive to the so-called "picture theory of meaning," believing that language always corresponds to the world in the same way.[30] Every word pictures some thing in the world and every true statement pictures some fact or state of affairs in the world. Indeed, he maintained that the world was simply the sum total of all true statements. In his later philosophy, however, he abandoned the attempt to discover a single logic that would relate language and reality and instead examined the diverse forms of life in which language is actually used.[31] By so doing, he came to see that there are a variety of "fits" between language and the world. Not all language has to "refer" to the world, nor does all referring language refer in the same way (think of the difference between a poetic and scientific description of a red rose).

In his later *Philosophical Investigations*, Wittgenstein came to see that there is no one correct way that language works. There are rather different "language games," whereby words are used in very different ways to do different things. The meaning of a word or sentence thus lies in the rules for its actual use in a real-life situation. These situations—building a house, playing football, learning to paint, worshiping— are always shared by a community of speakers. We will only understand a particular sentence, in Wittgenstein's view, when we see it in the context of its use.[32]

J. L. Austin: Ordinary Language at Oxford

J. L. Austin (1911–60) also believed that the study of language had been too focused on words rather than sentences (i.e., words put to a particular use). He held that the best way to study the word-world relation was to examine the situations in which we do (or do not) use certain expressions. Syntax, the study of a sentence's grammatical form, takes us only so far. "The cat is on the mat but I don't believe it" may be a syntactically correct sentence, yet it is nonsensical—*semantically* incorrect. Ordinary language philosophy analyzes what we say *when*; circumstances and specific situations are every bit as important as the words themselves.[33]

Traditionally, philosophers focused on whether language was true or false, but Austin suggests that many sentences that may look like statements do not really work as statements at all. Austin compares language to a toolbox; indeed, he entitled his most important book *How to Do Things with Words*.[34] Austin's main point is that *saying* is also a kind of *doing*; many utterances are *performative* ("I apologize"; "I bet you a dollar").[35] It is not that my words represent, much less picture, some physical or mental act; no, the utterance itself—performed in the right way in the appropriate circumstances—just *is* the performance of the apology.

Austin distinguishes three different things we do with words, three kinds of linguistic acts: (1) the locutionary act: uttering words (e.g., saying the word "Hello"); (2) the illocutionary act: what we do in saying something (e.g., greeting, promising, commanding, etc.); (3) the perlocutionary act: what we bring about by saying something (e.g., persuading, surprising).[36] Whereas locution has to do with a sign system or *langue*, illocutions and perlocutions have to do with sentences, with language in action or *parole*. The notion of the illocutionary act enables Austin to distinguish between the content of what we say (e.g., the sense and reference of our sentence) and its force (i.e., what we are using the content of our sentence to do). Austin's all-important notion of illocution requires us, I believe, to bring to the fore the speaker's (or author's) role as agent. The speaker is a *doer*. It is precisely this aspect of illocution—what is *done* in saying or writing something—that Undoers overlook. For the Undoer, a text is a code to be unraveled rather than a force to reckon with. For Austin, however, speech cannot be so easily dissociated from its speaker: "Our word is our bond."[37] William Alston underscores the importance of Austin's discovery: "If this is the line along which meaning should be analyzed, then the concept of an illocutionary act is the most fundamental concept in semantics and, hence, in the philosophy of language."[38]

John Searle: Speech Acts

If Austin is the Luther of speech act philosophy, John Searle may be considered its Melanchthon—its systematic theologian.[39] Both agree that the basic unit of meaning is not the word but the speech act. We get from the physics to the semantics, from noises in the air or marks on paper to meaning, only by assuming that these noises or marks were produced by beings who are using language in order to relate to others. Using language to communicate involves following certain socially agreed-upon rules. Accordingly, a theory of language must be part of a theory of action.[40]

How many things can we do with words? Whereas Wittgenstein believed there were countless ways of using language, Searle proposes a comprehensive typology of speech acts. There are, he says, five basic things we do with language: "We tell people how things are, we try to get them to do things, we commit ourselves to doing things, we express our feelings and attitudes and we bring about changes through our utterances. Often, we do more than one of these at once in the same utterance."[41] How can we perform such acts with sounds and signs? "Speaking a language is engaging in a (highly complex) rule-governed form of behavior. To learn and master a language is (*inter alia*) to learn and to have mastered these rules."[42] Each sphere of life in which language is used develops its own relatively stable types of use. In everyday speech, where speakers and hearers share the same context, there is usually little difficulty determining which language game is being played, what rules are in force. When there is uncertainty, one determines which rules are in force by locating the speech act in a particular context.[43]

How to Make a Promise. Consider the promise. How am I able to commit myself to a future course of action by speaking? In coming to see what a promise is, it is most important to distinguish propositional content, which involves predication and reference, from the stance a speaker takes towards it. For example, "Jesus feeding five thousand" predicates "feeding" of Jesus and refers to Jesus and the five thousand. Many philosophers believe that only assertions refer, but Searle insists that all speech acts do so. A proposition, then, is to be distinguished from an assertion or statement of it. Asserting a proposition means the speaker has taken up a particular stance towards it; to be precise, he or she is committed to its truth. However, a speaker can take up other stances towards the same proposition:

"Jesus fed five thousand."
"Did Jesus feed five thousand?"
"Jesus, feed five thousand!"
"Would that Jesus fed five thousand."

In other words, speakers can do more than one thing with the same proposition; they can assert, question, command, or wish. Searle calls what one *does* with a proposition the illocutionary act. "The illocutionary force indicator shows how the proposition is to be taken."[44] He represents the proposition by (p) and the illocutionary force by F. The symbolic form for a speech act is thus $F(p)$, where (p) stands for the propositional content and F for the stance adopted by the speaker toward it.

In order to make a promise, several conditions must be met. First, the proposition must specify a future act that is predicated of the speaker (we cannot make promises about the past, and we cannot make promises for others). There is, then, a "propositional content condition" for promises and for other speech acts as well. There is also a "sincerity condition," which specifies that the speaker intends to do act A. Last, and most important, the speaker intends that his or her utterance will place one under an obligation to do A. It follows that the speaker intends his or her hearer to recognize the utterance as *counting as* a promise. This is the "essential condition" of a speech act.

While Austin and Searle primarily study spoken sentences, a number of other philosophers and literary theorists apply and expand speech act philosophy to literary theory (and to biblical interpretation).[45] Texts, according to the literary critic Charles Altieri, "are best viewed as actions performed on a variety of levels for our contemplation."[46] It is important to determine what is being *done* with texts. There is no reason why we cannot view such literary forms as tragedy, history, story, and even Gospel as species of "rule-governed behavior."[47] Grammar and grammatology alike are only part of the story of meaning and interpretation. Alongside questions of form must be placed questions of function. Texts are meaningful acts and acts of meaning.

The Searle/Derrida Exchange. Searle takes communication to be the primary purpose of language. Meaning is a matter of intending to convey a message to another person. A speaker intends to produce certain effects—notably, understanding—on a hearer. In light of these emphases, it should come as no surprise to learn that Searle is one of the most persistent critics of deconstruction. Indeed, his exchanges with Derrida (partly conducted on the pages of the *New York Review of Books*) are both celebrated and infamous.

Derrida's essay "Signature Event Context" sets out to undo Austin's notion of the performative utterance, a concept that Derrida regards as a classic example of philosophy's tendency to privilege speech (presence) over writing (absence).[48] Derrida admits that ambiguity can be reduced by determining the context of a speech act, but he doubts whether the conditions of a context are ever absolutely determinable. Can Austin's analysis survive without a rigorous and scientific concept of context? Derrida invokes his grammatological point that language is not so much intentional as it is *iterable* and that signs are repeatable in diverse situations: "A written sign carries with it a force that breaks with its context."[49] Language is precisely that which can be taken *out of context*, which also means, out of the control of its author. Speech acts are ultimately swallowed up by writing, in Derrida's sense of "an economy of difference nowhere coinciding with the present intentions of individual speech."[50] Cut off from its author, the speech act means *other* than what it meant in its original context.

In his response, Searle accuses Derrida of willfully and perversely ignoring the plain drift of Austin's intentions by focusing on minor points of textual detail.[51] In a subsequent eighty-two page rejoinder, Derrida remains unrepentant. In fact, during the course of his word play he manages to quote the whole of Searle's text, mainly out of context, in order to demonstrate that authors cannot control their texts and limit the ways that they can be interpreted.[52]

Searle may not think that deconstruction is serious philosophy, but he does think that Derrida is addressing a serious problem and making a serious mistake.[53] The problem is whether knowledge, meaning, and morality have any foundations. Derrida correctly sees that the various candidates—sense data, logic, consciousness—fail to provide foundations insofar as they are always already "contaminated" by language. He believes that speech act philosophy relies on a number of distinctions (e.g., ordinary vs. abnormal use of language) that are undermined by the iterability of the sign. Yet Derrida's mistake is to conclude that, because there are no certain foundations for determining the author's intention, there is neither knowledge nor meaning. In other words, Derrida asks us to choose between the alternative of absolute certainty and utter skepticism. Searle berates Derrida for repeatedly committing the black or white fallacy: "Unless a distinction can be made rigorous and precise, with no marginal cases, it is not a distinction at all."[54] We may not be able to "verify" that a speaker has a particular intention, but, says Searle, we may know it "in all sorts of ways."[55] Our knowledge of text acts may not be founded on metaphysical certainties, but that does not mean that it has no basis at all. Literary knowledge is grounded rather in a complex network of linguistic and social practices.[56]

Common Sense Hermeneutical Realism. Derrida realizes that deconstruction is inappropriate for the purposes of everyday discourse; usually the conventions of language work. Yet he objects to philosophers building a theory of meaning on these everyday conventions as if they belonged to a proper or *natural* order of truth. This is precisely his dispute with speech act philosophy. Austin looks at abnormal cases to throw light on the "normal." Derrida protests that this hierarchical opposition (e.g., between the normal and abnormal, the "serious" and "non-serious"), like every other, is arbitrary and ideological. Derrida objects that what philosophers enshrine as "normal" or "common sense" are simply arbitrary institutional decisions, evidences of the corporate will to power.[57] What appears "normal," in other words, is always a function of a given interpretive context. This is Derrida's sober contribution to the debate about knowledge. He reminds us of the non-naturalness of our philosophy, our politics, our ethics: "I say there is no stability that is absolute, eternal, intangible, natural, etc. But that is implied in the very concept of stability. A stability is not an immutability; it is by definition always destabilizable."[58]

For his part, Searle insists that Derrida has culpably neglected some rather basic distinctions. First, Derrida confuses linguistic "types" and linguistic "tokens." A sentence type refers to the *form* of a sentence, for example, to the words "he's hot." A sentence token refers to a particular instance of those words (i.e., to their utterance in a specific context). The sentence type ("he's hot") could be a response to a forehand cross court, to someone's temperature, or to someone's angry outburst. Derrida mistakenly believes that the sentence "he's hot" is undecidable in meaning because it can be repeated in diverse contexts (e.g., the tennis court, the hospital, or the family argument). Searle makes a point that is as subtle as it is important, namely, that what is repeated is the sentence type; the sentence token is resolutely particular, tied to the speaker's context. Searle comments: "The fact that someone might perform *another* speech act with a *different* token of the same type . . . has no bearing whatever on the role of the speaker's utterance meaning in the determination of the speech act."[59] In other words, my using the same words ("he's hot") on one occasion to mean something different from what my friend meant on another does not evacuate my speech act (or his) of determinate meaning.

Searle draws a second distinction that is even more vital for the question of hermeneutic realism: "It is crucial to distinguish questions of what exists (ontology) from questions of how we know what exists (epistemology)."[60] Often we cannot absolutely know what someone may have intended, but this has no relevance to the question of whether there was a definite meaning to the text. It is one thing to be in interpretive trouble because of lack of evidence about the author's intention. In this case we are in an epistemic quandary and can look for more evidence. On the other hand, if we are in interpretive trouble because we think there *is* no fact of the matter about what the author meant, then that is an ontological problem of indeterminacy, and no amount of evidence can save us. Searle comments: "The standard mistake is to suppose that a lack of evidence, that is, our ignorance, shows indeterminacy or undecidability in principle."[61] Derrida mistakenly tries to derive ontological conclusions from an epistemological problem.

For the record, the Searle-Derrida exchange resulted in something of a stalemate, with neither side giving the least bit ground. As Norris rightly observes, Derrida denies at the outset what Searle presupposes, "that language is properly adapted to communicate meaning."[62] Perhaps Searle, the most preeminent speech act philosopher of his day, ought to reflect about what exactly Derrida is doing with his language. The answer, of course, is that Derrida is *undoing*: undoing the "normal," common sense assumptions about meaning, morality, and truth.

H. P. Grice, another ordinary language philosopher, admits that he is occasionally tempted by the demons of reductionism, naturalism, and skepticism. He resists their siren call by exposing their "minimalism." Such positions ignore phenomena whose presence calls for explanation and limit the philosopher's resources by forbidding the use of certain categories (e.g., intention).[63] Deconstruction, by refusing to take the sentence and the speaker as irreducible starting points, betrays a materialist tendency to reduce mind to matter. Indeed, poststructuralist literary theory as a whole tends to define the semantic in terms of the non-semantic: it tries to explain sentences in terms of something more basic, namely, signs. Many important common sense notions (e.g., about the relation between speakers and their speech) perish in this vainglorious attempt. My thesis, we may recall, is that the author and the sentence are basic particulars. Without these fundamental concepts we will simply be unable to talk about certain other things, such as speech acts and meaning. We may call the poststructuralist reduction of sentences and speakers to elements in a differential sign system the "semiotic fallacy."[64] This reductionistic move yields only an impoverished account of language as a medium for covenantal communion. The concept of illocution, however, puts the focus of attention "on the production of meaning by the author," as Daniel Patte correctly observes.[65] As we will see, however, illocution need not imply a return to the traditional psychological model of the author's intention. Viewed in the light of speech act philosophy, the author returns as a communicative agent.

Language: A Convention Made in Heaven? Wittgenstein, Austin, and Searle respond to the postmodern masters of suspicion by showing how language ordinarily works and by claiming that language ordinarily works well enough.[66] Their focus on how language is used in specific contexts for particular purposes allows these philosophers to anchor meaning elsewhere than in consciousness. To be exact, language and world come together not in the subject's mind but in inter-subjective interactions. Consider the phenomenon of marriage. For Searle, one marries by sincerely performing the speech act "I do" in the appropriate circumstances. In Western cultures, these circumstances involve two partners, of different sex, making public vows of lifetime fidelity. This is the rule or "institutional fact" that makes the speech act count as "marrying." To understand the speech act, one needs to look at the language, the social conventions, and the intentions of the speakers.

What if Derrida were to argue that this apparently "normal" custom is in fact a non-natural practice funded by a patriarchal ideology? Is marrying (or promising) *only* an arbitrary social convention? Might it not be that the institutional fact of marrying corresponds to something even more fundamental, to a *divine* convention perhaps, that is, to a structure of creation? Might this not be one way that, to use Steiner's phrase, God *underwrites* language? Our word may be our bond, but given deconstruction, does this bond not ultimately need to be forged by more than social convention? Deconstruction may be the death of God written into language, and Searle may ultimately be no better off in substituting society for God. Without a properly theological moment, it may be that even speech act philosophy cannot restore trust in language and authority to the author. Nevertheless, the ordinary language philosophers have been in the vanguard of those who oppose the deconstructor's attempt to undo the conditions of communication. Thanks to speech act philosophy, the author has begun to recover his or her voice.

Paul Ricoeur: Language As Discourse

Do the principles of ordinary language apply to literary texts? To help us see that they do, I turn now to my second philosophical resource: the interpretation theory of Paul Ricoeur. Despite Ricoeur's apparent dismissal of the author's intention as a ground and goal of interpretation, I believe there are important, often overlooked, clues in Ricoeur's work that indicate the author is very much alive.[67]

The Text As Written Discourse

We have already seen that Ricoeur refuses to reduce semantics to semiotics. To focus on sentences—on language used in specific contexts—is to focus on language as "discourse": *something said to someone about something*. The text is not a linguistic phenomenon only—a worldless and authorless object that could be explained purely in terms of its structural relations. This is an incomplete, reductionistic picture, for it eclipses discourse proper. When language constitutes a world of its own, it no longer appears as a mediation between mind and the world. It is noteworthy that Ricoeur defines the text as "any discourse fixed by writing."[68] Texts are able to communicate at a distance because writing preserves discourse. Writing, in other words, does not alienate authors from readers but makes shared meaning possible. Indeed, it is humanity's chief resource for overcoming spatial, temporal, and cultural distance.

Derrida and Ricoeur thus represent two contrasting poststructuralist options, two different ways of reacting to the structuralist view of language as a self-enclosed system of signs.[69] Ricoeur's interpretation theory has been called "the most effective hermeneutic counterpoint to deconstruction within post-structural criticism."[70] The basic issue between the two thinkers is the meaning of meaning.[71] Derrida sees language as a self-referential system without a center or stable structure. Ricoeur sees language as a structure that exists not for its own sake but for referring beyond itself to the world. *Discourse has a sense (something said), a reference (about something), and a destination (to someone).*

For Derrida, an author is not the cause of a text but its effect—a by-product of writing. Ricoeur, on the other hand, affirms speech act philosophy's emphasis on language as a communicative social practice. On the one hand, Ricoeur detaches meaning from authors. The written text is autonomous of its author; it sets out on a career of its own. On the other hand, he affirms the text as discourse. These two moves may, in the end, prove contradictory; nevertheless, my concern here is to develop Ricoeur's thesis that the text is a piece of discourse. As discourse, the text offers something to be appropriated by the reader. This is Ricoeur's "wager," his "second Copernican revolution": the idea that the self is not the source but the recipient of a meaning that comes from "beyond." Hermeneutics is not merely a matter of knowing things about texts, but of being affected by them. Indeed, it would be fair to say that Ricoeur's whole philosophy is an investigation into how language can exert a transforming effect on readers. Texts, insofar as they can move us, have a force—semantic rather than physical—of their own.[72]

Event and Meaning. Discourse for Ricoeur is a two-dimensional phenomenon. It partakes both of *langue* (the static system of language) and *parole* (the active use of language). It is both event (the "saying") and meaning (the "said"), though in writing the event aspect of discourse disappears. According to Ricoeur, the text fixes the meaning, not the event, of discourse. Furthermore, Ricoeur places the author's intention on the event side of discourse. The event is fleeting and cannot be recovered. Similarly, the intention—that is, the mental event in the author's consciousness—also disappears. Ricoeur thus prizes "meaning," the sense that the signs bear, apart from the author's intention, understood as a psychological event. What is written or "fixed" by writing is the meaning of the event, not the event of meaning: "The text's career escapes the finite horizon lived by its author. What the text means now matters more than what the author meant when he wrote it."[73] What is communicated is not the lived experience of the author but its sense. Discourse can be identified again and again and be shared because it preserves an identity of its own: the "said as such."[74]

Work and World. "Hermeneutics . . . remains the art of discerning the discourse in the work."[75] Ricoeur represents a mediating position between the traditional position that focuses on the author's intent and Derrida's undoing of it. There is a meaning in the text, but it is dissociated from the author. Because it is fixed in writing, discourse is both decontextualized from its original situation and depsychologized from its original author. Ricoeur develops the concept of discourse by means of a second pair of concepts: *work* and *world*. (1) As discourse, a text is a structured *work*, something that is crafted and produced. A text is a structured work of language that can be methodically examined and explained. The text, considered as work, has a principle of organization (form, genre) and a principle of individuality (style). Ricoeur acknowledges that the concept of the author reappears as the correlate of the individuality of the text. Indeed, the author returns as "the artisan of a work of language," though Ricoeur fails to build on this insight.[76]

(2) Discourse is always *about something*. Ricoeur calls that to which discourse refers the "*world* of the text." On the one hand, language is not self-referring. Yet what is understood is not the life or soul of the author either, but rather a world *of the text*. Whereas the text as work must be analyzed and explained, the world of the text must be understood or appropriated. What exactly does an interpreter appropriate? Not the intention of the author, not even the historical situation of the author and his or her original readers, but the meaning of the text itself, "conceived in a dynamic way as the direction of thought opened up by the text."[77] Interpretation uncovers not the mind of an author, but a perspective, a "way of looking at things," a proposed world.[78] In short, what a reader grasps is a possible way of being that is not merely a self-expression of the author. In this regard, Ricoeur speaks of the "narrative voice," the voice that commends the world of the text to the reader. Though cut off from its author, the text still has an "intention": the projected world that it proposes for our consideration and response.[79] The question remains whether we can discover this world without recourse to the notion of the author.

Ricoeur's analysis of discourse tacitly appeals to the author throughout: as originator of the event, as artisan of the work, as proposer of its world. His definition of
discourse, therefore, ought to be expanded in order to make these implicit appeals
more explicit. Discourse, I submit, is "something said *by someone* to someone about
something." After all, things do not get said on their own.

The Text as Meaningful Action

What Ricoeur rejects as the object of interpretation is the author's intention construed as a psychological event. Yet he admits that written discourse implies an
author: "It is impossible to cancel out this main characteristic of discourse without
reducing texts to natural objects, i.e., to things which are not man-made, but which,
like pebbles, are found in the sand."[80] To consider the text as an authorless entity is
to commit what Ricoeur himself calls the "fallacy of the absolute text."[81] Ricoeur goes
to some pains, however, to explain in just what way the author is of continuing relevance for interpretation. What he wants to say, I believe, is that authorial intention
becomes a dimension of the text, just as an artisan carves, paints, or otherwise projects oneself into one's handiwork. What Ricoeur actually does instead is to refer to
the "intention" *of the text*. Strictly speaking, however, texts do not have intentions,
nor do they act. We do not ascribe agency to texts, nor do we praise or blame books;
we rather direct our praise or blame to their authors. For only persons say something
to someone about something.

Interestingly, Ricoeur extends his theory of text interpretation into the human
sciences, most notably in an essay entitled "The Model of the Text: Meaningful Action
Considered As a Text."[82] He here compares discourse to other forms of human action.
Just as discourse can be fixed by writing, so action can similarly be objectified. With
Max Weber, Ricoeur defines the object of the social sciences as "meaningfully oriented behavior."[83] Action, like discourse, has a meaning aspect as well as an event
aspect. Intriguingly, Ricoeur explores the meaning aspect of action with distinctions
borrowed from speech act philosophy. (1) Action has the structure of a locutionary
act: it has a propositional content (e.g., s performs act y on the ball). (2) Action also
has illocutionary traits (e.g., in kicking the ball, s scores a goal). Like a speech act,
then, an action may be identified according to its illocutionary force (what x does in
y-ing). Finally, actions, like perlocutions, bring about certain results (e.g., winning
the game). Humans do things that leave "traces," which together make up a kind of
"document" of human action that can be "read" and reidentified.

Ricoeur explores the analogy between texts and actions at great length. Both texts
and actions, he argues, are plurivocal, capable of having many meanings. However,
as many philosophers of action have shown, we only know "what" has been done
when we know "why" it was done. In other words, we only understand what someone has done when we have some sense of what they thought they were doing and
their reasons for doing it. But is this not to invoke the agent's intention? Moreover, if
Ricoeur can consider meaningful action as a text, why cannot he consider a text as
meaningful action? The "something said" of discourse is also a "something done"; we
only know what has been said when we know what the author thought he or she
was saying and why. If the text is a meaningful action, and if the meaning of an action

depends on the intention of its agent, it follows that the meaning of the text as act depends on its author's intention. We can therefore have as much confidence in determining what an author is *doing* in a discourse as we can when we seek to determine what a person is doing in other kinds of action.[84] The author is as much an agent of meaning as the agent is an author of action.

Jürgen Habermas: Language As Communicative Action

Jürgen Habermas, a social theorist, offers a third philosophical resource for reconceiving language in terms of a covenant of discourse. Habermas accepts Derrida's critique of subject-centered meaning and of subject-centered reason, but not his nihilistic conclusions. Habermas offers a new paradigm for understanding that relies not on the subject-object dichotomy, as in Descartes and much modern philosophy, but on the structures of inter-subjectivity that are implicit in communication.[85] In so doing, he builds on speech act theory and develops an entire theory of rationality on what is necessarily implied by everyday communication.[86] Contra Derrida, language does not contaminate rationality but, in a way that remains to be seen, *contains* it.

It is the philosopher's task, Habermas believes, to reconstruct the norms implicit in discourse. He begins with an account of communicative competence. By competence he means a kind of implicit, intuitive knowledge that undergirds all successful communication.[87] Communicative competence involves far more than grammatical correctness. Competence pertains as much to *parole* as to *langue*, to the use of language, or to what Habermas terms "universal pragmatics": the general and unavoidable presuppositions of linguistic understanding.[88] What he has in mind is a kind of transcendental language game, with universal rules, that *all* competent speakers invariably play, regardless of what they are discussing. Specifically, every competent speech act must meet three "validity conditions":

1. It must be true (e.g., it must represent something in the external, objective world).
2. It must be truthful (e.g., it must sincerely express the inner, subjective world of the speaker's intentions).
3. It must be right (e.g., it must fit appropriately into the context of the social world).

For any speech act, "we understand its meaning when we know the conditions under which it can be accepted as valid."[89] Habermas extends the concept of validity beyond the truth of propositions to include the performative aspect of speech acts. In other words, there are standards not only for right reference but also for right use. Habermas thus enjoins interpreters not to separate speech acts from the context of their utterance or from their speakers. It is the expectation of communicative agents that they can, if challenged, defend the validity claims they implicitly make. In making a speech act, a speaker implies that he or she is willing to defend, if need be, the validity conditions it presupposes. A competent speaker, therefore, is able to "triangulate" the objective, subjective, and inter-subjective worlds: not only to form grammatically correct sentences, but also to relate the content of what one say to one's context in an appropriate fashion. Even stating the obvious obliges the speaker to consent to the requirement of rationality implicit in all communication. Far from disappearing from his discourse, then, every speaker on this view is responsible for justifying what is said.

Whereas for modern philosophers language is a means for representing the world, for Habermas language is primarily a means for coordinating human action: "Language is a medium of communication that serves understanding."[90] Meaning, one might say, is no longer an affair of consciousness, but of community. A sentence means "what the members of that linguistic community would intend it to mean were they to utter it."[91] Habermas thus treats language under the heading of social theory (as a medium for coordinating action) rather than epistemology (as a means for representing things in the mind).[92] So, while Habermas agrees with Derrida that the subject is no longer a sovereign consciousness, he does not dismiss the subject but reinstates it as a "commoner," that is, as a participant in communicative action.[93] This goes for authors and readers as well; all communicants must respect the norms inherent in language use.[94]

THE "WHAT" OF MEANING: TEXTS AS COMMUNICATIVE ACTS

The implications of the philosophical rehabilitation of speech (discourse) for a theory of interpretation are, I believe, immense. The rest of this chapter ties the three philosophical strands just reviewed together and argues that meaning is a matter of communicative action: both the "doing" and the resultant "deed." To be precise, meaning is a three-dimensional communicative action, with form and matter (propositional content), energy and trajectory (illocutionary force), and teleology or final purpose (perlocutionary effect). This "action" model of meaning provides the best account both of the possibility of stable meaning and of the transformative capacity of texts. It also entails a view of interpretation that gives primacy to the author as communicative agent. To inquire into what the text means is to ask what the author has done in, with, and through the text. *The goal of understanding is to grasp what has been done, together with its effects; the possibility of attaining such understanding is the presupposition of communicative action.*

This definition of meaning in terms of communicative action is well suited to the concerns of hermeneutic realism. Why is there something rather than nothing in texts? Because someone has said something about something to someone. Not just *anything*, but *something*. While elements in a language system are indefinite and unstable, words put to use in a specific time and place acquire specificity. Meaning is "there," inscribed in the text, prior to and independent of reading or interpretation, in much the same way that human actions are what they are prior to the investigative and interpretive work of the historian. To deny this would be to deny the reality of the past. The past, however, is real. Furthermore, what has been done, whether through corporeal or communicative action, is inseparable from the agent (or author) and his or her intention. The interpreter only recognizes the action for what it is. If meaning were a function of how readers respond to texts, then texts could never be misunderstood, and there would never be such a thing as false interpretation. It follows from hermeneutical realism, however, that it is possible to misinterpret. To impute a meaning to a text that an author could not have intended is to be guilty of the same lack of respect for the reality of the past that characterizes revisionist history. To read our ideas back into the biblical text may be the hermeneutical equivalent of denying that the Holocaust ever happened.

To inquire after textual meaning is essentially to inquire after what has been done by authors, together with the resultant effects. Understanding the nature and content of communicative acts (e.g., sermons, speeches, poems, novels) is the goal of interpretation. We may, of course, ask other questions about texts (e.g., "What do Shakespeare's plays teach us about the state of the English language in the Elizabethan era?"), but not all of these will be properly *interpretive* questions, as I am using the term. To the extent that our questions do concern interpretation, however, they will concern some aspect of the text as communicative action. *The basic unit of literary interpretation is thus the text considered as a complex communicative act.*

The Metaphysics of Human Action: The Writing on the World

There is a fourth dimension to the speech act: the interlocutionary. Language is the means of "social interaction through messages."[95] This last feature highlights the essential nature of the covenant of discourse, namely, that it is a means of personal communication and communion. Communicative interaction is quite different from causal interactions. Humans do not relate to one another solely in terms of necessity (i.e., cause and effect), but also in terms of freedom (i.e., action and reaction). How we use language makes a difference in the world ("the pen is mightier than the sword"): "To act, in its most general sense, means to take an initiative, to begin . . . to set something in motion (which is the original meaning of the Latin *agere*)."[96] Personhood is in large part a function of our dignity as communicative agents. From the viewpoint of Christian theology, persons are wholly determined neither by language (socio-linguistics) nor by genes (socio-biology). On the contrary, human persons are covenantal agents, whose stories, like that of Israel, depend in large measure on how they use their communicative freedom and assume their communicative responsibilities.[97]

"Action" can refer either to the doing or to the deed, either to the "energy" or to the "form and matter" of what one does. Moreover, something of the action remains even after the event of its doing is over—its "trace" and, possibly, its effect. These conceptual distinctions may help to show in what respect the author is an agent and in what respect the author is related to the text. Perhaps the most important of these distinctions, however, is that between "action" and "event."

Discourse: Action or Event?

Wilhelm Dilthey's (1833–1911) fateful distinction between the natural and the human sciences prepared the way for what we might call the "second coming" of hermeneutics.[98] The natural sciences aim to explain what happens in the natural world by formulating universal causal laws (e.g., laws of gravity, of motion, of the conservation of energy, etc.). The human sciences, on the other hand, aim at understanding human behavior. Dilthey argues that what we seek to grasp in the human order is not matter in motion but "mind," "spirit," or "lived experience." The movement of the human spirit—freedom—cannot be studied, he believed, with the tools of the natural sciences, for these ignore the volitional and intentional aspects of personal experience, thus reducing knowledge to the edicts of calculative reason. What the human sciences need, Dilthey claimed, was hermeneutical reason—a method for grasping what is distinct about human experience. History is the great "document" that expresses human life and thought, and hermeneutics is concerned with grasping the meaning of past human action. For Dilthey, this meant understanding the whole (of a life, of a text) in light of its parts, and vice versa.[99] Dilthey thinks, however, that the aim of understanding is to think oneself back into the mind of an author, to reproduce the author's psychology and so relive the author's experience. But this is to search for some meaning behind the discourse. It is to focus on human subjectivity rather than human action.

Dilthey is right to treat human action as qualitatively different from natural events, but he errs in orienting the human sciences towards subjective consciousness rather than inter-subjective communication. An overemphasis on subjectivity ultimately leads, as we have seen, to Derrida's attempt to deconstruct it. The hermeneutical focus must rather be on language as speech act. Speech acts are more than natural phenomena, more than a mere whiffling noise emitted through our windpipes, more than what can be explained by physics. Action does not "happen"; it is "done." We normally do not speak of what we do in terms of scientific causes and universal laws but in terms of reasons, desires, purposes, and motives. To the question, "What kind of action?" we respond with statements about the agent's intentions. To the question "Why did he or she do that?" we respond with statements about the agent's motives. Simply put: we explain and understand human actions with categories that are alien to the natural sciences. No scientist worries overmuch about the motives of billiard balls or the intentions of electrons when studying their movements. We approach the movements of human beings, however, with a wholly different set of questions. *For the human sciences have as their object meaningful human action.* Ironically, much contemporary literary theory studies texts with little reference to the agents who produced them. As I have argued, that is not merely an interpretive failure but an ethical one; much postmodern theory eclipses the very concept of the human person as a free and responsible agent. For if language speaks man, then the author is a mere link in a chain of semiotic causality, not an agent who can put the language system to work in new ways.

What happens in nature is a "process" that we explain by relating causes and effects by means of scientific laws. What happens in the human realm, by contrast, is a "project" that we understand by ascribing intentions to agents by means of historical deliberation. The mistake of much poststructural literary theory is to study texts as though they can be explained, not through a natural but through a kind of cultural necessity, namely, through ideological codes that are thought to govern all human thinking, language, thought, and behavior. As I have already argued, this is to reduce the sentence (and the self) to the level of the sign (and the system). The fundamental problem with such "semiotic materialism" is that it cannot account for communicative action or for humans as agents of covenantal discourse.

An agent has a kind of causality, a power to do, that is original and irreducible. To act means to take an initiative, to begin, to set something in motion; an action is an actualization of power.[100] To say "the devil (or my upbringing, or my genetic makeup, etc.) made me do it" is to say that one's choices have been caused by something outside oneself. Such a confession is nothing less than an abdication of agency, freedom, and responsibility. As we have seen, some postmodern thinkers believe that agency is indeed only an appearance, not a reality. While it would nevertheless be a gross exaggeration to say that Christians alone believe in freedom and responsibility, it is nevertheless the case that secular theories often struggle to give a convincing account of these essential human characteristics—hence the contemporary crisis in the humanities. My response to this crisis is to return to Christian doctrine and to think through, with the aid of certain philosophers, the question of meaning afresh.

Interpreting Action

Ricoeur, as we have seen, suggests that meaningful action is like a text. Conversely, meaningful action resembles the speech act.

(1) *The "doing" of an action corresponds to locution.* As the "said" of speaking is fixed by writing, so action is "fixed" by doing. The doing of an action leaves its "mark" on the world, in the past.

(2) *Actions have objects or "propositional contents."* In action, something is done to something by someone. If I open the door, for example, the door is the propositional content of my action. The content of my action (the door) may be shared with and identified by others; it is thus objective. People years later may visit the same door, commemorate my action, and perhaps open the door themselves.

(3) *Actions have a particular force.* In acting, the agent takes up a particular stance towards the object of his or her action. In my example, the agent takes up the stance toward the door of one who intends to open it (as opposed to slamming it shut, knocking on it, or painting it). What I *do* in taking up a particular stance toward the door thus corresponds to the action's illocutionary force.

(4) *Actions often have effects, both planned and unexpected.* In opening the door I may have surprised a mouse (my plan). This aspect of the action corresponds to the perlocutionary force of an utterance: to what I do *by* saying something. Not all effects are under an agent's control: by opening the door, for example, I may surprise a burglar and perhaps foil a crime.

Actions are thus like texts because they have a fixed propositional content, an illocutionary force, and a relevance that goes beyond what the agent could have foreseen. My point in drawing out this connection is, however, the opposite of Ricoeur's. Whereas he invokes the comparison to show that human action needs to be interpreted, I argue that understanding texts is ultimately a matter of interpreting human action. My point is twofold: (1) If we can interpret actions, then we can interpret texts; (2) we can only interpret actions in light of their agents.

The analogy between texts and actions is, of course, no interpretive panacea. There are difficulties in understanding actions too, but these do not normally prevent us from understanding what other people are doing. Working out what other people are doing is a large part of life, just as life itself is an ongoing negotiation between our actions and the actions of others. While there are certainly mystifying episodes (e.g., inexplicable behavior), we are usually able to figure out what people around us are doing. Four problems in the philosophy of action, however, complicate my proposal.

(1) When does an action begin and end? How *long* is an action?[101] These are important questions because actions take place in time and have the structure of a sequence. It is not enough to reply, thinking of texts, "They end on the last page." How then are we to tell the difference between an action and its results? Are the results "part" of an action? Would they be part of an action even if they were accidental? For instance, is it correct to say that the Bible "perpetuates patriarchy"? Is this part of what the Bible does—an unintentional effect—or is it a misconstrual of what the Bible is saying/doing?

(2) How are we to distinguish a unified action from its constituent parts? That is, what transforms an episodic sequence into a whole and complete action (e.g., how does moving one's arm up and down become incorporated into the whole and complete act of painting the house)?

(3) Where does the agent end and the action begin? To what extent should an agent be identified with his or her actions and their effects? Can we even discuss what counts as an action (the what) apart from the question of the agent (the who)? When, if at all, can a text be said to set out on a career of its own?

(4) In light of the above questions, how are we to describe or interpret actions? Is interpreting action merely a matter of describing bodily movements? Does interpreting an action also require describing the context of an action? Or should we seek to describe action with reference to the agent's intention as well? In what follows I will pursue this latter option. However, I transfer the concept of intention from its home in subjective consciousness to a new home in inter-subjective communicative action. The result of this move will be that interpreters gain knowledge of authorial intention not through intuition, as in the Romanticist conception of Dilthey and Schleiermacher, but rather through inference. *Intention is still the ground, goal, and guide of textual interpretation, but it is now an affair not of consciousness, but of communicative action.* I turn now to consider the notion of communicative action and to a redefinition of both text and author.

Communicative Action

Communication studies is now a well-established academic discipline in its own right. There are two main approaches.[102] The first sees communication as the transmission of messages. This approach stresses language as *parole* and focuses on acts of communication. Language here is the means of transmitting messages through space and time to others. Textual meaning is the "message in the bottle." The second sees communication as the textual and cultural production of meaning through sign systems. This model stresses language as *langue* and focuses on systems of communication—call it the "medium is the message" approach.

Where does meaning come from—personal action or impersonal sign systems? The first model understands meaning in terms of what message the sender intends to transmit. The second model understands meaning in terms of how the addressee decodes the sign system. At first glance, it might appear that my emphasis on communicative action predisposes me to favor the first model. In fact, I try to combine both models insofar as I view communication as the action that puts a language system into motion at a particular point in time by realizing certain possibilities offered by the code.[103]

Not all actions communicate, nor do all actions involve the transmission of messages. Some actions aim not to communicate but to manipulate. Reaching for the doorknob and turning it, for example, is not a communicative action but what Habermas calls a "strategic" action. Success here is measured in terms of an agent's ability to bring about a result in the world, to realize one's strategic aim. Communicative action, on the other hand, is action aimed at bringing about understanding. Specifically, communicative action aims at understanding in regard to some practical situation in order that speaker and hearer may freely coordinate their actions. Habermas believes this distinction between two kinds of action is essential for healthy social interaction, and this for two reasons. First, agreements reached through understanding are rational in a way that coerced agreements are not. Second, social justice is largely a matter of free, unimpeded communicative action. Rationality and justice alike demand that speakers use language not to distort but rather to enable the process of reaching understanding.

Habermas's theory of communicative action both aids and challenges my action model of meaning. His analysis of the norms implicit in all communication helpfully rounds out my account of the design plan of language. Yet his concern for rational conversation ultimately leads him to espouse an overly narrow view of understanding. His dichotomy between action oriented to "success" and action oriented to "reaching understanding" gives rise to a troubling question: When authors deploy rhetoric to achieve their aims (e.g., persuasion), is their action strategic or communicative? Do good authors aim to manipulate their readers or to produce understanding? This is no idle academic query, for Habermas knows that language is a form of power that can be used either to educate (when speakers reach for rational consensus) or to indoctrinate (when speakers use language as an ideological instrument).

According to Erich Auerbach, the Bible's claim to truth is "tyrannical": "The world of the Scripture stories is not satisfied with claiming to be a historically true reality— it insists that it is the only real world, is destined for autocracy. . . . The Scripture stories . . . seek to subject us."[104] If Auerbach's assessment is right, must we say that biblical literature resembles strategic rather than communicative action? To say yes would be to admit that the postmodern masters of suspicion are right. The interpersonal relation between author and reader would be neither rational nor oriented to understanding, but rather oriented to manipulation.

Habermas generally has a low estimate of strategic speech acts. Certain kinds of discourse (advertisements, logical fallacies, lies) treat persons as objects to be manipulated rather than as persons worthy of respect. Habermas insists, along with much of the Western philosophical tradition, that rhetoric is parasitic on logic—the dark side of discourse. He argues that the more original and proper use of language is that which is oriented to reaching understanding, where speakers and hearers acknowledge their implicit obligation to justify what they say.[105] Habermas's overriding concern for rationality leads him to define genuine communicative action in terms of a single effect: producing understanding, in the sense of a rationally agreed consensus. To elicit any other response would make one's speech act strategic rather than communicative.

Habermas reformulates Austin's distinction and says that illocutionary acts are communicative while perlocutionary acts are essentially strategic. It will be worth our while to examine this distinction in more detail. An illocutionary act aims solely at being understood for what it is: "By means of an illocutionary act a speaker lets a hearer know that he wants what he says to be understood as a greeting, command, warning, explanation, and so forth. His communicative intent does not go beyond wanting the hearer to understand the manifest content of the speech act."[106] By contrast, the perlocutionary aim tries to achieve *some other result besides understanding*. For instance, by saying "Hello" I may not only be giving a greeting but hoping for a dinner invitation. Habermas believes that it is possible to achieve one's illocutionary aim without producing a perlocutionary effect. One can *understand* my speech act as a greeting without having to return it (or without having to invite me to dinner). Habermas deduces that perlocutionary effects are *external* to the meaning of what is said: "The perlocutionary aim of a speaker, like the ends pursued with goal-directed actions generally, does not follow from the manifest content of the speech act; this aim can be identified only through the agent's intention."[107]

It is, of course, possible that illocutions can be used as the means to a perlocutionary end. Indeed, some authors openly acknowledge their perlocutionary aim: "These are written that you may believe that Jesus is the Christ" (John 20:31). What the Fourth Gospel does *in* its written discourse (the illocutionary act of narrating a story) is intended to achieve, besides understanding, an additional perlocutionary effect (persuading). When this happens, however, the actions are no longer communicative, in Habermas's strict sense, but strategic—oriented not to understanding but to success (e.g., bringing the reader to life in Christ). In sum, Habermas appears to be claiming that illocutions alone belong to the design plan of language: "The description of perlocutionary effects must therefore refer to a context of teleological action that *goes beyond* the speech act."[108]

Habermas's view results, I believe, in an overly narrow view of communicative action. Moreover, it is based on a confusion, for *the distinction between the illocutionary and the perlocutionary is not a distinction between communicative and strategic action.* It is a misconstrual of human communication to say that the point of language is solely to manifest one's illocutionary point. On the contrary, many illocutionary acts are designed to bring about effects beyond understanding. Indeed, Habermas himself is aware that illocutions can often be "strategic." He cites the following example: "*H* warned *S* not to give notice to his firm."[109] Given his exposition of communicative action in terms of illocution, one would expect Habermas to define illocutionary success in terms of *S* understanding *H* to have issued a warning. But do speakers really issue warnings in order to produce the understanding in their hearers that they have issued a warning? Of course not. In fact, Habermas gives a more liberal interpretation of illocutionary success: "If, for instance, *S* does not give notice, this is not a perlocutionarily achieved effect but the consequences of a communicatively achieved agreement."[110] Here, I think, Habermas departs from Austin's and Searle's analysis and confuses what is clearly perlocutionary success with illocutionary success because of his prior commitment to the distinction between communicative and strategic action. The fact of the matter is that speakers, and authors as well, are both perlocutionary and illocutionary agents. Interpreting texts is thus a matter of understanding purposive action—communicative *and* strategic.[111] When I speak of communicative action in relation to texts, therefore, I am referring to the full-fledged, four-dimensional reality described by speech act theory and not only to the illocutionary dimension, as is Habermas's practice.[112]

The Nature of the Text: Begotten or Made?

> The work of art, then, appears as an object of knowledge sui generis which has a special ontological status. It is neither real (like a statue) nor mental (like the experience of light or pain) nor ideal (like a triangle).[113]

"The most radical question of all in hermeneutics," writes Thiselton, "concerns the nature of texts."[114] In light of the preceding section, I now wish to define the text as *a communicative act of a communicative agent fixed by writing*. It may be helpful to recall that my goal in this chapter is to provide a stable ground for textual meaning. My proposal is that the proper ground for textual meaning is found in the communicative activity, not the subjectivity, of the author. Communicative action has two important features that give it a tremendous advantage over Hirsch's view that meaning is an affair of consciousness. First, one's communicative action, unlike one's consciousness, is publicly accessible. Second, past communicative action, like other acts done in the past, are fixed not only in writing but in history. It follows from my action model that the text, like other past human actions, has determinate meaning and that it is what it is independently of our theories about and interpretations of it. It also follows that, just as we can falsely ascribe an action to an agent, so it is possible to misinterpret a text.

The analogy between actions and texts prompts some difficult questions. What, for instance, is the nature of the connection between author and text? Let me propose another analogy in order to clarify the nature of human authorship. The church fathers, in the context of expressing the Son's relation to the Father, used the distinction between "begetting" and "making" to speak of that which is essentially "like" and "unlike" us respectively.[115] That which we beget is like us and deserves the respect that befits persons. That which we make, being unlike us, is not deserving of the same respect. Can we apply this distinction to the relation between authors and texts? Are communicative acts essentially "like" or "unlike" their agents? Are texts begotten or made?

Earlier I asked where the agent leaves off and action begins. To what extent is my action, my discourse, or my text the "same" as me? To some extent, this is a question of "identity." Ricoeur helpfully distinguishes two kinds of "identity." The first is the sameness of substance, the sameness that comes from sharing the same properties, the sameness that derives from begetting.[116] This kind of sameness clearly does not characterize the relation between authors and texts, for the simple reason that texts are not human, nor are they authors. Yet neither are texts wholly foreign to their authors: a work of art is not simply a physical or a mental phenomenon, but partakes of both. The ontology of works of art—literature, music, paintings—eludes the alternative "begotten or made." The work of art is neither the same as nor wholly different from its creator. Let us rather view the work of art as something *done*—neither *me* nor *made* by me, but rather *done* by me.

The nature of the work of art better corresponds, in my opinion, to Ricoeur's second sense of identity: self-constancy. Selfhood pertains not to the sameness of substance but to the continuity of persons over time. Ricoeur believes that personal identity—selfhood, not sameness—pertains to the pattern of the relationship between one's deeds and one's words. This second kind of identity helps to explain the connection between an agent and her act, an artist and his work of art, an author and her text. There is a continuity between an artist and the work of art, so much so that we can say "It's a Picasso" when clearly "it" is not a person but a painting. We say "It's a Picasso" because we perceive some continuity with other things Picasso has done. It is *his* work.[117] Of course, not everything the artist does is a work of art or a communicative act. Van Gogh no doubt walked extensively in Provence, but wearing out shoes is not a communicative act, though his painting a pair of peasant shoes was. We might identify Van Gogh with both pairs of shoes, but only the painted pair communicates something. What, then, is the difference between the two pairs of shoes? Just this: the painting of the peasant shoes is associated with Van Gogh's *thought*.[118]

Richard Wollheim, an art critic, locates painting "firmly within the domain of the theory of action" and argues that what constitutes the work of art as a communicative action is the thought that guides it, the thought that "both causes it and forms it character."[119] As I will argue below, one cannot even describe action without reference to the agent's intention. The artist makes raw materials meaningful by doing something with them—embodying thought. The Milton quote at the beginning of Part 2 suggests that books are created in the image of their reasonable creators just as rational creatures are in the image of God. Even those who, like Derrida, do not believe in authors, stand in continuity with their own communicative action. Derrida's *Glas* is a clever juxtaposition of texts by Hegel and Genet interspersed with Derrida's own playful reflections on copyright laws and on the place of proper names in writing. One commentator was sufficiently intimidated as to pass over the work since it "defeats the best efforts of descriptive analysis or summary."[120] However, A. D. Nuttall, a Shakespeare scholar, comments that "it is difficult to think of any way in which Derrida could have stamped his personality more firmly on a book than by such an idiosyncratic and wholly artificial withdrawal of authorial presence. Every page [of *Glas*] is clamorously eloquent of its author's identity."[121] Derrida ultimately cannot break the covenant of discourse; even deconstructive texts are communicative acts that image the identity of their communicative agents.

Text Acts

"Meaning," I have argued, can refer both to the doing (action) and to the deed done (act). If a project is "something to be done," then we may say that a text is a completed communicative project. Better said, a text is a complex communicative act done in the past that may nevertheless produce present effects. The text is both a completed communicative project and a projectile that has the potential to enter into and make a difference in the life-world of its readers.

May we stretch Searle's formula for speech acts—$M = F(p)$—so that it may apply to texts as well? Or is the formula for the meaning of text acts more complicated? Just a few years after the publication of Searle's *Speech Acts*, the literary critic Richard Ohmann appealed to illocutions in order to solve a notorious problem: how to define literature. Most attempts to define literature usually concentrate on form (locution) or effect (perlocution). Ohmann distinguishes literature from ordinary discourse, however, by suggesting that literary works only *pretend* to make illocutionary acts: "*A literary work is a discourse abstracted, or detached, from the circumstances and conditions which make illocutionary acts possible; hence it is a discourse without illocutionary force.*"[122] The alleged absence of a genuine illocutionary dimension to texts, however, challenges my claim that texts, like speech acts, are means of social interaction and thus part of the covenant of discourse. For Ohmann, literary texts do not really assert, warn, exhort, and so forth. Such a view fails, in my opinion, to do justice to the power of texts to affect and move us. On Ohmann's view, a text is an "act" only in the theatrical sense of the term, and the author is an actor, not an agent.

According to Mary Louise Pratt, however, the author of a literary work is not merely mimicking but making a real illocutionary act: not the act of asserting but rather the act of *displaying* a state of affairs. Pratt's point is that authors, in stories, are really doing something: "verbally *displaying* a state of affairs, inviting his addressee(s) to join him in contemplating it, evaluating it, and responding to it."[123] Stories, then, can have genuine illocutionary force; in what we could term the "narrative act," the author projects a world towards the reader. In narrative, (*p*) is best viewed not as propositional content but as the plot.

Susan Lanser finds speech act theory particularly helpful in studying point of view, that is, the author's perspective on the world displayed in the text: "In speech act theory I found a philosophical basis for understanding literature as communicative act and text as message-in-context, as well as exciting new tools for analyzing discourse."[124] It is one thing to display a world, quite another to take up some normative stance towards it (e.g., praising, commending, condemning, mocking, etc.). The author's stance, over and above the illocutionary force of the story itself (e.g., displaying), also communicates something to the reader: "Speech acts on the level of narration then become the equivalent of the character's actions on the level of *histoire* [story]."[125] Texts, in other words, not only display a world but communicate a way of viewing it: "*Much like the biblical parable, the novel's basic illocutionary activity is ideological instruction; its basic plea: hear my word, believe and understand.*"[126] Literary texts aim not simply to impart information, therefore, but to provide what Lanser calls "cultural communication": training in ways of being human. Readers can, of course, reject an author's point of view, but to mistake or ignore it is a signal failure in communication and understanding.

I agree with Charles Altieri that literary texts "are best viewed as actions performed on a variety of levels for our contemplation."[127] Speech act philosophy enables us to attend to at least three of these levels with a fair degree of precision. The distinction between locutionary, illocutionary, and perlocutionary acts creates a firm basis on which to pursue both poetics (the study of the various forms of text acts) and rhetoric (the study of the functions of text acts). Lanser comes close to offering a description of the various levels of "text acts": "Propositional content, illocutionary content, and speech act context together determine the conventional perlocutionary effects of the verbal performance, the rhetorical impact the discourse will have."[128]

Consider the Fourth Gospel as a complex communicative act. Let *p* stand both for the (literary) form and the (subject) matter of the text, both for the text as structured work and for the text as a world of people and events. This is the locutionary dimension of the Fourth Gospel: recounting (*p*)—the plot ("Jesus' passion for us"). The illocutionary dimension *F* stands for what the evangelist *does* in telling *p*: *displaying* a world and *testifying* to Christ. Matters again become more complicated when we consider the perlocutionary dimension. While it is clear that the Fourth Gospel was written in order to *persuade* others that Jesus is the Christ (John 20:31), it is still not clear whether this purpose is part of the meaning of the text. With Habermas, Searle denies any role to perlocutions in the constitution of meaning: "I will reject the idea that the intentions that matter for meaning are the intentions to produce *effects* on audiences."[129] The subsequent response and behavior of the audience are extrinsic, often unstable, factors and thus cannot be part of what makes a speech act what it is. The Fourth Gospel testifies to Jesus Christ regardless of how readers respond to it, but it only *persuades* if readers respond to its testimony with belief. Searle excludes the author's perlocutionary purpose from his definition of meaning. It would thus be mistake to define textual meaning as $M = F(p) + x$, where *x* stands for an author's ulterior purpose for his or her text act. Nevertheless, the distinction between illocution and perlocution is a valid one and will later prove indispensable for revising Hirsch's distinction between meaning and significance. To anticipate that discussion: the significance of a text act is a function of how the author's communicative act (including the perlocutionary dimension) bears on the reader's context (*R*).[130] My immediate concern, however, is not with significance, but with showing how the reality and determinacy of textual meaning follows from the nature of a text as a communicative act.

An Ark of the Covenant of Discourse

What is a text? We are now in a position to provide a definition. A text is a complex communicative act with *matter* (propositional content), *energy* (illocutionary force), and *purpose* (perlocutionary effect). This definition, while true as far as it goes, is too general. For we never simply act; rather, we do specific things: we invite, we record, we warn, we cook, etc. So too with texts: they are not simply instances of writing but stories, histories, parables, jokes, plays, novels, gospels, etc. Every text belongs to a certain kind of communicative action. My thesis is twofold: that texts have determinate natures, and that authors determine what these are. A text is a story (or a history, or a poem, or a parable) just because of what the author has done, just because of what the author has wrought in words. And because a text is one kind of communicative act rather than another, there will be some uses to which it may legitimately be put and others that may not be appropriate. The use to which a text may legitimately be put is a function of the kind of thing it is, which in turn is a function of its author's act.[131]

The author is not only the cause of the text, but also the agent who determines what the text counts as. In other words, the author is responsible both for the existence of the text (*that* it is) and for its specific nature (*what* it is). Nevertheless, the text remains what it is even in the absence of the author. A "last will and testament," for example, comes into its own *especially* in the author's absence. When an author pens a last will and testament, he or she puts a legal as well as a linguistic system into motion and lays an obligation on the reader not to ignore his or her intentions. How much more obliged are readers of the New Testament when, in the closing lines, the reader is enjoined neither to add to nor to take away any words (Rev. 22:18–19).[132] All texts, not only biblical ones, similarly invoke a certain debt that readers owe authors. In marked contrast to Derrida and Fish, then, I contend that it is neither individual readers nor even whole interpretive communities that determine what a text counts as. On the contrary: *What an act counts as is not a matter of how it is taken, but of how it was meant.* I agree with Nicholas Wolterstorff, another hermeneutical realist: "One act may count as another even though no one counts it as the other."[133] I may take Jane Austen's *Pride and Prejudice* as tragedy, but that does not make it so. I may have missed, as a thirteen-year-old reader, the element of social comedy and satire, but it was there nevertheless. The nature of communicative action, in other words, does not change at the behest of how it is interpreted. There is a kind of objectivity proper to the human sciences.

A text, then, is communicative action fixed by writing. Communicative "matter" (propositional content) and "energy" (illocutionary force) are inscribed. Moreover, texts also have a certain momentum; the communicative act generated by the author continues to have force wherever it is interpreted. *Genuine interpretation conserves textual matter and energy. Deconstruction lets it dissipate.* In the postmodern world, signs too often only meander; I say signs mediate. In his treatise on interpretation Augustine remarks that to worship the sign rather than the thing to which the signs point is idolatry. The postmodern textualist is in danger of worshiping the play of signs. For one who believes in meaning, however, the text is a semantic sacrament that mediates the other: the author's vision of the world, the testimony of the witness.

What is a text? Insofar as an author's personal identity is tied up with his or her word, the author can say of the text, analogically if not ontologically, "This is my body." My text is the concrete sign and seal of my communicative rights and responsibilities, the ark of the covenant of discourse. If the text is communicative action fixed by writing, then human authors are indeed "incarnate" in their texts. Just as an agent performs certain acts through bodily movements, so an author performs communicative acts through the body of his or her work. How else could written discourse be a means of social interaction (communication) and interpersonal relation (communion)? A text is an extension of one's self into the world, through communicative action. Thiselton rightly sees the connection between Christian doctrine and literary interpretation: "Theologically a hermeneutic of an *embodied* text reflects an incarnational Christology, in which revelation operates through the interwovenness of word and deed."[134] The divine author embodied his message in human flesh: "In Christ the truth of God is *spoken, embodied, and lived.*"[135] Is the word of human authors not incarnational too? Thiselton writes: "*The text is more than a 'docetic' or disembodied system of signifiers.*"[136] The text is instead a kind of "body" of the author. It is this body, this medium of authorial agency, that I have sought to resurrect. The "death" of the author is only the next to last word in contemporary interpretation.

THE "WHO" OF MEANING: AUTHORS AS COMMUNICATIVE AGENTS

Any theory of interpretation that misunderstands what an author is cannot hope to understand what a text is and how it conveys . . . meaning.[137]

What exactly is the problem of authorship? By and large, historical critics have treated authorship as the historical or apologetic problem of determining whether a given biblical book was really authored by the person whose name it bears (e.g., "The Gospel According to Matthew"). For biblical criticism, the problem of authorship refers to the identity of the writer: "Who is the author of this book?" I address a different question—call it the *hermeneutical* question of authorship: "*What* is an author?" "What does authorship *mean*?"[138] The short answer, to be expanded in what follows, is that the author is the one whose action determines the meaning of the text—its subject matter, its literary form, and its communicative energy.

History, psychology, and sociology alike direct their attention, in different ways, to the overall question of the meaningfulness of human action. *So too, I would add, should literary criticism*. The author, viewed as a communicative agent, is a proper object of study for the human sciences. As we saw in Part 1, there are many today who believe that the human subject—that is to say, an individual center of independent conscious thought—no longer exists. The postmodern turn to language displaces the speaking and thinking subject from the privileged position it enjoyed in modernity. However, the determinism of socio-linguistics leads, in my opinion, to the despair of human society. The author, previously considered in modernity to be the master of his or her words, has in postmodernity been thoroughly dispossessed. My claim is that there is a mediating position. Between the extremes of sovereign and slave stands the subject as *citizen* of language. Doing things with words involves intersubjective linguistic conventions and individual intentions, as well as literary inventions for engaging with the world and with one another in new ways.

The biblical narratives depict human beings as speech agents engaged in the covenant of discourse. Personhood, both human and divine, is to a large extent defined by the relation between the speaker and his or her words. A large part of Israel's history turned on promise-making and promise-breaking. In what follows I will show how the model of communicative agency leads to a more adequate view of the self than either the standard Cartesian picture, which dominated early modern philosophy, or its postmodern disintegration.[139] Furthermore, viewing the author as a communicative agent provides a corrective to the Romanticist attempt to recover the mental life of authors. I believe it is important to recover the author's thought, but this is best done not by psychological intuition but by historical inference—by an analysis of the author's *public* communicative action. In this section I will analyze the author's action from four complementary perspectives and return at the end to the question of the author's presence and inquire of the text, "Is anybody there?"[140]

"I Mean, Therefore I Do"

Cogito ergo sum ("I think, therefore I am"). As we have seen, Descartes' picture of the solitary sovereign subject dominated early modern philosophical thinking about human being.[141] It gave rise to several dualisms—subject/object, mind/body, thought/language—that had an adverse effect on hermeneutics and eventually invited deconstruction. Cartesian dualism—the view that the human mind is an altogether different kind of reality from all other things in the world—complicates both the human sciences and hermeneutics. When one begins with solitary thought (the *cog-*

ito), it is difficult to give an account either of action or of one's relationship to others: "If we make the 'I think' the primary postulate of philosophy, then not merely do we institute a dualism between theoretical and practical experience, but we make action logically inconceivable—a mystery . . . in which we necessarily believe, but which we can never comprehend."[142] One can explain neither individual action nor social interaction from the starting point "I think." The subject-object and mind-body dichotomies make it difficult to achieve understanding of human persons, for how can one study "mental substance"?

With regard to hermeneutics, Cartesian anthropology poses three problems:

(1) How can we recover mental intentions? It is one thing to say that the self-present subject knows its own mind, but how can we know other minds? Given the Cartesian understanding of the human person, Schleiermacher's hermeneutic quest—to relive the mental life of the author so that interpreters might know the author better than the author knows himself or herself—appeared at best quixotic and at worst deluded. And, as we have seen, the notion of a pure consciousness, uncontaminated by language, makes for an easy Derridean target. Derrida undoes the Cartesian picture and denies the possibility that the human mind exists in a mental realm somewhere beyond that of the material (e.g., the bodily, the historical, the social, and the linguistic).

(2) Is there a role for social conventions? Charles Taylor notes that one of the negative consequences of Cartesian dualism is atomism. The human person appears to be a disengaged individual "metaphysically independent of society."[143] Such a view not only makes social theory impossible; it makes it difficult to understand others.

(3) Is language anything more than an instrument of thought with which knowing subjects name objects and manipulate concepts? For much of the modern era, meaning was a matter of what ideas or things words stood for.

Hermeneutics and the human sciences appear to have reached a dead end (a dead author, to be exact) in postmodernity only because an alternative to the Cartesian subject was not forthcoming. A viable alternative, the communicative agent, is now available, however. Authorship should consequently be understood not in terms of sovereign subjective consciousness but rather in terms of inter-subjective (viz., communicative) agency. The crux of the matter is this: *communicative agents are not disembodied minds but embodied persons who form part of a language community*. Hence, to understand language, one needs to understand the social life of those who use it. As Fergus Kerr notes:

> It is our bodiliness that founds our being able, in principle, to learn any natural language on earth. In contrast to the metaphysical conception of the self, where our bodies supposedly get between us and prevent a meeting of minds, Wittgenstein reminds us of the obvious fact that the foundation of mutual understanding is the human body, with its manifold responsiveness and expressiveness.[144]

Language, spoken or written, creates what Charles Taylor calls a public space.[145] In spoken discourse, what a speaker does creates the context against which what he or she says makes sense. We understand that "Help!" is an urgent request for assistance when it is uttered by a speaker in what is clearly a dangerous situation. Of course, in the case of written texts one cannot see the author's body, reaction, or gestures in order to determine the context. Nevertheless, like all human action, communicative action ultimately only makes sense against some contextual background. We must wait until the next chapter when we examine the notion of literary genre to see how texts themselves resemble public practices. My point here is simply that authors are communicative agents who mean things by participating publicly in rule-governed behavior. Neither authorship nor interpretation makes sense if language is a merely private affair.

The author, lost as Cartesian thinking subject, thus returns as communicative agent—one who means, one who puts a language system and a literary form to work in a particular way for a particular purpose. We may therefore accept C. K. Barrett's definition of an author: "the man (or group) who would accept responsibility for the book as we read it in the ancient manuscripts."[146]

In ascribing the dignity of communicative agency to authors, I am by no means ignoring the revolution initiated by Saussure, who sees language as a differential system of signs (*langue*). Meaning is not a private party, an affair of subjective consciousness only. There are social conventions that communicative agents must respect in order to perform certain actions (e.g., promising). I am not denying *langue*, only situating it. Better, I am resituating the author as a historical agent vis-à-vis the system of language. It is the author who activates the system of language, the author who initiates an event of discourse, the author who *means*.[147] The meaning of a text is not an impersonal static property, but a dynamic personal act fixed by writing. And while not all forms of doing count as meaning, all forms of meaning are forms of doing. The concepts of textual meaning and meaningful action stand or fall together.

Authorial Agency: Four Perspectives

In one sense, of course, authors are absent from their texts. Yet on my view, presence is a secondary category, an implication of action—not a being-there, but a having-been-there. Human being is mediated by language: by communicative acts. Interpreters search not for the thinking subject or mind behind the text, but for the communicative agent implied in and by the text.

The Author As Historical Agent

It follows from the rejection of the Cartesian paradigm that we view authors as "embodied souls." Consciousness and corporeality belong together. This is not simply a rejection of Descartes, but a return to the anthropology of the Old Testament and of the apostle Paul: "The true man is the whole man—corporeal and incorporeal together, the incorporeal acting through the corporeal, each equally deficient without the other."[148] Material marks—the printed words on this page, for instance—do not stand for (or against) my mental life, but rather mediate it to others: "We interact with the physical and social dimensions of our world through our bodies and through speech."[149] According to Jerry Gill, language is "an extension of our embodied existence, for not only is it impossible without a body . . . but it frequently serves as a way of altering the environment (getting the door closed, making agreements, evoking feelings)."[150] Texts thus enable authors to do things, even at a distance. Authors are, perhaps most fundamentally, historical agents.

History, according to N. T. Wright, is the attempt "to plot, uncover, and understand from the inside the interplay of human intentions and motivations present within a given field of initial investigation."[151] It is the attempt to understand a sequence of events and intentions by means of an explanatory story. Central to Wright's account is the concept of historical agents; the meaning of history lies "in the intentionalities of the characters concerned."[152] The historian is interested in what actually happened and why. To answer these questions one has to know something of the agent and something of the world in which one left one's mark: the culture, the political situation, the social structure, and so forth. The search for "brute facts" or knowledge from a neutral point of view is not an option; historical knowledge involves interpretation. Yet the converse is also true, and of significance, for hermeneutics: *interpretation involves historical knowledge*.

Wright's own project is to understand Jesus. In particular, he wants to understand Jesus in such a way that does not merely reflect his (Wright's) values. There would be no genuine knowledge, and even less chance of personal communion, if Wright, like previous questers of the historical Jesus, managed only to discover himself and his own values. Whereas readers risk seeing themselves in the mirror of the text, historians are prone to see their own faces at the bottom of a deep well and mistake it for the face of Jesus. Wright's attempt to describe a face unlike his own is therefore of the utmost theological, as well as historical, importance.[153] For the way Christians know God is by coming to know Jesus Christ. Jesus—the Word made flesh—is God's embodied soul, the divine self-communicative action that allows us to know God at a distance. Unless we can have some knowledge about what Jesus did and why, his life will appear meaningless and God will remain forever hidden. What is the meaning of the Christ event? Not merely what contemporary interpreters want it to be. That way lies theological solipsism and idolatry. *No, the meaning of the Christ event is a function of what God, the divine communicative agent, was doing in the man Jesus of Nazareth*. Though we may have a hard time deciphering this meaning, it is nevertheless really there, rooted in the historical agency of God the Father.[154]

The study of history is the study of intentionality: "We are trying to discover what the humans involved in the event thought they were doing, wanted to do, or tried to do" (and, I might add, what they actually did do).[155] Wright is especially keen to discover a person's "aim" (the fundamental direction of a person's life) and "intention" (the specific application of the aim in a particular situation). What was Jesus seeking to do within Judaism? What was his intention in going to Jerusalem?[156] The realist believes that there is, in principle, an answer to such queries. As with Jesus, so with the Evangelists. Wright rightly exhorts New Testament historians to treat the Gospels as what they are and not as something else.[157] To inquire after the meaning of the Gospels is to inquire about what their authors have done.

To sum up: Understanding the text involves determining what an author has done, for a text is a communicative action fixed by writing. Jorge Garcia rightly makes the metaphysical point that there cannot even be texts without historical authors.[158] For there is meaning only where someone means, or meant, something. There is meaning only where someone *does* something with words. Meaning (the noun) exists only where someone has *meant* (the verb), for meaning is not a natural event but an intentional act. It follows that meaning is historical. What one does with language depends on the particular language, the state of that language, and the linguistic and literary resources one has at a given time and place. In order to understand the marks p-a-i-n, for example, one has to know, at the very least, whether the author was doing something with English or French. As Garcia comments: "Signs, like texts, are historical entities, the products of conventional uses whose meanings change from time to time."[159] Texts without authors count neither as historical nor as communicative action. Texts without historical authors are texts without meaning.

What the interpreter seeks to understand—whether in a text, a work of art, a piece of music, or in any other kind of meaningful action—is what the agent did, and why. Biblical interpreters, similarly, seek understanding of communicative action fixed by writing. Again, by communicative action I do not mean the impartation of information only, but all the things that authors do with words, sentences, and larger literary forms. Interpretation and historical knowledge thus go hand in hand; understanding communicative action is incomplete unless one has a sense of the agent's aims and intentions, for only these make an action what it is. The art critic Michael Baxandall argues that we unavoidably "think of pictures . . . as products of purposeful activity, and therefore caused."[160] We explain why a painting or a text is the way it is by inferring—from its structure, from the problem the painter was trying to solve, from the resources the painter had available to him or her, etc.—what the author was probably doing. If we simply used concepts drawn from the physical world (e.g., large, flat, red, pigment), it would be virtually impossible to explain how the work of art came to be or to say what it meant. We could describe our feelings when we look at it, but this would not take us beyond self-knowledge.

Why is there something—a text, a work of art—rather than nothing? Because a human author at a particular place and time activated the linguistic resources that were to hand, put a socio-linguistic system in motion, and *did* something in order to make a difference in the social world.[161] True, the author's face may be inaccessible to us; reading a book is not the same as face-to-face dialogue. What we have of the author is not a face but a trace, the mark of an action. What I hope to have established in this section is the thesis that meaning, mediated by texts, is the communicative activity of a genuine "other." There is meaning in this text because it is the product of communicative agency.

The Author As Aesthetic Agent

Whereas historians approach the author as the one who is responsible for the being of a text, rhetorical critics attend to the literary aspects of the author's communicative act, to what Roman Jakobson terms the poetic function of communication. Which words does an author choose, how are they structured or put together, and why does he or she choose just these? Authors are literary strategists, aesthetic agents who deploy words the way generals deploy troops. Rhetorical critics study the vast array of locutionary techniques authors use to inform, engage, and guide the reader (e.g., achieve perlocutionary effects).[162] The focus here is on the text's formal features; yet as I have already argued, interpreters must, at least tacitly, invoke the author as a historical agent as soon as they study the text in terms of a particular language as it has developed at a particular time. In other words, the perspective of the author as a historical agent grounds and controls the perspective of the author as an aesthetic agent.[163]

It is now widely acknowledged that each of the four Evangelists is an aesthetic agent.[164] Each composes his Gospel so as to make certain theological points and to produce certain effects and responses in the reader.[165] Each employs *logos* (the locutionary style and structure of the text) to create an underlying *ethos*, or sense of reliability, in order to achieve *pathos* (the perlocutionary effect on the reader). For instance, in John 4 the author employs the man-meets-woman-at-the-well betrothal type scene, familiar to readers of Genesis, to structure the encounter of Jesus and the Samaritan woman.[166] There is an encounter at a well, but no betrothal takes place. What is the author doing? What makes problematic sense as a statement—"whoever drinks the water I give him will never thirst" (John 4:14)—makes perfect sense as a rhetorical strategy. By invoking and then varying a well-known literary convention, the author leads the reader, and not only the Samaritan woman, through the puzzle of Jesus' identity. The adoption of this form, in other words, heightens the effect of the content of Jesus' announcement: that he is the one who can give living water. "The result is a very different betrothal—not in marriage but in worship (4:21–24) and mission (4:35–42)."[167]

The Author As Ethical Agent

Interpreters may also attend to a third dimension of communicative action. To ascribe authorship is to assign responsibility for what has been said and done.[168] For instance, Gundry argues that Matthew does several specific things in writing his Gospel besides telling a story or displaying a world. He "reminds true disciples of their duty to obey Christ's law and make it known despite persecution" and "warns false disciples and those tempted to follow their antinomian course of least resistance that everlasting torment awaits the disobedient."[169] The ethics of authorship pertains to the *illocutionary* form of an author's discourse, to the *what* rather than the how of communicative action.

Speech act theory has a strong ethical underpinning.[170] Austin takes the promise as the paradigm speech act, though "reminding" and "warning" can be ethical acts too. By emphasizing the performative nature of language (i.e., language as action, as work, as something we do), Austin reminds us that we are responsible for everything we say, and not just for promises. To some extent, therefore, all speech acts have a "commissive" dimension. And as Habermas argues, every speaker has a responsibility to redeem the validity conditions of his or her speech (viz., truth, truthfulness, rightness) if requested to do so. The phenomenon of libel, moreover, reminds us that our communicative action carries certain legal as well as ethical obligations.

Authors have the remarkable power to set a language system in motion, to do things at a distance, and to intervene in the life worlds of an infinite number of possible readers. The dignity of communicative agency implies a certain freedom as well as responsibility. The author, as the efficient cause of his or her text-act, is conditioned but not wholly determined by the social-historical context. Cultural and ideological forces may well be at work, but there is nevertheless room for the exercise of individual deliberation and imagination. This is precisely the point about authors being responsible citizens of language with the power to put language to work: "The blindness of all determinist models of the literary text is that they eschew the possibility of compatibilism."[171]

No one denies that speakers speak or that writers write, that is, that they are the historical causes of discourse. That the author is an aesthetic agent is also relatively uncontroversial. The conflict of interpretation usually centers on the question of what, if anything, has been done. Postmoderns deny the author's ability to accomplish anything in texts; the only aims and interests that count are those of the reader. When meaning is viewed as the effect texts have on readers, there is little room for the concept of the author as an ethical agent. On the other hand, some postmoderns, perhaps inconsistently, hold the author responsible not only for what is said but also for the ensuing consequences. It is all too easy to confuse the communicative action with its results. Austin was aware of the problem: "We have then to draw the line between an action we do (here an illocution) and its consequences."[172] How do we draw the line? By what criterion can we distinguish the author's act from, say, the reader's response?

A full answer to this last question must await the next chapter. Suffice it to say that this is a problem for the philosophy of action in general and that legal theory provides a vital clue. H. L. A. Hart, the legal philosopher, asks, "What is the difference between human action and mere bodily movement?" and replies that we ascribe responsibility to the former but not to the latter.[173] Hart believes that statements of the type "he did that" should be interpreted along the lines of judicial decisions. If we follow Hart's analysis, interpretation then becomes a deliberative process in which opposing descriptions of an action are confronted and defeated. Textual interpretation is fundamentally about imputation: the ascription of meanings and intentions to a communicative agent.

The Author As Religious Agent

There is, lastly, a religious aspect to the author's communicative agency. As communicative agents, humans have the capacity not only to intervene in the social world but to form themselves. Through our speech acts we not only do but *become* something. To "own up" to our words means accepting the project of becoming a self. We communicate, indeed we make, something of ourselves by the way in which our deeds (our actions in general) relate to our discourse (our communicative action). I am implicated in my discourse in ways that go far beyond the grammatical. Austin considers the case of Hippolytus ("my tongue swore to, but my heart did not").[174] One cannot get out of a promise simply by making a mental reservation. Promising is a public act that implicates the speaker. And selfhood is to a large extent a function of how we comport ourselves in relation to our words. The sum total of our speech acts, therefore, reveals who we are because they largely make us who we are. Our word is our bond: to the world, to others, to ourselves, and to God.

It need not follow, however, that what we encounter as readers in texts is primarily the personality of the author. C. S. Lewis is right to protest against this "personal heresy." Our attention as readers should be directed not to the personality of the author but to the subject matter of the text.[175] Does attention to communicative action, then, center on the author or on the thing said? In fact, I believe readers must attend to both. On the one hand, if all language use is performative, then all communicative action is a kind of personal testimony whereby the author is implicated in what is said. This is especially true of biblical discourse, but I believe it applies to everyday discourse as well. We have only to recall Habermas's first and third validity conditions: authors must be prepared to defend the objective truth of their testimony and their truthfulness or sincerity in saying it. On the other hand, no authors speak about themselves only. The author is first and foremost a *witness*.

Faithful speech means taking responsibility for one's words. Speech agents are religiously related to their words if they speak faithfully, if their testimony is true. The constancy of the self is not that of some unchanging metaphysical substance (e.g., Derrida's "being as presence"), but rather the dynamic constancy of faithful speech— of keeping one's word, of being faithful in and to one's communicative acts: "The constancy of faithful speech finds its paradigm in the spirit of the biblical God whose word . . . endures forever."[176] One need not subscribe to the metaphysics of presence, therefore, in order to believe in authors. We need only presuppose that the text is the result of a prior communicative action. The voice in the text embodies the author's spirit, not in a mystical but in a publicly accessible way.

Postmodern literary theory has, to a great extent, resulted in the eclipse of both the ethical and religious dimensions of communicative agency. For to pry author and text apart is to remove all responsibility for meaning. Jacques Ellul bewails the contemporary depersonalization of language: "The word has become anonymous and therefore has no importance, since its only reality involved the meaning of two living persons who needed . . . to exchange something."[177] He even speaks of a certain "hatred" of language on the part of some theorists who feel it necessary to detach themselves at all costs from what the other person meant, "since it might have import."[178] The question is whether the covenant of discourse can be maintained apart from some overarching theological context, or whether what is covenantal is reduced to the level of arbitrary social convention. Ellul is in no doubt about what is at stake: "The rupture between the speaker and his words is the decisive break. If a person is not behind his words, it is mere noise."[179]

Unless there is something in what we say, we will never be able to witness to what is other than ourselves. And unless we are faithful to what we say, our witness will be null and void. I have maintained that it is the privilege and responsibility of all speech agents, but preeminently of the witness, to set a language system in motion and so intervene in the life world of the other. The witness, says Ellul, is "one who introduces something new and unexpected into a given situation."[180] The witness, I believe, is the paradigmatic voice of the other, of the author. The biblical authors raise their combined voices to testify to the Wholly Other and to their vision of the world created and loved by God. Here we must speak of the death of the author in another sense, namely, in terms of martyrdom: the ultimate demonstration of the truth of one's testimony. As Ellul observes: "The word commits unto death the one who has spoken it."[181] This commitment unto death is precisely what gives communicative agency its religious aspect. Fidelity to our words exacts a sacred bond; only by owning up to one's words can the author achieve authenticity.

Real Presences? Word As Sacrament

A number of literary critics have compared the sense of authorial presence in the text to questions concerning the manner of Christ's presence in the Lord's Supper.[182]

Conversely, some sacramental theologians attribute the renewal of interest in the sacraments to twentieth-century developments in linguistic philosophy and interpretation theory.[183] This analogy is not as far-fetched as it might seem at first blush. John Milton, we may recall, spoke of the "potency of life" in books, which he saw as embodiments of the author's soul. The "elements" that mediate authorial presence, of course, are literary and linguistic, not physical, but they are nonetheless real for that. Texts may indeed be means of knowledge, perhaps even grace, but in what sense can we speak of the author's "embodied soul" in a text if the author is no longer physically "there"? For Foucault, we may recall, the author is merely a projection of the reader's way of interpreting texts. Can the analogy with the Eucharist enable us to conceive of the author as other than a "ghost in the machine"? What might it mean to speak of the author's "real presence" in a text?

Symbolic Presence: The "Implied Author"

Aristotle long ago pointed out in his *Rhetoric* that an orator creates an image of himself—a particular *ethos* or *persona*—that persuades listeners that he is, say, an intelligent or morally upright man. The same is true of authors. Wayne Booth names this projected *persona* the "implied author" in contrast to the real author. The "implied author" is a rhetorical construct used to convey a sense of authorial presence. This sense of a convincing authorial presence is, according to these rhetoricians, an effect of the text. That is, the "voice" that we think we hear in a text is not that of the real author, but rather part of the total fiction.

Alexander Nehamas adds a further distinction. He distinguishes the writer ("actual individuals, firmly located in history, efficient causes of their texts") from the author ("formal causes . . . postulated to account for a text's features and . . . produced through an interaction between critic and text").[184] The writer is a "creative author"; the implied author is a "created author." The writer accounts for the existence of the text, but the (implied) author accounts for its meaning. The real question concerns the genealogy of the implied author: Is the implied author the creation of the writer, the text, or the reader?

Barthes and Foucault follow Feuerbach, for whom "God" is simply the projection of humanity's highest thoughts, in claiming that the "author" is merely the projection of the reader's best interpretation. On this view, the author's presence is a fiction; though we may speak of the author, there is really nothing there. We might here draw an analogy with Zwingli, who believed that the bread and wine only symbolize Christ's body and blood. Or, to change theological metaphors, we can compare the denial of the author with the position of skeptics who claim that the resurrection tells us less about Jesus than about the faith of the first disciples. Similarly, the masters of literary suspicion argue that the historical author is not really present, but is only a veiled way of talking about the experience of the reader.

Immediate Presence: "Transubstantiation"

On the other hand, in an extreme restatement of the traditional view, William Gass still believes in the author's authoritative presence. The real author is a designer: atom by atom, word by word, the writer constructs a world. The historical author is creator, sustainer, and lord of this world and of its implied or created author. Gass claims that there is an identity between the historical and the implied author; indeed, the real author projects oneself into the implied author in a kind of literary incarnation. The writer is eternally present in the text; his or her "soul" is "transubstantiated" into the word.[185] What Ricoeur calls the narrative voice is here considered not an effect of rhetoric but the effect of the historical writer. Gass overlooks, however, the extent to which real authors can and do assume personae in their texts, as well as the extent to which texts *mediate* their authors' communicative acts.

Mediated Presence: The Inferred Author

Is it possible to avoid these two extremes, one that affirms and one that denies the author's presence in and control over the written text? Nehamas successfully resists identifying the writer (the historical individual who produced the text) with the author without dismissing the author as an effect of the text. He accepts Booth's point that different works by the same writer may have different implied authors, but goes on to define "author" in terms of what several texts written by the same person have in common. The "author" for Nehamas is the figure implied by diverse texts when taken together: the "author" is the agent postulated as the principle of unity behind a number of otherwise disparate texts. Thus, we may speak of the "implied author" of Tom Sawyer, of the "author " of all the books written by Mark Twain, and of the "writer" Samuel Clemens. What, then, is the relation of Mark Twain (a "created" author) to Samuel Clemens (the real author)? Can we read *Huckleberry Finn* as if it were written by Jane Austen, Charles Dickens, or for that matter, Norman Mailer? Not according to Nehamas: "The author is to be construed as a *plausible historical variant of the writer*, as a character the writer could have been."[186] Interpretation must be guided by a historically plausible answer to the question, "Who wrote this?" Hence "the author's intentions depend on what the writer *could have* meant."[187]

Nehamas's distinction clarifies the nature of the author's real presence. We can agree with Booth that the implied author stands somewhere between a fictional character and the historical writer. Yet, insofar as the author must be a historically plausible version of the writer, we may term the latter the "inferred" author. The historical author, I submit, must be inferred from the work itself, including its "created" or implied author. Booth rightly urges caution in identifying any one particular voice in the text as the historical author's. *Everything* we read is the product of the author's decisions: "We must never forget that though the author can to some extent choose his disguises, he can never choose to disappear."[188] The device of the implied author, therefore, need not exclude the notion of the historical author as communicative agent.

The real author necessarily makes choices as to what to do and how to do it: he or she chooses to follow or to ignore certain conventions, to be sincere or insincere. The intentions that interpreters seek to recover need not be equated with the psychology of the author, in the sense of the motives that prompted that person to write. In focusing on communicative action, I am interested not in the motives behind the act but rather in the nature, structure, and content of the literary act itself. Interpretation tries to understand what the historical author is saying and doing in the work, and this includes what the historical author is doing in and with the implied author.

Readers are free, of course, to attend to certain aspects of a story without raising the question of what the author was trying to do with it. However, insofar as this question is ignored, one's overall comprehension of what is going on in a text will be that much diminished.[189]

Though verbal marks may be all we have, it does not follow that meaning is nothing other than verbal marks. What a person does is more than the sum of one's bodily movements. Similarly, the sentence is more than the sum of its constituent signs. Meaning is more than vocabulary and syntax (it is "transcendent"), though it cannot be grasped apart from them (it is "immanent"). "Linguistic deeds and events are vital features of reality, as substantial and significant as chairs, jumps, persons, and ideas."[190] In other words, intangible reality (such as meaning) exists and is known in tangible reality (such as marks or sounds) without being reducible to or equated with it: "Meaning is neither read *off* nor read *into* language, but is rather *encountered in* it."[191]

The view I am here developing—that works mediate their author's intentions—resembles the Reformed tradition's solution to the problem of the mode of Christ's presence in the Lord's Supper. For the Reformers, Christ is not physically, but spiritually, present in the sacrament. Similarly, we might say that the author's "spirit" and thoughts are really "exhibited" by the text, considered as a kind of "sacrament."[192] In the Eucharist, according to Calvin, Christ is offered to humans who receive him in faith and repentance. The faith does not create the offer of Christ—the "communion"—but only receives it. The sacrament is not only sign but seal: an act regarded as a guarantee that there is something behind the words. For Calvin, the physical elements are instruments that *communicate* Christ's real presence to faith. Similarly, the linguistic elements mediate the author's presence to participants in the covenant of discourse—to those with the faith that seeks textual understanding. Unbelievers may consume the external signs, but they fail to participate in the thing (or presence) signified. Readers, too, may consume linguistic signs; but if they do not believe in authors, they fail to perceive the agency at work in the text and go away as empty as they came.

COMMUNICATIVE ACTION AND THE AUTHOR'S INTENTION

How do we get from physical movements to purposeful actions, from marks on the printed page to literary meaning? My answer, to this point, has been: by means of the author's communicative agency. The author, I said, is a communicative agent whose *parole* puts *langue* to work. The author is the condition for the possibility of determinate meaning. Stable meaning is grounded on past authorial action ("Paul meant *this*, not that"). Otherwise, textual meaning could not be independent of the interpreter's activity, and there would be as many meanings as there are communities of readers.

No account of past communicative action is complete, however, if it does not deal with the vexed question of intention. Meaning, I will argue, involves both material marks (signs, sounds) and mental direction (intentions). Yet neither bodily movements (sheer signs) nor psychological intentions (sheer consciousness) alone is enough. My intention in this section is twofold: to show why, and how, the author's intention matters for interpretation, and to offer a revised, non-fallacious account of this controversial concept.

Beyond the Intentional Fallacy

In Chapter 2 I referred to Derrida's "ugly ditch," by which I called attention to the gap between an author's intention and a sequence of words. I posed there metaphysical, epistemological, and ethical questions about the author's intention—where is it located, can we have access to it, why should we be interested in recovering it? Before turning to my own position, it might be helpful to review what has happened to the notion of the author's intention in literary criticism and speech act philosophy since Hirsch. It will also be helpful to recall that what is in view in this chapter is ontology or metaphysics, that is, the author's intention as the ground of determinate textual meaning. The epistemological question—how we can discover the author's intended meaning—will be taken up in the next chapter.

Intention in Recent Literary Criticism

Literary critics remain divided over the nature and the normativeness of the author's intention. W. K. Wimsatt, in an article written some twenty years after "The Intentional Fallacy," reasserted his earlier thesis that the author is irrelevant for determining textual meaning. Literary critics can choose to study "the Age, the Author, the Work."[193] Wimsatt himself holds that the meaning of words depends more on the *langue* of the age than the *parole* of the author. The most important alternatives to Wimsatt's New Criticism view meaning as a function either of *langue* (e.g., structuralism) or of the interaction of the text and reader (e.g., poststructuralist and most postmodern approaches). The following literary critics, however, represent a minority opposition and insist that the author's intention continues to be the ground and goal of interpretation.[194]

Juhl. P. D. Juhl complains that Hirsch's *Validity in Interpretation* is not so much an argument as a practical recommendation (or threat): read for the author's intention *or else* be prepared for anarchy in interpretation. Juhl proffers a more rational basis for making the author's intention the criterion for textual meaning. He argues that there is a *logical* connection between statements about textual meaning and statements about the author's intention.[195] For instance, to claim that a given passage is ironic simply *is* to claim something about the author's intention. Juhl furthermore claims that critics know this, though they may not all wish to admit it; he points out that every appeal to some feature of the text as evidence for one's interpretation is actually a tacit appeal to the author's probable intent. Why should this be so? Because, says Juhl, every interpretation tries to account for the text *as a whole*. To speak in terms of wholes, however, is to speak in terms of purpose—the author's intended purpose.[196] Interpretation provides explanations for textual features that must refer to some overall purpose in order adequately to explain the textual features. In other words, what ultimately has to be explained when seeking a coherent interpretation of a text is a human action: "How we construe a literary work is, if I am right, logically tied to what we think the author intended and hence depends on a large number of (usually implicit) assumptions about the author's beliefs, attitudes, interests . . . and so on."[197] Like it or not, critics must treat the text as a purposeful human action. In Juhl's words: "My contention has been that the meaning of a literary work is essentially like the meaning of a person's speech act."[198]

Knapp and Michaels. While Hirsch appeals to intention on the basis of ethics, and Juhl on the basis of logic, Steven Knapp and Walter Benn Michaels turn to ontology. Their thesis is as simple as it is breathtaking: meaning simply *is* intention, and interpretation just *is* the finding of intention. In their celebrated essay "Against Theory," they argue that a text means exactly what its author intended it to mean. It is only "theory" that imagines there can be "intentionless meaning" or some other source of meaning. Consequently, the idea that the author's intention has to be theoretically defended is nonsense, or worse than nonsense, since it "creates the illusion of a choice between alternative methods of interpreting."[199] The very idea of a meaningful sign or text (as opposed to an accidental or arbitrary configuration of marks and words) requires that one postulate conscious intention. If one saw John 3:16 written in the sand, one would either ascribe these marks to an intentional agent or consider them non-intentional effects. In the latter case—where the marks are considered to be accidents—they will no longer be words, but only seem to resemble them. There is no such thing as intentionless meanings.[200] Once one acknowledges this, the problem (and the need for further argument) disappears. As soon as marks are regarded as intentionless, they become meaningless as well. "Against Theory" is at once the most powerful argument for authorial intention and the most powerful argument against the practical usefulness of the concept of intention: "Once it is seen that the meaning of a text is simply identical to the author's intended meaning, the project of *grounding meaning* in intention becomes incoherent."[201]

In a second essay, "Against Theory 2: Hermeneutics and Deconstruction," Knapp and Michaels engage Ricoeur and Derrida, critics who each suggest, in different ways, that textual meaning may be something other than what the author intends.[202] Knapp and Michaels repeat their claim that only the author's intention could plausibly serve as an object of any coherent practice of interpretation. There is no other plausible criterion that would enable the would-be interpreter even to identify a string of marks as a text. One cannot even determine the language of a text without reference to the author's intention: "We have tried hard to find, or when we couldn't find it to *invent*, a reason why someone might insist that a text be read as meaning what it means in the language in which its author wrote it, even while at the same time insisting that it doesn't matter what the author intended."[203] Linguistic conventions, according to Knapp and Michaels, are not independent repositories of meaning, only ways of signaling one's intention.

There is much to admire in Knapp's and Michaels's brazen refusal to be tempted into theoretically defending the identity of the author's intention with the meaning of the text. For them, the decisive question is not, "Should I try to recover the author's intention?" but rather "Should I interpret or not?" If one decides to interpret, then one decides to examine a string of marks as counting as language, and thus counting as the product of an intentional agent. While I agree with their (ontological) identification of meaning with the author's intention, there is nevertheless something to be said for a continued theoretical defense of the concept. A defense of authorial intent is necessary, first, because many literary critics, especially postmodern ones, resist the identification. There is thus a continuing need for an *apologetics* of authorial intention. Second, though Knapp and Michaels insist that meaning is to be equated with intention, they do not explain what they mean by intention. There is thus a *systematic* task of defining author's intention—a task to which I will return below.

Intention in Speech Act Theory

Searle distinguishes his account of intention from that of another speech act philosopher, Paul Grice. According to Grice, to say a speaker S meant something by x is to say that S intended the utterance of x to produce some effect in a hearer H by means of the hearer recognizing the speaker's intention.[204] If I say "Hello," I intend that you recognize my intent to greet you. According to Searle, this account of meaning, while valuable, is defective in two important respects. First, by defining meaning in terms of the intention to produce effects on an audience, Grice risks confusing illocutionary with perlocutionary acts. For Searle, however, meaning is a matter specifically of illocutionary, not perlocutionary, effects. If I make a statement, I succeed in communicating if I achieve an illocutionary effect (viz., the hearer understands my utterance as a statement). My success in transmitting my intended meaning does not mean that a listener has to agree with me. As Searle rightly puts it: "*The characteristic intended effect of meaning is understanding.*"[205]

Second, Grice's account "fails to account for the extent to which meaning can be a matter of rules or conventions."[206] Speaker meaning is more than randomly related to sentence meaning. With the distinction between author's intention and linguistic convention, we come to a dispute between speech act theorists themselves. Some, like Grice, hold meaning to be primarily a matter of intention; others emphasize the role of conventions. The strength of Searle's theory, in my opinion, derives from its ability to include both factors; Searle's model is thus able to account for how a speech agent intentionally puts a language system to work.[207] Searle contends that authors get their readers to recognize their intention to do x by using linguistic conventions that readers associate with doing x. To cite a simple example, I signal my intent to marry my wife when, in the appropriate circumstances, I say "I do." Literary meaning is, of course, more complex, but the same combination of elements—intention and convention—still holds.

Conventions and Collective Intentions. What makes a communicative action what it is rather than something else? Intention alone is not enough. Intention alone is not enough, as Wittgenstein's challenge makes clear: "say 'warm' and mean 'cold.'" The fact is, we communicate our intentions by using recognizable linguistic conventions. I signal my intent to greet you by uttering "Hello" in the appropriate circumstances. In France I use a different linguistic convention: "Bonjour."

It is important to distinguish this modest role for conventions from a linguistic determinism that engulfs the author's intention, such as we saw in Part 1: "The individual author, or 'subject,' is assigned no initiative, expressive intention, or design in producing a work of literature. Instead, the conscious 'self' is declared to be a construct that is itself the product of linguistic conventions."[208] For postmoderns, the author is merely an empty space on which the impersonal system of literary conventions writes itself. Such a stress on socially constructed conventions makes the author an effect rather than an agent of language.[209] In my view, it is entirely possible, indeed necessary, to incorporate linguistic and literary conventions into a theory of communicative action and intention. Individual authors cannot determine the meaning of a word by intention alone, no matter how sincere or intense it may be. Indeed, many things that we do with words and with texts would not be possible without linguistic conventions. Language is a rule-governed form of behavior: conventional and covenantal.

Why isn't a language system an impersonal and autonomous second source of meaning, alongside intention? Because a dictionary describes neither a speaker's private intention nor an impersonal linguistic system but rather records "the intentions of the many different current speakers speaking on many occasions."[210] A dictionary definition is not a set of abstract possible meanings, but a record of how a term has actually been used in different contexts. Linguistic and literary conventions are tools developed by a group of people who come together to coordinate actions and to do things that, without language, would simply not be possible.[211] In the covenant of discourse, intention and convention are cooperative, not competitive, principles. Grammar does not drop from the sky, but rather reflects a social consensus on good usage: "Languages are human institutions and thus are intentionalistic through and through."[212] Indeed, a convention may be said to be a *corporate intention*.[213] This latter insight warrants further clarification, to which I now turn.

Constitutive Rules and Institutional Facts. Meaning is not a "brute fact," such as the fact that a physical object is made of stainless steel and weighs five grams. Meaning cannot be perceived by the physical sciences; there is no hermeneutic Geiger counter, no instrument that detects communicative activity instead of radioactivity. It does not follow, however, that meaning does not exist or that it is the reader's hermeneutic hallucination. *For there is more in the world than brute facts.* The stainless steel object that weighs five grams may be a fork. That it is a fork is an institutional fact—that is, a fact that depends on corporate intention. For it is not just my subjective opinion that the object is a fork; it really is a fork. Yet it really is a fork only in relation to a community that designates it as such. There may be primitive societies that use fork-like objects as weapons. My point is that institutional facts are what they are thanks to corporate intentionality, though they are nonetheless facts for that.

The distinction between brute facts and institutional facts is as crucial as it is subtle. It is the all-important distinction that enables Searle to explain how he gets from the physics to the semantics. It thus repays careful attention. Searle states the distinction as follows: "Brute facts exist independently of any human institutions; institutional facts can exist only within human institutions."[214] Consider the human institution of baseball. It is an institutional fact that when Hank Aaron sent the ball over the fence in center field, he hit a home run. Newspapers report such institutional facts: "Hank Aaron hit a home in the ninth inning to win the game." The physical sciences cannot account for this fact. The physicist can calculate the force and trajectory of the ball as it comes off the bat, but such a person looks in vain with his or her instruments for a home run. There is no set of statements about physical happenings or states of affairs to which statements of institutional facts can be reduced. "Institutional facts exist, so to speak, on top of brute facts."[215]

How do we get from the physics to the home run, from brute facts to institutional facts? The missing link is corporate intention. A round object is only a baseball thanks to a corporate intention to count it such, just as the word "baseball" designates the object thanks to the corporate intention to assign these marks the function of representation. Moreover, a baseball only becomes something more when a community assigns it a new status—a home run, for example—in the rule-governed activity we call baseball. Corporate intention is the means by which natural objects (and written marks) become something more than brute facts. *Whether there is meaning in texts is for Searle ultimately a question about institutional facts.*

Institutional facts are supported by systems of what Searle calls "constitutive rules." A constitutive rule has the form "X counts as Y in context C." Hitting the ball over the fence counts as a home run in the context of a baseball game. The rule states a corporate intention (to count X as Y in context C), and the rule is constitutive because without the rule there would be no home runs. Note that the rules are a necessary condition for there being certain activities (e.g., baseball), but which X counts as Y is a matter of convention and is therefore arbitrary (one can play baseball with softballs or hardballs of varying sizes). We may apply this analysis to meaning as follows. Speaking a language and writing a text are matters of institutional facts and constitutional rules, matters of authors' intentions and corporate intentions.

Constitutive rules create the possibility of new forms of behavior.[216] Behavior that is in accordance with a constitutive rule can be described in ways that would be impossible if the rule did not exist. Making a promise, hitting a home run, and taking communion are institutional facts. Language is a particularly rich institution whose varied constitutive rules make many types of action possible that could not otherwise be performed (e.g., marrying, baptizing, commissioning, etc.).[217] Which specific action is performed depends on the rules that are followed and the conventions that are intentionally invoked. We will not describe communicative action correctly unless we know something about the constitutive rules in force at the time of its performance, for we will not otherwise know what X (e.g., bodily movements, marks on paper) *counts as.*

The route from physics to semantics should now be clear. Written marks and physical events count as parts of communicative actions only against a background of constitutive rules that reflect a corporate agreement to count X as Y. Counting one thing as another is the heart of the process by which corporate intentions impose meaning onto linguistic phenomena. To define meaning in terms of author's intention ultimately involves us in a search for the constitutive rules and the institutional facts that make movements or marks *count* as communicative action.

We need to go beyond Searle, however, if we wish to apply the notion of institutional facts to literature and to the Bible. Biblical texts and works of literature in general, I will say, are themselves "institutions" with their own sets of constitutive rules.[218] Fully to understand Scripture involves grasping the rules that constitute such institutions as prophecy, law, psalm, wisdom, apocalyptic, gospel, and canon. Textual meaning is in large part a matter of the literary conventions that an author intentionally invokes and puts to work. An author decides to follow one set of rules rather than another—for example, the rules that constitute history or the rules that constitute fiction. The point is that literary forms, insofar as they are governed by rules, represent an institutional activity that has been collectively acknowledged and constituted by community agreement. To repeat, a convention is a rule that says a particular action counts as such and such in the appropriate circumstances. Literary conventions describe rule-governed patterns of social actions. A text is a communicative act that counts as such and such a literary genre because of the conventions an author puts into motion. It follows that the interpreter should be less concerned with his or her own subjective responses or with the brute fact of the text, and more concerned with textual meaning as an institutional fact.

Author's Intention: A Reconstructive Proposal

You cannot take the top of a man's head off and look into his mind and actually see what his intent was at any given moment. You have to decide it by reference to what he did, what he said and all the circumstances of the case.[219]

It is now time to offer a more precise account—using ingredients from philosophy of action, speech act theory, and the philosophy of law—of the relation between authorial intentions and communicative action. In order to do that, we first need to reformulate the concept of intention in such a way that avoids the psychologizing tendencies of earlier definitions. In particular, we need to distinguish between, on the one hand, what I will call "mapping intentions," which have to do with planning or plotting one's course, and, on the other, "meaning intentions," which have to do with deeds and actual destinations. What an author planned to write is not necessarily the same as what an author succeeds in doing. What is needed is an account that explains the author's intent in terms of action rather than psychology.

Intention and Action

Intention alone enables us to view actions as *counting as* more than mere bodily movements or written marks. While my account of the author's intention is not primarily a psychological one, it nevertheless resists reducing human actions to impersonal events.

Intention and Attention: Following Directions. A number of philosophers, Searle among them, define intentionality in terms of "directedness." To be conscious of something is to have one's mind directed towards an object.[220] Consciousness is always consciousness *of* something. Mental states are always directed: beliefs, fears, and hopes are always beliefs, fears, and hopes *of* something. Not all contents of consciousness actually exist (e.g., the bogeyman under the bed). To intend, then, is a matter of directing one's mind towards a certain object or idea. The etymology of "intend" (from the Latin *tendere*) is instructive: to "stretch or strain toward, to aim at."[221] One is reminded here of a poet's struggle to grasp the ineffable—the moment, the eternal—in words. Indeed, language is the chief means that the mind uses to direct its attention to objects, hopes, beliefs, fears, and so forth, whether one is a poet, philosopher, or for that matter, a farmer. Thinking, saying, and doing are equally intentional.[222] Intending—to think or to say or to do something—always has an object: a thought, in the case of thinking; a proposition, in the case of saying; a project, in the case of doing. I earlier defined the meaning of text acts with the formula

$F(p)$. Intention, most basically, has to do with what one does *in tending* to p—a proposition, a plot, even a projected world—in a particular way.

In short, the author's intention pertains to the "directedness" of his or her communicative action. It is a matter of what the author is doing *in tending* to his or her words. I use this phrase—*in tending*—to catch both the sense of "inclining" or "straining towards" on the one hand, and "taking care of" on the other. What does an author do *in tending* to words? Just this: the author intends both an object (e.g., the propositional content to which the author's activity is directed) and a disposition (e.g., the stance an author takes with regard to the object). Or, to use Searle's shorthand: the author intends $F(p)$—both a subject matter and the energy of an illocutionary force.

Searle considers speech acts to be the paradigm of what goes on in intentionality in general. In speech acts the speaker's attention is directed towards an object (e.g., the propositional content) in a particular manner (e.g., assertive, commissive, directive, etc.). To act with intention is thus *to attend to what one is doing*. I can "attend" the propositional content "Moses' going down" in various ways: I can give it the force of a statement, a question, a command, and so forth. The manner in which I attend to this proposition is my intention. Indeed, we would eliminate a considerable amount of confusion in hermeneutical debates by referring to the author's *attention* or to the "author's *attended* meaning."

We can nevertheless agree with Ricoeur and say that the intended meaning of the text is not the lived experience of the writer but rather what the text means for whoever complies with its "direction."[223] An author intends his or her text *as* a particular kind of communicative act, with a particular object and a particular force. The text's intention is "the direction which it opens up for life and thought."[224] According to speech act theory, it is an author's illocutionary force that determines the kind of directedness—what Searle calls the direction of fit—between the propositional content and the world.

Take, for instance, the propositional content "Jesus' walking on water." The distinction between different directions of fit is precisely the distinction between different kinds of illocution. Beliefs and assertions have a word-to-world direction of fit: "Jesus walked on water" aims to match the words to the world. Directives—illocutionary acts that attempt to get the hearer to do things—have a world-to-words direction of fit: "Jesus, walk on water!"[225] It is the author's intention that determines the direction (and manner) of fit between words and world.[226] Understanding takes place when both author and reader *attend* to the same matter in the same manner.[227] Interpretation, I conclude, is largely a matter of following directions: the direction of the author's attention (e.g., to a proposition), the direction of fit between words and world (e.g., the kind of illocution).

Basic Communicative Action: Meaning As an Emergent Property. I argued earlier that both the self and the sentence are irreducible entities. So too is human action. We experience ourselves acting in the world as agents with intentions. Thomas Aquinas described human action in terms of a voluntary movement towards some end. He distinguishes the voluntary from the violent: action that is forced onto an agent does violence, for it stems from an extrinsic, not intrinsic source. Intentional action is voluntary rather than violent. Actions are voluntary not because there is first some mental event (a volition) and then a bodily event (a movement), but rather because they come "with a certain context of belief, initiative, and desire on the part of the agent."[228] So it is with authors: there is no need to postulate some separate mental activity over and above what authors do with words. Intention is not a mental event that precedes communicative action. On the contrary, intention has to do with what the agent does *in tending* to the object of action.

Consider the wink. We wink involuntarily, though non-violently, many times an hour. Yet we also wink voluntarily, say, when we wish to make contact with a friend across a crowded room. How do we get from the physics to the semantics, from the involuntary to the voluntary, from the reflex to the intentional action? The same bodily movement—a rapid closing and opening of the eyelid—can be either an act or a non-act. What makes a wink a communicative act depends entirely on whether it was intended as such. Moreover, the wink, like the home run, is an institutional fact that cannot be explained away in terms of brute facts and lower-level causes without significant explanatory loss: "Thus no explanation of occurrences, if they are intentional acts, relying exhaustively and solely upon physical laws of cause and effect that eliminate any reference to the freedom of the human will, can adequately represent that 'part' of the real world in which action by agents takes place."[229] It is wrong to attempt to explain intentional action in terms of involuntary events, just as it is misguided to reduce communicative acts to semiotic laws.

I agree with the philosopher Edward Pols that agents execute intentions via infrastructures, which, taken by themselves, can be understood in reductionistic, non-intentional ways. One could explain the physiology of the wink, for example, in terms of reflexes and the nervous system. (The language system would be another such infrastructure, though Pols does not explicitly treat it.) Yet even a thoroughgoing physiological explanation of an eye movement may be incomplete; it may only get us as far as the blink, not the wink. Ultimately, it is the agent's intention that makes an action what it is: "This means that metaphysically one has reached the north pole of explanatory capacity when one has reached the act of an agent, or, more precisely, when one has reached the initiation of an act in the intention of its agent."[230]

Pols argues further that the unity of the act—that is, what makes it a whole and complete act—is the ultimate explanation of what that act unifies. This is a most important point. It means that one cannot understand an action by analyzing its constituent parts. To return to the example of the wink: by analyzing the various neural firings and muscular movements on the bodily level, we end up losing precisely that which unifies this sequence and makes it a wink; consequently, we lose the entire communicative act. As Blake puts it: "We murder to dissect." Furthermore, the unity of the act covers the whole temporal sequence necessary for carrying it out. When I intend a wink, I originate and unify all the infrastructural systems that I need to put in motion in order to enact my wink. Each of these stages could be examined in itself, but no one stage is the locus of the intention or of the wink. Yet if the wink is indeed a communicative act, then its explanation is incomplete and inauthentic unless reference is made to the intention that initiated and enacted it. Intention is not the first in a series of events that initiates an action, but rather the principle that unifies the whole act.[231] With regard to action, the whole is greater than the sum of its parts.

Let us now apply this analysis to communicative agency. The author's intention is the originating and unifying power that puts a linguistic system (the infrastructure) into motion in order to do something with words that the system alone cannot do. The author's intention is the real causality that alone accounts for why a text is the way it is. It is important to locate the cause of the text at the right level: not at the level of the infrastructure (the sign system) or at the level of the superstructure (e.g., the ideology), but at the level of the completed act—the level of that to which the author was attending. The author's intention is a necessary condition of the text taken as a unified and completed act.

My account of intention resists what I call "eliminative semiotics"—the tendency to reduce meaning to morphemes in motion or to explain meaning in terms of the immanence of the language system. My reformulation of the author's intention receives support, I believe, from recent work in the problem of consciousness.[232] Consciousness, and intentional action in general, requires a different set of predicates to describe it and a different type of explanation to make sense of it than those offered either by naturalists such as Darwin or by textualists such as Derrida. To use the rather technical language of the mind-body debate, we can say that meaning, like the mind, is an "emergent property." An emergent property is one that characterizes a higher order phenomenon (e.g., the brain) that has attained such a level of organizational complexity that it displays new properties (e.g., mental rather than physical) and requires new categories (e.g., the mind) to describe them.

Nancey Murphy draws an important corollary from the concept of emergence: "The new concepts needed to describe the emergent properties are neither applicable at the lower level nor reducible to (translatable into) concepts at the lower level."[233] Emergence may also be illustrated by biology. A cell is a complex phenomenon that emerges out of small infrastructures (molecules and atoms) and demands its own science (biochemistry). Similarly, mental properties depend on a biological infrastructure, yet they are irreducible to that substratum. Mental states, that is, "supervene" on physical states.[234] This way of conceiving of mind has the advantage of being the most adequate scientific explanation of consciousness and of conforming to a Christian understanding of human beings as created in the divine image.[235]

Both mind and meaning, the self and the sentence, are higher level phenomena—new beings, as it were—that are discontinuous, at least in some respects, with the lower forms (e.g., brain states, *langue*) from which they emerge. The theory of emergence is thus three things: a theory of explanatory adequacy, a theory of causal activity, and a theory of what exists (an ontology). Moreover, the theory of emergence is an effective counter to the postmodern tendency to reduce higher level phenomena (e.g., meaning) to lower, materialistic levels (e.g., signifying systems). I believe that the theory of communicative action yields a fuller explanation of how things at the lower linguistic levels get taken up into more complex literary forms and provides a better account of what we must postulate in order to account for the emergence of textual meaning. The author's intention, reconceived in terms of agency, explains how we get from the physics to the semantics. *I believe in the reality of the author's intention, for without it I cannot explain the emergence of meaning, that is to say, how meaning supervenes on written marks.*

Background and Context

Both Wittgenstein and Searle escape the trap of treating intentions as though they were mental processes that can be observed by introspection. Thiselton states: "'To intend' a linguistic meaning is emphatically *not to perform some action or process separable from the linguistic act or process itself*."[236] In Thiselton's view, even Schleiermacher, despite saying that we have to understand an author better than the author understood himself, is less interested in getting into the author's psyche than he is in understanding the life world or background of his communicative acts. As Wittgenstein notes, the grammar of meaning "is embedded in a situation from which it takes it rise."[237] In short, intended actions have contexts. However, the intention only emerges as a distinct phenomenon when one offers descriptions of a communicative act in the light of an appropriate context. In order to reconstruct the author's intention, therefore, we must "triangulate" the intention, the linguistic conventions, and the communicative context.

Attending to conventions and constitutive rules means knowing something about the state of a language system at a given time and about the circumstances of communicative action: "X counts as Y *in context C*." According to Moisés Silva, "the context does not merely help us understand meaning; it virtually *makes* meaning."[238] I earlier suggested that the golden rule for evaluating propositions and property alike is: location, location, location. What exactly is the role of context with regard to meaning construed as intentional communicative action? Three questions in particular stand out: What is a context? What do contexts do? How large is a context?

The Intentional Context. (1) What is a context? Context identifies the circumstances relevant to something under consideration. What is under consideration in interpretation is the nature of communicative action. In particular, we need to identify the relevant circumstances and the background rules that make a string of words or sentences count as such and such a communicative act. Let us define "context" as the various factors one has to take into consideration together with the text in order to understand the author's intention. Any number of circumstances or contexts might be relevant to this task: historical, linguistic, literary, canonical, sociological, and so forth.

(2) What do contexts do? Authorial intention is always located in a network of beliefs and practices that form the background for communicative action. Think of the background as the kind of board on which a rule-governed game will be played. A Monopoly board is different from a chessboard, and so, therefore, is what counts as a move. Michael LaFargue argues that biblical interpreters should try to recover not merely the mind of the author but the background, the *mind-set*: "the author's word- and image-associations, the linguistic and literary conventions governing his speech, the shape of his existential concerns, and his mode of engagement with his own text."[239] In other words, interpreters should recover not the only the author's intentions but the corporate intentions that constitute the state of linguistic and literary conventions at a given time, for the prevailing corporate intentions, by and large, are what structure an author's life world. As we come to know the context, we recover the ability to construe an author's words as he or she construed them, "to see reality as he saw it."[240] Wendell Harris speaks of "koinonoetic" interpretation in order to

emphasize the extent to which understanding relies on shared contexts: "Meaning is dependent on the author prospectively and the reader retrospectively sharing the context. . . . What others know and know we know are shared contexts."[241]

(3) How large is a context? That depends; the circumstances relevant to understanding texts can pertain to the author, to the form of literature, to general background knowledge, or to knowledge of specific situations. Searle argues effectively that intentions only make sense against a "background" of assumptions and practices that are not themselves intentions. For instance, a person's declaration "I am running for President of the United States" only makes sense against a background of non-intentional circumstances, such as there being a country called the United States that has periodic presidential elections. I suggest that the context of textual interpretation should be as broad (or as narrow) as it needs to be in order to make sense of the author's communicative act. The relevant circumstances are those that enable us to identify the game board and the game being played. Often the text itself—the literary context—is sufficient evidence of the author's intention to engage in such and such a form of rule-governed communicative behavior.

Legal Contexts. Determining an agent's intention is often literally a matter of life and death. Establishing intention in the courtroom, for instance, means ascribing actions and assigning responsibility. Traditionally, a person is not thought to have acted criminally without some consideration of *mens rea* ("the mental element of the act"). An act is not guilty unless the mind is also guilty. Yet bare intentions (what I called "mapping intentions") never put into action do not constitute legal guilt either. R. A. Duff, a philosopher of law, defines intention as "acting to bring about a result."[242] Intention is distinct from both "desire" and from "foresight." Intention is rather "acting in order to." Thus far, Duff's analysis is consistent with my own; the author's intention is not a matter of what the author wanted to do, nor of what the author believed might happen as a consequence, but rather of what the author was doing and actually did. The link between intentions and illocutions (what one *does* in saying) remains firm.

Intriguingly, Duff's distinction between the "result" of an action and its "consequence" corresponds precisely to the distinction between illocutions and perlocutions.[243] As Duff rightly observes, "I 'intend' what I have decided to bring about; but I cannot intend a result which is 'wholly beyond' my control."[244] A "result" is what occurs when the action is done (e.g., what one does *in* saying something). The result, one might say, is an aspect of the action: the food going down my throat is a result of my swallowing. If the food doesn't go down, I have not swallowed. "To discern an agent's intentions is to grasp the relation between her action and its context . . . what she will count as success or failure in what she does."[245] The "consequence" of an action, on the other hand, is an event that follows from or is *caused by* the action. As a consequence of my swallowing, I may appease my hunger. Then again I may not (I may want seconds). Consequences are not tied to actions as closely as are results. Consequences are not intrinsic, but extrinsic, to actions. Consequences have to do with ulterior, perlocutionary purposes. As such, they fall outside the purview of intended action.

Perlocutionary intentions, I suggest, are aimed at producing consequences. We discover what illocutionary act is being performed, on the other hand, by asking, "What are you doing?" and we answer that question by specifying what would count as a satisfactory result. Searle devotes an entire chapter in *Speech Acts* to analyzing the necessary and sufficient conditions for the successful performance of the illocutionary act of promising. The "propositional" condition of a promise is that the speaker must predicate a future act of himself or herself. The "essential" condition of a promise is that the utterance counts as a commitment to do the future act. These conditions must be satisfied in order for the action to have a "result," or to be performed at all.[246]

In a legal context, it is vitally important to describe the action correctly, as such descriptions ascribe responsibility—blame or merit—to the agent. The question is: What are we describing? Duff's answer is in line with the approach developed thus far: what we describe is an intended action—what the agent was attending to in doing *x*. Moreover, to describe what an agent is doing we need not postulate some prior psychological process. We discover intention by looking to the action itself. The author's intention is that intrinsic, emergent factor that constitutes a text *as* what it is (e.g., history, apocalyptic, parable, etc.). Understanding an author's intention is not a matter of recovering psychic phenomena but of reconstructing a public performance in terms that makes its nature as an intended action clear. Briefly, to understand an author is to understand what he or she was doing, his or her illocutionary act. This is no more difficult with texts than with any other kind of human action: "Human intercourse consists largely of making sense of people in their own terms while at the same time thinking about them in one's own terms."[247] Duff therefore rejects any mind-body dualism: intention is not some mental process that precedes bodily movement, but is rather intrinsic to the action itself.

Meaning As Embodied-Enacted Authorial Intention

In his intriguing essay on responsibility, "Three Ways of Spilling Ink," J. L. Austin suggests that intentionality pertains to the fact that agents usually have a general idea of what they are doing. Intention is like "a miner's lamp on our forehead which illumines always just so far ahead as we go along."[248] Austin's account agrees with Duff. An agent's intention is the way an agent thinks about what he is doing in his mind as he is doing it; an agent's purpose is something to be achieved as a result of what she is doing. It is this intentional stance toward her activity that makes an agent's bodily motion "count" as a wink to a friend rather than an involuntary bodily movement.

To sum up: the meaning of a text emerges only against the backdrop of the author's intended action and the background of the author's context.

(1) *Every text is the result of an enacted intention.* Every piece of writing has its agent and its time. Searle defines the "meaning intention" as the intention "with which the act is performed which makes it the act that it is."[249] I have argued that there is more to meaning than signs relating to other signs. The "more" is the author's intention, but this does not refer to hidden mental states so much as to the directedness of the text as a meaningful act. Intention is not something that can be reduced to simpler non-intentional events; it is rather an emergent property that is required to explain what illocutionary act has been performed in a text. What we see in the text is the author's intentional action: "Persons and action, that is, are logically *basic* categories; these concepts cannot be explained by an analysis which seeks to reduce them to supposedly simpler elements."[250]

(2) *Every text is an embodied intention.* Writing fixes the author's enacted intention in a stable verbal structure. It is only fallacious to appeal to intention when the appeal is to some mental, pre-textual event, rather than to the intention embodied in the text. According to Nathan Scott, "verbal meaning is constituted of those intentions of the author which are *embodied* in his text and which, under the prevailing conventions that control linguistic usage, are *shareable* by his readers."[251] My purpose in this section has been to lay the basis for a clear distinction between a mapping-intention and a meaning-intention, a distinction that serves to demarcate the work of the interpreter from the work of the psychologist.

Is there a meaning in the text? Properly to describe meaning requires us to describe the author's intended action—not the plan with which the author set out to write, nor the consequences that an author hoped to achieve by writing, but what the author was doing *in* writing, *in* tending to his words in such and such a fashion. The reality to which interpreters are accountable and to which their descriptions must correspond if they seek to be true is grounded in the author's embodied and enacted intention. This level alone allows us to achieve the most satisfactory possible explanation of why a text is the way it is. Understanding is a matter of recognizing the author's embodied and enacted intentions. It will be the burden of Chapter 6 to argue that readers can come to know the author's intention, at least in a provisional manner, and that they can offer relatively adequate descriptions of communicative acts. Here I have only wanted to argue that the concept of authorial intention, as recast from psychology into a philosophy of action, is the essential condition for any talk about both meaningful action considered as a text and about the text considered as meaningful action.

On the Definition of Meaning As Author's Intention: A Brief Excursus

Is the definition of meaning as "what the author intended (did)" an arbitrary definition? Or a stipulative one? Let us avoid the term meaning and review what interpreters are typically after as they read. If one is not reading for the author's intended message, what exactly is one doing?

(1) "I am trying to reconstruct the original historical situation." This is, perhaps, equivalent to saying, "I am using the text as evidence for something else." Specifically, this approach is more interested in the context than in the text itself. On my view, however, interpreters are not trying to recreate the background so much as to determine *what happened.* I would therefore contest the notion that "interpretation" is primarily a matter of trying to get back *behind* the text.

(2) "I am trying to reconstruct the history of the text's composition." Again, this is a laudable enterprise, but one that is only marginal to the task of interpretation and understanding. It is an instance of looking *at* the mirror instead of in it.

(3) "I am trying to uncover the ideological interests that motivated the author and to criticize them in light of what we now believe about human liberation, morality, and human rights." A most praiseworthy aim—but what is its connection to the task of interpretation? Does one not first have to recover "what is said/done" (by the author) in order to go on to criticize it? And is not the task of determining "what is said" precisely what I have acknowledged to be the goal of interpretation? If so, then

this position articulates not an alternative definition of meaning so much as a step beyond it, towards evaluating the author's enacted intention.

(4) "I am reading to see what I can get out of the text." But is interpretation purely a private matter? Is there no sense in which what one gets out of a text is to be shared— between author and reader, as well as between readers? This position, if taken to its extreme, is better classified as invention or creation, even "authoring." At the limit, this option treats the text as though it had been written by the reader. In other words, the meaning is the sense the words have borne had the *reader* written them.

(5) "I am exploring the sense potential of the text. I am reading for the text's intention, not the author's." This last option is, in my opinion, the most plausible alternative to the position defended in the present work. But is it cogent? What does it mean to speak of the text's "sense potential"? If it means the sense I think these words *now* bear (to me here and now), then this position dissolves into the preceding one. On the other hand, if it refers to the sense potential the words had in their original context, then we are determining what the author might, or *could have*, intended. But this is to make the author's intended meaning the goal of the interpretive process. In short, what appears to be a plausible alternative to my own view of meaning ends up affirming it.

Intentional and Unintentional Effects

What are the implications of the preceding analysis for what I have called the metaphysics of meaning? Textual meaning, I have argued, enjoys an independence and integrity of its own, apart from the process of interpretation, thanks to the nature and directedness of the author's communicative act. The author attends to a particular matter (the propositional content) in a particular way (the illocutionary act); the author's intention is what makes his or her words count as one kind of action rather than another. Hermeneutic realism is a matter of past communicative action. In subsequent chapters I will address two further questions: "Can what the author is doing in the text be known?" (ch. 6), and "Should readers care about what authors are doing?" (ch. 7). Before I turn to these epistemological and ethical problems, however, I want to explore further certain aspects of my view of meaning as communicative action. The most important of these concerns the *unintended* effects of communicative action. Are these part and parcel of textual meaning too?

Accidents and the Author's Intention

What is the relation between what the author intends to bring about and what actually happens when someone reads the text? In the context of legal theory, disputes about an agent's intention often concern the consequences of one's actions. For example, when Mrs. Hyam struck the match, did she intend to kill anyone or only to start a fire?[252] Do I "intend" whatever I foresee as a likely or probable consequence of my action? Could Nietzsche have intended (or be held responsible for) Hitler's appropriation of his notion of the Superman? Was it the intention of the author of the patriarchal narratives in Genesis to promote patriarchy? Should one hold the biblical authors responsible for all subsequent uses of their texts? It is precisely such questions that make the distinction between the author's intent and the reader's appropriation imperative.

Mrs. Hyam was convicted of murder because the court ruled that an agent's intention includes what is a likely or highly probable consequence of an action. Duff, for his part, distinguishes an action's intended effects (which an agent acts to bring about) from its foreseen side effects (which an agent expects but may or may not want). For legal and for literary reasons, I believe that it is also important to distinguish between intended results (illocutions), foreseen or desired consequences (perlocutions), and consequences neither intended nor foreseen (accidents). It is true that authors often hope to achieve something by their communicative acts over and above understanding. However, as we noted earlier, authors are not in control of these further, perlocutionary, effects. Moreover, the consequences of communicative actions are often unforeseen. The author's communicative act is never the sole causal factor in bringing about a perlocutionary effect. Only the illocutionary, therefore, refers to something intrinsic to the action. Strictly speaking, then, consequences should not be considered part of the internal structure of the action.

Are the patriarchal narratives guilty of patriarchy? Ethical "consequentialists" believe that the rightness or wrongness of an action depends solely on the goodness of badness of its outcome. The equivalent in literary criticism is to judge the goodness or badness of a text by reader responses. On this view, to take the patriarchal narratives as sexist is to *make* them sexist. Non-consequentialists such as Duff, on the other hand, believe that the moral significance of an action depends not on its outcome but on the intentions that structure it.[253] Here the question is not whether Genesis is taken to be sexist but whether its author intends to promote sexism. The meaning of a communicative act depends not on its outcome (e.g., how it is received by readers) but on the direction and the purposive structure of the author's action. Meaning, in other words, refers to the intrinsic action—to the illocution and its intended result—not to its unforeseen consequences. To display a world where men rule, as the patriarchal narratives do, is not necessarily to commend it. The difference between description and prescription is crucial in evaluating the biblical stories, if indeed the intrinsic action of narrative is "displaying a world." In any case, the main point of the patriarchal narratives is not to provide a blueprint for social order but to chart the history of God's covenant dealings with Israel. That the patriarchal narratives would be read as, and criticized for, promoting patriarchy is an unforeseen and unintended consequence of the text, and thus not part of its meaning (i.e., not part of what their authors were doing).

If the biblical narratives have come to be read as promoting sexism (or racism, for that matter), this should be seen as an unintended consequence of the authors' communicative action for which they ought not be held responsible. Accidents may form part of the observable process of our bodily movement, or in this case the history of a text's reception, but they are not "integrated" with the agent's action and cannot be considered part of the agent's intention. I may break a glass (unintended consequence) when I am washing the dishes (intended result), yet this is not my "act." If asked what I am doing in the kitchen, I would not answer "breaking dishes." In the final analysis, however, the distinction between act and accident cannot be determined by any inference from brute fact, but only by establishing the agent's intentions. The moral is clear: the best way to avoid interpretive accidents is to attend to authorial intention.

Ambiguity and the Author's Intention

"Ambiguity" refers to the uncertainty surrounding words or texts that seem to give rise to two or more senses. Garden-variety ambiguity—mere vagueness or confusion—is often considered a fault. True, some communicative acts may be performed sloppily. The status of literary ambiguity, however, is, well . . . more ambiguous. William Empson's 1930 study argues that ambiguity is a literary device that uses a word or expression to signify two or more things.[254] Ambiguous words have implications beyond their literal sense. Indeed, one might say that ambiguity is a catch-all term that covers all those forms of discourse that mean more, or other, than they apparently say (e.g., allegory, metaphor, irony, etc.).[255]

Multiple Meanings? According to Hirsch, appeals to the author's intention "disambiguate" textual meaning. Hirsch apparently assumes that ambiguity is an obstacle to valid interpretation. It is easy to see how it could be. Absolute ambiguity would render all interpretive efforts hopeless. If ambiguity is the last word, if it's ambiguity all the way down, then there is nothing in the text for the reader to approximate, or for that matter, to appropriate. A little ambiguity, however, might not be such a dangerous thing. Indeed, authors might actually *intend* to communicate something other than what they explicitly say.[256] In some cases, of course, ambiguity is accidental; the author, through negligence or incompetence, performs a clumsy communicative act.[257] In other cases, though, ambiguity is intentional. Indeed, far from working against my theory of communicative action, I believe that we can only account for certain forms of ambiguity by appealing to authorial intentions.

To act, communicatively or otherwise, is to attend to what one is doing. Can an author intend two things at a time or do two things at once? Does the author ever intend more than that of which he or she is explicitly aware? Some critics think so: "I'm certain that the only meanings that are worth anything in a work of art, are those that the artist himself knows nothing about."[258] I disagree. Those descriptions of the action—of its intrinsic structure, of its illocutions—that count as genuine interpretations depend on the author's awareness of what he or she is doing. I will illustrate this thesis by considering three areas of ambiguity in interpretation: allusion, irony, and the history/fiction distinction. All claims that a text alludes to some previous text, that it is ironic, or that it is fiction rather than history depend, logically and ontologically, on what the author was actually doing.

Allusion. To allude is to refer to something—a person, place, event, or other text—indirectly. Allusion is particularly important for biblical studies, given the complex relations between the Old and New Testaments. The New Testament both explicitly quotes and alludes to the Old Testament. Perhaps the most important of these allusive relations is typology, the study of how Old Testament events and persons prefigure events and persons in the New Testament. In typology, allusion can refer not only back, to something earlier, but forward, to something future. According to Paul and a number of the early church fathers, Adam is a "type" or "figure"—an indirect reference to Christ.

Umberto Eco, in his dual capacity as literary theorist and novelist, makes some interesting comments on how it feels as an author to be told by a reader what he meant. He relates how he called one of the characters in *Foucault's Pendulum*

"Casaubon," after a historical philologist. "I was aware that few readers would have been able to catch the allusion, but I was equally aware that, in terms of textual strategy, this was not indispensable."[259] Before he had completed *Foucault's Pendulum*, however, he discovered that Casaubon was also a character in George Eliot's novel *Middlemarch*. Coincidentally, the character in *Middlemarch* was fascinated by mythology, an important theme in Eco's novel too. Eco was thus led to wonder whether he had read *Middlemarch* years earlier and whether this was not an unconscious factor in his choosing the name Casaubon. Eco's thought experiment well illustrates the issue: Does meaning always coincide with what authors were aware of doing?

From the standpoint of the hermeneutic realism advanced in the present work, whether a text alludes to a previous text logically depends on what the author *could have done* in tending to his words. An author's knowledge of a name or a phrase is a necessary precondition for her being able to allude to it. Allusion without authorial intention is a logical contradiction. Were a New Testament author to produce an Old Testament phrase verbatim, it would be only an accidental coincidence, not an allusion, if he had not previously known it.

Irony. The phenomenon of irony is similarly instructive. A mere word sequence is not able to signal irony, for irony is, by definition, a mode of speech of which the meaning is contrary to the words: "the art of saying something without really saying it."[260] Irony is notoriously difficult to identify. Yet it is precisely the elusiveness of verbal irony that makes it a good test case for our thesis that meaning is a matter of communicative action. Wayne Booth notes that "irony is an extraordinarily good road into the whole art of interpretation."[261] Yet another reason to examine the role of authorial intentions in irony is that irony is the preferred mode of much deconstructionist criticism. Indeed, irony has become a virtual worldview in the postmodern era among those who believe that no text ever means what it says. The ironist is doomed to remain, like Nietzsche, in the uncomfortable position of one who is committed to the truth that truth is inaccessible. A closer examination of verbal irony, however, will show that even here—where the meaning is contrary to the words— interpretation is a matter of determining the author's intentions.

Irony is, I submit, a kind of communicative action. "Verbal irony implies an ironist, someone consciously and intentionally employing a technique."[262] Booth agrees that ironies are deliberately intended: "They are not mere openings, provided unconsciously, or accidental statements allowing the confirmed pursuer of ironies to read them as reflections against the author."[263] Whether a word or speech act is ironic depends "not on the ingenuity of the reader but on the intentions that constitute the creative act."[264] The words "Hail, king of the Jews" (Mark 15:18) are ironic because the reader knows the soldiers do not believe what they say. Yet, as reported in Mark's Gospel, this mocking designation illustrates not only verbal but dramatic irony, for unbeknownst to Jesus' mockers, he really is the king of the Jews. Mark 15:18 is a good illustration of the subtle results authors can achieve with words.

Booth cites Samuel Butler's statement as another example of irony: "I had indeed a hairbreadth escape; but, as luck would have it, Providence was on my side."[265] This sentence is hard to take literally; people who believe in luck do not normally believe in providence, and vice versa. Readers have to reconstruct the author's meaning in order to get the ironic point. Most readers experience no ambiguity whatsoever, for the author makes his ironic intent sufficiently evident. Indeed, any clue that readers care to give that a text is ironic "can be stated in the form of an inference about an implied author's intention."[266]

Coming to see a text as ironic involves three steps. (1) Reject the literal meaning because of the incongruity between the words or between the words and something else the reader knows (e.g., one cannot believe in luck and providence). (2) Decide about the author's knowledge and beliefs: Is he crazy? Is she being inconsistent? Is he intending to say something other than the surface meaning? (3) Choose a reconstructed meaning that will be in harmony with the unspoken beliefs that the reader has decided to attribute to the author.

One will only recognize a textual ambiguity as irony on the basis of one's beliefs about the author's intentions—about what an author is up to in the text. The author, similarly, has to depend on assumptions about what his readers will probably assume or know, both about the world and about how to read texts. Booth claims that authors and readers must share three kinds of commonality for irony to be successful: a commonality of language, a commonality of life world, and a commonality of literary experience. While it is true that authors sometimes mean other than what they appear to say, these three sets of commonalities or horizons make communication possible. They also match, more or less exactly, what Hirsch calls the "three horizons" of textual interpretation.

(1) There is, first, a linguistic horizon (e.g., the range of meanings that a word or text could have had at a particular time). The same words have different meanings when used by different people. At the very least, knowing a text's author allows us to situate the text at a particular point in the history of a language. Even the authors of the "intentionalist fallacy" knew that biographical evidence helps us to determine the meaning of an author's words. What does Hamlet mean when he says of his uncle, "I'll tent him to the quick"?[267] Knowing that "tent" was used in Elizabethan England to signify "probe" helps us to understand that Hamlet wanted to investigate his uncle for murder rather than send him on a hasty camping trip. "Not even the strongest opponents of the 'intentionalist fallacy' would deny that words can have identifiable meanings and that these meanings may be dependent in some respects on the identity of the author."[268]

(2) Hirsch also speaks of the author's horizon. Interpreters must familiarize themselves "with the typical meanings of the author's mental and experiential world."[269] That means being familiar with the corporate intentions that structure the author's world as well as the author's individual intentions. Juhl's comment on one critic's reading of John Donne is relevant: "No doubt, Donne was not thinking of all the associations Hough mentions, but surely they are the sort of thing Donne meant."[270] The critic draws out what may have been in the "back of Donne's mind."

(3) Lastly, there is the generic horizon, the set of literary expectations shared by author and reader that creates an implicit sense of the whole.

History or Fiction? To some extent, of course, literary genres are themselves ambiguous. Here too, however, must we not say that they are what they are thanks to the author's intention? Fiction, for instance, is ultimately determined by the author's awareness of what he or she is doing. Searle points out that there is no textual marker that infallibly identifies a work of fiction as fiction rather than history.[271] Michael Crichton's *Andromeda Strain*, a work of science fiction, begins with the notice: "This is a true story." The only factor that makes a story fiction rather than history is the manner of the author's attention, which dictates the "direction of fit" between the words and the world (or the partial suspension of the relation, as in fiction). Booth confesses that he is struck "by how often the critic's final court of appeal is explicitly to what the author—being such-and-such a kind of man—must have done or not done."[272] Reconstructing the intentions of the implied author relies on inferences about authorial intentions that in turn depend both on our grasp of the text as a whole and on our knowledge of facts outside the text.

To summarize: I have argued that the author's intention should be confused neither with what an author planned to write nor with what the author unintentionally brings about. Meaning is a matter of what the author is attending to and of the way he or she attends to it. How focused is the author's attention? Do not speakers communicate some things unintentionally—through their body language, for instance? Might not authors communicate some things—about their historical context, their social situation, the prevailing ideology—of which they are similarly unaware? Must we limit meaning to the author's focal awareness, or can it cover things of which the author was only tacitly aware (or unaware) too? In short, is it never appropriate for the reader to discover something in the text of which the author was not, *nor could have been*, aware? Such queries require us to take one more step in order to justify our identification of meaning with the author's communicative action.

MEANING AND SIGNIFICANCE *REDIVIVUS*

Hirsch, we may recall, contrasts what the author willed once-for-all, which is permanently fixed "in" the text, with the inexhaustible relations that this authorial meaning has to readers, texts, and contexts outside it. Textual meaning does not change because it is tied to what an author intended, and did, in the past. Juhl agrees: "The speech act which a man performs by producing a certain word sequence cannot change at all, regardless of changes in the language, culture, or whatever; for it is uniquely determined at the time it is performed."[273] A statement remains a statement, a promise remains a promise, and irony remains irony.

For Hirsch, the issue is clear: "Without the stable determinacy of meaning there can be no knowledge in interpretation."[274] The reality of meaning is grounded on past action: "Stable meaning depends, then, on pastness."[275] There is a determinate something "in" the text—intended meaning—that remains fixed and unchanging throughout the history of its interpretation. Yet many interpreters are more interested in the present than the past, and in the question, "What does it mean, here and now, to me?" The concern for relevance—for reading with the aim of bringing a text to bear on contemporary concerns—is a concern for what Hirsch calls "significance." Unlike meaning, the significance of a text can change, for significance pertains to the relation between the text's determinate meaning and a larger context (i.e., another era, another culture, another subject matter).

Booth defines significance as "the whole range of social and historical association and of approval and disapproval that a given sentence or a given work takes on as it moves out into space and time from its intending author."[276] A text's significance is a function of how the text comes to be explained and evaluated in terms of contexts not presumed by the author.[277] Significance corresponds more to *criticism* than to interpretation, that is, to "all of the indefinitely extendible interpretations that any work might be given by individuals or societies pursuing their own interests unchecked by intentions."[278] This is the object of criticism (e.g., political, feminist, Freudian). For instance, various readers may come to the argument in the present work with their own agendas. Some may believe that my attempt to draw a distinction between meaning and significance is indicative of some psychological dysfunction. Others may think that my desire to preserve determinate meaning is part of a sexist plot to render the author an authoritative father figure, the author as owner of meaning. However, these attempts to "explain away" my communicative acts should not be confused with attempts to understand it. To explain *why* I am doing something is not the same as understanding *what* I am doing.

Hence there are two tasks for readers, *communicative* and *strategic*: "We read with two purposes: to understand what the author means, and to relate that meaning to what we know, believe, seek to know, or might believe."[279] The goal of the first task, of interpretation proper, is "the reconstruction of intended meaning that attempts to take into account as far as possible the context in which the author assumed the anticipated audience would place the utterance or text."[280] The challenge is to "become competent to construe [the author's] words as he construed them, and so to see reality as he saw it."[281] The second task is secondary precisely because it depends on the successful completion of the first; one can only relate textual meaning to non-communicative purposes after one has first understood the communicative act for what it is. Hermeneutic realism ultimately rests on this distinction between meaning and significance, on the distinction "between an object of knowledge and the context in which it is known."[282]

How does my definition of meaning in terms of communicative action stand in relation to Hirsch's distinction between meaning and significance? I will address this question, first, by recasting the meaning/significance distinction in terms of the author's attention span. Second, Hirsch's notion of the "author's original context" has to be made more precise, especially so in the case of the Bible, where the possibility of divine-human authorship—of *God* speaking—seems, at first glance, to risk overturning the distinction between past and present meaning altogether. These corrections notwithstanding, I nevertheless agree with Hirsch that the author's intended meaning should remain the regulative principle for interpretation. I will conclude, then, that with regard to interpretation, the meaning/significance distinction continues to be both meaningful and highly significant.

The Author's Attention Span

Intention, as I have here defined it, should not be confused with "planning." Yet authors may have a plan for what consequences, other than understanding, they want to bring off by their communicative acts, though ultimately authors cannot control how people receive their texts. To produce a text that will be not only meaningful but significant requires not only communicative but *strategic* action. Whereas communicative action brings about its results—warning, promising, stating—regardless of the reader's response and aims only at achieving understanding, the consequences of a strategic action are not intrinsic to the action itself. As a first approximation, then, I suggest that meaning is a matter of illocutions, while significance concerns perlocutions.

An author can, of course, try to achieve a perlocutionary effect. My perlocutionary intent in this section, for example, is to convince the reader of the soundness of the meaning/significance distinction. I may or may not achieve this perlocutionary effect. Yet my success or failure on the perlocutionary level does not affect what I have said (the meaning) in this text. If you remain unpersuaded, that does not indicate (I hope) that the argument is meaningless, but rather that, having grasped the nature of the paragraph (an argument) and understood the premises, you judge the argument either to be invalid or to offer less than the conclusion requires. In that case, my perlocutionary intent will have failed and my text will be judged insignificant. Perlocutionary intents fail regularly, but this does not threaten the possibility of communication, *for perlocutionary intents pertain not to the act but to the effects of meaning*. If, on the other hand, I fail in my illocutionary intent, then the communicative act itself is defective. My statements are not statements; my promises are not promises; my arguments are not arguments. Illocutionary intent is thus constitutive of communicative action and of meaning in a way that perlocutionary intent is not.

Now for the complication. The meaning/significance distinction contrasts an author's past action either with desired effects over which the author has no control (e.g., perlocutions, intended significance) on the one hand, or with unforeseen consequences a text has on present readers (e.g., accidents, unintended significance) on the other. What are we to make, however, of cases where an author intends to address readers *in contexts other than the author's own*? Is such an intention a matter of mapping or meaning? We have seen that writing allows authors to communicate *at a distance*. Just what is the author's *attention span*?

Hirsch has recently put forward a case for what he calls "transhistorical intentions."[283] Though he wishes to preserve the meaning/significance distinction, he is uncomfortable with restricting the author's intended meaning to the original context or content alone. In a move that parallels Brevard Childs's treatment of "canonic intentionality," Hirsch now sees authors as intending to address *the future*: "We intend our meanings to transcend our momentary limitations of attention and knowledge."[284] Literature, like the biblical canon or a political constitution, is "an instrument designed for broad and continuing future applications."[285]

Behind Hirsch's modification of the meaning/significance distinction is a concern for relevance. Does pastness imply irrelevance? Some meanings do become dated; their original sense is of little significance today. Hirsch has no desire to *make* dated texts significant by creative interpretation, however, for this reduces the text to the mouthpiece of the interpreter. His strategy is rather to speak of open-ended authorial intentions. Shakespeare's sonnets, for instance, attend not only to Shakespeare's love, but to human love in general: "When I apply Shakespeare's sonnet to my own lover rather than to his, I do not change his meaning-intention but rather instantiate and fulfill it. It is the nature of textual meaning to embrace many different future fulfillments without thereby being changed."[286] Hence, if I were to apply the sonnets to my beloved, this is not an example of significance but of meaning, even if Shakespeare himself was not attending to her. A second example: When Joseph Priestly writes in his *Observations on Different Kinds of Air* (1772) about "dephlogisticated air," historians of science know that he intended to refer to what we now call "oxygen." In other words, Priestly was *attending to* oxygen, though in a less explicit way than scientists today. The point is that an author's intended meaning can tolerate a small revision in mental content and still remain the same. Hirsch contends, following Saul Kripke, that words can still refer even when the author's actual mental contents prove to be inadequate or dated.[287] Priestly "meant" oxygen because he was referring (i.e., directing his attention towards) to oxygen, even though the propositional content with which he was working—dephlogisticated air—was an inadequate description.

It follows from Hirsch's notion of transhistorical intention that certain applications may belong to the meaning rather than the significance side of the meaning/significance distinction. Indeed, Hirsch is even willing to countenance a modest form of allegorical interpretation in which present-day readers can read authors as meaning something *other* than they say (Priestly *said* "dephlogisticated air" but *meant* "oxygen").[288] Intriguingly, Hirsch calls for an "Augustinian" approach that avoids the extremes of, on the one hand, getting stuck in the past with the "originalists," and neglecting the past with the "non-originalists" on the other: "Interpretation must always go beyond the writer's letter, but never beyond the writer's spirit."[289]

In this chapter I have urged interpreters to rethink authorial intention in terms of communicative agency in order to escape the deconstructive undoing of the subject and the concomitant death of the author. Intention is enacted and embodied in the text; consequently, it is to the text that we must go in order to determine what an author has done in tending to his or her words. As we have seen, communicative acts, unlike other types of acts, have a clear beginning and end. *The meaning/significance distinction is fundamentally a distinction between a completed action and its ongoing intentional or unintentional consequences.* It is one thing to describe an action, quite another to describe its diverse effects. Hirsch's "allegories," I suggest, are neither new acts nor unintended effects, but rather applications of the original intended meaning. I would therefore be happier to speak of meaning in terms of the author's intended meaning and of significance in terms of the author's *extended* meaning.

When authors successfully enact their intentions, we can say *meaning accomplished*; when these meanings are brought to bear on other texts and contexts and so achieve perlocutionary effects, we should say *meaning applied*. To this point, however, I have said little concerning the criteria for legitimate applications (that is the task of subsequent chapters); I have argued only that meaning is to be equated with the author's intended communicative act. Whether readers are able to recover authorial intentions, and whether they should even try, raise epistemological and ethical issues that will be the subject of the next two chapters. This chapter aims only for clarity with regard to the metaphysics of meaning by defining meaning in terms of illocutionary action: *the meaning of a text is what the author attended to in tending to his words.*

The distinction between meaning and significance is, at root, a corollary of the belief in the reality of the past. For the realist, one cannot change the past simply by interpreting it differently. The way Jesus was in history, for example, does not change at the behest of our changing interpretations. The *meaning* of Jesus is independent of our attempts to express his *significance*. That is not to say that we cannot have new interpretive insights, but to insist that these insights, insofar as they enable a more adequate reading of the text, reveal something already there that had previously escaped notice.

It follows, then, that the author's authority partakes of the authority of the past, or better, of the authority of the *reality* of the past, which is in turn the authority of truth (e.g., Matthew did *this*, not that). Without this basic distinction between meaning and significance, subsequent distinctions—between exegesis and eisegesis, understanding and overstanding, commentary and criticism—will be difficult, if not impossible, to maintain. Without some such criterion for discriminating "what it meant" to the author from "what it means" to the reader, interpreters risk confusing the aim of the text with their own aims and interests. It is one thing to fuse horizons, quite another to *confuse* them. Contemporary readers who reject the meaning/significance distinction, refuse hermeneutic realism, and ignore the author's intended meaning as a goal and guide, condemn themselves to such confusion, and to interpretive narcissism besides. Bereft of intrinsic meaning, a text becomes a screen on which readers project their own images or a surface that reflects the interpreter's own face.

Inspired Intentions and *Sensus Plenior*

There remains a final objection to my reinvigorated distinction between meaning and significance that pertains to biblical interpretation in particular. Does not the *divine* author intend a fuller meaning (a *sensus plenior*) than what the human authors could have meant? If so, should we associate the "word of God" with the Bible's meaning, its significance, or both? In short, should the doctrine of biblical inspiration affect the way in which one interprets the Bible, and if so, how?

A belief in divine authorship lies behind the medieval practice of searching for multiple senses in Scripture: "All the meanings which can be found in scripture by human ingenuity, and which are consonant with orthodoxy of faith, may be taken to have been put there by God. No human interpreter can think of anything God has not intended."[290] Thomas Aquinas, for instance, believes that God arranges the events in history so that they too signify something. He here proceeds from a theological assumption, "that Divine providence could cause things to signify still other things."[291] It is not simply that the words have a fuller meaning, but that the text's referents signify things too. Aquinas controls the possible excesses of such "fuller" interpretation by according theological primacy to the literal sense: "Nothing necessary to faith is contained under the spiritual sense which is not elsewhere put forward by the scripture in its literal sense."[292]

Modern biblical scholars continue to wrestle with the tension between "what it meant" to the original author and "what it means" to the church today. The tension is most noticeable when one considers the "fuller meaning" that the authors of the New Testament were able to find in the Old Testament. Raymond Brown, a leading Roman Catholic biblical scholar, distinguishes between literal meaning (what it meant to its author), canonical meaning (what it meant to those who first accepted it as Scripture), and contemporary meaning (what it means today in the context of the Christian community). There are thus two ways in which meaning goes beyond what the author could have intended: (1) when the text is read in the context of the canon as a whole, and (2) when the text is read in the light of the church's ongoing tradition. Brown is thus willing to accept a "fuller" meaning, though he insists that the author's intended meaning must remain "a conscience and a control."[293]

To take a concrete example: Could the author of Isaiah 53 have intended to predict, allude, or otherwise refer to Jesus' passion, an event that had not yet taken place at the time of composition? This particular text serves as a particularly sharp instance of what Christian readers say more generally about the Old Testament, namely, that it is, somehow, about Jesus Christ. Is it possible to hold to a view of meaning as past communicative action and still affirm that the Old Testament has a "fuller meaning" than what its human authors could have intended? Perhaps it is, but only if one is willing to acknowledge the possibility of *divine* authorship.[294] Where is the divine intention enacted and embodied, and how does it relate to the intention of the human authors? The answer lies, I believe, in viewing the canon as a divine communicative act.[295] Let us now consider how divine authorship adds a new dimension to Hirsch's notion of transhistorical intention.

Hirsch now admits that even certain non-biblical texts (e.g., the American Constitution) seem to acquire a meaning that goes beyond anything that their human historical authors could possibly have intended. Yet Hirsch also believes that the framers of the Constitution may have willed their texts to have applications in situations that they knew to be beyond their explicit knowledge, "for some genres of texts the author submits to the convention that his willed implications must go far beyond what he explicitly knows."[296] Brevard Childs, similarly, claims that the canonizers intended Scripture to function authoritatively for future generations too. We must not forget that the individual human authors of Scripture often intended their readers to receive their words not merely as human words but as the Word of God.[297]

My thesis is that the "fuller meaning" of Scripture—the meaning associated with divine authorship—emerges only at the level of the whole canon. As Wolfhart Pannenberg has argued, meaning in general—whether of words or events—largely depends on the relation between part and whole.[298] The meaning of a historical event, for instance, does not become apparent immediately. However, if the whole of history is the ultimate context for deciding on the meaning of the parts, does it follow that the meaning of an act, communicative or otherwise, *changes* as history moves forward, or that it acquires a "fuller sense" beyond what could have been intended by its agent? With regard to history, Pannenberg accepts the implication that we will know the true meaning of an event only at the end of history, when the whole is complete. Interpreting from the end of history is, of course, an impractical requirement; hence our interpretations about the meaning of historical events are always partial, provisional, and "from below." Pannenberg nonetheless claims that judgments about meaning always involve an *implicit anticipation of the whole*.[299]

How then shall we address the problem of *sensus plenior*? Does the meaning of the biblical text go beyond what the human authors could have intended? The answer, I believe, depends on what—or rather, whose—intended act we are inter-preting. A text must be read in light of its intentional context, that is, against the background that best allows us to answer the question of what the author is doing. For it is in relation to its intentional context that a text yields its maximal sense, its fullest meaning. *If we are reading the Bible as the Word of God, therefore, I suggest that the context that yields this maximal sense is the canon, taken as a unified communicative act.* The books of Scripture, taken individually, may anticipate the whole, but the canon alone is its *instantiation.*

If God is taken to be the divine author, in other words, then it is the canon as a whole that becomes the communicative act that needs to be described. It is important to note that the canon is both a completed and a public act, and as such provides access to the divine intention. The problem of the "fuller meaning" of Scripture and of deter-mining the divine author's intent is precisely the problem of choosing the intentional context that best enables one maximally to describe the communicative action embod-ied in Scripture. That is, to say that the Bible has a "fuller meaning" is to focus on the (divine) author's intended meaning at the level of the *canonical* act. Better said, *the canon as a whole becomes the unified act for which the divine intention serves as the unifying prin-ciple.* The divine intention *supervenes* on the intention of the human authors. Inspira-tion, that is, is an emergent property of the Old and New Testaments.[300] That Jesus is the referent of the whole relies on, but cannot be reduced to, the intended meaning of the individual books; yet the unity of Scripture emerges only at the canonical level. The canon, like the cell, is a higher order phenomenon that displays new properties and requires new categories (e.g., divine intention) adequately to describe it.

In conclusion, the canon is a complete and completed communicative act, struc-tured by a divine authorial intention. *The divine intention does not contravene the inten-tion of the human author but rather supervenes on it.* In the same way, the canon does not change or contradict the meaning of Isaiah 53 but supervenes on it and specifies its referent. In speaking of the Suffering Servant, Isaiah was referring to Christ (viz., God's gracious provision for Israel and the world), just as Priestly, speaking of dephlogisti-cated air, was referring to oxygen. In short, the dual authorship of Scripture qualifies, but does not overthrow, my analysis of meaning in terms of communicative action.

Is the Word of God a matter of past communicative action only? Does God not speak to his people today?[301] Both those on the theological left and the theological right appeal to the Holy Spirit as a source that supplements the Word. Does the Spirit lead the community into a fuller meaning that goes beyond "what it meant"? An ade-quate response to that important question must await subsequent chapters. My the-sis will be that the Spirit is tied to the written Word as significance is tied to meaning. With regard to hermeneutics, the role of the Spirit is to serve as the Spirit of signifi-cance and thus to apply meaning, not to change it.[302] At the same time, the Bible is concerned with its own relevance, that is, with the extension of its meaning into new contexts. Between the contexts of the author and reader stand a number of textual contexts—narrative, generic, canonical—that enable us to extend biblical meaning into the present. We thus turn our attention to the question of how meaning can be known and to the possibility that the biblical text is itself the most appropriate con-text for interpretation.

NOTES

1. Augustine, *On Christian Doctrine*, 2.2.3.

2. Hix, *Morte d'Author: An Autopsy* (Philadelphia: Temple Univ. Press, 1990), 12.

3. John K. Sheriff, *The Fate of Meaning: Charles Peirce, Structuralism, and Literature* (Princeton: Princeton Univ. Press, 1989), 140.

4. Derrida, *Of Grammatology*, 7. See also the excellent article by Brenda Deen Schildgen, "Augustine's Answer to Jacques Derrida in the *de Doctrina Christiana*," *New Literary History* 25 (1994): 383–97.

5. Derrida is committed not only to a non-Christian view of language but also, according to John Searle, to one that is pre-Wittgensteinian and hence philosophically out of date. See Searle, "Literary Theory and Its Discontents," 639.

6. John Searle, *Intentionality: An Essay in the Philosophy of Mind* (Cambridge: Cambridge Univ. Press, 1983), 26.

7. John Searle, *Speech Acts: An Essay in the Philosophy of Language* (Cambridge: Cambridge Univ. Press, 1969), 12.

8. Cited in Burke, *Death and Return of the Author*, 13.

9. J. L. Austin argues that "properly speaking, what alone has meaning is a *sentence*" ("The Meaning of a Word," in *Philosophical Papers*, 3d ed. (Oxford: Oxford Univ. Press, 1979), 56.

10. Ricoeur, *Interpretation Theory*, 1.

11. Ibid. Cf. Richard Harland, *Beyond Superstructuralism* (New York: Routledge, 1993), who argues that deconstruction and ordinary language philosophy alike neglect the contribution of the syntagm (words taken together as a syntactic unit) to meaning. From another angle, John K. Sheriff claims that C. S. Peirce's triadic theory of the sign is more adequate than the structuralist and poststructuralist dualism of signifier-signified. See Sheriff, *The Fate of Meaning*, ch. 4.

12. Ricoeur, *Interpretation Theory*, 7.

13. Ibid., 8. For the distinction between semiotics and semantics, see the whole of ch. 1.

14. In *Individuals: An Essay in Descriptive Metaphysics* (London: Methuen, 1957).

15. Michael Edwards quotes Milton's comment to the effect that Adam "rightly named" because he "understood the nature" of the animals. Whether or not the actual names Adam chose are arbitrary signs or not is not at issue; the point is that Adam uses language to interact with the world in such a way as to yield knowledge of reality. See Michael Edwards, *Towards a Christian Poetics* (Grand Rapids: Eerdmans, 1984), 9.

16. Edwards's *Towards a Christian Poetics* is in large part an exploration of how to make sense of language in terms of the Christian schema of Creation-Fall-Redemption.

17. I am here relying on Plantinga's account of the design plan of the human mind, found in his *Warrant and Proper Function* (Oxford: Oxford Univ. Press, 1993), 11–17, 21–31: "A thing's design plan is the way the thing in question is 'supposed' to work" (21).

18. Ibid., ix.

19. For a spirited defense of an evolutionary account of language, see Steven Pinker, *The Language Instinct: How the Mind Creates Language* (New York: William Morrow, 1994).

20. Plantinga, *Warrant and Proper Function*, 198.

21. Plantinga's objection to the performative circularity of the naturalist's attempt to allay doubt by producing arguments also applies to Derrida: once one doubts the ability of language to communicate thought to others, why bother writing books about deconstruction?

22. I argue that communicative agency is an essential ingredient in theological anthropology in my "Human Being, Individual and Social," in Colin Gunton, ed., *The Cambridge Companion to Christian Doctrine* (Cambridge: Cambridge Univ. Press, 1997).

23. Edwards comments that Adam's naming of the animals was not a communication but "a response to reality" (*Towards a Christian Poetics*, 9).

24. Steiner, *Real Presences*, 93.

25. Ibid., 95.

26. I appropriate elements of these philosophies only insofar as they serve as handmaidens to my (theologically derived) picture of language as a covenant of discourse. Though Ricoeur is a professing Christian, neither Searle nor Habermas are believers. Indeed, Searle ultimately has difficulty getting beyond the physics. See his *The Construction of Social Reality* (London: Penguin, 1995).

27. For a thorough account of the origins of ordinary language philosophy, see J. O. Urmson, *Philosophical Analysis: Its Development Between the Two World Wars* (Oxford: Oxford Univ. Press, 1956), esp. ch. 11. See also Dan R. Stiver, *The Philosophy of Religious Language: Sign, Symbol and Story* (Cambridge: Cambridge Univ. Press, 1996).

28. Steiner, *Real Presences*, 149–50. Steiner goes on to say that the text is a phenomenon of freedom; it did not have to be the way it is. Interpretive freedom is secondary and derivative (see ibid., 151).

29. See Alan Montefiore, "Philosophy, Literature and the Restatement of a Few Banalities," *Monist* 69 (1986): 56–67.

30. Wittgenstein seemed to think that the logical structure of a true statement "pictured" a state of affairs in the world. See his *Tractatus Logico-Philosophicus* (London: Routledge & Kegan Paul, 1961). He later repudiated this view.

31. See Wittgenstein, *Philosophical Investigations*, 3d. ed., tr. G. E. M. Anscombe (Oxford: Blackwell, 1958).

32. For a fuller analysis of how Wittgenstein might fruitfully be applied in biblical interpretation, see Anthony Thiselton, *The Two Horizons*, chs. 13 and 14.

33. See Anthony Manser, "Austin's 'Linguistic Phenomenology,'" in Edo Pivcevic, ed., *Phenomenology and Philosophical Understanding* (Cambridge: Cambridge Univ. Press, 1975), 109–24. Austin asserts that our common stock of words "embodies all the distinctions men have found worth drawing, and the connexions they have found worth making" (Austin, "A Plea for Excuses," 182).

34. J. L. Austin, *How to Do Things With Words*, 2d ed. (Cambridge: Harvard Univ. Press, 1975).

35. See his "Performative Utterances," in *Philosophical Papers*, 233–52.

36. See Austin, *How to Do Things With Words,* esp. lectures 8, 9, and 10.

37. Ibid., 10.

38. William P. Alston, *Philosophy of Language* (Englewood Cliffs, N.J.: Prentice-Hall, 1964), 39.

39. See my "The Semantics of Biblical Literature," 85–92, in which I apply Searle's philosophy of speech acts to the question of biblical authority. I argue there that biblical genres are to be distinguished not only by their literary form but also by their illocutionary content (see esp. 87–104).

40. Note that for Searle, "the study of the meanings of sentences and the study of speech acts are not two independent studies but one study from two different points of view" (*Speech Acts*, 18).

41. Searle, *Expression and Meaning*, 29. Austin had also proposed a fivefold typology (*How to Do Things With Words*, 151–64), but Searle says it fails to employ a consistent principle of classification.

42. John Searle, *Speech Acts*, 12.

43. The Russian literary theorist Mikhail Bakhtin speaks of "speech genres." Each sphere in which language is used, he says, develops its own relatively stable types or "genres" (M. M.

Bakhtin, *Speech Genres and Other Late Essays*, tr. Vern W. McGee (Austin: Univ. of Texas Press, 1986), 60–102. I treat the role of genre in achieving literary knowledge in greater detail in the next chapter.

44. Searle, *Speech Acts*, 30.

45. See especially Sandy Petrey, *Speech Acts and Literary Theory* (London: Routledge, 1990); Mary Louise Pratt, *Towards a Speech Act Theory of Literary Discourse* (Bloomington: Indiana Univ. Press, 1977); Susan Snaider Lanser, *The Narrative Act: Point of View in Prose Fiction* (Princeton: Princeton Univ. Press, 1981); in biblical studies see Hugh C. White, "Introduction: Speech Act Theory and Literary Criticism," *Semeia* 41 (1988): 1–24 (the whole issue is devoted to speech act theory and biblical studies); Dietmar Neufeld, *Reconceiving Texts As Speech Acts: An Analysis of 1 John* (Leiden: E. J. Brill, 1994).

46. Charles Altieri, *Act and Quality: A Theory of Literary Meaning and Humanistic Understanding* (Amherst: Univ. of Massachusetts Press, 1981), 10.

47. J. Eugene Botha, *Jesus and the Samaritan Woman: A Speech Act Reading of John 4:1–42* (Leiden: E. J. Brill, 1991).

48. Derrida, "Signature Event Context," *Glyph* 1 (1977): 172–97.

49. Ibid., 182.

50. Norris, *Deconstruction: Theory and Practice*, 110.

51. Searle, "Reiterating the Differences," *Glyph* 1 (1977): 198–208.

52. See "Limited Inc. abc" in *Glyph* 2 (1977): 162–254. The whole of the debate, together with a valuable appendix by Derrida on the "ethics" of the discussion, may be found in Derrida, *Limited Inc.* (Evanston: Northwestern Univ. Press, 1988).

53. Searle, "The World Turned Upside Down," a review of Jonathan Culler's *On Deconstruction*, *New York Times Review of Books* (Oct. 27, 1983), 74–79.

54. Searle, "Literary Theory and Its Discontents," 638.

55. Searle, "The World Turned Upside Down," 79.

56. Thiselton agrees. Derrida abstracts language from inter-subjective judgments and practices. The biblical witness, however, was not by word alone, but by action and behavior. Wittgenstein observes: "The common behavior of mankind is the system of reference by means of which we interpret an unknown language" (cited in *New Horizons*, 591). Human agents choose to make this or that aspect of a potential system operational at any given moment. I will discuss this point at greater length in the following chapter. Searle's diagnosis of Derrida is open to dispute. In his own autopsy of the debate, Derrida suggests that it is Searle who wants to make things simple with his clear distinctions (e.g., serious, non-serious) whereas he, Derrida, tries to bring complication and complexity into the open ("Afterword: Toward an Ethic of Discussion," 127–28).

57. This is also the thrust of Norris's defense of Derrida against Searle, in *Derrida*, 178–80.

58. Derrida, "Afterword," 151.

59. Searle, "Literary Theory and Its Discontents," 660.

60. Ibid., 648.

61. Ibid.

62. Norris, *Deconstruction: Theory and Practice*, 112.

63. For a summary of Grice's position, see Richard E. Grandy and Richard Warner, ed., *Philosophical Grounds of Rationality* (Oxford: Clarendon, 1986), 1–44. See too Grice's response in the same work.

64. The implied analogy with the naturalistic fallacy—the attempt to define the ethical ("good") in non-ethical terms—refuted by G. E. Moore, the common sense realist, is intentional.

65. Daniel Patte, "Speech Act Theory and Biblical Exegesis" *Semeia* 41 (1988): 91.

66. H. P. Grice states that Austin believed ordinary language was an instrument "rather marvellously and subtly fitted to serve the multiplicity of our needs and desires in communication" (in Grandy and Warner, *Philosophical Grounds*, 57).

67. See ch. 3 above, where I criticize Ricoeur's attempts to formulate an autonomous "sense of the text."

68. Ricoeur, "What Is a Text? Explanation and Understanding," 145.

69. Anthony Thiselton and Wendell V. Harris criticize Derrida for the way he develops Saussure's distinction between *langue* and *parole*. According to Thiselton, Saussure only opens up the possibility of limitless interpretation when his linguistics is exaggerated into a world-view based on Freud's and Nietzsche's genealogical critiques: "The *use of a hermeneutic of suspicion as a method* is an entirely different matter from the *transformation of the principle of suspicion into a world-view*" (Thiselton, *New Horizons*, 126). Wendell Harris agrees: the use of signs is grounded in a pre-linguistic realm of shared practices that occur in specific contexts (Harris, *Interpretive Acts*, 158). Moreover, though the signs are arbitrary, the process by which sensation is carved up into words is not. We signify sensations and things in ways that are useful; distinctions serve human purposes. Moreover, change to *langue* stems from changes in *parole*, and these are often prompted by events that are not linguistic in nature. "The heart of deconstructionists' strategies . . . lies in conflating that which may be said of a word regarded under the aspect of *langue* with that which is true of it under the aspect of *parole*" (ibid., 25). For my part, I prefer to say that *parole* supervenes on *langue*.

70. *A Ricoeur Reader*, 17. Ricoeur attacks Derrida's attempt to conflate metaphorical and metaphysical discourse, literature, and philosophy (see his *The Rule of Metaphor*, 284–89, 294). Against Derrida, Ricoeur views both speech and writing as forms of discourse (*Interpretation Theory*, 26).

71. So Mario Valdes, "Introduction," in *A Ricoeur Reader*, 23.

72. S. H. Clark says the issue raised by Ricoeur's work is whether meaning emerges sacramentally or humanistically (*Paul Ricoeur*, 8–9).

73. *A Ricoeur Reader*, 325.

74. Ibid., 321.

75. Ricoeur, "The Hermeneutical Function of Distanciation," in *Hermeneutics and the Human Sciences,* 138.

76. Ibid., 137–38.

77. Ricoeur, *Interpretation Theory*, 92.

78. Ibid.

79. Ricoeur, "What Is a Text?" 161–62.

80. Ricoeur, *Interpretation Theory*, 30.

81. Ibid.

82. In Ricoeur, *Hermeneutics and the Human Sciences*, 197–221.

83. Ibid., ch. 8.

84. Ricoeur notes that the meaning of certain actions exceeds the intention of the agent, but as I argue below, this is to confuse the meaning of an action with its significance, its object with its unintended effects.

85. See his "Communicative Versus Subject-Centered Reason," in *The Philosophical Discourse of Modernity* (Cambridge: Polity Press, 1987), 294–326, and Thiselton's treatment in *New Horizons*, 385–91.

86. David Rasmussen notes the relevance for literary theory of Habermas's philosophy, but his bibliography does not list any studies that have applied Habermas for this purpose. To date, Habermas is discussed in relation to hermeneutics primarily on the strength of his criticisms of Gadamer and Derrida (see Rasmussen, *Reading Habermas* [Oxford: Basil Blackwell,

1990], 1). For Habermas's own foray into literary theory, see his "Excursus on Leveling the Genre Distinction Between Philosophy and Literature," in Habermas, *The Philosophical Discourse of Modernity*, 185–210.

87. Noam Chomsky develops a theory of linguistic competence that focuses on the mastery of certain universal grammatical rules. Chomsky only takes us as far as *langue*, whereas Habermas is interested in universal rules for the interactive use of language, in *parole*.

88. One of Habermas's aims is to escape Derrida's criticism of Austin, namely, that the conditions for a successful speech act were only conventional and hence arbitrary.

89. Habermas, *Philosophical Discourse*, 313.

90. Habermas, *The Theory of Communicative Action*, tr. Thomas McCarthy (Boston: Beacon, 1984), 1:101.

91. Freadman and Miller, *Rethinking Theory: A Critique of Contemporary Literary Theory and an Alternative Account* (Cambridge: Cambridge Univ. Press, 1992), 212.

92. Habermas, *Theory of Communicative Action*, 1:274.

93. Can Habermas account for this mutual accountability and the unity of human beings merely by appealing to what is implicit in communication? Helmut Peukert, in his *Science, Action, and Fundamental Theology: Towards a Theology of Communicative Action* (Cambridge, Mass: MIT Press, 1984) has argued that Habermas's conception of rationality must include a theological dimension if it is to be coherent. Theology alone, not some kind of social contract theory, can serve as a normative basis for a theory of action and its concomitant demand for universal solidarity (e.g., solidarity with the dead is unthinkable in modernity but not in Christian theology). The question is what unites humanity: Are similarities based on a shared biology, or even on a shared social situation, sufficient for a sense of universal solidarity?

94. Habermas recognizes that actual speech is corrupt. Ideally, however, speakers should be able to "redeem" their validity claims. This ideal is implicit in every speech act. Rationality is not a function of one's mental faculties but of how one conducts a conversation. Reason is embedded in language as communicative action. In this way, Habermas reinstates the ideals of the Enlightenment—truth, reason, freedom, justice—into the very practice of communication.

95. John Fiske, *Introduction to Communication Studies*, 2d ed. (London: Routledge, 1990), 2.

96. Hannah Arendt, *The Human Condition* (Chicago: Univ. of Chicago Press, 1958), 177.

97. I am thinking of the Deuteronomistic history (the OT books from Joshua to 2 Kings), which relates the history of Israel as a story of how the people responded to the Word of God.

98. The "first coming" was with Christian interpretation of the Old Testament (cf. Buber's comment "What Christianity gives the world is hermeneutics"). On the significance of Dilthey's work for hermeneutics, see Ricoeur, *Hermeneutics and the Human Sciences*, chs. 2–3, and Thiselton, *New Horizons*, 247–51. Dilthey's distinction reflects Kant's earlier distinctions between nature and freedom, fact and value.

99. This is one version of the so-called "hermeneutical circle."

100. According to G. H. von Wright, *Explanation and Understanding* (Ithaca: Cornell Univ. Press, 1971), agents can intentionally interfere with the course of nature. Agents can make things happen by putting "systems"—physical systems, semiotic systems—into motion. When they do, the notions of action and cause meet. Von Wright referred only to natural systems, but I believe we can expand his ideas and so speak of an agent's interference in a language system.

101. We will see below that the question of where meaning begins and ends is wrapped up with the vital distinction between meaning and significance.

102. I am indebted to John Fiske, *Introduction to Communication Studies*, for the material in this paragraph.

103. I here follow Roman Jakobson's (1896–1982) model of communication, which subordinates the code function to the overarching function of communication. Jakobson distinguishes six factors of discourse: the speaker, hearer, medium, code, situation, and message. See Jakobson's "Linguistics and Poetics," in T. A. Sebeok, ed., *Style in Language* (Cambridge, Mass.: MIT Press, 1960), 350–77.

104. Erich Auerbach, *Mimesis* (Princeton: Princeton Univ. Press, 1953), 14–15.

105. This is a problematic claim, as commentators of Habermas are quick to point out. See Stephen White, *The Recent Work of Jürgen Habermas: Reason, Justice and Modernity* (Cambridge: Cambridge Univ. Press, 1988), 45–46; David M. Rasmussen, *Reading Habermas* (Oxford: Basil Blackwell, 1990), 27–28, 38–41.

106. Jürgen Habermas, *Theory of Communicative Action*, 1:290.

107. Ibid.

108. Ibid., 1:291.

109. Ibid.

110. Ibid.

111. I will return to Habermas's worry below when I appeal to the distinction between illocutions and perlocutions in an attempt to go beyond Hirsch and put the distinction between meaning and significance on firmer ground.

112. The four dimensions are the locutionary, the illocutionary, the perlocutionary, and the interlocutionary. Against Austin, Habermas urges us not to confuse "acts of communication" with "communicative action." His anxiety on this point is a function of his overall concern to describe a social order that is characterized by rational consensus rather than rhetorical manipulation. Indeed, his worry—that rhetoric will corrupt rationality—is essentially that of Plato's as expressed in the *Republic*, a work similarly devoted to social theory. For a fuller discussion of these points, see Jonathan Culler, "Communicative Competence and Normative Force," *New German Critique* 35 (1985): 135–37.

113. René Wellek and Austin Warren, *Theory of Literature* (London: Jonathan Cape, 1949), 157.

114. Thiselton, *New Horizons*, 49. See pp. 55–58 for a review of various options, including the text as expression of author, as autonomous object, and as invitation to the reader.

115. The phrase "begotten, not made" was used in the Nicene Creed (A.D. 325) to indicate that the Son was *homoousios* with ("of the same substance as") the Father.

116. Paul Ricoeur, *Oneself As Another*, tr. Kathleen Blamey (Chicago: Univ. of Chicago Press, 1992).

117. We may here recall Ricoeur's comment that the author is the ground for a work's individual style.

118. For a very different analysis of Van Gogh's painting, see Martin Heidegger, "The Origin of the Work of Art," in *Poetry, Language, Thought*, tr. Albert Hofstadter (New York: Harper & Row, 1971), 33ff.

119. Richard Wollheim, *Painting As an Art* (Princeton: Princeton Univ. Press, 1987), 17–18.

120. Norris, *Derrida*, 46.

121. A. D. Nuttall, *A New Mimesis: Shakespeare and the Representation of Reality* (London: Methuen, 1983), 37.

122. Richard Ohmann, "Speech Acts and the Definition of Literature," *Philosophy and Rhetoric* 4 (1971): 13 (italics his). Cf. Ohmann, "Literature As Act," in Seymour Chatman, ed., *Approaches to Poetics* (New York: Columbia Univ. Press, 1973), 81–107.

123. Pratt, *Toward a Speech Act Theory*, 136.

124. Susan Snaider Lanser, *The Narrative Act*, 7. Both Pratt and Lanser reject the distinction between ordinary and literary discourse. Pratt declares her aim to be the development of

a "unified theory" of discourse (*Towards a Speech Act Theory*, vii). According to Lanser, "literature is communicative both in usage and intent, and the distinction between 'literary' and 'ordinary' language which poeticians have tended to assume is not supported by linguistic research" (*The Narrative Act*, 65). Again, this is far from being a merely academic dispute. Whether one reads Scripture with a general or a special hermeneutic will depend on whether one thinks that the Bible should be read as ordinary discourse or as literature.

125. Lanser, *The Narrative Act*, 227.

126. Ibid., 293 (italics mine). According to Lanser, the author cannot help but express the worldview of his or her historical context: "The voice of the text, then, is endowed with the authority of its creator and of the community in which it is published and produced" (122).

127. Charles Altieri, *Act and Quality*, 10.

128. Lanser, *The Narrative Act*, 73.

129. John Searle, *Intentionality*, 161.

130. If *S* stands for significance, we can represent the relation of textual meaning and its bearing on the contemporary context as follows: $S = (R)[F(p) + x]$.

131. Every text is a kind of communicative action; every text belongs to a specific literary genre. In the next chapter I examine how readers determine what specific communicative actions have been performed.

132. A similar formula occurs in Deut. 4:2. Meredith Kline points out that ancient treaties often concluded with an inscriptional curse directed at those who would change its terms (meaning!). He then suggests that both the OT and the NT share a number of characteristics with these ancient treaties and concludes: "'Testament,' or 'covenant,' denotes more than a prominent element in the contents of the Bible. The documents which combine to form the Bible are in their very nature—a legal sort of nature, it turns out—covenantal" (*The Structure of Biblical Authority* [Grand Rapids: Eerdmans, 1972], 75). To put it in terms of speech act philosophy: "testament" is not only the propositional content of the Bible but its illocutionary force as well.

133. Nicholas Wolterstorff, *Works and Worlds of Art* (Oxford: Clarendon, 1980), 205. Cf. the important discussion of this point in Thiselton, *New Horizons*, 615–16.

134. Thiselton, *New Horizons*, 75.

135. Ibid., 68.

136. Ibid., 75.

137. Hix, *Morte d'Author*, 12.

138. For a fuller treatment of how this question bears on biblical interpretation, see my "The Hermeneutics of I-Witness Testimony: John 21:20–24 and the 'Death' of the 'Author,'" in A. Graeme Auld, ed., *Understanding Poets and Prophets* (Sheffield: JSOT, 1993), 366–87.

139. See my "Human Being, Individual and Social," 158–88.

140. N. T. Wright uses this question to introduce a brief reflection on the role of the author's intention. I reserve that important discussion to the next section.

141. For a brilliant analysis of how this picture has affected modern theology too, see Fergus Kerr, *Theology After Wittgenstein* (Oxford: Basil Blackwell, 1986), ch. 1.

142. John Macmurray, *The Self As Agent* (London: Faber & Faber, 1957), 73.

143. Charles Taylor, *Human Agency and Language: Philosophical Papers 1* (Cambridge: Cambridge Univ. Press, 1985), 259.

144. Kerr, *Theology After Wittgenstein*, 109.

145. Taylor, *Human Agency and Language*, 259.

146. C. K. Barrett, *The Gospel According to St. John*, 2d ed. (London: SPCK, 1978), 5.

147. I am here referring to the use of non-natural signs or symbols. A natural sign, like the smoke that accompanies fire, is not a communicative act (unless it's a native American smoke signal, in which case it becomes a non-natural sign).

148. Robert H. Gundry, *Soma in Biblical Theology, With Emphasis on Pauline Anthropology* (Cambridge: Cambridge Univ. Press, 1976), 84. Gundry argues that the Pauline view of human being is best described in terms of "an anthropological duality, a functional pluralism, and an overarching unity" (84).

149. Jerry Gill, *Mediated Transcendence. A Postmodern Reflection* (Macon, Ga.: Mercer Univ. Press, 1989), 60. For Gill's analysis of meaning, see ch. 5.

150. Ibid., 127.

151. Wright, *The New Testament and the People of God* (London: S.P.C.K., 1992), 91.

152. Ibid., 95. Wright acknowledges that "meaning" may be held to lie in the contemporary relevance or consequences of past actions or, at another level, in the divine intention revealed by a larger pattern. I will deal with levels of communicative intentionality in the next chapter.

153. For Wright's claim that he has achieved this, see his *Jesus and the Victory of God* (Minneapolis: Fortress, 1996), xv. I return to the theme of the face in the Conclusion to the present work.

154. The answer of the New Testament is that God was in Christ, reconciling all things to himself (Col. 1:20; cf. 2 Cor. 5:19).

155. Wright, *The New Testament and the People of God*, 109.

156. For Wright's answer to these vital questions, see his *Jesus and the Victory of God*, 99–109 and chs. 11–12.

157. If the author is the one responsible for the final form of the text, then there is no problem expanding my definition of author to include editors, or indeed anyone who may have had a hand in shaping the text's form and matter. Interestingly, Wright does not really coordinate his remarks on the significance of aims and intentions for the study of history with his hermeneutical reflections on authors.

158. See Garcia, "Can There Be Texts Without Historical Authors?"

159. Ibid., 251.

160. Michael Baxandall, *Patterns of Intention: On the Historical Explanation of Pictures* (New Haven: Yale Univ. Press, 1985), vi.

161. Cf, Baxandall: "The account of intention is not a narrative of what went on in the painter's mind but an analytical construct about his end and means, as we infer them from the relation of the object to identifiable circumstances" (ibid., 109).

162. See C. Clifton Black, "Rhetorical Criticism," in Joel Green, ed., *Hearing the New Testament: Strategies for Interpretation* (Grand Rapids: Eerdmans, 1995), 256–77. Black notes that both James Muilenburg and Amos Wilder, leading exponents in the field of biblical rhetorical criticism, believe that the study of a text's formal features should be historically grounded, with due attention paid to the author's intention, cultural context, and social situation.

163. There is another school of rhetorical criticism that is more interested in the reader than the author, on praxis rather than poetics. I will treat this approach in ch. 7.

164. The contention that the Gospels were modified by editors or perhaps written by a whole school of disciples does not affect my argument; by "author" I mean the individual or group responsible for the text as we now have it.

165. Cf. Robert Gundry: "By noting Matthew's emphases we can infer the situation in which he wrote and purposes for which he wrote" (*Matthew: A Commentary on His Literary and Theological Art* [Grand Rapids: Eerdmans, 1982], 5). In my terms, by carefully observing Matthew's locutions and illocutions (especially as these differ from the other Evangelists), we may infer things about his perlocutionary purposes.

166. See Robert Alter, *The Art of Biblical Narrative* (New York: Basic, 1981), 47–62.

167. Black, "Rhetorical Criticism," 271. For more on the rhetoric of John 4, see Lyle Eslinger, "The Wooing of the Woman at the Well: Jesus, the Reader and Reader-Response Crit-

icism," in Mark W. G. Stibbe, *The Gospel of John As Literature: Twentieth Century Perspectives* (Leiden: Brill, 1993), 165–79, and my "The Reader in New Testament Interpretation," in Joel B. Green, ed., *Hearing the New Testament*, 318–24.

168. The historical dimension focuses on the *that* of communicative action, the aesthetic on the *how*, and the ethical on the *what*.

169. Gundry, *Matthew*, 9.

170. See Henry Staten, *Wittgenstein and Derrida*, ch. 3 (esp. 113–14).

171. Burke, *The Death and Return of the Author*, 156.

172. Austin, *How to Do Things With Words*, 111.

173. I treat Hart's position in more detail in the next section in relation to the question of the author's intention. Interestingly, Austin thinks that it is easier to draw the line between an action and its consequences when the action in view is an illocution, a saying something. Terms for physical action often embrace their natural consequences (e.g., breaking bread, washing the dishes, walking to town), whereas the vocabulary of names for acts of saying something "seems expressly designed to mark a break at a certain regular point between the act (our saying something) and its consequences (which are usually not the *saying* of anything)" (*How To Do Things With Words*, 112).

174. Austin, *How to Do Things With Words*, 9–10.

175. See C. S. Lewis and E. M. W. Tillyard, *The Personal Heresy: A Controversy* (Oxford: Oxford Univ. Press, 1939).

176. Hall, *Word and Spirit*, 191.

177. Jacques Ellul, *The Humiliation of the Word* (Grand Rapids: Eerdmans, 1985), 157.

178. Ibid., 173.

179. Ibid., 157.

180. Ibid., 110.

181. Ibid., 107.

182. Steiner entitled his book *Real Presences* but does not explore its associations with the Christian sacraments in any detail.

183. See Geoffrey Wainwright, "Sacraments/Sacramental Theology," in Donald W. Musser and Joseph L. Price, ed., *A New Handbook of Christian Theology* (Nashville: Abingdon, 1992), 421–27.

184. Nehamas, "What an Author Is," *Journal of Philosophy* 83 (1986): 686.

185. See Gass, "The Soul Inside the Sentence," in *Habitations of the Word* (New York: Simon & Schuster, 1986). The Roman Catholic Church in 1215 made the doctrine of transubstantiation—the change in substance of the bread and water into the substance of Christ's body and blood—part of official church teaching.

186. Nehamas, "Writer, Text, Work, Author," in Anthony J. Cascardi, ed., *Literature and the Question of Philosophy* (Baltimore: Johns Hopkins Univ. Press, 1987), 285 (italics mine).

187. Nehamas, "The Postulated Author: Critical Monism As a Regulative Ideal," *Critical Inquiry* 8 (1981): 145.

188. Booth, *Rhetoric of Fiction*, 20.

189. P. D. Juhl agrees. It is not the implied but the real author who affirms the propositions expressed by a work and who is committed to their truth. When Huck Finn decides to go against his conscience and rescue his black friend, even if it means going to hell, the author is saying "that Huck is not committing wrong, and that his so-called inner conscience is in reality only the arbitrary social values of his society" (see Louis D. Rubin, *The Teller of the Tale* [Seattle: Univ. of Washington Press, 1967], 18; cited in Juhl, *Interpretation*, 190).

190. Gill, *Mediated Transcendence*, 120.

191. Ibid., 126.

192. For Calvin's trinitarian development of this idea in the sacraments, see Francis Wendel, *Calvin* (London: Collins, 1965), 345–55. The Latin *exhibeo* bore a twofold sense: conveying and disclosing.

193. W. K. Wimsatt, "Genesis: A Fallacy Revisited," 137.

194. Cf. Denis Dutton, "Why Intentionalism Won't Go Away," in Anthony J. Cascardi, *Literature and the Question of Philosophy*, 192–209. Literary critics are not the only intentionalists. Ben Meyer's "95 theses on general and biblical hermeneutics" defines communication as "the will to transmit intended meaning" (Ben Meyer, *Critical Realism and the New Testament* [Allison Park, Pa.: Pickwick Publications, 1989], 18). Meyer, a New Testament scholar, declares his hermeneutical realism: "the text has a primary claim on the reader, namely, to be construed in accord with its intended sense" (17). The intended sense is the "formal cause" of the text's unique configuration and coherence. Meyer believes that Hirsch failed to distinguish the extrinsic intention of the author (e.g., the author's plan in writing) from the intention of the author as intrinsic to the text (e.g., the author's performance in writing). The object of interpretation is not the author's plan but the nature of the communicative act itself. Meir Sternberg agrees. Wimsatt's and Beardsley's "intentionalist fallacy" attacks interpretations that rely on "external" intentions about the author's purpose and psychology. Sternberg comments: "As interpreters of the Bible, our only concern is with 'embodied' or 'objectified' intention" (*The Poetics of Biblical Narrative*, 9). "Intention" is "a shorthand for the structure of meaning and effect supposed by the conventions that the text appeals to or devises: for the sense that the language makes in terms of the communicative context as a whole" (9).

195. For Juhl, the relation between the meaning of a text and the author's intention is *analytic*: the one concept implies the other.

196. "More explicitly, coherence and complexity are criteria of what a text means *only insofar as* they are criteria of the author's intention" (P. D. Juhl, *Interpretation*, 87).

197. Ibid., 216.

198. Ibid., 240.

199. Knapp and Michaels, "Against Theory," 18. Knapp and Michaels criticize Juhl as well for thinking that intention has to be theoretically defended, as if it were possible to interpret without it (19–20).

200. Knapp and Michaels reject the distinction between speaker-meaning and sentence-meaning, between *parole* and *langue*. On their view, the language system—represented by a dictionary—is an index of frequent usages of words, not a matrix of abstract, preintentional possible meanings (cf. 20n.12).

201. Ibid., 12.

202. Knapp and Michaels, "Against Theory 2: Hermeneutics and Deconstruction," *Critical Inquiry* 14 (1987/88): 49–68.

203. Steven Knapp and Walter Benn Michaels, "Reply to John Searle," *New Literary History* 25 (1994): 671.

204. H. P. Grice, "Meaning," *Philosophical Review* 66 (1957): 377–88; see also H. P. Grice, "Utterer's Meaning and Intentions," *Philosophical Review* 78 (1969): 147–77.

205. Searle, *Speech Acts*, 47 (italics mine).

206. Ibid., 43.

207. Petrey accuses Searle, for whom the philosophy of language is a subset of the philosophy of mind, of underemphasizing the role of social conventions. As I shall argue below, Searle does do justice to the role of social and linguistic conventions, especially in his later book, *The Construction of Social Reality* (London: Penguin, 1995). For an overview of the tension between intentionalists and conventionalists in speech act theory, see Hugh C. White, "Introduction: Speech Act Theory and Literary Criticism," *Semeia* 41 (1988): 1–24. See also

P. F. Strawson, "Intention and Convention in Speech Acts," in his *Logico-Linguistic Papers* (London: Methuen, 1971).

208. Abrams, *A Glossary of Literary Terms*, 189.

209. A few speech act theorists themselves are anti-intentional in their analysis of speech acts. Sandy Petrey criticizes Searle's claim that whether a text is fiction or history depends solely on the author's intention: "When it comes to the things words do, we are quite mistaken to concern ourselves in any way with what's happening inside while language is performing outside" (Petrey, *Speech Acts and Literary Theory*, 84).

210. Freadman and Miller, *Rethinking Literary Theory*, 131.

211. The English word "convention" comes from a Latin root—*convenire*—which means "to convene, to come together."

212. Searle, "Structure and Intention in Language: A Reply to Knapp and Michaels," *New Literary History* 25 (1994): 680.

213. Searle prefers to speak of "collective intentions." Examples would be playing baseball, playing chess, worshiping God—all cases where the participants share a set of beliefs about what they are doing and acknowledge the same set of rules for doing it properly. See Searle, *The Construction of Social Reality*, ch. 1.

214. Ibid., 27.

215. Ibid., 35. Though Searle does not mention it, I believe that his remarks about the irreducibility of institutional facts resemble what scientists refer to by the notion of "supervenience." See below for more on meaning and supervenience and emergent properties. Petrey insists on the reality of institutional facts: "Although the distinction between getting married and getting hit in the head is certainly that between the conventional and the non-conventional, is one more real than the other?" (*Speech Acts and Literary Theory*, 18).

216. Searle, *Speech Acts*, 35.

217. Searle asserts that "language is essentially constitutive of institutional reality," the reason being that institutional facts mean or symbolize something beyond themselves (*Construction of Social Reality*, 59).

218. I discuss literary genre in some depth in the next chapter.

219. Cited in R. A. Duff, *Intention, Agency and Criminal Liability: Philosophy of Action and the Criminal Law* (Oxford: Basil Blackwell, 1990), 29.

220. The term intention was used to explain the directedness of consciousness by the German philosopher Franz Brentano in his 1874 work, *Psychology From an Empirical Standpoint*. Brentano's work eventually gave rise to phenomenology (the study of the contents of consciousness), to Husserl's theory of intentionality, and thus, through Husserl, to Hirsch's *Validity in Interpretation*. Hirsch used the metaphor of directedness as well, but for him the emphasis is on consciousness rather than action. Hirsch defines intention as the "relation between an act of awareness and its object" (*Validity*, 218).

221. J. L. Austin comments: "No word ever achieves entire forgetfulness of its origins" (J. L. Austin "Three Ways of Spilling Ink," in *Philosophical Papers*, 283).

222. Thiselton rightly notes that "intending" is not a distinct act. With Wittgenstein, he asks how one should respond to the imperative "Intend to. . . ." The point is that intending is not a separate act, but rather a quality of action. Intention is thus best understood "adverbially" (see Thiselton, *New Horizons*, 559–60).

223. Ricoeur, *Hermeneutics and the Human Sciences*, 161–62.

224. It is perhaps not entirely a coincidence that *sens*, the French word for "meaning," also means "direction."

225. Promises also have a world-to-words direction of fit. Expressive speech acts such as, for example, apologies, thanks, and congratulations, have an empty direction of fit, while

declaratives (e.g., "You're fired"; "I surrender") have a double direction of fit insofar as the world matches the words when someone uses the words to bring about a change in the world. For more on direction of fit, see Searle, "A Taxonomy of Illocutionary Acts," in *Expression and Meaning*, and Daniel Vanderveken, *Meaning and Speech Acts*, vol. 1 *Principles of Language Use* (Cambridge: Cambridge Univ. Press, 1990), 103–10.

226. Sometimes the author signals his or her intent in this matter with conventional signs, such as exclamation points or question marks. The question mark gives a very different illocutionary force to propositional content: "Jesus walked on water?"

227. My ontological analysis of the author's intention carries with it an epistemological implication: good interpretation is a matter of *paying attention* to what the author was attending to. Indeed, there may be an ethical implication as well. Iris Murdoch borrows the concept of attention from Simone Weil to express the idea of "a just and loving gaze directed upon an individual reality" (Iris Murdoch, *The Sovereignty of Good* [London: Routledge and Kegan Paul, 1970), 34). Murdoch believes that it is only when one gives one's full attention to what is actually there that it becomes clear what one is to do in a particular situation. Though she is referring to ethics, I believe a similar process takes place in textual interpretation. The ethical response of the reader is the one that attends, lovingly and justly, to what is there.

228. Brian Davies, *The Thought of Thomas Aquinas* (Oxford: Clarendon, 1992), 221.

229. Frank G. Kirkpatrick, *Together Bound: God, History and the Religious Community* (Oxford: Oxford Univ. Press, 1994), 60.

230. Ibid., 68.

231. See Edward Pols, *Meditations on a Prisoner: Towards Understanding Action and Mind* (Edwardsville: Southern Illinois Univ. Press, 1975).

232. I am indebted for many of the ideas in this paragraph to Philip Clayton, *God and Contemporary Science* (Edinburgh: Edinburgh Univ. Press, 1998), ch. 9. It is significant that my account of meaning should return to the problem of consciousness, though with different philosophical resources than those used by Hirsch.

233. Nancey Murphy, *Anglo-American Postmodernity: Philosophical Perspectives on Science, Religion, and Ethics* (Boulder, Colo.: Westview, 1997), 20.

234. Though drawn from technical discussions concerning emergent properties in the natural sciences, I believe the concept of supervenience is also the answer to Searle's question of how we move from the physics to the semantics. For a rather technical discussion, see Elias E. Savellos and Ümit D. Yalçin, ed., *Supervenience: New Essays* (Cambridge: Cambridge Univ. Press, 1995).

235. See W. Mark Richardson, "The Theology of Human Agency and the Neurobiology of Learning," in W. Mark Richardson and Wesley J. Wildman, ed., *Religion and Science: History, Method, Dialogue* (New York: Routledge, 1996), 356–59. See also Arthur Peacocke, *Theology for a Scientific Age*, rev. ed. (London: SCM, 1993), 300–302.

236. Thiselton, *New Horizons*, 559 (italics his).

237. Ibid.

238. Moisés Silva, *Biblical Words and Their Meaning: An Introduction to Lexical Semantics* (Grand Rapids: Zondervan, 1983), 139 (italics his).

239. Michael LaFargue, "Are Texts Determinate? Derrida, Barth, and the Role of the Biblical Scholar," *Harvard Theological Review* 81 (1988): 354.

240. Ibid., 356.

241. Wendell V. Harris, *Interpretive Acts*, 158.

242. R. A. Duff, *Intention, Agency and Criminal Liability*, 43.

243. Ibid., 42.

244. Ibid., 50.

245. Ibid., 131.

246. Searle, *Speech Acts*, 57–61.

247. F. E. Sparshott, "Criticism and Performance," in *On Literary Intention*, 113.

248. J. L. Austin, *Philosophical Papers*, 284.

249. Searle, *Intentionality*, 164.

250. Duff, *Intention, Agency and Criminal Liability*, 130. Duff briefly relates his treatment of intention to literary theory on p. 132.

251. Nathan A. Scott Jr., "The New *Trahison des Clercs*: Reflections on the Present Crisis in Humanistic Studies," *The Virginia Quarterly Review* 62 (1986): 418–19.

252. Duff rehearses the facts of the case: Mrs. Hyam, in a fit of jealousy, poured petrol through the letterbox of her lover's door, set it alight, and returned home. The fire killed two children, and Mrs. Hyam was charged with their murder. She realized, she later admitted, that her action was dangerous, but she insisted that she did not *intend* to injure or kill the children, only to frighten their mother into leaving town. See Duff, *Intention, Agency and Criminal Liability*, 1–3.

253. Duff, *Intention, Agency and Criminal Liability*, 111.

254. William Empson, *Seven Types of Ambiguity* (London: Chatto and Windus, 1930).

255. M. H. Abrams suggests "multiple meaning" or "plurisignation" as alternate terms that avoid the pejorative associations of the term "ambiguity" (*A Glossary of Literary Terms*, 8–9).

256. Authors may intend a whole range of senses in a metaphor, for instance. Nevertheless, I believe we are still justified in speaking of the author's intention. In the case of figurative language, however, the author intends an indeterminate range of "associated commonplaces." For example, Jesus' self-designation as "the bread of life" is rich in its associations, but nonetheless directed on a particular subject matter (e.g., Jesus as life-giving bread). Moreover, some of these associations are not as relevant as others. We can be fairly confident, I believe, that Jesus intended some associations (e.g., nourishing) and not others (e.g., sliced).

257. Both Searle and Austin realize that speech acts can fail. Austin says that utterances can "misfire," and when they do, "the act purported to be done is null and void, so that it does not take effect" (*How to Do Things With Words*, 25). Searle, similarly, speaks of "defective" performances (*Speech Acts*, 54).

258. Roger Fry, cited in David Newton de Molina, ed., *On Literary Intention*, 14.

259. Eco, *Interpretation*, 82.

260. D. C. Muecke, *The Compass of Irony* (London: Methuen, 1969), 5.

261. Booth, *A Rhetoric of Irony* (Chicago: Univ. of Chicago Press, 1974), 44.

262. Muecke, *The Compass of Irony*, 42.

263. Booth, *A Rhetoric of Irony*, 5

264. Ibid., 91.

265. Ibid., 19.

266. Ibid., 52. Booth notes that one nineteenth-century critic suggested that ironists use a special punctuation mark, resembling an inverted question mark, "as a textual sign that a passage was meant ironically" (55).

267. Shakespeare, *Hamlet*, Act 2, scene ii.

268. Tuckett, *Reading the New Testament*, 161.

269. Hirsch, *Validity in Interpretation*, 223.

270. Juhl, *Interpretation*, 132

271. Searle, "The Logical Status of Fictional Discourse," *New Literary History* 6 (1975): 319–32.

272. Booth, *A Rhetoric of Irony*, 121.

273. Juhl, *Interpretation*, 166.

274. Hirsch, *Aims of Interpretation*, 1.

275. Hirsch, "Meaning and Significance Reinterpreted," *Critical Inquiry* 11 (1984): 216.

276. Booth, *Irony*, 20.

277. Harris, *Interpretive Acts*, ix.

278. Booth, *Irony*, 19. Ben F. Meyer, in similar fashion, distinguishes "interpretation" from "analysis." Interpretation aims at recovering authorial intent. "Analysis" refers to all secondary readings (e.g., structural, socio-economic, form-critical) that aim to solve some problem other than that of determining the nature of the author's communicative act.

279. Harris, *Interpretive Acts*, 169.

280. Ibid., viii–ix.

281. LaFargue, "Are Texts Determinate?" 356.

282. Hirsch, *Aims of Interpretation*, 3.

283. E. D. Hirsch, "Transhistorical Intentions and the Persistence of Allegory," *New Literary History* 25 (1994): 549–67.

284. E. D. Hirsch, "Meaning and Significance Reinterpreted," 202. I will treat Childs below. Suffice it to say that, on his view, those who shaped the canon did so with the distinct intention of enabling it to function authoritatively for future generations.

285. Ibid., 209.

286. Ibid., 210.

287. Kripke propounds a "causal theory" of reference, which claims that reference is established not by a definite description but by a causal chain that links the speaker to the intended referent; Priestly was referring to the same thing that later scientists refer to, though under a different name. See Kripke's *Naming and Necessity* (Cambridge, Mass.: Harvard Univ. Press, 1972). For an alternate view, see Searle, *Intentionality*, 249.

288. Hirsch may here be lapsing into speaking of intention in psychological terms, that is, in terms of mapping intentions.

289. Hirsch, "Transhistorical Intentions," 558. The relation of letter and spirit in biblical interpretation will be the special subject of ch. 7 below.

290. Evans, "Medieval Interpretation," *Dictionary of Biblical Interpretation*, 439.

291. Cited in John Hilary Martin, "The Four Senses of Scripture: Lessons from the Thirteenth Century," *Pacifica: Australian Theological Studies* 2 (1989): 100n31.

292. *Summa Theologica*, Ia I.10. I examine the concept of the literal sense in the next chapter.

293. Raymond E. Brown, *The Critical Meaning of the Bible* (London: Geoffrey Chapman, 1981), 33. Cf. Brown, *The "Sensus Plenior" of Sacred Scripture* (Baltimore: St. Mary's Univ. Press, 1955). For an analysis and critique of Brown's position, see Douglas Moo, "The Problem of Sensus Plenior," in D. A. Carson and John D. Woodbridge, *Hermeneutics, Authority, and Canon* (Grand Rapids: Baker, 1995), esp., 201–4. As will become apparent, I accept the first of Brown's extensions of literal meaning but not the second. The way the church reads the Scripture does not affect its meaning, only its significance.

294. I agree with Paul Noble's judgment about Brevard Childs's notion of "canonical intentions": "Only *divine* authorship could account for the meanings that Childs wishes to find in the Bible" (Noble, *The Canonical Approach*, 206). Neither collective authorship nor later editorial activity can adequately explain how the canon of the Old Testament, as a human document, could be about Jesus Christ.

295. The precise means by which God could be considered the author is not at issue. There are several possibilities, ranging from the traditional thesis of double agency (e.g., concurrence) to Wolterstorff's more recent view that the Bible is "divinely appropriated" discourse (see Wolterstorff, *Divine Discourse*, 51–54).

296. Hirsch, *Validity in Interpretation*, 123.

297. See, for example, 1 Thess. 2:13.

298. Wolfhart Pannenberg, *Theology and the Philosophy of Science* (Philadelphia: Westminster, 1976), ch. 3. Pannenberg draws particularly on Dilthey for his understanding of hermeneutics and the human sciences.

299. With regard to history, Pannenberg says that the resurrection of Jesus anticipates the end of history and so discloses the meaning of the whole.

300. Does it follow that the divine intention contradicts that of the human authors? I avoid such an incoherent position in the following way. If we return to the concept of supervenience, we can see the divine intention as an "emergent property" of the diverse human communicative acts that comprise Scripture. I explore this option in the following chapter at greater length, in which I distinguish between different *levels* of communicative action.

301. I treat these questions at greater length in "The Bible—Its Relevance Today," in David W. Torrance, ed., *God, Family and Sexuality* (Carberry: Handsel, 1997), 9–30.

302. Exegesis can give us knowledge of textual meaning, but the Spirit gives us wisdom.

CHAPTER SIX

Redeeming the Text: The Rationality of Literary Acts

It is a logical mistake to confuse the impossibility of certainty in understanding with the impossibility of understanding.

E. D. Hirsch Jr.[1]

Protests . . . against the postmodern readings of the Bible are likely to be ineffectual. Unless, that is, those who care about serious reading of the gospels set about exploring ways in which to articulate a better epistemology.

N. T. Wright[2]

To someone who believes in determinate meaning, disagreement can only be a theological error.

Stanley Fish[3]

The results of the preceding chapter established the "metaphysics" of meaning. There is meaning—intended communicative action—in the text. This assurance is small comfort, however, to those engaged in actual interpretive disputes. For it is one thing to affirm *that* a text has determinate meaning, quite another thing to determine just *what* that meaning is. At the same time, it is important to avoid what Searle calls the "standard mistake" of supposing "that lack of evidence, that is, our ignorance, shows indeterminacy or undecidability in principle."[4] Many ambiguities, resulting from distance of the reader in time or cultural context, can often be dispersed by good scholarship.

This chapter explores a number of epistemological issues that arise from the notion of meaning as communicative action. Is interpretation a form of knowledge? If so, is it knowledge based on evidence? What kind of evidence? What remains of rationality after the Undoer's thoroughgoing critique of Cartesian objectivity? Is there really such a thing as validity, and invalidity, in interpretation, and if so, how may we articulate it? Are interpretations right or wrong? Is this something we can demonstrate? Merely to affirm the reality of meaning in texts would be an empty achievement if nothing about this meaning could be known. At stake, then, is the possibility of an epistemology of meaning and the intelligibility of the idea of "literary knowledge."

The reader is not, of course, entirely passive in the process of knowing, for the mind is not a blank slate on which the object of literary knowledge simply inscribes itself. Yet it would be grossly overstating the case to say that an interpreter, in engaging the text, can come to know only his or her own mind. I wish to argue, on the contrary, that the text can be a source of evidence and a means of knowledge not only about an author (i.e., what he wrote, what she did), but also about what the author feels, knows, observes, and imagines.[5] Indeed, much of what we have in texts is *testimony to something other than themselves or their authors*. To be sure, neither authors nor texts can control a reader's interpretation. It does not follow, however, that the author's intention is inaccessible or that the text means anything its readers take it to mean. The text stands between author and reader as an embodied intention that, through various textual strategies, extends the matter and mode of the author's attention to the world into the world of the reader, enabling the reader to respond to the same matter in an appropriate fashion. In particular, there are a number of textual contexts—narrative, generic, canonical—that enable present-day readers of the Bible to move from "what it meant" to "what it means." My thesis is that the text itself constitutes the most appropriate context for interpretation, provided that readers attend to the text on the level of the literary and canonical act. Literary knowledge, I suggest, is largely a matter of what in another context has been called "thick description."[6]

In order to redeem the text as a source of knowledge and interpretation as a means of knowledge, we need to address four questions. (1) First, what is the *nature* of literary knowledge? Neither fideism nor foundationalism alone provides an adequate account of the morality of literary knowledge. Though readers must begin with faith, they need not end there. On the other hand, interpretation is not solely a matter of appealing to incontrovertible evidence either. Textual knowledge, I contend, is rather a matter of believing testimony, and such belief is well within the interpreter's epistemic rights.

(2) I look next at the main *problem* of literary knowledge, namely, the conflict of interpretations. The despair of ever achieving literary knowledge has reached a near fever pitch in our society. Believers in interpretation are today regarded with the same pity (or scorn) usually reserved for fundamentalists; in postmodern literary criticism, skepticism is next to godliness. Interpretations may be useful for this or that purpose, for this or that interpretive community; they can no longer be said to be "true." In order to speak of literary knowledge, then, it is necessary to clarify the nature of the conflict and to find a way through it, avoiding relativism on the one hand and absolutism on the other.

(3) This leads to my third question, concerning the *norms* of literary knowledge. Interestingly, contemporary positions mirror those deployed in fourth-century and sixteenth-century debates over biblical interpretation, for the possibility of valid interpretation is tied to the controversial concept of the literal sense, which in turn is related to how interpreters view the significance of Jesus Christ. I here present a new defense of a reconstituted literal sense and argue that literary knowledge is to a large extent a matter of giving appropriately "thick" descriptions of communicative acts.

(4) The final question treats the *method* of literary knowledge. I argue that one's interpretive approach should be dictated by the object of literary knowledge, which is none other than a particular kind of literary act. Implicit in each kind of literary act is a rationality proper to that practice. The best way to come to know what has been done is to attend to the *whole* act or, in the case of texts, the literary genre.

The burden of this chapter is to sketch a model of interpretation that answers to the requirements of hermeneutic rationality and yields literary knowledge, which, while not absolute, is nevertheless adequate. My contribution to the epistemology of meaning is to stress the extent to which literary criticism is not simply a problem of the morality of knowledge, but a problem that ultimately demands theological resources—specifically, the virtues of faith, hope, obedience, and love: *faith*, that there is a real presence in the text that demands a response; *hope*, that the community of interpreters can reach, at least ideally, a reasoned agreement; *obedience*, that the interpreter will observe the context of the text itself and follow the literary sense where it leads; *love*, that the interpreter will indwell the text and attend to it on its own terms.[7]

BELIEF IN MEANING AS PROPERLY BASIC: THE NATURE OF LITERARY KNOWLEDGE

David Hume once inquired, "Are morals derived from knowledge or from sentiment?" We can ask the same of meaning: "Is meaning derived from a reader's knowledge of the text, or from the reader's experience (emotional, ideological, aesthetic) of the text?" Obviously, the text itself is the most important source of literary knowledge, but how does one's encounter with the text lead to literary knowledge? The first step is to offer a preliminary definition of "literary knowledge."

Literary Knowledge

Many contemporary critics treat "literary knowledge" as an oxymoron rather than dignify it with a definition. The study of literature, they object, is not sufficiently "scientific." Others dismiss this attitude—call it "scientism"—as a positivist prejudice. Explanation is not limited to the Book of Nature. There is, however, a second objection to the idea of literary knowledge, namely, that the question behind the whole interpretive enterprise—"What does it mean?"—is simply too vague. Such an imprecise query cannot hope to found a "discipline" of knowledge. What, then, is the proper object of literary knowledge?[8]

Knowledge and the Literary Critic

"Literary knowledge" can refer to one of two things: either *knowledge about the text* (e.g., its circumstances of composition) or *knowledge of what the text is about* (e.g., its subject matter). The latter understanding prevailed in classical Greece and in the humanist tradition in general, where it was common to view literature as a medium of moral instruction. Good literature is about good people, their values, and their virtues. The study of the humanities was traditionally the means for cultivating the finest qualities in humanity. Literature—stories and histories alike—gives us greater knowledge of the human condition.[9] It is the laboratory of human possibilities.[10]

Other literary critics prefer to obtain knowledge *about* a text: about its socio-historical conditions and consequences, about its linguistic, literary, and aesthetic features. On this view, the text itself is the object to be described and explained. What kind of explanations are appropriate for literary objects? According to Paisley Livingstone, "to explain is to give reasons why a given state of affairs obtains; this providing of reasons is achieved by relating the particular case under explanation to a more general pattern."[11] Ironically enough, many literary critics never raise what I call a "properly interpretive question"; in their haste to analyze and explain the text, they forget to seek understanding of what the text is about. What else can we make of a critic who discusses the way in which a novel reflects the social-historical conditions of its production, the unconscious psychoses of its producer, or the patriarchal ideology of the era, but never that to which the author is primarily attending? While one or all of the above might be true descriptions, are they descriptions of communicative action? Knowledge *about* the text is not necessarily the same as knowledge of *what the text is about* (viz., its meaning).

"What does it mean?" need no longer remain a vague question. The burden of the previous chapter has been to specify the nature of textual meaning in terms of communicative action. The primary *interpretive* questions thus become questions about the text's matter and energy: about the subject matter and illocutionary force of a text, about what and how the author attended to his or her words. While there are many ways of studying texts, many of these are at best peripheral to the task of determining their meaning. What defines the intellectual effort of interpretation is best summed up by Gilbert Ryle's notion of "thick description."[12] For Ryle, this meant, appropriately enough, describing actions so as not to lose their intentionality. *A description is sufficiently thick when it allows us to appreciate everything the author is doing in a text.*[13]

Commentary and the Biblical Critic: Descriptions Thick and Thin

We can quickly relate these issues to biblical interpretation by asking a simple question: What is a commentary? Are commentaries sources of background knowledge, handbooks of linguistic information, aids to faith, creative interpretations? J. L. Houlden's definition provides a starting point: "A commentary on a biblical book sets out to help the reader with various kinds of explanatory material, so that the text may be better understood."[14] He immediately adds, however, that commentaries are often more aggressive in pushing their own agendas than his definition suggests. Richard Coggins, similarly, concedes that a certain amount of ideological bias is inevitable: "Almost every feature of every commentary will be value-laden."[15] Impartial biblical scholarship, in which the commentator remains studiously objective, strikes today's postmodern exegete as an antiquated myth. Typically, commentaries try either to reconstruct the original context or to establish the relevance of Scripture in the contemporary context. Neither of these concerns, however, is necessarily more conducive to objectivity than the other. According to Robert Carroll, the multiplicity of different commentary series now on the market "represents a wide-ranging set of choices of approach, treatment and purpose for different interpretative communities and guilds. It also highlights what some would see as a 'crisis' in the biblical commentary genre."[16] The crisis is largely epistemological: a crisis about the nature, method, and criteria of literary, or in this case biblical, knowledge. In short: Does a biblical commentary *invent* or does it *discover*?

The crisis in biblical interpretation affects both the academy and the church. Since the Enlightenment, most biblical scholars in the university adopted a strictly historical approach to the biblical texts in order to concentrate on "facts" rather than "values."[17] Among both liberal and conservative exegetes, the text came to be seen as a means to a historical end, namely, the reconstruction of what really happened. In particular, biblical critics spent considerable intellectual energy in a valiant, though ultimately vain, attempt to reconstruct the history of a text's composition. Increasingly, the historical-critical method displaced other methods of reading the Bible and, at least in the university, was thought to be the only rational approach to the text. The net effect was that biblical texts were read in isolation from their literary and theological contexts as part of the canonical Scriptures. In other words, the task of interpreting, say, Genesis in the context of the Old Testament as a whole, or of the Christian Bible as a whole, was no longer considered academically acceptable.[18]

Karl Barth, in a famous defense of his overtly theological interpretation of the book of Romans, states: "My complaint is that recent commentators confine themselves to an interpretation of the text which seems to me to be no commentary at all, but merely the first step towards a commentary."[19] Barth accuses historical critics of not being critical enough because, in their eagerness to explain word derivations or to imagine which bits of the text are the oldest, they stop short of grappling with the subject matter of the text. Barth comments: "For me, at any rate, the question of the true nature of interpretation is the supreme question."[20] Whether historical criticism qualifies as an example of genuine interpretation is a disputed point. What we can say, with a fair amount of confidence, is that much modern biblical scholarship is an example of what Ryle calls "thin description." For Ryle, a thin description of, say, a wink would be one that offered a minimal account only ("rapidly contracting his right eyelid"). The description is thin because it omits the broader context of the event that alone enables it to appear as an intended action. In consequence, thin descriptions suffer from a poverty of meaning. As an example of a thick description, Ryle imagines a boy who parodies another boy's wink. The movement is the same, but the action is altogether different—neither blinking nor winking, but mocking—and the context that forms the background for this description is altogether more complex. The point is that interpretation—whether in cultural anthropology, history, or literary criticism—is a matter of offering "thick" descriptions of what people are doing.

Fortunately, some biblical scholars continue to believe that the purpose of the commentary is to enable readers better to appreciate what an author did and that to which an author attended. According to Gundry, "What the biblical authors intended to say should exercise a magisterial role over our interpretation of the Christian faith."[21] The purpose of a commentary is to examine what was said/done in order to apprehend the author's communicative intent—in order to follow the author's thought, not back into his mind, but outwards toward the matter of his discourse. It is not necessary to assume that an Evangelist always thought out or planned in advance what he was going to do; in this direction lies the intentional fallacy. Gundry admits that it is impossible to decide what was deliberate and what was spontaneous on Mark's part. But this need not distract the interpreter from the goal of discovering what Mark has actually done.[22]

It follows from the nature of interpretation that the principal task of the biblical commentator is to comprehend the nature and content of the author's communicative act. A commentary that ignores this aspect will be less an interpretation of the text than a critical study of some incidental or fragmentary aspect of the literary act. The genuine commentary is an analysis of one or more of the dimensions of the text's total communicative act. Commentaries, then, aim at different types of knowledge: of the immediate situation of the act (the occasion of biblical texts), of the broader contexts of the act, and of the consequences of the act (the history of reception).[23] This knowledge *about* the text serves the purposes of interpretation only when it puts us in a better position to know what the text is *about*. The good commentary both reduces our puzzlement and enriches our appreciation of what is going on in a text: "The success of any interpretation depends on its explanatory power, on its ability to make more complex, coherent, and natural sense of textual data than other interpretations do."[24]

Foundationalism or Fideism?

Can we justify our belief that there is a determinate meaning in the text, that texts are about something other than themselves? Can Christians justify their belief that what the Bible is about is the knowledge of God? Most readers may feel no need to justify their belief in determinate meaning. They hold a common sense view that simply assumes that texts express the thoughts—about the world, or human nature—of their authors.[25] That there is meaning, and what that meaning is, is for these readers usually obvious. As we have seen, however, the Undoer claims that the "obvious" meaning is not discovered but invented by the interpreter. What is undone is the authority of common sense itself. Common sense—the way we think, speak, and experience the world—is a function of the language system we are in. In the light of the postmodern suspicion of hermeneutics, it is a live question whether interpretation deals with facts. Do interpreters ever find, or is it fabrication all the way down?

Interpretive Foundationalism

Philosophers have struggled, long before deconstruction, to distinguish discovery from invention, knowledge from mere opinion. What must one add to belief or to interpretation in order to justify it? Mere opinion becomes knowledge, according to the common modern account, when there is sufficient reason or sufficient evidence. We may recall Clifford's dictum that it is always and everywhere wrong to believe something on insufficient evidence. For Harvey too, the "morality" of knowledge is a matter of fulfilling one's epistemic obligations. Unsubstantiated belief is not only irrational but immoral. A judgment has intellectual integrity for modern thinkers only if it is based on sufficient evidence or reasons, and this applies to literary as well as to historical interpretations.

Modern biblical criticism, by and large, is an attempt to respond to Clifford's challenge. For many biblical scholars, sufficient evidence meant critically reconstructed *historical* evidence. The so-called "introduction" to a biblical book, a standard fixture in modern commentaries, gathers historical data (especially extrabiblical evidence from archaeology or other ancient texts) that helps in reconstructing the history of a text's composition.[26] The first reflex of biblical critics was to act on Lord Acton's assumption that "the beginning of wisdom in history is doubt," to distrust the surface appearances of the text and to press behind the appearances to the historical reality.[27] While Genesis appears to be a unified work written by a single author (Moses), the "true" (e.g., historically reconstructed) story of its composition and authorship is a different matter. The task of the critical commentary is to provide a sufficient foundation of hard facts about a text that can then be used to form reasonable interpretive judgments. Modern biblical scholarship, I suggest, is a good example of "foundationalist" epistemology.[28]

The present crisis in the idea of the biblical commentary is best viewed in light of the undoing of the epistemological foundations with which modern scholars have traditionally worked. For the critical sense is no less prone to attack by postmodern thinkers than its common sense predecessor. If there is no such thing as neutral or objective criticism, then all scholars stand accused of tampering with the evidence; the autonomy of the individual is only an Enlightenment disguise for an institutional ideology.[29] Clearly, foundationalism cannot survive the loss of the fact/value distinction. Far from being universal, the morality of critical knowledge, like all other values, turns out to be a matter of personal preference: "Exegetical methods and their theoretical underpinnings are not univocal, natural or self-evident."[30] Fish's point that knowledge is the result of our interpretive practices, practices that ultimately derive from values and beliefs, can be applied equally to the practices of biblical criticism. Our beliefs "have no possible justification outside the practices, contexts, or language-games that happen to prevail at present."[31] What was once thought to be a universal foundation for knowledge turns out to be only a temporary, makeshift political platform.

Interpretive Fideism

Faced with such theoretical onslaughts to modern strategies of justification, it is little wonder that some have abandoned the search for sufficient evidence or reasons. Many Bible readers prefer a more direct approach—"The Bible tells me so"—as if interpretation were not a problem. Literary knowledge, if it is knowledge, is here a matter of immediate apprehension. N. T. Wright suggests that some Bible study groups have inadvertently blessed ways of reading that bear an uncanny resemblance to certain relativistic strands of postmodernity: "The devout predecessor of deconstructionism is that reading of the text which insists that what the Bible says to *me, now,* is the be-all and end-all of its meaning. . . . There are some strange bedfellows in the world of literary epistemology."[32]

Even professional literary critics, however, have returned to something like a "faith seeking understanding" approach. For, as George Steiner admits, deconstruction, on its own terms, is irrefutable. Yet this does not stop Steiner from believing in meaning; on the contrary, he proceeds to wager on the meaningfulness of meaning. Indeed, Hirsch appeals explicitly to Pascal's wager: "Let us weigh the practical gain and loss in calling heads—that is, that objective historical truth exists. . . . If you win, you win something. If you lose, you lose nothing. Do not hesitate, then, to gamble on the existence of objective truth."[33] Is this a form of interpretive easy-believism, of fideism transposed to hermeneutics? Can we really do nothing better than place our bets? I believe we can. For the wager of faith is not incompatible with rationality, or at least not with a species of rationality that is neither Cartesian nor foundationalist.

Fortunately, we are not obliged to choose between two options only—between finding certain foundations on the one hand, or floundering in fideism on the other.

The New Reformed Epistemology

Alvin Plantinga and Nicholas Wolterstorff have been at the forefront of efforts to approach traditional philosophical questions from a specifically Christian point of view.[34] How might Christian philosophy (and theology) make a difference to literary epistemology? Plantinga argues that, from a Christian perspective, the design plan of the human mind is to produce true beliefs. I wish to apply this notion to hermeneutics in order to argue that the belief in determinate textual meaning (viz., communicative action), far from being "immoral," is instead "properly basic." Once we can establish this important belief about the text, we can then go on to examine properly basic beliefs about what the text is about.

Is Interpretation Properly Basic?

Plantinga sees three competing worldviews "vying for spiritual supremacy in the West": perennial naturalism, creative anti-realism, and Christianity.[35] Naturalism views the human condition as on a par with non-human reality; it is prone to evolutionary and socio-biological explanations of all human experience, from love to language. Apart from a few philosophers of language, however, this view has not attracted many literary theorists, and we will have no more to say about it, other than to repeat Steiner's observation that meaningful language is ultimately underwritten by God.[36] The second view, creative anti-realism, is much more relevant to our discussion, for it maintains that it is human beings who are ultimately responsible for structuring the "natural" as well as the cultural world. Creative anti-realists ascribe to the human rather than to the divine mind the role of ordering reality. Humans cannot say "let there be light," but they can and do shape the world by naming it in different ways. In literary theory, both Undoers and Users are creative anti-realists. There is no such thing as "the" correct meaning of a text, only different interpretations: "Thus does anti-realism breed relativism and nihilism."[37] Neither naturalists nor anti-realists can believe in the author's mind: intended meaning is either reduced to physical events on the one hand, or deemed a matter of the interpreter's creative projection on the other.

How might Christian theism bear on the subject of literary knowledge? Plantinga's explanation of what turns belief into knowledge represents an important alternative to the options of foundationalism and fideism, naturalism and creative anti-realism. Just as the design plan of language is to serve as a medium for covenantal relations, so the human mind has also been designed by God for a particular purpose: "The purpose of the heart is to pump blood; that of our cognitive faculties (overall) is to supply us with reliable information."[38] Human beings have several belief-producing mechanisms—perception, memory, intuition—that are designed to produce true beliefs when they are functioning properly in a cognitively clean environment. Following on from Plantinga, my thesis is that the mind is designed to *interpret* when it is functioning properly in an appropriate *linguistic* and *literary* environment. When confronted with human behavior or with written texts, that is, we do not have to prove intentionality but can legitimately assume it. *Interpreting— that is, ascribing intended meanings to discourse—is properly basic.*

Belief in Other Minds and Authors' Minds

The problem of how to prove the existence of other minds has long plagued philosophers. This problem too has a bearing on literary theory, and it is just here— in arguments about authors' minds—that the advantages of the new Reformed epistemology can best be appreciated.

Following Thomas Reid, Plantinga argues that some beliefs are held not on the basis of evidence or argument but rather on the basis of "intuition," or what Reid calls "common sense."[39] Reid's common sense insight amounts to this: we have no practical alternative but to assume that our cognitive faculties (e.g., perception, memory) are basically reliable.[40] We do not have to *prove* the reality of the external world; we simply find ourselves with a conception of it as a result of our perceptions. Belief in the reality of the external world is thus a "basic" belief, one that does not depend on prior beliefs. Belief are "properly" basic when our belief-producing faculties are functioning properly in the right cognitive environment. Upon being asked what I had for lunch, I do not have my stomach pumped to observe the contents; I rather find myself with the appropriate belief, thanks to memory, and say, "Pastrami on rye." The point is that we do not have to appeal to foundationalist evidence in order to justify our basic beliefs.

With regard to texts, the question becomes: "Is belief in intended meaning 'properly basic'?" On the one hand, belief in textual meaning does not appear to be like beliefs that stem from self-knowledge, memory, or perception. However, there is an interesting parallel between the belief in intended meaning and the belief in other minds. And indeed, it is under just this heading that we find Plantinga addressing, all too briefly, the question of meaning.[41] When our cognitive faculties are working properly, we should not have to produce evidence or attempt to justify the existence of minds in our neighbors. Similarly, we need not prove that there is meaning (e.g., the intentional agency of another person) in a text. When reading a book, we just find ourselves ascribing things to the author. The belief that there is something there—"in" the body, "in" the book—does not have to be demonstrated; it is a properly basic belief.[42] With regard to human action, we properly impute intentionality; in the case of texts, we properly impute communicative intention. From a Christian perspective, we can say that *God created us with linguistic faculties in order to communicate with and understand one another (and with him).* Such is the "design plan" of *homo interpretans.*

How to demonstrate the existence of other minds is not exactly a literary critical problem. Nor should it be. My argument is that exegetes just find themselves believing in the author's mind (and intentional action) as a result of reading a text. A commentary, whether on the Bible or some other book, proceeds on the basis of "a belief in the possibility of meaningful dialogue."[43] Calvin, too, held that the first act of understanding is belief.[44] The contemporary reluctance to believe in authors or to talk about their intentions is thus a sign either of interpretive malfunctioning or of faulty epistemology.

It is important not to mistake talk about other minds as implying a dualism between mind and body (or mind and text). The dualist takes external behavior (or textual data) as *evidence* from which something about the agent's (or author's) inner states could be inferred. But this is not how we make sense of people's actions (or texts). Instead of inferring intention from external behavior, we simply interpret bodily movement (or textual data) *as* basic actions. That is, when our cognitive faculties are functioning properly in the right sort of cognitive environment, we do not infer from bodily movement or textual marks what someone is doing, we just find ourselves with the belief that a person is, say, pouring a cup of tea or telling a story. Similarly, we do not have to infer from black marks on white paper that there is a text; we simply find ourselves reading stories, histories, gospels. "We must claim instead that we *begin* with people and their actions: that these are what we can directly observe, and directly know; that these are not reducible by philosophical analysis to such supposedly simpler or more basic constituents as bodies and their colorless movements."[45] In short, we do not first observe bodily movements from which we then infer intentions; we simply observe intentional action. Similarly, we do not read one word after another and then infer a pattern; we simply read poetry. When our interpretive faculties are functioning properly, in a clean interpretive environment, we simply find ourselves contemplating purposeful communicative action. My belief "that there is a meaning in this text" is a properly basic belief.

Testimony

Our trust in the word of others is fundamental to the very idea of serious cognitive activity.[46]

One of the most important sources of basic beliefs, according to Reid, is testimony. "The wise author of nature hath planted in the human mind a propensity to rely upon human testimony before we can give a reason for doing so."[47] Or, as Plantinga puts it, our design plan leads us to believe what we are told by others. This is his reformulation of Reid's "principle of credulity"—"a belief-forming process whereby for the most part we believe what our fellows tell us."[48] Human intellectual powers have been designed to produce true beliefs on the basis of what we are told. Credulity—the predisposition to believe others—is a "gift of Nature." It is the indispensable condition of inter-subjectivity and of community.[49] It is also a crucial notion for literary epistemology, for it is the chief means by which we come to know that *about which* texts speak.

The Principle of Credulity: Belief in Others' Words

Credulity is not gullibility, as John Locke and other modern critics seem to think.[50] Locke defines faith as an assent to propositions made not on the basis of sufficient reason or evidence but only upon the credit of the proposer, which for Locke is no proper basis at all. Modern biblical critics, by and large, tend to agree.[51] According to Dennis Nineham, the biblical critic must exercise a hermeneutics of suspicion: "His very integrity and autonomy as an historian prevent his taking his 'sources' at face value."[52] This applies to the question of authorship as well as to the question of truth. As we have seen in earlier chapters, this hermeneutics of suspicion is taken to the limit by deconstructors who deny the very existence of determinate meaning. Obviously, texts with no determinate meaning cannot be sources of knowledge; they can neither witness, report, or confess.

For Reid, maintaining an attitude of distrust (a hermeneutics of systematic suspicion) is the equivalent of doing violence to our constitution. If our minds were not inclined toward believing what we are told, we would almost never accept anything, for few beliefs come with sufficient evidence. Such an ascetic and exacting standard, moreover, would leave us epistemically impoverished, for it would remove the main source of literary knowledge: testimony. The philosopher C. A. J. Coady has recently argued that testimony is as reliable a source of knowledge as memory and perception.[53] To restrict belief to that which we see for ourselves would eliminate most of what we know: "It is testimony and learning from others that makes possible intellectual achievement and culture; testimony is the very foundation of civilization."[54] Testimony is a properly basic form of knowledge. For Nineham and other biblical critics, however, the only eyewitness testimony that is wholly reliable is one's own. Coady shrewdly observes that the tendency to privilege perception over testimony is really "a hankering after a primacy for my perception."[55] This is precisely what interpreters who create rather than attempt to discover textual meaning do; they prefer their own observations to the testimony of authors.

Testimonies and Testaments

Like the promise, testimony establishes a connection between what one says and the way things actually are. Indeed, in many cases, testimony is the only access one has to what a text is about. Testimony is an illocutionary act whereby a witness's say-so is itself evidence for the truth of what is said.[56] We are oriented to reality as much by others as by our own observation. It is often impossible to verify testimony by going beyond or behind what is written. Reporting, says Coady, "is probably the dominant form of assertion."[57] A person's stating "that p," under normal circumstances, is reason enough for believing it. Testimony is thus a reliable and indispensable source of knowledge.

An appropriately thick description of the Gospels will interpret them as testimonies to something other than themselves. The historical critic's reconstruction of the text appears, in this light, conspicuously thin; to attempt to get behind testimony is not to gain literary knowledge but to lose it. For the knowledge we gain from testimony is not inferential but properly basic. In the case of the Gospels, the texts are the only access we have to the events in question. It should be evident that the skeptical critic stands at a distinct disadvantage to the believer when it comes to apprehending the subject matter of the Gospels: "The attempt to get behind these testimonies does not enable us to say more but to say less than they do."[58]

For too long, biblical critics have sought to understand the biblical text by ignoring its plain testimony and instead attempting to cross-examine extra-textual witnesses (e.g., other ancient literary sources, archaeological evidence, etc.). This, as I have argued, takes us as far as thin description only; for, inasmuch as one distrusts testimony, one removes the most important means of knowing what the Bible is about. One salutary effect of revitalizing testimony as a source of literary knowledge, therefore, is that biblical interpreters can once again attend to the text and to what it is about, rather than to what purportedly lies behind it. Trust rather than suspicion is more fruitful when it comes to interpreting testimony. Our interpretive faculties are designed to produce belief in the words of witnesses in the absence of compelling reason to the contrary.

Plantinga makes the intriguing point that most of our beliefs are such "that the very possibility of our forming them is dependent on testimony. For if there were no such thing as testimony, as a source of belief, then, in all likelihood, there would be nothing but the most rudimentary sorts of language."[59] The corollary of this suggestion is that many of our beliefs are dependent on sophisticated sorts of language, say, literary texts. And this is precisely what I wish to argue in relation to the Gospels and, indeed, in relation to the Old and New Testaments as a whole. The Bible is the corporate testimony of the Jewish and Christian communities to God's self-revelation in history and in Jesus Christ. Taken as a whole and as a divine communicative act, the Bible is God's self-attestation. However, the subject matter of the Bible is not discovered by treating the Bible as evidence for historical reconstruction, but by treating it as testimony. Only by reading the Bible as testimony and by offering thick descriptions of testimony as a communicative act will one gain not merely knowledge about the text, but knowledge of what the text is about: God's reconciliation with humanity through Jesus Christ.

We have established a number of important points this section that go some way towards an adequate literary epistemology. Most important, we have seen that literary knowledge admits of two senses: knowledge about the text (e.g., what kind of communicative act) and knowledge of what the text is about. We then saw the importance of thick description for forming an adequate view of what the text is (e.g., communicative action). The best kind of knowledge about the text—the kind of knowledge relevant for the purposes of interpretation—is knowledge of what the author was doing. I argued that interpretation is a properly basic cognitive activity, for it is entirely proper to ascribe intended meaning to written texts. We then turned our attention to testimony as the linchpin that connects what the biblical authors are doing (testifying) and what the text is about (testaments). Finally, I claimed that the biblical texts, as testimonies, are legitimate sources of literary knowledge and ultimately of the knowledge of God. My objective has been to show the cultured despisers of literary knowledge that belief in authors and in authors' words needs no further justification. Is "conflict" the last or only the penultimate word to be said about interpretation?"

THE CONFLICT OF INTERPRETATIONS: THE PROBLEM OF LITERARY KNOWLEDGE

> To give an interpretation is to make a claim. To make a claim is to be willing to defend that claim if challenged by others.[60]

If, as I have argued, it is part of our design plan that we impute intended meaning to texts in order to understand them, then why is there so much misunderstanding in the world? More to the point: why do interpreters disagree about the meaning of everything they read, from the simplest children's fable on the one hand to Galatians on the other?[61] Is it because of some defect in the text (e.g., indeterminacy), or of some defect in the interpreter (e.g., partiality), or perhaps both? The present chapter, on the rationality of the text as literary act, treats only the first part of this query. Is there any evidence, with regard to literary knowledge, that the history of biblical interpretation is progressing rather than degenerating? Given widespread and perennial conflict, is it ever appropriate to use the term "knowledge" of interpretation? Is "conflict" the last or only the penultimate word to be said?

The Problem Stated: Can Determinate Meaning Be Determined?

Readers clearly differ in their interpretations. What, precisely, is the nature of an interpretive disagreement? If I claim, "Matthew's Gospel portrays Jesus as the Messiah promised in the Old Testament," what kind of claim have I made? How do I defend it? Do disputes in interpretation concern conflicting knowledge claims, and if so, claims about what—properties in texts? the purpose of the author? the experience of the reader? Perhaps there are many different types of interpretive claims, depending on what one regards as the purpose of interpretation. At the very least, however, we should be able to distinguish between descriptive and evaluative interpretive claims. The former make some claim about the way things (e.g., authors, texts) are, while the latter makes a claim about their value or worth. Strictly speaking, only descriptions can make knowledge claims and thus be susceptible of truth or falsity.

According to the present account, a claim to literary knowledge is a claim about what a text is and what it is about. We want to know how correctly to describe a communicative act. *The primary object of interpretation is thus to specify the what, whys, and wherefores of the text considered as communicative action.* Who, when, and where are secondary questions that may nevertheless serve to illumine the primary ones. At issue is the extent to which good scholarship can reduce conflict and adjudicate rival answers to these questions.

Is biblical interpretation a form of rational inquiry? This query takes on a certain urgency in our present postmodern climate. Is it possible to recognize, and to reject, false interpretations (knowledge falsely so called), or is meaning relative to the interpretive community? What is the alternative, on the one hand, to cognitive anarchy (where everyone believes what he or she wants about a text), and cognitive totalitarianism (where the individual's belief is dictated by the powers that be, that is, the institutions of Church or State), on the other? Our belief that there is indeed meaning in the biblical text would be small comfort if we could not say, however tentatively, *what* that meaning is. Of course, part of the problem in resolving interpretive disputes is that different interpreters work with different definitions of meaning. It is impossible to answer the question "Can we determine determinate meaning?" until we first determine whether readers are engaged in the same enterprise. I have already presented my case for defining meaning in terms of communicative action. Even so, it is possible for interpreters to agree with this definition and still talk past one another, for communicative action itself can be described in many ways. In the final analysis, however, the conflict of interpretations owes more to the complexity of communicative action than to the inherent indeterminacy of language and textuality. It therefore follows that deconstructive despair about the possibility of correct interpretation need not be the last word on the matter.

Options in the Conflict: Between Dogmatism and Skepticism

There are a number of possible responses to the phenomenon of interpretive disagreement. Whether in literary criticism or in religious studies, the crucial question concerns our knowledge of the transcendent: in the case of religion, to what extent can human beings determine the meaning of what transcends the world; in the case of hermeneutics, of what transcends the linguistic signifiers?

Hermeneutic Exclusivism: From A(theism) to Z(ealotry)

One common response to the conflict of interpretations is to judge one's own interpretation correct and all others wrong. The most radical believers in determinate meaning posit not only the possibility of a single correct interpretation, but claim to possess it. Interpretation on this view becomes a form of absolute knowledge, with clear-cut "right" and "wrong" answers. However, it is precisely this claim to absolute knowledge that invites the Undoer's skeptical response.

Cognitive Zealots: Certain Literary Knowledge. On one end of the spectrum, then, are those—call them "cognitive zealots"—who believe in a single correct meaning that interpreters can attain. They believe in the possibility of certain literary knowledge, a knowledge gained by dint of hard work. The hard work in question involves careful observation and thorough consideration of the evidence. The epistemology underlying such an approach to texts is surely a form of foundationalism, though neither the term, nor perhaps the full-blown position, is often mentioned in the context of literary criticism. Kermode states what is perhaps the obvious objection: "But what we are waiting for now is an instance of a literary work with one and only one correct interpretation."[62]

Cognitive Atheists: No Literary Knowledge. At the other end of the spectrum are the radical skeptics who exclude the possibility that any single interpretation can be correct. The skeptic does not have to reject all evidence; he or she needs only to insist that the evidence is insufficient to prove any one interpretation better than the alternatives. As we have seen, Derrida deduces the "conditions of impossibility" for literary knowledge by maintaining that every interpretation is underdetermined, and thus undermined, by the text. I have argued that what deconstruction undoes is the pretense to have absolutely certain foundations for knowledge. Undoing foundationalist certainty, however, is not the same thing as undoing all literary knowledge.

Critical Believers: Possible Literary Knowledge. Others—and here we can include Hirsch and Juhl—are more mild-mannered exclusivists. They concede Kermode's point that dogmatism in interpretation is unwarranted. While they believe there is a single correct interpretation, they acknowledge that it is difficult to know that we know it. Juhl contends that "a theory of interpretation must account for the fact that we do draw a distinction between a possible and a correct interpretation, even if we may not agree in any given case what the correct reading is."[63] In theory, then, they are staunch exclusivists; in practice, their arguments are nuanced with qualifications.

Hermeneutic Inclusivism

Another response, growing in popularity, is that there may be several correct interpretations. This stems from a recognition that the text is only a potential of meaning that readers actualize in various ways. There are textual constraints as well as openings for the reader. In consequence, there are a (finite) number of correct interpretations. Paul Ricoeur likens the text to a finite space of possible meanings: "A text is a space of variations that has its own constraints; and in order to choose a different interpretation, we must always have better reasons."[64] Interestingly, hermeneutic exclusivism is oriented towards the author, while hermeneutic inclusivism is text-oriented. Hermeneutic pluralists, as we will see, view both authors and texts as effects of various strategies of reading.

Hermeneutic Pluralism

Whereas the exclusivist believes that only one interpretation is correct and the inclusivist believes that several may be correct, the pluralist believes that many, perhaps all, interpretations may be equally valid. Textual meaning is undecidable, talk of literary "knowledge" a mere subterfuge for institutional power. What a text means, therefore, depends on the location and identity of the reader. We cannot know the text as it is in itself, only the interpretive scheme we bring to it (e.g., patriarchy, dispensationalism, feminism, etc.). Instead of describing the meaning inherent in a text, then, the focus shifts to "descriptions of social interests and institutions or of the 'forces' that shape the discursive formations that determine knowledge."[65] According to Foucault, all talk about knowledge serves only to misdirect one's audience. Individuals, together with their opinions and their knowledge claims, are actually only effects of institutional power. We see only what we have been trained to see.

Conflict, Consensus, Community: How to Account for Interpretive Difference

Each of the above options has its own way of explaining interpretive disagreement. "To someone who believes in determinate meaning, disagreement can only be a theological error."[66] From the perspective of the hermeneutic exclusivist, that is, those who disagree with one's interpretation are either ignorant of the evidence or consciously flaunting the rules of interpretation. One way or the other, they have "missed the mark"; they have committed interpretive sin. Not all exclusivists, however, need be so dogmatic. For Juhl, interpretive disagreements are inevitable because the facts about authorial intent are often inconclusive: "Thus when the evidence is inadequate, it is often easy to convince oneself that the author 'must have' meant a certain passage in the way that our own beliefs would require."[67] At the same time, however, Juhl and Hirsch observe that much of what passes for interpretive disagreements are actually disagreements about a work's significance, not its meaning.

The Authority of Interpretive Communities

Fish gives a very different account of how to interpret the conflict of interpretations. In "What Makes an Interpretation Acceptable?" he argues that disagreements can never be resolved by a better study of the facts, "because the facts emerge only in the context of some point of view."[68] One cannot appeal to the text to adjudicate interpretive disagreement, for the text is itself a product of interpretation. In other words, we never read the text as it is in itself, but only the text as construed by the practices and procedures of an interpretive community. Within a community that follows the same interpretive procedures, we find not relativism but consensus. Indeed, for Fish, literary knowledge is simply the name for interpretive consensus. We may decide to rule out a eco-feminist-Eskimo reading of Ephesians, not because the text does not permit it, but because "there is at present no interpretive strategy for producing it."[69] While there are, therefore, procedures for ruling out certain far-fetched readings (nobody wants to be a silly relativist), "their source is not the text but the presently recognized interpretive strategies for producing the text."[70]

For Fish, literary knowledge is a matter of community consensus. The "correct" interpretation is the interpretation we are warranted to assert in light of our community's interpretive practices and procedures. There are different interpretations of the same text because it is read by different interpretive communities. This is not a silly but a sophisticated relativism—a cultural relativism. There *are* standards in interpretation on this view, but they are neither universal nor determined by the text. The hermeneutic realist's belief that the text has a determinate meaning, however, is for Fish merely illusory. Seen from his neo-pragmatist perspective, the interpretive agreements of both conservative exclusivism and liberal inclusivism are simply a matter of consensus politics—an institutional rather than an intellectual achievement.

Kathleen C. Boone tests Fish's hypothesis by studying the ways in which Protestant fundamentalists interpret the Bible. "Fundamentalist" here stands for a distinct interpretive community whose members share a theology—indeed an ideology—that determines how they read. Though they think they are reading the text, the whole text, and nothing but the text, they are actually "writing" or constructing it. Fundamentalist doctrines, such as inerrancy and creation, generate "a host of strained interpretations" that attempt, sometimes desperately, to provide readings that correspond to a set of prior beliefs. For example, fundamentalist biblical scholars reconcile differences among the Gospels through harmonization, occasionally with odd results (e.g., the cock crowing *six* times).[71] Boone poses an interesting question: Can fundamentalists simultaneously "control" interpretation and claim "that nothing but the text itself is authoritative"?[72] According to her, fundamentalists face the following dilemma: either they grant interpretive legitimacy to any reader who espouses the inerrancy doctrine, or they resort to some form of institutional authority. "Fundamentalists are caught in the very trap they try to avoid. They must resort to some form of institutional authority, unless they want to grant authority to the interpretations of any reader whatsoever who espouses the inerrancy doctrine."[73] In fact, says Boone, fundamentalists, like everyone else, have traditions and institutions that shape their interpretive results. The irony is painful, for fundamentalism sets its belief in the ultimate authority of the Bible over against, say, the Roman Catholic position of authoritative tradition. Yet it is just this distinction between Scripture and tradition, text and interpretation, that Boone and Fish reject.

Stanley Hauerwas agrees with Fish that biblical interpretation is more a matter of politics than philology. For Hauerwas, the key issue is whether or not individuals are reading the Bible in believing communities. The Bible should be read only by those *"who have undergone the hard discipline of existing as part of God's people."*[74] Both fundamentalists and biblical critics, he says, "make the Church incidental" to the process of biblical interpretation.[75] Hauerwas too rejects the distinction between text and interpretation (and interpretive realism with it), for it assumes "that the text of the Scripture makes sense separate from a Church that gives it sense."[76] As we will see, however, the distinction between text and interpretation is vital if we are to maintain hermeneutic realism and rationality and thus the possibility of deeming a particular reading false.

Theological Explanations of Interpretive Conflict

Fish mentions in passing, but nowhere seriously pursues, the suggestion that one might account for the plethora of errant interpretations by appealing to the doctrine of original sin. How, in fact, do theologians account for the diversity of biblical interpretations? The problem is hardly new. Douglas Jacobsen rightly states that interpretive diversity "is the Protestant hermeneutical problem *par excellence*."[77] He contrasts "Calvinistic" and "Arminian" answers to this question to illuminate contemporary evangelical thinking on this question. The problem is practical as well as theoretical: either one keeps to one's community of truth and excludes all others (which Jacobsen takes to be the Reformed position of "monistic separation"), or one talks and learns from those who read the Bible differently (which he associates with the Arminian tendency towards "pluralistic conversation"). We may again note the parallel between debates in the theology of religion and those in what we might call the theology of literary knowledge: How does one stake any claim to knowledge, in biblical interpretation or in religious studies, in a pluralistic, postmodern world—a world in which epistemology is in crisis, requiring intensive care?[78]

Old Reformed. Francis Turretin, not Calvin, is Jacobsen's preferred choice to represent the Calvinistic approach. Turretin believes that the true meaning of the text will be clear to those who read it properly (e.g., with attentiveness, prayer, and the illumination of the Spirit); "those who misunderstand the Scripture do so because they sinfully will to misread the text."[79] The correct interpretation, by contrast, is the one that discovers what is there in the text. Fish is scathing in his criticism of such an approach, scornfully dismissing every attempt to let the text speak for itself as "a move drenched in humility."[80] Jacobsen's assessment of Turretin is similarly caustic: "This is a neat trick. Turretin's claim is that others interpret the Bible; the orthodox, by contrast, merely uncover the true meaning of Scripture."[81] Since, for Turretin, the clear teaching of Scripture is set forth in the Reformed confessions, it is tempting to take disagreement with Reformed orthodoxy as a sign that the Bible itself is being culpably misread.

Arminian. Jacobsen draws three morals for coping with interpretive diversity from a brief consideration of Arminius. First, it should be acknowledged that interpretation is hard work. We need not always impute evil motives to others: "Ignorance, not malice, is the primary cause of difference and error."[82] Second, because interpretation is hard work, people tend to be proud of their results and to force them on others. Arminius called interpreters to acknowledge the inevitable subjective element in their work and thus to recognize the possibility of learning from others. Lastly, instead of excluding those with whom we disagree, we should engage in dialogue. Even where differences remained, Arminius was unwilling to break fellowship: "In the final analysis,

Arminius seems to have valued peace among Christians who held divergent views about Scripture . . . more highly than he valued conformity in faith or purity in dogma."[83]

Liberal and Ecumenical. What Jacobsen calls the "Arminian" approach to the conflict of interpretations has become, in its secularized modern form, the dominant stance in the Western world—and not only with regard to biblical interpretation. Wolterstorff notes that the liberal solution to the problem of religious diversity—tolerance—is essentially that of John Locke. It is a solution seen particularly in American polity (e.g., in the division of church and state), but it is also characteristic of European societies. For Locke, our common life is to be based on reason, which in modernity is a source of common knowledge. Wolterstorff observes: "Fundamental to the liberal solution is the distinction between the private sphere and the public."[84] With regard to public truth there can be rational consensus, but with regard to religion and one's private opinions there is to be tolerance. This solution, modified by Kant, turned into the fact-value dichotomy; reason, especially science, gives us knowledge of the facts, whereas values are private and should not be imposed on others.

Back to interpretation and literary knowledge. In our post-Kantian and postmodern day, facts have largely been restricted to the physical world. Every other aspect of reality is always already interpreted by some conceptual framework or other (are tomatoes a fruit or vegetable, and what makes them one rather than the other?). Western thinkers are least tolerant when it comes to the natural sciences. Disagree here and you risk being marginalized from the academy. Everywhere else, however, we find tolerance, because we are aware that we are all in the same Kantian boat—alienated from things as they are in themselves, obligated to look at things through conceptual frameworks. Since we cannot escape our Kantian frameworks, even in our churches, let us at least tolerate each other's perspectives without going to war. Such is the liberal-ecumenical consensus. *In short: the liberal solution to the conflict of interpretations is to place interpretation on the value side of the fact/value distinction.* What knowledge claims are made in literary and biblical studies are confined to "facts" about the composition of the text—that is, to *thin* description. Historical critics who speak of the "assured results" are still clinging to the myth of objectivity, namely, to the idea that their historical reconstructions are value-neutral and their observations theory-free. By and large, however, "interpretation" is no longer seen as a matter of public truth but rather of personal preference.[85]

New Reformed. Must we choose between a passion for knowledge and a passion for tolerance? I for one would be most reluctant to choose between truth and peace, or between Calvinist objectivity and Arminian subjectivity. For it is one thing to believe that there is a correct interpretation of the text, quite another to believe that only your community has got it right.

At first blush, it would appear that the new Reformed thinkers are as exclusivistic as their predecessors. For Plantinga, Christian philosophy in its Augustinian mode recognizes an antithesis between belief and unbelief, between the city of God and the concern of the world. Moreover, Plantinga likens the current intellectual debates to a battleground for the soul of Western civilization.[86] The conflict of interpretations is at root a spiritual conflict: "Christian philosophers must discern the spiritual connections of the various philosophical and quasi-philosophical currents that swirl around us."[87] It may be that interpretive disagreement arises not because of some defect in the text, but rather because of a defect in us—all of us. What else is the doctrine of original sin but a statement of the universality of cognitive malfunction, a confession that our design plan has been flawed through illicit tampering? Not only do our cognitive functions not always function as they ought, but we interpret in an environment strewn with cognitive and moral pollution. Cognitive malfunction can be corporate as well as individual.[88]

With this insight, we can easily spot the flaw in a Fish-eye view of the world. For Fish, what is authoritative is the interpretive community operating with "normal" procedures under "normal" conditions. But functioning normally is not at all the equivalent of functioning *properly*, as Plantinga convincingly demonstrates. Proper function is a matter of design plan; normal function is a matter of statistics.[89] This is a crucial distinction, though it is missing from Fish's account of the interpretive situation, and with good reason. For to acknowledge that the *normal* interpretive procedures may not be *proper* interpretive procedures is to call into question the authority of the interpretive community, Fish's sole defense against a thorough-going relativism.

So whose cognitive functions are working properly? The new Reformed philosophers would be well-advised to keep their hands down in response to this query, remembering Luther's dictum that Christians are both saints and sinners—especially so when they are reading the Bible. After all, even members of the same community of faith, or even the same denomination, have interpretive disagreements. What, then, does a Reformed account of cognitive malfunctioning contribute to the discussion about the sources and norms of interpretive disagreement? Just this: that it is precisely those who are aware of the pervasive possibility and true source of cognitive malfunction who will be most attuned to the dangers of ideological distortion. Deconstruction is valuable precisely as a diagnostic device for such malfunction. For the powers and principalities against which we struggle are not of flesh and blood. Ideas—a misleading picture, a false theory—can bind the imagination as tightly as any chain its captive. No individual or community is immune from error. It is precisely for this reason that excommunication should never be our first reflex, but rather our last resort. As far as is possible, we should strive to be at peace with other interpretive communities. Yet we must never go so far towards peace that we become indifferent to the truth of the textual matter.

Beyond Conflict? Interpretation and Critical Realism

Does peaceful dialogue guarantee that we will attain truth in interpretation? Can we hope for reconciliation, or at least progress, in the conflict of interpretations? To this point I have argued, first, that the mere presence of interpretive disagreement does not imply that there is no correct interpretation; second, that the mere presence of interpretive agreement is no guarantee that correct interpretation has been reached. I now hope to account for both of these points by developing a "critical realism" of interpretation.

Objections to Naive Hermeneutic Realism

Naive realism—a view that is oblivious to the problems of interpretation and that tends to identify the way things are with the way they appear—has been effectively refuted from a number of quarters. The notion that the mind simply apprehends the world as it is overlooks the way in which theories shape our observations, not to mention the possibility of cognitive malfunctioning. What is vital for our purposes is the recognition that objections to naive realism do not overthrow realism as such. Both critical realism and regulative realism, I believe, escape the charges laid at the naive realist's door.

Kant, as we have seen, exposed the tempting, though overly simplistic, identification of appearance and reality. Our concepts, he argued, do not correspond to the way the world (text) is in itself, but only to the way in which we experience the world (text). Both the Users and the Undoers have appropriated Kant's idea that the knower/reader comes to the data with an interpretive framework already in place. Indeed, postmodern thinkers have radicalized Kant by rejecting his suggestion that everyone comes to the data with the same conceptual framework, the same vocabulary. Contemporary thinkers have, by and large, espoused the view that these conceptual and linguistic frameworks are culturally relative.[90]

Derrida makes what is essentially a Kantian point: there is no object of knowledge—no text—as it is in itself. The fundamentalist naiveté that knowers are objective subjects who do not intrude into the process of knowing must be rejected for the dangerous deception it is. Derrida's clearsighted repudiation of the myth of neutrality is admirable. Yet he, like other skeptics, seems unable fully to let go of just this craving for objectivity. If he cannot have "perfect" knowledge, then he won't have any of it. Yet the move from naiveté to stubborn skepticism is at best a dubious achievement. Perhaps Derrida, and other postmoderns, should take heed of Wolterstorff's advice: "Kant is not a terminal disease. It's possible to get over him."[91] Humans are neither like angels, knowing things immediately, nor are they dumb brutes, who are unable to work out their differences except through force. We do not have absolute knowledge, only *human* knowledge—the kind of knowledge humans were designed to have. We have, that is to say, *adequate* knowledge—all the knowledge we need to fulfill our vocation as human beings and interpreters. In the context of hermeneutics, this means that we have the epistemic abilities to respond to the communicative overtures of an author enacted in the text in the appropriate manner. Skepticism, insofar as it dissents from this view in its all-or-nothing insistence on knowledge, resembles an epistemological tantrum that refuses to accept the human condition.

Critical Hermeneutic Realism: Fallible Knowledge

It is possible to believe in a single correct interpretation without believing that one has full possession of it. There is conflict in interpretation because literary knowledge, like all knowledge, is provisional and open to correction. Yet it is only open to correction because there is an independent standard: determinate textual meaning. This is good news. In principle, there is an end to the conflict; in practice, the conflict itself may speed us towards the resolution. The new challenge for dealing with interpretive conflict is to arrive at a model of interpretive rationality that does not presuppose either absolute foundations or a value-free standpoint, on the one hand, or arbitrary and value-laden readings, on the other. We can agree with Derrida that interpreters do not enjoy any privileged, non-contextual standpoint from which they can recover meaning apart from its mediation through signs. If things were that simple, Derrida wryly notes, word would have gotten round. What needs to be demonstrated is that knowledge of determinate meaning is possible *without* such a privileged position.[92] The critical realist must be able to say: "There is literary knowledge (viz., determinate meaning and correct interpretation), but I am not certain that I have it."[93]

Can we have knowledge without certain starting points or sacred vantage points? Literary knowledge may be likened in this respect to navigation. As the readers seeks to orient themselves with regard to the text, so sailors seeks to orient themselves on the seas. A schooner has a determinate position even though one may not be able to pinpoint the position with absolute accuracy. Significantly, the captain can establish his position without having recourse to some foundation. Spatial location is relative and can be determined by using any number of possible objects as landmarks (e.g., sun, stars, lighthouses, land, etc.): "There are no particular objects or locations which are the ultimate, fundamental landmarks or base-lines for the location of all other objects."[94] We can establish determinacy, in the text or on the high seas, not because we orient ourselves by means of absolutely fixed epistemological landmarks, but by means of points that are *fixed in relation to one another*. The meaning of a word may not be unchanging and absolute, but this does not mean that it has no determinate meaning. A language may have no one absolute center or foundation (e.g., no one interpretive key), but its terms are nevertheless in a determinate relation to one another.

Interpretations are attempts to take our bearings. While some literary critics are more interested in the conditions or consequences of communicative action, I have argued that the prime interpretive questions concerns the how, what, and why of the text considered as a communicative act.[95] While one can indeed study the socio-historical conditions and consequences of communication, these bear only indirectly (and thinly) on the question of meaning and understanding. Interpretation, I have argued, is primarily directed at understanding the communicative act itself: its "matter" (viz., propositional content), "energy" (viz., illocutionary force), and "momentum" (viz., perlocutionary effect). An interpretation is a hypothesis about the nature of communicative action, not—at least not in the first instance—about its consequences. Interpretations can, therefore, be correct or incorrect, for the intended results of a communicative action are determinate in a way that its consequences are not.

Rationality in interpretation is not a matter of having absolute evidential foundations, either of the history of the text's composition or of the author's strategic intentions. Nor is there any one point of view that is so privileged that it escapes the obligation critically to test its hypotheses. Indeed, hermeneutic rationality is a matter of putting one's interpretations to critical tests, not of putting them on secure foundations. Hermeneutic rationality, like its scientific cousin, is essentially the process of critically testing one's hypotheses as to the nature and purpose of literary acts.[96] The rationality of an interpretation is essentially a function of its ability to endure critical inquiry. Both the belief in determinate meaning and the conflict of interpretation are compatible with such a view of hermeneutic rationality.

With regard to the methods by which we arrive at a comprehensive understanding of determinate meaning, therefore, I am a pluralist. Some methods describe certain aspects of the communicative act particularly well, other methods are more appropriate for other aspects. I will return to this theme in due course. I am also an inclusivist, because I believe that the one determinate meaning encompasses more than one level of description. Thick description, that is, may require more than one interpretive approach. However, with regard to the meaning of the communicative act itself, I am an exclusivist. There is one determinate meaning in light of which the many interpretations must be judged inadequate or incorrect.[97]

Must people who believe in determinate meaning become dogmatic about it? Not if the believers are also critical realists; for the claim that there is knowledge is not the same as the claim that one possesses it or that the possession of such knowledge allows one to impose one's opinion on others. There is always something more that can be said in an argument. Interpretations can always be questioned; few proofs (outside mathematics and geometry) are ever exhaustive. Participants in a conflictual discussion may eventually come to believe there is no more point in talking. This, however, is a moral failure. The Christian morality of literary knowledge stresses the following virtues that, if cultivated, allow the conversation to continue and advance: self-criticism, clarity, consistency, patience—"the faith and courage to follow the argument where it leads."[98] If we cooperate with each other and with the text, we may hope for a provisional consensus, if not the truth itself.

Regulative Hermeneutic Realism

While Kant did not think we could know the world as it is in itself, he postulated the idea of the world as it is in itself (viz., truth) as the transcendental condition of scientific thinking. A "regulative" idea accounts for the coherence of a practice. Truth, for Kant, is a "regulative" idea that accounts for the coherence of scientific practice. Scientific research would be nonsense unless some such ideal as "the way the world is" were presupposed. The situation in textual interpretation is, I believe, similar. Even Derrida concedes that interpretive practice presupposes something like truth: "The reconstitution of a context can never be perfect and irreproachable even though it is a *regulative ideal* in the ethics of reading, of interpretation, or of discussion."[99] The attempt to discover the author's intended meaning is similarly an open-ended process that may require a variety of descriptive frameworks: "To say that a certain text has 'one' meaning need not imply that this meaning is a monad—a single, invariant, unitary statement which the reader need simply extract and paraphrase."[100] As Michael Fox observes, one reason for the conflict of interpretations is that authors often *intend* it: "Much of what is called indeterminacy is actually effective mimesis of a determinate but complex reality."[101] Hermeneutic realism does not mean that everything will necessarily be simple and clear. For reality, and this includes the reality of the communicative act, may be extremely complex.

Meaning, on my view, is a regulative idea that orients interpretation and accounts for its coherence as a practice. The idea of a meaning—a determinate and complex authorial act that is independent of the interpreter's activity—is needed in order to make sense of the interpreter's activity *and* of the conflict of interpretations. Neither meaning nor truth should simply be equated with our best interpretations. For meaning may outrun our best interpretations, and truth certainly does. Human knowledge remains on the level of the fallible and the provisional. Consensus alone is no guarantee that an interpretive community is correct. In the final analysis, the ideal of the single correct interpretation must remain an eschatological goal; in this life, we cannot always know that we know. Stated more positively, *meaning is a regulative idea, one that orients and governs interpretive practice.* While we cannot assume that the history of biblical interpretation is progressing, we can at least insist that the ideal of meaning should regulate the conflict of interpretations, provided that interpreters adhere to the mission of redeeming the text and recovering meaning: "The only way to go beyond the struggle, or at least to make it productive, is to constitute a community of interpreters sharing a primary concern for the book's verbal meaning."[102] What exactly is this regulative ideal of "verbal meaning"? Towards what kind of norm are our interpretations striving? I suggest that the regulative ideal of literary interpretation is none other than the literal sense.

HOW TO DESCRIBE COMMUNICATIVE ACTS: THE NORM OF LITERARY KNOWLEDGE

> Every discourse on the freedom of interpretation must start from a defense of the literal sense.[103]

> Whenever Christians have attempted to give to the scriptures a sense other than the plain sense intended by those who wrote them, Christianity has been in danger of running out into the sands of Gnosticism.[104]

In the previous section I asked, "Is it rational to believe in determinate meaning in the presence of interpretive disagreement?" We must not conclude from the diversity of present opinion, I argued, that there is no correct interpretation. Everyday life constantly requires us to "read" situations—laughter, gestures, the eighteenth green—correctly if we are to prosper in our sundry activities. If, for instance, a golfer thinks the ball will break left when actually it breaks right, he has not created meaning; he has misread the green (and failed to sink the putt). And just because some golfers misread a green does not mean that the green does not have a single correct interpretation.[105] Moreover, it is possible to have a rational discussion about correct interpretation by forming and testing hypotheses against the text. The present section turns from the problem of literary knowledge to the criteria used to arbitrate disagreement. *If the author's intention is embodied in the text, then the ultimate criterion for right or wrong interpretation will be the text itself, considered as a literary act.*

Body, Text, History: Literal Meaning and Christology

> As . . . the begotten Word of God hath two natures, the one human and visible, the other divine and invisible; so the written word of God hath a twofold sense: the one outward, that is historic or literal; the other, inward, that is mystic or spiritual.[106]

What do we mean by the "literal sense"? Can it serve as an interpretive norm? What does it have to do with Christology? These are by no means straightforward queries. As James Barr notes: "There is no field of human thought in which the concept of the 'literal' is as much used as in the understanding of the Bible."[107] In Chapter 3 I contrasted the literal and allegorical ways of reading the Bible. We saw there that the literalists emphasized historical reference, whereas allegorists were more concerned with symbolic and philosophical truths. The present task is to define the literal sense more carefully and to specify how it may serve as a norm for interpretation. For too long the literal sense has been identified with "the sense of the letter," which in turn has been identified with the objects to which individual words refer. I propose that we instead define literal meaning as "the sense of the literary act." On my view, literal interpretation is less a matter of identifying objects in the world than it is specifying communicative acts—their nature and their objects.

Perhaps nowhere else does the theological dimension of interpretation so come to the fore as in the debate about the literal meaning of Scripture. For as I argued earlier, meaning is as determinate or indeterminate as the conception of ultimate reality one presupposes. Either meaning (and God) is above the letter and conceptual determination, as the tradition of negative theology maintains, or else meaning (and God) can be known (not exhaustively, but adequately for the purposes of making wise unto salvation) in and through a determinate communicative act (e.g., the Word), as a positive theology of revelation maintains. In short, there is a correlation—at least in biblical interpretation, perhaps in general—between the doctrine of God and the literal sense. For if Jesus (the Word become flesh) "exegetes" the Father (John 1:18), then ultimate reality has determinate meaning.[108]

The Incarnation, according to Scripture and Christian tradition, is the literal embodiment of God. The Logos, that is, did not simply *appear* to take on a physical body but really did so.[109] Jesus is the "exact representation of [God's] being" (Heb. 1:3), "of the same substance" (*homoousios*) as the Father.[110] "God," one could say, has a literal sense—"Jesus Christ"—and so, in consequence, does the world. I wish to explore the following parallel: the body of Jesus is to his meaning ("Christ") as the letter is to the meaning of the text. In both cases, everything depends on the context of description. What is the sense of the letter? What is the sense of the body of Christ? A full-fledged Christology is, of course, beyond the scope of this chapter. What is of interest, however, is the way in which the body of Jesus progressively acquires determinate meaning in a series of expanding contexts of description. Such an approach allows me to resist reducing the significance of the body of Jesus to the physical level, just as I will later resist reducing the literal sense to its most primitive level, namely, the empirical objects named by individual words.

The body of Jesus is, first, a *physical* body—a body of flesh, blood, and bone.[111] But we can be more specific, more definite, than that. Jesus had a body of *Jewish* flesh, presumably with typically Jewish physical characteristics, and with a genetic lineage that could be traced back to royalty: "who was descended from David according to the flesh" (Rom. 1:3, RSV). This much biochemistry could, in principle, confirm. Yet the next qualification of Jesus' body is just as important and just as real. His body is considered "sinful flesh" (Rom. 8:3, RSV) and was made a sin offering (Heb. 10: 5–10). Finally, Jesus' body was raised "a spiritual body" (1 Cor. 15:44), though according to Paul, the spiritual body was just as real and historical as the physical body (15:3–11).

Jesus' flesh, therefore, was physical, Jewish, sinful, and spiritual. To limit what we can predicate truly of Jesus' body to the physical level only would be an unnecessary reductionism. Everything depends, of course, on the context in which Jesus' body is described. My point here is that the scientific and physical aspects do not exhaustively describe every important feature about Jesus' body. We learn other important truths about the body of Jesus from the narrative context that connects the story of Jesus to the story of Israel, to the story of the Levitical priesthood and the temple, and to the story of God's supreme plan for creation. The narrative contexts—not only the Gospels but the Old Testament as well—are necessary if we are to give a "thick description" of the body of Jesus. Only when we consider all four descriptive levels can we say *what God was doing in Christ*: revealing himself to the world (Jn. 1:18), reconciling the world to himself (Col. 1:20). Similarly, only when we consider the text as a literary act requiring a number of levels of description can we give an account of what the author is doing in the text; and *only when we give an account of what the author is doing can we give a sufficiently "thick description" of the literal sense.* How do we know when a description of what the author is doing is sufficiently thick? I believe that the text itself usually provides sufficient evidence. Indeed, one of my aims in this chapter is to reclaim a Reformation insight: "The infallible rule of interpretation of Scripture is Scripture itself."[112] This statement of what we might call the "hermeneutical sufficiency" of Scripture implies that the text itself contains those contexts necessary for determining the literal sense.

The Literal and the Historical: Modern Biblical Criticism

Those who invoke the literal sense as a possible norm for contemporary hermeneutics run the risk of being mistaken for "literalists." "She takes the Bible literally" is, as often as not, a criticism, if not an outright dismissal of one's reading. This hostility to "literality" is, however, far from new. James Barr's effort to define "literality" may help us see why this is so.

Barr suggests "physicality" as a first approximation for the meaning of "literality": "Physicality affords a simple, commonsense, one-to-one correspondence between the entities referred to and the words of the text."[113] Second, "literal" connotes "historical," though Barr acknowledges that this too is somewhat ambiguous. "Historical" interpretation, as Barr points out, may mean different things to the modern biblical scholar: focusing on what the writers intended at the time of writing or editing, focusing on the earliest known form of the text, or using the text to determine what really happened.[114] Historical interpretation refers, in the context of the Reformation, to respecting the sense that words would have had for their authors. Calvin, for example, stresses the importance of the interpreter's task "to unfold the mind of the writer . . . the more he leads away from the author's meaning so the more he leaves his own purpose and is certain to wander from his goal."[115]

Calvin's exposition of 2 Corinthians 3:6 ("for the letter kills, but the Spirit gives life") is also germane to his understanding of the literal sense. He takes issue with Origen's influential interpretation of this passage. Origen argued that by "letter" we should understand the grammatical and plain sense of Scripture, and not, as Calvin thinks, the old covenant:

> This passage has been distorted and wrongly interpreted first by Origen and then by others, and they have given rise to the most disastrous error that Scripture is not only useless but actually harmful unless it is allegorized. This error has been the source of many evils. . . . The terms 'letter' and 'Spirit' have nothing to do with methods of expounding Scripture but with its force and fruit.[116]

As this quote clearly shows, what Calvin meant by literal interpretation should by no means be confused with a wooden "literalism." The literal sense of the word "letter" in 2 Corinthians 3:6 depends, in Calvin's view, on the broader narrative, indeed canonical, context. Calvin, acquainted as he was with the scholarship of Renaissance humanism, was well-versed in rhetoric and had no difficulty in recognizing figures of speech or literary connections. Indeed, we might say that for Calvin, *the literal sense was the literary sense.*[117] I will return to this suggestion below.

Who today practices literal interpretation: fundamentalists or modern biblical critics? Before we can answer that, we must examine what has become of the literal sense in the modern era. Hans Frei suggests that the meaning of "literal" undergoes an important shift during the Age of Enlightenment, at which time "literal" came to be contrasted not with "allegorical" but with "apparent." The literal meaning, that is, has become in modernity the *critical* meaning, namely, the historical reality behind the textual appearance.

The biblical critic seeks the historical reality behind the textual appearances. The goal posts of historical reality, however, have moved. In the modern world, reality tends to be defined by the natural sciences (and by naturalism as a worldview). Frei charges biblical critics with prying the meaning of the text apart from its literary form in order to relocate it in the facts *behind* the text, or alternately, in some universal mythological truth *above* the text: "In either case, history or else allegory or myth, the *meaning* of the stories was finally something different from the stories or depictions themselves."[118] The critic, then, uses the literal sense as a means to some other end. Historical interpretation has become a critical method for trying to get *behind* the letter in order to reconstruct its original historical context or the process of its composition. Biblical critics are not the rightful heirs of literal interpretation.

Interestingly, Christology continues to be the touchstone of the literal sense of Scripture, and this in two ways. With regard to the Old Testament, the critical question is whether or not the Hebrew Scriptures refer to Christ. According to the historical critics, for whom the original meaning is paramount, they could not have done so (assuming, as many anti-supernaturalist critics did, that the texts are purely human documents). To read historically in this sense, therefore, is to deny that the Old Testament is the church's book. Second, with regard to the New Testament, if God did not actually become man, then what are we to make of the Gospel narratives? Intriguingly, Barr suggests that modern biblical critics were not really committed to the literal sense, for they saw that the Bible, if taken literally, appears untrue.

The standard critical reflex, much like that of their premodern forebears, is to conclude that the Bible's basic truth lies on another level than that of the literal sense. Rudolf Bultmann, for instance, interprets the resurrection of Jesus not as an event in history but as a symbolic expression of what happens to present readers when they put their faith in the crucified Jesus. Perhaps Barr is right to conclude that modern biblical scholarship has certain affinities with allegory.[119] Biblical critics have two options vis-à-vis the sense of the letter: to identify textual meaning with historical reference and conclude that the Bible is sometimes untrue, or to locate textual meaning on some other level than the literal, in which case the Bible would have symbolic or mythic but not historical truth. This dilemma, however, begs the question of the literal sense. Must we assume, with the biblical critics, that the literal sense is the historical sense, and that the historical sense is one that can be empirically verified? The root confusion, I believe, stems from the modern tendency to identify the literal with the empirical. Such a "positivism of the literal," I contend, mistakenly reduces historical reality to what can be established within the limits of historical reason alone.[120]

Who's Afraid of the Literal Sense? Contemporary Approaches

Given its checkered history, can the literal sense still be the norm that governs biblical interpretation today? I will consider three varieties of literal interpretation before presenting my own view.

Literal Sense As Historical Reference. The first option is one shared, strangely enough, by fundamentalists and modern biblical critics alike, though with varying results. I refer to the view that the literal meaning of the biblical text should be identified with what the words employed commonly designate. This view tends to equate meaning with historical reference—with the *empirical* sense of the letter. "Taking the Bible literally" here means identifying the events and persons to which it refers. Fundamentalists believe that the biblical narratives accurately (i.e., empirically, physically, historically) describe what actually happened, even when this includes understanding creation in terms of six twenty-four hour days. The biblical critic is similarly concerned with history, but with a particular interest in what the authors thought, in how the text came to be the way it is, or in what actually happened. Unlike the fundamentalist, however, the biblical critic may conclude that what it means, if taken literally, is false. That is to say, what the Bible literally affirms is not necessarily "what actually happened."

Barr protests that neither fundamentalists nor critics practice literal interpretation consistently; both escape to another level of meaning—in the one case, when inerrancy is threatened, or in the other, when liberal values are threatened. Others object that this type of liberal approach relies on a non-spiritual, individualistic manner of reading, as if the interpreter could be an autonomous knower. Bernard Ramm, for instance, charges fundamentalism with espousing an "abbreviated" Protestant principle to the extent that they believe they can interpret the Word without benefit of the Spirit.[121] Perhaps the most serious problem with identifying the literal sense with historical reference, however, is its inadequate view of the way that language and literature actually work. Reference to historical or empirical reality is only one of the things language does. Indeed, it is precisely this consistent identification of meaning with reference that ultimately prompts the charge of *literalism*. In this respect, empirically minded fundamentalists share something in common with demythologizers such as Origen and Bultmann, namely, an inability to appreciate the *literary* dimension of the text. According to Wiles, "Origen was totally lacking in poetic sensitivity The literal sense of scripture is for him the literally literal meaning of the words."[122] Such literal-mind-edness in text interpretation approximates a functional illiteracy.

Fundamentalists and liberal critics find themselves, surprisingly, in the same pro-crustean bed: modernity. Both are guilty of what Rowan Williams terms the "disas-trous shrinkage" of the literal sense.[123] Neither approach, that is, gets beyond the thinnest of descriptions of the literal sense. Literal interpretation, however, is more than a univocally descriptive and exact presentation of historical factuality. Further, fundamentalist and modern critics share the belief that reason can be used both to interpret Scripture (e.g., identify its historical referents) *and* to confirm or falsify its meaning. A positivist view that sees truth as that which can be empirically designated and verified thus controls the content of "literal" meaning.[124] In sum: a modernist epistemology not only eclipses but fatally distorts the literal sense, condemning inter-pretation to offering only thin, literalistic descriptions of empirical referents.

Literal Sense As Storied Reference. Frei sees a clear connection between the Christian community's decision to assign primacy to the literal sense on the one hand, and their recognition that God was in Christ on the other. The plain or consensus read-ing in the Christian community recognizes the unsubstitutable identity and particular-ity of Jesus Christ. It is the literal reading of the Gospels that ensures they are stories about Jesus rather than something else: "I am persuaded that . . . theological reading is the reading of the *text*, and not the reading of a source, which is how historians read it."[125] The tie between hermeneutics and Christology could not be stronger. Jesus is the one who is described by the narrative when the latter is interpreted literally.

Frei brilliantly demonstrates that the meaning and truth of the Gospels is eclipsed whenever one seeks to interpret them in terms of an independent (e.g., extra-textual) description of their subject matter. This happens in Gnosticism and demythologiz-ing alike when biblical narratives are interpreted "without ascribing primacy or cen-trality to those narratives in deciding about truth."[126] It happens in any interpretation in which the Gospel is not a story about Jesus, but a story about something else: exis-tential possibilities, social liberation, the rights of women, etc. In short, the literal sense of the Gospels is eclipsed whenever one interprets the texts "through an inde-pendent description of their subject matter."[127] One cannot discern the matter of the text without going through its form. Bruce Marshall makes the connection between literal meaning and Christology explicit: "If the moderns made a mistake in biblical interpretation with regard to the narratives, it was ultimately because they made a christological mistake: they failed to see the narratively identified Jesus as epistemi-cally primary and in that sense as logically basic to and decisive for all of our talk about God and ourselves."[128] And Frei adds: "It was largely by reason of this central-ity of the story of Jesus that the Christian interpretive tradition in the West gradually assigned clear primacy to the literal sense in the reading of Scripture."[129] Instead of interpreting the text with our categories and conceptual schemes, Frei proposes that we let the text itself interpret everything else, including its readers. To interpret the Bible literally means letting the biblical text "swallow up the world" rather than the world the text.[130]

Frei's own view is that the Gospel narratives, when interpreted literally, identify Jesus in his relation to God, as the risen Christ. How does this literal identification relate to the historical Jesus (e.g., to the literal Jesus of biblical criticism)? Frei is hard pressed to answer, for the relation of Jesus to God is not part of the domain of "historical facts." Frei affirms the Gospels as "literally" true of Jesus, but he is wary of explaining "literally true" in terms of some extra-textual framework, such as critically reconstructed history. For Frei, the literal sense of the Bible, like its subject matter, is something *sui generis*. While insisting on a determinate literal sense of the Gospels, Frei is content to leave their reference somewhat indeterminate. The point is that there is no other way to describe the referent apart from the text. The Gospels are testimonies, not sources or resources for historical reconstruction. In terms that I will explain more fully below, we may say that *we have the reality of Jesus only under a narrative description*.[131]

Literal Sense As Canonical Sense. Brevard Childs argues that historical criticism's inability to read the Bible as Scripture follows from a faulty view of the literal sense: "For the Reformers, the literal sense was a *literary* sense; but for critical scholars it became 'literalistic.'"[132] According to Childs, the literal sense of the Bible is a function neither of its historical nor of its storied context, but rather of its *canonical* context.[133] He wishes to recover the original unity of the literal and historical sense, characteristic of the Reformers' interpretation, prior to the "ugly ditch" between the "original" and "canonical" senses that bedevils modern criticism. The key for Childs, as for Frei, is that the text itself, and only the text, renders its referent. What the texts are about is not something behind the text or over the text, but rather something in the text. Whereas the critical-literal sense looks behind the text, the canonical-literal sense of the Old Testament looks through the text and points to Christ. Childs believes that the literal sense will have religious value only in the context of the canon. Specifically, Childs wishes to recover the Reformers' sense that, in reading Scripture, they had to do with the Word of God. Taking the Bible literally for Childs means reading it in the context of the Christian canon.[134]

Literal Meaning: A Proposal

Each of the three preceding approaches—the historical, the narrative, the canonical—focuses on a valid, though partial, dimension of the literal sense. The task now is to weave these three dimensions of "literality" together by means of the concept of communicative action.

The Logos or the Letter? Let me begin with a reminder, a caveat, and a correction. I have suggested that the author's intention, that determinate textual reality to which all interpretation is accountable, is a "regulative idea." I also noted the ways in which various literary critics (viz., Steiner, Fish, Derrida) considered this to be a quasi-theological claim, having to do with transcendence, proper meaning, and logocentrism. Finally, we have just observed the striking correlation between one's understanding of the literal sense and one's Christology.

Now, for the caveat. There are at least two strategies for avoiding the authority of the literal sense. One denies its reality altogether. For the hermeneutic non-realist, the literal sense is merely the product of our literary theories.[135] Whatever *logos* inhabits the letter has been breathed into it by the interpreter. Such interpretive atheism characterizes Fish's neo-pragmatism, for whom meaning is a product of our practices. *Fish is to literary theory what Feuerbach is to Christology; for these masters of suspicion, the transcendent (Christ for Feuerbach, meaning for Fish) is always only a human projection.* There may be norms for ruling out meanings (e.g., we can say "this is a false reading"), but their source, as Fish reminds us, is "not the text but the presently recognized interpretive strategies for producing the text."[136] The false reading, in other words, is not the one that reads against the grain of the letter but the one that reads against the grain of the present consensus.

There is a second, more theological, way of forestalling the *logos* from uniting with the letter. This is the way not of atheism, but of negative theology, a tradition that views God as beyond all philosophical and linguistic determinations. How can the Bible refer literally to God if language is finite and God is infinite?[137] Negative theology, then, affirms (to use Tillich's phrase) a "God beyond God": a God, that is, beyond the reach of literal language and metaphysical concepts.[138] We have already observed the similarity between Derrida's grammatology and the rabbinic fascination with the sacred letter of the Torah. From this perspective, the sacredness of the letter entails that the text can neither be translated nor "de-ciphered": "Yet where the rabbis look to the inexhaustible fullness of God's word to sponsor their exegeses, Derrida appeals to a mode of negativity, *la différance,* which ceaselessly generates meaning."[139] Derrida attends only to the signifiers, not the signified. In negative theology, the sacred letter does not disclose, but endlessly postpones, the *logos.* Thus, faced with the prospect of the literal sense as one's interpretive norm, one can either deny its existence (Fish) or its knowability (Derrida).

Lastly, the correction: "The Word became flesh and made his dwelling among us" (John 1:14). The doctrine of the Incarnation corrects both atheism and negative theology; the cloud of unknowing is dispersed on Christmas morning. The transcendental signified has become a sign; God's Word has taken human form.[140] The "body" is therefore no longer an obstacle to but the condition of revelation. As the Logos indwelt the flesh of Jesus, so meaning indwells the body of the text. "In positive theology the Father is revealed by the Son in and through the Spirit, thereby establishing a God that can be described, albeit imperfectly, in positive and negative predicates."[141] Truth lies, both hidden and revealed, under the veil of Jesus' humanity. Similarly, under the veil of letters, there is meaning.[142] The literal sense should not, of course, be simply equated with the physical body of the Word or with the dictionary definition of the words. To employ a familiar concept once again: the literal meaning *supervenes* on the letter but cannot be reduced to it.[143]

Literal Versus Literalistic. Instead of pitting the three definitions of the literal sense we considered above against one another, I will view them as aspects of communicative action. We may begin with the physical level of the letter, its "materiality." Letters and words are the "raw materials" of literary acts. "Literal" must not, however, be reduced to *langue* (e.g., the place of a word in a language system), for literal meaning is not a matter of words taken in isolation but of communicative acts taken in their communicative context. It is important to distinguish the locutionary act (the act of using words to say something intelligible) from the illocutionary act (the act performed in saying the words). The literal sense, I maintain, is not a matter of locutions alone; every utterance has an illocutionary force as well (e.g., assertive, directive, expressive, etc.). To treat the literal sense as a matter of locutions or dictionary definitions is to be guilty of offering only the thinnest of descriptions.

It is all too easy to equate the literal meaning of a word with its dictionary definition. The problem with such a move is twofold. First, a dictionary is simply a compendium of how people ordinarily use words; definitions are not, therefore, unchanging and absolute, but only relatively determinate. Second, and more important, the basic unit of meaning is the speech act, not the individual words. The literal meaning of Jesus' statement "I am the door" is a function of his speech act (a metaphorical assertion), not of the words taken individually (and thus out of context). Where, then, is the literal meaning: in *langue* or *parole*? Before they are used in particular communicative acts, words have only a potential (e.g., a limited number of possibilities) for meaning. Hence, it is only at the level of the sentence act that we can speak of an actual literal sense. Literal meaning is always a joint product: of semantics *and* pragmatics, of *langue and parole*, of convention *and* intention.

We must avoid the twin heresies that over- and underestimate the letter: that the literal sense has *nothing* to do with the letter, or that the literal sense has *only* to do with the letter. The letter is the indispensable means for performing the communicative act and for signaling the intention, but it is only a necessary, not a sufficient condition for meaning. Interpretation is "literalistic" only if one overlooks this dual parentage and reduces the literal to the sense of the letter (i.e., to *langue*).[144] By no means do I wish to advocate literalistic reading, the hermeneutic equivalent of the cult of the body. Rather, I am arguing that literalistic reading is less than fully "literal"—that it is insufficiently and only "thinly" literal—insofar as it ignores the role of authorial intentions and communicative acts. To ignore the role of illocutions is to succumb to "letterism," or to what could also be called "locutionism."[145] Those, on the other hand, who seek the author's enacted intention in the text attend to the communicative act, to what we might call the "spirit of the letter."

What is "letterism"? It is a wooden, thin interpretation that fails to go beyond the standard meanings of words and expressions (the locutions) or to discern the manner in which an author attends to these meanings (the illocutions). Hence literalism short-circuits the literal sense insofar as it fails to appreciate the author's intention to give his or her utterance a certain kind of force. It is most important to distinguish literalistic from literal interpretation. The former generates an unlettered, ultimately *illiterate* reading—one that is incapable of recognizing less obvious uses of language such as metaphor, satire, and so forth. By contrast, the latter attends to what authors are doing in tending to their words in a certain way. "Literalistic" interpretation is like a word-for-word translation that yields verbally exact or "formally equivalent" versions but that also runs the risk of overlooking the main (illocutionary) point. Literal interpretation, on the other hand, is more like a translation that strives for dynamic equivalence and yields the literary sense. The distinction, then, is between "empirically minded" interpreters, who, in their zeal for factual correspondence, take an unimaginative, almost positivist, view of things, and "literate-minded" readers, who are sensitive to context and familiar with how literary texts work. Interpreters err either when they allegorize discourse that is intended to be taken literally or when they "literalize" discourse that is intended to be taken figuratively.

Consider, for example, the literal meaning of "the eyes of the LORD are on the righteous" (Ps. 34:15). According to Donald Davidson, the literal sense specifies the truth conditions to which the speaker, if serious, is committed. We cannot establish these conditions, however, without establishing the context of the discourse and, I would add, the nature of the communicative act. The psalmist is here saying something about divine knowledge, about God's "oversight" of his people. The truth condition of the psalmist's statement has nothing to do with divine ocular body parts but with divine omniscience. Note that the author does not intend two meanings, one literal and one metaphorical, but only one. The author intends that the reader recognize his expression as a metaphor. He thus performs the communicative act of metaphorical assertion. The word "eye," as an element in *langue*, has a normal, everyday designation. But *langue* does not define the literal sense of a term; only actual usage can do that. "Metaphorical meaning is always a speaker's utterance meaning."[146]

Literal interpretation seeks understanding by determining the nature and content of the literary act. Literalistic interpretation, on the other hand, disregards the illocutionary intent and focuses rather on the conventional meanings of isolated words. Hence my proposal: *the literal sense is the sense of a literary act.* On my view, the body of the text—the material with which a communicative agent works—is a necessary but, in itself, insufficient condition for a literary act. The body of the text mediates the spirit, but the spirit cannot be reduced to the body. Rather, the spirit (read: illocutionary intent) supervenes on the body (the locutionary event). Literal, that is to say, *literate,* interpretation grasps the communicative context and is thus able to identify the communicative act. We grasp the literal meaning of an utterance when we discern its propositional matter and its illocutionary force—that is to say, when we recognize what it is: a command, assertion, joke, irony, parable, etc.[147]

Taking the Bible Literally. Taking the Bible literally means reading for its literary sense, the sense of its communicative act. This entails, first, doing justice to the propositional, poetic, and purposive aspects of each text as a communicative act and, second, relating these to the Bible considered as a unified divine communicative act: the Word of God.[148]

(1) Propositional reference. Literal meaning, I have argued, should not be equated with historical reference. Nevertheless, reference is an aspect of communicative action and thus of literal sense. For every communicative act has an object, namely, the propositional content, and the propositional content specifies the referent—the object of the communicative act, what the act is about. Of course, not all referents need be historical, nor are all historical referents susceptible to empirical verification. It is a major part of my argument that we have some referents only "under a description."[149]

(2) Poetic form. "Poetic" here refers not to poetry but rather to the fact that a text is a composition, a thing "made" or "done" (Gk. *poiēsis*), a *formed* matter. Later in this chapter I will relate the literary form to the kind of literary act an author performs. Here I want only to suggest that, if the literal sense is the literary sense, we must attend to the literary form of the literary act. Literal sense is as much a matter of poetic form as it is reference; indeed, our main access to what a text is about is the text itself, the form in which the matter is described. For Frei, the literal meaning of narrative

is the story itself, and the literal reference is the *story's* world, not the historian's. To locate the meaning or reference of the Gospels in some other world (viz., the historical reconstruction of the biblical critic, or the demythologized reconstruction of the existentialist) is to depart from a literal reading. We can generalize Frei's point and say that the reality of which the Bible speaks is mediated to us through a variety of literary forms. This is an epistemological point that is part and parcel of a critically realist hermeneutics: to affirm that the reality of Jesus Christ is mediated to us only through the biblical texts is not at all equivalent "to the ontological claim that there is nothing outside the text."[150] We have the referent of a text, that is, only under its textual description.

(3) Pedagogical nature and function. This third aspect of the literal sense, unlike the two previous categories, is specific to the Bible. What I have in mind is the Bible's character as "Scripture" and "canon"—its nature as a guidebook for the believing community. Iain Provan maintains that we cannot do justice to the Old Testament texts, either as academic critics or as believers, unless we recognize that each text was intended by its authors to be read as Scripture along with other Scriptures: "To ignore the Scriptural context in which the book now sits is to ignore something which is fundamentally important about its nature."[151] It also means that "writing Scripture" is an aspect of the overall literary act. If the literal sense is the sense of the literary act, then the canonical context may well provide the most embracing descriptive framework in which to specify its nature and content as "Scripture." The canonical intent is both "pedagogical" and "eschatological," directed towards guiding the people of God in the present and future alike.[152]

(4) Taking the Bible literally means, finally, taking it as testimony to Jesus Christ. The canon is a corporate communicative act of witness to something real and historical: the revelatory and redemptive acts of God in the history of Israel and, above all, in the history of Jesus Christ. Is the Old Testament literally testimony to Christ? Are the Gospels literally true? I argued in the last chapter that the so-called "fuller sense" of some biblical passages can be attributed to divine authorship. Building on that insight, I now want to suggest that *this "fuller sense" is in fact the literal sense, taken at the level of its thickest description.*

This notion of a "fuller literal sense" has received a sort of secular confirmation in the work of Mikhail Bakhtin. Bakhtin offers an interesting account of how a work can grow in meaning. According to Bakhtin, literary forms carry meaning potential that writers may sense but never fully command. A work's potential is its capacity to function in future circumstances, a capacity that for Childs is precisely the canonical function. The sense that a literary act has implicit potential guides the author's work, as does one's desire explicitly to express what one means. To focus solely on what the author (or original reader) explicitly realizes is for Bakhtin to "enclose" the work "within the epoch."[153] Yet it is precisely the function of canon to serve as a guide for future generations and to provide the descriptive framework within which to understand new events (e.g., the event of Jesus Christ). The latent potential of a text is really there, buried in the cumulative wisdom carried by a literary form.[154] What this means is that the literal sense—the sense of the literary act—may, at times, be indeterminate or open-ended. However—and this is crucial—the indeterminacy we are considering is intended; moreover, it is a definite feature of the meaning of the text.[155] Old Testament prophecy and apocalyptic, for example, were intended as descriptions of what the original authors only dimly understood. To give a thick description of the literal sense, say of Isaiah 53, therefore requires an expansive account of the literary act. What often appears to be figural or typological interpretation may actually be an attempt to describe a determinate, though complex, literary act: testifying to the history of salvation.

If there is a *sensus plenior*, then, it is on the level of God's gathering together the various partial and progressive communicative acts and purposes of the human authors into one "great canonical Design."[156] Noll's definition of "canonical intentionality" is suggestive: "that cooperative inspiring work of the Holy Spirit and traditioning work of the community of faith which produces a final text of Scripture normative for all future generations of believers."[157] The Old Testament Scriptures testify to God's gracious activity. Putting them together with the New Testament testimony does not "spiritualize" but "specifies" their reference. Jesus Christ—the fullest embodiment of God's gracious activity in Israel and in the world—is the literal referent of biblical testimony.[158]

Through a Class Darkly? Determining the Literal Sense

And if the bugle gives an indistinct sound, who will get ready for battle? (1 Cor. 14:8 RSV)

Does the Bible have something definite or determinate to say—about history, about God, about the human condition—or does it make an "indistinct sound"? What is at stake in the debate over the reality and knowability of literal meaning is ultimately biblical authority and, indeed, the ability of any text to address and transform us. In this respect, the parallels between our time and that of the Reformation are particularly striking.[159] On the one hand, modern "enthusiasts" claim that meaning is new each day, a result of the encounter of text and reader, an encounter governed as much by the spirit of the age as by the Holy Spirit. Modern "papists," on the other hand, claim that the text can be interpreted correctly only in the church. Fish represents a kind of secular catholicism that ascribes interpretive authority not to one privileged reading community (e.g., the Roman), but to interpretive communities in general.[160] The Reformers, on the other hand, argued that reason, tradition, and experience do not guarantee understanding; yet, at the same time, they claimed that the Bible's meaning was both "perspicuous" (clear) and "simple" (single).[161] But for whom—the scholar? the poor? the Spirit-led believing community? Who, if anyone, is qualified to determine the literal meaning of the text?

As the sixteenth-century Reformers redeemed the text and thus the possibility of literary knowledge, so we have to redeem the text in our time. Redeeming the text means rescuing it from obscurity and from the vagaries of interpretation (Kierkegaard's 30,000 different interpretations), and that means recovering the knowability of the literal sense. The normativeness of the literal sense is once again under threat, and this in two ways: (1) by the assumption that the text is "dark" and obscure, an endless labyrinth with no issue; (2) by the assumption that the process of interpretation sets up obstacles—schemes, screens, interests, ideologies—that keep textual meaning as it is in itself forever out of understanding's reach.

Is there anything "there" in the text, prior to the process of interpretation, to which we should attend and for which we are accountable? If meaning resides in the encounter of text and reader, it necessarily follows that meaning does not reside in the text itself and, consequently, that meaning will change and develop as it encounters new readers and enters new contexts. In order to tackle this question I will first discuss what the clarity or perspicuity of Scripture can mean in our postmodern era. I will then move from perspicuity to community and offer a critique of Fish's thesis that it is the authority of the interpretive community, not the text, that regulates the process of interpretation. Is it indeed the case, as Fish might say, that we only see the text, if at all, through a class darkly?

The Clarity of Scripture: Philology and Psychology

To begin with, it is important to note what the clarity of Scripture does not mean. It does not mean, first of all, that interpretation is unnecessary—that biblical meaning will be delivered up by some mystical process of hermeneutical osmosis. Nor does it mean that an autonomous individual can, by employing critical techniques alone, wrest the meaning from the text. Rather, clarity means that the Bible is sufficiently unambiguous in the main for any well-intentioned person with Christian faith to interpret each part with relative adequacy. In the context of the Reformation, the perspicuity of Scripture was the chief weapon for combating the authority of the dominant interpretive community: Rome.

Thiselton helpfully distinguishes three different uses of the Reformers' concept of perspicuity. In relation to the claim that the meaning of the Bible is in principle unstable and indeterminate, the perspicuity of Scripture acts as a hermeneutical principle.[162] In relation to the claim that the Bible can only by interpreted by an authoritative interpretive community (viz., the magisterium of the church), perspicuity functions as a critical principle.[163] Finally, in relation to the claim that the determinate meaning of Scripture cannot be sufficiently known to inform and challenge Christian practice, perspicuity acts as an epistemological principle.

Luther speaks of "external" clarity, which means that any well-intentioned interpreter who follows the rules of language (and, I would add, literature) can discover the author's intended message.[164] Ramm calls this the "philological" principle of Protestantism. Philology is not just the study of words, but the "total program in understanding a piece of literature."[165] Philology—the love of learning and literature, the love of words in context, the love of speech acts!—serves as a control on Protestant biblical interpretation.[166] For the philologist, words are instruments of light and truth; for the grammatologist, we may recall, words darken and deceive. Luther's appeal to external clarity should not be confused, however, with a naive objectivism; the interpreter's mind is never a mere passive observer, as if neutrality were the guarantee of knowledge. On the contrary, philology speaks of the love of words, and the clarity of Scripture always assumes a well-intentioned interpreter—presumably one who belongs to the community of faith.[167]

The external clarity of Scripture means that, in principle—that is, if our cognitive and interpretive capacities are functioning properly—the literal meaning of the basic plot or message of Scripture can be understood.[168] Or, to put it in terms of the present work, the external clarity of Scripture means that the interpreter can correctly grasp the object of literary knowledge, namely, the author's locutionary and illocutionary acts.

Does it follow from the external clarity of Scripture that intelligent individuals can interpret it for themselves? Need one add faith to reason, or belong to a community of faith, to make sense of the Bible? While Luther located ultimate authority in the canon rather than church councils, "he did not seek to substitute individual opinion for tradition in a way akin to the mood of post-Enlightenment rationalism."[169] The reason for this is that the individual sees through a glass darkly (1 Cor. 13:12). The real problem is not with the text but with the heart and mind of the interpreter. Luther, therefore, speaks of the need for "internal" clarity, a result of the Spirit's illumination of the interpreter, which enables readers to see the Bible for what it is, namely, testimony to Christ. Given the blinding effects of sin, both Luther and Calvin believed that the things of God could be understood only by those illumined by the Spirit of God, that is, by those who have the right presuppositions.[170] Luther's concept of "internal clarity"—the requirement that an interpreter be properly "attuned"— is as insightful a critique of the knowing subject as anything the postmoderns have since come up with. The knowing subject of the Enlightenment has properly been exposed as a fiction, and with it, the notion that external clarity is sufficient for understanding. No one comes to the text with "pure reason"; understanding is a matter of having the right prejudices, or rather, of having what I refer to in the next chapter as the interpretive virtues. *It is highly misleading to charge the text with obscurity when in fact the unclarity resides in the psychology of the human knower.*

Calvin formulated the doctrine of the "inner witness" of the Spirit to counter three alternative explanations—church tradition, new revelations from the Holy Spirit, and rational (foundationalist) evidences—as to how one gains certainty that the Scriptures are the Word of God. Can we relate Calvin's notion of internal witness to Luther's concept of internal clarity? It is most important not to mistake the Reformers' emphasis. The internal clarity and inner witness have an epistemological role, to be sure, but it is not that of providing independent and immediate evidences for, or subjective certainty of, the correct meaning. On the contrary, internal clarity has to do with the cognitive faculties of the interpreter working properly in the right environment. Internal clarity is not a way of short-circuiting interpretive rationality, therefore, but of fulfilling its requirements.

"No prophetic writing is a matter for private interpretation . . ." (2 Peter 1:20 RSV). This text does not forbid individuals from interpreting the Bible, says Calvin, but rather states that "it is not godly for them to come out with something out of their own heads. Even if all men in the world were to agree and be of one mind, the outcome would still be private, of their own."[171] In Luther's opinion, interpreters of Scripture often shut out its clear message, exchanging the truth for a lie. The problem with the Enlightenment ideals of individual autonomy and objective knowledge is that actual knowers are corrupt. Subjective readings are to be tested, says Luther, "in the presence of the Church at the bar of Scripture."[172]

Is the interpreter better off in a community? That depends. The Reformers are hermeneutic realists; for Luther and Calvin, consensus alone does not guarantee the correctness of interpretation. Indeed, there is a real danger of thinking too highly of one's own interpretive tradition. Thus, while they did not oppose tradition as such, they did resist any self-serving appeal to tradition as authoritative.[173] To elevate an interpretive tradition over Scripture is ultimately to follow Fish and to admit that the community creates the text. This is to make tradition supplementary to Scripture rather than a commentary on it.

The idea that the Bible is clear does not obviate the need for interpretation but, on the contrary, makes the work of interpretation even more important. The clarity of Scripture means that understanding is possible, not that it is easy.[174] Redeeming the text does not mean reconciling all interpretive conflicts. *The clarity of Scripture is neither an absolute value nor an abstract property, but a specific function relative to its particular aim: to witness to Christ.* The clarity of Scripture, in other words, does not mean that we will know everything there is to know about the text, but that we will know *enough* to be able, and responsible, to respond to its subject matter. The clarity of Scripture is not a matter of its *obviousness* so much as its *efficacy*; the Bible is clear enough to render its communicative action effective.

So much for the objective aspect of literary knowledge. The external clarity of Scripture is a necessary but not a sufficient condition for literary knowledge, for as we have seen, there is a subjective component as well: the psychology of the interpreter, the readiness of the reader to engage with the subject matter. We will see in the following chapter that there is an ethical and a relational component to literary knowledge as well. To anticipate: *the theological virtues are also epistemological virtues, in which case we should speak of faith, hope, and love seeking textual understanding.* And it may well be that the greatest of these is love.

Interpretive Scheming: The Relativity of Descriptive Frameworks

Fish takes an important step towards "de-regulating" the process of interpretation by refusing to accept the notion of a literal meaning that is independent of the reader's activity. Such de-regulation is now part and parcel of postmodern pluralism; the Bible is an "open text" that calls for multiple interpretations rather than a "closed book" that licenses only a single, restricted interpretive paradigm (e.g., the historical-critical).[175] Kant previously took the crucial epistemological step by claiming that we cannot know reality as it is in itself, only reality as processed by a conceptual scheme. Admittedly, for Kant, all rational thinkers interpret nature with the same categories (the Newtonian). By denying Kant's premise that all rational thinkers interpret experience with the same conceptual scheme, however, Fish and other postmodern thinkers have made relativism philosophically respectable.[176] Today, there are as many interpretive schemes as there are interpretive communities, and none has the right to say that its way of approaching the world, or the text, is more rational than any other.

As we have noted, postmodern thinkers refuse to equate any one perspective, even that of reason, with a God's-eye point of view.[177] Perhaps God does employ a conceptual scheme for interpreting reality, but if so, humans do not have access to it. This is forcefully brought out in Barry Unsworth's novel, *Morality Play*, in which a troupe of medieval players decide to stage a rendition of a real event—a local murder, it so happens—rather than a biblical story, as was their practice. A monk who has temporarily joined the troupe is alarmed, because the transcendent meaning of the event has not been revealed to them, as has the meaning of Adam's sin or Christ's birth and death (through Scripture). The monk protests: "Players are like other men, they must use God's meanings, they cannot make meanings of their own, that is heresy, it is the source of all our woes, it is the reason our first parents were cast out."[178] One of the players counters this (theo)logic: "Men can give meanings to things. . . . That is no sin, because our meanings are only for the time, they can be changed." In the absence of absolute knowledge, that is, we are all interpreter-players, obliged to give meanings that, at best, will be interesting and useful relative to particular situations and communities. But can such "plays" be dignified, even for a time, with the epithet "knowledge"?

Literal meaning itself, Fish claims, is always a product of some interpretive practice, some way of reading. Does not the plurality of descriptive frameworks make a mockery of the very notion of literary knowledge? If meaning and truth are relative to a scheme, then are there as many texts and as many "realities" as there are schemes? When interpreters differ, are they disagreeing about the same text or creating different texts? It follows from Fish's relativism that, if he and Hirsch were to differ in their interpretations of Milton's *Paradise Lost*, he might say (if he were being consistent) they were reading different texts. Were they ever to co-teach a course on Milton, it would doubtless be appropriate to inquire, "Are there *two* texts in this class?"

Is the history of interpretation a matter of the growth or progress of literary knowledge or does it simply reflect a change in cultural fashions? How does Fish account for the change in scholarly consensus, for instance, concerning *Paradise Lost*? Is it because experts discovered something "there" in the text that had been previously overlooked, some new "fact"? Not at all; in Fish's opinion the new consensus rather reflects a change in scholarly values, practices, and ideologies. The same is true of knowledge in general: "There is no discipline, however 'scientific' its credentials, which does not take rise within a given context of agreed-upon values and beliefs, or against some backdrop of enabling assumptions which provide its only possible ground of appeal."[179] Whereas Bultmann famously declared that the Gospels tell us more about the disciples (e.g., the authors) than they do about Jesus, Fish might say that our interpretations tell us more about ourselves than they do about either Jesus or the Evangelists.

"To see oneself in the text"—to the extent that this means projecting oneself onto the text, it hardly seems to qualify as an instance of literary knowledge. Yet even scientific terms—the words we employ to say what we see—have meaning only relative to particular theoretical frameworks. For example, Kepler and Tycho Brahe, two sixteenth-century astronomers, observed the same object in the eastern sky at dawn but did not *see* the same thing.[180] There was a similarity in their optical inputs, but these were filtered through different conceptual schemes: "People, not their eyes, see."[181] What we see—in Scripture, in the sky—is a function of the conceptual scheme we inhabit. Fish and Hirsch, like Kepler and Brahe, are members of different interpretive communities. If my Milton is different from your Milton, then it follows that our respective interpretations are incommensurable (incomparable); because they cannot be compared, they cannot come into conflict. Of course, the price to be

paid for such hermeneutic pacifism is the loss of genuine dialogue. Is knowledge relative to conceptual frameworks and interpretive schemes? This impasse returns us
to our initial query: Do we create the Milton we read or the sun we see?

The philosopher Donald Davidson argues against the very idea of a "conceptual
scheme."[182] Reality cannot be relative to a scheme because, in the first place, there is
only one reality.[183] It makes sense to say that you and I experience *the same reality differently*, but not that we experience *different realities*. Second, how can we even know
that someone has a different conceptual scheme? To say that a person's beliefs are so
different from ours that they cannot be compared is to imply that we know what
these beliefs are (because we understand them and know them to be different). If I
can understand others by translating their languages into my own, however, then our
conceptual schemes must not be radically incommensurable.[184] In fact, people with
different conceptual schemes are often able to reach understanding, if not agreement;
how else could Marxists and capitalists, structuralists and post-structuralists,
Reformed and Arminians debate with one another?[185]

That there are diverse communities employing diverse conceptual schemes seems
incontrovertible. Davidson's argument is that diversity need not imply that these
schemes cannot be compared with, or corrected by, one another:

> Even if we do not know the world aside from our interpretation of it, this
> does not mean that the world is our interpretation of it. If it were, our inter-
> pretations would never change and would never undergo successful and
> persuasive refutation; but change they do, as we change and refine our the-
> ories in accord with our changing experience.[186]

Davidson's model thus "allows for the possibility of learning from experience, something Fish's model of interpreters, always certain of their interpretations, does not
and cannot."[187] Similarly, the possibility of learning from texts "is the most important
reason to read and to study literature: to break out of our own circle of beliefs and
assumptions and to encounter another point of view."[188] All that Fish can acknowledge is that we encounter different interpretations: "Nowhere in his system does he
allow us to assign any otherness to the text itself."[189] Indeed, Fish's non-realism commits him to the position that, with respect to texts, "to be is to be interpreted." To be
in an interpretive community is, for Fish, to see only what its conceptual scheme
allows one to see. On Fish's view, the authority of an interpretive community is, for
all intents and purposes, absolute. In this context, to insist on normative literal meaning is to issue a counterblast against the authority of interpretive communities.

Other points can be raised about Fish's view of the role of interpretive communities and about the hermeneutical relativism that apparently ensues. First, he both
asserts and denies that there are any universal categories for interpretation. On the
one hand, he denies that any one scheme has categories that correspond to the way
things are; on the other, he maintains that *his* account of the interpretive situation
corresponds to the way things are (e.g., in interpretive practice). Furthermore, he
presents his account of interpretation to those in other interpretive communities, and
he clearly expects them to follow his argument. If, however, we only see what our
own interpretive schemes allow us to see, how does Fish expect to communicate with

and convince us? Is not such a relativism *self-refuting*, or at the very least, inconsistent? For the relativist "regularly participates in communication and evaluation of other conceptual systems while implying that it has no basis for doing so."[190]

Second, is not interpretive relativism *self-perpetuating*? If interpretive communities rather than texts are the locus of authority, then texts cannot challenge the tradition of their interpretations. Why is it, then, that so many communities feel the need to ban certain books that they consider dangerous? Is not the very existence of an Index eloquent testimony to the ability of texts to make their own voice heard over that of interpretive communities?

The above represent significant reasons for withholding authority from interpretive communities. Nevertheless, might there not be some sense in which the interpreting community is conducive to literary knowledge? More pointedly, is there any advantage in belonging to a church when interpreting the Bible? If so, it is not for the reasons that Fish suggests. It is not because the church somehow constructs better meanings, nor is it because the church's conceptual scheme is necessarily more adequate than the academy's. I suggest that it is rather because the church represents that community of interpreters who share a primary concern for the Bible's literal meaning.[191] It may also be because the church is that community in which the interpretive virtues—intellectual, ethical, and spiritual—are cultivated. For it is not only a community's interests but also its *virtues* that make it an appropriate environment for obtaining literary knowledge. In short, *literary knowledge is not simply a matter of having the right descriptions but also of having the right dispositions.* Literary knowledge, like knowledge in general, is ultimately related to ethics, to epistemic rights and duties, and to intellectual virtues.[192]

Critical Hermeneutical Realism and the Role of Descriptive Frameworks

To this point I have argued that there is meaning—enacted communicative intention—in the text. The "world of the text" is not some free-floating indeterminate referent, but is directly related to what its creator—the author—has said and done. What about nature, the "text of the world"? Does it follow from scientific realism that there is a "single correct interpretation" of physical reality, that is, a single correct interpretive framework for describing the cosmos? To link science and literary theory in this way is not arbitrary; non-realism strikes at the heart of *all* interpretation—literary and scientific—and the notion that descriptive frameworks are relative to interpreting communities arose in the context of the history and philosophy of science.[193] Indeed, a number of philosophers of science argue, with Fish, that what science discovers depends on the particular "scheme" with which the scientist views the world. What we see (our observations) is conditioned by our theories (our ways of seeing; our "views" of the world).[194]

Interpretation is at the heart of all our attempts to make cognitive contact with reality, including physical reality. In science and textual interpretation alike, we come to the data with an interpretive scheme and look for feedback.[195] In response to creeping relativism, a number of recent philosophers of science have proposed a kind of realism that avoids reductionism on the one hand and relativism on the other. The difference between these newer, moderate realists and earlier naive realists is that the former are aware of the inevitability of descriptive frameworks. The difference between moderate realists and non-realists is that the former believe that, far from distorting reality, at least some descriptive frameworks are indispensable for knowing certain aspects of reality. Many, though not all, of these arguments for scientific realism apply equally well, I believe, to literary knowledge.

Like the world, the text is "there," independent of our attempts to interpret it. The question I have been examining throughout this chapter is whether the world and the text have a stable meaning—a differentiated structure, an intrinsic nature—and whether it can be known. The older foundationalists believed that there was a structure, that the mind could mirror it, and that such reflection counted as knowledge. The newer realists continue to hold that the world exists and behaves independently of how we describe it, but add that we can only know the world under particular descriptions that are themselves historical and provisional. They are provisional because the world can "kick back"; it can resist our attempts both to manipulate it and to describe it in certain ways. Some descriptive frameworks, therefore, enable us to "read" the world better than others, thus "improving the legibility of nature."[196] Texts may not kick back in the same way, but they too can resist descriptions and uses that violate their natures.

The issue is not whether we can interpret without schemes or descriptive frameworks (we cannot), but whether such frameworks necessarily distort the reality they seek to describe. The more moderate realism I am here commending acknowledges the inevitability of descriptive frameworks but claims that these may nonetheless allow us to discern the real, however dimly. Theories for Fish, on the other hand, can never do more "than reproduce existing consensus-ideas of what counts as a competent, qualified reading."[197] The difficulty with defining truth as consensus—the way a particular community sees and describes reality—is that nothing is allowed to count as a reason for critiquing the status quo. Fish refuses to admit "that beliefs may change . . . as the result of *discoveries*."[198]

It is one thing to say that all interpretation is theory-laden, quite another to say that all textual evidence in literary criticism is "totally determined by the reader's perspective, theory, or prejudices."[199] Interpretations are not true, correct, or justified merely because some interpreters believe them to be so; "what we are after are discoveries, not inventions."[200] *Sola scriptura* is a reminder that textual meaning is independent of our interpretive schemes and, hence, that our interpretations remain secondary commentaries that never acquire the status of the text itself. The notion that readers make or *construct* meaning rejects *sola scriptura* and is ultimately non-realist: "On matters ontological, it [non-realism] preaches abstinence (no knowledge constructs should be thought to refer . . .) or promiscuity (there are as many realities as there are constructs)."[201] The new morality of knowledge no longer values fidelity to the real. The realist, on the other hand, stands within the covenant of discourse and practices *fidelity*; the purpose of interpretive schemes is not to obscure meaning but to mediate and release it. The interpretive scheme plays the ministerial role of the midwife; it is not the parent of meaning, only the helper in its delivery.

While some of our interpretive approaches may be mutually contradictory, not all of them need be so. It may be that a number of different interpretive schemes are complementary, each representing a valid insight into a common text. So, while there may be no single correct interpretive scheme, it does not follow that any scheme is as good as another. Each scheme can only be considered bad or good relative to its particular purpose. If the purpose is to determine how the Gospel of Matthew came to be written, then source criticism may be the best interpretive scheme. However, if the purpose is to determine what Matthew's own particular theological slant was, then redaction criticism is the better tool. What is important to note is that the source critic and the redaction critic use different schemes to describe different aspects of the same text. So do the feminist, Freudian, structuralist, reader-response, and even deconstructionist critics. At the same time, not all descriptive attempts count as genuine interpretation. I reserve the term "interpretation" for the attempt to understand literary acts. Whether this reservation is justified or arbitrary will be seen, I hope, in the next section.

Bhaskar helpfully distinguishes between (1) the notion that all beliefs are produced in some social context ("epistemic relativity"), and (2) the notion that all beliefs are equally valid in the sense that there are no rational grounds for preferring one over another ("judgmental relativism"). One can accept (1) (so avoiding epistemological absolutism) but reject (2) (so avoiding epistemological relativism). Relativists, says Bhaskar, mistakenly infer (2) from (1).[202] The Reformers would agree that all interpretations are provisional (*semper reformata* presupposes the corrigibility of our interpretations), but not that all interpretations are equally valid.

Critical realism maintains both that theories describe things that exist (hence "realism") and that theories can be true or false (hence "critical"). Critical realism does not maintain that our theories or descriptions have to be "absolutely" correct. Indeed, it is precisely this "all or nothing" approach to knowledge that gives rise to skepticism. Fortunately, however, there is a third option by which we can break out of the debilitating dichotomy of "all or nothing," namely, *some*. *Some* descriptive frameworks may yield *some* interpretive knowledge. "There is a red ball," under some circumstances, is an acceptable assertion about what one sees rising in the east on a winter's morning. On the other hand, this sentence can undergo "referential refinement"; one can offer more and more comprehensive descriptions. The person who says, "There is an enormous gaseous ball of fire," is not talking about another sun, only using a different framework of description.

I do not wish to be misunderstood with regard to this vital point. The critical realist sees no contradiction between, on the one hand, believing in "the way things are" independently of our descriptions of them and, on the other, employing a number of different interpretive frameworks to describe "the way things are." To say that there is a truth to the world or a meaning in the text is not necessarily to commit oneself to one interpretive scheme only. As Harty Field rightly asks: "How could there be only one true and complete description of the way the world is? The concepts we use in describing the world are not inevitable."[203] For the critical or moderate realist, the world is there, independent and determinate, yet it is indescribable apart from interpretive schemes and only partially accessible to any one scheme. Yet the concepts we use in describing the world or the text are not wholly arbitrary either: "It is not as if any interest at all on our part will do if we are investigating what reality is like."[204] Neither the world nor the text are wholly indifferent to our descriptions. As Frank Farrell states: "Reality itself 'educates' our sensibility towards it so that we come to recognize, for example, that an interest in the mechanical operations of very tiny particles will let us understand nature's articulations better than an interest in the magical control of substances."[205] And though Farrell does not draw a connection between "educating our sensibility" and the ethics of knowledge, I do: the biblical text will only guide our attempts to describe it if we are patient, attentive, and genuinely open-minded about what it is.

It is not that our descriptive frameworks *construct* reality, then, but rather that certain aspects of reality only emerge or come to light under particular descriptions. Some things we wish to talk about, that is, "can emerge as determinate only when we put a particular set of concepts to work."[206] One cannot describe the workings of Parliament, for example, with the categories of particle physics. The moderate realist thus acknowledges "that we need a pluralism of vocabularies in order to give an adequate account of how matters stand."[207] While we inevitably come to the text with an interpretive scheme, it may nevertheless be the text's meaning that comes to us, and not only our own reflection. Our knowledge of what is there—in the world, in the text—though partial, can still be true. Critical realism thus stands as a middle position between epistemological absolutism ("there is only one correct interpretive scheme") and epistemological relativism ("every interpretive scheme is as good as any other").

In sum, while we can never dispense with interpretive schemes and descriptive frameworks, it is nevertheless true that the text itself can "educate our (literary) sensibilities." Indoctrination by interpretive communities, whereby we see through a class darkly, need not be the final word. On the contrary, if the text educates our interpretive sensibilities, then the Bible itself can be a kind of "class." Indeed, this is precisely the image Calvin uses to illustrate biblical authority: the Scriptures are the schoolroom, the Spirit is the teacher, and the Son is the subject. We need the interpreting community not because it alone has the single correct conceptual scheme, but rather because the church is, or should be, the community that (1) displays the interpretive (ethical, spiritual) virtues, and (2) shares a concern for textual meaning and a desire to hear the Word of God. The community's role is interpretation is not magisterial, therefore, but ministerial.

Sola Scriptura: Thick Descriptions and Interpretive Truth

Look thou on the text whether I interpret it right. . . .[208]

The success of any interpretation depends on its explanatory power, on its ability to make more complex, coherent, and natural sense of textual data than other interpretations do.[209]

The norm of literary knowledge, I have argued, is the literal sense: the sense of a literary act, what an author has done in a text. I defined the perspicuity of Scripture and claimed that there is no contradiction between affirming the clarity of the text on the one hand, and acknowledging the necessary mediation of descriptive frameworks on the other. I now wish to unpack the notion that "Scripture interprets

Scripture" and show in more detail how the Bible itself calls for some types of description rather than others. I first consider what is involved in describing literary acts, then turn to three subsidiary questions: (1) Can our descriptions be rationally compared? (2) Can our descriptions be defeated or shown to be false? (3) Can our descriptions be completed or shown to be true?

Describing the Object of Literary Knowledge

The philosopher Arthur Eddington once gave, in a well-known example, two very different accounts of his desk. The "ordinary story" described its color, weight, style, and solidity. The "scientific story," on the other hand, described a host of tiny particles and electrical charges. The first description uses the framework of everyday perception; the second, that of subatomic physics. Which is the better, the truer, description of Eddington's desk? Should either one serve as the standard of all our other stories?[210] No—not because both are false but rather because both descriptions are true. Truth here is less a matter of *perfect correspondence* than of *adequate response*; there is a desk in this class, and both descriptions are relatively adequate responses to that fact. It is not that there are two different desks; rather, there is one desk, described in two different ways for two different purposes.

What do literary critics describe? Stein Haugom Olsen believes that textual interpretation is a matter of describing textual parts; there is no further "meaning" over and above the "body" of the text.[211] Literary criticism, that is, is limited to describing aesthetic features that make the text noteworthy. Paisley Livingstone, by contrast, prefers to describe the socio-historical situation of a text and to use the text, in turn, to illumine certain aspects of its socio-historical situation.[212] On my view, what interpreters should describe is the text *as a literary act*. I will not repeat the argument for defining the text in this manner. Instead, I will focus on what one actually describes if the object of literary knowledge is indeed the author's intended *meaning* of the text.

The primary goal of interpretation is textual understanding. Understanding, however, involves more than knowledge about the text. *Understanding is a matter of getting into cognitive contact with what the author was doing in a text and with what the text is about.* Further, understanding involves an appreciation of the whole, of how the fragmentary parts of a text fit together; understanding involves the comprehension of "the pattern of a whole chunk of reality."[213] Merely to describe a text's aesthetic features or its socio-historical background is not enough to account for what a text is or why it is the way it is. On the contrary, we grasp the meaning of the text when we understand, not some fact about the text, but the text itself.

My thesis, briefly put, is that the most adequate descriptions of texts are those that seek to understand the text as a complex communicative act. To be sure, this is not always what readers or exegetes do. Is there, then, any prescriptive force in my preferring descriptions that focus on the text as communicative action? I believe there is. Most important, we must have recourse to an agent's intention in order adequately to describe his or her action.[214] We must know, for instance, that a person's not eating was intended as fasting if we are to understand the act as a political gesture. What we are trying to describe, says Altieri, is intention enacted in the work.[215] The intention in the work "is a purposiveness that has a public determinacy, like that of conventions

... which warrants the full force of person predicates."[216] Again, any account that omits the level of authorial intention will achieve no more than "thin" description.

One possible objection to my thesis might be stated as follows: "Is not the claim that there is indeed a single correct descriptive framework a form of epistemological absolutism?" While I acknowledge the apparent similarities, I nevertheless beg to differ. In the first place, to say that the literary act is the norm for interpretation is not yet to privilege a single descriptive framework; as we will see, communicative acts admit of, indeed require, more than one descriptive framework. That is because our descriptions are not direct representations so much as descriptions that are "framed" in different ways and trained on different aspects of the literary act. Second, while it is possible to attend to texts in different ways, and while each of these ways may be the result of a valid interest, it is virtually impossible to attend to the text without reducing it to the status of a natural object unless one gives descriptions under which the text is intentional. Of course, there is nothing to stop a critic from giving impersonal descriptions of texts or from reporting on one's own reactions as a reader. However, the former descriptions do not yield literary knowledge (unless this includes such facts as the size, weight, and color of books), and the latter descriptions are not descriptions of the text, but of something else. I conclude that *the text's existence and nature alike are ultimately inexplicable apart from some consideration of communicative agency.*

The text as a literary act, then, is the principal norm for valid interpretation.[217] Like the physical world, the literary act has an intrinsic nature and determinate shape; it is a structured work (Ricoeur). What exactly is determinate about a literary act? There are various aspects: (1) the words and sentences of a text as they stand in a fixed relation to one another, and the relation between these words and words outside the text that have been written at the same time in the same language (the locutionary aspect); (2) the life world or context of the historical author, in which persons, things, and events stand in determinate relation to other persons, things, and events; (3) the mind-set of the author, that is, the way in which the author engages with the world through words (the illocutionary aspect).[218]

Can Our Descriptions Be Compared?

Let us now assume that what the literary critic describes is a literary act. Is there a single correct interpretation of an act, or might there be several compatible descriptions? Can diverse interpretations be compared, or are they so radically different as to be incommensurable?[219] Hermeneutic rationality detests an "anything goes" pluralism. Accordingly, I contend that descriptions of the same kind may be compared, while descriptions of different kinds, though incomparable, may nevertheless be compatible. It may well be that some conflicting interpretations are simply describing different aspects of the same text.

Describing Complex Actions. Even simple acts can be described in a variety of ways: flipping a switch, turning on a light, scaring a burglar—all are ways of describing the same act. Or are they? If I did not know a burglar was downstairs but was merely on my way to the kitchen for some water, I would not, I think, subsequently describe my act of turning on the light as "scaring a burglar." Why not? Because I was not thinking about scaring away burglars when I flipped the light switch (though I was thinking about turning on the light). Richard Wollheim explains: "Corresponding to each description of an action is a thought, and an action is intentional under a certain description if what guides the person's action is the corresponding thought. A thought guides an action when it both causes it and forms its character."[220] That the burglar was scared away was an unintentional consequence of my turning on the light. One cannot accurately interpret actions, we may recall, either by describing an agent's bodily movements or by describing accidental effects. Such thin descriptions lose sight of the act itself.

What of speech act categories—do they provide for thick description? Some critics charge speech act theory with relying on a simplistic view of intention, whereby a single mental state accounts for the meaning of an entire text.[221] Others charge Searle with adopting a "one sentence–one speech act" model that ignores the broader social (and literary) context.[222] Take, for example, the act of writing a letter. How should one describe it? Consider the various possibilities: he gripped the pen; he moved the pen in straight and circular motions; he spelled the word "predestined"; he sent his greetings; he addressed the Ephesians; he strung a number of sentences about "election" together; he explained the significance of the event of Jesus Christ. How many of these descriptions are necessary for understanding the literary act we know as Ephesians? How many of these acts can be described with the conceptual scheme of speech act philosophy?

It may be that speech act philosophy is ultimately inadequate to the descriptive task.[223] There is no reason, however, why communicative action has to be described atomistically, word by word or sentence by sentence. On the contrary, one of my main goals has been to demonstrate that literary acts represent a higher level of communicative complexity than signs and sentences and thus call for new concepts to describe them, concepts appropriate to forms of literature—to speech acts of a higher order.[224] I did claim, it is true, that the sentence is the basic unit of meaning, but sentences can become complex communicative acts, just as other basic actions (e.g., hammering, sawing, drilling) can become ingredients of a complex act (e.g., building a bookcase).

Do whole texts, like utterances, have meaning? Does it make sense to ask not only, "What is the meaning of the 'eternal life' in John 3:16?" but also, "What is the meaning of the Fourth Gospel?" Indeed, it does. A text, though made up of many parts, is nevertheless a whole and complete action. For Aristotle, the *mythos* or "plot" of a text is the means by which "goals, causes, and chance are brought together within the temporal unity of a whole and complete action."[225] Like the plots they recount, then, texts too are unified actions that require a new set of concepts with which to describe them. A text is thus a large-scale communicative act, a complex project of meaning.

Describing and Prescribing Reactions. Not every interpretation aims at describing what the author was doing in tending to his or her words. Some describe the way a reader feels when reading, the way a text has been used to sustain unjust social structures, the way a text has been used in order to liberate the oppressed, or even how to read a text as though someone else wrote it. There are study groups in the Society of Biblical Literature devoted to the History of Interpretation, Semiotics and Exegesis, Women in the Biblical World, Ideological Criticism, Psychology and

Biblical Studies, and the Bible in Mediterranean Culture and Tradition, to name but a few. Each group has its own interest and its own descriptive, or prescriptive, framework. Do all such varied approaches count as genuine interpretations? Can they be counted as true? How many of these can we construe as describing the literary act?

Annette Barnes has a broad view of what it is for interpreters to describe a literary act:

> I have been relying here on what I take to be an uncontroversial truth, namely, that there are many ways of correctly characterizing an action, not all of which will exhibit or accord with the way the action was intended . . . Artists in creating works do something, they are agents, and what they do is not merely what they intend to do even when they are successful in carrying out their intentions.[226]

Interestingly, Barnes herself inadvertently grants a priority to what I have called the "literary sense" of communicative acts, for she says that not all acceptable interpretations are necessarily "true." For example, we know that Grant Wood intended his "American Gothic" to be a picture of a man and his daughter, but it is not unacceptable to regard it as a painting of a man and his wife. Why not? Because, says Barnes, the "false" interpretation is more interesting (and thus acceptable for that reason) than the "true" one (e.g., the one that corresponds to the author's communicative intent). Her criterion for truth in interpretation is admirably clear: "Exhibiting successfully executed artistic intent is sufficient for establishing interpretive truth."[227] Yet she goes on to suggest that not all interpretive remarks need to have truth as their aim. After all, why should "true" be a more important criterion for assessing interpretations than "interesting"?[228]

Why indeed? For hermeneutic non-realists, the truth question is a moot point. As we have seen, pluralists deregulate interpretation by abandoning the norm of the literal sense. Readers can, of course, talk about their own experience of a text. That is their privilege, and I do not contest it. "What it means to me" is a virtually irrefutable formula, like "the way I see things" or "I feel like." It is difficult, perhaps impossible, to verify or to disagree with such statements, for they are reports of a subjective experience other than one's own. What I do contest is the claim, often unspoken, that this sort of report yields textual understanding; indeed, I question whether such reports ought even to count as examples of genuine interpretation. Descriptions of the reader's experience, while they may indeed be "interesting," are less than normative unless it can be shown that they have the potential to illumine the literal sense of the text. In my view, a reader's experience generates an interpretive insight only if it enhances textual understanding, for that reader and, in principle, for all others as well.

Other literary critics describe still other aspects of the text. Which of these may be said to yield literary knowledge? To what extent, for instance, must we describe the socio-historical conditions that provide the setting for the text? Should we describe the consequences of literary acts, and if so, which ones: the immediate or long-term? Again, while these are valid queries, they should not be confused with, or be substituted for, an understanding of the text itself. They may yield knowledge, but is it literary knowledge—knowledge about what the author was doing with his or her words, knowledge of that to which the author was attending? The *sense* of communicative action should not be mistaken for a description either of its initial *setting* or of its subsequent *significance*.

Levels of Description. What's in a literary act? As we have seen, the author acts on different levels: locutionary, illocutionary, and perlocutionary. The text is a propositional, poetic, and purposive authorial act with three validity conditions: truthfulness (sincerity), truth (correspondence), and fittingness (coherence). Hence, there are several levels and dimensions of the literary act that can be examined. Take, for example, the book of Jonah. The author says many things about a man named Jonah and his misadventures, including a famous encounter with a fish. He puts these statements into the form of a narrative. One can thus describe the "narrative act": the relation between the narrator and the content of the story (point of view), as well as the way the story is put together (rhetoric).[229] In narrative texts, we can further distinguish between "a level of represented courses of action and a level of representing and interpretive acts."[230] In other words, one can describe what happens in the story (*p*—the propositional content, the plot), or one can describe what the author was doing in tending to his narrative in just this way (the illocution). What kind of literary act is the book of Jonah: history, fiction, satire, theology, or some combination thereof? What is it doing, and what kind of truth claim does it make?

It is difficult to say which of the above questions is most vital in order to describe the meaning of the literary act we know as Jonah. Many biblical interpreters would not like to choose. We may here recall Stout's proposal to abandon the term "meaning" and speak instead about interpretive interests: "Good commentary is whatever serves our interests and our purposes."[231] Similarly, for Barton, the various methods of biblical interpretation reflect different underlying aims and interests: "Biblical 'methods' are theories rather than methods: theories which result from the formalizing of intelligent intuitions about the meaning of biblical texts."[232] Stout correctly perceives the issue: "At the heart of the current debate over literary theory is the question of which normative aims one ought to have in studying literature."[233] Much confusion could indeed be eliminated if interpreters would stop speaking of meaning and instead say what exactly they are describing (or prescribing), and why. It would be helpful, for instance, to learn that the aim of an approach was to interpret a text as though the reader had written it. One might question the value of such an enterprise, but at least it would be clear what some forms of reader-response criticism were doing. For my part, I have explicitly stated my aim as an interpreter of the Bible: to gain literary knowledge, to discover what an author is doing in tending to words as well as what those words are about. This, I contend, is a proper response to the text as a communicative act, for it respects the design plan of language (and literature) and increases my self-understanding precisely by giving me knowledge about something other than myself.

Another important reason to focus on literary acts is to resist reductionist approaches that yield only thin descriptions.[234] The present work resists ontological reductionism by insisting that meaning is not merely a matter of relations between signs; authorial intention, as we have seen, supervenes on signs to create a higher level of organization and purpose. Second, it resists methodological reductionism by insisting that one cannot do justice to literary acts by explaining them in terms of one descriptive framework only. The object of interpretation and of literary knowledge is the literary act, and this object calls for a number of descriptive frameworks, some of which operate on different explanatory levels. This last point merits further consideration.

The parallel between literary and scientific theory is again instructive. Contemporary science views the world as a hierarchy of complexities. Arthur Peacocke writes: "Corresponding to the different levels in these hierarchies of the natural world there exist the appropriate sciences which study a particular level."[235] Each level requires its own science and its own set of concepts. Peacocke distinguishes four clearly demarcated levels: the physical world, living organisms, the behavior of living organisms, and human culture. Only humans, he notes, span all four levels. There is a similar hierarchical order, I submit, in communicative action: sign systems, speech acts, literary acts. The Bible, we may note in passing, spans all three levels.

As long as each method confines itself to the level that corresponds to it, the ensuing descriptions will be compatible. All too often, however, champions of a certain method transgress the limits and imperialistically attempt to subordinate other levels. Structuralism, for instance, attempts to explain speech acts and literary acts alike with concepts that more properly belong on the level of sign systems—on the level of *langue* rather than *parole*. The issue is whether the descriptions and concepts of one interpretive method can be reduced to or swallowed up by the descriptions and concepts of another. One example of such reductionism in science is the attempt to explain the human person—everything from one's lymph nodes to one's loves—at the level of evolutionary biology or genetics.[236]

The most vigorous form of the tendency to explain higher-level phenomena in terms of lower-level descriptive frameworks is what we may call "nothing but" reductionism—as in the claim that "higher complexes are 'nothing but' atoms and molecules and their processes."[237] Such physicalism consigns immaterial phenomena (such as thoughts, hopes, and desires) to the bin of unreality, as Hume had earlier consigned metaphysics to the flames. The parallel between such reductionistic moves and deconstruction is striking: both radically analyze (= take apart) wholes in terms of their constituent parts in order to collapse them in upon themselves. The undoing of the self by evolutionary biology finds its parallel in literary theory in the undoing of the sentence by semiotics. The reduction of mental categories to physical ones corresponds to the deconstructors' claim that texts are "nothing but" differential sign systems. This semantic "undoing" recalls other famous attempts at reducing the human—for example, B. F. Skinner's explanation of human behavior in terms of conditioning (nurture), or Freud's explanation of human behavior in terms of the unconscious (and the nursery). *Deconstruction and pragmatism alike are examples of what we might call socio-semiology, a reductionist approach that eliminates communicative agency by viewing meaning and interpretation in terms of ideological sign systems and interpretive communities.* The closest parallel in science to the postmodern reduction of literary theory is perhaps socio-biology, which posits a biological basis to all social behavior.[238] Both approaches—socio-biology and "socio-semiology"—effectively eliminate both meaningful acts and acts of meaning.

Arthur Peacocke argues, against reductionism, that concepts appropriate for one level cannot always be explained in terms of another: "There is no sense in which subatomic particles are to be graded as 'more real' than, say, a bacterial cell or a human person or a social fact."[239] Similarly, with regard to literary theory, there is no sense in which signs or socio-historical conditions are to be deemed "more real" than the communicative intentions and actions of an author. *Each level of description refers to something irreducibly real.* To focus on meaning as communicative action is ultimately to opt for an *expansionist* rather than reductionistic approach to descriptive frameworks and literary knowledge.

The tendency to reduce the richness of human experience to one level of description is dangerous, for it explains less, not more, of reality. Indeed, reductionistic theories, strictly speaking, do not explain, but *explain away.* They do not save the phenomenon, but sacrifice it on the altar of unified theory. What exactly do we lose if we view communicative action as an epiphenomenon, a secondary symptom, of ideology? What we lose, I believe, is the purpose of language, its design plan. From a Christian point of view, language provides the matrix within which freedom and responsibility operate, as well as the most important medium through which human beings interact.[240] Again, from a Christian perspective, language does not merely condition our thought but gives us the capacity for free thought as well. To replace communicative action with a description of social and institutional power structures is not only to miss the hermeneutic mark, but to eliminate communicative freedom and responsibility—what we do with our words.

Is there a normative level of description? Can we order the various levels in hierarchical fashion? Is there a "ground level" description of texts that would be truer than others? Derrida, we may recall, argues against the notion that any one context is more privileged than another. Peacocke agrees: "No one description at any one level can ever be adequate . . . no one level has ontological priority."[241] At the same time, he wants to avoid a thoroughgoing fragmentation of the various levels. For Peacocke, then, the ultimate aim "is a description that takes account of all levels of investigation, analysis and description and integrates them into a unified perspective."[242] The human being calls for biological description, but as Peacocke observes, what is *distinctively* human transcends the biological level.[243] Similarly, a text is semiotic, yet what is distinctively hermeneutical transcends that level too. The text is the product of a particular person in a particular culture; consequently, our methods of description must do justice to the intentional aspect of the text.[244] Peacocke argues that one cannot account for persons with categories drawn only from the natural sciences. As Peter Morea puts it: "As yet, the experience of being human cannot even be captured other than by poets, novelists and dramatists; it certainly cannot be described scientifically."[245] Peacocke concurs: it is precisely "this multiply-levelled character of humanity [that] actually constitutes the very essence of *being a person.* . . ."[246] In the same way, my model of communicative action does justice to the varied layers that constitute the very essence of *being a literary act.*

If the object of our description is a communicative act, we would do well to attend to what Searle terms its "essential" condition.[247] The *raison d'être* of language and literature is social interaction. The so-called "communicative principle" holds that if people talk or write, "they do this with the intention to communicate something to somebody."[248] Communication lies at the heart of the producing and consuming of texts. This principle of communication indicates that social interaction is the essence of speech and literary acts alike. Communication is the unifying act that orders all the other acts that go into producing a piece of written discourse. If we miss the communicative focus and go wrong here, we go wrong everywhere.

Scripture Interprets Scripture. What might "Scripture interprets Scripture" mean in the light of the preceding discussion? It means that Scripture itself indicates what kinds of descriptions might be most appropriate. Let us return to Jonah. The book of Jonah is a complex reality that requires a variety of descriptive frameworks, operating at different levels, in order to interpret it fully. To begin with, though at a fairly elementary level, one may analyze the text sentence by sentence, in fragments. This may yield information, but probably not understanding. Such reading is a bit like viewing an impressionist painting from too close-up; all one sees is sundry color patches. Only when one steps back does the pattern (e.g., the Rouen cathedral at sunrise) emerge. So it is with most literary acts; their sense emerges only when one "steps back" and surveys the whole. It follows that the text itself, in its complete and final form, is the best evidence for determining what the author is doing.

At the level of the whole, then, Jonah is a narrative with a beginning, middle, and end, which can be analyzed in terms of its literary structure. At this narrative level, Jonah is best described as a story—but a story about what: God, Jonah, the people of Nineveh, the great fish? What is the author doing besides "telling a story"? What kind of narrative act is Jonah? One plausible answer, supported by a number of commentators, is that Jonah satirizes Israel's religious complacency and criticizes Israel's ethnocentrism.[249] Indeed, at the level of the whole, when one begins to ask, "What *kind* of narrative?" it is difficult not to see the story as satire. It is also harder to maintain that the author of Jonah was primarily making truth claims about certain forms of sea life that swim in the Mediterranean. Interpretations that never rise above the level of the reported events of the story, whether to affirm or to deny them, offer no better than thin descriptions. In contrast, the illocutionary act of "satirizing religiosity" only emerges at the level of interpretation that employs a new set of literary-critical concepts. Finally, at the canonical level, the book of Jonah forms part of the ongoing testimony to God's justice, compassion, and generosity toward those who repent and toward those who do not.

To summarize: first, while there are various ways in which to describe texts, our ultimate aim in interpretation is to take account of as many of these levels as possible. These levels are arranged in a hierarchy of complexity, where the higher (literary) levels emerge out of or supervene on the lower (linguistic) ones. *Integration* rather than reduction is the watchword. Second, our descriptions should aim at what is *distinctive* about texts as opposed to other types of entities. Finally, we must focus on what is *essential* about texts. Describing texts as communicative action admirably meets, I believe, these three conditions for valid interpretation—the kind of interpretation that yields literary knowledge.

Can Our Descriptions Be Defeated?

Critical hermeneutic realism—the notion that there is determinate meaning in texts that can be discerned through interpretive schemes—entails that there are correct and incorrect ways of describing the object of literary knowledge. To begin with, an interpretation is "defeated" if a further consideration of the evidence shows that the author *could not have done* or *probably did not do* what an interpretation implicitly or explicitly ascribes to him or her. In the second place, the implication of my earlier comments on reductionism is that some interpretive approaches, because they offer only thin descriptions of literary acts, will ultimately be seen to be inadequate and perhaps self-defeating. Indeed, this may be happening at present to the historical-critical method of biblical interpretation.

Critically to interpret a text "means to read it in order to discover, along with our reactions to it, something about its nature."[250] Because the author's communicative intent supervenes on the text, the text itself is public evidence of the author's intent. Consider the following interpretive claims about Matthew's Gospel: "It is an anti-Semitic racist tract"; "It is a polemic for male-only ordination"; "It is a fictional re-telling of Jesus' life inspired by Old Testament prophecies"; "It is a literary and theological representation of Jesus as the promised Messiah." How might one adjudicate among or defeat these conflicting descriptions of Matthew's literary act? Can we determine which of these claims is probably true and which is probably false? The norm for interpretation, to repeat my central thesis, is the sense of the literary act; the true interpretation is the one that correctly describes the communicative intention enacted by the text. What we wish to avoid above all are reductionistic or thin descriptions. An adequate interpretation will be one that, at the very least, does not suffer from the limitations and partialities of lower-level descriptions—one that at least takes a stab at stating what kind of literary act has been performed.

According to the present argument, an interpretation counts as literary knowledge when it accounts for the author's enacted communicative intent under certain thick descriptions of the literary act. Correct interpretations describe the beliefs, thoughts, and feelings that guided and shaped the text as a communicative act.[251] *Interpreting texts involves, in large part, ascribing illocutions to an author.* Such an enterprise is far from being quixotic; on the contrary, something similar lies at the heart of the judicial process. According to legal theorists, intentions are not inaccessible but can be inferred through a process of critical testing, in which our hypotheses as to what the author did are examined against the evidence—especially against the evidence of the text.[252]

H. L. A. Hart, the legal philosopher, states the difference between human action and mere bodily movement in the following terms. We readily ascribe intentionality and responsibility to the former but not to the latter. Ascribing intentions and describing illocutions are operations that employ higher-level concepts (e.g., ascription) in order to give thick descriptions of texts as literary acts. What is interesting for our purposes is Hart's proposal that statements of the type "he did that" are comparable to judicial decisions. "Ascribing" is the result of a deliberative process in which opposing descriptions of an action are confronted and debated.[253] In order to describe one's intention, the thought process embodied in the act must be reconstructed. Agents act for a reason, and communicative acts are no exception; authors do things in tending to their words for a reason. Thick descriptions of literary acts similarly ascribe intentions to an author. Whenever we describe a literary act as something or other, we are therefore making inferences about an author's intentions: "You cannot take the top of a man's head off and look into his mind and actually see what his intent was at any given moment. You have to decide it by reference to what he did, what he said and all the circumstances of the case."[254]

Altieri likens the work of the interpreter to a jury that must decide on "competing descriptions of action."[255] The "jury" is any reader or group of readers faced with competing interpretations of the same text.[256] Specifically, what the jury needs to decide is why the text is the way it is. A text is the result of an author's choices, and there are probable grounds for deciding what the choices were and why they were made. "To discern an agent's intentions is to grasp the relation between her action and its context . . . what she will count as success or failure in what she does."[257] Intended actions are done for reasons. Intended communicative actions are those done for communicative reasons. These communicative reasons determine which descriptions are appropriate, for these reasons specify the kind of result a particular communicative act intended to bring about.

Are communicative acts always so transparent, susceptible to easy descriptions and uncontroversial ascriptions? Not necessarily. Frank Kermode argues that Nathaniel Hawthorne purposely set out to write an equivocal text, one that was open to a number of different interpretations. Altieri is surely right, however, when he draws a distinction between an equivocal text and a "determinate textual act."[258] We can describe, with a good deal of precision, Hawthorne's literary act as "making an ambiguous point." There are other examples of books written to confound rather than to communicate (e.g., James Joyce's *Ulysses*). It is more often the case, however, that books considered indeterminate (and perhaps undescribable) are rather works that do something complex, something that may need to be described on several levels. This is not to claim that every aspect of the text is the result of the author's intentional action. Authors may not intend to reflect their intellectual and social history, or for that matter, the state of a given language at the time of writing, but they inevitably do so. To read a text only for the evidence it yields about the state of the language at a given time, however, does not yield understanding of the text; only an interpretation that describes it as a literary act does that.

Sternberg effectively rebuts those who say we cannot recover the author's original intention, separated as we are by time and culture: "It does not follow that we cannot approximate to this state by imagination and training—just as we learn the rules of any other cultural game—still less that we must not or do not make the effort."[259] No one has yet proposed that students of the Old Testament invented biblical Hebrew! Sternberg therefore asks: "Is the language any more or less of a historical datum to be reconstructed than the artistic conventions, the reality-model, the value system?"[260]

Hermeneutic rationality—the quest for literary knowledge—may perhaps be best viewed as a form of inference to the best explanation (abduction), rather than a species of deduction or induction.[261] The interpreter seeks literary knowledge, an explanation as to how and why a text is the way it is and what it is about. One does this by imputing intentions to the author that account for the way the text is, in its parts and in its wholeness. Critical interpretation proceeds by making conjectures or hypotheses about what the author was doing in tending to his or her words. On this view, one does not validate interpretation by "proving" the existence of the author's intention; one rather shows its explanatory power and fruitfulness by asking questions about the text to which certain descriptions of the literary act represent possible answers. Most serious interpretations cannot usually be falsified or dismissed simply by appealing to the lexical evidence. Interpretive conflicts generally pit one interpretive scheme against another, each of which claims best to account for the same data. Peter Lipton's account of scientific explanation correctly grasps the conflictual nature of interpretation: "What gets explained is not simply 'Why this?', but 'Why this *rather than* that?'"[262] The successful interpretation is the one that provides the best account as to why a text is the way it is rather than another way.

Who determines which explanation is "best"? Is "best," like beauty, in the eye of the beholder? Lipton considers two options: "the explanation best supported by the evidence" (the "likeliest") or "the explanation that would provide the most understanding" (the "loveliest").[263] Lipton thinks that the former begs the question and hence claims that we should prefer instead the loveliest explanation, the one "which would, if true, provide the most understanding."[264] In the context of hermeneutics, the "loveliest" theory provides the most understanding only if it accounts for the literary act as a complex whole, that is, only if it adequately describes what is happening on each of the important levels (e.g., locutionary, illocutionary, literary). We infer, for example, that Matthew is claiming that Jesus is the Messiah promised in the Old Testament, not by citing one verse, but rather by applying the same criteria that science uses to appraise theories—correspondence, comprehensiveness, coherence, and compellingness—to the whole of the Gospel.

The best explanation of a text is one "whereby the occurrence of a phenomenon is explained as brought about by a rational agent doing some action intentionally."[265] In order to satisfy the criterion of correspondence, our descriptions must avoid anachronism; the best interpretation must be one that describes what *this* author living in *this* culture *could* have done. Historically implausible explanations are less satisfactory, and hence less rational, than those that are probable. In order to satisfy the criteria of comprehensiveness and coherence, the best interpretation must describe the whole text as well as the text as a whole. Finally, in order to satisfy the criterion of compellingness, the best interpretation must describe the literary act in such a way that enables us to understand more about the text than do other interpretations. Note that the best explanation does not have to be an absolute explanation; it can be improved. For example, according to Alasdair MacIntyre, we can make rational judgments between traditions of hermeneutic inquiry—between competing interpretive schemes, traditions, and communities—by judging their progress in solving interpretive problems over time.[266]

Can Descriptions Be Completed?

In saying that we cannot attain absolute truth in interpretation, have we slid down the slippery slope of relativism into the outstretched arms of Derrida? Not at all. For the argument, "If no absolutes, then skepticism," is fallacious. Between "all" and "nothing" stands "some." Hermeneutic rationality yields *some* literary knowledge.

Our descriptive frameworks need not be barriers to understanding but rather its enabling conditions. At the same time, it is important not to take the "critical" out of critical realism. No single theory or interpretive scheme gives us the whole truth or complete description. It does not follow, however, "that no theory gives us any of the truth, and still less . . . that there is no truth to give and to receive."[267] *It is possible to give true, though not exhaustive, descriptions of literary acts.* Critical realism, both in science and literary theory, is the middle way between absolutism and relativism. "Scientific explanations are successful . . . insofar as they refer—partially and with approximate truth—to mind-independent nature not entirely caused, constituted, constructed, or overdetermined by the framework of science itself."[268]

With regard to the morality of literary knowledge, the crucial point is surely that we can achieve interpretive adequacy without having to achieve interpretive absolutism. By adequate knowledge, I mean sufficient for the purpose at hand. What is this purpose? Communication and understanding. What we are after as readers is not an interpretation that *perfectly corresponds* to the text (whatever that might mean), but rather an interpretation that *adequately responds* to it. In responding to the text we allow the text to complete the purpose for which it was sent. The fact is, human beings communicate successfully with one another and understand what they read every day.[269] Yet the Bible is different, for the kind of response it enjoins is more demanding. Consequently, responding appropriately to Scripture is as much an ethical as an epistemological task. Indeed, knowledge is ultimately an ethical, indeed spiritual, affair. Dogmatism and skepticism alike are as much moral failures as they are epistemological mistakes. In the light of human fallibility and fallenness, Derrida's iconoclastic protest against totalizing interpretations, however one-sided, may nevertheless be pastorally apt.

The final context, in light of which alone the proper meaning of all things will be seen, is an eschatological, theological horizon.[270] All human knowing is thus partial until the end of history, when the final judgment will be given. *Différance*, therefore, is not the final word; the deferral is not endless. Eschatology means only that the end is postponed. Interpreters live, of course, on the hither side of the eschaton, and truth outruns interpretation precisely for this reason. Our best explanations may still fall short of the absolute truth. This should not disturb us. To be human is to be an interpreter, a communicative agent, a citizen of language. We know things not immediately, as do the angels, but mediately: through our bodies, our senses, our language. Yet we know in part. We know enough—enough to go on with our reading, enough to go on with lives. There is something to be known, though our knowledge of it will remain only partial, fallible, incomplete. *Sola scriptura* expresses the adequacy and sufficiency of the literary knowledge we may glean from Scripture. Yet *semper reformata* reminds us that the interpretive work of the theologian and literary critic alike is never-ending.

GENRE AND COMMUNICATIVE RATIONALITY: THE METHOD OF LITERARY KNOWLEDGE

Language is in essence a medium of communication. If the hearer takes words in a sense not intended by the speaker, that is not an enlargement of meaning but a breakdown of communication.[271]

Many people who have an excellent command of a language often feel quite helpless in certain spheres of communication precisely because they do not have a practical command of the generic forms used in the given spheres.[272]

Every piece of writing is a kind of something.[273]

How one approaches an object of study depends, in large part, on the nature of the object to be known. We might call this the material condition of knowledge: the method must be appropriate to the subject matter.[274] One does not study the moon with a microscope or Monet's "Water Lilies" with a stopwatch. Nor should one study words, speech acts, literature, or Scripture with the same set of tools, for they represent varying levels of increasing complexity that call, at each new level, for new descriptive concepts. We may illustrate this as follows:

Object of knowledge/data	*Method of knowledge/discipline*
Canon	Canon criticism, biblical theology
Genre	Genre criticism, literary criticism
Parole	Speech act philosophy, discourse analysis
Langue	Linguistics, semiotics, syntax

In this hierarchical arrangement, the more complex objects supervene on the simpler ones. Thus, the canon is made up of a variety of literary forms, which are in turn made up of a variety of utterances, which are in turn made up of a variety of words.[275]

This section introduces a crucial interpretive concept that is vital to correct reasoning about literary acts, and thus vital to hermeneutic rationality: *genre*.[276] A "genre" (from the Latin *genus*, "kind") is a species of literature. Since Plato and Aristotle, critics have ordered the domain of literature into various classes. Though all texts are literary acts, not all acts are of the same kind. The ancient classification scheme distinguished poetry, epic, and drama. Aristotle wrote treatises on comedy and tragedy.[277] From the Renaissance through the eighteenth century these genres were regarded as fixed types, somewhat like biological species that could neither mix nor evolve. More recently, Northrop Frye has proposed a fourfold theory of genre in which the major types—comedy, tragedy, romance, irony—represent permanent forms of the human imagination.[278]

The concept of genre, however, is more than a device for literary classification. The notion that there are diverse forms of literature is not just a useful tool of the librarian. Nor should one mistake an interest in literary form with what is called "form criticism" in New Testament studies. Form critics such as Bultmann study short passages (e.g., in the Gospels) and trace them back to earlier, oral traditions, which served particular social functions (e.g., instructive sayings, proverbs, etc.). The effect of form criticism, however, has been to separate these passages from their literary context in order to relate them to a historically reconstructed social or religious setting. To focus on genre, on the other hand, is to treat texts as literary wholes—unified communicative acts—though this need not rule out their having a social function as well.

Literary acts have subject matter, illocutionary energy, a perlocutionary trajectory, and a particular literary form. It is essential to attend to this last aspect—the "generic"—for, as we established earlier, the literal sense of a text is its literary sense, and this can only be determined by identifying the genre. Understanding, I have argued, is a matter of grasping what an author is doing in a text. For one cannot simply "do"; one must do something or other. We may note in passing that the tendency among theological conservatives to offer "proof texts"—a method of abstracting individual statements from their larger literary context—is every bit as detrimental to understanding the literary act as a whole as is form criticism. Though they may inhabit different ends of the theological spectrum and though their doctrines of Scripture may be vastly different, the interpretive practice of both form critics and theological conservatives is equally atomistic, equally unlettered—equally capable of short-circuiting the process of interpretation.

Communicative Competence: Genre As Rule-Governed Form of Social Behavior

Language, said Searle, is a rule-governed form of behavior. Words behave differently in various contexts. We gain grammatical knowledge when we understand the rules that govern a particular communicative act in a particular context. "Love" in the context of a tennis match, for example, does not mean what it does when associated with candlelight dinners. Wittgenstein's great contribution was to point out that there are different "grammars" associated with different forms of life. Speaking a language and understanding it are matters of practical mastery, of learning what to say when and where, and how to say it.

When we engage someone in dialogue, we automatically follow a number of rules: we let a person finish his or her sentences; we take the context of the dialogue into account; we respond when asked a clarification question. Paul Grice's "cooperative principle" formulates the implicit rules that typically govern the conversation of competent speakers. The principle states that speakers should always provide the suitable amount of relevant information, given the context, that they should be as clear as the situation demands, and that they should speak truly: "Communication is not a matter of logic or truth, but of cooperation; not of what I say, but of what I *can* say, given the circumstances, and of what I *must* say, given my partner's expectations."[279] Why should speakers cooperate? Because non-cooperative behavior would be antisocial and irrational. If one departs from the "cooperative principle," one makes communication impossible. Meaning is located neither on the level of the language itself nor on the level of the individual, but in rule-governed interpersonal interaction.

What I wish here to explore is the possibility of a "cooperative principle" in the realm not only of spoken conversation but of written texts as well. My contention is that literary genres are communicative acts of a higher order, existing on a level of greater organizational complexity. Just as we must develop linguistic competence in order to understand how words are used in everyday contexts, so we must develop literary competence in order to understand different types of texts. In the context of linguistics, Chomsky uses "competence" to refer to the implicit knowledge that speakers have acquired of their native language.[280] Jonathan Culler extends the term to include an understanding of literary conventions and rules as well.[281] The literary theorist aims to describe, explicitly and theoretically, the rules that govern a given literary form, understood as a patterned communicative action. Literary competence is thus related to what I term "generic rationality," where "generic" means not "general," but rather "characteristic of a specific literary type." The rules that govern a particular literary genre are not extrinsic to the text but are rather embodied within it. Understanding texts, I submit, is a matter of learning these rules to the point of being able to follow them. Writing and reading alike thus involve "communicative competence": the practical know-how that grasps grammatical and generic rules. Literary theory is simply the attempt to provide a theoretical account of what competent readers already do.

Literary genres, then, are like language games. The interpreter's task is to determine which game (e.g., epic, history, chronology, prophecy, parable, etc.) is being played; only then will the individual "moves" make sense. Hirsch agrees: "Coming to understand the meaning of an utterance is like learning the rules of a game."[282] As Wittgenstein has shown, language games are related to forms of life; no one language game represents the essence of language, just as no single form of life represents the essence of life. On the contrary, there are as many language games as there are human activities, and many have developed their own rules, not to mention a distinct vocabulary. If words are like tools, as Wittgenstein suggests, then genres may perhaps be thought of as the projects on which the tools are put to work.[283]

Genres facilitate interpersonal interaction by offering relatively stable types of communicative forms. They are distinguished according to their primary communicative function (e.g., political speech, political commentary, sports commentary): "Genres are the conventional and repeatable patterns of oral and written speech, which facilitate interaction among people in specific social situations."[284] Literary genres are best understood, I suggest, as communicative *practices* rather than as isolated communicative acts: "A practice is any form of socially established cooperative human activity that is complex and internally coherent . . . and is done to some end."[285] In particular, genres are literary practices that enable complex ways of engaging reality and of interacting with others. It follows, therefore, that understanding is not only a matter of identifying language games, but of participating in a communicative practice.[286] Jeanrond suggests that text genres demand appropriate "reading genres."[287] For example, a text whose primary communicative intent is historical is misunderstood if read as fantasy (and vice versa). Understanding is a matter of communicative competence, a practical skill much like learning a language, which enables the interpreter to recognize and participate in various forms of communicative activity. Readers who grossly mismatch text genres and reading genres should be deemed hermeneutically *incompetent*.

Ways of Meaning: The Level of Genre

If the project of redeeming the text depends on recovering the author's enacted intention, then many might deem the task hopeless. It is one thing to speak of a "cooperative principle" between interlocutors in a face-to-face conversation, but how can readers be said to "cooperate" with authors long since departed? A text, Ricoeur observed, is distanced from its author as soon as it is written and launches out on a career of its own. It is precisely its capacity to float freely through other contexts that, for Derrida, renders textual meaning indeterminate. Cut off from its author, the text is also cut off from any fixed context. Or is it? There is, I believe, at least one context that remains relatively fixed: the literary context. The thesis I wish now to defend is that literary genre has its own resources with which to resist Derrida's attack on the idea of stable context. I hope to show that what writing pulls asunder—author, context, text, reader—genre joins together. Furthermore, it may be, as Berkouwer suggests, that the Reformers' serious attempt to do justice to literary types "was motivated by the desire to deal correctly with the *sui ipsius interpres* [its own interpreter]."[288] By attending to the level of literary genre, in other words, we may gain further insight into how "Scripture interprets Scripture."

Literary Genres As Historical Formations

Derrida's main point, we may recall, is that writing breaks from its original situation and drifts from context to context. Consequently, interpreters can never get a "fix" on the text. There is no way to anchor meaning or to plot its location. Moreover, because no one descriptive framework is privileged in interpretation, the very idea of context is indeterminate. The so-called new historicists, on the other hand, lie on the opposite side of the scale of textual determinacy. They stress the importance of historical context to the point that what a text says is not only determinate, but *determined* by its socio-historical location. Some feminist critics, for instance, contend that traditional genres are the historical products of a patriarchal social order.[289]

The concept of literary genre allows us to escape this dichotomy between contextual indeterminacy on the one hand and contextual determinism on the other. In the first place, literary genres have, as communicative practices, a social and historical location. That is, literary genres themselves have determinate historical contexts. We can chart, for instance, the rise and development of the novel in the eighteenth century and relate it to changing social circumstances and changing worldviews. Literary forms, unlike Platonic forms, develop and have histories. One can study the history of a literary form (e.g., tragedy) over time, or one can study a literary form as it exists at a particular time (e.g., Greek tragedy, Elizabethan tragedy). A given literary form, then, has a determinate historical context.

In the second place, precisely because writing does not assume a shared situational context, genre creates the possibility of a shared *literary* context. Alistair Fowler says genre compensates for the lack of a shared situational context in two ways: "First, it provides a situation of *literary* context; second, it reinforces the signal system with additional coding rules."[290] A literary form is not a "restraint" on what an author can say, but an enabling means of being able to say something about something to someone *at a distance*.

Third, the rules that govern literary forms are flexible. According to Fowler, "Every literary work changes the genres it relates to."[291] This accords with what I have previously said about communicative agents who put the language system to work by making initiatives of meaning. Fowler eloquently captures the freedom genres give their authors: "Far from inhibiting the author, genres are a positive support. They offer room, as one might say, for him to write in—a habitation of mediated definiteness; a proportioned mental space; a literary matrix by which to order his experience during composition."[292] An author enjoys freedom within limits; the author is a citizen of literature. *Literary genre holds communicative freedom and determinism in constructive tension.* An author can modify some conventions of a given genre, but not all of them. Just as the meaning of a word is relatively fixed at a given point in time in relation to its language system, so genres, as historical formations, are similarly determinate. The significance of genre as a historical formation for interpretation is that it provides a strong case for recognizing and eliminating anachronistic interpretations on the level of literary acts.

What of texts whose authors and original contexts are unknown? Yet again, genre is the way forward to literary knowledge. In his discussion of the anonymous letter to the Hebrews, Thiselton notes that what the interpreter wants to discover is not the name or biography of an author, but rather the sense of textual wholeness, "*which represents the vision of a human mind and which belongs to some larger context or life-world.*"[293] What we reconstruct is the *kind* of thought and life-situation that finds expression in the text. Such thought, like the genre that expresses it, has a historical context that conditions but does not determine it. Understanding the historical formation of literary genres allows the interpreter to make an initial guess as to what kind of literary act has been performed, but we should not forget that genres also enable authors to make new initiatives of meaning.[294] The literary act is not only shaped by the historical context but may in turn affect it.

How to Do Things With Texts: Generic Illocutions

Just as triangles and squares are kinds of geometrical figures, each with their own rules of composition, so literary kinds—histories, epics, gospels, chronologies, etc.—have their own distinctive features too (e.g., structure, length, mood, style, subject matter). However, it would be wrong to think of genres in terms of necessary properties. Fowler prefers to speak in terms of "family resemblances."[295] The basis of a generic resemblance, moreover, is a function of literary tradition: "What produces generic resemblances . . . is tradition: a sequence of influence and imitation and inherited codes connecting works in the genre."[296]

Given my earlier identification of the literal sense with the literary sense, it is perhaps not surprising that the theory of communicative action should give pride of place to literary genres *and to their illocutions*. Some approaches, such as new criticism, focus on genre but then concentrate on its locutionary aspect: its form and structure. Other approaches, such as reader-response criticism, focus on perlocutions—the effects on readers. I have argued, however, that a true description of a literary act must focus on what the author is doing with a genre. That means specifying illocutions: the intentions enacted in following conventional procedures. Examples of such descriptions will be something like, "He's telling a story"; "She's satirizing an attitude of religiosity"; "He's giving religious instruction," and so on. Is it legitimate to describe the text of Jonah as a whole in any of these ways? The logically prior question is: Do texts as wholes have an illocutionary force over and above that of their constituent parts? Richard Ohmann denies this, arguing that works of literature do not really perform speech acts, but only pretend to do so. Literature is hence "*a discourse without illocutionary force.*"[297]

Ohmann's objection has been answered, in my opinion adequately, by literary theorists who have introduced new concepts into speech act philosophy. For the most part, the discussion has centered on narrative, but similar points could be made in relation to other literary forms. Let us, then, take narrative as an example of a complex literary act. Is there such a thing as a narrative illocution? On one level, the illocution would be "telling a story." This is indeed an accurate description as far as it goes, but ultimately it needs to be supplemented, for authors can do various things in telling stories. What they do, says Mary Louise Pratt, is something both important and wonderful: they *display worlds*.[298] This is not simply to say that narratives make assertions, for the world displayed in the text may not correspond to any actual state of affairs. No, a narrative displays an interpreted world. Yet a narrative may nevertheless make an assertion of a higher order; it may assert a worldview. For instance, the implicit message of Camus's novel *The Stranger* (*L'Étranger*) is (roughly), "Life is absurd." Camus makes this assertion by displaying a world in which people make choices and do things without any clear idea of why they do so. The assertion "Life is absurd" thus supervenes on the story; it is a higher-level illocutionary act, a *generic illocution*. There is no need, of course, to reduce every literary work to an assertion. For this reason, it is preferable to view the generic illocution of narratives as "displaying the world as. . . ."

Pratt's analysis has been taken further by Susan Snaider Lanser, who says that in addition to displaying a world, authors of narrative take up a *stance* toward it.[299] Lanser's study examines what she terms the "narrative act": the perspective established by the author by means of which the world of the text is presented to the reader.[300] In other words, the way the story is told communicates the author's perspective on the world of the text. To speak of "point of view" in narrative is to acknowledge that the author's voice and vision is communicated indirectly, in and through the displaying of a world.[301] In choosing to write in the narrative genre, authors choose to take up a stance toward their displayed worlds, hence to communicate an ideology, a "worldview." Lanser is especially interested in the ideological function of point of view, in particular, with how values and evaluations are communicated.[302] The literary act of a narrator is indeed "displaying," but it is also accompanied by *evaluative* illocutionary acts—praising, snubbing, mocking, questioning. The illocutionary force of narrative includes not only displaying imagined worlds but commending, or condemning, them as well. Lanser argues that the purpose of literary acts is not to impart information about the here and now (i.e., the author's immediate context), but rather to provide "culture communication," namely, information vital to understanding the human condition and to knowing how to contribute to its flourishing. According to Lanser, culture communication operates through four modes: instruction, suggestion, information, and example (narrative fiction). Her summary is worth quoting in full: "Much like the biblical parable, the novel's basic illocutionary activity is ideological instruction; its basic plea: hear my word, believe and understand."[303] *The canon of literary works thus serves much the same purpose as the biblical canon: to guide future generations.*

The concept of genre, I suggest, describes the illocutionary act *at the level of the whole*, placing the parts within an overall unity that serves a meaningful purpose. It follows that genre is the key to interpreting communicative action. It is not enough to know the meaning of words; one must have some sense of the illocutionary point of the whole utterance: "Our stance about the literary genre of the book determines our entire interpretation of the book."[304] To invoke the notion of genre is to acknowledge a tacit agreement on how a text should be written and how it should be read. A text only communicates, that is, if the reader is able to follow the rules of the literary game being played by the author. Genre is nothing less than the "controlling idea of the whole."[305] In Hirsch's words: "All understanding of verbal meaning is necessarily genre-bound."[306]

Genre theory is especially important for biblical interpretation.[307] For the Bible is not one book but many books of different kinds, with a wide repertoire of illocutions. The illocutionary force of Paul's letters, for instance, is not so much "displaying the story of Jesus" as "explaining the story of Jesus."[308] One commentator suggests that the illocutionary force behind 1 John is "confessing Christ."[309] Other literary forms may have their own characteristic illocutionary forces: wisdom ("commending a way"), apocalyptic ("displaying the *end* of the world," "exhorting"), psalm ("celebrating a created world," "addressing God"). And the various literary forms, taken together as Scripture, may on the canonical level have yet another illocutionary force: "proclaiming God's salvation"; "testifying to Christ." These are only approximations, for genres too have rough edges. Much work needs to be done on this level of discourse, a level that, I believe, has great potential in aiding the recovery of biblical theology.[310]

The Ways of Meaning: Varieties of Cognitive Contact With Reality

Genre is much more than a device for classifying forms of literature. According to Bakhtin, the forms of literature represent not only communicative strategies with diverse illocutionary forces but also cognitive strategies with diverse ways of envisioning the world. A genre, in other words, is not only a mode of communication but a mode of experiencing and thinking about the world. Furthermore, the concept of genre coordinates three related aspects of communicative action: the enactment of the author's intent, the engagement with the world, and the encounter with the addressee. Genre is a way of engaging with reality and with others through words.[311]

Each genre makes possible a distinct way of thinking about and experiencing the world. Narratives, for instance, enable us to experience and reflect on the temporal connectedness of human existence and personal identity unlike any other form of literature (or thinking).[312] In this respect, a genre is like a descriptive framework that allows certain aspects of reality to shine through more than others. We may only have reality "under a description," but it is still reality that is being described. It follows, then, that there is no such thing as a "foundationalist" genre into which all other genres can be translated.[313] To have a repertoire of genres—wisdom, apocalyptic, parable, etc.—at one's authorial command is to be able to engage the world and others in different ways that would not otherwise be possible. In this respect, genre is a learning device, not simply a means for expressing something one already knows. The parallel with metaphor is instructive. Until recently, philosophers have felt that metaphors were simply a way of decorating discourse. Metaphors would be dispensable if one could say the same thing non-metaphorically. Ricoeur, as we have seen, has argued on the contrary that metaphors are indispensable cognitive instruments.[314] So too, I believe, are genres.

Literary genres make indispensable cognitive and practical contributions to human experience and social interaction. Indeed, Bakhtin believes that genres are bearers of traditional wisdom that allow one generation to share its experience with others: "Genres . . . accumulate forms of seeing and interpreting particular aspects of the world."[315] The author, in binding himself or herself to a genre, is thus a beneficiary of its considerable cognitive resources.[316] Each genre is a form of thinking "adapted to conceptualizing some aspects of reality better than others."[317] To relate genre to our previous discussion of narrative illocutions, we can describe genre as "form-shaping ideology."[318]

Think of the various biblical genres—prophecy, apocalyptic, hymn, narrative, law, etc.—as different kinds of maps. Each map highlights certain features of the world more than others and accomplishes different tasks: informing, warning, encouraging, commanding, assuring, etc. Each genre has its own "key" and "scale." The "key" explains what a text is about. Just as different maps highlight different aspects of reality (e.g., roads, geological characteristics, historical events), so different literary genres select and attend to some aspects of reality more than others. Similarly, each genre has its own "scale," that is, its own conventions for thinking and its own manner of fitting words to the world. The "key" and "scale" of history, for instance, is to make words fit or correspond to the world ("what actually happened"); that of utopia, by contrast, is to make the world (the future) conform to our words.

Ricoeur has tentatively begun to explore the significance of the Bible's many genres for interpretation and theology. The many forms of biblical discourse each mediate revelation in irreducible ways, such that if we abandon the form, as in demythologizing, we lose the content. Why? Because genre is not simply a device for classifying forms of literature, but a cognitive tool for generating worldviews. The crucial point, again, is that the *form is not incidental but essential to the content*. This insight highlights the shortcomings of the proof-texting method; biblical texts yield not only propositional information, *but ways of interpreting and processing the information* as well. Biblical interpreters need to develop the skills to recognize and to participate in the various forms of communicative activity found in the Christian canon.

Hermeneutic Rationality: Genre and the Covenant of Discourse

Understanding texts, we may now claim, is a matter of achieving *generic competence*. We will only understand a text correctly when we grasp *what it is* and *what it is about*, for the proper function of a text follows from its form and content. Competence, as we have seen, refers to the implicit know-how that enables us to perform successful communicative acts. Communicative rationality, on the other hand, is Habermas's term for the process of validating those truth claims that are implied in every speech act. Rationality for Habermas consists of "redeeming" these claims by achieving mutual understanding through reason-giving rather than by coercion. In this section I will examine how the diversity of literary forms complicates this project. Whereas Habermas focuses on the universal rules for rationality implied in all discourse, I will speak of "generic rationality," referring to the process by which the rules that implicitly govern a particular literary form are explicitly reconstructed. With regard to literary acts, the genre of a work specifies the context in which the "cooperative principle" functions. *Genre creates a cooperative context, and generic competence requires that one attend both to the universal rules that govern all discourse as well as to the particular rules that govern particular literary forms.*

Global Rationality: Universal Validity Conditions

It is fitting that we conclude this chapter on the epistemology of meaning with reference to a philosopher who turns to speech acts in order to uncover the rationality inherent in all communicative action.[319] As we have seen, Habermas believes that he has discovered universal standards of rationality that are embedded, not in the mind of the subject (as Descartes, Kant, and most modern philosophers believed), but in language itself. Rationality is implied in communicative action, that is, in action oriented to mutual understanding and agreement. Habermas is interested in what we might call the "transcendental conventions" of communication: the necessary conditions for the very possibility of linguistic communication among human beings. The philosopher's task is to make explicit the universal bases of communicative action.[320] They do so by a process that Habermas calls "rational reconstruction," whose goal is "an explicit description of the rules that a competent speaker must master in order to form grammatical sentences and to utter them in an acceptable way."[321]

"Everyday communicative practice, in which agents have to reach an understanding about something in the world, stands under the need to prove its worth."[322] What exactly do speech acts have to prove? What are the conditions for a valid speech act? Speakers must be ready to show not only that their act is comprehensible, but that it is *sincere, true, and appropriate*. If we cannot rely on these conditions being met, the possibility of communication breaks down. Communicative competence involves more than grammatical competence; it involves the ability to situate sentences vis-à-vis external reality and the social world. It is not only a matter of matching words to the world, but rather a matter of *using* the words in the right way in the appropriate context; it is a matter of "universal pragmatics." Every speech act implicitly claims that it has met, or could meet if challenged, these universal validity conditions.

I said earlier that the concept of genre coordinates three aspects of communicative action: the enactment of authorial intention, the engagement of words with the world, and the encounter through words with the addressee. These three aspects of genre correspond to Habermas's three validity conditions. The meaning of a communicative act—from the lowliest speech act to the most sophisticated literary genre—is not a matter of its propositional content only, but of the way it engages reality and establishes interpersonal relations as well. Every communicative act implies that it *truthfully* expresses its author's intention (subjective condition), that it *truly* represents something in reality (objective condition), and that it establishes *right* interpersonal relations (inter-subjective condition). The competent speaker will be able to meet each of these conditions.[323]

Habermas believes that, by uncovering the inherent rationality implied in communicative action, he has escaped Derrida's criticisms that interpretation is only conventional and thus arbitrary. On the contrary, ideals such as truth (relation to external world), truthfulness (relation to inner world), and fittingness (relation to social world) are embodied in the very structure of speech itself. Hence, rationality is located not in the knowing subject but in the very structure of communicative action.

"Generic" Rationality: Particular Validity Conditions

Up to this point, we have been dealing with universal pragmatics, that is, with those validity conditions that Habermas believes are implied in all communicative acts. I want now to suggest that different genres respond to these validity conditions in different ways and that interpreters may need to attend to *local pragmatics* too. As we have seen, literary genres constitute different forms of thinking; there are as many types of communicative competence as there are types of communicative practice. This is not to say that some literary genres are absolved from, say, the criterion of truth. On the contrary, I affirm Habermas's procedural approach to rationality. What I suggest, rather, is that *the way in which the validity conditions are met will vary from genre to genre.* All texts will have to be comprehensible, but the rules by which texts make sense are not invariant.

Our aim, following Habermas, is systematically to reconstruct the intuitive knowledge of competent authors and interpreters. We wish to provide explicit theoretical knowledge of their implicit, pre-theoretical "know-how"—of the rationality presupposed by all communicative action. Yet we also wish to make explicit the genre-specific, local rationality of diverse literary forms: How do they construct their discourse? What conventions do they follow? How do they engage reality? Our project is thus related to what Meir Sternberg calls "poetics": the study of the rules of literary composition.[324] *Our method for gaining literary knowledge is thus the rational reconstruction and explicit formulation of the "local" rationality that governs a particular genre.* We understand the sense of a communicative act when we understand what it is and what rules govern its successful performance.

What happens to the universal validity conditions when we examine them in the light of particular generic rationalities? To what extent do Grice's "cooperative principle" and Habermas's "universal pragmatics" admit of local variation? The sincerity condition—that one's discourse be truthful, a sincere expression of one's subjectivity—is, I believe, unaffected. The way in which texts engage with the world and with others, however, is relative to the kind of literary act performed. Generic competence means using sentences correctly in the context of a particular literary form; the standards of generic correctness thus are subject to local variation. What relation a sentence bears to external reality, for instance, depends on the kind of literary act being performed. History and fiction both aspire to truth—correspondence to the world—but in different ways, under different descriptive frameworks. The historian, in writing history, leads the reader to expect a discourse that conforms to events that happened in the past; the novelist, on the other hand, defends a different kind of claim: "Life is like that." All forms of discourse enact intention, are about the world, and engage the reader—but not in uniform fashion.

Habermas's third validity requirement—that a discourse be appropriate to or fit its social setting—raises special problems for literary genre. Have we not seen that it is the unique effect of writing to break the contextual chain that binds speakers to their hearers? Texts, we may recall, become distanced from their authors. Clearly, the author and reader do not always share the same situation, much less the same culture, country, or century. It would appear, then, that literary acts cannot meet the validity claim that pertains to the social world: fittingness. This appearance, however, is deceiving; my argument is that the world of the text is indeed a shared world. The context that authors share with readers is a literary context: to be precise, a generic context the comprises specific rules and conventions for discussing, describing, and discerning certain aspects of the real world. The author engages the reader and reality not in spite of but thanks to the mediation of the text, together with its distinctive mode of viewing the world. Literary knowledge here acquires a new sense: not only knowledge about genre, but a kind of knowing that can be learned and shared with others through literary genres.

Authors signal their generic intent (and thus how the validity conditions are to be met) in different ways. Fowler discusses several "generic signals." Generic markers at the beginning of a work are particularly important in guiding the reader into the particular rule-governed communicative activity represented by the text: "The beginning of the gospel about Jesus Christ, the Son of God" (Mark 1:1); "Paul, a servant of Christ Jesus, called to be an apostle . . ." (Rom. 1:1); "In the days when the judges ruled . . ." (Ruth 1:1 RSV); "The proverbs of Solomon . . ." (Prov. 1:1); "The vision that Isaiah son of Amoz saw concerning Judah and Jerusalem . . ." (Isa. 1:1). These opening statements call to mind other literary works of the same kind: Gospel, letter, moral fable (history?), wisdom, and prophecy respectively. Titles provide another clue. Booth remarks that titles "are often the only explicit commentary the reader is given."[325] Another signal is "generic allusion": "Apart from explicit labelling, the most direct form of indication is reference to previous writers or representatives of the genre."[326] Through a number of other means as well, stylistic and thematic, the author sends signals, in the text itself, that identify its genre. Of course, to readers familiar with a given genre, understanding is not a problem; they follow the rules and conventions intuitively. If, however, the work is of an unfamiliar kind, the interpreter must reconstruct this intuitive knowledge and make it explicit.

Literary Genre As Communicative Covenant

A genre is a covenant, a covenant of discourse. Just as authors implicitly accept the validity conditions of communicative rationality when they begin to write, so readers implicitly accept the validity conditions of understanding when they begin to read. Meaning and understanding involve generic "agreements" between author and reader and generic "agreements" between words and the world. These two covenantal dimensions correspond to the two basic functions of language: to engage other persons (through illocutions) and to engage reality (through propositions). It is interesting to note that, in the history of literary criticism, it was the Romantics in the nineteenth century who rebelled against the perceived rigidity of generic rules. Some Romantic writers rejected generic norms "as tyrannical constraints upon individual feeling."[327] Benedetto Croce, for example, rejected the idea that texts displayed family resemblances and insisted instead that each work was a genre unto itself. In this regard, it seems that the postmodern rebellion against fixed meaning is incurably "Romantic."

Between Author and Reader. Entering into a covenant is a sign that a relationship between two parties has been established and that mutual obligations have been pledged. To engage in communication is similarly to enjoy privileges and incur responsibilities. I treat these communicative privileges and responsibilities more fully in the next chapter. Here I am primarily interested in how the ethical stance of the reader is an aid to gaining literary knowledge.

The first step towards understanding is to determine a text's genre, that is, the kind of communicative action being considered. The next step is to reconstruct the particular rationality—the distinct form of thinking and experiencing the world—that both structures and governs the genre in question. A literary act is a unified whole, thanks to its belonging to a specific genre: "The theme of the work is the theme of the whole utterance as a definite socio-historical act. Consequently, it is inseparable from the total situation of the utterance to the same extent that it is inseparable from linguistic elements."[328]

Genre, therefore, acts as a bridge between the author's and reader's horizon of meaning. An author intends a particular set of generic rules and intends the reader to recognize them. For their part, interpreters, in coming to a text, have a preunderstanding—what Davidson calls a "prior theory."[329] The prior theory is a guess as to the text's genre; it may or may not correspond to the author's interpretive framework. One reader, for instance, may read *Pride and Prejudice* as historical tragedy, another may read it as social comedy. The competent reader, however, will adjust his or her prior theory in the course of reading through a process like that of inference to the best explanation. To identify the genre of a piece of writing is to know what "text game" is being played, what rules are in force, and how the words fit with the world. Only the whole bestows meaning on the parts. Genre is thus that integrative level of textual description that recovers the enacted intention, the distinctive nature, and the essential function of a communicative act.

Textual understanding is the hoped-for result of a generic cooperative principle whereby authors and readers agree to abide by the same set of rules. Understanding a text means approaching it in a "fitting" way, according to the kind of act it is. It is for this reason that the process of understanding a text has a covenantal dimension to it. Authors and readers must at least agree about the kind of act being performed, though they may disagree about many other things (e.g., whether the content of the text is accurate, whether it is good, etc.). Authors usually expect their illocutionary intent to be recognized (or else why write?). Readers usually assume that authors know what and how much their audiences know, and so compensate for any anticipated deficiencies within the text. Genre facilitates the process of communication precisely by orienting authors and readers to a shared literary context. The covenant of discourse is not entirely reciprocal, however: the original text is a "norm-kind," while the interpretation is a "performance-kind."[330] When a pianist performs a Mozart sonata, for instance, he or she follows the composer's norms (and the norms for the genre "sonata"). The performance, though essential to interpretation, is subordinate to the score. So too with texts and interpretations. Covenant faithfulness to what is written is the necessary condition for receiving the covenant blessing: understanding. Understanding is a covenantal agreement between competent authors and competent readers about the rule-governedness of every kind of text.

Between Words and the World. Let us now expand our account of the covenant of discourse to include the word-world relation. Implied in communicative action is the claim that our words are about something. The first point to recall is that this "aboutness" is not limited to empirical reference. We must not repeat the error of the logical positivists, for whom every meaningful sentence had to represent some empirical state of affairs. At the same time, I do believe that every speech act and every genre engage with the world in some way. Searle, we may recall, says that some words fit the world (e.g., assertives, expressives) while others aim to make the world fit our words (e.g., commissives, directives). This distinction, while correct, is too stark to be helpful when it comes to discriminating the many ways in which different genres engage reality.

That genres are "word-views"—selective perspectives, finite frameworks—does not subvert the possibility of real reference, only "the myth of a total and full re-presentation of the real."[331] We earlier compared genres to maps. Typically, maps single out only some properties or features of the total object domain. Moreover, the way maps refer to the world varies, sometimes quite radically. We have only to compare a road map, for instance, with a historical atlas or a geological survey to see how maps can differ while still referring to the world. In the same way, texts need not all correspond to reality in a one-to-one fashion. A hermeneutics sensitive to the variety of communicative action need not make that fateful reductionistic assumption. Words do not "naturally" represent reality. If they did, then meaning would indeed equal reference. I have argued, by way of contrast, that literary acts operate with generic conventions. It does not follow, however, that reality itself is conventional. The way through this paradox is to affirm, with A. D. Nuttall, that "all reference to reality (including pointing with the finger) is conventionally ordered."[332]

There is a profound difference between saying that texts are governed by conventions and saying that our concept of reality is merely conventional. To say that texts are ordered by conventions is simply to reaffirm that communicative acts are rule-governed. There are many ways that narratives can represent the world. We do not need to choose between mimesis as a mirror of nature and mimesis as a mere social convention. As with the choice between absolute knowledge and skepticism, here too we must refuse the dichotomy: there is neither *one* way that words "agree" or correspond to the world, nor *no* way. Rather, every genre works out its own ad hoc arrangement with regard to the word-world relation: "We can use words merely to summarize or refer to known material. Or we can use words to elicit an imaginative awareness of the known material."[333] Some genres (e.g., history, reporting) add to our stock of propositional knowledge; other genres (e.g., poetry, novel) increase our knowledge by deepening or intensifying our awareness of what we already know. Nuttall suggests that fiction contributes to experiential knowledge (*connaître*) rather than to intellectual knowledge (*savoir*): "The notion of experiential knowledge accounts at once for our preferring a Rembrandt to a photograph."[334] Are the Gospels more like photographic records or portraits? Neither genre is "truer" than the other; each aims for its own kind of engagement with reality and its own kind of precision. But the question must be asked, if for no other reason than to avoid interpretive mistakes. We should not expect historical knowledge from fictional texts or scientific knowledge from historical texts. The kind of literary knowledge we glean from reading depends on the kind of literature we read.

In the final analysis, of course, we must say that authors and readers share not only the world of the text, but the real world as well. The shared world of the text allows authors to engage with others and to say something about reality (under a particular descriptive or generic framework). Literary knowledge is thus a matter of knowing something about a text (e.g., its literary form) and, consequently, something of what the text is *about* (e.g., its subject matter). Interpreters gain both kinds of knowledge, I suggest, by "dwelling" in the text. According to Michael Polanyi, "All knowing is personal knowing—participation through indwelling."[335]

We need not seek far for the reason. If genres are communicative practices, then the best way to learn the rules is to become an apprentice. This is the best way to educate our literary sensibilities and to achieve not only generic competence but also excellence. Such knowing, however, comes at a cost. For indwelling demands that interpreters pour themselves out, at least temporarily, for the sake of understanding the other. It demands that we abandon ourselves and our own ways of seeing for the sake of the other. Perhaps this is what N. T. Wright means when he describes his critical realism as an "epistemology of love."[336] It is surely what C. S. Lewis was referring to in his discussion of good reading, which involves "putting ourselves in the other person's place and thus transcending our own competitive particularity. In coming to understanding anything we are rejecting the facts as they are for us in favour of the facts as they are."[337] In knowledge, as in love, the dominical paradox holds true: "He that loseth his life shall save it." Understanding genre is thus a matter of indwelling the author's literary acts. Literary knowledge is ultimately a matter not only of theoretical but also of personal knowledge, not only of *savoir*, but also of *connaître*.

Between Words and the Word. My case for literary knowledge rests to a great degree on the centrality of literary genre. However, the previous treatment does raise the following question for interpreters of the Bible: Is the canon also a genre? This is a subtle query. On the one hand, some dispute my suggestion that the individual biblical books represent distinct genres. David Aune, for instance, lists twenty different genres that he finds in the Gospels alone, including sayings of Jesus, proverbs, parables, miracle stories, genealogies, and prayers.[338] These are best described, however, as "sub-genres," for they are embedded within an overarching narrative and are subordinate to the text as a whole; they have a relative independence only. On the other hand, the various literary genres in the Bible themselves have only a relative independence, for they are taken up or appropriated into a larger communicative purpose. In the context of Scripture, each of the literary genres of the Bible has an additional illocutionary force, namely, "confessing faith" or "testifying to Christ." Being part of the canon, in other words, allows yet another level of complexity to emerge: the level of "bearing witness."[339] The genres of the Bible, though diverse in form, overlap in content and function. I suggested earlier that with respect to canonical intention, we may have to invoke divine authorship. Accordingly, we could say that the canon represents divinely appropriated human discourse; taken together, the various books of the Bible constitute the Word of God.

In conclusion, genres engage the reader and render reality in different ways. The presence of rules and conventions does not preclude real reference, though the way in which a text "maps" the world varies from genre to genre. Texts have many kinds of objects and can render them in many different ways. The diversity of genres is yet another confirmation of critical realism. No one form of discourse, no one descriptive framework, exhausts all that can be said about the world, humanity, or God. The diversity of biblical genres has a twofold benefit: Scripture can render various aspects of reality, and it can address the reader in different ways (e.g., the mind, the will, the heart). Access to the reality of Jesus or to anything else of which Scripture speaks is textually mediated. The process of mediation, however, is not guaranteed. For though the communicative act may be successfully performed, and though meaning may really be "there," there is no guarantee that the interpreter will behave in a rational, or indeed moral, way. The covenant of discourse may be broken. Communicative action calls not only for hermeneutic rationality but also for communicative ethics. Literary knowledge requires not only the right interpretive methods but also the right interpretive virtues. For the reader too is a covenantal agent, and the communicative act remains in suspended animation until the reader responds.

NOTES

1. Hirsch, *Validity in Interpretation*, 17.
2. N. T. Wright, *The New Testament and the People of God*, 61.
3. Stanley Fish, *Is There a Text in This Class?* 338.
4. Searle, "Literary Theory and Its Discontents," 648.
5. C. S. Lewis contends that the literary critic should attend, in the first instance, to the subject matter, to the "real things," that texts are about, rather than to the style or personality of the author (see his *The Personal Heresy*).
6. By the philosopher Gilbert Ryle and, after him, the anthropologist Clifford Geertz (see below).
7. I am in agreement with N. T. Wright's call, similar to my own, for an "epistemology of love": "What I am advocating is . . . an epistemology or hermeneutic of love as the only sort of theory which will do justice to the complex nature of texts in general, of history in general, and of the gospels in particular" (*The New Testament and the People of God*, 64).
8. On these and related matters, see Paisley Livingstone, *Literary Knowledge: Humanistic Inquiry and the Philosophy of Science* (Ithaca: Cornell Univ. Press, 1988).
9. Altieri suggests that literature enables us to make more complex and varied discriminations about human action, thus expanding our knowledge of the human condition (*Act and Quality*, ch. 8).
10. Matthew Arnold, perhaps the greatest of the Victorian humanists, held that literature exposes us to "the best that is known and thought in the world"; poetry in particular is essentially "a criticism of life." Livingstone believes that literary knowledge has something to contribute to other disciplines. Literary knowledge serves "to challenge and to refine, to complexify and perfect hypotheses within the other anthropological disciplines" (*Literary Knowledge*, 260). We might add, from a Christian perspective, that the biblical texts serve to challenge and to refine our idea of what it is to be genuinely human.
11. Livingstone, *Literary Knowledge*, 230.
12. See "Thinking and Reflecting" and "The Thinking of Thoughts," in Gilbert Ryle, *Collected Papers*, vol. 2 (1971).
13. Clifford Geertz has famously applied the notion of "thick description" to the practice of cultural anthropology in his *The Interpretation of Cultures* (London: Fontana, 1993 [first published 1973], esp. 3–13). My own treatment is much indebted to that of Geertz, though he only mentions literary interpretation in passing.
14. J. L. Houlden, "Commentary (New Testament)," in *Dictionary of Biblical Interpretation*, 129.
15. Richard Coggins, "A Future for the Commentary?" in Watson, ed., *The Open Text*, 166.

16. Robert Carroll, "Commentary (Old Testament)," *Dictionary of Biblical Interpretation*, 134.

17. See, for example, Hans W. Frei, *The Eclipse of Biblical Narrative*, 5: "There is now a logical distinction and a reflective distance between the stories and the 'reality' they depict. The depicted biblical world and the real historical world began to be separated at once in thought and in sensibility, no matter whether the depiction was thought to agree with reality (Cocceius and Bengel) or disagree with it (Spinoza)." The fact-value dichotomy is distinctively modern: we can have public knowledge about facts, but values are a private affair. The problem is determining whether interpreting the Bible is a matter of facts or values. For modern biblical critics, the dilemma is between historical facts that have no religious value and religious values that have no factual backing.

18. It follows from this that biblical scholars could not abide by the Reformation rule that "Scripture interprets Scripture." One of my aims in the present chapter is to reclaim this important interpretive principle by means of the notion of "thick description."

19. Barth, *The Epistle to the Romans*, 6th ed. (Oxford: Oxford Univ. Press, 1968), 6.

20. Ibid., 9.

21. Robert Gundry, *Matthew*, 638.

22. Robert Gundry, *Mark: A Commentary on His Apology for the Cross* (Grand Rapids: Eerdmans, 1993), 24.

23. See, for example, the six-volume Paternoster/Eerdmans series on the book of Acts in its first-century setting, which includes separate studies of its ancient literary setting, its Palestinian setting, its Diaspora setting, its Graeco-Roman setting, and its setting in the history of theological ideas.

24. Gundry, *Mark*, 4.

25. Catherine Belsey terms this approach "expressive realism": "This is the theory that literature reflects the *reality* of experience as it is perceived by one . . . individual, who *expresses* it in a discourse" (*Critical Practice*, 7). She argues that expressive realism is a product of the same forces that produced industrial capitalism in the nineteenth century.

26. For fuller treatments, see F. Gerald Downing, "Historical-Critical Method," in *Dictionary of Biblical Interpretation*, 284–85; Edgar Krentz, *The Historical-Critical Method* (Philadelphia: Fortress, 1975); Morgan and Barton, *Biblical Interpretation*, chs. 2–4, 6.

27. Cited in Harvey, *The Historian and the Believer*, 111.

28. Foundationalism is the theory that knowledge rests on a foundation of indubitable or highly probable beliefs, from which further beliefs can be inferred. In modern times, these foundations were either empirical (e.g., sense experience) or rational (e.g., logic, geometry). Only the former, of course, would be of interest to the historical critic. I discuss criticisms of foundationalist epistemology below.

29. According to Phillips, "criticism of the Bible today . . . can no longer be thought apart from the institutional and ideological agendas which . . . often as not remain undisclosed, suppressed" ("Introduction," *Semeia* 51 [1990]: 2); cf. Moore's comment that today it is our methods of exegesis, not the text, that need to be demythologized.

30. Phillips, "Exegesis As Critical Praxis," 11.

31. Christopher Norris, *What's Wrong With Postmodernism?* 95.

32. Wright, *The New Testament and the People of God*, 60.

33. Hirsch, "The Politics of Theories of Interpretation," 243. Kathleen Boone objects to this analogy on the grounds that Hirsch's wager, unlike Pascal's, is not susceptible to verification—"unless Hirsch has postulated some literary-critical afterlife of which I'm unaware" (*The Bible Tells Them So: The Discourse of Protestant Fundamentalism* [Albany: SUNY Press, 1989], 68]). And if we cannot verify objective meaning, then indeterminacy remains lodged in the heart of our literary theory, a stubborn fog that refuses to lift.

34. For an introduction to this approach, see Kelly Clark, *Return to Reason* (Grand Rapids: Eerdmans, 1990).

35. Plantinga, "Augustinian Christian Philosophy," 296.

36. The outstanding representative of naturalism in philosophy is Willard Quine, who has applied his theory to the question of language often, most notably in *Word and Object* (Cambridge, Mass.: Harvard Univ. Press, 1960) and *Pursuit of Truth* (Cambridge, Mass.: Harvard Univ. Press, 1990). See also Steven Pinker, *The Language Instinct: How the Mind Creates Language*.

37. Plantinga, "Augustinian Christian Philosophy," 303. "There is no such thing as *the* way the world is; there are instead many different versions" (ibid.).

38. Alvin Plantinga, *Warrant and Proper Function*, 14. See ch. 5 above on the design plan of language.

39. For a helpful introduction, see Keith Lehrer, *Thomas Reid* (New York: Routledge, 1989). Reid was an eighteenth-century Scottish thinker who sought to refute his compatriot David Hume's skepticism.

40. Lehrer comments: "It is as a first principle of our nature that we trust our faculties" (*Thomas Reid*, 18).

41. See Plantinga, *Warrant*, 75n16 and 135n18. Plantinga argues that in normal circumstances, we do not have any trouble learning what someone means when he or she points to a rabbit and says "rabbit." Meaning is only indeterminate if (a) one's cognitive faculties are not functioning properly or (b) one's cognitive environment is polluted.

42. Plantinga acknowledges that it is possible (though highly improbable) that I am the victim of a deceiving demon. It need not follow that I am unjustified in my beliefs, only that I do not have "the sort of certainty Descartes sought" (*Warrant*, 76). Yet Plantinga's whole point is that knowledge does not require Cartesian certainty.

43. Gundry, *Mark*, 17.

44. Calvin's note on 2 Pet 1:20, in Joseph Haroutunian, ed., *Calvin:Commentaries*, The Library of Christian Classics (Philadelphia: Westminster, 1958), 89.

45. Duff, *Intention, Agency, and Criminal Liability*, 129–30.

46. C. A. J. Coady, *Testimony: A Philosophical Study* (Oxford: Clarendon, 1992), vii.

47. "Essay on the Intellectual Powers of Man," in *Thomas Reid's Inquiry and Essays*, ed. R. Beanblossom and K. Lehrer (Indianapolis: Hackett, 1983), 281.

48. Plantinga, *Warrant*, 33.

49. Credulity works best when people tell the truth. Indeed, God's design plan for our cognitive faculties involves the whole human community.

50. There are other factors involved in trust besides gullibility: "We may simply recognize that the standard warning signs of deceit, confusion, or mistake are not present" (Coady, *Testimony*, 47).

51. For a fuller exposition of this point and of the argument that follows, see my "The Hermeneutics of I-Witness Testimony," 366–87.

52. Dennis Nineham, "Eye-Witness Testimony and the Gospel Tradition. III" *Journal of Theological Studies* 11 (1960): 258.

53. C. A. J. Coady, *Testimony*.

54. Plantinga, *Warrant*, 77. Of course, we learn to qualify our inclination to believe on the basis of experience or because of our judgment that the cognitive environment is polluted (e.g., we learn to distrust the campaign promises of politicians). Plantinga admits that testimony alone is not the strongest warrant for belief. If no one has non-testimonial evidence for the claim in question, then the whole believing community is in trouble: "A testimonial chain is no stronger than its weakest link" (*Warrant*, 84).

55. Coady, *Testimony*, 148.

56. For a complete analysis of testimony as an illocutionary act, see Coady, *Testimony*, ch. 2.

57. Coady, *Testimony*, 154. It is important to remember that both history and fiction can be forms of testimony: the one to what has happened, to the world as it was; the other to a vision of what could be, to the world as it might or ought to be.

58. Francis Fiorenza, *Foundational Theology: Jesus and the Church* (New York: Crossroad, 1986), 41.

59. Plantinga, *Warrant*, 78.

60. David Tracy, *Blessed Rage for Order*, 25.

61. A recent academic conference attributed some thirty meanings to the story of "Little Red Riding-Hood."

62. Cited in Juhl, *Interpretation*, 209.

63. Ibid., 213.

64. Ricoeur, "World of the Text, World of the Reader," 496.

65. Livingstone, *Literary Knowledge*, 150.

66. Fish, *Is There a Text?* 338.

67. Juhl, *Interpretation*, 233.

68. Fish, *Is There a Text?* 338.

69. Ibid., 346. Fish's original example refers to an Eskimo reading of Faulkner's "A Rose for Emily."

70. Ibid., 347.

71. Boone, *The Bible Tells Them So*, 64. James Barr has criticized fundamentalism for similar reasons (see his *Fundamentalism*, 55–72, on harmonization).

72. Boone, *The Bible Tells Them So*, 73.

73. Ibid., 72.

74. Hauerwas, *Unleashing the Scripture*, 9.

75. Ibid., 26.

76. Ibid., 27.

77. Douglas Jacobsen, "The Calvinist-Arminian Dialectic in Evangelical Hermeneutics," *Christian Scholar's Review* 23 (1993): 72.

78. I have dealt with this general issue in "The Trials of Truth: Mission, Martyrdom, and the Epistemology of the Cross," in Andrew Kirk and Kevin Vanhoozer, ed., *To Stake a Claim: Christian Mission in Epistemological Crisis* (Maryknoll, N.Y.: Orbis, forthcoming).

79. Jacobsen, "Calvinist-Arminian Dialectic," 74.

80. Fish, *Is There a Text?* 353.

81. Jacobsen, "Calvinist-Arminian Dialectic," 76–77.

82. Ibid., 79.

83. Ibid., 80. Cf. David Tracy's proposal in *The Analogical Imagination* that rationality should take the form of conversation.

84. Wolterstorff, "Between the Pincers of Increased Diversity and Supposed Irrationality," in William J. Wainwright, ed., *God, Philosophy and Academic Culture: A Discussion Between Scholars in the AAR and the APA* (Atlanta: Scholars, 1996).

85. A point driven home to me in a seminar on Ricoeur when I had the temerity to suggest to a class of comparative literature students that there might be wrong ways to read certain texts. The unanimous response: "I can read any way I like."

86. Plantinga, "Augustinian Christian Philosophy," 295.

87. Ibid., 307

88. Much of the work of Jürgen Habermas is directed at an analysis of the ideological distortions of communicative action. The history of Israel as recounted in the Deuteronomistic history is a good example of the spiritual roots of corporate cognitive malfunction.

89. See Plantinga, *Warrant*, 9, 199ff. "Perhaps most male cats have been neutered; it hardly follows that those that haven't are abnormal and can't function properly" (201). Plantinga argues that the explanations of proper function work best in conjunction with supernatural theism.

90. Michael Dummett, for instance, believes that truth is whatever we are now warranted in asserting. Truth is relative in the sense that what we assert as true today may be false tomorrow. See his "Realism," *Synthese* 52 (1982): 55–112.

91. Wolterstorff, "Between the Pincers," 20.

92. LaFargue argues convincingly that elements in a differential system (e.g., a text) can have a determinate relation to each other even if there is no absolute "center" or foundation to the system. See his "Are Texts Determinate?" 349–54.

93. Grant Osborne also speaks of "interpretive realism," but by this he means we should be realistic about the interpretive process. Specifically, we must view the process of interpretation as "an ongoing dialogue between . . . reading communities" (*The Hermeneutical Spiral*, 413). At this point, the all-important question becomes, "How can discussion between interpretive communities be rational?" It is not at all clear how rational discussion among interpretive communities could proceed on Derridean or Fishian grounds.

94. I owe this quote, with its analogy, to Renford Bambrough, *Reason, Truth and God* (London: Methuen, 1969), 94. See also his extended use of the analogy of the landmark in his *Moral Scepticism and Moral Knowledge* (London: Routledge and Kegan Paul, 1979), ch. 8.

95. Livingstone proposes that literary critics focus on the conditions and consequences of texts. In so doing, he hopes to integrate literary studies with the other human sciences: "To arrive at even an approximately accurate understanding of the place of a work within concrete interactional systems requires a reliable knowledge of the social history in question" (*Literary Knowledge*, 255).

96. See for instance, Karl Popper, *Conjectures and Refutations: The Growth of Scientific Knowledge* (London: Routledge and Kegan Paul, 1963), and especially Imre Lakatos, ed., *Criticism and the Growth of Knowledge* (Cambridge: Cambridge Univ. Press, 1970). For two different applications of Lakatos to theological explanation, see Nancey Murphy, *Theology in an Age of Scientific Reasoning*, and Philip Clayton, *Explanation From Physics to Theology* (New Haven: Yale Univ. Press, 1989).

97. To say there is one determinate meaning is to make an "ontological" point about what meaning is. But it does not follow from the unity of meaning that there is only one method of discerning it.

98. Bambrough, *Moral Scepticism and Moral Knowledge*, 160.

99. Derrida, "Ethic of Discussion," 131 (emphasis mine); cf. LaFargue, who cites Derrida's remarks about "doubling commentary" as another example of his assumption that determinate textual meaning is accessible ("Are Texts Determinate?" 350).

100. Fox, "The Uses of Indeterminacy," 175.

101. Ibid., 190.

102. Ibid., 180.

103. Umberto Eco, *The Limits of Interpretation*, 58.

104. G. B. Caird, *New Testament Theology*, ed. and completed by L. D. Hurst (Oxford: Clarendon, 1994), 422.

105. A correct interpretation of the green's "meaning," if we can speak in such terms, is a description of the way the green really is. Good golfers are invariably hermeneutical realists.

106. Robert Bellarmine, cited by William Whitaker, *A Disputation on Holy Scripture Against the Papists*, tr. W. Fitzgerald (Cambridge, 1849), 404.

107. James Barr, "The Literal, the Allegorical, and Modern Scholarship," in *Journal for the Study of the Old Testament* 44 (1989): 3.

108. Cf. John Macquarrie's free rendering of John 1:1 "Fundamental to everything is meaning . . ." ("God and the World: One Reality or Two?" *Theology* 75 [1972]: 400). To believe in God is to believe that the world is set within a wider context in which it has determinate meaning.

109. The notion that Jesus Christ only appeared to have a physical body is known as the "Docetic heresy," from the Greek verb "appear" (*dokeō*).

110. Alternate translations of Hebrews 1:3 include "the express image of his person" (KJV), "the stamp of God's very being" (NEB), "the very stamp of his nature" (RSV), and "the exact representation of his being" (NIV). The Greek term *homoousios* comes from the Nicene creed, which affirmed the Son's literal deity.

111. Paul speaks of "his body of flesh" (Col. 1:22, RSV), John of his coming "in the flesh" (1 John 4:2). There are also numerous other proofs of Jesus' real physical existence, such as his eating, sleeping, tiring, bleeding, and dying.

112. *Westminster Confession of Faith*, 1.9.

113. Barr, "Literality," *Faith and Philosophy* 6 (1989): 415.

114. Barr, "The Literal, the Allegorical, and Modern Scholarship," 9.

115. Cited by Richard C. Gamble, "*Brevitas et facilitas*: Toward an Understanding of Calvin's Hermeneutics," *Westminster Theological Journal* 47 (1985): 2n5. Cf. Joseph Haroutunian, who argues that Calvin's "literalism" is oriented to recovering the author's intention; see "Introduction" to *Calvin: Commentaries* (The Library of Christian Classics; London: SCM, 1958), 27–28.

116. *Calvin's Commentaries: The Second Epistle of Paul the Apostle to the Corinthians*, tr. T. A. Smail (Edinburgh: Oliver and Boyd, 1964), 43.

117. William Whitaker, speaking for the Reformed English church in 1588, wrote: "We affirm that there is but one true, proper and genuine sense of scripture, arising from the words rightly understood, which we call the literal: and we contend that allegories . . . are not various senses, but various applications and accommodations of that one meaning" (*Disputation on Holy Scripture*, tr. W. Fitzgerald [Cambridge, 1849], 404).

118. Frei, *Eclipse of Biblical Narrative*, 11. Barr disputes this characterization of critical scholarship. He contends that biblical critics have used the literal sense as a means for getting to the "theological sense," that is, "the theology that operated in the minds of those who created the biblical literature" ("The Literal, the Allegorical, and Modern Scholarship," 12).

119. Barr goes so far as to compare biblical criticism with allegorism, though "critical" allegorical interpretation must be (1) contextually defensible and (2) culturally appropriate, rather than arbitrary, as was its ancient counterpart (see his "The Literal, the Allegorical, and Modern Scholarship").

120. My argument is that, just as historical critics cannot read off the divine intention from a reconstruction of the events of Jesus' life, so they cannot read off the author's intention from a reconstruction of the text's original situation and history of composition. In both cases, the context that alone delivers the literal sense (the sense the words or acts had for the agent doing them) is the final form of the text itself. *Scripture* interprets Scripture.

121. I will return to Ramm's charge in ch. 7 below.

122. Maurice Wiles, "Origen As Biblical Scholar," *The Cambridge History of the Bible* (Cambridge: Cambridge Univ. Press, 1970), 1:470.

123. Rowan Williams, "The Literal Sense," *Modern Theology* 7 (1990): 124.

124. Frei's verdict is clear: "It cannot be said often and emphatically enough that liberals and fundamentalists are siblings under the skin in identifying or rather confusing ascriptive as well as descriptive literalism about Jesus at the level of understanding the text, with ascriptive and descriptive literalism at the level of knowing historical reality" (*Types of Christian Theology* [New Haven: Yale Univ. Press, 1992], 84).

125. Ibid., 11. Frei notes that the consensus covers this basic identification of Jesus as the ascriptive subject of the Gospels, but not the "reality status" of Jesus. That is, while the tradition is clear that the Gospels are about Jesus (and not something or someone else), it is not clear about what kind of subject "Jesus" is (e.g., a historically factual person or a character in a narrative plot).

126. Bruce Marshall, "Meaning and Truth in Narrative Interpretation: A Reply to George Schner," *Modern Theology* 8 (1992): 176.

127. Ibid.

128. Ibid., 178–79.

129. Frei, "The 'Literal Reading' of Biblical Narrative in the Christian Tradition: Does It Stretch or Will It Break?" in *The Bible and the Narrative Tradition*, ed. Frank McConnell (Oxford: Oxford Univ. Press, 1986), 39.

130. Frei, following George Lindbeck, terms this "intratextuality," and he opposes it to "extratextuality." See Lindbeck, *The Nature of Doctrine*.

131. Ultimately, Frei appeals in his defense of literal interpretation to community consensus; throughout Western church history, the literal sense has been accorded primacy. It was the community that agreed not to deny literal ascriptions to Jesus (e.g., that Jesus came in the flesh). Frei acknowledges that, had Gnosticism won the day, the spiritual reading would be the "plain" meaning. Frei thus comes close to endorsing Fish's account of how interpretations are generated. In this case, the church's rule of faith functions as a rule for interpretive practice. It was only at the time of the Reformation, Frei avers, that the literal sense became authoritative in its own right apart from an interpretive tradition ("Literal Reading," 42).

132. Paul Noble, "The *Sensus Literalis*: Jowett, Childs, and Barr," *Journal of Theological Studies* 54 (1993): 15.

133. See Brevard Childs, "The *Sensus Literalis* of Scripture: An Ancient and Modern Problem," in H. Donner et al., ed., *Beiträge zur alttestamentlichen Theologie* (Göttingen: Vandenhoeck and Ruprecht, 1977), 80–93.

134. Cf. Ramm, who contends that the systematic teaching of Scripture "is in its final intention" (*Protestant Biblical Interpretation*, 175).

135. Fish, *Is There a Text?* 338.

136. Ibid., 347.

137. Much has been made recently of the inadequacy of language to speak of God. In an important sense, however, we can say more than what our individual words can name. The noun is not the basic unit of meaning; this privilege goes to the sentence, which has been described as the infinite use of finite means. Where individual words cannot "name" or identify God, sentences can succeed in referring beyond empirical boundaries. The Gospels, for example, use ordinary human language to tell the story of God made a human being.

138. Crossan suggested that Derrida's thought lends itself to negative theology (*Cliffs of Fall* [New York: Seabury, 1980]). Kevin Hart, on the other hand, argues that Derrida is neither a positive nor a negative theologian (*The Trespass of the Sign*, 184–86).

139. Hart, "Poetics of the Negative," 317.

140. According to Charles Martindale, the doctrine of the Incarnation corresponds to the central paradox about interpretation, namely, "that any text has to be treated *both as transhistorical and as contingent on a particular moment of history*" (*Redeeming the Text* [Cambridge; Cambridge Univ. Press, 1993], 104).

141. Hart, "The Poetics of the Negative," 286. I am indebted to Stephen Noll for calling my attention to the trinitarian aspects of the literal sense, in his "Reading the Bible As the Word of God," *Churchman* 107 (1993): 227–53.

142. Cf. Morris Inch, "The Place of the Incarnation in Biblical Interpretation," in Samuel J. Schutz and Morris A. Inch, ed., *Interpreting the Word of God* (Chicago: Moody, 1976), 162–77.

143. Christology is, again, the key. One cannot read divine revelation off of the body of Jesus. It is only in other contexts, on higher descriptive levels, that we can see Jesus as the Christ and as the Son of God. "Christ" supervenes on "Jesus." His divinity cannot be reduced to his humanity, but it cannot be discussed apart from it either.

144. "The heart of deconstructionists' strategies . . . lies in conflating that which may be said of a word regarded under the aspect of *langue* with that which is true of it under the aspect of *parole*" (Wendell Harris, *Interpretive Acts*, 25).

145. Conversely, to ignore the role of linguistic conventions is to succumb to hermeneutic "spiritism," a charge leveled by some of his critics at Barth, for whom the Bible only becomes the Word of God through a gracious movement of the Spirit. Yet there is also contrary evidence that Barth does not bypass the letter of the text altogether. See the section on perspicuity below.

146. Searle, *Expression and Meaning*, 77.

147. A parable—an extended metaphor—"always has a literal meaning and an intended figurative meaning that is supposed to be as plain to the initiates as the literal meaning" (Mark Gaipa and Robert Scholes, "On the Very Idea of a Literal Meaning," in *Literary Theory After Davidson*, 169–70).

148. I am indebted to Stephen Noll's threefold treatment of the literal sense in "Reading the Bible As the Word of God," though I have modified it somewhat. The three aspects also correspond to Sternberg's three main categories in his *Poetics of Biblical Narrative*: the historical, aesthetic, and ideological, as well as to the speech act concepts of propositional content, illocutionary force, and perlocutionary significance.

149. Francis Watson concurs. Our knowledge of reality is often mediated through texts; our knowledge of Jesus Christ always is. Watson labels this position "intratextual realism" (*Text, Church, and World*, 152).

150. Ibid., 152.

151. Iain Provan, *1 & 2 Kings* (Sheffield: Sheffield Academic Press, 1997), ch. 6 (esp. 99–107).

152. Stephen Noll suggests that those interested in the literal sense should ask not only, "What happened?" but "Where is it all headed?" ("Reading the Bible," 237). Rowan Williams agrees: "We might try reconceiving the literal sense of Scripture as an eschatological sense. To read diachronically the history that we call a history of salvation is to 'read' our own time in the believing community . . . as capable of being integrated into such a history" ("The Literal Sense of Scripture," 132).

153. M. M. Bakhtin, *Speech Genres and Other Late Essays*, 4.

154. See esp. Gary Saul Morson and Caryl Emerson, *Mikhail Bakhtin: Creation of a Prosaics* (Palo Alto: Stanford Univ. Press, 1990), ch. 7.

155. In considering the relation of the two Testaments, Calvin says that the Old Testament is "literal" and the New Testament is "spiritual" (*Institutes*, 2.11.7–8). Yet he also maintains that the substance of the testimony (e.g., to the covenant of grace) is the same in both Testaments, though the New Testament makes what is implicit and indeterminate in the Old Testament more explicit and specific, and hence more glorious (see *Institute*, 2.10.2, 23).

156. Noll, "Reading the Bible As the Word of God," 234.

157. Ibid., 232.

158. Unlike Barth, I do not believe the Bible refers to Jesus Christ only by a miracle of God's grace. The human illocutionary act, at the level of the canon, is already "testifying." Barth confuses, I believe, the illocutionary and perlocutionary aspects of communicative action (see my "God's Mighty Speech Acts: The Doctrine of Scripture Today," in Philip E. Satterthwaite and David F. Wright, ed., *A Pathway Into the Holy Scripture* [Grand Rapids: Eerdmans, 1994] 143-81).

Hunsinger observes that for Barth, the subject of the biblical narratives is the living presence or address of God (*How to Read Karl Barth*, 49; cf. p. 172 for a formulation of the relation of the cognitive and performative dimensions of Scripture that is closer to my own). Note, however, that if critical interpretation means, as Barth suggests, penetrating to what the text is really about, then we can say, in this sense only, that the literal sense is the critical sense.

159. Indeed, the burden of the present chapter is to redeem characteristic Reformation themes—the priority of the literal sense, the clarity of Scripture, the priesthood of all believers, *sola Scriptura*—by recasting them in terms of a theory of communicative action.

160. Stanley Hauerwas correctly sees the parallel between the so-called "papists" and Fish's authoritative interpretive communities. See Hauerwas, "Stanley Fish, the Pope, and the Bible," in *Unleashing the Scriptures*, ch. 2.

161. Luther spoke of the *claritas Scripturae*, Calvin of its one (*simplex*) meaning.

162. Luther objects to Erasmus's claim that it is impossible to reach firm interpretive conclusions that can lead to action because the teaching of Scripture is indeterminate and uncertain. In particular, Luther is reacting to Erasmus's skepticism concerning the clarity of the Bible's teaching concerning free will. According to Thiselton, "what Luther attacks is the denial of the possibility of making *truth-claiming assertions* on the basis of the biblical writings" (*New Horizons*, 182).

163. Thiselton notes that for the Reformers, the belief in the clarity of Scripture implied neither an indifference to interpretive theory nor an indifference to interpretive tradition (Thiselton, *New Horizons*, 179).

164. Berkouwer speaks of a shift after the Reformation by which clarity came to be associated with words rather than the message: "In this manner Scripture is isolated from its context of salvation, and perspicuity is no longer religious clarity . . . [but] a theoretical and verbal perspicuity that the natural mind can appreciate and perceive. . . . According to the Reformers, the force behind this connection of message and words was the power of the Spirit" (*Holy Scripture* [Grand Rapids: Eerdmans, 1975], 275). I will discuss the all-important relation of Word and Spirit in the following chapter.

165. Ramm, *Protestant Biblical Interpretation*, 114.

166. Today it pertains to the scientific study of languages, but historically it had to do with the broader program of understanding literary texts: "The true philological spirit . . . in biblical interpretation has its goal to discover the original meaning and intention of the text. Its goal is *exegesis*—to lead the meaning out of the text, and shuns *eisegesis*—bringing a meaning to the text" (Ramm, *Protestant Biblical Interpretation*, 115).

167. Luther admits that many texts in Scripture are obscure, but this is so not because of the unclarity of their author or their subject matter, but rather "because of our ignorance of their vocabulary and grammar" ("On the Bondage of the Will," in E. Gordon Rupp and Philip S. Watson, ed., *Luther and Erasmus: Free Will and Salvation* [Philadelphia: Westminster, 1969], 110).

168. Thiselton (following Beisser, Berkouwer, and Ramm) distinguishes Luther's view of the clarity of Scripture from a context-free "obviousness" of meaning. External clarity is relative to the goal of mediating Christ. It is a functional capacity for mediating Christ (*New Horizons*, 184–85). Berkouwer thinks the discussion about perspicuity later became a matter of words instead of salvific function (*Holy Scripture*, 275). For a fuller discussion of Luther's understanding of the perspicuity of Scripture, see Friedrich Beisser, *Claritas Scripturae bei Martin Luther* (Göttingen: Vandenhoeck & Ruprecht, 1966).

169. Thiselton, *New Horizons*, 182.

170. "It is true that for many people much remains abstruse; but this is not due to the obscurity of Scripture, but to the blindness or indolence of those who will not take the trouble to look at the very clearest truth" (Luther, "On the Bondage of the Will," 111).

171. *Calvin: Commentaries*, Library of Christian Classics, 88.

172. Luther, "On the Bondage of the Will," 159.

173. The Council of Trent asserted the church's right "to judge regarding the true sense and interpretation of holy Scriptures" (Denzinger, *The Sources of Catholic Dogma* [1957], sec. 786).

174. Berkouwer comments: "Concerning the confession of perspicuity, one can state without exaggeration that in practical life many would feel more at home with the statement in II Peter 3:16 about Paul's letters: 'There are some things in them hard to understand . . .'" (*Holy Scripture*, 269).

175. See Watson, ed., *The Open Text*, 3–4.

176. A conceptual scheme is a set of concepts that serve as a framework or mental map for interpreting human experience, the world, or in the case of hermeneutics, the text.

177. Hilary Putnam expresses it well: "There is no God's Eye point of view that we can know or usefully imagine; there are only the various points of view of actual persons reflecting various interests and purposes that their descriptions and theories subserve" (*Reason, Truth and History*, 50). Putnam proposes a "realism with a human face," an "internal realism," which maintains that we have access to reality (and truth) but only from inside a theory of description. For Putnam, objects do not exist independently of descriptive schemes. The notion that meaning is the result of a reader's encounter with a text may find philosophical support from Putnam's theory of internal realism.

178. Barry Unsworth, *Morality Play* (London: Penguin, 1996), 64.

179. Norris, *What's Wrong With Postmodernism?* 93.

180. Norwood Hanson, *Pattern of Discovery* (Cambridge: Cambridge Univ. Press, 1958).

181. Cited in Livingstone, *Literary Knowledge*, 93.

182. Donald Davidson, "On the Very Idea of a Conceptual Scheme," in *Relativism: Cognitive and Moral*, ed. Michael Krausz and Jack W. Meiland (Notre Dame: Univ. of Notre Dame Press, 1982).

183. According to John W. Cooper, God's created order is the common context within which various interpretive schemes take shape. Understanding the created order, however, is not an exercise of pure reason but involves commitment-based perspectives. Cooper advocates a "perspectival realism" ("Reformed Apologetics and the Challenge of Post-Modern Relativism," *Calvin Theological Journal* 28 [1993]: 108–20).

184. See Thomas Kent, "Interpretation and Triangulation: A Davidsonian Critique of Reader-Oriented Literary Theory" in *Literary Theory After Davidson*, 37–58.

185. Davidson's remarks on "triangulation" are relevant here. We only know our own minds—our language and our concepts—through "triangulation" with other language users and the objects that constitute our shared world (see Kent, "Interpretation and Triangulation"). Davidson's philosophy is only now beginning to be appropriated by literary theorists. For an overview of how Davidson's critique of relativism has been applied in literary theory, see Michael Fisher, "Davidson and the Politics of Relativism: A Response," in *Literary Theory After Davidson*, 286–94.

186. Reed Way Dasenbrock, "Do We Write the Text We Read?" in *Literary Theory After Davidson*, 29.

187. Ibid., 28.

188. Ibid., 31. Cf. C. S. Lewis' comment that we read in order to seek "an enlargement of our being. . . . We want to see with other eyes, to imagine with other imaginations, to feel with other hearts, as well as with our own" (*An Experiment in Criticism*, 137). Encountering another point of view is only possible if there is a point of view in the text other than my own. That, in turn, implies that *all* texts have something of the character of the witness about them.

189. Ibid.

190. Cooper, "Reformed Apologetics and the Challenge of Post-Modern Relativism," 115.

191. Because, as Frei points out, they share a primary concern for the unsubstitutable significance of Jesus Christ, the subject of the Gospel narratives.

192. I rely here especially on Linda Trinkhaus Zagzebski, *Virtues of the Mind: An Inquiry Into the Nature of Virtue and the Ethical Foundations of Knowledge* (Cambridge: Cambridge Univ. Press, 1996). In ch. 7 I will treat the ethics of interpretation at greater length. In the present chapter I am primarily concerned with the ethical aspects of literary knowledge. My account of what I call the "interpretive virtues," however, bridges both chapters.

193. I have in mind Thomas Kuhn's work, especially his notion that particular scientific communities work with diverse "paradigms" or descriptive frameworks. See his *The Structure of Scientific Revolutions*, 2d ed. (Chicago: Univ. of Chicago Press, 1970). For Kuhn's significance for hermeneutics, see Vern S. Poythress, *Science and Hermeneutics* (Grand Rapids: Zondervan, 1988), chs. 3–4.

194. Paul Feyerabend makes a case for epistemological anarchy. Knowledge is "an ever-increasing ocean of mutually incompatible . . . alternatives" (*Against Method*, 30). We do not have visions of the world so much as versions, versions dictated by whatever assumptions happen to prevail at a given time.

195. Hirsch, following the philosopher of science Karl Popper, is clear that validity in interpretation is a function of testing and correcting our interpretive schemata. For Popper, science is a critical method insofar as it tests these preunderstandings or "conjectures" (see his *Conjectures and Refutations*). Hirsch, too, compares textual interpretation to the process of testing conjectures (see his *Aims of Interpretation*, 32–33).

196. Roy Bhaskar, *Philosophy and the Idea of Freedom* (Oxford: Blackwell, 1991), 30–31. Bhaskar divides his book into two parts: "Anti-Rorty" and "For Critical Realism."

197. Norris, *What's Wrong With Postmodernism?* 108.

198. Ibid., 106.

199. Livingstone, *Literary Knowledge*, 82.

200. Ibid., 63.

201. Ibid., 87.

202. Roy Bhaskar, *Scientific Realism and Human Emancipation* (London: Verso, 1986), 54.

203. Harty Field, "Realism and Relativism," *Journal of Philosophy* 84 (1982): 553.

204. Farrell, *Subjectivity, Realism, and Postmodernism*, 167.

205. Ibid., 169.

206. Ibid., 167.

207. Ibid., 129.

208. *The Work of William Tyndale*, ed. Gervasse E. Duffield (Philadelphia: Fortress, 1965), 337.

209. Gundry, *Mark*, 4.

210. This example is taken from Paul Churchland, *Scientific Realism and the Plasticity of Mind* (Cambridge: Cambridge Univ. Press, 1979), 44.

211. Stein Haugom Olsen, *The End of Literary Theory* (Cambridge: Cambridge Univ. Press, 1987), 53–72.

212. Livingstone, *Literary Knowledge*, ch. 7.

213. Zagzebski, *Virtues of the Mind*, 49.

214. Annette Barnes concurs: "I have assumed in anti-Derridean fashion that what an artist intended is relevant information if one wants to determine what's in a work, what the point is" (*On Interpretation: A Critical Analysis*, 166).

215. Altieri here follows Quentin Skinner, who recognizes the difference "between the achievement of a meaning which reveals intentions and the intention to mean which may not be realized" (Altieri, *Act and Quality*, 146).

216. Ibid., 146.

217. Note that this formulation depsychologizes Hirsch's account of the author's intention as a norm for interpretive validity.

218. LaFargue makes the interesting observation that the cause of interpretive conflict is not the indeterminacy of the biblical texts "but rather the fact that their meaning is so determinate and particular that no paraphrase can substitute for engagement with the words themselves and their particular background" ("Are Texts Determinate?" 354). No paraphrase quite captures the matter and energy of the original. Description will never be a substitute for an engagement with the texts for oneself.

219. "Incommensurable" means that two descriptions or theories are so different that no one standard of measurement or evaluation could be applied to both.

220. Richard Wollheim, *Painting As an Art*, 18.

221. Livingstone, *Literature and Rationality*, 78.

222. Jacob L. Mey, *Pragmatics: An Introduction* (Oxford: Blackwell, 1993), 148.

223. I myself am not as pessimistic about this as others seem to be, however. Lanser and Pratt have made a good start in applying speech act theory to texts, and Neufield has applied some of their techniques to 1 John.

224. I discuss some of these in the next section, on literary genre.

225. Paul Ricoeur, *Time and Narrative* (Chicago: Univ. of Chicago Press, 1984), 1:ix.

226. Barnes, *On Interpretation*, 57.

227. Ibid., 56.

228. Fully to answer this question would require us to compare, and perhaps rank, different values. I cannot here review the ethical and theological reasons here for preferring "truth" to "entertainment." In the present context, I am assuming that knowledge is a value. In the following chapter I will support my theory of interpretation by appealing to justice (toward the author) as well.

229. See Snaider, *The Narrative Act*.

230. Altieri, *Act and Quality*, 257.

231. Stout, "What Is the Meaning of a Text?" 6. Livingstone, similarly, believes the question, "What does it mean?" is too imprecise (see his *Literary Knowledge*, ch. 6).

232. John Barton, *Reading the Old Testament: Method in Biblical Study*, 205.

233. Stout, "The Relativity of Interpretation," 112.

234. See "Reductionism," in Ted Hondreich, ed., *The Oxford Companion to Philosophy* (Oxford: Oxford Univ. Press, 1995), 750–51.

235. Peacocke, *Theology for a Scientific Age*, 39.

236. A 1996 *Time* article explored attempts to explain adultery in terms of evolutionary biology. If infidelity could be exhaustively explained in terms of one's biochemistry, then a whole level of discourse—that of morality—would effectively be eliminated.

237. Peacocke, *Theology for a Scientific Age*, 40.

238. For a fuller discussion of socio-biology, see ibid., 226.

239. Ibid., 41.

240. Sin corrupts this medium along with all other aspects of the human being. Satan, insofar as he interprets God's speech for his own devices, may perhaps be viewed as the first radical reader-response critic—the first to replace the author's voice with his own: "Did God say?" Theological non-realism is ultimately a rebellious protest against having to answer to any other voice than our own.

241. Peacocke, *Theology for a Scientific Age*, 224–25.

242. Ibid., 225.

243. Ibid., 244.

244. A text may be a joint product, or even an international one, but this only serves to complicate, not contradict, the essential picture I am here sketching.

245. Peter Morea, *Personality: An Introduction to the Theories of Psychology* (London: Penguin, 1990), 154–55).

246. Peacocke, *Theology for a Scientific Age*, 246.

247. The essential condition of a speech act is that which makes it *count as* a promise, assertion, warning, etc.

248. Mey, *Pragmatics*, 55. Possible exceptions to this would include people who talk to or write for themselves only. Even here, however, I would maintain that language fulfills a communicative purpose, insofar as it allows a speaker or writer to relate to himself or herself as another.

249. See, for instance, James S. Ackerman, "Jonah," in Alter and Kermode, ed., *The Literary Guide to the Bible*, 234–43.

250. Eco, *Limits of Interpretation*, 57.

251. J. I. Packer states that his goal is "a total, integrated view built out of the biblical material in such a way that, if the writers of the various books knew what I had made of what they taught, they would nod their heads and say that I had got them right" (Packer, "In Quest of Canonical Interpretation," in Robert K. Johnston, ed. *The Use of the Bible in Theology: Evangelical Options* [Atlanta: John Knox, 1985], 47). For a slightly different account of the relation of text, descriptions, and intentions, see Michael Baxandall, *Patterns of Intention: On the Historical Explanation of Pictures*.

252. Extra-textual tests for the accuracy of our descriptions and ascriptions might include: consistency with other literary acts by the same author; statements the author may have made about his or her intention; capacities and resources of the culture to which the author belongs (i.e., to eliminate anachronistic descriptions).

253. On the differences between description and ascription, see Joel Feinberg, *Doing and Deserving*, 139ff.; see also J. R. Lucas: "To be responsible is to be answerable. . . . I can equally well say I am answerable for an action or accountable for it. And if I am to answer, I must answer a question; the question is 'Why did you do it?' and in answering that question I give an account of my action" (*Responsibility* [Oxford: Oxford Univ. Press, 1993], 5).

254. Cited in Duff, *Intention, Agency and Criminal Liability*, 29.

255. Altieri, *Act and Quality*, 158.

256. Altieri assigns to the jury the task of determining what the meaning (e.g., intended action) was. "Significance" is analogous to the kinds of factors a judge might take into account in deciding the appropriate sentence (ibid., 159).

257. Duff, *Intention, Agency, and Criminal Liability*, 131.

258. Altieri, *Act and Quality*, 231.

259. Sternberg, *Poetics of Biblical Narrative*, 10.

260. Ibid.

261. I rely heavily in what follows on Peter Lipton, *Inference to the Best Explanation* (London: Routledge, 1991). Annette Barnes proposes something similar, namely, that interpretive claims can be defeated by pointing to relevant counter-possibilities (*On Interpretation*, 116).

262. Lipton, *Inference to the Best Explanation*, 35.

263. Ibid., 59.

264. Ibid., 186.

265. Peacocke, *Theology for a Scientific Age*, 106. Peacocke is here speaking of the postulate of a Creator God as the best explanation of all that is, but in relation to the world of the text, authors are creators too.

266. See Alasdair MacIntyre, *Whose Justice? Which Rationality?* (London: Duckworth, 1988), esp. chs. 18–20. MacIntyre can be seen as adapting a fallibilist epistemology and apply-

ing it to the history of social traditions. Nancey Murphy notes the parallels between Lakatos and MacIntyre in her *Beyond Liberalism and Fundamentalism: How Modern and Postmodern Philosophy Set the Theological Agenda* (Valley Forge, Pa.: Trinity International, 1996), ch. 4.

267. Bambrough, *Moral Scepticism*, 104.

268. Livingstone, *Literary Knowledge*, 34.

269. Cf. Wendell Harris: "I began to ask what sort of theory might be erected by asking not *whether* communication is possible, but, given that we do communicate, *how* this occurs" (*Interpretive Acts*, viii).

270. According to Pannenberg's version of the hermeneutical circle, the part-whole dynamic in which understanding seeks to orient itself also characterizes human history.

271. G. B. Caird, *New Testament Theology*, 423.

272. M. Bakhtin, *Speech Genres*, 80.

273. Gabel and Wheeler, *The Bible As Literature*, 16.

274. In theology, Karl Barth and T. F. Torrance have insisted that objectivity is a matter of allowing our inquiry to be guided by the nature of the reality under study. Literary knowledge, as I am presenting it, works both with such a material condition and with a formal procedure (viz., critical testing and the logic of abduction). I will argue below that biblical testimony is a form of literary and theological knowledge that responds to both conditions.

275. So Alistair Fowler: "In receiving a work, the reader has to construct every feature in its level, by interpreting signals at a lower level of organization. From ink marks we infer letters . . ." (*Kinds of Literature: An Introduction to the Theory of Genres and Modes* [Oxford: Clarendon, 1982], 257).

276. Note that Fowler, in his authoritative study, acknowledges the centrality of authorial intention: "It is simply the realized intention that construction aims to recover" (ibid., 256). It is also worth noting that Fowler dedicated his book to E. D. Hirsch!

277. Sadly, only his work on tragedy, the *Poetics*, survives.

278. See the article on "Genre" in M. H. Abrams, *A Glossary of Literary Terms*, 70–71.

279. Mey, *Pragmatics*, 57.

280. Chomsky believers that speakers possess an innate grammatical ability, though he attributes this mental capacity to human biology rather than to the design plan of language. See Maria-Luisa Rivero, "Chomsky," in *Encyclopedia of Contemporary Literary Theory*, 271–73.

281. See Jonathan Culler, *Structuralist Poetics*.

282. Hirsch, *Validity in Interpretation*, 70.

283. Bakhtin coins the term "speech genre" to refer to the everyday uses of language that fill everyday life. The nature and forms of speech genres are as diverse as the forms of social activity with which they are associated (e.g., grocery lists, military orders, parliamentary motions, medical diagnoses, etc.). Whereas for Wittgenstein genres may be considered language games of a higher order, for Bakhtin languages games may be viewed as genres of a lower order. See Bakhtin, *Speech Genres and Other Late Essays*.

284. James L. Bailey, "Genre Analysis," in Joel Green, ed., *Hearing the New Testament*, 200.

285. David Kelsey, paraphrasing Alasdair MacIntyre, in *To Understand God Truly: What's Theological About a Theological School* (Louisville, Ky.: Westminster/John Knox, 1992), 118.

286. This is a very different form of play from that advocated by deconstruction. There the "play" had no rules; the play I am describing is rule-governed.

287. See Werner Jeanrond, *Text and Interpretation*, 94–119.

288. Berkouwer, *Holy Scripture*, 131.

289. See the survey of ancient and contemporary approaches to genre in Frans de Bruyn, "Genre Criticism," *Encyclopedia of Contemporary Literary Theory*, 79–85.

290. Fowler, *Kinds of Literature*, 22.

291. Ibid., 23.

292. Ibid., 31.

293. *New Horizons*, 261 (italics his).

294. There is a long-standing dispute about the genre of the Gospels. Could it be that they represent a distinctive and unique literary form—that they are *sui generis*, a genre to themselves—because something distinctive and unique had to be said? See C. H. Talbert, *What Is a Gospel? The Genre of the Canonical Gospels* (Philadelphia: Fortress, 1977); P. L. Shuler, *A Genre for the Gospels: The Biographical Character of Matthew* (Philadelphia: Fortress, 1982); David Aune, *The New Testament in Its Literary Environment* (Philadelphia: Westminster, 1987).

295. Fowler, *Kinds of Literature*, 41.

296. Ibid., 42.

297. Richard Ohmann, "Speech Acts and the Definition of Literature," 13 (italics his).

298. Pratt, *Toward a Speech Act Theory of Literary Discourse*, 136–49.

299. Lanser explicitly acknowledges her indebtedness to speech act theory in *The Narrative Act*, 7–8.

300. On point of view, see the classic work by Wayne Booth, *The Rhetoric of Fiction*, and M. H. Abrams, "Point of View," in *A Glossary of Literary Terms*, 142–45. No matter what we are told or shown by narrative, says Booth, "the author's judgment is always present" (p. 20). The aspect of point of view means that storytelling is also testifying.

301. The communication is indirect, for the real author's views may not coincide with those of the implied author. Nevertheless, the real author does communicate with readers, thanks to the textually mediated voice of the implied author.

302. Indeed, it is precisely its focus on the tie between an utterance and its social context that commends speech act philosophy to Lanser's examination of point of view in literature. A speech act analysis reveals that point of view "expresses and structures the relationship of speaker to the verbal act, the audience, and the propositional material" (*The Narrative Act*, 79). However, in my opinion Lanser overestimates the extent to which the author's social situation *determines* the ideological point of view.

303. Ibid., 293. Meir Sternberg comes to much the same conclusion with regard to the literature of the Old Testament in his *The Poetics of Biblical Narrative*.

304. Ramm, *Protestant Biblical Interpretation*, 145.

305. Hirsch, *Validity in Interpretation*, 79.

306. Ibid., 76; cf. Mary Gerhart, "Generic Competence in Biblical Hermeneutics," *Semeia* 43 (1988).

307. On the centrality of genre for biblical interpretation, see Grant Osborne, *The Hermeneutical Spiral*, Part Two; and Longman, *Literary Approaches to Biblical Interpretation*, 76–83.

308. Richard B. Hays detects a "narrative sub-structure" to Paul's thinking in *The Faith of Jesus Christ* (Chico, Calif.: Scholars, 1983).

309. Neufeld, *Reconceiving Texts As Speech Acts*, 135. The act of confession involves a commitment both to factual content and to a religious stance. The act of confessing Christ "is instrumental to the formation of the self and sets in motion the overall communicative design of 1 John" (58).

310. I am currently engaged in a study of literary genre as that level of discourse that best mediates the concerns of biblical and systematic theology. See D. A. Carson and K. J. Vanhoozer, *The One, the Two, and the Many: Unity and Plurality in the Relation of Biblical and Systematic Theology* (Eerdmans, forthcoming).

311. We will return to these three aspects below. Bakhtin himself is primarily interested in the development of the novel, and the implications that the creation of this genre has for engaging with, and thinking about, human existence. Bakhtin compares Dostoyevsky with

Einstein: each enriched humanity with a whole new conceptualization of the world. See Bakhtin, *Problems of Dostoyevsky's Poetics*, ed. Caryl Emerson (Minneapolis: Univ. of Minnesota Press, 1984).

312. See Paul Ricoeur, *Time and Narratives*, 3 vols. (Chicago: Univ. of Chicago Press, 1984–88).

313. This raises problems concerning the status of philosophy and systematic theology alike. Do these represent further genres, or do they escape the generic constraints and speak about things as they are? The answer to this important question lies beyond the scope of this essay, but see Carson and Vanhoozer, *The One, the Two, and the Many* (forthcoming). Paul Ricoeur sees philosophy's task as *coordinating* between the various genres.

314. See Paul Ricoeur, *The Rule of Metaphor* (Toronto: Univ. of Toronto Press, 1977).

315. M. Bakhtin, *Speech Genres and Other Late Essays*, 5.

316. One Bakhtin commentator prefers to speak of "paradigms of communication" (see Walter L. Reed, *Dialogues of the Word: The Bible As Literature According to Bakhtin* (Oxford: Oxford Univ. Press, 1993), 47.

317. Emerson and Morson, *Mikhail Bakhtin: Creation of a Prosaics*, 276.

318. Ibid., 283.

319. Here, too, I must register a certain caution or proviso. As with Reid, Plantinga, Bambrough, and others, so Habermas too is not explicitly concerned with literary understanding as such, though interpretation could certainly be counted as "action aimed at reaching intersubjective understanding." Note too that communicative competence involves certain pragmatic features of utterances (e.g., illocutions), unlike linguistic competence, which pertains only to *langue* (e.g., locutions).

320. See especially Jürgen Habermas, "Philosophy As Stand-In and Interpreter," in *After Philosophy*, 296–315 (esp. 310).

321. Habermas, "What Is Universal Pragmatics?" in *Communication and the Evolution of Society*, tr. Thomas McCarthy (London: Heinemann, 1979), 26.

322. Habermas, *The Philosophical Discourse of Modernity*, 199.

323. Habermas intends his analysis to fund a social theory whose centerpiece is a concept of justice based on the universal norms inherent in communicative action. See Habermas, *Justification and Application: Remarks on Discourse Ethics* (Cambridge, Mass.: MIT Press, 1993).

324. "Poetics is the systematic working or study of literature as such" (Sternberg, *Poetics of Biblical Narrative*, 2).

325. Cited in Fowler, *Kinds of Literature*, 92.

326. Ibid., 88.

327. Frans de Bruyn, "Genre Criticism," 80.

328. Medvedev, cited in Emerson and Morson, *Mikhail Bakhtin*, 273.

329. See Davidson, "A Nice Derangement of Epitaphs," in *Truth and Interpretation: Perspectives on the Philosophy of Donald Davidson*, ed. Ernest LePore (Oxford: Basil Blackwell, 1986), 433–46.

330. So Wolterstorff, *Works and Worlds of Art*.

331. Livingstone, *Literary Knowledge*, 207.

332. A. D. Nuttall, *A New Mimesis: Shakespeare and the Representation of Reality*, 53.

333. Ibid., 74.

334. Ibid., 78. Cf. C. S. Lewis on the difference between "tasting" and "seeing" ("Myth Become Fact," in *God in the Dock* [Grand Rapids: Eerdmans, 1970]). Literature for Altieri adds to our stock of real knowledge about the world insofar as it helps us to make more complex and varied discriminations about human actions: "Texts afford knowledge not because they describe particulars but because they embody ways of experiencing facts" (Altieri, *Act and Qual-*

ity, 12). Livingstone, for his part, says that texts afford knowledge because they throw light on socio-historical situations.

335. Michael Polanyi and Harry Prosch, *Meaning* (Chicago: Univ. of Chicago Press, 1975), 44.

336. N. T. Wright, *The New Testament and the People of God*, 64.

337. C. S. Lewis, *An Experiment in Criticism* (Cambridge: Cambridge Univ. Press, 1961), 138.

338. See David E. Aune, *The New Testament in Its Literary Environment* (Philadelphia: Westminster, 1987).

339. Ricoeur makes a similar proposal: Scripture contains multiple genres, which, in various ways, are all doing the same thing: "naming God" (Ricoeur, *Figuring the Sacred: Religion, Narrative and Imagination* (Minneapolis: Fortress, 1995), 224.

CHAPTER SEVEN

Reforming the Reader:
Interpretive Virtue, Spirituality,
and Communicative Efficacy

Even to judge against the text's grain, you must first judge with it:
receptivity before resistance, competent reading before liberated
counterreading, poetics before politics.

Meir Sternberg[1]

I take it to be a moral and pragmatic fact that the poem, the painting, the sonata, are prior to the act of reception, of commentary,
of valuation.

George Steiner[2]

The question, What is within the Bible? has a mortifying way of
converting itself into the opposing question, Well, what are you
looking for, and who are you, pray, who make bold to look?

Karl Barth[3]

In the two previous chapters I presented the case for hermeneutic realism and hermeneutic rationality. Hermeneutic realism claims that the author's intended meaning is "there," enacted in the text. Hermeneutic rationality maintains that the form and content of a communicative act—what it is and what it is about—can be known with relative adequacy. The author is a communicative agent and the text a communicative act with matter (propositional content) and energy (illocutionary force). Texts also have, like arrows, a certain trajectory and direction (perlocutionary aim). With respect to this third aspect, however, everything hinges on the reader's response.

"For every communicative action there is an equal and opposite communicative reaction." Well, not quite. Readers do not always behave according to Newton's third law of motion. But some kind of response is inevitable in the process of reading, even if it is only apathy. Interpretations that fall short of the reader's personal engagement with the matter and form of the text remain incomplete, short-circuited. To invoke Aristotle's concept of rhetoric: I will be interested in this chapter not with the *ethos* of the author's discourse or with the *logos* of the discourse itself, but with the *pathos* associated with reading—with the way in which texts *affect* readers.[4] If there is a meaning in the text, is there a right (and a wrong) way to respond to it? This question concerns not the production of the communicative act but its consumption or reception, not communicative agency so much as communicative efficacy. Accordingly, the focus of this chapter will be on application rather than explication, on perlocution rather than illocution, on God the Spirit rather than God the Word. After metaphysics and epistemology come the ethics of meaning and the notion of "interpretive right."

Literary knowledge is not a matter of disinterested factuality. Most authors do not write simply to convey information, but to affect their readers in some other way besides. Understanding is not simply an intellectual affair whereby one mentally registers the sense and reference of disjointed sentences. The covenant of discourse includes a moment of personal appropriation. One can read for the illocutionary point (intellectual recognition) or for the perlocutionary effect (existential transformation). In either case, the reader is never simply passive. A text is both a communicative act and the object of subsequent interpretive acts. The meaning of the text, I will claim, is something for which readers are responsible.

Do readers really have obligations towards texts, and if so, what kind? The answer to this query depends on whether or not one believes that meaning is independent of the reader's activity. Accordingly, this chapter explores the implications for the ethics of interpretation of the divide between hermeneutical realists and nonrealists. Dostoyevsky once commented, "If there is no God, then everything is permitted." A similar ethical vacuum accompanies the death of the author. If meaning is the creation of the reader, how can the text ever be something "other," with the power to affect us? If there is no fixed meaning apart from the reader's interpretive activity, then there is nothing prior to that activity to respect.

Some of the radical reader-response critics have concluded, consistently enough, that the role of the reader is to play, and to create. There is no need, they urge, to go beyond aesthetics to ethics. I resist this unhappy dichotomy between a meaning that is absolutely knowable and one that is absolutely undecidable. Neither option allows for a responsible response on the part of the reader. *My thesis is that in reading we encounter an other that calls us to respond.* With Steiner, I view this call as the moment of transcendence in interpretation; responding to the call of a voice beyond our own is precisely what makes reading a theological activity. Interestingly, deconstruction too assumes, at least rhetorically, the role of the other's champion and protector. Derrida's recent works repeatedly return to the theme of ethics. As we will see, Steiner and Derrida represent two different ways—the one theological, the other countertheological—of doing "justice" to the otherness or "alterity" of the text.

This chapter contrasts rival ethics of interpretation, each of which is inspired by a different "spirit" of interpretation—of play, of power, of peace. Reforming the reader (that is, approaching the ethics of interpretation from an explicitly theological point of view) involves five steps. First, I distinguish between the reader's using, criticizing, and "following" a text. The true reader is a disciple of the text and follows its illocutions and perlocutions in order to gain understanding. Second, I address the question of whether the reader, as one who inevitably comes to the text with certain ideological biases, can ever have a properly interpretive interest other than one motivated by some aim beyond understanding. Is there a "categorical imperative," a universal moral rule, for reading? This question leads me to distinguish, third, between interpretive goods and interpretive right, between the ethics or aims and the morality or norms of interpretation. Our reflection on the ethics of interpretation then leads us to inquire to what extent interpretive responsibility presupposes the freedom of the interpreter. Just what might interpretive freedom mean? To what extent do texts foreordain their interpretations, and to what extent is textual meaning contingent on what interpreters do? Can readers be obedient to texts and simultaneously preserve their freedom to read with a variety of aims and methods?

Finally, to what extent must a discussion of the ethics of interpretation be rooted in a theology of interpretation? To what extent, in other words, does the morality of literary knowledge presuppose a *spirituality* of literary knowledge as well? In short: to what extent is understanding—of the Bible or of any other communicative action—genuinely possible, given human fallenness, without the aid of the Holy Spirit? Can readers avoid doing interpretive violence without the aid of the Spirit of peace, without that peculiarly Pentecostal (and perlocutionary) power that Barth called the "Lord of the hearing"? Postmodern interpreters who seek to do justice to the other—to the Word—must read in the right spirit. For good readers need to have the right desires, not simply the right devices—the right interpretive virtues, not merely the appropriate hermeneutical techniques. Interpretation is ultimately a matter not only of technology or even of ethics, but rather of religion and theology. Only from the vantage point of Christian faith, perhaps, does language appear not as a system of differences that reflects political power but as a form of divinely instituted communicative action that can be performed responsibly or irresponsibly, to the glory of God or to the undoing of humanity.

THE READER AS USER, CRITIC, AND FOLLOWER

What should readers do? The following parable suggests the beginning of an answer. Hauerwas relates, in a sermon on the Emmaus road story, an anecdote about following Jesus to the cross but not onto the cross.[5] The one who follows Jesus to the cross (but no further) is an admirer; the one who takes up the cross is a disciple. The admirer, unlike the disciple, follows Jesus only up to a point. Hauerwas uses this distinction to illustrate the reaction to Jesus of the two men on the Emmaus road as well as the reader's response to the written Gospel; in both cases it is a matter of following only up to a point. The Emmaus road admirers did not recognize Jesus; he was a stranger to them. They were incapable of reading the Scripture or the situation rightly. Accordingly, the perlocutionary effect—namely, "that you may believe that Jesus is the Christ" (John 20:31)—misfires. Admirers of Jesus are able to follow the biblical testimony only up to a point; they are able neither to recognize what it means for them nor to appropriate its perlocutionary effect. Similarly, for many readers, the text is a "stranger," to be admired or followed only "up to a point." Like the Emmaus travelers, the itinerant reader may be familiar with the text without ever having a moment of recognition, without ever coming to a personal knowledge of the "strange new world of the Bible," without ever deciding whether the stranger is friend or foe.

Hauerwas's example forms part of his argument that Christians read the Bible rightly only as members of the believing interpretive community. Just as we cannot recognize Jesus simply by looking, so we cannot get the meaning of the text simply by reading: "To claim that if Jesus had joined us on the Emmaus road, we should have recognized him is not unlike claiming that in order to understand the Scripture all we have to do is pick it up and read it."[6] As Hauerwas pointedly notes, the men on the way to Emmaus knew the biblical text. They were, however, unable to apply or to appropriate it in a new situation: Jesus' risen presence. Hauerwas contends that only those who are already following (viz., members of a believing interpretive community) will have the necessary training to follow the text not only up to a point, but to the point where the text transforms the way one sees and follows.

Are readers to be admirers and followers but never critics? Should responsible readers turn off their critical faculties and willingly suspend their disbelief? Or might it not be that responsible reading requires the reader to judge the content of what is read? Is it not the case that certain texts should neither be admired nor followed, but rather rejected in disgust? And might not some perlocutionary effects prove harmful to the reader and so work against the good of humanity? How then should we read? Are some ways of reading more ethical and more responsible than others?

J. A. Appleyard argues that the ways in which we read develop from childhood to adulthood.[7] Adolescent readers read to get the message or to acquire a role model. They do not, strictly speaking, "see" the text; it is like a transparent window that looks out onto a world. The college student approaches literature and develops an interest in how it works (e.g., in poetics or rhetoric); that is, he or she comes to see the text as a screen that lets one see only this or that aspect of the world. The adult or "pragmatic" reader self-consciously chooses to use a text in one way rather than another (e.g., to escape into fantasy, to search for truth, to experience the pleasure of the text, to challenge oneself). One of the most powerful motives for reading is the desire for self-understanding, for integrating our individual experiences with the collective wisdom of our culture: "Reading begins as a social activity, as an initiation into a community and into a communal vision of human life . . . a reader changes and develops through a dialectic of self and culture."[8] Adult readers, that is, seek not only literary knowledge but wisdom. Let us now examine the ways of reading in more detail. Are there indeed right and wrong, wise and foolish, ways to read?

The Reader As User

When I use a word . . . it means just what I choose it to mean—nothing more, nothing less.

Lewis Carroll

Humpty Dumpty's comment is the epitome of the interpreter's will to power over language. It is a sentiment with which many readers can identify: "When I read a text, it means just what I choose it to mean." Such a position fails, however, to provide a sufficient rationale for reading. Why read if one already knows what one will find, namely, oneself?

In the third age of criticism, many contemporary critics are happy to reassign most moral rights to the reader rather than the text. The copyright stipulation whereby writers "assert their moral right to be identified as the author of this work" only prohibits citing the author's language without permission. Evidently, the moral rights of the author do not extend to the interpretation or use that readers make of a text. As Robert Morgan so bluntly puts it: "Texts, like dead men and women, have no rights, no aims, no interests. They can be used in whatever way readers or interpreters choose. If interpreters choose to respect an author's intentions, that is because it is in their interest to do so."[9] On this view, how to read a text is not a moral but a pragmatic question.

Is reading, therefore, neither moral nor immoral, but amoral? In postmodernity, the only ethical criteria that are regularly applied in interpretive discussions are those of a utilitarian sort. For example, "Prefer those readings that best serve the interests of a particular group." As Rorty observes, there is nothing to be responsible *to* except historical communities.[10] The difference between a good and a bad reading is relative to the particular purpose for which it is offered. Indeed, Rorty defines the "good" as "that which serves human purposes." The good—in interpretation or anything else—is relative to human aims and interests. As for criteria, they "are temporary resting places constructed for utilitarian ends."[11] The question is whether, on the one hand, the interpreter ought to find a universal criterion that is distinct from community interests, or whether ethics is a matter of comparative interpretation only, on the other.

Rorty acknowledges that his view of interpretation goes hand in hand with a larger vision of human beings and society in which no one group can lay claim to a privileged perspective. In such a culture, interpreters "would not be those who knew a Secret, who had won through to Truth, but simply people who were good at being human."[12] This is, however, somewhat disingenuous, because Rorty has definite beliefs about what counts as the "good" for human beings. What is good for humans is ultimately a function of our view of humankind. Rorty prefers (it can be no more than a personal preference, given his theory of truth) the description of human beings as "alone, merely finite, with no links to something Beyond."[13] If this is truly the human condition, he reasons, interpreters should abandon the search for right answers and turn instead to sharing as many ideas as possible. His ethics of interpretation clearly follow from his prior interpretation of what it is to be human.

Once again, the crucial issue is realism: Do our interpretations approximate a meaning that precedes and is independent of them? Is it possible to get it right (or wrong)? Or can we do whatever we like with texts, so long as it serves some purpose, even when that purpose is something other than reaching understanding? For instance, can the pragmatist ever criticize a community interest as improper or immoral? It appears not, if indeed "there is nothing deep down inside us except what we have put there ourselves, no criterion that we have not created. . . ."[14] Rorty apparently even considers it acceptable for readers to read as if they were the authors of the text. While this may be an interesting exercise (what could I have meant if I had written *Ulysses*?), it is not a particularly edifying one. More seriously, there is ultimately nothing that provides the User with resources that permit one to critique a potentially abusive interest or to prevent oneself from becoming a textual abuser.

The Reader As Critic

In early modern times, "criticism" referred to a method for obtaining knowledge about texts: "a descriptive pursuit, analysing, explaining and codifying the questions that perceptive readers put to the text; not a prescriptive discipline laying down rules about how the text ought to be read."[15] In late (post?) modernity, however, it describes the reader's claim to enjoy a privileged perspective from which the text may be evaluated (e.g., feminist, womanist, Marxist, gay criticism, etc.). What was once epistemological, a matter of knowledge, is now considered ideological, a matter of power and privilege.

Steiner draws a slightly different distinction between critics and readers. The critic establishes a certain distance from the text and views it from a particular angle.[16] For the critic, the text is an object, an impersonal thing onto which one's mental judgments may be imposed. The critic becomes a text's judge and master. "Any suggestion that a text has rights is a deception concealing someone else's interests."[17] The reader, on the other hand, views the otherness of the text not as some objective datum or as a blank slate, but rather as a kind of personal presence. The reader becomes both shepherd and servant of the text preeminently when one learns it by heart and thus allows the text to be an efficacious presence in one's life.

Both critics and readers claim to practice ethical interpretation. On the one hand, critics claim to be ethical insofar as they are concerned with the contemporary situation and with the text's influence on society. Textual visions of what life should be like, they point out, may be distorting. Consequently, a critique of the text, even its deconstruction, may be the most ethical response and the best means for liberating humanity. Readers, on the other hand, claim to be ethical because they seek to do justice to the text and allow the text's moral content into their lives. Literature deals with the question of the meaning of life and displays visions of what that meaning may be. One way or another, then, interpretation has of late become an ethical concern for readers and critics alike.

Wayne Booth, like Steiner, favors readers over critics. To begin with doubt and distance is to destroy the datum. We read in order to be transformed; transformation is stultified by a hermeneutics of suspicion. Booth therefore suggests "friendship" as the principal metaphor for reading.[18] Steiner's preferred metaphor for reading is "hospitality."[19] The real presence of an "other," of a voice and a communicative agent that impinges on us, requires, at least initially, a courteous welcome. Arthur Quiller-Couch, believing that all great literature is edifying, encourages reader to "*trust* any given masterpiece for its operation, on ourselves and on others."[20] Of course, it is possible to become an unthinking slave of the text. Not all texts deserve to be so admired, however. For feminists, the deep patriarchal bias of texts needs to be challenged. "The reader's human and ethical and political responses, having been shaped by a social context . . . ultimately require a critique of the themes of the text or a critique of the codes out of which a given text has been constructed."[21]

There is a second sense in which interpretation is ethical, one that has to do not with the moral content of the texts but with the process of interpretation itself. Some forms of criticism focus not on texts but on traditional methods of reading texts. Elisabeth Schüssler Fiorenza contends, for instance, that traditional biblical scholarship, far from being a disinterested scholarly endeavor, is actually conditioned by its social location. Granting that objectivity in interpretation is impossible, Schüssler Fiorenza advocates an "ethics of accountability," which takes responsibility for the ethical consequences of the biblical texts and their meanings.[22] In other words, the critic must judge the presumed effects of the text and its interpretation with *political* criteria. Specifically, the ethical critic must ask: "What does the language of a biblical text 'do' to a reader who submits to its world of vision?"[23] Frances Young agrees; ethical reading involves respecting the otherness of the text *and* evaluating its possible effects: "A responsible reading must invite attention both to past meaning and future potential."[24]

Increasingly, even deconstructive critics are claiming the high moral ground in debates about reading.[25] Deconstruction, as we have seen, is not so much a method of interpretation as a strategy for undoing interpretations. Deconstructive critics claim to be ethically responsible because they respect the otherness of the text. For the "other" is that which escapes human mastery, that which cannot be assimilated by human reason or conceptual schemes without remainder. The other is that which interrupts interpretation. Deconstruction is thus "a critical reminder of the obligation literary texts impose upon readers to respond to the Other through a hands-on engagement with the particular text."[26] Deconstruction is ethical, that is, insofar as it safeguards otherness by exposing the workings of power in interpretation.

The deconstructive reader is ultimately a critic of complacent interpretation. Deconstruction teaches one to ask, "What does such and such an interpretation omit?" Though deconstruction is text-centered, it denies that there is a center to the text. Any interpretation, then, insofar as it stabilizes the text, ultimately does the text an injustice. Deconstruction exposes the lie; interpretations do not find but create a unified, coherent text. Deconstruction compels us to acknowledge the ways in which ideologies and institutions exert power over our readings. Rather than bow the knee to dominant interpretations, the deconstructive reader plays the text. Since meaning is not fixed, the reader is free to explore endless alternatives: "For deconstruction, the text retains the power to elude and overturn every reading—while the reader retains the power endlessly to rewrite the text."[27] What is ultimately at stake, therefore, is how one views ethics: "Ethics used to be a coercive, customary manner of ensuring the cohesiveness of a particular group through the repetition of a code. . . . Now, however, the issue of ethics crops up wherever a code (mores, social contract) must be shattered in order to give way to the free play of negativity, desire, pleasure. . . ."[28]

The Reader As Follower

Reading, says Ricoeur, is first and foremost "a struggle with the text."[29] Why should this be so? Perhaps because the reader is trying to use the text in ways that are inappropriate—in ways that go against the textual grain, as it were. One can, of course, do many things with texts. One can use them as kindling, as booster seats, or as a means of legitimizing oppressive social structures such as apartheid. It is also true that one can ask many questions about texts that are inappropriate for the purpose of interpretation (e.g., how much Moby Dick weighs, what *Macbeth* reveals about the state of the English language in the sixteenth century, what Genesis tells us about ancient Near-Eastern cosmology, etc.). Such questions do not help us to understand the text as communicative act any better. Readers who use or question the text in inappropriate ways will find reading a struggle, for they are reading against the textual grain. Yet there may also be properly interpretive reasons why reading is a struggle with the text.

Letting the Text Have Its Say: Following Illocutions

"The first demand any work of any art makes upon us is surrender. Look. Listen. Receive."[30] We "receive" a work, according to C. S. Lewis, when "we exert our senses and imagination and various other powers according to a pattern invented by the artist."[31] The true reader "reads every work seriously in the sense that he reads it whole-heartedly, makes himself as receptive as he can."[32] A person should read in the same spirit as the author writes: "What is meant lightly will be taken lightly; what is meant gravely, gravely."[33] Unfortunately, however, many readers *use* texts; relatively few receive them. To use texts rather than to receive them is to read in bad faith. Users take the text as a pretext for some activity of their own. Users resist what the text, as a specific literary act, can do for them. A text that is merely used rather than received, however, prevents one from ever getting beyond oneself. The User is condemned to the narcissistic hermeneutics of Socrates: *read thyself.*

When Lewis speaks of "reception," on the other hand, he is referring not to a state of passivity or impassivity, but rather to a state of active obedience. The reader responds to the call of the text: "Look. Listen." An ethical critic will accept the text as a genuine other—not as a mere reflection or projection of the reader. If there were more ethical criticism, Lewis suggests, there would be less evaluation: less talk, that is, of the reader's own prejudices and predilections. "Can I say with certainty that any evaluative criticism has ever actually helped me to understand and appreciate any great work of literature or any part of one?"[34] His answer is a resounding no: "Find out what the author actually wrote and what the hard words meant and what the allusions were to, and you have done far more for me than a hundred new interpretations or assessments could ever do."[35]

Lewis acknowledges that his view will not please the "vigilant" critics for whom criticism is "a form of social and ethical hygiene."[36] Such is the case in much postmodern criticism, for instance, in which reading is an exercise of the will to power, whereby texts are made to conform to the prevailing vision of a community's values. It is important, now more than ever, to be clear about what concept of the "good" lies behind the critic's evaluations. Lewis's caution is salutary: "You must . . . accept their (implied) conception of the good life if you are to accept their criticism. That is, you can admire them as critics only if you also revere them as sages."[37] Many so-called "ethical" readers assume that their wisdom is superior to that of the author's.

A more appropriate ethical approach is one that acknowledges the right of the text to have its own say first. Such an approach begins by inquiring about the illocutionary aspect of texts. We judge a communicative act primarily on the basis of its intrinsic aim and interest, by the work it does or fails to do. To quote Lewis: "The first qualification for judging any piece of workmanship from a corkscrew to a cathedral is to know what it is—what it was intended to do and how it is meant to be used."[38] But one can only judge a work if one first receives it and lets it have its own say. To cite Lewis again: "The necessary condition of all good reading is 'to get ourselves out of the way.'"[39] For no text will yield its secret to a reader "who enters it regarding the poet as a potential deceiver. . . . We must risk being taken in, if we are to get anything."[40]

Steiner agrees. Reading is ultimately ethical because a communicative act requires a response. "Responsible response, answering answerability make of the process of understanding a moral act."[41] The text is not to be contemplated so much as lived; what the text offers us may be welcomed or refused. Steiner notes that in many cultures, showing hospitality to the stranger is a religious act. The stranger is not us, and for this very reason may have something vital to teach or to bring us. For Lewis and Steiner, ethical reading is a struggle to hear a voice that is genuinely other than our own: the voice of an other, of an author. Simply to engage in dialogue need not imply approval. Recognizing an illocutionary act or imaginative vision for what it is, is only the first step in appropriating its meaning. There is an obvious difference between, on the one hand, acknowledging an illocutionary act for what it is, and doing what it says, on the other. At the very least, the ethical reader must be prepared to acknowledge communicative acts as what they are—especially those from which one ultimately dissents.

Letting the Text Have Its Way: Following Perlocutions

To this point we have discussed following in the sense of recognizing illocutionary action (e.g., following a story or following an argument). There is another sense of following, however, that goes beyond recognizing the illocutionary point. We speak, for instance, of following directions. When Jesus says "Follow me," we follow what he is saying when we recognize that his speech act is a directive, though we only follow Jesus in the second sense when we not only let him have his say but begin to walk his way, that is, when we modify our behavior. The difference is that between explication and application. The text can become more than a dialogue partner; it can become a pedagogue that illumines one's existence and opens up new ways of living in the world. Most authors want not only to be understood, but also to have some further effect upon their readers. Must interpreters follow a text's perlocutions as well as illocutions in order to attain understanding? Must interpreters be not only hearers but doers of the word?

Ricoeur describes the last stage of understanding as a personal appropriation in which readers expose themselves to the effects of the text. It is not enough to explain what a text meant; one must decide what it means today, how it impinges on the individual and on society. The difference is between explanation (analyzing locutions and illocutions) and application (appropriating illocutions and perlocutions). At this stage, criticism is not merely a matter of determining what the text says, but of deciding whether or not what the text says is good or true and worthy of being followed. Application pertains to bringing the reader into personal involvement with the claims of the text. For Ricoeur, the text is the medium through which we gain self-understanding. This is not Socrates' idea of knowing oneself, but rather the notion that we come to understand ourselves in new ways in the light of the text. Indeed, far from being a projection of the reader, the text actually projects a sense of self onto the ego. Ricoeur refers to the "dispossession" of the ego in the process of reading: "It is the text, with its universal power of unveiling, which gives a self to the ego."[42] This is, perhaps, the ultimate perlocutionary effect. According to Ricoeur, what is finally understood in reading texts is oneself, one's situation as a finite temporal being with certain possibilities. In reading texts we come to understand the human condition.

I earlier likened literary genres to maps that "plot" the world in different ways. We can follow a map by recognizing what it is, but we can also follow it by allowing it to provide our orientation in the world. Lewis and Ricoeur use another metaphor; they compare reading to a musical performance. "The poem . . . is like a score and the readings like performances."[43] "Reading is like the execution of a musical score; it marks the realization, the enactment, of the semantic possibilities of the text."[44] To "perform" a map is to submit to its guidance and direction, to walk in its way. As we know a person by the company he or she keeps, so we know the text by keeping company with it. Readers must be willing to follow a text at least part of the way in order to understand it. At the same time, we must be willing to part company with texts that we conclude are potentially harmful. Readers must remain themselves, even when opening themselves up to potential friends (or enemies). To follow a text's perlocutions, then, is to allow it to keep us company and to set our course.

The Interpretive Virtues

Ethically minded readers must decide whether texts should be followed in the second sense. However, before one decides whether or not to befriend a text, one must first recognize it for what it is. "We must look, and go on looking till we have certainly seen exactly what is there."[45] My claim is that only the interpretive realist can truly respect the text as a genuine other. To say, with Fish, that the text is the product of a community's reading conventions ultimately fails to safeguard textual otherness. A text that has no meaning independent of a community of readers cannot, I suggest, be followed. In the last analysis, the Fishian reader is not following an other, only chasing his tail. Pannenberg speaks for the hermeneutical realist: "All exposition presupposes that the content of the text which is to be expounded is a given for the expositor. . . . Without this presupposition fidelity to the text could no longer be distinguished from the freedom of poetic composition."[46]

Only the realist, I submit, can respect what is there, for the non-realist does not believe that there is anything to be respected. As Plantinga puts it: "Commitment goes with the idea that there really *is* such a thing as truth."[47] To be committed to something "is to think it is *true*, not just true relative to what you or someone believes."[48] There is a deep connection, on the other hand, between non-realism and intellectual (or ethical) indifference. Christian interpreters, I suggest, are interpretive and ethical realists. It is the way of Christian wisdom to live according to God's created order, revealed and redeemed in Christ. Folly, on the other hand, consists in living against the grain of creation.

Respect for what is there in the text (viz., its enacted intention and its implicit invitation) is a moral virtue. There are other virtues that further characterize readers who follow the text rather than their own inclinations. Let us refer to these as the "interpretive virtues." *An interpretive virtue is a disposition of the mind and heart that arises from the motivation for understanding, for cognitive contact with the meaning of the text.*[49] An interpretive virtue, in other words, is one that is conducive to literary knowledge. When readers display interpretive virtue, their cognitive capacities exemplify not merely proper function but *excellence*. I have already discussed the importance of faith, hope, and love for hermeneutics. To these theological virtues we can add four others:

(1) *Honesty*. Honesty in interpretation means, above all, acknowledging one's prior commitments and preunderstandings. Readers need to be clear about their own aims and interests (in this regard honesty is a form of internal clarity). A dishonest interpreter is less likely to be receptive to those texts that appear to challenge one's most cherished beliefs or habits or desires. A dishonest interpreter is more likely to drown out the voice of the other.

(2) *Openness*. The open-minded reader is willing to hear and consider the ideas of others, including those that conflict with one's own, without prejudice and without malice. Closed-mindedness is an interpretive vice; closed-minded readers are either unwilling or unable to go beyond themselves. They thus thwart the ability of the text to transcend and transform the reader. Readers display interpretive openness when they welcome the text as other, with courtesy and respect, and when they entertain other interpretations as well. Note that openness implies a willingness to change; literary knowledge is provisional, not certain.

(3) *Attention*. The virtuous reader, far from being self-absorbed, is rather focused on the text. Paying attention to the text is itself a form of respect and involves a number of related virtues, such as patience, thoroughness, and care. The attentive reader must be observant, which means attending to the details, being sensitive to the various levels of the literary act, and having insight into the nature of the whole.

(4) *Obedience*. The obedient interpreter is the one who follows the directions of the text rather than one's own desires. This does not necessarily mean doing what the text says, but it does mean, minimally, reading it in the way its author intended. It means adopting a reading genre that corresponds to the genre of the text. It means reading history as history, apocalyptic as apocalyptic, and so on. Only obedient readers can indwell the text and so gain whatever other knowledge it has to give.

How can readers cultivate these interpretive virtues? For C. S. Lewis, the purpose of great literature is to train our feelings and our imaginations to perceive the world and ourselves correctly. Literature trains us to see, for example, the difference between right and wrong, between the noble and the naughty, between the real and the fanciful. We meet here yet another version of the hermeneutic circle: reading develops the interpretive virtues; the interpretive virtues help us to become better readers. Developing interpretive virtues is not a matter of following, say, "thirty-six steps to better exegesis." It is not a matter of following rules or procedures, but of acquiring skills and learning good practice.[50] To this end, readers must be apprentices of texts and of their authors. Right reading—reading that both fosters and exemplifies virtue—is ultimately a matter of cultivating good judgment, of knowing what to do when. This is as much a spiritual as an intellectual and interpretive task. Indeed, moral and interpretive virtues alike are ultimately in the service of wisdom.[51] Wisdom, in turn, is the virtue whereby human beings live as they ought, in a way that fits into the created order, resulting both in human flourishing and in the glory of God. The wise reader knows not only how to interpret, but more importantly, what interpretation is for. Wise readers see themselves in the mirror of the biblical text as they actually are, and they respond appropriately.

The Reader As Believer: Reading the Bible "Like Any Other Book"

Readers follow some texts not only as friends with whom they keep company, but as authorities in relation to whom they are disciples. What stance should readers take towards the Bible—that of User, critic, friend, disciple?

Can Unbelievers Read Rightly?

Can one read the Bible like any other book? The question is ambiguous: Can one, that is, can an individual reader, interpret the Bible correctly? Or does one need to belong to an interpretive community? In addition, can a community read the Bible as it would any other book, or must it employ a special hermeneutic?

Jowett: The Scholarly Community. Is right reading dependent upon one's belonging to a church? Benjamin Jowett's 1860 essay "On the Interpretation of Scripture" vigorously rejects this suggestion.[52] The Bible, he argues, should be read with the tools of historical and literary scholarship, "like any other book." Reading the Bible "like any other book" is, for Jowett, the "master principle" of interpretation. Implicit in his essay is an assumption that the critic who stands apart from traditional beliefs and practices is in a superior position to see what is really going on in the text. The critical approach allows readers "to combat the obscuring of the true meaning of the biblical texts through traditional interpretation being forced upon them."[53] On Jowett's view, only readers who suspend belief in the text (i.e., who refuse to follow its per-locutions) are qualified to attend to it. The "critical spirit" will rescue the literal (= original) sense and cast out "the seven other senses" that have taken up their abode therein.

Is it, however, possible to be completely disinterested? Have not biblical critics simply substituted "Enlightenment" interests (e.g., neutrality, objectivity, indifference) for "Christian" ones? Jowett's prescription "like any other book" already presupposes some general theory about the aims of interpretation. Jowett's "critical spirit," like its parent, the spirit of modern individualism, needs to be tested against the interpretive virtues and against the Holy Spirit.

Hauerwas: The Believing Community. Stanley Hauerwas, at the other extreme, argues that the Bible should not be read like any other book: "The Bible is not and should not be accessible to merely anyone, but rather it should only be made available to those who have undergone the hard discipline of existing as part of God's people."[54] What is needed, says Hauerwas, are not scholarly tools but saintly practices. In Francis Watson's words:

> What is at issue is whether the interpretative task is best undertaken on the basis of a relative or complete separation from the beliefs, values and practices of the ecclesial community, or whether it could be possible to take seriously, from the start, the expectations that accord with the genre of the biblical texts as the holy scripture of a worshipping community.[55]

In other words, the Bible is more likely to be misunderstood by an unbelieving and unaffiliated individual than by a believing and practicing member of the church. Jowett mistakenly believed that it was enough to have the right scholarly tools. This overlooks the ethical and spiritual dimension of interpretation. For Hauerwas, the interpretive virtues are distinctly Christian, that is, specific to the community of Christian readers.

Hauerwas challenges the two "dogmas" of criticism: that biblical scholarship is objective and that biblical scholarship is apolitical. He maintains that the whole endeavor to interpret the Bible "on its own terms" is vain nonsense. The Bible does not make sense independently of a church that gives it sense. However, in his zeal against objective knowledge, Hauerwas approaches Fish's non-realist position, where meaning is a matter of the way in which a community reads. This is unfortunate and unnecessary. We can agree with Hauerwas that spiritual training is a vital part of biblical interpretation, not because it creates the meaning of a text, but because it helps us to discover and to recognize the meaning that is already there.

Stephen E. Fowl and Gregory Jones argue, similarly to Hauerwas, that faithful reading of Scripture is a moral and spiritual activity.[56] To read the Word of God rightly is to allow it to work its transforming effects on the interpreting community. The basic criterion for right biblical interpretation, therefore, becomes holy living. People learn to become faithful readers by acquiring Christian virtues through participating in the Christian community. While the emphasis of Fowl and Jones on the reader's following and embodying the meaning is most welcome, there are certain problems in their account, an account that perhaps concedes too much to the spirit of postmodernity. First, even interpreting communities can get it wrong. This seems to be Jesus' point against the religious leaders of his day: they searched the Scriptures, yet they did not follow their reference to Christ (John 5:39–40). This leads, second, to the obvious question: *which* interpretive community? As church history amply attests, the conflict of interpretations is nothing less than a conflict between interpretive communities. One cannot arbitrate this conflict simply by preferring one community over another. Third, what exactly does it mean to read *as* or *in* the church: that one must be baptized, or be a church member, or be reading during a worship service? Finally, we observe that "faithfulness" seems to be understood by Fowl and Jones in primarily moral terms. There is little place in their account for a specifically theological moment in the interpretive process. In short, they fail to relate interpretive discipleship to the nature and effect of the Spirit's work in the community.

The Community of Saints (And Sinners). No interpretive community is infallible. If we let the biblical text inform our thinking about the church as an interpretive community, we should rather say that it is a community of saints *and* sinners. Christians attribute their correct interpretations (their descriptions and applications of biblical meaning) to the guidance of the Spirit and not only to their academic discipline, and certainly not to their own interpretive *works*. This follows both from a theological anthropology and from an understanding of the Spirit's work by grace through faith. Christian doctrine, I have claimed, has hermeneutical significance. I prefer to say, not that we should read the Bible like any other book, but that we should read every other book as we have learned to read the Bible, *namely, in a spirit of understanding that lets the text be what it is and do what it intends.* John Owen's rule for right biblical interpretation should be extended to general hermeneutics as well: "Let reading follow prayer." Right reading *in general* demands an explicitly theological hermeneutic and calls for resources that exceed the religion of Socrates. The interpretive virtues, as we will see, are none other than the fruit of the Spirit.

Reading the Bible As Canonical Scripture

Finally, to address fully the question of whether we should read the Bible "like any other book" requires a consideration of its status as canonical. As we have seen, acknowledging the Bible as "canon" entails recognizing a unity of a higher order (i.e., not merely of *parole* or of genre, but of "Scripture"). The absorption of a text (e.g., Job, Luke-Acts) into the Old or New Testament does indeed affect how it is read, namely, by expanding the context of interpretation beyond the original historical and literary contexts. It also adds a new level of illocution: "providing guidance for future generations," "testifying to Christ," etc. Childs insists that canonical interpretation is just as descriptive as its historical counterpart. What is being described in Childs's case, however, is the way the text has been structured in order to function authoritatively for future generations. According to the historical critic, in contrast, the object of description is the text in its original situation. But this is manifestly not a description of canon. Historical critics analyze how the text came to be (the text's pre-history), but canonical critics describe the text as it was *meant* to be (the history of the text as Scripture). The point is that "description always presupposes a prior construction of the object in terms of a given interpretive paradigm."[57]

Some will object that "canons" are themselves only constructions of an interpretive community, whose function is to legitimate the authority of community opinion. The postmodern worry is that canon all too easily becomes an ideological tool, a product of the corporate will to power. I do not share this view. On the contrary, the canon has often proved to be an effective check against the hegemony of human institutions and traditions (cf. the Reformation!). The canon, in other words, functions as an instrument of ideology critique. The canon, moreover, calls for continued interpretation, a call that again puts into question the finality of human formulations (and institutions). Last, the canon provides an interpretive framework by which the past can illumine the present. The canon generates not an absolute, unchanging static tradition but rather a dynamic tradition of critical reinterpretation.

Of course, only those within the context of a believing community will read the Bible as "Scripture," that is, as the supreme authority for life and thought. Does reading the Bible as Scripture change or develop its meaning? To say that it does is to make the interpretive community into an authoring, and authoritative, community. On my view, to view the Bible as "Scripture" best accords not with the illocutionary but rather with the perlocutionary aspect of communicative action. That is, Scripture intends, by and through its communicative action, to function in a way that leads to Christ and to the righteousness of God. To call the Bible Scripture does not make its warnings or its promises something other than warnings and promises, but rather reorients them to the larger purpose of "making wise unto salvation."

All texts, I have argued, have a certain claim on the reader. Reading a text is like an "I-Thou" encounter. This encounter, as Lévinas has eloquently described it, is fundamentally ethical: the implicit plea "Thou shalt not kill" is inscribed in the face of the other. Parallel to the other's face is the author's voice, which also represents a plea not to be oppressed, not to be swallowed up or used merely as a means for some end chosen by the reader. We "kill" a text by suppressing its voice; "we murder to dissect" (Wordsworth). "As with people, so with books, both the subjectivist and the objectivist reveal a desire to dominate, the one by imposing *his or her* (supposedly subjective) meaning, the other by imposing *the* ("true") meaning."[58] In either case, the other is not allowed to be or to speak for itself. The implied reader of *Scripture* has, in addition to the negative obligation not to kill, a further, properly positive obligation—to be a follower, a believer, and a doer. Genuine understanding entails going the second mile: "The reader is challenged to enter this world by becoming a disciple, a hearer of the word, a follower of Jesus."[59] In short, the ideal reader of Scripture must be a disciple. "As scripture . . . Luke and Acts have implied readers who are [actually or potentially] Christian."[60] The reader is invited, even summoned, to dwell in the world of the text, to abide in the Word of God.

Our ultimate aim in reading and following the Bible as Scripture should be the knowledge of God.[61] Note that this is also the level of understanding in which we find true self-knowledge; as Calvin says, there is no knowledge of self without knowledge of God. Yes, one may read the Bible "like any other book," but the present question concerns how readers should respond if it is indeed the Word of God. Perhaps the clue is on the road to Emmaus. The disciples on that road only recognized Jesus after he revealed who he was "according to the Scriptures." His identity, that is, was textually mediated.[62] Good interpretation is similarly demonstrated only by recognizing and by following. Attaining understanding is a matter of knowing how to respond to something (or someone) according to its (or his) nature. We show that we understand a text when we exercise the right capacities in responding to it. We show that we understand a hammer, for instance, when we "recognize" it and use it correctly. Similarly, we show that we understand Scripture when we recognize Christ, the wisdom of God, and follow him.

All textual understanding is a theological matter—an encounter with something that transcends us and has the capacity to transform us, provided that we approach it in the right spirit. Such is the fundamental thesis of my argument. The interpretive virtues are in reality spiritual virtues: without faith—an openness to transcendence—we would never find something in the text that is not our own creation, or our own reflection. Hence the struggle with the text is ultimately a *spiritual* struggle—with the text and with ourselves. Readers may have reasons for wishing not to encounter the meaning of the text; it may be too challenging, a threat to our lifestyle, if not to life itself. For the Gospels call us to die to self, to former practices, to previous self-understandings. The reader's struggle with the text, then, is sometimes a struggle to death. It is at the very least a wrestling match in which we may ask for a blessing but receive a dislocated hip.

IS EXEGESIS WITHOUT IDEOLOGY POSSIBLE?

> Biblical scholars have been slow to awaken . . . to the realization that our representations of and discourse about what the text meant and how it means are inseparable from what we *want* it to mean, from how we *will* it to mean.[63]

To this point, we have asked what readers ought to do. But does ought imply *can*? Can readers "follow"? Can the reader ever have a pure interpretive interest, that is, an aim simply to understand the text as it is, without pressing it into some self-serving use? Or does ideology infect the whole set of relations between readers, language, and the world? Is there an alternative to claiming absolute disinterestedness (e.g., objective knowledge) and absolute interestedness (e.g., subjective preference)? I argue for a mediating position that recognizes both the knowability of the text (e.g., a reality principle) and the partiality of the reader (e.g., a bias principle).

Can Readers Ever Get Beyond Themselves?

Good commentary is whatever serves our interests and purposes.[64]

No one reads in a vacuum. Every reading is a contextualized reading. Moreover, the reading conventions that are in force in a given interpretive community are not arbitrary but are related to broader patterns of social power. These interpretive conventions even shape our so-called common sense.[65] Reading, for many postmoderns, has less to do with literary knowledge than with political power. On this view, interpretation appears less a strategy for comprehending than for conquering the other. The commentator becomes a kind of exegetical conquistador, interpretation the process of ideological colonization. If this is what interpretation truly is, one can begin to sympathize with the political motivation behind much deconstructive criticism. At its best, deconstruction is a strategy for undoing privileged hierarchies—linguistic and social, philosophical and theological—a way of releasing the "other" from its ideological bondage to an interpretive community.

David Clines agrees that exegesis is contextual but draws an economic rather than a political analogy. He espouses a market philosophy or "end-user" theory of interpretation, according to which an interpretation is considered legitimate if it "sells," if it meets the need of some reader-consumer.[66] The hottest sellers in the contemporary marketplace of biblical interpretation are ideological readings that criticize the text for being politically incorrect. Cline wonders whether traditional interpretation, in which readers strive for the author's intended meaning, can rightly be considered ethical. For if a reader's ethical and ideological values truly lie outside the text, "understanding" would mean negating one's own commitments. Does not the very assumption that the task of biblical scholars is to interpret the text in fact represent "a systematic repression of our ethical instincts"?[67]

Does it indeed follow from the notion that every interpretation is contextual (an indisputable fact about human finitude) that "there is no one authentic meaning which we must all try to discover, no matter who we are or where we happen to be standing"?[68] True, we can neither eradicate ourselves from the process of reading nor separate our personal identity from our interpretations. But does it follow that we can "explain" (or explain away) someone's reading simply by pointing to his or her social location? Does interpretation tell us only about readers, never about texts?

To prefer readings that "sell" is merely to prefer an updated, uptown version of the consensus theory of truth. Market forces are hardly satisfactory criteria, however, for right interpretation. I suspect that Clines does not really believe that either. For on purely market-driven grounds, how could he ever argue against fundamentalist readings of biblical texts, readings that he would surely wish to contest? Instead of advocating a free market in which readers are purveyors of ideological readings, should we not rather acknowledge that every choice about how to read implicitly makes a normative claim concerning interpretive aims? The relevant question then becomes, "Why should I buy *your* interpretation rather than another?" In a pluralistic age, every reader ought to be prepared to give an account, not only of the hope, but of the hermeneutics within him or her (1 Peter 3:15).

Norman Holland, one of the founders of reader-response criticism, uses a Freudian psychoanalytic approach to argue that readers ultimately never get beyond themselves: "All of us, as we read, use the literary work to symbolize and finally to replicate ourselves."[69] According to Holland, each individual has an "identity theme" that he or she "discovers" in every text. This is the hermeneutics and religion of Socrates—"know thyself"—with a vengeance. For to have knowledge of oneself only is ultimately to be condemned to self-confinement. Self-transcendence is not a Socratic option. Robert Fowler's approach to the Gospel of Mark is similar to Holland's in that he too sees the comments and commentaries of biblical critics "as disguised reports of the critics' own experience of reading biblical texts."[70] Fowler attributes his insight to Fish and to the notion that talk about the author's intention (e.g., meaning) is really talk about ourselves. "To see oneself in the mirror of the text" here receives what is perhaps its most extreme narcissistic reduction.

Can interpreters ever get beyond themselves? This is ultimately a question not only about psychology, but about philosophy and ethics. Emmanuel Lévinas expresses the more general concern: Can the self ever encounter the other, or do reason and interpretation alike ultimately result in self-absorption? Lévinas accuses traditional philosophy of taking every thought captive with a "totalizing" method that acknowledges only what conforms to its prior interpretive scheme.[71] Reason necessarily discovers itself—its own system, its own conceptual scheme—whenever it think about objects or, for that matter, texts. Thought processes the "other" by transforming and absorbing it into the "same"—into "me." For Lévinas, epistemology is essentially reductionistic and hence *unethical*; knowledge represses rather than recognizes otherness.[72] For Lévinas, "ethics" refers to a way of relating to the other that refuses to reduce it to the same (e.g., the self, the system) by *letting the other be*. We here approach the crux of the postmodern crisis in interpretation, namely, how for the hermeneutic non-realist the other can truly be other, if interpretation is ultimately a matter of one's self-projection.

The task of an ethics of interpretation, I submit, is to guard the otherness of the text: to preserve its ability to say something to and affect the reader, thus creating the possibility of self-transcendence. Neither biblical hermeneutics nor hermeneutics in general can afford to follow Feuerbach's suggestion that what we find—God, meaning—is merely a projection of ourselves. The hermeneutical equivalent of Feuerbach's suggestion that theology is really only anthropology would be to say that reading is really only authoring, that exegesis is really only eisegesis. The postmodern suspicion of hermeneutics is also a suspicion of transcendence, that is, a suspicion of our ability as readers to be addressed by what is beyond us. It is the postmodern suspicion of hermeneutics that threatens to reduce the other (the author) to the selfsame, that is, to oneself.

"Meaning . . . is always realized at the point of reception."[73] If meaning is an event, then a focus on reading will undermine the notion that meaning is objectively "there," a potential item of objective knowledge. The authors of *The Postmodern Bible* clearly articulate this belief: "Deconstruction rejects all 'container' theories of meaning. Meaning is not in the text but is brought to it and imposed upon it."[74] If there is no hard and fast distinction between what is in the text and what is in the reader, how can different readers of the same text get the same meaning out of it? Can we even say that two readers have read the same text? Certain groups may not be ready to receive a certain message at a particular time (e.g., an Aboriginal tribe is not yet ready for Einstein's special relativity theory; the nineteenth-century bourgeois European was not ready for Nietzsche's announcement of the death of God, etc.). If meaning is the product of our interpretive aims and procedures, then the text is only an alter ego of the reader.

To give pride of place to the reader is ultimately to subscribe to hermeneutic non-realism. In an essay published in 1946, Wimsatt and Beardsley defined the "affective fallacy" as the error of evaluating a poem on the basis of its effects—particularly its emotional effects—on the reader. The fallacy rests on "a confusion between the poem and its *results* (what it *is* and what it *does*)."[75] Restated in terms of the present argument, *the affective fallacy confuses illocutions with perlocutions*. The question is: Does recent reader-response criticism not make a similar mistake? Can critics who give pride of place to the reader's response continue to distinguish between what a text says and how it affects the reader? As Wimsatt and Beardsley saw all too well, the consequences of the affective fallacy are far-reaching: the text itself, as an object of literary knowledge, tends to disappear, and commentary "ends in impressionism and relativism."[76]

Is the meaning of a text a matter of the interpreter's impression? Is the Bible's authority in danger of becoming a subjective impression? Perhaps so. The authors of *The Postmodern Bible*, however, believe that most biblical interpreters who focus on the reader continue, paradoxically, to privilege the text. The reader in question is the "implied reader," a creation of the text: the model reader who follows all textual directions. Whether or not this correctly describes the situation in biblical studies is not the issue; the point is that the authors of *The Postmodern Bible* wish to challenge such conservative reader-response criticism in the name of ethics. Only if one abandons the belief in the text-in-itself and in a meaning that transcends the act of reading, they argue, will one be able to examine the practices by which readers make meaning, and hence the relation of these practices to the larger socio-political situations in which they are embedded. For many postmoderns, the ethics of interpretation is a matter not of guarding the integrity of the text so much as insisting on its unknowability.

The Reader As Traitor: Is Translation Without Ideology Possible?

With few exceptions biblical scholars have not yet acquiesced to the collapse of the text-reader dichotomy.[77]

Is the phenomenon of translation not a counterexample to the claim that readers never get beyond themselves? Or do translators too reduce the other to the same?

Is translation an ideology-free zone? Ideology, we may recall, is "meaning in the service of power."[78] To say that all approaches to meaning are ideological is to insist that translations and interpretations alike are fundamentally political, that is, entangled in relations of social power. Is it indeed the case that ideology inevitably betrays every attempt at interpretation or translation? If so, then not only is every biblical commentary also *political* commentary, but every translation of the Bible also serves some master other than meaning.

The Confusion of Horizons

If certain texts display, say, a patriarchal bias, should the ethical translator redress the balance? Does justice demand that we sometimes substitute feminine for masculine pronouns? May we, for example, address the Lord's Prayer to "Our Mother (or Parent) who art in heaven" with impunity? If we may, then is the reader free to make other changes to texts that are considered politically incorrect? If so, can we continue to sustain the distinctions between translating, commentary writing, and censorship? We may here recall Coggins's urgent query: "Can the commentary be kept distinct from the propaganda weapon?"[79]

Judith Fetterley's *The Resisting Reader* contends that the great works of American literature are patriarchal and that, in reading them, men and women alike are indoctrinated "to identify as male."[80] A feminist reader must learn to resist, rather than assent to, this oppressive ideology.[81] In a similar vein, some feminists also take issue with the notion that the cross is part of God's salvific plan:

> Christianity is an abusive theology that glorifies suffering. Is it any wonder that there is so much abuse in modern society when the predominant image or theology of culture is of "divine child abuse"—God the Father demanding and carrying out the suffering and death of his own son? If Christianity is to be liberating for the oppressed it must itself be liberated from this theology.[82]

Frances Young admits that parts of the Pastorals have functioned as "texts of terror": "The theology of the Pastorals presents us with a whole culture of subordination."[83] An ethical reading, she suggests, is one that takes seriously both the need to be "true" to the text and the need to be "true" to oneself. Can readers simultaneously respect, and suspect, the text?[84]

Sternberg helpfully distinguishes the ideology of the text, which is the job of *poetics* to uncover, from the ideology of the reader, which is a matter of *politics*. Sternberg readily grants that no reading is free of ideology. Poetic competence, however, requires that one be attuned to the ideology of the text. With regard to the Bible, the implication is that "a reader unable or unwilling to postulate the articles of faith (from God down) will forfeit competence as a hopeless counterreader."[85] Readers must ultimately choose between hermeneutic realism and non-realism: "Either we reconstruct the whole as best we can in the light of the writer's presumed intention . . . or we fashion—in effect reinvent—everything as we please."[86] In the final analysis, it is not much of a choice: "Even to judge against the text's grain, you must first judge with it: receptivity before resistance, competent reading before liberated counterreading, poetics before politics."[87]

It may be tempting to identify textual meaning with its effects, but it is ultimately unethical and dishonest. Readers are, like everyone else, sinners who tend to suppress the truth in unrighteousness. This is true, sadly, even of those who belong to the church—the believing interpreting community. A certain hermeneutics of suspicion, not only of the text but also of habits of reading, can be healthy. A *little* deconstruction may not be such a dangerous thing; indeed, it may be therapeutic. At the same time, I reject the notion that our social location determines what we see in texts. If readings were indeed "predestined" by our social location, then the notion of responsible interpretation is a chimera and a sham. *What we may call "the confusion of horizons"—that blurring of text and reader, poetics and politics, illocutions and perlocutions—is fundamentally a confusion of text and commentary* (in effect, another version of the affective fallacy).

"Translator, Traitor": Betraying the Text?

As there is no such thing as an innocent reading, we must say what reading we are guilty of.[88]

We thus return to our original question: Can readers discover the meaning of the text or do they find themselves only? For Steiner, translation is the model of all understanding and interpretation. Every reading is a translation, every reader a translator, someone who takes something (viz., meaning) from the text (the source language) and moves it somewhere else (the receptor language). Translation is about the transfer of meaning from one language to another. Hermeneutically speaking, to fail here, in translation, is to fail everywhere. What happens in translation, traditionally conceived, is that a semantic content (a kernel) is handed on in another signifying form (a husk). The assumption is that meaning is transferable. The problem is that every language maps the relations between words and the world differently. Some languages have more color words than others, for instance. Every language thus represents "a unique system of experience."[89] Translation risks *transforming* meaning in the process of transferring it.

"*Traduttore, traditore*" ("translator, traitor"). This aphorism expresses the "law of Babel," namely, that no text can be translated without fundamental loss. All transferring of meaning is a handing over of meaning (as in Judas's "handing over" of Jesus). Translation begins with a kiss but ends in betrayal. The problem is that the same words, when repeated in another context (e.g., five minutes later, five centuries later) may mean something else. The problem is even more acute, for isn't the translator's ambition just a special instance of that totalizing thought that assimilates the "other" to the "same," an act that Lévinas believes to be essentially unethical?

Derrida, we may recall, bases deconstruction on "iterability," the notion that the same words can be repeated in different contexts. It follows from iterability that my words cannot mean exactly the same thing in someone else's mouth as they do in mine. "Iterability alters."[90] As Steiner puts it: "Strictly considered, no statement is completely repeatable (time has passed)."[91] And since the context is not exhaustively determinable, there is no way to recreate the original context and so repeat the self-same speech act. Because the context of reading is never the same, neither is the text.

In Derrida's words: "A text, I believe, does not come back."[92] For Derrida, then, translation is less about communicating the meaning of the original so much as "the survival, which is to say the growth, of the original."[93] In a stunning reversal, the original is indebted to the translation as the power that enables it to live on. Is Derrida right? Can texts survive only by adapting (mutating) to fit new situations? Can the translator never transfer the same meaning to a different language?

Whether or not the translator is also a traitor finally depends on the sense one gives to "the same." Towards what kind of sameness does the translator work: the sameness of "equivalence" or the sameness of "identity"? The debate over two kinds of sameness dominates contemporary translation theory. Is sameness a matter of verbal equivalence? Must a good translation preserve the same number, or order, of words? Those who seek such sameness aim for "formal" equivalence. What matters most in formal equivalence is verbal consistency, that is, a word-for-word correspondence. The 1384 version of Wycliffe's translation of the Latin Vulgate was a word-for-word translation that made no attempt to put the words into a correct English idiom. "This method reflects the belief, current during the Middle Ages, that a translation had to be absolutely literal if it was to preserve the sacred quality of the original."[94] Saint Jerome reacted against earlier forms of such an exaggerated literalism, claiming instead to translate "sense for sense and not word for word."[95]

There is a second strategy for producing accurate translations. "Dynamic" equivalence aims for sameness of *effect*. It is also important to communicate not only the propositional content of the message but also its speech act character, so that the text makes the same kind of impact (i.e., performs the same communicative act) in a new situation. What matters here is the *illocutionary* and *perlocutionary* rather than the locutionary correspondence. On this view, the goal of translation is to produce an "equivalent response" in a new context.[96] In order to preserve the nature and content (proposition and illocution) of the message, however, it is often necessary to change the form (locution).

Is there some reason to believe that two communicative contexts—for example, first-century Palestine and twentieth-century Paris—can be equivalent? Eugene Nida lists four factors that form, he believes, an underlying common basis for human communication. All human beings have similar mental processes, similar bodily reactions, a similar range of cultural experience (e.g., material, social, linguistic, religious), and the capacity to adjust to the behavioral patterns of others. In other words, we are agents who share a world; we are speech agents who relate to others in similarly social ways. What dynamic equivalence translation tries to preserve is the overall *illocutionary* force of the communicative act. A good translation accurately contextualizes a communicative act in another language.

Is "equivalence" a realistic goal in interpretation or translation? According to Steiner, the experience of the translator is first and foremost the experience of the *non-identical*, the irreducible singularity, the stubborn otherness, of the text. As Steiner reminds us, Saint Jerome likens translation to the conquest of cities and the taking of slaves, to "meaning brought home captive."[97] This brings us back to Lévinas's concern about interpretation in general: in order to make sense of a text, we must take it prisoner. If, however, translation is to be an ethical activity, the translator must *nego-*

tiate with the other, with that which cannot be subsumed into one's own interpretive schemes (the same). Translation is a struggle with the text—a struggle to preserve the soul of meaning while embodying it anew. Steiner believes that texts resist the impulse to render them propositionally transparent; language is "difficult." The successful translation is a kind of "impossible possibility," a hermeneutic miracle.

Prospective miracle workers, says Steiner, must follow four steps. One begins a translation in trust, with the belief that "there is 'something there' to be understood."[98] Interpretation begins with a leap of faith that there is "something there," that there is meaning in the text ("I believe in order to understand"). The second step is aggressive: we crack the code, hunt the meaning, penetrate the surface. Next, we import the form and content into our own context; we domesticate it. With the fourth step— that of restitution—we arrive at the heart of the ethics of interpretation, for the translator here restores the voice of text and hence its ability to continue affecting its readers.[99] Through translation, we set the text free from its original context and prolong its career. Translation greets the text with a kiss, not of betrayal but of life. "'Interpretation' [is] that which gives language life beyond the moment and place of immediate utterance or transcription."[100] Thanks to this last step, translation preserves the potential of texts to have meaning in new contexts.

Creative Fidelity: Understanding As Free Yet Faithful

The best translations are those that are both creative and faithful. Successful translations do not annihilate but preserve the identity of both text and reader.

Faithful Translation: Reproductive Interpretation?

What is a faithful translation? Fidelity should not be confused with reiteration. It is the literalist who attempts what we might call a "reproductive" translation. The literalist tries to erase himself or herself from the interpretive process, to be so obedient to the text that the first step—submission—is also the last. The literalist "does not aim to appropriate and bring home . . . [but] to remain 'inside' the source."[101] Perhaps the most obvious example of this kind of repetition is the interlinear translation. Yet as Steiner archly observes, the interlinear is less a translation than a translation help: "It sets a dictionary equivalent from the target-language above each word in the source-language. Strictly defined, a word-for-word interlinear is nothing else but a total glossary, set out horizontally in discrete units and omitting the criteria of normal syntax and word-order in the language of the user."[102] The notion that only word-for-word translations are faithful rests on a faulty view of semantics that sees words, rather than speech acts, as the fundamental unit of meaning. Faithful translation, however, is not a matter of matching *locutions* so much as finding equivalent *illocutions*. As we have seen, the literal sense is the sense of the literary act (an illocution).

Creative Understanding: Dialogical Interpretation

Even translations that aim for dynamic equivalence are still concerned with reproduction: reproducing a communicative act that elicits the equivalent response in the contemporary reader to that of the original audience. However, we can never really go back; try as we might, we cannot quite get out of our own skins. Despite our best interpretive efforts, something of our own, and of our age, will remain in our experience of all literature. We can call this the "bias principle." Readers may nevertheless approximate the author's intended meaning in spite of the bias principle. We can, for example, eliminate "the grosser illusions of perspective."[103] Such was the burden of the previous chapter, in which I argued for the possibility of a relatively adequate literary knowledge. But there is a second, more positive way to construe the bias principle, namely, in terms of a *productive* rather than a reproductive understanding. Good translation and good reading, I submit, is a matter of *creative* fidelity to the text. The New Revised Standard Version translators, for instance, were guided by the principle, "As literal as possible, as free as necessary." This principle raises a question for hermeneutics in general, namely, how free can readers be before becoming irresponsible?

According to Bakhtin, the ideal reader is much more than a passive mirror. Mirrors simply image the original, and mirrored reading achieves only reproductive or "duplicative" understanding. In Bakhtin's view, however, authors typically expect more of their readers. Reading, he believes, should never be monologic; neither the text nor the reader is a "voiceless thing" with nothing to contribute. Understanding (the goal of the human as opposed to the natural sciences) is thoroughly dialogic.[104]

An interpretation stands to its original not as an exact copy but as a kind of metaphor: "Instead of dissimulating the otherness of the original, a translation establishes a relationship, between two texts . . . two languages, ultimately two cultures and perhaps two historical moments."[105] Michael Edwards draws an analogy between the change wrought by translation to the change wrought by redemption. Translation is a "re-creative possibility": "Just as language, rather than duplicating the world, operates upon it, so translation, rather than duplicating a work, may operate on the work and on the world of the work."[106] The "misery" of the translator is that he or she can never equal the original; the "glory" of the translator is that one can make it greater (e.g., one can prolong it, enhance it). Christian interpreters, above all, should be people who hope for re-creation.

Creative understanding results in the transformation of the other's word into one's own without simply collapsing the one into the other, that is, *without losing* either the horizon of the text or of the reader and *without confusing* the horizons. Historical criticism, we observed, tends to reduce the meaning of a text to the time of its production, thus rendering the reader's creative insights null and void. To "enclose" a work within its own epoch is to restrict it to what Bakhtin calls "small time." On the other hand, if textual meaning simply were what the reader made of it, this would similarly enclose the meaning within the single epoch of the present—"small time" again. Would translation not be more accurate if we could completely eliminate the contribution of contemporary readers? Bakhtin thinks not: "There exists a very strong, but one-sided and thus untrustworthy, idea that in order better to understand a foreign culture, one must enter into it, forgetting one's own . . . but if this were the only aspect of this understanding, it would merely be duplication."[107] Creative understanding, however, does not renounce its own place in time or culture and precisely for this reason can understand what is foreign about the other. "A meaning only reveals its depths once it has encountered and come into contact with another, foreign meaning: they engage in a kind of dialogue, which surmounts the closedness and one-sidedness of these particular meanings, these cultures."[108] Significantly, this dialogue does not result in a merging or fusing (confusing) of these horizons into some third thing that is neither one nor the other. Contra Gadamer, a "fusion of horizons" is not yet a true dialogue, for instead of preserving two voices in their integrity, it collapses them into one.

Bakhtin is not saying that creative readers impute to texts something that is not there. It is possible, of course, to distort a text; it is possible creatively to *misunderstand*. In genuine understanding, on the other hand, one encounters the author as other. The solution to the paradox of creative fidelity is to be found, for Bakhtin, in the nature of the literary act and of literary genre. Meaning can grow over time, thanks to the potential inherent in communicative practices: "Semantic phenomena can exist in concealed form, potentially, and be revealed only in semantic cultural contexts of subsequent epochs that are favorable for such disclosure."[109] This was the point of Steiner's fourth step, where the translator provides restitution to the text. Fidelity, either in translation or interpretation, is neither literalistic nor duplicative: "Where it surpasses the original, the real translation infers that the source-text possesses potentialities, elemental reserves as yet unrealized by itself."[110] Booth agrees: "What determines which values emerge in each . . . new community of discourse, is not *only* what the community chooses to do with the stuff but also what the stuff 'chooses' to do."[111] *King Lear* will just as surely remain a tragedy even as it develops, just as a human fetus will remain human as it grows. Yet the meaning of *King Lear* develops because of what creative readers have discovered and continue to discover in it.

It is precisely the reader's distance from the text that creates the possibility of dialogue and the condition for discovering the full meaning potential of a text. It is important, however, to root meaning potential in the text. The link between locutions, illocutions, and perlocutions is neither arbitrary nor absolute; not just any illocution can be associated with a particular locution, nor can just any perlocution follow from a given illocution. "It is only what the text actually says that can, in truth, transformatively engage the spiritually motivated reader."[112]

Identity in Interpretation: Two Kinds of Sameness of Meaning

This insinuation of self into otherness is the final secret of the translator's craft.[113]

I wish to conclude this discussion of faithful interpretation and sameness of meaning by returning to the concept of identity. Nida posits "equivalence" rather than "identity" as the goal of translation in acknowledgment of the impossibility of repeating the selfsame speech act.[114] There may nevertheless be a role for the concept of identity. The identity the translator seeks is not, I suggest, the identity of an unchanging substance but rather the identity of a historical tradition. I draw on Ricoeur's distinction between two modes of personal identity—*idem* and *ipse*—to illustrate two kinds of semantic identity.

"Idem" Identity. *Idem* is the Latin term for sameness. We speak, for instance, of numerical identity, of something being "one and the same." Clearly, reading cannot be "one and the same" as authoring; neither the time nor the context of interpretation is the same in the two cases. What about, in the second place, material identity, that is, substantial sameness? Here the interpretation may be so similar to the original as to be virtually interchangeable; like identical twins, there is real commonality, though not numerical identity. The goal of interpretation would be to substitute a commentary for the text without essential semantic loss. What these two definitions of *idem* share is the notion of permanence through time—a perpetuation of the same. It is difficult, however, given the realities of interpretation (e.g., the fact that interpreters do not share the same place and time as the original communicative act), to speak of permanence through time. For as we have seen, with the passing of time goes the passing of context. *Idem* identity seems more appropriate for the natural sciences, where two events can be said to be identical if they are repeated under exactly the same conditions. The problem with textual interpretation, of course, is that the conditions—the contexts of author and reader respectively—are never the same.

"Ipse" Identity. Must "sameness of meaning" ("semantic identity") imply unchanging permanence through time? Ricoeur turns to another model of permanence in time to distinguish personal identity or selfhood (*ipse*) from the sameness of impersonal things. *Ipse* suggests a model of permanence in time that applies to persons rather than things. My claim is that the sameness of meaning is more like personal identity than impersonal sameness.[115] When a person keeps a promise, this is a matter not of self-sameness but of self-constancy. Self-constancy is not simply the perpetuation of the same. As Ricoeur notes: "The continuity of character is one thing, the constancy of friendship is quite another."[116] A full-orbed concept of personal identity must include an account both of character and of self-constancy. Insofar as the promise is the paradigm instance of a person's keeping one's word, we may conclude that personal identity is related to *illocutionary* continuity. In return, we may say that sameness of meaning is, in large part, a matter of *ipse* identity—of constancy, not numeric identity.

Earlier I argued that texts, as communicative acts, have an implicit aim. This aim is, moreover, twofold: every communicative act wants to be recognized for the kind of act (illocution) it is; every communicative act wants to produce some further effect on the reader (perlocution). Of course, as we have seen, the text, unlike a person, is unable to take the initiative in interpretation. The text-reader relation is asymmetrical. To the extent that the text is a "helpless other," all it can do is call us to attention. Can the reader respond to the call responsibly? Keeping in mind the twin notions of dynamic equivalence and *ipse* identity, we can now resolve the paradox of creative fidelity by offering the following definition of creative understanding: *interpretations that are creative and faithful demonstrate not identity but constancy with regard to the text.* Specifically, a faithful interpretation must reflect the same matter, force, and direction that characterized the original communicative action.

Can we carry the analogy between texts and personal identity (selfhood) even further? Why do some texts affect various readers in different ways? Perhaps for the same reason that I affect people differently. Though I remain myself, I relate to different people in different ways. Most important, what makes me *me* is a matter of how I relate to others, so much so that my personal identity is revealed only in and by my relations to others.[117] So it is, perhaps, with texts. A text remains what it is, but it can affect and relate to others in different ways. Further, the text cannot be itself without the mediation of others—without readers. The reader is necessary in order to receive and to realize the communicative capacity of the text. Interestingly, the mediating role of others is discussed by Aristotle in his *Nichomachean Ethics* under the rubric of friendship. Friendship brings to the forefront the question of reciprocity. One does not love a friend for the sake of utility or even pleasure. In friendship, giving and receiving are mutual. In the case of interpretation, however, the reader must take the initiative; for the text is potentially a helpless victim as well as a potential friend.

Rudolf Bultmann famously asked: "Is exegesis without presuppositions possible?" Simply to pose the question is to suggest the obvious answer: interpretation is always biased. The interpreter never stands in the same place as the author. Readers can never wholly recover the selfsame meaning of the original. However, though exegesis without ideological presuppositions may not be possible, it does not follow that the interpreter cannot exegete (i.e., "lead meaning out of") the text. Indeed, I have argued that it is *because* of the reader's ideology, because the reader is an "outsider" with regard to the text, that he or she is able to be an other, to recognize the text for what it is in its difference, and thus is able to develop its full potential. As with persons, so with texts: their true identity only becomes apparent in the full range of their relationships. It is because the reader occupies a different place that he or she can be a friend to the text, or an enemy.

Is the translator, then, friend or foe of the text? There is a kind of "handing over" that is not a betrayal. Or, to be exact, there is a "handing down," a *traditio*, that is not a "handing over," a *traditore*. Whereas Judas handed Jesus over, the other apostles handed Jesus on to subsequent generations.[118] Faithful interpretation is, I believe, more like apostolic tradition; it is a matter not of betraying but of continuing the communicative act, of passing it on. One who stands in a tradition attends to and is affected by the past. We receive something that we did not make and pass it on to others. Interpreters, by mediating the past to others, repay their debt to what has gone before. What interpreters ultimately must give to the text is attention, justice, and memory. *Like tradition, then, translation does not simply repeat the past but rather develops it.* Like tradition, interpretation helps the text survive the passing of its original context in order to live on. The text does not preempt dialogue but opens it through an overture of meaning that invites a responsible response. Handing on need not be a guilty handing over. The ethical interpreter seeks the sameness not of the self-identical but of the self-constant; *the translator is one who preserves the efficacy of past communicative action.*

READER RESPONSE AND READER RESPONSIBILITY

A text is an overture of meaning that invites a responsible response on the part of the reader. Ethical interpretation may refer, in the first instance, to the reader's evaluation of a text's moral worth. Yet reading is itself an interpretive act, an integral part of the covenant of discourse, for which the reader is in turn responsible. Like other human acts, that is, the way one reads is also open to evaluation, including moral assessment. In particular, the reader is responsible for what he or she does with meaning. In this section I distinguish interpretive ethics, which has to do with the variety of interpretive aims and reader rights, from interpretive morality, which has to do with universal interpretive norms and reader obligations. The question is whether the reader's response is more a matter of interpretive rights or of interpretive duties, and of how and where one draws the distinction between the two.

Realism and Responsibility

It would be all too easy to contrast a hermeneutics of responsibility with the playful, aesthetic posture of certain postmodern thinkers. It would also be an oversimplification, for a number of recent works, including some by Derrida himself, challenge the view that deconstruction results in a kind of nihilistic textual freeplay. The real issue is rather the contrast between different senses of "responsibility." There *is* an ethics of deconstruction, though it is not perhaps self-evident, for how can there be a responsible response if texts have undecidable meanings? Over against the ethics of deconstruction stands the ethics of the covenant of discourse, with its emphasis on attending to meaning rather than deferring it. Hence our question: *which ethics? whose responsibility?*

Non-realist Conceptions of Reader Responsibility

Those who do not believe that textual meaning is "there" may feel free to invent it. Fish, for instance, argues that the reader's response is not *to* the meaning; it *is* the meaning. Vincent B. Leitch takes it for granted that reading is more a matter of creation than discovery.[119] Indeed, he believes that critics are being dishonest when they pretend to have got "the meaning" of a text. For hermeneutic non-realists, the primary obligation is to keep the "play" of meaning going—to resist closure. For Roland Barthes, readers take their "pleasure" of the text whenever they make it mean something new or different. His goal as a literary critic is not to reduce the text to a stable signified (e.g., a determinate meaning) but rather "to keep its signifying power open."[120] Here we can perhaps speak of the "will to play" rather than the "will to power." The main point about non-realism, however, is that nothing limits the powerplay of interpretation. If meaning is not there, then there is nothing to which one can respond or be responsible.

A number of deconstructors have recently claimed the moral high ground, however, and if they continue to commend play, it is now play with a political purpose.[121] Undoers, they contend, show respect for the otherness of the text by *resisting* conventional readings and methods of interpretation. Responsible reading, that is, seeks to free the text (and the reader) from the control of ideological interpretation. Undoing liberates the text from its "Babylonian captivity" to the "single correct interpretation." Deconstruction is ethical insofar as it reads *against* the standard readings in search of what they have left out or suppressed. "Deconstruction is neither corrective surgery carried out on a diseased text nor autopsy performed on a deceased text. Rather, it is active engagement—an ethical engagement, a signing on—by the reader *with* a living text and the Other that comes to the reader as a gift and a challenge."[122] One might say that deconstruction is a search for signs of textual *life*.

At its best, deconstruction calls our attention to how institutional configurations of power suppress otherness. It asks us to be attentive to the "alterity" of the text. "It calls me to be on guard against reinscribing the other in my image for my purposes."[123] Deconstruction resists textual and interpretive structures and systems that repress what does not comfortably fit: "Postmodern readings function as political and ethical responses to other readings which claim that their own foundations exist outside of a field of power."[124] For many postmoderns, the only real ethical question concerns the formation of interpretive conventions: Whose interest do they serve?

Postmodern readings of the Bible share one important family resemblance: a suspicion of the claim to "mastery" that often characterizes traditional readings, including those of modern biblical criticism. I have already commended deconstruction for its iconoclastic tendencies. With the Undoers, I too resist Marxist, feminist, psychoanalytic, and so forth theories of interpretation that reduce a text to its political, social, or psychological conditions. In the context of resisting such reductionism, even playful interpretations (e.g., those that undo interpretive privilege by exposing the power play) are ultimately political acts. As I argue below, however, it is far from clear what positive ethical or political action emerges from a non-realist ethics of interpretation. Responsibility *for* the other shades into freedom *from* the other, for an other that has no concrete form and content can make no determinate demands on the reader.

Realist Conceptions of Reader Responsibility

The non-realist claim about what is "good" for human beings—a freedom that consists in resisting closed orders—inescapably involves certain beliefs about reality and about the nature of human beings. But this is a metaphysical query. Metaphysics may be defined as the discourse about the underlying intelligible structure of our commitments, about "what constitutes them as more than arbitrarily willed options."[125] At the bottom of many non-realist approaches to interpretation, I suggest, is the assumption that language, and human being itself, is essentially a struggle for power. This is the metaphysics of neo-Darwinian naturalism, however, rather than a view of reality informed by the doctrines of creation and redemption. Behind every ethics of interpretation, including the deconstructive, lies a set of assumptions concerning the way things really are.

The basic problem with the postmodern liberation of the reader from dominant interpretations is that it fails to free readers from themselves. The irony of this liberation from fixed orders is that the postmodern self becomes free and responsible only by emptying out everything that opposes it. That meaning is not "really" there, but only an imposition of institutional ideologies and practices, is a liberating insight for the postmodernist; for if nothing is really there, then nothing can make a claim on my life. Must we say, amending Derrida, that there is nothing outside oneself? This does seem to be the logic behind much postmodern thought. An independent reality with its own intrinsic order would limit my creativity and call my freedom into question.

Theological hermeneutics, on the other hand, is unabashedly realist about meaning. A theological interpretation of interpretation contends that there is something in the text that transcends me. It believes that readers can receive something from the communicative act of another that can engage, and perhaps enlarge and enhance, their being. How do hermeneutic realists deal with the phenomenon of textual otherness? If there is indeed a meaning in texts that transcends the process of interpretation, what is the reader's obligation toward it? Just this: the reader ought to acknowledge it as other, to respond to what is there, to what Steiner terms its "real presence." Concretely, this means acknowledging a communicative act for what it is, namely, a verbal work whereby an author says something about something to someone. It means acknowledging the text's matter (the sense and reference), energy (illocutionary force), and teleology (perlocution). For example, with regard to Jesus' parables, one must acknowledge that these texts metaphorically describe the kingdom of God and challenge the reader to espouse a way of life commensurate with it. Thiselton rightly highlights the speech act nature of the parables: "They attack, they rebuke, they claim, they defend."[126] Jesus' parables are complex actions that elicit further actions (e.g., of interpretation, evaluation, following, etc.). They display narrative worlds that collide with the world of the reader. How is it that reading a parable can affect a reader's life as powerfully as any physical encounter? Is it not because in reading we encounter a proposal that is not merely of our own making? The ethics of the interpretive realist is characterized by responsibility *to* another, not freedom from it.

In fact, readers have a twofold responsibility towards the text: to determine to what kind of communicative act a text belongs, and to respond to this communicative act in an appropriate manner. The ethical response to a text will be "fitting." Jeanrond concurs: "A text whose primary communicative perspective is aesthetic can be expected to provoke an aesthetic genre of reading. A text whose primary communicative perspective is theological can be expected to provoke a theological genre of reading."[127] Responsibility for the text is thus a matter of responding appropriately to the text. Indeed, as Richard Niebuhr suggests, with an eye to the etymology of the term, the responsible self is an *answerer*.[128] To be a responsible human being is to be one who can answer back. To be responsible is to be engaged in a dialogue with what is not oneself: "Meaning is neither read *off* nor read *into* language, but is rather *encountered in* it. . . . Meaning is 'encountered' in the sense that we are engaged by it rather than merely exposed to it."[129] The encounter with the text is an encounter with the work and with the "face" of the author—a face to which the reader must respond and a work with which the reader must grapple. The responsible reader walks a middle way between conformity and creativity, neither slavishly repeating nor freely inventing. In the covenant of discourse, one's response to the text's overture of meaning must be one that is fitting—a creative obedience.[130]

Reading As an Ethical Activity

What criterion decides which reader response is "fitting"? Is the ethical reader more like the "master" or the "slave" of the text? Jeanrond classifies conservative reader-response critics (like Iser and Sternberg) as slaves of the text and radical reader-response critics (like Fish) as masters.[131] A theological approach that gives centrality to the covenant of discourse, however, will define text and reader not in terms of rival power centers but rather as centers of communication.

Inactive Reading

Some readers, of course, are not responsive enough. Like those who listen only for the tune, inactive readers read only for the plot or for the point. The form and style of the text as a communicative act pass by largely unnoticed. Consequently, they miss entire dimensions of meaning. Eco mentions reading Kafka's *Trial* stupidly, as if it were only a crime novel. Is it also possible to read the Bible stupidly, say, as merely a cleverly designed myth (or alternately, as a meticulously researched history)?

In fact, the Bible is an ensemble of many different kinds of literary acts, each demanding *different kinds* of reader response. Law, prophecy, parable, story, parable—each calls for a different kind of engagement on the part of the reader. Inactive readers typically read for the proposition and overlook the varieties of illocutionary force. The inactive reader, by remaining on the level of explanation and never getting to the level of appropriation, short-circuits the process of interpretation. Preoccupation with the locutions may replace genuine interaction with the subject matter on an existential level. Unresponsive readers remain unmoved by the matter because they fail to feel its (illocutionary) force. We can perhaps better appreciate Barth's reproach to the historical critics of his day as an attack on insufficiently *responsive* reading.

Reactive Reading

Reactive readers, on the other hand, resemble freedom fighters, whose resistance to the text or to standard interpretations is the resistance not of inertia (as is typical of inactive readers) but of indignation. The ethical question for the reactive reader is: "When should real readers decide to read against the conventions of the text or of the interpretive community, and how is that resistance to be enacted."[132] Reactive readers read against the text or against the history of its interpretation. They are responding, but not to the text as such but to the ways in which texts and interpretations have served the ideological interests of class, gender, race, or religion.

Reactive readers may even *rebel* against the text in the name of social justice. The rebellious reader refuses to accept meanings or interpretations that serve a sociopolitical interest that oppresses others: "Resistance reading means different readings that resist the oppressive use of power in discourse. . . . Better ideological readings are those that support and encourage positive social change that affirms difference and inclusion."[133] But this will simply not do. Who determines which changes are "positive," what differences should be affirmed, and how wide the gate of inclusivism should be thrown open? Is any marginal reading to be welcomed simply because it is on the margins?

Hyperactive Reading

Both the inactive and the reactive reader tend to be hermeneutic realists. That is, they are largely content to acknowledge that there is a meaning in the text, though they might differ with regard to what they take to be an appropriate response to it. Hyperactive readers, on the other hand, are non-realists. Their burden is to create meaning, as much meaning as possible perhaps, in order to realize the full potential not only of the text but also of the reader. On this view, the reader's response is what interpretation is largely about. There is no transcendent logos that indwells the text; the text is simply a pretext for an endless series of decodings in and for different contexts.

The hyperactive reader is abnormally active; his or her response, in other words, is excessive. Barthes describes a kind of reading where one keeps stopping and looking up, not because of boredom (inactivity) but because of the flow of ideas and associations that keep interrupting the text.[134] In such hyperactive reading, the reader's train of thought is not deductive but associative, busily reading the text in light of other ideas, other contexts, other codes. Hyperactive interpretation is a frenetic allegorizing that finds associations never intended by the author by superimposing various decoding devices (e.g., psychoanalytic, structuralist, feminist, Marxist, etc.) on texts that were otherwise encoded. Such creative decoding yields a pleasure all its own, which Barthes calls "writing." This is the pleasure that comes from creating something that will attract attention to itself and call for yet more writing (more interpretation). The hyperactive reader "does not decode; he *overcodes*."[135] It is the hyperactive reader, not the author, who creates the world of the text. The problem, once again, is that such readers never get beyond themselves. Piaget's verdict on egocentric children applies equally well to the hyperactive reader: "He makes his own reality . . . magic on the ontological plane. . . . At the root [of the magic] . . . lies the same egocentric illusions, namely . . . confusion between the self and the external world."[136]

Deconstruction represents another type of hermeneutic excess. It is an overreaction to reason's pretentious claim to have attained absolute certainty or closure. As I have already argued, there is an alternative to the dire choice that deconstruction gives us between absolute knowledge and absolute undecidability. The alternative is that we have, and are responsible for acting on, relatively *adequate* knowledge about texts—adequate for specific communicative purposes. The hyperactive reader, however, suffers from hyperbolic doubt. Undoers believe there are no facts, only interpretations, or as Derrida puts it, that there is nothing outside the text. Derrida questions all settled interpretation by an excessive, almost perverse, attention to the details (including the margins) of texts. In my opinion, the deconstructor errs in attending overmuch to the inconsequential. Such exaggerated attention is a form of *misdirection*; it is a classic case of not seeing the forest for the trees or, for that matter, being unable to see the trees because of an excessive preoccupation with the texture of the bark. To take another image: the radical Undoer is like a petulant child, invariably a literalist, who ignores a parental directive by pointing out some minor verbal infelicity: "'Wait a moment, please.' 'It's been a moment.'"[137]

Proactive Reading

The "proactive" reader takes an initiative on behalf of the text. Responsibility *for* the text as other requires, first and foremost, accountability *to* the text. As Steiner puts it: "We are answerable to the text . . . in a very specific sense, at once moral, spiritual and psychological."[138] Steiner notes that in many cultures, hospitality is a religious obligation. Similarly, our duty to receive the textual stranger as a welcome guest is an obligation implied in the covenant of discourse. Moreover, we can only judge the moral worth of a text after we get to know it. To judge the ethical effect of a particular communicative act, we need to judge the quality of response invited by the whole work: "What will it do to us if we surrender our imagination to its paths?"[139] The proactive reader is willing to make an initial step of faith and open himself or herself up to the effects of the text: "I believe in order to understand." There is no way to achieve textual understanding if one refuses to follow and respond to the initiatives of the text.

Readers have an infinite debt, not to the face, as Lévinas would have it, but to the *voice*. Every text confronts its reader with an ethical demand: "Thou shalt not kill." One may "kill" a voice by extinguishing it or by assimilating it to one's own agenda, forcing it to say only what one wants to hear. According to Morgan, the moral right of authors to be understood as they intended is only short-term; "that right dies with them or with the occasions for which the utterance was intended."[140] As I have already argued, however, the text as communicative act is an extension of its agent, a projection of the author's voice through space and over time. We owe a debt to authors and to the past, not to forget or to falsify their voices, even when we disagree with them.[141] *The existence of a voice other than my own presents an absolute command: "Thou shalt not bear false witness."*

The Aims and Norms of Reading: From Interpretive Goods to Interpretive Right

Not all readers read the same way, of course, nor do readers who read the same way always get the same results. Must we then conclude that some of these readers have borne false witness with regard to the text? We must first consider a preliminary question: What kind of readings count as instances of bearing false witness? To answer this latter query, we need to distinguish between the aims and norms of interpretation. The question then becomes: Are all interpretive aims ("goods") equally normative ("right")? In distinguishing ethics (the discourse on the "good") from morality (the discourse on the "right"), I am following a convention represented by, among others, Ricoeur: "I reserve the term 'ethics' for the *aim* of an accomplished life and the term 'morality' for the articulation of this aim in *norms* characterized at once by the claim to universality and by an effect of constraint."[142]

Interpretive Goods

Aristotle defines the "good" as "that at which things aim."[143] Mark Brett helpfully distinguishes between "interpretive interests" (e.g., the aims that guide particular interpretive methods) and "ideological interests" (e.g., the aims that reflect a reader's broader ethical and political commitments).[144] I am here concerned, however, with the ethical significance of a reader's interpretive aims. Brett observes that "a method is not, in itself, an ethic," but goes on to say that particular interpretive interests—he does not specify which—can and should be given ethical defenses. Now for the difficult question: Which interpretive aims, or "goods," are normative, morally defensible? Is, for instance, the interest in reconstructing the history of a text's composition a legitimate interpretive interest, or does it fall on the side of the *immorality* of literary knowledge? (And who can say?)

Different interpretive communities have disparate interpretive aims. What one deems "good" in interpretation depends to some extent on the community of readers to which one belongs. Historical critics have one idea of interpretive "good," reader-response critics quite another, and deconstructive readers yet another. To suggest that a particular interpretive interest—for example, an interest in reconstructing the history of a text's composition—is somehow immoral is, at first blush, most peculiar. For it is a commonplace in our postmodern context that the search for universal foundations—in ethics or anything else—must be abandoned. Values, in interpretation and ethics alike, are relative to particular communities.

Interpretive Right: The "Hermeneutical" Imperative

Morality is, as Wilfred Sellars has said, a matter of "we-intentions." But how large is the communal "we"? Is it a community that has a history and tradition or a community that shares the same political agenda? Or can the communal "we" be just you and me? Where do hermeneutical values come from? Why move from a description of diverse interpretive aims to a prescription of some aims rather than others? The answer to this last question is basic yet massive: violence. It is the possibility of interpretive violence—of repressing the otherness of the text—that calls us to supplement a reflection on the various aims of interpretation (hermeneutic "goods") with a reflection on the valid norms of interpretation (hermeneutic "right"). *The morality of literary knowledge has to do with the checks on interpretive aims and interests*. Not every interpretation of the text is as legitimate or appropriate as another. If it were, there would be no such thing as a misreading.

Historical critics stake out the moral high ground in biblical interpretation by claiming to have rescued the text from dogmatic interpretations that had been foisted upon it. Whereas theologians press a text into the service of their respective denominations, the biblical scholar acts as champion of the "oddness and specificity" of the text.[145] On the other hand, Karl Barth charges biblical critics with avoiding the real matter of the biblical texts in their preoccupation with the history of the text's composition. What are we to make of these diverse assessments of the morality of biblical criticism? Do critical methods protect or neglect the otherness of the biblical text?

It is difficult to fault historical criticism for its interest in determining as much as possible about the original context, for this is an aspect of the quest to discover what a communicative act meant to the author and the first addressees. Barth may nevertheless have a valid point when he says that biblical critics are not critical enough. They attend to one aspect of the text to the detriment of others. Historical critics have become fixated on one level of description only, to use categories drawn from our last chapter. It is a mistake to think that one has grasped the nature and aim of a communicative act when one has clarified its prehistory only. To confine interpretation to one level of meaning is ultimately to reduce it. And this is precisely where the category of hermeneutic right and wrong is useful, *to combat interpretive reductionism*. What is immoral about certain interpretive interests is not what they do but what they fail to do. To reduce the fullness of textual meaning to this or that aspect of the communicative act is to commit a form of interpretive violence. Specifically, it is to reduce interpretation itself to something sub-hermeneutic—a kind of thin description that may yield limited knowledge, but not understanding. What is immoral about an interpretive interest, then, is not so much what it does but what it leaves out or overlooks. *Reduced* interpretations produce only half-hearted responses. Theirs is the sin of omission, of not telling the whole truth.

Another form of interpretive violence is that which willfully reads against the grain. The problem here is not so much reduction as abduction, where meaning is kidnapped—carried off by force or deception. The phenomenon of revisionist history is a good case in point. Revisionists make historical judgments on the basis of ideological commitments. For example, Robert Gnuse suggests, on the basis of an evolutionary approach to the history of religion, that the distinction between Israelites and Canaanites, with regard to religious issues, may be "bogus."[146] The discontinuity between Israel and the other nations that so marks the Pentateuch and the historical books is, says Gnuse, a fiction. Israel's distinctive monotheism was a "mutation" in the evolutionary development of religion. What actually lies behind Gnuse's whole historical reconstruction is, in fact, process theology. He believes that God works not through intermittent mighty acts but through constant "pressure." What this means for contemporary Christians is that we should not view ourselves in opposition to the world, but as catalysts in the evolutionary advance of monotheism. In short, Gnuse's theology (an ideological interest) guides his approach to the biblical text (an interpretive interest). The same temptation that beset earlier dogmatic theologians has ironically come to roost in the house of biblical criticism, namely, the desire to conform the biblical text to one's prior theological agenda.

Is the norm of authorial intention an arbitrary one, as some of Hirsch's critics have suggested?[147] Hirsch responds to this criticism and strives for a degree of universality in his prescriptions by grafting his discussion of interpretive norms onto Kant's discussion of the moral law. For Kant, any rational person should come to see that persons should be treated always as ends, never as means. Respecting other persons was, for Kant, a universal rational requirement.[148] Hirsch invokes Kant in defending the rights of the author: "To treat an author's words merely as grist for one's own mill is ethically analogous to using another man merely for one's own purposes.[149] Hirsch posits the following "fundamental ethical maxim for interpretation": "*Unless there is a powerful overriding value in disregarding an author's intention (i.e., original meaning), we who interpret as a vocation should not disregard it.*"[150] When we use an author's words for our own purposes we transgress the norms of interpretation, "just as we transgress ethical norms when we use another person merely for our ends."[151] An interpreter stands under "the basic moral imperative of speech, which is to respect an author's intention."[152]

For the most ambitious attempt to formulate a universal moral norm for communicative action, however, we must return to Habermas.[153] He recognizes that we live in a time where there is a plurality of visions concerning the "good." If we do not want to settle the ethical question by force, then we must raise the question of what is good for all. To adopt the moral point of view requires us to transcend our particular socio-historical contexts and to adopt the perspective of all those possibly affected by a discussion.[154] A norm is valid when it corresponds to a general interest and is therefore subject to "universalization": "Universalization, the basic principle of a discourse ethic, implies a specific procedure whereby contested norms are accepted once their consequences are understood by all without coercion."[155] The ideal of dominance-free communication is implicit in every speech act. No one communicates, either in speech or writing, except on the assumption that one will eventually be understood, that one's discourse will be received as it was intended rather than distorted and made into something else. *To act communicatively is to hope that one will not fall prey to interpretive violence.*

Interpretive right designates the norm that is in *everyone's* interest insofar as it prohibits interpretive violence: "Do unto others' discourse what you would have others do unto yours." Habermas neither invents this interpretive norm arbitrarily nor deduces it, as did Kant, from the abstract idea of duty. On the contrary, rationality and morality alike are always and already embedded in communicative action. Habermas's "transcendental-pragmatic" approach calls attention to the rules that are implicit in the covenant of discourse. The norm is "transcendental" because it cannot be denied without pragmatic self-contradiction. Even deconstructors read reviews of their books and protest when they have been misunderstood. They contradict themselves when their practices deny what their theories necessarily assume. Take, for instance, the assertion, "No statement is meaningful." It is difficult, if not impossible, to utter this sincerely or coherently. Such a speech act results in a performative contradiction. By contrast, an interpretive norm is justified by showing that it is a necessary condition for the very possibility of understanding. What we might call the "hermeneutical imperative" makes explicit the norm inherent in communicative action.

We can marry Hirsch's arbitrary recommendation to respect the author's intention to Habermas's universal moral requirement by showing that *it is in everyone's interest to respect authors* together with their literary acts. As we have seen, the implicit goal of communicative action, the principle that not only regulates but constitutes action as communicative, is to reach understanding. *Understanding a communicative agent's intention is, therefore, in everyone's interest insofar as it is an intrinsic aspect of communicative action.* The search for understanding is, likewise, in everyone's interest, for to abandon the search is to undermine everyday communicative practice. In reaching this conclusion, we need not claim to have attained some ahistorical, neutral standpoint—a "God's-eye point of view," as it were. The hermeneutical imperative, far from being a "view from nowhere," is actually the view from everywhere, for there is a general consensus on this matter, at least in practice if not in theory. Our very engagement in communicative action is concrete (though often tacit) evidence of our agreement with this principle. The voice of the communicative agent confronts us with a moral demand: "Heed me. Hear me. Understand. Do not bear false witness."[156]

UNDERSTANDING AND OVERSTANDING

To be understood is in itself a source of joy, not to be understood a source of unhappiness.[157]

Seek ye first the original meaning, and all these relevant applications will be added unto you.[158]

"Seek ye first understanding" may be the interpretive norm, but it need not exhaust the reader's interpretive aims. The hermeneutical imperative—to respect the author's intended act—is nevertheless a sieve through which all interpretive aims must pass. Some readers, however, are more concerned with "overstanding" a text than with understanding it. Can "overstanding" ever be moral? Is it ever right for readers to "lord it over" the text? I believe we can apply Luther's paradoxical formula for Christian freedom to interpreters: the reader is "a most free lord of all, subject to none . . . and a most dutiful servant of all, subject to all." I contend that responsible interpretation not only permits, but even requires, both understanding and, to a certain extent, overstanding.

Understanding: The Reader As Servant

The contrast between using and understanding texts signals the crucial difference between interpretive aims and interpretive right. Whereas readers may have various uses in mind as they approach a given text, the task of communicative rationality (and ethics) is precisely to achieve understanding. Understanding a text should not be equated with slavish obedience so much as with the initial honor and respect one owes a stranger. All communication involves vulnerability: the risk that one's overture of meaning will be ignored or rejected. The obligation to hearken to a person's voice stems from the fact that the hearer is in a position to refuse, or even to abuse, an overture of meaning—to turn a deaf ear. Significantly, it has been suggested that the historical origin of communicative ethics may well be the parable of the Good Samaritan.[159] Who is our neighbor? Anyone—speaker or author—who initiates a communication.

The first response of a responsible reader should be respect: acknowledge the text for what it is. Specifically, readers must respect the aim of the text as communicative act. The hermeneutical imperative—to reach understanding—means that readers must first treat the text not as a means (i.e., as something to be used), but as an end (i.e., something to be received). To understand a text is to recognize its locutions and illocutions for what they are, not for what one thinks they ought to be. The moral interpreter grasps the true nature and content of the text as communicative act. The understanding reader "attends to" the same matter that the author "intended." To "stand under" a text means to acknowledge its propositional content and to expose oneself to its illocutionary force. This is our primary responsibility as readers. Understanding means grasping the sense potential of the text, what I have been calling its matter and energy. Insofar as readers acknowledge what is there in the text, they are the text's dutiful servants.[160]

"Subject to all." Given the complexity of the literary act, readers must be willing to acknowledge that many different interpretive methods may in fact contribute to the search for understanding. The Christian interpreter must be prepared to recognize that other interpreters may well have seen something that he or she has missed.[161] Because we are ultimately servants of the text, we must not take the text captive to any one interpretive scheme only.

"Subject to none." It follows from the incompleteness of interpretation that we are free from subscribing unreservedly to any one reading. Interpretive freedom from the tyranny of our immediate contexts derives from our unconditional commitment to understanding the text, insofar as it is possible, on its own terms.[162] Ethical interpreters, therefore, must resist becoming a slave to any single interpretive method while at the same time admitting that every interpretive method may describe an aspect of textual meaning.

Overstanding: The Reader As Lord

Readers, according to Booth, ask three kinds of questions of texts: "those that the object seems to *invite* one to ask; those that it will *tolerate* or respond to, even though perhaps reluctantly; and those that *violate* its interests or effort to be a given kind of thing in the world."[163] All texts set boundaries for appropriate questions: "However indeterminate the work, it will still ask us to rule out certain inappropriate questions."[164] Examples of inappropriate questions might include: "Where's the punch line (of Job)?" "What happens after the end (of Revelation)?" "What can we learn about weather patterns in ancient Israel (from the Gospels)?" And, though one can perform Freudian analyses of texts as diverse as Jane Austen's *Emma* and the Fourth Gospel, we can reasonably guess that the texts themselves would reply, "That is your concern, not mine." Even Derrida's texts ask us to rule out certain questions as inappropriate, such as, "To what traditional literary genre should I assign you?"[165]

Some inappropriate questions may nevertheless need to be asked. Because readers have their own aims and interests, it is unlikely that they will want to ask only the questions the text invites or insists on. Booth cites the example of a forgery, to which the question "Are you a fake?" is improper—that is, a question that the text resists— but important nonetheless. Whereas the understanding reader recognizes what the text demands, the overstanding reader must judge which "violations" of the text may prove necessary.[166] To lord it over a text is to believe that one's own views or one's own questions are superior to those of the text. But not every "standing over" need be a lording over. Indeed, overstanding is sometimes a way of respecting texts by allowing them to address one's contemporary context. I will argue below that overstanding the Bible is a responsible response insofar as it aims at uncovering the text's *significance*.

It is possible, of course, to recognize, even respect, otherness and at the same time contest it. Understanding does not necessarily imply agreement; if it did, there would be no real disputes, only misunderstandings. We must therefore articulate our differences. We cannot know whether or not to agree or disagree with a text until we understand it. For instance, we must determine whether a text offers itself seriously or ironically before disputing its message. Again, this is a matter of recognizing its illocutionary act. We must first determine the kind of communicative act (genre) to which a text belongs before we can ask the *proper* improper questions!

It is all too common among biblical interpreters to overstand before reaching understanding. Interpreters often prefer their own superior understanding of an issue to what the text apparently says. Consider, for instance, the phenomena of genocide in the conquest narratives or slavery in the patriarchal narratives. Many critics decry and condemn the Old Testament stance on these issues. But does the text ever advocate either genocide or slavery *tout court*? Does accusing the Old Testament of promoting mass murder really do justice to the aim of the text itself, taken in context as a literary whole, or does this charge not rebound on the reader and betray a rather peremptory (and premature) judgment? Those who seek textual understanding will appraise the quality of response invited by the *whole* work: "What will it do to us if we surrender our imagination to its paths?"[167] We must ask what the text is really saying/doing with regard to such matters as slavery and genocide. After keeping company with texts for a time, we may indeed feel that it is right to part, and we may even shake the dust from our feet as we do so. But one can only properly make such a judgment after accompanying texts for a time. In short, it is only legitimate to *overstand* a text once one has properly *understood* it.

Attention and Answerability

The solution to the apparent paradox of interpretive servanthood and interpretive freedom is that readers must both *respect* and *relate to* the text's illocutions. The moral interpreter must be both attentive and answerable to the text.

To attend the text means, first and foremost, to let it be. Every text wants to survive in order to fulfill its communicative mission. Understanding occurs when author and reader attend to the same object. The nuances of the term "attention" are instructive: to give care to, to tend, to escort or accompany, to wait on or serve. To attend the text is thus both a positive aim and a constraining norm: "Pay attention." This is our primary debt toward the textual other.

Readers can only pay attention, of course, to what is there. Iris Murdoch criticizes the non-realist notion that ethics has to do with the imposing, rather than the discerning, of form and value on the world. Neither the good in the world nor the meaning in the text is merely the effect of the interpreter's will to power. Murdoch pleads for a moment of attention prior to willing, for "a just and loving gaze directed upon an individual reality."[168] It is only when one gives one's attention to *what is really there* that the fitting possibilities for response become apparent. Murdoch suggests that when a situation is truly understood, then it will be obvious how we should respond. Indeed, a genuine attentiveness to what is there compels the fitting response, a response that Murdoch likens to "obedience." For Murdoch, reality has an inherent structure. So, I would add, does a text. Attending to the text, on different levels and with different descriptive frameworks, brings its intrinsic rationality progressively to light.

It is only by first attending to the text's communicative aims that we can later go on to articulate our differences. Deconstructive ethics ultimately fails to engage the other, and this despite its frequent rhetorical celebrations of "difference." As Gillian Rose rightly comments: "'The Other' is misrepresented as sheer alterity."[169] If the other is *so* other that nothing can be said (or done) about it, then it can make no concrete difference to our lives. If the text endlessly defers meaning, as Derrida claims, then the reader's response may be permanently delayed too. This seems a highly inappropriate manner of respecting otherness. The postmodern rhetoric in favor of the other apparently leads to the postmodern ethic of indifference to the other. Deconstructive readers "wait" on the text, but only in the sense that Vladimir and Estragon waited on Godot: always waiting, never meeting; always reading, never responding. While deconstruction is an effective remedy for interpretive pride, it easily degenerates into interpretive sloth: to avoiding rather than attending to the text. The slothful reader fails to respond to that meaning which can, however dimly, be discerned. *Différance* is neither final, an exaltation of the other, nor reducible, a cancellation of the other.[170] Interpreters should neither feel complacent on the one hand nor abandon hope on the other; meaning is neither bobbing on the surface of the text nor sunk in an impenetrable abyss. It is rather there, suspended *in* the text, ready to yield to those who approach it with attention and respect.

The attentive interpreter reads Scripture as a complex communicative act that involves a historical or referential dimension, an aesthetic or formal dimension, and an ideological or evaluative dimension. According to Sternberg, there is no more reason to project an ideology on the text than there is to project a grammar: "Either we reconstruct the whole as best we can in the light of the writer's presumed intention . . . or we fashion—in effect reinvent—everything as we please. . . . It accordingly becomes incongruous to stipulate attention in the process of invention."[171] Ethical interpreters, therefore, pay attention to what is there: the language, the literary conventions, the reality model, and the value system. The alternative is to substitute inventions of our own, a choice that makes a mockery of the notion of attention.

Properly to attend the text requires more than a fascination with its locutions (*langue*). The responsible interpreter is answerable to illocutions and perlocutions, the matter and energy of the text, as well. Interpretations are not simply projections or first-person reports on our own feelings, but attempts to describe and to respond to communicative acts. What response should readers give? That depends, of course, on what we encounter when we attend to a given text. Refusing to obey an order may demonstrate our understanding (e.g., our recognition of an illocutionary act) and our overstanding (e.g., our judgment that it does not deserve to be obeyed). The reader's response, I argue below, is ultimately a matter of interpretive virtue. Augustine defines "virtue" as an "ordered love": "the ordinate condition of the affections in which every object is accorded that kind and degree of love which is appropriate to it."[172] All texts demand an initial respect. But what further response a reader gives the text depends on the kind and quality of textual meaning and the reader's own affections.

Understanding Scripture: Discipleship and the "Death" of the Reader

Apply thyself wholly to the text; apply the text wholly to thyself.[173]

Understanding is not easy, but neither is it impossible. Readers can indeed respond to a text in a manner befitting its intention, but often only after a considerable struggle, both with the text and with oneself. For to acknowledge the direction of thought opened up by the text often obliges us to look at our own lives differently. The reader thus struggles with the question of how best to respond to the meaning of the text. Such a struggle is often a wrestling with oneself and with the sense that the text is reading *me*.

Ricoeur discusses the reader's appropriation of the text, the last stage in the interpretive process, not in terms of a "making one's own," as we might have expected, but rather in terms of the unmaking or dispossession of the reader. The understanding reader does not simply assimilate the text to old ways of seeing; the text rather gives to the reader a new mode of seeing the world and oneself. Indeed, the text invites the reader to inhabit its world, to live according to its values and in the light of its vision. It is therefore by reading that one escapes the circularity of Socrates' "Know thyself," for the text gives the reader a new capacity for self-understanding: "It is the text . . . which gives a self to the ego."[174] Of course, not all readers yield so graciously. Not all readers go quietly into the world of the text. Some resist or refuse outright the text's proposals. Like the sower's seed, so texts fall on different kinds of soil.

It has been my aim throughout this work to get beyond the hermeneutics of Socrates, in which one sees only oneself—one's own values or the ideology of one's own community—in the mirror of the text. With Lewis, Steiner, Sternberg, and Ricoeur, I maintain that all genuine reading for understanding, for the *other*, carries with it the risk that the reader will be changed in the process. The search for under-standing is potentially a struggle between sense and self. For to understand the Bible as Scripture means not only acknowledging the Bible's illocutions, but also laying oneself open to its intended effects, its perlocutions. To follow this text means to die to self in order to regain it.

Biblical interpretation is undoubtedly one of the chief means of character for-mation in the church. Character—and community—are formed by hearing and doing the Word. Indeed, the theological aim of biblical interpretation is to grow in the knowledge of God, as well as in wisdom and righteousness. This is the *telos* of reading the Bible as Scripture (2 Tim. 3:16). It follows that readers respond to Scrip-ture as Scripture by *following*, that is, by applying its meaning according to its intent. The church is a community of readers who acknowledge an infinite debt toward the Scriptures, for what the Bible demands of its readers is nothing less than their whole-hearted attention.

According to John A. Darr, reading the Gospels is a character-forming activity—both in the sense that literary characters (e.g., Peter, Judas) are filled out and, more important, in the sense that the reader's character is formed as readers adopt the implied author's outlook on whatever subject matter (actions, attitudes, or ideas) is under consideration. Even the reader's affections are cultivated through reading the Scriptures, which train them to discern "whatever is true, whatever is noble, what-ever is right, whatever is pure" (Phil. 4:8). In gaining a new worldview, readers come to see themselves in a new light too. Competent readers of Luke-Acts, for instance, come to see themselves as believing witnesses of the events surrounding the life of Jesus Christ. The text thus teaches readers how to be faithful disciples: "Theophilus will represent the ideal reader, that potential/incipient believer ('friend of God'), whose very name implies that he is well-disposed toward, receptive of and, indeed, eager to witness and understand."[175] In similar fashion, readers of the Fourth Gospel, insofar as they understand and adopt the perspective offered or imposed by the text, come to play the role of believing disciples and are charged with continuing the role of the beloved disciple who bears faithful witness.[176]

To read the Bible with Christian understanding is to have the ability to use a word, a concept, or a text "according to the Scriptures." Readers schooled in the com-munity of faith acquire the skills to read the Bible as Scripture, that is, to follow its illocutions and its perlocutions so that its meaning is both accomplished and applied. This specifically Christian understanding has as its goal knowledge of the God of Jesus Christ: a dynamic, personal knowledge that leads ultimately to righteousness (2 Tim. 3:16). To read the Bible for Christian understanding is to engage the texts in a dialogue about, and ultimately with, God. The biblical text thus creates the space wherein the reader lays himself or herself open to divine communicative action. Inter-preting Scripture entails a personal encounter from which no responsive reader emerges unchanged. Indeed, responsive readers die to old patterns of interpreting God, the world, and themselves and, to use words of the apostle Paul, are "trans-formed by the renewing of [the] mind" (Rom. 12:2). Far from celebrating the birth of the reader, then, those who seek Christian understanding know that biblical inter-pretation requires the reader's death. The desire to project oneself onto the text, so prevalent in the age of the reader, forestalls the possibility of genuine transformation. In his study of Calvin's hermeneutics, T. F. Torrance observes that it is at the point where we most feel ourselves under attack from Scripture (where our reason is most offended) that genuine interpretation can take place. For it is here "that we can let ourselves be told something which we cannot tell ourselves, and really learn something new which we cannot think up for ourselves."[177]

Is understanding, or appropriating meaning, simply a matter of following hermeneutical rules? Can readers work out their own transformation through interpretive works? If so, then Socrates' "Know thyself" becomes an imperative to "save yourself." On the contrary, genuine understanding involves more than following rules; it involves cultivating response-ability—and "interpretive virtue." As Thiselton rightly comments, the idea that the reader contributes everything "does not seem to fit easily with a theology of divine gift and grace."[178] The morality of interpretation may be a matter of universal procedures, but biblical interpretation involves more; it demands attention and answerability. The truly responsible response is the one that attends to the particular in an appropriate manner. Those who read with creative fidelity must be prepared to follow the particular direction of thought opened up by a particular text, as well as abide by the hermeneutical imperative presupposed by the universal pragmatics of communicative action. To go beyond oneself in order to respond to the text's "Follow me" ultimately requires a responsible response that is not only moral but *spiritual*.

THE SPIRIT OF UNDERSTANDING: DISCERNING AND DOING THE WORD

Reading, says Ricoeur, is "first and foremost, a struggle with the text."[179] But what kind of struggle: an honest struggle to understand a stranger, a "loving struggle" between friends who are trying to overcome their differences, or a violent struggle between two value systems and ways of viewing the world? Reading is essentially the struggle to overcome the various kinds of distance—linguistic, historical, cultural, and moral—that prevent the reader from encountering and appropriating the message of the text. In the course of this study we have encountered various spirits that inform hermeneutics: spirits of play and power, the ubiquitous spirit of the age, and occasionally even the Holy Spirit. I want here to suggest that the struggle with the text, to discern and do the word, is ultimately a matter of spirituality. One's struggle with the text must be conducted in a "spirit of understanding"—not some vague spirit of peace but the Holy Spirit.

The role of the Holy Spirit in biblical interpretation is a justly famous problem. My problem is even more difficult, for I wish to explore the possibility that the Spirit plays a role in general hermeneutics as well. If I am right that genuine interpretation affirms transcendence (e.g., an encounter with something in the text not of our own making)—that all hermeneutics is ultimately theological hermeneutics—then it is only fitting that we consider the Spirit in a chapter dealing with the reader and with the ethics of interpretation. I earlier suggested that the text can be truly respected only when we are prepared to die to self in order to embrace the other. Now we must ask whether such a disposition is not merely ethical (much less natural), but rather the result of spiritual exercise, and perhaps a fruit of the Spirit.

Reader-Reception of Scripture, of Spirit

Nehemiah 8 presents a provocative case study of the kind of "spiritual" reader-reception I have in mind. It depicts Ezra standing on a wooden pulpit made specifically for the purpose of reading the law of Moses to the exiles just returned to Jerusalem. When Ezra opened the Scripture, the people, below him, literally "stood under" the text.[180] Their subsequent response to the reading showed that they understood: they worshiped. Contrast that response with that of earlier kings and priests who had failed to understand or to follow the law (Neh 9:34). A habit of disobedience had made it difficult to understand the biblical text. Under Ezra, however, there was a week-long feast of reading, followed on the eighth day by a solemn assembly. The Scriptures were read for a quarter of the day, and for the next quarter of the day the people responded, confessing their sins (9:2) and worshiping (9:3). Here was no dead letter, but a text that spoke directly to the people's hearts and minds. Significantly, their reception of the text was the occasion for reformation and renewal. Nehemiah 8 thus serves as a paradigm for viewing reader-reception in terms of spiritual renewal. Acts 2 depicts another interpretive "feast," one that involved receiving the Spirit as well as the Scriptures.[181] There is another text reception (of Joel and some Psalms as preached by Peter), followed, as in Nehemiah 8, by an act of corporate repentance: "When the people heard this, they were cut to the heart" (Acts 2:37). In the case of Acts 2, the readers' response includes undergoing baptism.

Nehemiah 8 and Acts 2 raise an intriguing question about how reader-reception of the Word is related to believer-reception of the Spirit. On the basis of these two passages alone, one might conclude that right understanding is a matter of reading in community and in a spirit of repentance. Yet the connection between a past text and its present effect is also a matter of the history of the text's reception. Some critics suggest that we come to know a text only by its effects. Does the community's reception of the text, then, whether guided by the Spirit or not, *change* the meaning of the text or generate new meaning?

According to Gadamer, participation in a tradition is the condition for *all* understanding. A text may have matter and energy, but it also occupies a particular place at a particular time, and its position may change. Both texts and readers are thoroughly historical; each shows the signs of their cultural conditioning. Gadamer insists, against the myth of objectivity, that the reader's place in history and tradition is a vital ingredient in the whole process of understanding. One's prejudices, far from being a skeleton in the reader's closet, are what connects one to the past. Meaning for Gadamer is thus neither in the text nor a mere projection by the reader. It is rather the result of the interaction between the two. Hans Robert Jauss, cofounder of the Constance School of Reception Theory and former student of Gadamer, has made the history of a text's reception his special field of study. For Jauss, the historical significance of a work is determined not by its intrinsic qualities or by the genius of its author but by its reception from generation to generation through history.[182] Past meanings/readings are understood as the prehistory of present meanings/readings.

The situations depicted in Nehemiah 8 and Acts 2 are just two examples of a universal phenomenon, namely, of understanding through participation in community tradition. The "spirit of understanding" is, for Gadamer, thoroughly historical—the spirit of living tradition, the spirit of the "fusion of horizons."

Two problems bedevil this approach. First, Habermas points out that readers are unable to criticize their tradition if participation in the tradition is a condition for understanding. Could Gadamer ever appeal to the text *against* the tradition of its interpretation, and if so, how? If not, then it is far from clear how to stop an interpretive community from being not merely authoritative but authoritarian, or even fascist. For if the text itself cannot be used as a critical principle, what can be? Second, to "confuse" a text with its history of interpretation is to abandon realism in favor of pragmatism. C. S. Peirce's summation of pragmatism all too closely resembles Gadamer's account of meaning: "Consider what effects, that might conceivably have practical bearings, we conceive the object of our conception to have. Then, our conception of these effects is the whole of our conception of the object."[183] The confusion of horizons ultimately succumbs to the affective fallacy: "The Affective Fallacy is a confusion between the poem and its *results* (what it *is* and what it *does*), a special case of epistemological skepticism"[184]

For Gadamer, understanding is always "traditioned"; that is, readers never come to the text as it is in itself, only to the text as received by a particular community. The interpreter is always already part of the history of the text's effects. It is unclear, however, whether the effects that the text produces in its community of readers are part of its objective meaning or of its ongoing significance. The problem with Gadamer's approach is precisely that he is unable to draw this distinction. The meaning-significance distinction is even harder to maintain in biblical interpretation, for the church's understanding is thought to be not only "traditioned" but "spirited." Hence we return to our initial query: Is it the Spirit's role to develop or create new meaning from the text in the history and tradition of its reception? The role of the Spirit in interpretation hangs on the answer one gives to this question. Today, there is a danger of demeaning the literal sense (what it meant to the author and the original audience) in favor of an *ecclesiastical* sense (what it means to us today in the community guided by tradition or by the Spirit).[185] Should we follow Gadamer and identify the Word of God not with the text in itself but with the "traditioned" text, that is, "the text as read by the church in the Spirit"? Do we have any practical alternative? I believe that we do: the spirit of understanding is, as we will see, the Spirit of God's Word.

Mission and Meaning

He will guide you into all truth. (John 16:13)

Communication, like revelation, has an objective and a subjective component. Karl Barth divides his discussion of revelation into two parts: the first focuses on Jesus, the "objective reality of revelation"; the second on the Holy Spirit, "the subjective reality."[186] Similarly, "communication" can refer to the act of transmitting a message and to the event of its reception. Is the meaning of Scripture, or of any other text, objectively there, or is it there only when it is received?[187] Is the Bible objectively the Word of God, or does it only become the Word of God when the Holy Spirit enables hearers and readers to receive it as such? As in the Reformation, so in our time some of the most pronounced disagreements over theological hermeneutics concern the relation of Word and Spirit. Biblical interpretation here becomes entwined with biblical authority as readers attempt to locate the Word of God in the church today. Because of both hermeneutic and theological influences, there is increasing pressure on Reformed churches to abandon the Reformers' position on *sola scriptura* in favor of a view that makes Scripture an inseparable aspect of the church's Spirit-led, living tradition.

I propose rethinking the relation of Word and Spirit with the aid of speech act theory. The third term in speech act theory—perlocution—has a special affinity with the third person of the Trinity. The perlocutionary effect, we may recall, refers to what the speech act aims to accomplish in the reader, over and above the illocutionary effect of producing understanding. For instance, one of my perlocutionary aims in writing this book is to *convince* readers that general hermeneutics is properly theological. Now it is of the utmost importance to note that the intended perlocutionary effect of my text is not arbitrarily related to its illocutionary act. Indeed, the trinitarian language of "procession" is apt: as the Spirit proceeds from the Father and the Son, so the literary act proceeds from the author, and so too does the perlocution (persuading, convincing) proceed from the illocution (claiming, asserting).[188] A text, then, has a *mission* of meaning, that we may provisionally define in terms of illocutionary success: the goal of a literary act is to accomplish the purpose for which it was sent (Isa. 55:11). The Word of God in Scripture, similarly, has a mission, and this in turn determines the mission of the Spirit. Just what is the mission of the Spirit with regard to the Word?

The Spirit-Led Interpretive Community

Donald Bloesch notes that the church fathers and the Reformers alike viewed the Word of God as more than a text: the Word of God is powerful and alive.[189] It is the Spirit, he claims, that breathes life into inert letters. Furthermore, when God speaks through Scripture, he does not merely repeat himself. How are we to understand this divine communicative action? If God says new things, does God not contradict himself or mean something other than what the text says? Exegetes and theologians alike should take care, I believe, not to exaggerate the dichotomy between "what it meant" and "what it means"; one must beware of pitting Word *against* Spirit. The Spirit is not some kind of Derridean supplement that adds to or improves upon the written Word. What, then, is the Spirit's relation to the written Word? In particular, how does the Spirit render the Word relevant?

On the basis of his reading of Acts 2, James McClendon argues that Scripture is addressed directly to readers today: Peter declares "this" (the event of Pentecost) is "that" (the meaning of the prophecy of Joel).[190] Such an interpretation is not merely Peter's human projection but a product of the Spirit's guidance. Only his sharing in the life of the believing community, however, allowed Peter to see "this" as "that." Richard Hays generalizes the point: it is the Spirit who enables Paul to interpret the Old Testament as articulating the promises of which the church is the ultimate fulfillment. Paul, that is, read Scripture in light of his experience of the Spirit rather than vice versa.[191] To read in the Spirit is thus to declare "this" (e.g., promises and prophecies about Israel) as "that" (e.g., promises and prophecies about the church). Only a prayerful reading that invokes the Spirit can perceive the true meaning in what is otherwise a dead letter. Such Spirit-led exegesis "restores the interpretive activity of the spiritual community as the connecting link between text and reader."[192]

Hauerwas agrees. Scripture can be read and interpreted correctly only from within a believing and practicing community—the church.[193] It is not some objective "meaning of the text" that interests the church "but rather how the Spirit that is found in the Eucharist is also to be seen in Scripture."[194] What the interpreter needs in order to read the Bible correctly is not scholarly tools but saintly training. The very attempt to interpret the Bible "on its own terms" is vain nonsense—an attempt to know Jesus "after the flesh." For Hauerwas, there is no such thing as "the real meaning" of Paul's letters to the Corinthians, once one understands that they are not Paul's letters but the church's Scripture. Making it useful is more important than getting it right: "The 'meaning' is that use to which I put these texts for the upbuilding of the Church."[195] The question that such an approach raises is both important and troubling: *How can the church know what God is saying through Scripture if what God is saying fails to coincide with the verbal meaning of the text?* Hauerwas appeals, of course, to the leading of the Spirit. The problem with this solution is (1) that the Spirit's leading is often difficult to discern or to distinguish from a merely human consensus, and (2) that it relocates the Word of God and divine authority from the text to the tradition of its interpretation.

Hauerwas's view hearkens back to the early church's use of the apostolic tradition as a hermeneutical principle. In settling interpretive disputes with heretical groups, the prime criterion was the "rule of faith." According to Tertullian and Irenaeus, Scripture is rightly understood only in the context of the living tradition handed down via apostolic succession. Tradition was seen as providing not only *content* (e.g., the unanimous mind of the church, what had been held from the beginning) and *continuity* (e.g., with the original apostles) but *context* (e.g., an interpretive community). In other words, only in the context of the church, the interpretive community of faith, would readers have the right set of interests (and sympathies) necessary for a correct reading.[196] Georges Florovsky, an Orthodox theologian, states that ultimately the criterion for right interpretation is the consensus of the catholic church, best represented by the earliest creeds. On this view, the arbiter of right interpretation is the church, which enjoys not canonical but "*charismatic* authority, grounded in the assistance of the Spirit: *for it seemed good to the Holy Spirit and to us.*"[197]

Stephen Fowl argues that the way one interprets the Scriptures is related to the way one interprets the Spirit's work in the community. In the book of Acts, for example, Peter comes to a new understanding of the Old Testament and of Jesus' words as a result of the gift of the Spirit to the Gentiles: "Experience of the Spirit provides the lenses through which Scripture is read rather than *vice-versa*."[198] Hays agrees and adds that Paul too opts for the "hermeneutical priority of the Spirit-experience" as over against the text of Scripture.[199] James Dunn maintains that for the early Christians, the authoritative Word of God was not the biblical text itself, nor was it their own perception of God's will, but rather the interaction of both past revelation (Word) and present revelation (Spirit).[200] What matters is not the original sense of the text but the sense of the text when interpreted in the light of the event of Jesus Christ. The gap between past text and present context is thus bridged by the notion of "the continuity of living tradition."[201]

If "what it means" is only discerned in the light of Spirit-led tradition, how should we explain the response of the readers in Nehemiah 8 to a text that had been forgotten? Bloesch speaks for many today in stating that the Bible's revelatory status "does not reside in its wording as such but in the Spirit of God, who fills the words with meaning and power."[202] The Bible is *not* like any other book, for its words are filled with meaning by the Holy Spirit. This picture, attractive though it may be, is incomplete in one important respect: What actually happens to the sense of the words when the Spirit quickens them? Is "what it means" a function of the Spirit's *use* of the text, for example, to direct us to Christ?

There are interesting parallels between Bloesch's "historical-pneumatic" hermeneutics and the dichotomy between the Jesus of history and the Christ of faith. Bultmann, for instance, distinguished *Historie*, the knowledge of what Jesus was actually like (which can be gained through historical research), from *Geschichte,* a perception of Jesus' significance that is open only to faith. Similarly, Bloesch distinguishes a historical investigation of the text from the Spirit's illumination, which alone "can bring us the revelational meaning of what has transpired in history."[203] The basic question for Bultmann and Bloesch alike amounts to this: To what extent is the revelational meaning (the Word, Christ) more than arbitrarily connected to the historical meaning (the human words, the man Jesus)? The stakes are high, for in separating the historical Jesus from the Christ of faith, Bultmann ultimately has difficulty preserving the former. There is, I believe, a similar danger of losing, or at least of subordinating, the literal sense of Scripture ("what it meant") to its use by the Spirit in the community ("what it means"). To what extent, then, do both conservatives and liberals err in separating the historical meaning of the biblical text from its spiritual message?

The spirit of the age is, I have argued, virulently non-realist. Meaning and truth alike are widely thought to be the product of human reasoning or cultural practices. I return once more, then, to the question of hermeneutic realism, only this time under the rubric of pneumatology. Is meaning "in" the text, or is it the product of the encounter between the text and the Spirit-led reader? More pointedly: Should the meaning of a text include the history of its effects? The oddness of the question surfaces when one rephrases and refines it: Does the meaning of a communicative act include its unintended effects? If "what it means" is only discerned in the light of Spirit-led tradition, how should we explain the response of the readers in Nehemiah 8, who no longer belonged to a living tradition, or the response of the readers in Acts 2, whose reception inaugurated a new tradition? Furthermore, how can we distinguish Spirit-guided community interpretation and practice from other, more mundane, interpretive practices, imposed perhaps, by less holy spirits? Finally, how can we avoid reducing the apostolic confession in Acts 15:28, "It seemed good to the Holy Spirit and to us," to Fish's abbreviated, User-friendly formula: "It seemed good to us"?

The Spirit of Reception: Illuminated Manuscripts

The Spirit, says Barth, is the "Lord of the hearing." For readers to understand and to appropriate the biblical text as they ought, more than sheer exegetical effort is required. When we struggle to reach understanding, we are not contending "against flesh and blood, but against the principalities, against the powers" (Eph. 6:12 RSV). Reading is a struggle with the text against those powers that would distort understanding. We are also struggling against ourselves, against our lust for power, against the tendency to totalize and to lord it over others. It is for this reason that a Pelagian hermeneutics, one that simply stresses the hermeneutical imperative and urges the interpreter to try hard, is inadequate. The spirit of understanding is not a spirit of works or of power, but of peace: a spirit of prayer. If, as I maintain, the Spirit does not create new meaning, then what is his role? *The Spirit's role in bringing about understanding is to witness to what is other than himself (meaning accomplished) and to bring its significance to bear on the reader (meaning applied).* For the sake of clarity, we may distinguish three aspects of the Spirit's work in bringing readers to understanding.

(1) The Spirit *convicts* us that the Bible is indeed a divine as well as human locution (and thus to be read as a unified text). This is the so-called "internal witness" of the Spirit, by which the reader comes to accept the Bible as the Word of God.[204]

(2) The Spirit *illumines* the letter by impressing its illocutionary force on the reader. Thanks to the illumination of the Spirit, we see and hear speech acts for what they are—warnings, promises, commands, assertions—together with their implicit claim on our minds and hearts. In so doing, the Spirit does not alter but *ministers* the meaning: "The spiritual sense is the literal sense correctly understood."[205] The distinction between "letter" and "spirit" is precisely that between reading the words and grasping what one reads. Likewise, the difference between a "natural" and an "illumined" understanding is that between holding an opinion and having a deep sense of its profundity.

(3) What precisely does the Spirit illumine: head or heart? Paul Noble, in his study of Childs's canonical hermeneutics, argues that epistemic progress is possible only if one is first willing to admit that one might be mistaken. For critical realism to work in practice, "the interpreter must possess certain affective qualities, such as teachableness."[206] The Spirit's illumination of our minds is therefore dependent on his prior transformation of our hearts. *Sanctification* is thus the final aspect of the Spirit's work in interpretation. Negatively, the Spirit progressively disabuses us of those ideological or idolatrous prejudices that prevent us from receiving the message of the text. The Spirit purges us, first, of hermeneutic sin, of that interpretive violence that distorts the otherness of the text. Positively, the Spirit conforms our interests to those of the text. To read in the Spirit does not mean to import some new sense into the text, but rather to let the letter be, or better, to let it accomplish the purpose, illocutionary and perlocutionary, for which it was sent: "[My word] will not return to me empty, but will accomplish what I desire and achieve the purpose for which I sent it" (Isa. 55:11). In short, the Spirit convicts, illumines, and sanctifies the reader in order better to minister the Word.

We can agree nevertheless with Hauerwas that the Bible is best read in the context of a community of disciplined readers, not because there is no meaning in the Bible apart from its reception by the Spirit-led community, but because the church is the place where the Spirit cultivates righteousness and the willingness to hear the Word. There is no contradiction between calling for spiritual reading and affirming a realism of meaning. Indeed, as Nehemiah 8 suggests, it is precisely through the Word that the Spirit works to discipline the community. Scripture itself is profitable for training in righteousness (2 Tim. 3:16). It functions most profitably toward that end in a community of virtuous interpreters whose primary aim is to expose themselves to the effects of the text.

The Spirit and General Hermeneutics

To what extent does the Holy Spirit exercise a "ministry of the word" with regard to other, non-biblical, texts? Put differently: What is the relation between special and general hermeneutics?[207]

Ricoeur describes the general process of interpretation in theologically charged terms. A text, he says, both "reveals" and "transforms." That is, it both displays new ways of looking at oneself or the world and thereby transforms the reader's existence. All texts, not only the Bible, have the potential to be both revelatory and transformative. We can learn lessons for hermeneutics in general, Ricoeur believes, by attending to how we interpret the Bible in particular. I have argued elsewhere, however, that Ricoeur's hermeneutics lacks an adequate role for the Holy Spirit. Transformative reading is for Ricoeur ultimately an innate human capacity that is more related to the power of the imagination than to the Holy Spirit.[208]

Barth too acknowledges that the way one reads the Bible should provide principles and rules for reading all other texts: "It is from the word of man in the Bible that we must learn what has to be learned concerning the word of man in general."[209] He accepts the notion that all interpreters bring their biases to the task of interpretation. Yet the Bible, perhaps more than other books, demands that we be open to its peculiar subject matter, for there is no other access to the Word of God except through the biblical texts. "Is it not the case that whatever is said to us by men obviously wants . . . to make itself said and heard? It wants in this way to become to us a subject matter."[210] The lesson Barth drew from his experience of writing his commentary on the book of Romans was to attend to the subject matter of the text: "For if a text is to speak, it must have hearers who are willing to be confronted by what the text has to say."[211] Barth says that this "biblicist" method is equally applicable to the study of Lao-Tse and to Goethe.[212] Barth asks: "Is there any way of penetrating the heart of a document—of any document!—except on the assumption that its spirit will speak to our spirit through the actual written words?"[213] His surprising conclusion, with which I am in full agreement, is that those schooled in biblical interpretation are best able to appreciate what it is to do justice to textual otherness. General hermeneutics is, as it were, a subset of biblical hermeneutics. Does it then follow that the Spirit is Lord of the hearing, not only of the Scriptures, but of all texts?

Bultmann distinguishes the philosopher from the theologian by saying that while the former can analyze the conditions for authentic existence, only theology can announce their fulfillment. Similarly, it is one thing to formulate principles for understanding, quite another to follow them. On a Christian view, what authenticity there is in human beings—in existence or in understanding—is a gift of God. Derrida rightly exposes the many sources of coercion and distortion in the process of communication. Our polluted cognitive and spiritual environment darkens understanding of *all* texts. Self-centered readers do not wish to understand the other, particularly when the other has a claim on them. Self-love perverts the course of interpretation as it does every other human activity. Of course, not every text lays claim to us; not every text challenges our self-understanding as does the Bible. If there is no perceived threat, there may be less reason for readers to resist the meaning of the text. Nevertheless, it is the Spirit's unique role to bridge distances that impede understanding. Not just any distance—hard historical and philological effort is still needed—but moral and spiritual distance in particular. The Spirit enables us to avoid falling prey to self-deception, not by working a miracle on our rational faculties, but by shedding grace abroad in our hearts. The Spirit's work in interpretation does not represent a new faculty or capacity in the reader so much as a reorienting of those faculties that we already have. The Holy Spirit aids understanding in general, not least by cultivating the interpretive virtues in individuals and in the believing community. It is in this sense that the "renewing of our minds" (Rom. 12:2) is a help to receiving textual meaning.

Pentecostal Plentitude: How to Be a Responsible Pluralist

The appeal to the Holy Spirit's role in interpretation takes two very different forms. One approach appeals to the Spirit's ongoing work in building up the church through discovering new meanings in the biblical text. The Spirit that enables Peter to say of "this" (the phenomenon of Acts 2) that it was "that" (the fulfillment of Joel 2) is the same Spirit who continues to lead the church into new readings that will speak to the situation today. For proponents of this first approach, spiritual interpretation enables the text to mean something other than it says ("this means that") and so renders Scripture of continuing relevance to the church. On this view, the Spirit is the creative power behind the fusion of the text's and reader's horizons.

A second approach—represented by the present work—appeals to the Spirit as the minister of the Word, the one who leads the community into the single correct interpretation: the literal sense. The locus of the Spirit's recreative work, however, is not the letter of the text but rather the life of the interpreter, who, as sinner, is inclined to distort the text insofar as its message is perceived as threatening to the status quo. In recognizing the priority of the literal sense, I am neither neglecting the role of the Holy Spirit nor reducing the Bible to a book of inert propositions. For Bloesch, the latter reduction is the inevitable consequence of identifying the Word of God with the Word written. I believe that Bloesch has been misled at this point (and he is not alone) by a false picture of language. On a speech act view, there is a built-in safeguard against reducing meaning to propositional information. As we have seen, speech acts have matter *and* energy, propositions *and* illocutionary force, not to mention aims and objectives. When contemplating the Spirit's role in interpretation, then, it is important not to forget the second half of John 16:13: "He will not speak on his own; he will speak only what he hears." The truth into which the Spirit guides us is itself shaped by and received from the Word.

Both of the above approaches hold that the Spirit is necessary for the ongoing richness and relevance of the written Word, though this is explained in different ways.

These two pictures of the Spirit's role in the reading community give rise to two different ethics, indeed spiritualities, of interpretation: on the one hand, an Antiochene preference for the original meaning (viz., the historical communicative act) and an Alexandrian predilection for the spiritual sense on the other. We have seen that interpretive ethics means respecting the text as "other." Can we do so if we interpret the text as meaning other than what it says?[214] The tendency of spiritual interpretation to generate multiple readings raises not only moral but theological problems for the biblical interpreter. The apostle Paul, when faced with dissension in the churches, exhorted his readers to "keep the unity of the Spirit" (Eph. 4:3). Christians are members of the one body of Christ (1 Cor. 12:12). At the same time, Paul recognizes variety in the church, that is, a diversity of gifts (12:4–6).

The present pluralistic situation calls for an ethics of interpretation, informed by the doctrine of the Spirit, that avoids both absolutism and arbitrariness in interpretation. The church is one, yet its readings are many. We therefore need to define unity and plurality as these pertain to biblical interpretation. What is the status of interpretations that emerge from a community that is both one and many? How is the Spirit of understanding related to the Word and to the community of the Word's interpreters? I believe that the concept of a *plural unity* is compatible with the critical realism and the trinitarian theology defended in these pages. To anticipate: the biblical text can have diverse, even inexhaustible significance, and yet have determinate meaning. The alternative to absolutist or arbitrary readings of Scripture, in other words, is one that celebrates its *abundance*.

The One and the Many: Do Texts Have Single or Plural Meanings?

How should we account for the incontrovertible fact that a single text often generates a multitude of readings, many of which conflict with one another and some of which are mutually exclusive? In the previous chapter I argued that "the meaning of the text" admits of various levels of description and that these should be integrated into an attempt to understand what the author was doing. According to Ricoeur, the historical question, "What did the text say?" is under the control of the hermeneutical question, "What does the text say to me?"[215] Is this correct? To what extent does "what it means" depend less on the author's act than that of the reader or, for that matter, that of the Spirit?

"The One": Monists. The interpretive monist contends that there is one single correct interpretation of a text that readers everywhere, regardless of their context or method, should acknowledge as valid and true. It may appear that the present work advocates interpretive monism, and in a sense this is true. However, much depends on the way one defines monism. Lévinas, as we have seen, mounts a sustained attack on philosophies and interpretations that "totalize" their subject matter with methods that acknowledge only what already conforms to their schemes. "Greek" thought, typical of ancient and modern philosophy alike, suppresses differences through a process of systematic thought that reduces the "other" to the "same." Lévinas calls for an ethical relation to the world (and, by extension, to texts) that recognizes an other which eludes the grasp of reason. The other constitutes an ethical appeal to continual openness and responsibility, which is for Lévinas an "infinite" ethical requirement.

Similarly, deconstruction's ethics of resistance is a plea for a continuing conversation among many voices rather than a premature end to the conversation and an institutionally enforced consensus.

The monism I seek to defend is not the metaphysical doctrine that "meaning is simple" (i.e., a matter of one level or of a single descriptive framework) but rather the epistemological doctrine that, when all is said and done, the text has a true, and thus unified, interpretation. As we will see in due course, my version of monism, like the realism that begets it, leads not to a totalizing oneness but to a critical and multifaceted unity. A naive monism that too quickly identifies one particular interpretation with the single correct interpretation (a regulative ideal) falsifies the complexity of texts. Some, like David Hoy, a Gadamerian, fear such simplification and thus do not wish to posit a single correct meaning even as a regulative ideal for interpretation. Such an ideal amounts "to the recommendation that interpreters avoid inconsistency and keep testing their interpretations against other interpretations with more readings that take more aspects of the text into account."[216] Hoy sees no reason, however, to think that there will be an end to this process or that critical monism is the only rational stance. Postmodern critics harbor no illusion or hope that they can rise above the conversation and conflict of interpretations. Does it follow that an indiscriminate tolerance is the only ethical stance vis-à-vis interpretive plurality?

"The Many": Pluralists. We can distinguish, for the sake of clarity, four kinds of interpretive plurality.

(1) First, there is a plurality of authorial intentions. No one denies that there are a number of possibilities for what a given author might have intended in a particular text. Indeed, the monist sees his or her task as reducing the number of possibilities to the most likely one. As we have seen, however, literary acts are complex and can be described as "doing" things on various levels. With regard to Scripture, however, the case is even more complicated. Aquinas acknowledges God as the author of the literal sense, but he adds that God can use the referents to mean something too. Hence "what it means" is as much a matter of providence as propositions. God can say any number of things through "what the text says."[217] Even those for whom the author's intention is an interpretive norm, then, must continue to reckon with plurality.

(2) With regard to the Bible in particular, we can distinguish a second kind of plurality *on the level of the text.* Modern historical critics, for instance, treat each stage in the history of a text's composition as a quasi-text to be interpreted. These earlier stages of tradition are distinguished from the text in its final form, from the text considered as a unified canon, and from the text considered as a church's Scripture. In other words, there is a plurality of intratextual relations and intertextual contexts. For example, with regard to the formation of the canon, Dunn sees a continuing interaction of what was already in the canon and the community's new experience of God's presence. Psalm 22 is heard differently, for instance, thanks to its inclusion in a canon that includes the Passion narrative. "To recognize the different levels of canonical authority and their diversity is to accept that God may well speak differently from one generation to another."[218] And it is precisely this diversity of how God speaks "which exalts the Spirit above the Bible."[219]

(3) We may also discern a plurality of readers and of readers' contexts. Multiculturalism is now a phenomenon of biblical interpretation as it has been of ethics. A number of studies have been conducted into how one's gender, race, or class (or combination thereof) affects one's reading of texts.[220] In the words of one literary critic: "In order to serve the various needs and desires of various readers, texts *ought* to have plural meaning."[221] Again, the question is how there can be a single correct sense if meaning is the result of the encounter between text and reader—particularly when this encounter may involve the Spirit of diversity. "For a faith which professes belief in the Holy Spirit the perception and exercise of canonical authority can never rest solely on the assertion 'The Bible says.'"[222]

(4) Last, there is a plurality of reading methods. Robert Tannehill states that "methodological pluralism is to be encouraged, for each method will have blind spots that can only be overcome through another approach."[223] The same text can be studied in a number of legitimate ways, each corresponding to different interpretive aims, questions, and interests. Thiselton rightly observes that many of those who call for a proliferation of interpretive methods seem to presuppose "that these strategies cannot be ordered and ranked . . . in relation to different tasks or to the nature of different texts."[224] Reading strategies, he says, reflect interests and worldviews (and, as I have been at pains to point out, theologies as well). Some interests, of course, are too narrow to be deemed properly interpretive; that is, they do not yield understanding of the text as communicative action. Hence, while the fact of a plurality of ways of reading is incontestable, the burden of Part 2 has been to claim that not all interpretive interests are equal.

One should not confuse evidence of plurality with evidence for pluralism. Plurality describes the complexity of the interpretive situation; pluralism prescribes a certain attitude towards it. Pluralism is an ideology that sees mutually inconsistent interpretations as a good thing. I believe, on the contrary, that pluralism is, as an ideology, a bad thing. On the one hand, as N. T. Wright observes, pluralism encourages our culture's glorification of self-fulfillment—a danger in pietistic and postmodern readings alike, insofar as both see meaning as a function of what the Bible says to me right now. Pluralism encourages egocentric readings insofar as it makes "whatever seem good in your own eyes" into a legitimate hermeneutic principle. On the other hand, if one interpretation is really as good as another, readers are not necessarily motivated to "consider well." The conflict of interpretations seems less troubling to the pluralist, and there is less motive (or hope) either to arbitrate or to resolve it. If differences do not really matter, it would seem that the natural attitude towards the conflict of interpretations would be *indifference*.

Pluralism can, however, be as intolerant as any other ideology. Those who insist on inclusivity and pluralism as ethical goals in their own rights often coerce others to share their goals, or else exclude them! And pluralists are ironically inconsistent insofar as they themselves remain "closed" to the possibility that there may indeed be a single correct interpretation. As an ideology, therefore, pluralism is as totalitarian as other forms of absolutism.

Finally, pluralism is unable to establish a meaningful ethics of interpretation. As William Schweicker observes in his review of Daniel Patte's *Ethics of Biblical Interpre-*

tation, the only check on the reader's creative interpretations that can be given (since the text cannot serve as a criterion) is a vague concern for the "other," that is, for anyone affected by our interpretations (except the author!).[225] As Schweicker rightly points out, such a concern is impractical; the pluralist is unable to say what criteria we should use in order to decide whether our interpretations affect others for better or for worse. Any such judgment would impose a normative grid on diversity and so negate the concern for plurality.

"Pentecostal" Plurality. Unlike both monists and pluralists, however, Christian readers have reasons for believing in a final unified truth and for thinking, moreover, that this truth may not be monistic. As Colin Gunton has recently argued, the Christian doctrine of the Trinity presents a unique solution to the problem of the one and the many, namely, the notion of the three-in-one, *a unity of a plural kind*.[226] It is not enough, then, to declare oneself for or against plurality in interpretation. One must clarify what kind of plurality one rejects or supports. I reject any plurality that assumes the meaning of a text changes at the behest of the reader, at the influence of an interpretive community, or as a result of the Spirit's leading. On the other hand, *I affirm a "Pentecostal plurality," which maintains that the one true interpretation is best approximated by a diversity of particular methods and contexts of reading*. The Word remains the interpretive norm, but no one culture or interpretive scheme is sufficient to exhaust its meaning, much less its significance.

Wayne Booth, in his excellent work *Critical Understanding: The Powers and Limits of Pluralism*, tempers interpretive pluralism with three interrelated criteria: *justice, understanding, and vitality*.[227] These three values are best viewed, in my judgment, as interpretive virtues—qualities or habits of the spiritual reader.

(1) *Justice*. Doing justice to texts means, first, letting the other (viz., the author's intended act) "be" (i.e., be what it is) rather than trying to shape it into an image of oneself or one's desires. To do justice to texts means, second, to examine it as fully as it demands. In order to render a text its due, that is, one must do justice to the various levels that constitute the text as a communicative act. Just as an analysis of human being is incomplete if it remains on the level of chemical analysis, so an interpretation of texts is incomplete if it remains on the semiotic, linguistic, or historical levels and does not proceed to the semantic and intentional levels. Justice, then, involves making fair and reasonable judgments. Reasoned discourse—about the world or about the world of the text—proceeds on the assumption "that one view of a given matter is better than competing views, and that argumentation, if carried out properly, will show us in the long run which it is."[228] A thoroughgoing pluralist denies this. A critical pluralist, however, accepts the necessity of reasoned discourse, but notes that the best explanation or description of a text may be multifaceted or plural.

(2) *Understanding*. Understanding occurs whenever one person succeeds in grasping what another person is saying/doing. Hermeneutics formulates the principles and methods for grasping the nature and content of communicative action. Understanding texts means inferring the intention and information mediated by the text. Booth offers a "Hippocratic Oath" to would-be literary critics: "I will *try* to publish nothing about any book or article until I have *understood* it, which is to say, until I have reason to think that I can give an account of it that the author himself will rec-

ognize as just."[229] Ethical interpretation thus hearkens to the hermeneutic imperative and to the Golden Rule; these set the parameters to interpretive plurality. In this sense, the Spirit of understanding is a restraining influence. The reader works within certain parameters, of a metaphysical, rational, and ethical nature. "Metaphysically" the reader is constrained by the text, by what is there; "epistemologically" the reader is constrained by the canons of communicative rationality and good argument; and "ethically" the reader is constrained by the obligation to do justice to and understand the other.

(3) *Vitality*. Readers are indeed involved, even creatively, in making sense of texts and applying them to new contexts. Alongside justice and understanding is the virtue of "vitality." This third criterion carries clear theological overtones, though Booth himself does not pursue them: the Spirit is not only a restraining, but also a quickening influence. I submit that it is the Spirit that enlivens the text, yet without supplementing the letter and without going beyond the literal sense. A simple example of such "quickening" would be a successful (e.g., *dynamically* equivalent) translation. A fresh translation in contemporary terms can make an ancient text "come alive," and this without altering its meaning. Such vitality in interpretation is perhaps best illustrated by church tradition. Church tradition grows as a result of the community's attempt to preserve the message of the text and to develop its implications. The development of doctrine, for instance, can be seen as a *growth* in biblical understanding. Lively tradition is not at odds with a love for the written Word. Indeed, we might say that the Spirit makes the Word come alive by inciting readers to *love* it. Pneumatology and philology are far from being incompatible.

The Spirit's vitality in interpretation is also seen in the diversity of readings. Particular interpretations may make valuable contributions without needing to make the further claim that they have said everything that needs to be said. Just as many members make up one body, so *many readings may make up the single correct interpretation*. Is it really the case that hermeneutic realists must kill off certain commentators in order to eliminate the variety of interpretations? Would we be better off without, say, Rudolf Bultmann's reading of the Fourth Gospel, or Raymond Brown's, B. F. Westcott's, Augustine's, or for that matter, Origen's allegorical fancies? Booth reminds us that as we go about the business of interpretation, we should try to understand not only texts but their various readers too: "Seek critical truth—and incidentally, while you are at it, try to be fair, try not to kill off critics unnecessarily, try to understand them."[230]

Diversity as such is not a curse but a gift. Why else should we have four Gospels, four "interpretations" of the one event of Jesus Christ? We would be the poorer were we to have only one, two, or three rather than four. It is nevertheless possible to assert both that there is a single correct meaning to the event of Jesus Christ *and* that it takes all four Gospels *together* to articulate it. If this is so, can we not also say that, while there may be a single correct interpretation of the Fourth Gospel, it might take several (many?) interpreters to articulate it too? A critical hermeneutic realism, highlighting as it does the multileveled nature of literary acts, should lead us to expect that the single correct meaning may be richer than any one interpretation of it. Yes, the Spirit is the Spirit of unity, but this unity is both a gift and a task. It is a *vital* union, a harmonious union of many voices, not a unity of unison. It is a dialogical rather than a monological unity. It is, in short, an ethical unity—a unity of love—that welcomes legitimate differences without seeking to reduce them to uniformity.

Christ's statement to the disciples at the end of John 16:13 that the Spirit will declare "what is yet to come" might seem, at first glance, to substantiate the claim that the Spirit leads the reader beyond the literal sense of the text. However, a number of exegetes believe that Jesus' words refer to the Spirit's interpreting "in relation to each coming generation the contemporary *significance* of what Jesus has said and done."[231] George R. Beasley-Murray, for instance, sees the phrase as a reference to the Spirit's clarification of the significance of Jesus' teaching in a future context beyond the ability of the disciples to imagine.[232] Similarly, Bultmann interprets the clause as simply stating "the essential significance of the word."[233] The Spirit, in other words, discloses the significance of the (past) Word of God as it relates to all times. Vitality—the Spirit's enlivening of the letter—requires us to read not only for meaning but for *significance*, or, to be more exact, for one multilayered meaning and for an abundance of significance.

Reading for Relevance: The Spirit of Significance

How does the original sense of a text give rise to abundance? One popular response appeals to evolutionary development: a text has to adapt—mutate, even—as it enters new environments if it is going to survive. "Survival" means, in this context, continuing to be read and continuing to be relevant. This is Gadamer's view: textual meaning is inseparable from the history of its reception and effects. I am presenting a different account of the abundance of biblical meaning—one compatible with hermeneutic realism and with hermeneutic rationality. By speaking of "abundance" I wish to emphasize how the original meaning continues to be *meaningful* today. The Spirit's role, I will argue, is not to change the meaning but to *charge* it with significance. Scripture remains relevant (1) through the continuation of its illocutionary and perlocutionary effects, and (2) by relating the original content to new contexts. I will here treat the latter reason first and reserve the issue of efficacy for the following section.

To read for the original meaning only is to confine the text to its own time. Understanding, we have seen, is more than mere duplication or repetition. At the same time, reading something into the text that was not originally there is too high a price to pay for relevance. Understanding is not the same as authoring or invention, nor should reading be confused with what is effectively rewriting. What Childs and Bakhtin and even Hirsch point out is that authors intend their works to be relevant in the future, and not only in their immediate present. The Word of God must not be confined to the past, even when we identify it with the Word written. The Spirit's leading readers into all truth is a matter of nurturing a Pentecostal conversation about the correct interpretation of the Word's past meaning *and* present significance.

There is no contradiction between asserting that a text has a single, though not simplistic, determinate meaning on the one hand, and a plurality of significances on the other. Juhl, for instance, states: "Given a certain meaning, a work may be inexhaustible in that readers of many different periods are able to relate that meaning to their own personal experiences or to changing historical, social, or political circumstances."[234] I have argued that the primary object of understanding is not the present significance of a text but a text construed as a past communicative act. But interpretation, I have also suggested, may go beyond understanding. Texts written in the past continue to *affect* us. For instance, once I understand the Fourth Gospel and grasp its invitation to believe in Christ, I must still respond to its invitation and explore how my believing will affect the rest of my life. Interpretation remains incomplete without an appreciation of a text's significance, its meaningfulness. Only in this way can Scripture truly serve as supreme norm for the believing community's faith and life.

Hirsch, we may recall, refined his meaning-significance distinction and now thinks that authors regularly intend to address future readers and so transcend their original situation: "Literature is typically an instrument designed for broad and continuing future applications."[235] At the same time, he continues to hold fast to hermeneutic realism: "Stable meaning depends ... on pastness."[236] The pertinent question now becomes: Is past meaning necessarily dated? Does pastness imply irrelevance? Some meaning are indeed dated; their original sense is of little significance today. Dated meanings, however, usually have a narrow scope; they do not treat universal human themes. By contrast, Hirsch gives the example of a Shakespeare sonnet: "When I apply Shakespeare's sonnet to my own lover rather than to his, I do not change his meaning-intention but rather instantiate and fulfill it. It is the nature of textual meaning to embrace many different future fulfillments without thereby being changed."[237] Because love is a universal human theme, sonnets that explore love have continuing significance.

Interestingly, relevance is not always a virtue. It is possible to be too relevant. Some texts may speak so specifically to a particular situation that they have little to say to another. To be too topical is to risk being confined to one's era. At the other extreme, what often passes for relevance is often only fashion. A text that fits in too easily to the contemporary cultural horizon may find itself trapped at the other end of the temporal spectrum: in the present. Both past and present meanings can be "dated" and rendered quickly obsolete.

Just as authors often intend to address future generations, so readers read to get something of present significance out of past texts: "Analogizing to one's own experience is an implicit, pervasive, usually untaught response to stories."[238] Hirsch calls for an Augustinian approach that avoids the extremes of the "originalists" and "non-originalists" alike: "Interpretation must always go beyond the writer's letter, but never beyond the writer's spirit."[239] Hirsch names allegorical those interpretations that respect a real connection between the original referent (e.g., love) and the way that reality is understood today. Strictly speaking, however, Hirsch's allegories are not new meanings but rather applications or accommodations of the original meaning. The urge to make the text relevant by allegorizing it need not be at the expense of the author's intention, but may rather be a way of respecting it. What was once called the "spiritual sense" of the text may now be seen to be an expression of the letter's *significance*. This conclusion, if correct, has far-reaching implications for biblical interpretation. It means that one does not have to make the text mean other than what it says for the text to be relevant.

A text is relevant insofar as it has an important bearing on a certain problem or task. There are, of course, many questions and activities for which the Bible is not rel-

evant (e.g., making a kite, splitting the atom). On the other hand, the Bible may be relevant to activities or problems that its human authors never envisaged (e.g., making
a nuclear weapon, splicing human genes). Because its overall subject matter is Christ—
God's intention for the human creature—the Bible's content is of universal, and therefore permanent, relevance. That the Bible can address and affect readers today, then,
follows not only from its canonical form but especially from its christological content.

The Bible itself provides guidance for moving from "what it meant" to "what it
means." This is part and parcel of the Bible's being able to function as Scripture for
future generations. The Christian canon itself encourages the reader to recontextualize the content. Indeed, the very relation of Old Testament and New Testament is a
case study in recontextualizing. The authors of the New Testament had to answer the
question of what the Old Testament meant in light of the Christ event. However,
when the New Testament recontextualized the Old Testament in light of Christ, it
did not change its meaning but rather rendered its referent—God's gracious provision for Israel and the world—more specific. What is of continuing relevance across
the two Testaments is God's promise to create a people for himself and the divine
action that fulfills that promise. The promise that created Israel later came to be
applied to the church. Hence, what God says to us today through the Old Testament,
in the Spirit, is nothing other than the significance of the text, its *extended* meaning.
Significance just is "recontextualized meaning." Just as Jesus Christ recontextualizes
the meaning of the Old Testament, so the church is called to recontextualize the
meaning of Jesus Christ.[240] *In sum, the Word of God for today (significance) is a function
of the Word of God in the text (meaning), which in turn is a witness to the living and eternal Word of God in the Trinity (referent).*

The meaningfulness of the Bible is thus a matter of the Spirit's leading the church
to extend Scripture's meaning into the present; in this way it displays its contemporary significance. We can state my thesis in the following formula: *biblical relevance =
revelatory meaning + relative significance.* The meaning of Scripture is revelatory and
fixed by the canonical context; the significance of the Word is relative and open to
contemporary contexts. The content of the Bible is revelatory: it informs us of things
that we would not have otherwise known. Note that the revelation, like the meaning,
is a matter of past communicative action (its reception, of course, takes place in the
present). Significance, on the other hand, is relative to particular contexts and particular readers. The same meaning may be brought to bear on different situations in
different ways. "Objectivity" with respect to significance is thus misplaced, even as an
ideal. But relativity is not arbitrariness; it is still the same determinate meaning, or an
aspect thereof, that is being extended or applied in new situations. It is precisely
because the Bible speaks meaningfully to the present that we can see the relativity of
significance not as a problem but as a *perfection* of the biblical text.[241]

Ascertaining the significance of a text is an indispensable aspect of interpretation.
It should not be confused, however, with grasping the intended meaning. The latter
is a matter of historical and literary knowledge; discerning significance, on the other
hand, is a matter of wisdom, for it concerns not the achieving of knowledge but the
appreciation of knowledge and its right use. Now, perhaps, we can see why biblical
interpretation is best conducted in the context of the believing community—not

because the community makes new meaning with the Spirit's help, but because the getting of wisdom is a corporate enterprise that requires the interpretive virtues, virtues that are best cultivated by the Spirit of understanding in the context of community.

Pentecostal plurality is not to be despised. It is easy to mock the diversity of opinion among biblical commentators and theologians and to conclude, "They have had too much wine" (Acts 2:13). My argument has been that such diversity need not always be negative. First, with regard to meaning, it may be that we need to attend to many voices in order to appreciate the fullness of the text's unified determinate sense. It is salutary to be reminded that the way one looks at a text may not be the only legitimate way to do so. The plurality of perspectives from African and Asian Christianity may help Western Christians to discover hitherto unknown aspects of what is nevertheless really there in the text. Second, with regard to significance, the many voices confirm the relevance of the text in many different situations. Wisdom is cumulative; many generations and many cultures may be needed to mine the treasures of biblical significance. But the plural unity of interpretations should not be confused with a disordered pluralism; not all readings are equally legitimate. The Spirit of abundant understanding is first and foremost a vital minister of a determinate Word of which he is not the author but the hearer ("for he will not speak on his own authority," John 16:13 RSV).

Word and Spirit: "Why I Am Not a Fundamentalist"

Take . . . the sword of the Spirit, which is the word of God. (Eph. 6:17)

A recent Pontifical Biblical Commission document identifies *sola scriptura* as one of the distinguishing characteristics of fundamentalist interpretation. Such a maxim implies that it is possible to separate out the real meaning of the text from the tradition of its interpretation. On the one hand, I have defended a version of *sola scriptura*. On the other hand, I have acknowledged that plurality is to be expected, both with regard to meaning (because we need a plurality of descriptive frameworks) and with regard to significance (because we have a plurality of contemporary applications). We have reached a puzzling state of affairs: on my view, the Bible may be significant in different ways to different readers who nevertheless agree that there is a single meaning in the text. An astute critic might say that I am a fundamentalist with regard to meaning and a liberal with regard to significance, for the former is not dependent on Spirit-led tradition while the latter clearly is. Is such a theological hermeneutic inconsistent?[242]

An Abbreviated Protestant Principle

Let me first clarify the objection. First, is mine the approach of a fundamentalist who craves objective certainty and encourages individuals to interpret the Bible for themselves, using their own common sense?[243] Not exactly. On the contrary, I have espoused a critical realism that aims for adequate knowledge and suggested that such knowledge depends on a person's having cultivated the interpretive virtues.

Second, is mine an approach that assumes that the truth of the Bible is a matter of its correspondence to historical fact? Not necessarily. On the contrary, I have argued that literary genres engage with reality in different ways, with other illocutionary forces besides the assertive. This, to my mind, represents a decisive parting of the ways, for it means that not all parts of Scripture need be factually true. For most of the twentieth century, however, fundamentalists have distinguished themselves from other Christian groups by the phrase "Bible believers," by which they mean to affirm "the authority of a literally interpreted Bible."[244] Ramm claims that fundamentalists "never realized how much they were children of the scientific era."[245] Ironically, fundamentalist interpretation was held captive by a misleading, and *modern*, picture of meaning and truth: "Fundamentalist interpreters . . . tend to draw their understanding of truth only from the canons of scientific empiricism."[246] In their zeal to uphold the truth of the Bible, fundamentalists tend to interpret all narratives as accurate historical or scientific records.[247] In the previous chapter, however, I distinguished between a literalistic interpretation, which operates with a theory of meaning as reference, and a genuintly literal interpretation, which reads for the literary sense and operates with a theory of meaning as communicative act.

Third, do my proposals for a critical realism and a critical pluralism uncritically privilege the community to which I belong? Or worse, have I implied that only *I* know which interpretations are appropriate? I hope not. Kathleen Boone expresses what she takes to be the essence of what is wrong with fundamentalist hermeneutics: "What we commonly hear from fundamentalists is that they alone apprehend the true, objective, absolute, determinate meaning of the Bible."[248] Boone's criticism is a deconstructive one; though fundamentalists cry "Back to the texts themselves!" in reality they tend to confuse the text with their way of reading it. "What it meant" becomes "what it means to us now." *Fundamentalism thus preaches the authority of the text but practices the authority of the interpretive community.* Thus what appeared as one of the most conservative approaches to the text (fundamentalism) ironically turns out to have more in common with one of the most radical, for in privileging their own interpretive community, fundamentalists discover a strange bedfellow in Stanley Fish. The irony is acute and painful: while professing to stand under the Word, the fundamentalist is actually a *User*. In Boone's opinion, fundamentalism is the *reductio ad absurdum* of the Reformation claim that "Scripture interprets itself."

It is true that fundamentalism offers a way to end the wanderings that all too often characterize the process of biblical interpretation. Yet the way out leads not to the Promised Land but back to Egypt; the certainty they desire can only be achieved by resorting to some kind of institutional authority. As we have seen, however, to confuse one's own words with "The Bible says . . ." is to worship a golden calf of one's own making. Boone rightly grasps the fundamentalist's dilemma: "How does the fundamentalist control interpretation, while claiming at the same time that nothing but the text itself is authoritative?"[249]

Fundamentalists are, I believe, right in their concern to preserve a realism of meaning and in their desire to let the Bible speak for itself. Theirs, however, is a somewhat naive realism that tends to equate the meaning of the text either with the foundational proposition to which it is thought to refer or with the way it is read (by fundamentalists, that is). As we have seen, realism on the level of the "metaphysics" of meaning need not imply an objectivist epistemology. We must not simply approve but go on to *prove* our interpretations, in the sense of putting them to the test. Specifically, we test our interpretations, first, by submitting them to the text, and second, by entering the broader conversation with other interpreters about the text. Fundamentalists typically forgo the latter test, in effect ignoring the hermeneutical problem altogether. They sometimes give the impression that the main interpretive difficulty is coming to "accept" the Bible, not determining what it says and deciding how to apply it.[250] With regard to the spectrum of the morality of literary knowledge, fundamentalists tend to slide towards dogmatism. Hauerwas attacks fundamentalists for assuming that their interpretations are objective and neutral and for thinking they can extract the truth from Scripture without the hard discipline of living in the Christian community. One of the purposes of Part 1 was to temper such interpretive complacency by suggesting that one's exegetical discoveries may actually be projections, and hence symptomatic not of faith but of Nietzsche's "will to power."

Fundamentalists sometimes affirm a monism with regard to significance as well as meaning. How could there be certainty in matters pertaining to the faith if one did not know absolutely "what it means today"? As we have seen, however, the significance of the text must be discerned rather than deduced. To contextualize or extend the meaning of the text into new situations requires more than a willingness to follow a certain number of exegetical steps; it requires wisdom. The fundamentalist is overeager to say "I know" when he or she should say "I believe."

An inordinate desire for objective certainty ultimately affects the way some read the Bible.[251] A misplaced desire to honor "Holy Scripture" leads many fundamentalists to read the Bible as a book of true statements. The problem, in my opinion, is not so much their identification of the Bible with the Word of God as it is their theory of meaning and reference. A picture of meaning holds fundamentalists captive. This picture equates the meaning of a text with its referent, that is, with its empirical or historical correspondence.[252] It is this essentially *modern* theory of meaning and truth that generates literalistic interpretations and harmonizations where all parts of the Bible are read as though the primary intent were to state historical facts. Whereas Bultmann dehistoricizes historical material, fundamentalists may historicize unhistorical material. I have been at pains throughout this work, however, to contrast literalistic with literal (or literary) interpretation, where the latter is sensitive to the diverse genres in Scripture and to the various forms of communicative action. Though the Bible contains propositions (as do all speech acts), it is much more than a collection of proof texts.

In striving for objective certainty and neutrality, in treating the text as a series of propositional statements, and in assuming that the significance of the text can be deduced rather than discerned, fundamentalists display what Bernard Ramm terms an "abbreviated Protestant principle."[253] It is abbreviated because it attends to the Word and relegates the Spirit to the theological and hermeneutical margins. "Scripture interprets Scripture," in the context of fundamentalism, become a charter for a religion of the book. In the context of Reformed theology, by contrast, "Scripture interprets Scripture" may be paraphrased, "God, speaking in and through Scripture, interprets Scripture."[254] My thesis is that a view of Scripture as composed of divine-human speech acts is better able to account for the relation between Word and Spirit that was so important to the Reformers. The next three subsections—on efficacy, eschatology, and ecclesiology—constitute a fuller response to the criticism that the position defended in this book ultimately falls prey to the fundamentalist flaw. Let me now examine these further reasons why I am not a fundamentalist.

Efficacy

The word of God is living and active. (Heb. 4:12)

The *unabbreviated* Protestant principle acknowledges the Holy Spirit speaking in the Scriptures as the supreme authority for life and faith. The Westminster Confession of Faith states: "The Supreme Judge, by which all controversies of religion are to be determined . . . can be no other but the Holy Spirit speaking in the Scripture" (I.10). John Owen called the Holy Spirit the "primary efficient cause" of our understanding of Scripture. D. F. Strauss speaks for many who object to this principle when he says that the appeal to the Holy Spirit is "the Achilles' heel of the Protestant system."[255] This would only be the case if the appeal led to a dualism of Word and Spirit. I have argued, however, that the Holy Spirit is the Spirit of understanding—the Spirit of the letter correctly understood—not a rival author. Indeed, the one who inspired Scripture cannot contradict himself when he illumines it. A dualism that pits Word against Spirit and Spirit against Word must be avoided at all costs. The Spirit is neither a supplement nor a second source to the Word in Scripture. A speech act model of divine communication helps us to view the Word-Spirit relation in terms not of the sufficiency, but rather of the *efficacy*, of the Word.[256] By "efficacy," I refer to the power to produce effects. In brief, the Spirit renders the Word *effective*.

What is it that the Word does efficaciously? As communicative act, it addresses us in diverse ways. It tries our hearts and minds. The Word exposes—exegetes!—us, the interpreters. Calvin believed that even readers whose hearts were closed to its message could not completely evade the Bible's claims. Otto Weber criticizes the seventeenth-century Reformed orthodox theologians who argued that the Bible's efficacy was an inherent property rather than an empowerment by the Spirit. But Weber's criticism is imprecise; the notion of communicative action allows us to distinguish two kinds of efficacy, illocutionary and perlocutionary, and to associate the Spirit particularly with the latter.[257]

Illocutionary Efficacy. Illocutionary efficacy is a matter of meaning. The effect in question concerns the reader's recognition of the author's illocutionary intent. Another word for this effect is simply "understanding" (e.g., a metaphor is recognized as a metaphor, a warning as a warning, etc.). It is on this level that Luther's affirmation of the "external clarity" of the Word ought to be located. The "communicative presumption"—namely, that illocutionary intent is usually recognizable—is something shared by all texts, not only the Bible. The suggestion that either the church *magisterium* or the Spirit's illumination is a prerequisite for understanding would call this presumption into question.

On the level of meaning, then, the Spirit renders the Word efficacious by impressing on us the full force of a communicative action: its illocution. In so doing, the Spirit does not alter the literal meaning but brings it home to the reader. The Spirit accompanies the various illocutionary acts, including the act of testifying to Christ, and thus ensures that they are recognized for what they are. The Spirit enables understanding. But surely, one might object, this proves too much. Is the Spirit's work really necessary for readers to understand the Bible, much less novels, newspapers, and traffic signs? In response to this objection, we should recall how common it is for readers to let their prejudices or ideologies distort their readings. Distortion is a real possibility whenever readers are faced with texts that require behavioral change, not to mention the death of the old self and the end of self-love. Interpretation never takes place in a cognitively and spiritually clean environment. The gospel is rejected because its message has been grasped, however dimly, and then let go. Yet even here the Word achieves "the purpose for which [God] sent it" (Isa. 55:11), insofar as it is recognized for the communicative act it is. The image of God in humanity enables us to continue functioning, often despite ourselves, according to our design plan. The Spirit's work in interpretation is not to change the sense but to restore us to our senses.

Perlocutionary Efficacy.

The Spirit of God maketh the reading, but especially the preaching, of the Word an effectual means of convincing and converting sinners.[258]

The Spirit's present-day leading of the community into all truth is best viewed, I believe, under the rubric of perlocutionary effects. A perlocution, we may recall, is what happens as a *result* of speaking. Perlocutionary effects refer to what speech acts accomplish in the addressee, *beyond* the (illocutionary) effect of producing understanding. For example, by *stating* something (an illocution), I may *persuade* someone (a perlocution). Perlocutions have to do with an author's ulterior intentions (e.g., "These were written . . . that you may believe that Jesus is the Christ" (John 20:31). By warning someone not to cross the road, I may achieve a perlocutionary effect, prevent an accident, and thus save a life. Understanding *matters*.

The distinction between illocution and perlocution casts a different light on Paul's teaching: "A natural man does not accept the things of the Spirit of God" (1 Cor. 2:14 NASB). If this verse concerns perlocutionary effect, then the sense is that the unspiritual person does not "accept" the implications of what the Bible says; the "natural man" fails to believe its truth or to see its significance.[259] The Spirit thus opens readers' minds and hearts so that the words can produce all their intended effects: effects of illocutionary understanding and effects of perlocutionary obedience. Again, the Spirit's role is not to add a new sense to the Word, but to energize and empower the sense—the speech act—that is already there.

The Spirit's agency consists, then, in bringing the illocutionary point home to the reader and in achieving the corresponding perlocutionary effect—belief, obedience, praise, and so on. The Word is the indispensable instrument of the Spirit's persuasive (perlocutionary) power.[260] On the one hand, the Spirit is "mute" without the Word; on the other hand, the Word is "inactive" without the Spirit. Word and Spirit together make up God's active speech (speech act). As Ramm rightly observes, the Word does not work *ex opere operato*.[261] That is the mistake of subscribing to the abbreviated Protestant principle that transfers the life and power of the Spirit to the text itself. It is the mistake of overlooking the role of the reader and the importance of personal appropriation. The abbreviated Protestant principle thus leads to a short-circuited or abbreviated process of interpretation as well.

The Holy Spirit is the Spirit of the Word—the Spirit of Christ—and ministers Christ, the matter of Scripture, to its readers. The Bible is the instrument of the Spirit's persuasive power, the means by which he brings persons to faith in Christ. To repeat my thesis: the Spirit does not alter the semantics of biblical literature or add to the stock of revelation. Meaning—the good news about Christ—is already there, in the Word. The Spirit is the "Lord of the hearing" not because he makes the words of the Bible mean something other than they say but because he guides and directs the effects of Scripture's communicative action. We might say, to paraphrase Barth, that the Spirit is "Lord of the perlocutionary effect." Thanks to the Spirit, God's Word does not return to him empty but accomplishes the purposes for which it was sent (Isa. 55:11). The Spirit may blow where, but not *what*, he wills. The trinitarian doctrine of the *filioque* thus has an important hermeneutic parallel: as the Spirit proceeds from the Father and the Son, so perlocutions proceed from locutions and illocutions. The Spirit, then, is a witness to what is other than himself—to the Logos, to meaning *accomplished*—and enables readers to respond to this Word so that it can achieve its intended effect: significance, meaning *applied*. It follows that the Spirit's work is not to supplement the author's intention but rather to sustain and to fulfill it. Accordingly, the Spirit is most properly conceived as the *effective presence of the Word*, or as the *Word's empowering presence*.

Eschatology

The second reason why I am not a fundamentalist concerns eschatology, and in particular the tension between the "already" and the "not yet." To begin with, eschatology puts into question a fundamentalist (foundationalist) epistemology that aspires to absolute truths and objective certainties. Pentecost celebrates "firstfruits," not the whole harvest. The unity that should characterize Christ's church is both a gift and a task. The Spirit of unity is a present gift to the church, yet the church must work towards realizing this unity too.

We might make a similar point about truth. The truth of Christ is both gift and task. On the one hand, we have the Word written; on the other hand, we must interpret it. While its meaning has been fixed by the past, our grasp of that meaning is partial, and its significance is incomplete. There is an eschatological tension that must not be ignored, a tension that prohibits us from thinking that the truth—the single correct interpretation—is our present possession. It is a mistake, in other words, to confuse the content of tradition with any one moment of tradition. Truth, it has been said, is the daughter of time. It can neither be rushed nor coerced: "Nearly all the most discreditable actions of church institutions . . . flow from an improper anticipation of eschatology."[262] Yes, it is difficult to wait, but it is worse to bring the quest for truth, for a final interpretive solution, to a premature conclusion.

The second way in which eschatology raises questions about fundamentalist interpretation is more subtle. It has to do with the fundamentalist tendency to resist figural interpretation and with their insistence that passages about Israel concern the physical nation Israel and never the church. The hermeneutics of dispensationalism is insufficiently sensitive, I believe, to the literary sense of the text (in this case, to the literary genres of prophecy and apocalyptic). I do not intend to retrace old debates about the future of Israel, but to raise a more general point about how the Bible can be read in such a way as to have a continuing significance for the church.

In my view, the continuing relevance of the Bible stems from typological interpretation that sees the church (the interpreting community today) as both directly addressed by Scripture and as one of the main themes of the biblical texts. According to Richard Hays, what Paul discovers in Scripture "is a prefiguration of the *church* as the people of God."[263] Through typological interpretation, the Spirit discloses the eschatologically intended referent of the Old Testament: a people of God who correspond to the image of Christ. There is thus a narrative continuity that links the story of Israel in the Old Testament to the story of Jesus Christ and of the church in the New Testament and to the church today. The continuity derives from the fact that the history of the church today is a continuation of the story of Israel, Jesus, and the New Testament church: "Reading Scripture at the culmination of the ages, Paul discovers himself and his readers at the center of God's redemptive purposes."[264] In short, the reader of Scripture discovers himself or herself part of the drama of redemption.[265] The Spirit ministers the Word by enabling present-day readers to see themselves not only addressed by, but inscribed in, the biblical story line.

Ecclesiology

While I continue to affirm the principle of *sola scriptura*—the authority of the text against the tradition of its interpretation—I do not wish to underestimate the importance of interpreting the Bible in the church. My intent is not to deny the role of the community in interpretation but to clarify it. What reading Scripture in the church does is to provide a context for cultivating the interpretive virtues and a conducive environment in which to discern and to do the Word. I agree with Ellen Davis: "Reading the Scriptures as the Word of God is the basic identifying activity of the Christian community."[266] The church is the community dedicated to discovering the Bible's meaning and to *attesting* its continuing significance. It is, above all, the *significance* of Scripture that cannot be discerned apart from the receiving, believing community. While biblical scholars can write commentaries about "what it meant," it takes the congregation—a living commentary—to display "what it means." The interpreting community does therefore have an important hermeneutic role, but (as we will see below) it is not that of producing but of *witnessing* to meaning.

There are two reasons for the perceived inaccessibility or difficulty of the Bible. The first reason is its *distance*—historical and *moral*—from the interpreter. Understanding requires not only reason but repentance, not only scholarship but faith. It follows, second, that our habits of thinking and seeing need to be reformed. We must learn to view our world in the light of the Word rather than trying to force the Word into secular worldviews, where it fits often only uncomfortably. The Bible is often inaccessible, that is, because we lack the *imagination* to enter into it. As we have seen, the church is that community that sees itself in narrative continuity with the story of Jesus. The church is the community that believes that no matter how strange or unappealing a given passage may be, "there is something in it for us, something to be gained from the work of painstaking, acute *listening*, which is the fundamental act of obedience (cf. Latin *ob-audire*)."[267] The church should be that community of readers whose hearts, minds, and imaginations are open to receive what is there in the text and who strive to embody it—the story, the promises, the commands, the law—in new contexts.

"What it means" is ultimately not a matter of theory only but of practice, not a matter of sheer knowledge but of wisdom. How do we know which interpretation best grasps the significance of the text? How can we evaluate various judgments as to what the text means in today's context? I suggest that we may find a criterion in the demonstration of wisdom, in the *right use* of literary knowledge. Those whose minds and visions have been shaped by the biblical story and by the other types of communicative action will develop a Christian *habitus*—a way of life that forms habits of the head, habits of the heart, and habits of the hand. To read with understanding is to develop a Christian worldview, a spiritual orientation, and a loving way of life. The Spirit's power is demonstrated in wisdom. *Those who rightly apply "what it meant" attest the efficacy of the Word.* We can go further. I propose the following four criteria for discerning the Spirit's "ministry of the Word" among contemporary readers. We should prefer those interpretations of the Bible's significance that demonstrate

(1) faithfulness: interpretations that *extend* the meaning of the text into new situations;

(2) fruitfulness: interpretations that *enliven* the reader and show forth the Spirit's fruits;

(3) forcefulness: interpretations that *edify* the community, resolve problems, foster unity;

(4) fittingness: interpretations that *embody* the righteousness of God and contextualize Christ.

The testimony of the Spirit is not only to individuals but primarily to the church as a whole.[268] Yet the church is not the judge that arbitrates interpretive conflict so much as the *permanent witness to Scripture's meaning and significance.* One of the Second Vatican Council documents describes the church reading Scripture as the "Pupil of the Holy Spirit."[269] The Reformers had earlier likened the church to a schoolroom, in which believers become competent in the Christian way. What Christians study in Scripture is God's interpretation of reality, summed up in the story of Jesus Christ. Christians, then, have a schoolroom (the church), a subject (the way of Jesus Christ), and a teacher (the Spirit). And yes, there *is* a text in this class.

THE VOCATION OF THE READER: INTERPRETATION AS DISCIPLESHIP

How then should we read? How ought readers to respond to texts? Important choices must be made, *are* made, whether consciously or not. I have argued that the major dichotomy facing interpreters today is between various forms of realism and non-realism. To choose to invent rather than to recover meaning is a choice that determines not only one's reading, but to some extent one's very *being*. For what it is to be a self is, as we will see, a function of how we relate to words: our own words, the words of others, and the Word of God. Do we believe that meaning is there? How can we interpret ethically and attend to the testimony of others if we do not? And can we ever get beyond ourselves if we do not hearken to what others tell us?

Either/Or: Carnivalesque Versus Covenantal Interpretation

Kierkegaard's works were attempts to prompt the nominal Christians of his day to make a genuine choice for faith. Kierkegaard's nineteenth-century context was a paradoxical one: in the midst of Christendom, he could find few committed Christians. Our twentieth-century culture of interpretation presents us with a similar situation, in which there are more *nominal* interpreters than *genuine* ones. Our time too confronts us with the need for urgent decisions. There is no neutral ground in the culture wars, for what is contested is the territory of the human spirit. In his *Either-Or*,[270] Kierkegaard sketches two "stages of life"—the aesthetic and the ethical. These continue to be live options for the interpreter. Many of those apparently on a quest for understanding spend the bulk of their efforts overstanding texts instead. Whereas Kierkegaard's aim was to awaken his readers' sense of responsibility for self, my aim is to awaken my readers' sense of responsibility for *sense*: for the meaning in a text.

Aesthetics: Carnival and the Pleasure Principle

According to Kierkegaard, the "aesthetic" way of life is marked by a preoccupation with one's immediate environment and with one's own pleasure. By *aesthetic* Kierkegaard meant to signal a way of being devoted to the life of the senses. The aesthetic is the uncommitted life, the life of the moment, the life that recognizes no universals but seizes pleasure from moment to moment. This existence at bottom is one of despair, however, marked by skepticism and a growing weariness with life. Kierkegaard calls it "the sickness unto death." It is what Barth called, with respect to hermeneutics, "the sickness of an insolent and arbitrary reading *in*."[271]

Nietzsche is one of modernity's preeminent "aesthetic" thinkers. He aligned himself with the Dionysian spirit of riotous self-abandon rather than with the Apollonian spirit of order and self-discipline. As we have already seen, he believed that the most effective way to unsettle authorities and hierarchies was through "play." He believed that the proclamation that "God is dead" would result in a liberation of humanity and in an "affirmation of life." Since God is dead, there is no truth to be told. It follows, then, that "he speaks most truthfully who recognizes the illusory nature of his speech." Nietzsche's so-called "Superman" is thus able to create his own values, his own world. The idea of God (or of determinate meaning) simply represses human creativity. For Nietzsche, then, an aesthetic existence is the only human option, and he worked hard to make it appear a liberating one.

Derrida too thinks that the critique of logocentricity leads to liberation, to the "play of signs." As we have seen, the endless play of signs undoes any attempt to achieve a stable meaning. Like Nietzsche, Derrida tries joyously to affirm "the play of the world . . . a world of signs without fault, without truth, and without origin."[272] Nietzsche and Derrida capture the spirit of much postmodern interpretation—what I call the "spirit of carnival."[273] In the festivities associated with the medieval carnival, hierarchies are turned on their heads (fools become kings and kings fools) and the sacred is profaned. Everything authoritative or serious is mocked and subverted. Indeed, one critic has suggested that Derrida's most important, though perhaps unintentional, effect has been the "carnivalesque impetus" that has taken hold of and overturned the humanities.[274] To view the world, with Nietzsche and Derrida, as a Dionysian carnival is to celebrate its openness and indeterminacy. Yet the spirit of carnival is ultimately a *rebellious* spirit, one that undoes authority by mocking it: "Deconstruction subverts from within the system that liberation seeks to change from without. . . . Carnival as a social event is the mockery by the oppressed of the structures of oppression, through an ironic mimicry by the subordinate of the dominant, a reversal of roles."[275] *Carnival is thus an apt metaphor for the postmodern condition.*

Among the most significant carnivalesque role reversals that we have considered in the course of this study, two stand out. The first is the exchange of roles between author and reader. That readers "write" the meaning of the text has become a common postmodern refrain. The second role reversal, that between Creator and creature, is even more far-reaching. The modern and postmodern masters of suspicion imply that God, or talk about God (e.g., the Bible and theology), is merely a projection of the human creature. According to Cupitt, the real meaning of God-talk is that humanity is divine; it is we who shape the world, we who create values, we who "make believe." Consequently, the spirit of carnival is a spirit of abandon, revelry, and negation.

The carnivalesque spirit of aesthetic interpretation is, however, nothing to laugh at. Ronald Hall compares it to a self-destructive demonic spirit. Thiselton agrees: the carnivalesque self of postmodernity is not an active agent but a passive victim, doomed to be tossed this way and that by conflicting ideological forces and vocabularies. If the truth-stating function of language cannot be taken seriously, and if all argument can be reduced to rhetoric, then the self is ultimately unable to reach understanding of the world, of others, or of texts. Carnival offers no means of distinguishing true from false; the word is no sword, only a sore of the spirit. Furthermore, it is impossible to keep one's word in the context of carnival. We can neither take each other seriously nor expect others to take us seriously. Hall takes deconstruction to be "a project that is deigned to invade, attack, and destroy the legitimacy, efficacy, and authority of the speech act."[276] To deny speech acts is ultimately to deny one's responsibility for what one says. In undoing the tie that binds the word to the world and me to my word, postmodern thinkers permit—nay, compel—speakers and writers to *disown* their words.

Ethics: Covenant and the Promise Principle

Kierkegaard opposes ethics and religion to aesthetics, the spirit of *covenant* to that of carnival. The covenant of discourse recognizes the possibility of a proper relation between words and the world, between speakers, and between words and those who produce them. The promise, it may be recalled, is perhaps the paradigmatic speech act. It is the supreme instance of that act whereby one person gives his or her word to another and engages to do something in the world. In giving my word to another, I engage the world and enter into relation with another, with myself, and ultimately with God. The ethical question is: Will I keep my word and so be faithful to myself? Similarly, covenantal interpretation recognizes a right way to relate to the words of others and especially of authors.

The manner in which we engage in communicative action—in speaking and in understanding—says something not only about our view of interpretation but about how we view our *vocation* as human beings. On a Christian view of communicative action and interpretation, an individual is neither an absolute will to power nor the site of a conflict of discourse, but rather a communicative agent in covenantal relation.[277] To be in covenantal relation is to be bound to others by means of words; it is to call to another and to respond to another's call. Faith, too, is fundamentally a covenantal relation, mediated largely by words ("faith comes by hearing"). That the self has a narrative shape follows largely from the covenant of discourse; one's present is constituted by one's past and one's future, especially by the way in which one owns up to one's word.

For ethical speakers and interpreters, our word is our bond: a bond between persons, a bond between language and the world. In the light of the covenant of discourse, we see that the tie between language and the world is not a permanent metaphysical fixture but is rather due to the constancy of reliable speech. Without some sense of constancy, we go mad; it is impossible to live (or to communicate) in a state of permanent flux. An ethical relation to language, on the other hand, enables "a continuity of historical consciousness; it is the continuity of a promise, a covenant, that establishes a stability in time and across time and in the midst of contingency."[278] In other words, it is the sense of a reliable ethical relation between speakers, words, and interpreters that prevents the self from being swallowed up in the play of language. With this insight, we have come full circle in our study. We are back to metaphysics, only this time with a (non-deconstructive) difference. The answer to the question, "Why is there something rather than nothing?" is "because God has spoken." The distinctions that ultimately structure the world are not natural givens nor man-made constructions but rather expressions of the Word of God. For the Christian, the divine promise is more reliable than any metaphysical foundation in the world. Truth is ultimately a matter of reliability, of the Word that endures forever. "Heaven and earth will pass away, but my words will never pass away" (Matt. 24:35).

Interpretive Freedom

One's either-or choice between carnivalesque and covenantal interpretation leads to two opposing conceptions of interpretive freedom.

Carnivalesque Freedom

Those who interpret in the spirit of carnival stress freedom *from*. To some extent, the Reformers, historical critics, and the postmodern Undoers share a certain anti-establishment, iconoclastic zeal. Each group seeks to liberate the interpreter from the fetters of interpretive tradition. The Undoers go farthest, however, in seeking an unconstrained freedom.[279] Carnival, after all, is an antinomian social ritual that celebrates a release from all law-like structures. Deconstructive freedom is the freedom of license and licentiousness, the freedom of play without rules, without goals, and ultimately without satisfaction.

The postmodern suspicion of hermeneutics assumes that all organizing principles are socio-political constructions and thus so many expressions of the will to power. Freeplay is the disruption of transcendence, of any kind of order that "puts things in their place." Derrida attempts to undo legitimating orders by playing with them, by teasing them out, or rather inside-out. Carnival is anarchic: the celebration of freedom without origin, without form—the empty freedom of nullity and nihilism. Those who participate in carnivalesque interpretation are free only to negate, not to create meaningful form. As Thiselton rightly observes, the postmodern view of the self as "free to create" is unequally yoked to the view that the self is endlessly decentered by language and by unconscious forces.[280]

What is such an interpreter free *for* but self-expression or self-indulgence? In the end, the joyous affirmation of the play of signs celebrated by Nietzsche and Derrida leads to carnivalesque ridicule and derision. It also leads to the hollow laughter of the individual sentenced to freedom, as Sartre says, in a world that neither instructs nor rewards it. The human comedy on this view is a parody, a theater of the absurd. *For in carnivalesque interpretation there is ultimately no point to communicative agency.*

Covenantal Freedom

Freedom with no constraints is empty. True creativity requires certain forms and boundaries. We would not be able to say anything new, for example, unless we used the resources of a structured language that preceded us.

Intriguingly, Barth suggests that it is in fact interpreters of the Bible who are the freest thinkers of all. Reading the Bible teaches us, says Barth, that we are free to use systems of thought and descriptive frameworks critically: "Even from a human point of view, it is possible to regard scriptural exposition as the best and perhaps the only school of truly free human thinking—freed, that is, from all the conflicts and tyranny of systems in favor of this object."[281] Reading Scripture also frees us from the tyranny of the present. The text contains a "dangerous memory" that has the potential to liberate us from the confines of our epoch and to orient our action, in hope, to the future.

What does interpretive freedom mean positively? Do interpretive realists have simply to submit to what is there in the text, or is there scope for creativity? We saw earlier that readers may need to wrestle with the text in order to secure a blessing from it: "Transformative interpretation . . . is not blind submission to the text as answer but an in-depth engagement of the subject matter, of its truth claims."[282] Indeed, readers are *required* to be creative when it comes to applying or extending the word to new situations. Most important, perhaps, the interpreter is free *for* the other. Interpretation is itself an exercise of the reader's freedom for the text: "This readiness and willingness to make one's own the responsibility for understanding of the Word of God is freedom under the Word."[283]

Readers are free, finally, to receive or to reject a message not of their own making. The world of the text invites, but does not coerce, the reader to inhabit it. Moreover, in our encounter with the text as other, we escape from ourselves and our everyday world and are freed to enter new worlds and so to be transformed. *It is simply unwarranted to say that my freedom is diminished rather than enhanced by recognizing an author's intended meaning.* We do not lose our freedom by understanding others.

Indeed, true freedom occurs when we are able to go beyond ourselves, when we are open to transformation. As we have seen, the Spirit is the effective presence of the Word of God. And where the Spirit is, there is true freedom (cf. 2 Cor. 3:17).

Interpretation is thus not a task to which we have been sentenced, but a privilege and a responsibility for which we have been set free. The laughter that accompanies covenantal interpretation is not derisive or jaded but joyful. It is the laughter that accompanies fellowship and friendship. Indeed, Booth suggests that the best metaphor for reading is friendship. In friendship there is a meeting of the minds. True friends treat each other as ends, never as means; friends are not used, but enjoyed.

The story of interpretation need not have a tragic ending; postmodern despair is only the penultimate word. The story of interpretation can have, if not a happy ending, then at least a *comic* one. J. A. Appleyard notes that comedy "is above all a view of community transformed and redeemed from its limitations."[284] Comedy focuses on the integration of individuals into a community. A divine rather than a deconstructive comedy pictures interpreters who delight in understanding and in being understood.

Interpretive Obedience

Genuine interpretive freedom is never unconstrained. Only a non-realist imagines (and it is always only imagined, never a serious option) that there is nothing outside the self that limits our freedom. Such constraints as there are must be respected rather than rejected. The ethical interpreter displays an obedient freedom, a free obedience, towards the text as the work of another. The reformed reader will honor interpretive duties and not merely assert interpretive rights.

A "Constrained Freedom"

We owe a debt, perhaps inexhaustible, to other communicative agents. Ricoeur writes:

> We may have to repay a debt owing to the authors we read. So we cannot say whatever we like. . . . Perhaps we should say that a text is a finite space of interpretations: there is not just one interpretation, but, on the other hand, there is not an infinite number of them. A text is a space of variations that has its own constraints; and in order to choose a different interpretation, we must always have better reasons.[285]

Booth agrees: "Even the freest interpretations are finally parasitical upon modes that insist on the possibility of justice and understanding."[286] Obedience and freedom are not necessarily contradictory. One way to exercise our freedom is to respond in obedience to the word. Obedience means placing oneself under or behind another; it means *under-standing* and following. I have argued that the meaning of the text is known only to one who complies with its injunction and follows its directions.

Material Constraints

In an earlier chapter I considered methodological constraints on interpretive freedom.[287] To these constraints we must now add two others: a material and a spiritual constraint, to be precise.

According to Hays, the constraints on the apostle Paul's interpretation of the Old Testament were not methodological but material (e.g., theological). Hays maintains (following Barth) that one's interpretive method must never take precedence over the subject matter of the text. This is perhaps best illustrated by music. Performers "obey" the score by playing the right notes in the right order. Interestingly, my piano teacher regularly urged me to "love" the notes. My argument is that, insofar as concerns interpretation, loving and obeying the text may amount to much the same thing. The ethical interpreter must first of all *let the text be*.[288] This is true of all texts, not just the Bible. In Barth's words: "Is it not the case that whatever is said to us by men obviously wants . . . to make itself said and heard? It wants in this way to become a subject matter. It wants us for our part to bring it a true objectivity, i.e., interest for its own sake."[289] Interestingly, Barth notes that the written nature of the Bible contributes to its freedom. Only as discourse fixed by writing can the Bible have a determinate, public meaning that resists efforts to domesticate it or to subsume it under some ideology.[290]

For Barth, the hermeneutical question about Scripture entails "the ultimate material question of theology: Who is God and who am I?"[291] The Bible says all sorts of things about God and humanity, certainly, but for Barth it says in truth only one thing: "Jesus Christ." In this name it "proclaims God in his richness and mercy, and man in his need and helplessness."[292] Testimony, by its very nature, is the word of another. True freedom in interpretation means subordinating all human concepts and ideas to the biblical witness. True freedom is freedom *under* the Word.

Spiritual Constraints

Ethical interpretation must do justice to the text in order to attain understanding: "Part of acquiring competence as a biblical scholar is learning both what must be done and what may not be done in relation to different kinds of texts."[293] But the competent interpreter of Scripture has to learn more than how to handle texts. Biblical interpretation requires a more demanding apprenticeship. Why? Because a casual reading fails to disclose the subject matter of the text. The reader is in need not only of hermeneutical methods but of *holiness*. This requirement casts new light on the notion that reading is a struggle. Could it be that faith without works—without the *obedience* of faith—may seek understanding but not reach it? The faith that gains understanding, we may now say, is the faith that follows the Word. Indeed, we could perhaps define faith as the ability to follow the Word.

Is it possible that the Gospels were written to be understood only by spiritually "qualified" readers? Timothy J. Geddert suggests that "the requisite qualifications were related to discipleship more than scholarship."[294] Stephen Fowl argues that Acts 10–15 mentions a number of habits, dispositions, and practices that must be displayed by Christian communities as they struggle to read and respond, in the Spirit, to the Scriptures. For it is one thing to acquire knowledge of the text, quite another to respond to it rightly. The ability to follow the word, from page to practice, is ultimately a matter of wisdom. Wisdom, I have suggested, is "knowledge appropriated": *lived* knowledge. Wisdom and understanding are thus linked. Literary knowledge that does not affect life stops short of wisdom and achieves only an abbreviated understanding.

Wisdom is, therefore, the point at which our reflections on the metaphysical, epistemological, and ethical dimensions of meaning all come together. Wisdom is a matter of learning to live well in the world. The wise person flourishes in all that he or she does. Interpretation both requires wisdom and contributes to it. On the one hand, wisdom helps rid us of foolish assumptions that distort our approach to the text. Biblical wisdom, for instance, recognizes the reality of the Creator and the distinction between Creator and creature. Similarly, wisdom in literary criticism means recognizing the distinction between author and reader. To go wrong here—in one's presuppositions about authorship—is to go wrong everywhere.

Wisdom also enables one to dwell in the world as one ought, in a way that corresponds to the Creator's intention and to the structure of creation. John Yoder notes an important link between wisdom and discipleship: "Only he who is committed to the direction of obedience can read the truth so as to interpret it in line with the direction of God's purposes."[295] Interpreters in the Anabaptist-Mennonite tradition consider obedience to be a valid hermeneutical principle. The Holy Spirit is the Spirit of understanding and wisdom alike, the Spirit that guides the believing community into the right use of its literary knowledge, into living the literary sense. Just as the notion of a Spirit-cultivated interpretive virtue links knowledge and obedience, so spiritless reading and disobedience to the letter leads to interpretive and ethical vice. What is the right use of Scripture, its lived meaning? To make wise unto salvation and to create a community that is for "training in righteousness" (2 Tim. 3:16). To understand the Bible is ultimately to begin walking its way.

Interpretive Martyrdom

No man understands the Scriptures, unless he be acquainted with the cross.[296]

Every text contains an implicit call: "Follow me." The vocation of the reader is to respond to that call. Those who heed the call begin a journey of encounter with another that involves making, or rather receiving, sense. Interpretation is, in the final analysis, a form of discipleship: a discipline that seeks to follow the text ("what it meant") where it leads ("what it means"). Ricoeur observes the dual meaning of the French word *sens*: "meaning" and "direction." Intentionality too is a matter of the *directedness* of consciousness. If meaning opens up a certain direction of thought and life, the task of the interpreter is to follow its itinerary. Every meaning is a tacit call to the interpreter to *follow*, at least with one's attention. The reader is a disciple—one who discerns, deliberates over, and does the Word. The interpreter is ultimately neither slave to the text nor lord over it, but rather its witness. Readers who respond in covenantal freedom and obedience to the text are nothing less than "martyrs" to the Word.

The Interpreter As Witness to the Word

What we learn from studying biblical interpretation can be of value to hermeneutics in general. This is especially true, I believe, of the picture of the reader as a witness to meaning. The concept of "witness" has rich theological connotations. The Father witnesses to the Word (1 John 5:9); Christ is the witness to God the Father;

the Scriptures are a witness to Christ (Luke 24); the Spirit is the witness to the Scriptures and to Christ (1 John 5:7); the church is a witness to Word and Spirit. To witness to the meaning of Scripture is thus to participate in a divinely initiated communicative activity that embraces canon, church, and world.

It was Calvin who stressed the role of the Holy Spirit as the witness *par excellence* as well as the enabler of all witnessing: "The office of the Spirit [is] . . . to seal to our minds the same doctrine which the Gospel delivers."[297] Barth proposes thinking of Scripture as the "witness" to revelation. "A real witness is not identical with that to which it witnesses, but it sets it before us."[298] Every text is a testimony to its author's beliefs, desires, visions, etc. Barth insists that the text does not point to itself but to its subject matter. If the reader sees only "an empty spot" instead of that to which the author points, "that indicates something about either the extraordinary nature of the content of what they say or the state of the reader."[299]

Can we not take the model of the witness one step further and use it to characterize the relation between Scripture and interpretation? I believe we can. *A text is a communicative act, and interpretation is a witness to its meaning.* An interpretation, in other words, is a testimony to the communicative act of the author. The Evangelists are themselves examples of the interpreter witness. Each of the Evangelists writes what is essentially an interpretation of the story of Jesus, the communicative act of God-with-us. Each Gospel seeks to interpret the meaning of "Jesus Christ," the significance of the life, death, and resurrection of One the writers took to be the true referent of Old Testament law, prophecy, and wisdom alike. As ethical interpreters and truthful witnesses, then, the Evangelists are exemplars of interpretive freedom and obedience. Though they were constrained by the Old Testament Scriptures and by the reality of Jesus Christ, they were free to highlight different aspects of God's self-communicative act as well as its significance.

Each of the Gospels encourages its readers to side with the witnesses inside the story. Luke's text is designed "to persuade its readers to become believing witnesses of and to 'the things which have been fulfilled among us' (Luke 1:1)."[300] The Fourth Gospel is written "so that you may believe . . ." (John 20:31): "The ideal readers of the narrative are those who can play the role of the narratees in believing that Jesus is the Christ."[301] The Gospel of Mark is interested in telling not only the story of Jesus but in showing "what will (or should) happen to disciples."[302] And the Gospel of Matthew devotes a whole chapter to instructions for discipleship, in which Jesus states: "He who receives you receives me" (Matt. 10:40). Jesus here identifies his own person, the object of testimony, with those who testify about him.[303] The Gospel of Matthew closes with the Great Commission, a call to witness to the objective meaning of Jesus' teaching and to the significance of his life. *The vocation of a witness is to give testimony: to speak not on his own authority, but only what he hears* (John 16:13). (It would be ironic indeed if human interpreters were able to exercise greater freedom in their interpretations than the Spirit of understanding can in his.) In the light of the category witness, a category that I believe applies to general hermeneutics as well as theological hermeneutics, we may formulate the mandate for the ethical interpreter as follows: "Do not bear false witness." *An interpreter, then, is one who bears true witness to textual meaning.*

Churches in the tradition of the Reformation distinguish their own confessional statements from the written Word, which is considered supremely authoritative. Biblical interpretation is second-order discourse; it is present-day testimony about apostolic testimony.[304] The notion that meaning is produced by the encounter of text and Spirit-led tradition ultimately undermines the all-important distinction between text and commentary. Without some such distinction, there would be no means to impeach a witness's false testimony. Thiselton rightly claims that "a radical or exclusive emphasis on the role of the reading-community in *constructing* meaning *collapses 'the two horizons' of hermeneutics into one single horizon.*"[305] It should now be clear why hermeneutic non-realism, for which meaning is made rather than discovered, is unethical; non-realist interpretation may provide interesting reading, but it is ultimately unreliable as testimony, for it cannot point to what is other than itself.

The interpreter witness is not an observer of the past (not an *eye*witness) but one who testifies to the reality, intelligibility, and efficacy of past communicative action. The proper vocation of the interpreter is to be a true and faithful witness to the meaning of the text. Such a witness, like the Good Samaritan (who responded to the other lying injured in the ditch), tends to and attends to the needs of the text as an other. In this sense, everyone who opens a text has an ethical obligation to bear faithful witness to it. Testimony to textual meaning is, of course, only as trustworthy as the witness. False testimony—misinterpretation, misunderstanding, certain forms of strong overstanding—abounds. At the end of the Fourth Gospel, we see what form authentic following must take. Peter's following Jesus eventually leads him to undergo crucifixion too (John 21:25). In similar fashion, the true witness to Jesus' story—to what it means as well as to what it meant—testifies to it by living, and perhaps dying, in such a manner as communicates its sense.

The Interpreter As Bearer of the Word

Interpretation, we have seen, is a spiritual exercise. Reader struggle with themselves, with historical distance, and with the matter of the text as they seek to appropriate its meaning. The text aims at producing real effects on readers: at transforming them into the image of the Word. It wants not only to be followed, but to be, as it were, incarnated. The end of interpretation, I submit, is *embodiment*.

Jesus Christ is the preeminent interpreter of God's self-communication, the unique and definitive embodiment of God's self-communicative act or "Word." The church, as Christ's body, is a secondary and derivative embodiment. The Word seeks, by the Spirit, to be taken to heart, to be embodied in the life of the people of God. Scripture's warnings call for attention, its commands call for obedience, its promises call for faith. *The vocation of the biblical interpreter is not simply to point at biblical meaning, but to embody it—to walk the way the Word goes.* In engaging with the name "Jesus Christ," we respond to a testimony that concerns our own existence. Interpreting this message ultimately means becoming a witness oneself: to the text's meaning, significance, and truth. Such is the "martyrdom of life."

To a great extent, texts make up the context of our lives, as Ricoeur passionately attests: "For me, the world is the ensemble of references opened up by every kind of text, descriptive or poetic, that I have read, understood, and loved."[306] George Steiner says, similarly, that the text can become "the informing 'context' of our being."[307] The interpreter's response to texts is ultimately not only a matter of reading but of being. The way we live is also our "interpretation" of the texts we read. Just as a musician interprets a text by performing, so the church is a communal performance of the Scriptures. The church—the sum total of those who bear the name of Christ—bears the responsibility of bearing, of doing, indeed of *being* the Word of God. Intended meaning must be continually extended—embodied in the words, deeds, and lives of its readers. Lesslie Newbigin calls the church to be a "hermeneutics of the Gospel." The task of theology, as Barth saw it, was to evaluate the life of the church with the criterion of the Word of God. This is why the meaning of the text and its interpretation must be distinguished; the church is not the Word but a *living commentary*.

"Let the word of Christ dwell in you richly" (Col. 3:16). Understanding and appropriating the Scriptures, Paul believes, produces effects. Those who follow the Word, who make following the Word their chief aim in life, begin to embody the righteousness of God. Readers who "bear" the Word—those in whom the Word grows, those who witness to the Word by doing it—will also bear fruit. This was precisely the point of Jesus' parable in which he likens his words to seeds that fall on different types of soil (Matt. 13:18–23). Those who hear the Word and do not understand are held responsible for their incomprehension (13:19). Those whose attention is distracted and whose reception of the Word is either temporary or shallow (13:20–22) ultimately prove unfruitful. (We are spared a description of what happens to the seed when it is sown into the abyss of the Undoers.) By contrast, one who understands the Word bears fruit and flourishes (13:23).

The parable of the sower, together with its dominical interpretation, is of vast hermeneutical importance, for it explicitly links the theme of discipleship to understanding. To follow the Word is to grow in understanding. Growth demands endurance, the prime requirement of the test of time. Understanding God's Word is a vocation: a call to mission and discipleship. To follow this Word may become a matter of death; it is certainly a matter of life and of living. Cyprian, the third-century bishop of Carthage, saw the hundredfold yield of the seed that fell on the good soil as realized in the martyrs of the church. The martyr is the one who counts his witness more important than his life (cf. Rev. 12:11). The martyr is the one whose witness endures to the end. The martyr gives her life for the sake of the meaning she has come to embody. Thus the privilege of hermeneutics—the Protestant insistence on the "priesthood of all believers"—leads on to the responsibility of hermeneutics, to the call directed at interpreters to become "martyrs"—witnesses and sufferers—on behalf of meaning.

NOTES

1. Meir Sternberg, "Between Poetics and Sexual Politics: From Reading to Counterreading," *Journal of Biblical Literature* 111 (1992): 473.

2. George Steiner, *Real Presences*, 149–50.

3. Karl Barth, *The Word of God and the Word of Man*, 32.

4. The aim of a literary act is to affect a potential reader. Note that a frequent perlocutionary aim of a literary act is to incite the reader to further action.

5. Hauerwas, *Unleashing the Scripture*, 47–62.

6. Ibid., 49.

7. J. A. Appleyard, *Becoming a Reader: The Experience of Fiction From Childhood to Adulthood* (Cambridge: Cambridge Univ. Press, 1990).

8. Ibid., 190.

9. Morgan and Barton, *Biblical Interpretation*, 7.

10. Rorty, *Objectivity, Relativism, and Truth*, 198.

11. Rorty, "Pragmatism and Philosophy," in *After Philosophy*, 59.

12. Ibid., 56.

13. Ibid., 61.

14. Ibid., 60.

15. Barton, *Reading the Old Testament*, 6.

16. Steiner, "'Critic'/'Reader,'" *New Literary History* 10 (Spring 1979): 423–52

17. Morgan and Barton, *Biblical Interpretation*, 7.

18. See Wayne Booth, *The Company We Keep: An Ethics of Fiction* (Berkeley: Univ. of California Press, 1988).

19. Nathan Scott, for his part, calls Steiner a "veritable priest of reading" (Nathan Scott, *Reading Steiner*, ix).

20. Cited in Frank Gloversmith, ed., *The Theory of Reading* (Sussex: Harvester Press, 1984), x.

21. Appleyard, *Becoming a Reader*, 117.

22. Elisabeth Schüssler Fiorenza, "The Ethics of Biblical Interpretation," 15.

23. Ibid.

24. Young, "The Pastoral Epistles and the Ethics of Reading," *Journal for the Study of the New Testament* 45 (1992): 120.

25. See Simon Critchley, *The Ethics of Deconstruction*.

26. Gary A. Phillips, "The Ethics of Reading Deconstructively, or Speaking Face-to-Face: The Samaritan Woman Meets Derrida at the Well," in Elizabeth Struthers Malbon and Edgar McKnight, ed., *The New Literary Criticism and the New Testament* (Sheffield: Sheffield Univ. Press, 1994), 287.

27. *The Postmodern Bible*, 131.

28. Julia Kristeva, *Desire in Language: A Semiotic Approach to Literature and Art* (New York: Columbia Univ. Press, 1980), 23.

29. Ricoeur, "World of the Text, World of the Reader," in *A Ricoeur Reader*, 494.

30. C. S. Lewis, *An Experiment in Criticism*, 19.

31. Ibid., 88.

32. Ibid., 11.

33. Ibid.

34. Ibid., 121.

35. Ibid.

36. Ibid., 124.

37. Ibid., 127.

38. Lewis, *A Preface to Paradise Lost* (Oxford: Oxford Univ. Press, 1942), 1.

39. Lewis, *Experiment in Criticism*, 93.

40. Ibid., 94.

41. Steiner, *Real Presences*, 90.

42. Ricoeur, "Appropriation," in *Hermeneutics and the Human Sciences*, 193.

43. Lewis, *Experiment in Criticism*, 98.

44. Ricoeur, "What Is a Text? Explanation and Understanding," in *Hermeneutics and the Human Sciences*, 159.

45. Lewis, *Experiment in Criticism*, 19.

46. Pannenberg, *Systematic Theology* (Grand Rapids: Eerdmans, 1991), 1:15.

47. Plantinga, "Augustinian Christian Philosophy," 304.

48. Ibid.

49. I here adapt the definition of intellectual virtue taken from the excellent account of Zagzebski, *Virtues of the Mind*, 165–96.

50. Zagzebski states: "No specifiable procedures tell a person how to recognize the salient facts, how to get insight, or how to think up good explanations, much less how to use all three to get to a single end" (ibid., 226).

51. Zagzebski describes wisdom as the virtue that integrates and coordinates the other virtues (ibid., 224–26).

52. Benjamin Jowett, *The Interpretation of Scripture and Other Essays* (London: George Routledge & Sons, 1907).

53. Noble, "The *Sensus Literalis*: Jowett, Childs, and Barr," 3.

54. Hauerwas, *Unleashing*, 33–34.

55. Watson, *Text, Church and World*, 229.

56. Stephen E. Fowl and Gregory Jones, *Reading in Communion: Scripture and Ethics in Christian Life* (Grand Rapids: Eerdmans, 1991).

57. Watson, *Text, Church and World*, 33.

58. Martindale, *Redeeming the Text*, 32.

59. Schneiders, *The Revelatory Text: Interpreting the New Testament as Sacred Scripture* (San Francisco: Harper, 1991), 168.

60. William S. Kurz, "Luke and Acts As Canonical," *Reading Luke-Acts: Dynamics of Biblical Narrative* (Louisvillem Ky.: Westminster/John Knox, 1993), 105.

61. Charles Wood, *Formation of Christian Understanding: An Essay in Theological Hermeneutics* (Philadelphia: Westminster, 1981), 30.

62. Interestingly, the actual moment of recognition was delayed until they broke bread together (Luke 24:30–31). This "reading in communion" may be what Fowl and Jones have in mind.

63. *The Postmodern Bible*, 14

64. Stout, "What Is the Meaning of a Text?" 6.

65. So Belsey, *Critical Practice*, 5–7.

66. See Clines, "Possibilities and Priorities of Biblical Interpretation in an International Perspective," *Biblical Interpretation* 1 (1993): 80.

67. Ibid., 87.

68. Ibid., 78.

69. Cited in *The Postmodern Bible*, 28; see Holland, "Unity Identity Text Self," *PMLA* 90 (1975): 813–22. See also Gregor Campbell, "Holland, Norman N.," in *Encyclopedia of Contemporary Literary Theory*, 362–63.

70. Robert Fowler, *Let the Reader Understand* (Minneapolis: Fortress, 1991), 1.

71. Lévinas says that "Greek" (philosophical, logocentric) thought seeks "to *reconcile* oppositions and differences through a movement of thought that would finally reduce them to aspects of a single comprehensive vision" (see Norris, *Derrida*, 230). See also Critchley, *The Ethics of Deconstruction*, 4–9.

72. The argument of the present work is that there is an epistemology of meaning that aims at literary knowledge without reducing the other to the knower. Epistemology itself, that is, can have an ethical dimension. In subsequent sections, I discuss what such an epistemology would look like under the rubric of spirituality and the interpretive virtues.

73. Martindale, *Redeeming the Text*, 3.

74. *The Postmodern Bible*, 130.

75. W. K. Wimsatt and Monroe C. Beardsley, "The Affective Fallacy," in W. K. Wimsatt, *The Verbal Icon* (Lexington, Ky.: Univ. of Kentucky Press, 1954), 21. This was the companion piece to the authors' essay on the intentional fallacy, cautioning against equating the meaning with the author.

76. One of the chapters in Fish's *Is There a Text in This Class?* is entitled "Literature in the Reader: Affective Stylistics." Fish's thesis is that meaning inheres in the experience of reading.

77. *The Postmodern Bible*, 52.

78. John B. Thompson, *Ideology and Modern Culture*, 7.

79. Coggins, "A Future for the Commentary?" in Francis Watson, ed., *The Open Text*, 174. Coggins's own view is that every translation involves subjective choices that make of every version a kind of commentary.

80. Judith Fetterley, *The Resisting Reader: A Feminist Approach to American Fiction* (Bloomington: Indiana Univ. Press, 1978), xii.

81. It is noteworthy that this position grants a realism in the realm of meaning; one has to resist only because of a matter and force that is actually there.

82. Joanne Carlson Brown and Rebecca Parker, "For God So Loved the World?" in *Christianity, Patriarchy, and Abuse: A Feminist Critique* (New York: Pilgrim, 1989), 26–27.

83. Young, *Theology of the Pastoral Epistles* (Cambridge: Cambridge Univ. Press, 1994), 147.

84. Young's answer to this question takes the following line: "What we need to do is to look for the 'spirit' of the text as it relates to the specific particularities of the historical moment of its production" (ibid., 149).

85. Sternberg, "Biblical Poetics and Sexual Politics," 469.

86. Ibid.

87. Ibid., 473.

88. Louis Althusser, "From Capital to Marx's Philosophy," in *Reading Capital* (New York: Verso, 1970), 14.

89. Michael Edwards, *Towards a Christian Poetics*, 166.

90. Derrida, *Limited Inc.*, 200.

91. Steiner, *After Babel: Aspects of Language and Translation* (London: Oxford Univ. Press, 1975), 244.

92. Derrida, *Ear of the Other*, 157. What are we to make, however, of the fact that Derrida's works have been translated from French into English? As a matter of fact, a whole volume has been written on the issue that deconstruction raises for the practice of translation (Joseph F. Graham, ed., *Difference in Translation* [Ithaca: Cornell Univ. Press, 1985]).

93. Derrida, *Ear of the Other,* 122.

94. G. Lloyd Jones, "Translation (to the KJV)," in *Dictionary of Biblical Interpretation*, 704.

95. Cited in Eugene A. Nida, *Toward a Science of Translating* (Leiden: E. J. Brill, 1964), 13.

96. Eugene A. Nida and Charles R. Taber, *The Theory and Practice of Translation* (Leiden: E. J. Brill, 1974).

97. Steiner, *After Babel*, 298.

98. Ibid., 296.

99. The translator does his or her utmost to "retrieve the balance of forces," to aim at a "conservation of the energies of meaning," because "both formally and morally the books must balance" (ibid., 302–3).

100. Ibid., 27.

101. Ibid., 310. For some striking examples of the dangers of word-for-word translations, see pp. 306–7 on various attempts to translate Gen. 1:3.

102. Ibid., 308.

103. Lewis, *Experiment in Criticism*, 101.

104. Bakhtin asks: "Is there anything in the natural sciences that corresponds to 'context'?" (*Speech Genres*, 167).

105. Edwards, *Towards a Christian Poetics*, 167.

106. Ibid., 169–70.

107. Bakhtin, *Speech Genres*, 6–7.

108. Ibid., 7.

109. Ibid., 5.

110. Steiner, *After Babel*, 302.

111. Booth, *The Company We Keep*, 86.

112. Schneiders, *The Revelatory Text*, 14.

113. Steiner, *After Babel*, 359.

114. Nida and Taber, *The Theory and Practice of Translation*, ch. 2.

115. Ricoeur does acknowledge that "character"—one's settled dispositions and acquired habits—assumes a kind of sameness of the self, but he denies that the sameness of character is the whole story of personal identity (*Oneself As Another*, 119–23).

116. Ibid., 123.

117. See my "Human Being, Individual and Social," esp. 173–75

118. It is interesting to note that in the New Testament the same Greek word is used for the faithful deliverance of tradition as for Judas's betrayal of Jesus (*paradidōmi*: e.g., Mark 3:19; 1 Cor. 15:3).

119. Vincent B. Leitch, "Reflection on the Responsibility of the Literary Critic," appendix to *Deconstructive Criticism*.

120. Roland Barthes, "Wrestling With the Angel: Textual Analysis of Genesis 32:23–33," in Barthes, *The Semiotic Challenge* (New York: Hill and Wang, 1988), 260.

121. See Critchley's *The Ethics of Deconstruction*, Phillips's "The Ethics of Reading Deconstructively," and J. Hillis Miller's *The Ethics of Reading* (New York: Columbia Univ. Press, 1987).

122. Phillips, "The Ethics of Reading Deconstructively," 287.

123. Ibid., 317.

124. *The Postmodern Bible*, 3.

125. So Rowan Williams, "Between Politics and Metaphysics," 6.

126. Thiselton, *The Responsibility of Hermeneutics*, 99.

127. Jeanrond, *Theological Hermeneutics*, 116.

128. H. Richard Niebuhr, "The Meaning of Responsibility," in James M. Gustafson and James T. Lancy, ed., *On Being Responsible: Issues in Personal Ethics* (London: SCM, 1969), 31.

129. Gill, *Mediated Transcendence*, 127.

130. I note in passing that "fittingness" is a theme not only of ethical interpretation but also of biblical wisdom.

131. Jeanrond himself seeks a mediating position: both self-criticism and criticism of the text's content are necessary if texts are to transform readers (*Text and Interpretation*, 114).

132. *The Postmodern Bible*, 66.

133. Ibid., 302.

134. Roland Barthes, "Writing Reading," in *The Rustle of Language*, 29.

135. Barthes, "On Reading," in *The Rustle of Language*, 42.

136. Jean Piaget, *Child's Conception of the World*, in Gareth B. Matthews, *Philosophy and the Young Child* (Cambridge, Mass.: Harvard Univ. Press, 1980), 47.

137. I owe this real-life example to my daughter Emma.

138. Steiner, *Real Presences*, 8.

139. Booth, *The Company We Keep*, 399.

140. Morgan and Barton, *Biblical Interpretation*, 270.

141. This is particularly important for the genre of testimony, especially the testimony of an eyewitness. See my "The Hermeneutics of I-Witness Testimony: John 21:20–24 and the 'Death' of the 'Author,'" 366–87.

142. Ricoeur, *Oneself As Another*, 170.

143. Aristotle, *Nichomachean Ethics*, 1094a1. Ethics is here characterized by a teleological perspective that views the good in terms of ends and purposes.

144. Brett, "The Future of Reader Criticisms?" in Watson, ed., *The Open Text*, 13–31.

145. So Walter Brueggemann, *The Bible and Postmodern Imagination* (London: SCM, 1993), 57–58.

146. Gnuse, "New Directions in Biblical Theology: The Impact of Contemporary Scholarship in the Hebrew Bible," *Journal of the American Academy of Religion* 62 (1994): 893–918.

147. Eagleton complains that Hirsch, "like most authoritarian regimes . . . is quite unable rationally to justify [his] own ruling values" (*Literary Theory*, 69). Even P. D. Juhl, a friendly critic, acknowledges that Hirsch's definition of meaning is a stipulative one—a recommendation rather than a necessity (*Interpretation*, 12, 23–27).

148. Interestingly, with regard to biblical interpretation, Kant worked an Enlightenment variation on Augustine: read in such a way so as to encourage moral progress. For Kant, the highest aim for biblical interpretation—the aim of practical reason (e.g., reason's directions for human freedom)—was moral usefulness. In much ideological criticism, there is a similar Kantian drive: choose the reading that best fosters quality and justice among neighbors. However, the apparent universality of this rule is overstretched and breaks up over the dispute concerning that in which the human good consists.

149. Hirsch, *Aims of Interpretation*, 91.

150. Ibid., 90 (italics his).

151. Ibid.

152. Ibid., 92.

153. Habermas also distinguishes ethics (e.g., what a community believes to be the "good") from morality (e.g., what everyone believes to be "right")

154. Habermas, *Justification and Application*, 24.

155. Rasmussen, *Reading Habermas*, 61.

156. Many texts, of course, do not aim at being understood by, but rather at manipulating, their readers (e.g., propaganda). Do readers need to respect the covenant of discourse where the texts themselves do not? I do not know how Habermas would reply to this query. For the most part, he has focused on argumentative discourse. For my part, I believe it is necessary to admit that much of what humans say and write *is* manipulative, an attempt to influence people's thoughts and actions through the instrumentality of language. Nevertheless, I would still consider such discourse as communicative action and would insist that interpreters should determine precisely what a given discourse is doing before condemning it.

157. Niels Thomassen, *Communicative Ethics in Theory and Practice*, tr. John Irons (London: Macmillan, 1992), 79.

158. Clark Pinnock, *The Scripture Principle* (San Francisco: Harper & Row, 1984), 204.

159. By Thomassen in a discussion of K. E. Løgstrup, a Danish theologian, *Communicative Ethics in Theory and Practice*, 117.

160. Jeanrond collapses the distinction between under- and overstanding when he insists that understanding must include criticism, both of the text and of the situation in which interpretation takes place. On my view, understanding includes evaluation only if by the latter we mean the attempt to determine how successful the text is in executing its author's intentions (e.g., how excellent a particular kind of communicative act it is). Excellence, however, only has

reference to what we might call the text's implicit "mission statement": its inherent aims and objectives as a communicative act aimed towards a particular end. To criticize a text's "mission" as immoral is always an act of overstanding.

161. Booth makes a similar point: "Since any one critical mode will inevitably leave out, ignore, or distort danda [= data] revealed by other modes, I *must* respect many modes if I am not to reduce the wonderful variety of human achievement—of both 'literary' and critical texts—to the monotony of perceptions dictated by one particular mode"(*Critical Understanding*, 247–48). Critchley espouses his own version of the interpretive imperative: ethical interpretation acknowledges and affirms an irreducible alterity that can be neither excluded nor included within a logocentric conceptuality (*Ethics of Deconstruction*, 41).

162. I discuss interpretive justice and freedom in a pluralistic age more fully in the next section.

163. Booth, *The Company We Keep*, 90.

164. Booth, *Critical Understanding*, 241.

165. Booth notes that while modern texts intentionally violate conventional generic expectations, they continue to have a central thrust, namely, to defy conventional labels, and can be understood accordingly (ibid.).

166. For a fuller example, see Booth's often hilarious list of improper questions one might raise about the story of the three little pigs (ibid., 243).

167. Booth, *The Company We Keep*, 309.

168. Iris Murdoch, *The Sovereignty of Good* (London: Routledge & Kegan Paul, 1970), 34.

169. Gillian Rose, *Judaism and Modernity: Philosophical Essays* (Oxford: Blackwell, 1993), 8.

170. So Williams, "Between Politics and Metaphysics," 3–22.

171. Sternberg, "Biblical Poetics and Sexual Politics," 469.

172. C. S. Lewis, *Abolition of Man* (New York: Macmillan, 1947), 26.

173. Attributed to Johann Albrecht Bengel (1687–1752).

174. Ricoeur, *Interpretation Theory*, 95.

175. Darr, *On Character Building: The Reader and the Rhetoric of Characterization in Luke-Acts* (Louisville, Ky.: Westminster/John Knox, 1992), 55.

176. See my "The Hermeneutics of I-Witness Testimony," 384–85.

177. T. F. Torrance, *The Hermeneutics of John Calvin* (Edinburgh: Scottish Academic Press, 1988), 158.

178. Anthony C. Thiselton, "On Models and Methods: A Conversation with Robert Morgan," in David Clines, Stephen Fowl, Stanley Porter, ed., *The Bible in Three Dimensions: Essays in Celebration of Forty Years of Biblical Studies in the University of Sheffield* (Sheffield: JSOT Press, 1990), 345.

179. Ricoeur, *A Ricoeur Reader*, 494.

180. "Ezra opened the book. All the people could see him because he was standing above them; and as he opened it, the people all stood up" (Neh. 8:5).

181. The Feast of Pentecost was a harvest festival, and Jewish tradition held that the law of Moses was given on this day. Acts 2 raises interesting questions for a theory of text interpretation. What is the significance of the gift of "tongues"? Were these foreign languages? If so, the story may suggest that the curse of Babel has been reversed.

182. Hans Robert Jauss, *Toward an Aesthetic of Reception* .

183. *Collected Papers of Charles Sanders Peirce*, ed. Charles Hartshorne and Paul Weiss (Cambridge, Mass.: Harvard Univ. Press, 1931–35), 5:401.

184. W. K. Wimsatt Jr. and Monroe Beardsley, "The Affective Fallacy," in Wimsatt and Beardsley, *The Verbal Icon*, 21.

185. Cf. James Dunn, "Levels of Canonical Authority," in *The Living Word* (Philadelphia: Fortress, 1988), 152; R. E. Brown, "'And the Lord Said'? Biblical Reflections on Scripture As the Word of God," *Theological Studies* 42 (1981): 3–19.

186. See the table of contents in Karl Barth, *Church Dogmatics* I/2.

187. Metaphysical idealists such as Bishop Berkeley said "to be is to be perceived." Hermeneutic idealists might say "to mean is to be received."

188. I am well aware that not all theologians affirm the *filioque* clause ("and from the Son"). The issues are complex. I do not wish to stake my entire hermeneutical theory on the *filioque*. I believe the same point about perlocutions following from illocutions could be made with the aid of Barth's analysis of revelation in terms of revealer–revelation–revealedness as well.

189. Donald G. Bloesch, *Holy Scripture: Revelation, Inspiration & Interpretation* (Downers Grove, Ill.: InterVarsity, 1994), 21–22.

190. James W. McClendon Jr., *Ethics: Systematic Theology* (Nashville: Abingdon, 1986), 1:31–33.

191. Richard B. Hays, *Echoes of Scripture in the Letters of Paul* (New Haven: Yale Univ. Press, 1989), 108.

192. Curtis Freeman, "Toward a *Sensus Fidelium* for an Evangelical Church: Postconservatives and Postliberals on Reading Scripture," in Timothy Phillips and D. Ockholm, ed., *The Nature of Confession: Evangelicals and Postliberals in Dialogue* (Downers Grove, Ill.: InterVarsity, 1996), 170 and n. 42, citing Fish and Hauerwas in support.

193. Hauerwas, *Unleashing the Scriptures*, ch. 2.

194. Ibid., 23. Hauerwas observes that the Orthodox are equally insistent that Scripture only makes sense within the traditions and practices of the church. In this light, it would be interesting to hear Hauerwas explain Luther's ability to read the text against a tradition that had begun to misconstrue the sacraments.

195. Ibid., 41.

196. See Georges Florovsky, "The Function of Tradition in the Ancient Church," in *Bible, Church, Tradition: An Easter Orthodox View* (Belmont, Mass: Nordland, 1972), ch. 5.

197. Ibid., 103.

198. Stephen Fowl, "How the Spirit Reads and How to Read the Spirit," in *The Bible in Ethics*, ed. John W. Rogerson, Margaret Davies, and M. Daniel Carroll, JSOT Supplement Series 207 (Sheffield: Sheffield Academic Press, 1995), 358.

199. Hays, *Echoes of Scripture*, 108.

200. Dunn, *The Living Word*, 119.

201. Ibid., 154.

202. Bloesch, *Holy Scripture*, 27.

203. Ibid., 200.

204. See Bernard Ramm, *The Witness of the Spirit: An Essay on the Contemporary Relevance of the Internal Witness of the Holy Spirit* (Grand Rapids: Eerdmans, 1959).

205. Charles Wood's comment on Luther, "Finding the Life of a Text," in *An Introduction to Theological Study* (Valley Forge, Pa.: Trinity Press International, 1994), 102.

206. Noble, *The Canonical Approach*, 298.

207. See my "The Spirit of Understanding: Special Revelation and General Hermeneutics," in Roger Lundin, ed., *Disciplining Hermeneutics: Interpretation in Christian Perspective* (Grand Rapids: Eerdmans, 1997), 131–65.

208. This is one of the major reasons why I believe Ricoeur's hermeneutics aligns more naturally with Bultmann rather than Barth (see my *Biblical Narrative in the Philosophy of Paul Ricoeur*, ch. 9).

209. Barth, *Church Dogmatics* I/2, 466.

210. Ibid., 471.

211. Jüngel, *Karl Barth: A Theological Legacy* (Philadelphia: Westminster, 1986), 75.

212. Barth, "Preface to the Second Edition," *The Epistle to the Romans*, 12.

213. "The Preface to the Third Edition," *The Epistle to the Romans*, 18.

214. This is Frances Young's definition of allegory in "Allegory and the Ethics of Reading," *The Open Text*, 111.

215. Ricoeur, "Between the Text and Its Readers," in *A Ricoeur Reader*, 409.

216. David Hoy and Thomas McCarthy, *Critical Theory* (Oxford: Blackwell, 1994), 200.

217. See Eugene F. Rogers, "How the Virtues of an Interpreter Presuppose and Perfect Hermeneutics: The Case of Thomas Aquinas," *Journal of Religion* 76 (1996): 80.

218. Dunn, *The Living Word*, 156.

219. Ibid., 131.

220. Cf. R. S. Sugirtharajah, *Voices From the Margin: Interpreting the Bible in the Third World* (Maryknoll, N.Y.: Orbis, 1971); Cain Hope Felder, ed., *Stony the Road We Trod: African American Biblical Interpretation* (Minneapolis: Fortress, 1991); Daniel Smith-Christopher, ed., *Text and Experience: Towards a Cultural Exegesis of the Bible* (Sheffield: Sheffield Academic Press, 1995).

221. R. Crossman, "Do Readers Make Meaning?" in S. Suleiman and R. Crossman, ed., *The Reader in the Text* (Princeton: Princeton Univ. Press, 1980), 162.

222. Dunn, *The Living Word*, 159. Dunn continues to believe that the task of exegesis is to recover the author's intended meaning.

223. Robert Tannehill, *The Narrative Unity of Luke-Acts* (Philadelphia: Fortress 1990), 2:4.

224. Thiselton, *New Horizons*, 549.

225. See Schweicker's review of Daniel Patte's *Ethics of Biblical Interpretation*, in *Journal of Religion* 76 (1996): 355–57.

226. See Colin Gunton, *The One, the Three, and the Many: God, Creation and the Culture of Modernity* (Cambridge: Cambridge Univ. Press, 1993).

227. Booth, *Critical Understanding: The Powers and Limits of Pluralist*, 219–32.

228. Hoy and McCarthy, *Critical Theory*, 241.

229. Booth, *Critical Understanding*, 351.

230. Ibid., 346.

231. Raymond Brown, "The Paraclete in the Fourth Gospel," *New Testament Studies* 13 (1966–67): 116 (italics mine).

232. George R. Beasley-Murray, *John*, Word Biblical Commentary (Dallas: Word, 1987), 283.

233. Rudolf Bultmann, *The Gospel of John* (Oxford: Blackwell, 1971), 575.

234. Juhl, *Interpretation*, 226.

235. Hirsch, "Meaning and Significance Reinterpreted," 209.

236. Ibid., 216.

237. Ibid., 210.

238. Hirsch, "Transhistorical Intentions and the Persistence of Allegory," 553.

239. Ibid., 558.

240. See below on the vocation of the interpreter.

241. See my "The Bible—Its Relevance for Today," 9–30.

242. A critic may also ask what practical difference it makes to distinguish between a community led *beyond* the literal sense by the Spirit-in-tradition and a community led by the Spirit *into* the abundance of the literal sense itself, since in each case there will be a plurality of interpretations. The answer, which follows from my commitment to hermeneutical realism, is that the former possibility risks cutting interpretive tradition off from the Word and thus from the possibility of correction by the Word.

243. See Freeman's description of fundamentalism in "Toward a *Sensus Fidelium* for an Evangelical Church," 166.

244. C. T. McIntyre, "Fundamentalism," in *Evangelical Dictionary of Theology*, 435.

245. Ramm, *The Witness of the Spirit*, 126.

246. Mark Corner, "Fundamentalism," *Dictionary of Biblical Interpretation*, 244.

247. James Barr states that what is characteristic of fundamentalist hermeneutics is the presupposition of biblical inerrancy: "The typical fundamentalist insistence is not that the Bible must be interpreted literally but that it must be so interpreted as not to admit that it contains error" (*The Bible in the Modern World*, 168; cf. his *Fundamentalism*, 46–55).

248. Kathleen C. Boone, *The Bible Tells Them So: The Discourse of Protestant Fundamentalism* (Albany: SUNY Press, 1989), 69.

249. Ibid., 73.

250. Mark Corner, "Fundamentalism," 245.

251. Nancey Murphy argues that both conservative and liberal theology have been influenced by modern philosophy, not least in their theories of knowledge (foundationalism) and meaning (propositionalism vs. expressionism). See her *Beyond Liberalism and Fundamentalism*.

252. Cf. Gundry: "Our identification of the kind of literature an author intended to write governs the criteria by which we judge the truthfulness as well as the meaning of his work," in "A Theological Postscript," *Matthew*, 638.

253. Ramm, *The Pattern of Religious Authority*, 29.

254. I take this paraphrase from the Leiden Synopsis, cited in Heinrich Heppe, *Reformed Dogmatics*, 35.

255. Cited in Berkouwer, *Holy Scripture*, 40.

256. In describing the Spirit as the "efficacy" of the Word, I am following Calvin's example, though developing it with categories from speech act philosophy. See *Institutes*, 1.9.3. For a discussion of the seventeenth-century Reformed orthodox discussion of the efficacy of the Word, see Otto Weber, *Foundations of Dogmatics*, tr. Darrell L. Guder (Grand Rapids: Eerdmans, 1981), 1:284–86.

257. The Spirit is also the locutionary efficacy of the Word, for, as its inspirer, the Spirit guides the human authors to employ the right, divinely intended words.

258. Westminster Shorter Catechism, Question 89.

259. For a more complete defense of the use of "accept" as adopted here, see Daniel Fuller, "The Holy Spirit's Role in Biblical Interpretation," in W. Ward Gasque and William Sanford LaSor, ed., *Scripture, Tradition, and Interpretation* (Grand Rapids: Eerdmans, 1978), 189–98. For a contrary view, see Millard Erickson, who says the problem is that unbelievers do not accept because they do not understand (*Christian Theology*, 249).

260. Ramm notes that fundamentalism "lost the perspective of the instrumental character of Scripture, and gave Scripture an independent life of its own. . . . Thus among fundamentalists the expression 'the Word' became theologically equivalent to the expression 'Word and Spirit' among Reformed theologians" (*Witness of the Spirit*, 125).

261. Ramm, *The Witness of the Spirit*, 125.

262. Gunton, *A Brief Theology of Revelation* (T. & T. Clark, 1995), 97n19.

263. Richard Hays, *Echoes of Scripture in the Letters of Paul*, 86.

264. Ibid., 173.

265. N. T. Wright sees the biblical story as consisting of five "acts," with the writing of the NT forming the first scene of the fifth act, and with the church today in the process of performing the final scenes. See his *The New Testament and the People of God*, 141–43.

266. Ellen F. Davis, "Holy Preaching: Ethical Interpretation and the Practical Imagination," in Ephraim Radner and George R. Sumner, ed., *Reclaiming Faith: Essays on Orthodoxy in the Episcopal Church and the Baltimore Declaration* (Grand Rapids: Eerdmans, 1993), 198.

267. Ibid., 198.

268. Florovsky, *Bible, Church, Tradition*, 26.

269. *Dei Verbum*, par. 23.

270. S. Kierkegaard , *Either/Or*, tr. Howard V. Hong and Edna H. Hong, 2 vols. (Princeton: Princeton Univ. Press, 1987).

271. Barth, *Church Dogmatics*, I/2, 470 (italics mine).

272. Derrida, *Writing and Difference*, 292.

273. My analysis of carnival is drawn from Mikhail Bakhtin's analysis of the concept in his study of Rabelais's novels.

274. Dominick LaCapra, *Rethinking Intellectual History: Texts, Contexts, Language* (Ithaca: Cornell Univ. Press, 1983), 22.

275. Jobling, "Writing the Wrongs of the World," 103, 107.

276. Hall, *Word and Spirit*, 168.

277. See my "Human Being, Individual and Social."

278. Hall, *Word and Spirit*, 192.

279. Stephen Moore singles out poststructuralism as harboring the strongest anti-authoritarian instincts (see *Poststructuralism and the New Testament*, 117).

280. Thiselton, *Interpreting God and the Postmodern Self: On Meaning, Manipulation and Promise* (Edinburgh: T. & T. Clark, 1995), 107.

281. Barth, *Church Dogmatics* I/2, 735.

282. Schneiders, *The Revelatory Text*, 177.

283. Barth, *Church Dogmatics* I/2, 696.

284. Appleyard, *Becoming a Reader*, 189.

285. Ricoeur, "World of the Text, World of the Reader," 496.

286. Booth, *Critical Understanding*, 235.

287. See ch. 6 above.

288. I have adapted Barth's point for my own purposes. The freedom of the Word, on my view, does not mean that the Word of God floats free from the words of the human authors of Scripture, but rather that God the Spirit is free to use or not to use these words to witness to himself or to make the words efficacious in a perlocutionary manner.

289. Barth, *Church Dogmatics* I/2, 471.

290. "Therefore if [the church] would see Jesus Christ, it is directed and bound to His primary sign and therefore to the sign of this sign . . . it is directed and bound to Scripture" (Ibid., 583).

291. Werner G. Jeanrond, "Karl Barth's Hermeneutics," in Nigel Biggar, ed., *Reckoning With Barth: Essays in Commemoration of the Centenary of Karl Barth's Birth* (London: Mowbray, 1988), 84.

292. Barth, *Church Dogmatics* I/2, 720.

293. Schneiders, *The Revelatory Text*, 165.

294. Geddert, *Watchwords: Mark 13 in Markan Eschatology*, Journal for the Study of the New Testament Supplement Series 26 (Sheffield: Sheffield Academic Press, 1989), 180.

295. Yoder, "The Hermeneutics of the Anabaptists," in Willard M. Swartley, ed., *Essays on Biblical Interpretation: Anabaptist-Mennonite Perspectives* (Elkhart, Ind.: Institute of Mennonite Studies, 1984), 27.

296. Luther, *Table Talk*, 29

297. Cited in Ramm, *Witness of the Spirit*, 16.

298. Barth, *Church Dogmatics* I/2, 463.

299. Ibid., 469. C. S. Lewis agrees that the personality of the author is not what counts; what matters is the subject matter of the text. Cf. his argument with Tillyard in *The Personalist Heresy*.

300. Darr, *On Character Building*, 53.

301. Margaret Davies, *Rhetoric and Reference in the Fourth Gospel* (Sheffield: JSOT Press, 1992), 373.

302. Geddert, *Watchwords*, 180.

303. Gundry comments on this verse: "These sayings indicate that willingness to risk danger to oneself by harboring fleeing disciples characterizes true discipleship. Only the false disciple will refuse" (*Matthew*, 202). By extension, we might say that only those who protect the apostolic testimony may be regarded as true disciples.

304. Cf. Ebeling's notion that church history is the history of biblical interpretation.

305. Thiselton, *New Horizons*, 546.

306. Ricoeur, *Interpretation Theory*, 37.

307. Steiner, *On Difficulty*, 17.

CONCLUSION

A Hermeneutics of the Cross

The questions: "What is poetry, music, art?" "How can they not be?" "How do they act upon us and how do we interpret their action?" are, ultimately, theological questions.

George Steiner[1]

The sign and divinity have the same place and time of birth. The age of the sign is essentially theological.

Jacques Derrida[2]

CHAPTER EIGHT

A Hermeneutics of Humility and Conviction

The conclusion, as a literary genre, traditionally provides an opportunity for authors to pull the arguments of their texts together and to demonstrate their overall coherence. To this end, I want to suggest three ways in which readers may relate Parts 1 and 2 of the present work. A conclusion should, after all, be fitting; and I take it for granted that readers may feel the need not only to digest the individual arguments presented herein but also to interpret the whole. Accordingly, each of these ways offers a descriptive framework that focuses on a different level of meaning and so proffers an answer to the question, "What am I *doing* in this text?"

TRINITARIAN HERMENEUTICS

In the first place, I have sought to expose the philosophical, and ultimately theological, presuppositions that underlie debates, ancient and modern, about biblical interpretation. Theology is obviously hermeneutical, insofar as it seeks to interpret Scripture. Yet I have argued throughout this work that the converse is also true. Hermeneutics is theological, insofar as the interpretation of texts *in general* rests on beliefs about God and humanity. Specifically, beliefs that have to do with God, the world, and ourselves are implicit in the views interpreters take on the nature of the author, text, and reader. The present work represents a sustained plea to literary theorists and philosophers to make their implicit theologies *explicit*.

From Theological to Trinitarian Hermeneutics

The belief that there is something "in" the text, a presence not of the reader's own making, is a belief in transcendence. To read in order to encounter something beyond the mere play of signs is, to use Steiner's phrase, a "wager" on transcendence and a hope in the possibility of transformation. Both the believers (e.g., Steiner) and the unbelievers (e.g., Derrida) agree at least on this, though the former affirm the reality of such a meaning while the latter deny it. The unbelievers—Undoers and Users—deny the existence of a determinate message that transcends the surface play of the text. Disputes about the nature of interpretation are ultimately theological, therefore, insofar as they revolve around the possibility of transcendence.

On the one hand, then, we should read the Bible like any other text, though due consideration must be given to those factors that set it apart (e.g., its divine-human authorship, its canonical shape, its function as Scripture). On the other hand, we should read every other text with the same theological presuppositions that we bring to, and discover through, our study of the Bible. To argue that interpretation is theological is already an ambitious thesis, but it does not go far enough. In this book I have made the further claim that *the best general hermeneutics is a trinitarian hermeneutics*. Yes, the Bible should be interpreted "like any other book"; but *every* book should be interpreted with norms that we derive and establish from trinitarian theology.[3]

I do not wish to be misunderstood. The Trinity is not merely an illustration of a general intellectual process. I am not beginning with a philosophical framework and saying, "The Trinity is like that." Nor am I using the Trinity to justify a particular interpretive approach, as did Origen in relation to his tripartite distinction between the body, soul, and spirit of a text. *My appeal to the Trinity arises rather from the perception that the literary crisis about textual meaning is related to the broader philosophical crisis concerning realism, rationality, and right, and that this crisis, summed up by the term "postmodern," is in turn explicitly theological.* After all, it was Nietzsche's announcement of the "death of God" that eventually led to the "death of the author." Deconstruction, we may recall, is the death of God put into hermeneutics.[4] However, Nietzsche's was essentially a theological mistake that followed from a misleading view of God—a non-trinitarian view, to be exact. My recourse to a specifically trinitarian hermeneutics thus reflects my attempt to coordinate the remedy with the diagnosis. The degenerative disease that is slowly destroying Western civilization is a result of its denial of the Christian God and the Christian Gospel.

I have appealed to a number of threefold distinctions in the course of this study:

(1) to the literary triad of author–text–reader;
(2) to the traditional triadic division of philosophical labor: metaphysics–epistemology–ethics;
(3) to the three key interpretive issues that follow from these branches of philosophy: hermeneutic realism, hermeneutic rationality, and hermeneutic responsibility respectively;
(4) to the three components of the speech act: locution, illocution, perlocution;
(5) to three central Christian doctrines: creation, Incarnation/revelation, sanctification;
(6) to the triunity of God: the Father, Son, and Spirit.

What exactly has been the role of trinitarian theology in my analyses? I have been at pains not to use the Trinity merely as an illustration of a point obtained elsewhere. On the contrary, I have accepted Steiner's fascinating premise that God somehow "underwrites" language and attempted to clarify it from an explicitly Christian point of view. *The Trinity thus serves the role of what Kant calls a "transcendental condition": a necessary condition for the possibility of something humans experience but cannot otherwise explain, namely, the experience of meaningful communication.* From a Christian perspective, God is first and foremost a communicative agent, one who relates to humankind through words and the Word. Indeed, God's very being is a self-communicative act that both constitutes and enacts the covenant of discourse: speaker (Father), Word (Son), and reception (Spirit) are all interrelated.[5] Human communication is a similarly covenantal affair, though we cannot pour ourselves into our communicative acts and ensure their effects as God can through his Word and Spirit. Humans have the dignity of communicative agency, though not its perfection.

Contemporary literary theory is bound up with the modification or the outright rejection of orthodox Christian positions. We can readily see the effect that the loss of a Christian doctrine of God has on theories of textual interpretation by working backwards through the six triads listed above. To deny that God speaks into being what is other than himself is to refuse to ascribe locutions and illocutions to God; it is to reject the notion of the Creator's *parole*. But this is to reject the idea that the created order has meaning and authorial intention. This in turn leads to metaphysical non-realism, to the denial that there is an inherent order or structure in the "book" of nature. Metaphysical non-realism, next, spawns other forms of non-realism, including the hermeneutic variety. If meaning is not there, then there is nothing to be known and nothing for which interpreters are responsible. As a result, the author is pronounced "dead" on the reader's arrival. The death of the author "thus liberates an activity we may call counter-theological . . . for to refuse to halt meaning is finally to refuse God."[6]

Such is the postmodern "a/theology" that has led to readers becoming writers and to the ideology of pluralism. Postmodern skepticism thus represents an antithesis, not only to modernity, but to Christian theology as well. The thesis underlying the present work takes God's trinitarian communicative action as the paradigm, not merely the illustration, of all genuine message-sending and receiving. God is a speaking God. The Father is the one who, in the words of the creeds, *est locutus per prophetas*. Most of what God does—creating, warning, commanding, promising, forgiving, informing, comforting, etc.—is accomplished by speech acts. Moreover, God's speech agency is the epitome of clarity and efficacy.

Speech act theory serves as handmaiden to a trinitarian theology of communication. If the Father is the locutor, the Son is his preeminent illocution. Christ is God's definitive Word, the substantive content of his message. And the Holy Spirit—the condition and power of receiving the sender's message—is God the perlocutor, the reason that his words do not return to him empty (Isa. 55:11). The triune God is therefore the epitome of communicative agency: the speech agent who utters, embodies, and keeps his Word. Human speakers, created in God's image, enjoy the dignity of communicative agency, though as sinners their speech acts (and interpretations) are subject to all the imperfections and distortions that characterize human fallenness.[7]

True and False Religion

Current debates over right and wrong ways to read quickly become debates about true and false religion, about the nature of ultimate reality, and about distinguishing the divine voice from the dumb idol. Indeed, this would be one way to construe the relation of Parts 1 and 2 of the present work. The two parts describe two *theologies* of interpretation—the hermetic and the hermeneutic—and so confront the reader with a choice: to approach the theory and practice of interpretation with explicitly non-Christian theological assumptions or to work with assumptions drawn from Christian faith. What makes this dispute a religious one is that each side accuses the other of idolatry—of constructing false images of God.

In suggesting that general hermeneutics is a predicate or subset of theological hermeneutics, I have been aided, in a backhanded sort of way, by several secular philosophers and literary theorists (most notably, Derrida) who recognize the counter-theological quality of their own proposals. Only by reviewing contemporary trends and current developments in some detail could I hope to convince readers that many of the basic issues in literary theory and criticism depend on positions that are philosophical and ultimately theological. To repeat: the essential difference between the various postmodern approaches to interpretation and the approach represented here is to be found on the level of one's worldview, which is to say, theology. For me, interpretation is the positive attempt to recover the author's enacted intention, in all its complexity, and to relate it to the present. The doctrines of creation, Incarnation, revelation, and reconciliation are the main theological ideas that inspire and govern my approach. Postmodern critics, on the other hand, generally treat claims to have grasped objective meaning as illusory and view interpretation that is oriented to transcendence as idolatrous. The unbelievers of our time therefore urge various moralities of disbelief that are funded by negative theologies and a/theologies. For Derrida, God is less a presence than an absence, interpretation a matter of what is purely immanent to language.

The a/theology of deconstruction predisposes one to look at the world and at texts as a sea of indeterminate forces that lacks any transcendent ground or meaning. Contemporary non-realists follow Feuerbach in explaining belief in God and meaning alike in terms of human projections and the will to power. I readily acknowledge the partial truth of this position; I grant the inevitable role of subjectivity. We do not see the world or a text as God sees it, but through finite and fallible interpretive frameworks. I have argued that some frameworks—in particular, the literary frameworks or genres of Scripture—let more reality through than others. The Undoers, however, acknowledge neither the possibility nor the actuality of a genuine cognitive contact with reality. Postmoderns are unable to account either for literary knowledge or for biblical revelation. According to the Scriptures and Christian tradition, however, God is a speaking, revealing God, whose Spirit accompanies his Word from inspiration through inscripturation to appropriation.

Ultimately, Undoers and Users only bruise the heel of hermeneutics. The postmodern suspicion of hermeneutics can only be partial; in fact, even postmoderns believe they sometimes encounter what is more than their own projections in texts. Suspicion cannot become a consistent worldview; that way madness lies. Consequently, the postmodern bite is most effective when directed at the prideful interpreter; the wound need not be mortal so long as one heeds its moral. Undoers and Users helpfully expose the lie behind interpretations that too quickly claim to have attained the "plain" meaning. After Derrida, every honest interpreter will have to acknowledge that his or her interpretation always falls short. I therefore agree with Jeanrond's assessment: "One of Derrida's main contributions to hermeneutics lies precisely in his powerful warning against any form of absolutist or authoritarian reading of texts."[8] But postmodern theories have *not* succeeded in showing that interpretation is impossible. For while our knowledge of textual meaning may never be absolute, it may nevertheless be adequate. Against Feuerbach, atheism is not the secret of religion, nor is meaninglessness the secret of interpretation. There is something in texts to recover, a presence that is more than the reflection of my own face. In reading, we confront a mediated immediacy and meet with a face or a voice of an other, of an author. This brings us to my second integrative theme.

THE VERBAL ICON AND THE AUTHORIAL FACE

William Wimsatt, in his 1954 book *The Verbal Icon*, set forth the credo for New Criticism, an approach to literature that focused, as we have seen, on the text itself, independent of its origins or effects, as a source of knowledge in its own right. I have considered but rejected this approach in favor of a view that sees texts as communicative acts characterized by intention, illocution, and efficacy. Nevertheless, the image of the "verbal icon" is a rich and suggestive one. Indeed, we could view the positive argument in Part 2 as an apology for the verbal icon, as opposed to the more negative treatment in Part 1 of the text as a verbal idol.

The Empty Place: The Verbal Idol

I have already conceded that interpretations can become idolatrous. Insofar as they have pressed this point home, the Undoers and Users deserve our thanks. However, I have resisted their further claim that the text is an idol, a dumb object rather than a communicative act, a void rather than a voice.

"You shall not make for yourself an idol. . . . You shall not bow down to them or worship them" (Ex. 20:4–5). The biblical prohibition against idolatry is well known. What, however, does it have to do with hermeneutics? Just this: in both cases, religion and reading, the idol in question is a social construction. The unbeliever considers "God" and "meaning" to be the *effects* of adoration or interpretation respectively, not their prior conditions. The implications of treating the text as an idol—as the social construction of a community of readers—are, I believe, far-reaching. The most important of these implications is the one that leads to hermeneutic non-realism: to see the text as an idol is to suggest that it is the worshiper (e.g., the reader) who endows it with whatever power it has. Meaning is "graven" by the reader, not "given" by the author. For idols, as the biblical authors well knew, are dumb; they cannot speak or communicate anything new.

The idol, to return to the metaphor with which I began this work, is a *mirror* in which one sees only oneself: one's own beliefs, one's own values, one's own image. The divinity of the idol is a measure of oneself. Idols are projections of the human will to power. The idol confines the divine to the measure of the human gaze; precisely because idols are man-made, they cannot help us see or get beyond ourselves. Readers treat the text as an idol whenever they see in it only what they themselves have produced. On this view, the reader is the author, writer, or creator of the text-as-received. What the idol images is ultimately its maker—its reader-god. The idol thus acts "as a mirror, not as a portrait."[9]

Insofar as postmodern Undoers and Users resist the temptation to turn interpretations into idols, well and good. But insofar as their iconoclasm breeds indifference to the text, insofar as their suspicion renders every text dumb and mute, unable to speak, they go too far. And insofar as their cleansing of the temple lets in other spirits or enshrines self in the place of the other, their iconoclasm is damaging and dangerous. To say that the reader creates meaning is ultimately to give the reader only himself or herself, which is the same practical outcome of all forms of idolatry. Because the idol has nothing to give beyond what the idolater has put into it, any time spent tending and attending to idols is futile. In the end, it is the idolater who is deceived and ultimately undone.

A Meaningful Space: The Verbal Icon

Seen from an explicitly Christian point of view, the text is more like an icon than an idol. While the icon is also an "image," it is an image that opens onto an infinite depth to which one's gaze has ultimately to surrender, not a surface on which the reader writes. For Jean-Luc Marion, on whose analysis of iconicity this section largely relies, the difference between "idol" and "icon" is not the difference between two kinds of objects but of two different ways of regarding the same object.[10] Where the idol is a projection, the icon is a revelation; in the icon, that is, something comes to us from beyond.

Christ is the "icon" (Gk: *eikon*) of the invisible God (Col. 1:15). Marion notes that an icon lets the visible image be "saturated" by the invisible. Christians do not project divinity onto Jesus; rather, divinity shines *through* (at least to those with the faith, spirituality, and interpretive virtue to perceive it). The historian Norman Davies states that religious icons are the most enduring genre of European art.[11] The icon summons the human gaze to surpass itself by not remaining on the level of what is merely visible. Icons do not call attention to themselves, much less to their surface; they are rather "gates of mystery" and "doors of perception" to transcendence, to what lies beyond the surface level. Neither does the body of Jesus call attention to itself or exhaust his meaning. As in iconology and Christology, so it is with texts. The picture of postmodern interpreters as those whose gaze remains "frozen" on the surface—the level of the semiotic, of *langue*, of the play of signs—is a compelling one.

Let us take the notion of the verbal icon a step further. The Greek fathers, in particular St. John of Damascus (c. 675–749), distinguished between worship, which one directs to God alone, and reverence, which one may give to persons or objects. This reverence is directed not to the icon as an object, but rather to that which the icon represents or attests.[12] *The icon is a witness to transcendence from transcendence.* But this is precisely what we earlier concluded about texts: the task of interpretation is to get beyond oneself by attending to the form of a literary act in order to encounter an embodied intention. Interpretation is the attempt to bear true witness to what an other has said or done. Similarly, the posture demanded by the icon is that of "watchful calm." One cannot wrest its meaning from it; one does not master an icon or a text so much as attend, and pay attention, to it. To claim that the Bible is a verbal icon thus leads not to bibliolatry, but to the idea of *Holy* Scripture and to the idea that the text points away from itself.

One last feature of the icon is worth mentioning. Religious icons typically highlight the face (of God, of Christ, of saints), a potent visual symbol. What sense, then, does it make to speak of a "verbal" icon? The text is a verbal icon that represents the "implied face" of the author and mediates the author's presence. Marion states: "The body of the text does not belong to the text, but to the One who is embodied in it."[13] This sentence indicates how great is the distance between Wimsatt and the New Critics on the one hand, and Marion on the other, regarding the use of the term "icon." For Marion, the icon is a face that resists attempts to "master" it as one would an object of theoretical knowledge. It is a commonplace that, while we have no difficulty in recognizing faces, it is well-nigh impossible to explain how we know that we know them. Recognizing faces involves a form of personal knowledge, not merely a technical mastery of a person's physiognomy. Might there be an analogy between recognizing faces and interpretation? Could it be that the goal of reading Scripture is to have our gaze drawn and directed to the face of Christ?

The Second Council of Nicea in 787 states: "He who venerates the icon venerates in it the *hypostasis* of the one who is inscribed in it."[14] What matters, above all else, in the icon is the subject matter: the sense of a personal presence. The church fathers, of course, had in mind a pictorial face. Yet something similar holds for the text that mediates a personal presence in the form of a *voice*. To attend to the *hypostasis* of a visual or a verbal icon need not imply the substantial presence of a person, only a person's *intentional* presence.[15] In the visual icon, it is the gaze that emanates *from* the icon that counts: "Instead of the invisible mirror, which sent the human gaze back to itself . . . the icon opens in a face that gazes at our gazes in order to summon them to its depth."[16] Every face, says Marion, is like an icon; it is the public sign of a person's innermost being. The face, then, is both symbol and sacrament of the other to whom we owe an infinite ethical obligation.

The Authorial Face: Practicing the Presence of an Other

Le vrai lecteur est presque toujours un ami.[17]

I have argued that a text has an identity that is more like a person than a thing. Thanks to Marion, we can now see why. An icon—whether verbal or visual—shows us a face "that gazes at our gazes in order to summon them to its depth."[18] Like Marion, Emmanuel Lévinas links the visual to what knowers are able to grasp and to exhaust. Neither the face nor the icon, however, can be exhausted by our gaze or by our interpretations. For the face represents the singularity of the person to whom we owe an infinite obligation. We can never say that we have ever done all our duty towards the other. If I am right in linking Marion and Lévinas in this way and in relating the verbal icon to the face of the author, then ethics has been successfully established at the heart of interpretation theory. The reader's first obligation is to recognize in the text a face or voice *other* than one's own. Lévinas writes: "Face and discourse are tied. The face speaks."[19] The verbal icon shows us an implied face, and an explicit voice. I believe that this voice, like the face, summons the reader to responsibility.

Albert Schweitzer, at the end his *The Quest of the Historical Jesus*, compares scholars who believe they have discovered the historical Jesus to people looking down a deep well and discovering their own reflections at the bottom.[20] It is all too easy to project one's own values and interests onto the gospel. Postmodern thinkers are right about that. Interpreters who seek literary or historical knowledge must thus beware of Schweitzer's well. Interpretation requires belief in transcendence—a belief in a face or a voice that the text mediates *and is not our own*. Interpretation is a deeply ethical act: we have a duty to respect the voice of another, not to crush it. And when that voice testifies to the acts of God, readers should not only respect but revere it.

HERMENEUTIC HUMILITY AND LITERARY KNOWLEDGE

We have now characterized the relation between Parts 1 and 2 in terms of the debate between true and false religion and in terms of the difference between idols and icons. My final attempt to bring out the coherence of the two parts highlights the "morality of literary knowledge." Just how confident can we be as interpreters that we have discovered the meaning of the text rather than ourselves and our own projections? The short response is to say both that *our knowledge (Part 2) must be tempered by humility (Part 1), and that our skepticism (Part 1) must be countered by conviction (Part 2)*.

There are two sorts of responsibility in interpretation: a negative requirement not to exceed one's epistemic grasp and claim knowledge of what *cannot* be known, and a positive responsibility to make the effort to know what *can* be known. There must be a recognition of givens and of limits; the morality of literary knowledge demands both. If we are to live this tension, we must avoid absolute knowledge and absolute agnosticism alike. To be an interpreter, which is our vocation as humans and Christians, is cause both for dignity and for humility; we can know, but not as God knows.

Can we "prove" the realist's intuition that we have heard the voice of an other— the voice of the author or, for that matter, the voice of God? No, I am a critical realist, chastened by the conflict of interpretations and by the undoing of interpretive pride and prejudice. Readers with a healthy sense of the limits of interpretation need not fall prey to interpretive idolatry. Here, too, what we discover in Scripture holds true for hermeneutics in general. As Sternberg brilliantly observes, the Scriptures themselves inscribe the cognitive difference between God and humankind into the very fabric of the biblical story, a narrative with so many gaps and reversals that "the only knowledge perfectly acquired is the knowledge of our limitations."[21] At the same time, readers with a healthy sense of the givens of communicative agency need not fall prey to interpretive skepticism. As we saw in chapter 6, God designed the human mind to seek, and to attain, understanding of communicative action.

Two Deadly Interpretive Sins

The sins of the interpreter are two: pride and sloth. This book will have succeeded if it has established the possibility of a reading that yields knowledge while resisting both temptations, a reading that would be both humble yet confident.

We have repeatedly encountered, during the course of this work, the interpretive sin of pride in its various guises. It is the sin of conservative and liberal alike, for pride knows neither party nor denominational boundaries. Pride is a corrupting influence on the interpreter for a number of reasons. First, it encourages us to think that we have got the correct meaning before we have made the appropriate effort to recover it. Pride typically does not wait to listen; it knows. Indeed, at the limit pride is certain; it encourages claims of absolute knowledge. In Taylor's words: "The deconstruction of the Western theological network discloses the recurrent effort of human beings to achieve a position of domination. This struggle appears to grow out of the conviction that mastery results from the ability to secure presence and establish identity by overcoming absence and repressing difference."[22] Readers who take pride in their readings seek to "master" the text and so risk elevating their commentary over the text in importance. Pride neglects the voice of the other in favor of its own. It may therefore be the preeminent temptation of the fundamentalist, insofar as he or she craves certainty.

However, pride is, as I have said, non-partisan. Those on the radical left of hermeneutic theory are not immune to its pull. Oddly enough, it is possible to take pride in one's skepticism as well as in one's certainty. Indeed, it is sometimes hard to tell the two apart—particularly when the skeptic *insists* that one cannot know anything. Some of the more sophisticated Undoers adopt a superior tone even as they inform us (through texts!) that the author is dead. To ignore the reality of the author's claims on us, however, is ultimately to refuse to recognize the otherness of the text. There is something troubling about the more extreme expressions of this defiance. To be preoccupied with one's ego and one's own pleasure is, according to Piaget, one of the lowest levels of child development. The refusal to respond to the genuine otherness of the text may be the hermeneutical equivalent of sucking one's thumb. Finally, the skeptic signals a tendency toward pride by his or her laughter—the laughter of debasement and ridicule, and perhaps of the madness of despair. Interpretive pride at its ugliest leads not to humility but to humiliation.

Interpretive sloth is a kind of shadow image of interpretive pride, its evil twin. Whereas pride claims knowledge prematurely, sloth prematurely claims the *impossibility* of literary knowledge. Whereas interpretive pride ignores the reader's finitude, interpretive sloth ignores the reader's freedom and responsibility. Make no mistake: interpretive sloth is every bit as deadly a sin as pride, for sloth breeds indifference, inattentiveness, and inaction. Sloth is another name for what Kierkegaard called the "aesthetic" stage of existence: the way of the unconvinced and uncommitted. Specifically, interpretive sloth leads the reader to forgo the effort of attending to the text. Those on the theological right are slothful when, instead of interpreting for themselves, they rely on someone else—the Spirit, a television preacher, a teacher—to tell them what the text means. Those on the theological left are similarly slothful when, instead of working towards the best interpretation, they remain satisfied with a plethora of conflicting, often contradictory, readings. Interpretive sloth thus ignores the voice of the other every bit as much as does interpretive pride.

What Christianity Gives the World

"What Christianity gives the world is hermeneutics" (Buber). More to the point: I suggest that the distinctively Christian contribution to the debate about meaning and interpretation is best presented under the rubric of a "hermeneutics of humility and conviction."

Why humility? First, because humility is the solution to many postmodern objections to the notion of literary knowledge. Given the ever-present temptation to make idols of our interpretations, humility appears as a prime interpretive virtue. In recognizing real limits, humility is pride's defeat. In recognizing that interpreters are not makers but receivers of meaning, humility is realistic about the aims and objectives of hermeneutics and a natural ally of hermeneutic realism. Humility is also significant for epistemology (i.e., for a critical rationality that acknowledges one's fallibility) and for ethics (i.e., for a sense of responsibility that acknowledges one's obligations to others). In short, humility is the virtue that constantly reminds interpreters that we can get it *wrong*. More positively, humility enables the reader to wait upon the text, to participate in the covenant of discourse, and, if need be, to empty oneself for the sake of the text. C. S. Lewis describes such interpretive "kenosis" in a justly famous passage: "But in reading great literature I become a thousand men and yet remain myself. . . . Here, as in worship, in love, in moral action, and in knowing, I transcend myself; and am never more myself than when I do."[23]

Deconstruction, together with the varieties of hermeneutic suspicion, performs a valuable service in checking interpretive pride. I readily grant this point. Yet I have also argued that the humiliation of meaning and interpretation that results from this undoing is not the same as interpretive humility. Humility, I have suggested, is a specifically Christian contribution to hermeneutics. This last observation warrants further comment.

As we have seen, late twentieth-century interpretation is rife with ideological warfare. The ideological aims and interests of readers and interpretive communities seem to have taken precedence over the aims and interests of either authors or texts. The postmodern crisis in interpretation is actually a legitimation crisis. Whose voice, which interpretation, what aim counts, and why? Cultural theorists increasingly warn us that all knowledge claims are really instances of institutional power. For Foucault, to cite but one case, the "morality of literary knowledge" may be a contradiction in terms. Set against this backdrop of suspicion, the Bible stands out for its profound *anti-ideological* thrust. The Bible has a number of built-in strategies that challenge and resist the will to power. Indeed, a number of the high points in the biblical story line involve, at least implicitly, the critique of pride and prejudice. Moreover, it is largely through the hard exercise of interpreting the Bible that readers acquire the anti-ideological virtue of humility. Perhaps this is what Barth had in mind when he noted that biblical interpreters are the freest thinkers.

Is it really the case that the Bible represents an exception to Nietzsche's rule that sees truth as in thrall to the will-to-power—that Scripture propounds, as it were, an anti-ideological ideology? I have already commented on the importance of the Creator-creature distinction for hermeneutics. It was the willful ignorance of this distinction that led both to the Fall and to the tower of Babel, and thence to the will-to-power and to the confusion of tongues—in short, to distorted communication.[24] The climax of the Old Testament critique of ideology is the second commandment against idolatry, which reinforces the absolute distinction between God, the Creator-Author, on the one hand, and human being, the interpreting animal, on the other.

In the New Testament, Jesus consistently teaches that it is the lowly and the meek who will inherit the earth. For example: "I praise you, Father, Lord of heaven and earth, because you have hidden these things from the wise and learned, and revealed them to little children" (Matt. 11:25). In light of humanity's utter dependence on God, humility is clearly the most honest and appropriate attitude—and the most fitting—to adopt. The apostle Paul states that the foolishness of human beings is the wisdom of God (1 Cor. 1:18–25). Indeed, it is Paul's theology of the cross that provides the most compelling safeguard against the human will to power and its product, ideology. Ideology is the preeminent idol of the mind and of the illusion that meaning, like the ill-fated Tower, is ultimately a matter of social construction. The cross of Jesus contains counter-cultural wisdom; it teaches us that we must die to self in order to find self. This is especially true in the case of interpretation, in that it is only when we surrender our previous understandings that we are open to receive new ones.

What Christianity gives to hermeneutics is the contrast between a "hermeneutics of the cross" and a "hermeneutics of glory."[25] Those who read according to the hermeneutics of glory revel in their own interpretive skills, impose their interpretive theories on texts, and eclipse the text's own meaning. Such "glory" is, of course, short-lived. According to the hermeneutics of humility, by contrast, we will only gain understanding—of God, texts, others, and ourselves—if we are willing to put ourselves second and our interpretive theories to the test of the text.

One last doctrine completes the case for hermeneutic humility. It is eschatology, which we have already examined. Here I need only add that one should pursue the quest for the single correct interpretation under the aegis of hope and its reminder "not yet." That the meaning and significance of a text are never a present possession, but a partially fulfilled promise, is perhaps sufficient antidote to the poison of prideful interpretation.

To speak only of a hermeneutics of humility, however, would be a one-sided description of what Christianity gives hermeneutics. Humility must be balanced by conviction. Why? Here it may perhaps be best to start with eschatology—with the theme of Jesus' own preaching that the kingdom of God is already among us.[26] The "already" is as important an eschatological theme as the "not yet." There is a similar eschatological qualification that could be made of epistemology: while absolute knowledge is not a present possession, adequate knowledge is. Some things about God, that is, may be known on the basis of the revelation we already have in Christ. Indeed, we might here speak of "realized epistemology." God has already staked his truth claim in the cross of Christ. He has already redeemed his claim in resurrection. Of course, this is another aspect of verification that is "not yet"; only at the last day will we know more than provisionally. Nevertheless, the apostle Paul urged his interpreters to boldness on behalf of the gospel message. While there may be more light on the Bible's meaning to come, we have a firm enough grasp of the overall story line as to encourage boldness in our witness. Only such confidence, commitment, and conviction about what can be known can serve as the corrective to interpretive skepticism and sloth. The uncommitted interpretation is not worth hearing.

As I have argued, God created humans in his image with the dignity of communicative agency. The design plan of the human creature includes the ability to achieve understanding through verbal communication. Is it not the case that we only communicate with others because we presume that they will understand us? The despair of language's frailties must not engulf the delight in language's capacities. The "hermeneutics of conviction" encourages readers to have the courage of their communicative convictions. All knowing begins in commitment, but it need not end there. The hermeneutics of conviction thus stands for the belief that the same interpretive virtues that arise from the motivation for literary knowledge are also reliable means for attaining cognitive contact with meaning.[27] Faith not only seeks understanding but often gets it.

A hermeneutics of humility *and* conviction. We must hold these two aspects together in a constructive tension. Emphasize one without the other, and you quickly fall prey to one or the other of the two deadly interpretive sins. Emphasize the two together, and you are able to avoid hermeneutic dogmatism and skepticism alike. The situation of the reader thus parallels that of the believer who is *simul justus et peccator*, saint *and* sinner. As in soteriology, so in hermeneutics; the pastoral challenge is to balance the themes of assurance and perseverance. When the saints are besieged by doubts, the good pastor reminds them that they are in Christ. When, on the other hand, they begin to think too highly of themselves, he or she will minister an imperative word: *remain* in Christ. Both assurance and perseverance are necessary for the believer. So it is with the interpreter: he or she must be assured that literary knowledge and understanding are possible, but not led to think that reaching understanding is easy. On the contrary, one must be encouraged to keep on persevering after meaning and significance in light of one's infinite obligation to the voice of the other. A similar dynamic characterizes the work of the scientist as well. Michael Polanyi perfectly captures the tension between humility and conviction that constitutes the Christian morality of knowledge: "The principal purpose of this book [*Personal Knowledge*] is to achieve a frame of mind in which I may hold firmly to what I believe to be true, even though I know that it might conceivably be false.[28]

"Here I Stand"

The history of biblical interpretation includes a precursor to Polanyi's picture of the responsible scientist. Martin Luther summed up the hermeneutical virtues when he confessed, in a context fraught with political and ideological power, "Here I stand." Luther's brief confession sums up much of I want to say about the interplay between humility and conviction.[29] "Here": not there, not everywhere, but here. I stand *here*. This is an acknowledgment of finitude. I am here in space and time, here in culture and tradition, here in this body with this history. In this sense, "Here I stand" is a confession of hermeneutic humility. At the same time, Luther did not simply find himself placed, but occupied a place. He stood where he stood because he believed it to be the right place. "Here *I* stand." Luther was passionately committed to his interpretation of Scripture because he believed it to be faithful to the meaning of the text itself. That is, Luther stood *by* and stood *with* the text, and stood *against* the tradition of its interpretation. Luther's stance thus manifests hermeneutic conviction.

"Here I stand." This was Luther's answer to a difficult hermeneutical question. He stood before the Holy Roman Emperor at the Diet of Worms, accused of heresy and threatened with excommunication and death. His interrogator asked: "Martin, how can you assume that you are the only one to understand Scripture?" perhaps anticipating the postmodern suspicion that interpreters see only themselves in the text. In response, Luther asserted that interpretive tradition alone would not sway him. Only Scripture could convict: "My conscience is captive to the Word of God."[30] Luther insisted that it was "through the Word, and not by force, wisdom governs."[31] He believed that speech was God's special gift to humanity; for it is by speech—by reading and preaching Scripture—that faith and understanding come. Ultimately, Luther stands for the possibility that the text and its meaning remain independent of the process of interpretation and hence have the ability to transform the reader. Indeed, one reliable indicator of a good Protestant hermeneutics is whether it enables reformation. A hermeneutics of humility and conviction may well be a necessary condition for reforming individual self-understanding and interpretive traditions. Perhaps it is even a sufficient condition. It is certainly the condition for authentic interpretation, that is, for bearing true witness to textual meaning.

Neither standing nor understanding, however, is the final word in interpretation. The final word belongs to following. The church should be that community of humbly confident interpreter-believers whose consciences, seared and sealed by the Spirit, are captive to the Word, and whose commentaries and communities seek progressively to embody the meaning *and* significance of the text. Readers who work and pray over the text, who interpret freely and responsibly, and who follow its itineraries of meaning, will be progressively transformed into the image of him who is the ultimate object of the biblical witness. Those who stand in this dynamic way understand and *withstand*, and so fulfill their vocation as witnesses and martyrs to the Word. These are the interpreter-believers who, like the psalmist, take up their book and walk:

Your word is a lamp to my feet and a light for my path (Ps. 119:105).

NOTES

1. Steiner, *Real Presences*, 227.
2. Derrida, *Of Grammatology*, 14.
3. Only on such a basis can we secure the possibility of meaningful interpersonal communication. The alternative—a naturalistic, evolutionary account—sees language as an instrument of domination and manipulation, not communication.
4. There is a growing literature analyzing modernity in terms of its rejection of a certain, non-trinitarian view of God. See esp. Gunton, *The One, the Three, and the Many*.
5. Karl Barth famously arrives at the doctrine of the Trinity by analyzing God's revelation in Jesus Christ (see his *Church Dogmatics* I/1).
6. Barthes, "Death of the Author," 54.
7. On my view, the human speech agent has real freedom and responsibility with regard to his or her words. According to the Undoers, however, the self is less a speaker than a cipher of a language, a mere pawn of a linguistic system that shapes the way it talks and thinks.
8. Jeanrond, *Theological Hermeneutics*, 104.
9. The analogy of the icon is put to striking use by Jean-Luc Marion, *God Without Being* (Chicago: Univ. of Chicago Press, 1984), 12. Marion is concerned not with hermeneutics so much as theology. He believes that the attempt to think God as a metaphysical reality with the concepts of being falls prey to a form of conceptual idolatry.

10. For a somewhat different analysis of "iconological interpretation," see Erwin Panofsky, *Meaning in the Visual Arts* (Chicago: Univ. of Chicago Press, 1955) ch. 1.

11. Norman Davies, *Europe: A History* (Oxford: Oxford Univ. Press, 1996), 247.

12. See Symeon Lash, "Icons," in *New Dictionary of Theology*, 275.

13. Marion, *God Without Being*, 1.

14. Cited in ibid., 18.

15. Ibid., 19. Marion actually defines the icon as over against the idol according to the "aim of the intention," 19.

16. Ibid.

17. A quote by Pagnol: "A true reader is almost always a friend."

18. Marion, *God Without Being*, 19.

19. Lévinas, *Ethics and Infinity*, 87.

20. Albert Schweitzer, *The Quest of the Historical Jesus*, 3d ed. (London: A. & C. Black, 1954).

21. Sternberg, *The Poetics of Biblical Narrative*, 47.

22. Taylor, *Erring*, 15. The kind of presence that we can achieve as readers, I have argued, is an iconic presence that mediates but does not surrender its meaning without remainder.

23. Lewis, *An Experiment in Criticism*, 141. "Kenosis" refers to the Son of God's "emptying" himself for the sake of the human other in his incarnation (cf. Phil. 2:5–11).

24. Cf. Augustine on Moses' intent in Genesis 1 (*Confessions*, 12.24–25) and how to deal with the plurality of interpretations. Pride is the prime hermeneutical sin. See also Calvin's remark that the conflict of interpretations serves to keep us humble and in communication with other interpreters (*Calvin: Commentaries*, 75–6).

25. I am amending Luther's contrast between the theology of the cross and the theology of glory as found in his "Heidelberg Disputation."

26. I am referring to the "realized eschatology" associated with C. H. Dodd's interpretation of Jesus' parables in his *The Parables of the Kingdom* (London: Nisbet, 1961). See also N. T. Wright, *Jesus and the Victory of God* (Minneapolis: Fortress, 1996), chs. 6–8.

27. I am here borrowing (and amending) Zagzebski's definition of knowledge as "a state of cognitive contact with reality arising out of acts of intellectual virtue" (*Virtues of the Mind*, 270).

28. Polanyi, *Personal Knowledge: Towards a Post-Critical Philosophy* (Chicago: Univ. of Chicago Press, 1962), 7.

29. My interpretation of Luther's confession is largely an example of overstanding on my part. Yet I believe Luther would agree that I have correctly caught the "spirit" of the letter of his remark (that is, if it is authentic!).

30. For a fuller account of the incident, see Roland H. Bainton, *Here I Stand: A Life of Martin Luther* (New York: Abingdon–Cokesbury, 1950), ch. 10.

31. Luther, *Table Talk*, 25.

BIBLIOGRAPHY

Abrams, M. H. "The Limits of Pluralism: The Deconstructive Angel." *Critical Inquiry* 3 (1977): 425–38.

_____. *A Glossary of Literary Terms*. 4th ed. New York: Holt, Rinehart and Winston, 1981.

Adam, A. K. M. "The Sign of Jonah: A Fish-Eye View." *Semeia* 51 (1990): 177–91.

_____. *What Is Postmodern Biblical Criticism?* Minneapolis: Fortress, 1995.

Alston, William P. *Philosophy of Language*. Englewood Cliffs, N.J.: Prentice-Hall, 1964.

Alter, Robert. *The Art of Biblical Narrative*. New York: Basic, 1981.

Alter, Robert, and Frank Kermode, ed. *The Literary Guide to the Bible*. Cambridge, Mass: Harvard Univ. Press, 1987.

Altieri, Charles. *Act and Quality: A Theory of Literary Meaning and Humanistic Understanding*. Amherst: Univ. of Massachusetts Press, 1981.

Appleyard, J. A. *Becoming a Reader: The Experience of Fiction from Childhood to Adulthood*. Cambridge: Cambridge Univ. Press, 1990.

Arendt, Hannah. *The Human Condition*. Chicago: Univ. of Chicago Press, 1958.

Arnold, Matthew. "The Function of Criticism at the Present Time." Pp. 1–41 in *Essays in Criticism*. London: Macmillan, 1865.

Ateek, Naim Stifan. "A Palestinian Perspective: The Bible and Liberation." Pp. 280–86 in Sugirtharajah, *Voices from the Margin*.

Attridge, Derek. "Derrida and the Questioning of Literature." Pp. 1–29 in Derrida, *Acts of Literature*.

Auerbach, Erich. *Mimesis: The Representation of Reality in Western Literature*. Princeton: Princeton Univ. Press, 1953.

Augustine. *Confessions*. Tr. R. S. Pine-Coffin. London: Penguin, 1961.

_____. *On Christian Doctrine*. Tr. D. W. Robertson, Jr. Indianapolis: Bobbs-Merrill Educational Publishing, 1958.

_____. *The Literal Meaning of Genesis*. Tr. John Hammond Taylor. New York: Newman, 1982.

Augustine: Earlier Writings. Ed. J. H. S. Burleigh. The Library of Christian Classics. Philadelphia: Westminster, 1953.

Austin, J. L. *How to Do Things with Words*. 2d ed. Cambridge, Mass: Harvard Univ. Press, 1975.

_____. *Philosophical Papers*. 3d ed. Oxford: Oxford Univ. Press, 1979.

Bakhtin, Mikhail. *Rabelais and His World*. Tr. H. Iswolsky. Cambridge, Mass: MIT Press, 1968.

_____. *Problems of Dostoyevsky's Poetics*. Ed. Caryl Emerson. Minneapolis: Univ. of Minnesota Press, 1984.

_____. *Speech Genres and Other Late Essays*. Tr. Vern W. McGee. Austin: Univ. of Texas Press, 1986.

Bambrough, *Reason, Truth and God*. London: Methuen, 1969.

_____. *Moral Scepticism and Moral Knowledge*. London: Routledge and Kegan Paul, 1979.

Barker, Margaret. "Pseudonymity." Pp. 568–71 in Coggins and Houlden, ed., *A Dictionary of Biblical Interpretation*.

Barnes, Annette. *On Interpretation: A Critical Analysis*. Oxford: Basil Blackwell, 1988.

Barr, James. *The Bible in the Modern World*. London: SCM, 1973.

_____. *Fundamentalism*. Philadelphia: Westminster, 1978.

_____. "The Literal, the Allegorical, and Modern Scholarship." *Journal for the Study of the Old Testament* 44 (1989): 3–17.

_____. "Literality." *Faith and Philosophy* 6 (1989): 412–28.

Barth, Karl. *The Epistle to the Romans*. 6th ed. Oxford: Oxford Univ. Press, 1968.

_____. *Church Dogmatics*. Edinburgh: T. and T. Clark, 1956–69.

Barthes, Roland. *S/Z*. New York: Hill and Wang, 1974.

_____. *The Rustle of Language*. Tr. Richard Howard. New York: Hill and Wang, 1986.

_____. "The Death of the Author." Pp. 125–30 in Burke, ed., *Authorship from Plato to Postmodernity*.

Barton, John. *Reading the Old Testament: Method in Biblical Study*. London: Darton, Longman and Todd, 1984.

_____. "History and Rhetoric in the Prophets." Pp. 51–64 in Warner, ed. *The Bible As Rhetoric*.

Baxandall, Michael. *Patterns of Intention: On the Historical Explanation of Pictures*. New Haven: Yale Univ. Press, 1985.

Baynes, Kenneth, James Bohman, and Thomas McCarthy, ed. *After Philosophy: End or Transformation?* Cambridge, Mass. and London: MIT Press, 1987.

Berg, Temma F. "Reading In/to Mark." *Semeia* 48 (1989): 187–206.

Berkouwer, G. C. *Holy Scripture*. Studies in Dogmatics. Grand Rapids: Eerdmans, 1975.

Belsey, Catherine. *Critical Practice*. London and New York: Routledge, 1980.

Bhaskar, Roy. *Scientific Realism and Human Emancipation*. London: Verso, 1986.

_____. *Philosophy and the Idea of Freedom*. Oxford: Blackwell, 1991.

Bloesch, Donald G. *Holy Scripture: Revelation, Inspiration and Interpretation*. Christian Foundations. Downers Grove, Ill.: InterVarsity, 1994.

Bloom, Harold. *A Map of Misreading*. Oxford: Oxford Univ. Press, 1975.

_____. *Kabbala and Criticism*. New York: Continuum, 1975.

Boone, Kathleen C. *The Bible Tells Them So: The Discourse of Protestant Fundamentalism*. Albany: SUNY Press, 1989.

Booth, Wayne C. *The Rhetoric of Fiction*. Chicago: Univ. of Chicago Press, 1961.

_____. *A Rhetoric of Irony*. Chicago: Univ. of Chicago Press, 1974.

_____. *Critical Understanding: The Powers and Limits of Pluralism*. Chicago: Univ. of Chicago Press, 1979.

_____. *The Company We Keep: An Ethics of Fiction*. Berkeley: Univ. of California Press, 1988.

Bordwell, David. *Making Meaning: Inference and Rhetoric in the Interpretation of Cinema*. Cambridge, Mass.: Harvard Univ. Press, 1989.

Botha, J. Eugene. *Jesus and the Samaritan Woman: A Speech Act Reading of John 4:1–42*. Leiden: E. J. Brill, 1991.

Brown, Raymond E. *The Critical Meaning of the Bible*. London: Geoffrey Chapman, 1981.

_____. "'And the Lord Said'? Biblical Reflections on Scripture As the Word of God." *Theological Studies* 42 (1981): 3–19.

Brueggemann, Walter. *The Bible and Postmodern Imagination: Texts under Negotiation*. London: SCM, 1993.

Bruns, Gerald L. "Midrash and Allegory: The Beginnings of Scriptural Interpretation." Pp. 625–46 in Alter and Kermode, ed., *The Literary Guide to the Bible*.

Bultmann, Rudolf. "The New Testament and Mythology." Pp. 1–44 in Hans Werner Bartsch, ed. *Kerygma and Myth: A Theological Debate*. 2d ed. London: S.P.C.K., 1964.

Burke, Seán. *The Death and Return of the Author: Criticism and Subjectivity in Barthes, Foucault and Derrida*. Edinburgh: Edinburgh Univ. Press, 1992.

_____, ed. *Authorship from Plato to Postmodernity: A Reader*. Edinburgh: Edinburgh Univ. Press, 1995.

Calvin: Commentaries. Ed. Joseph Haroutunian. The Library of Christian Classics. Philadelphia: Westminster, 1958.

Caputo, John D. *Radical Hermeneutics: Repetition, Deconstruction, and the Hermeneutic Project*. Bloomington: Indiana Univ. Press, 1987.

Carroll, Robert. "Authorship." Pp. 72–74 in Coggins and Houlden, ed., *A Dictionary of Biblical Interpretation*.

_____. "Ideology." Pp. 309–11 in Coggins and Houlden, ed., *A Dictionary of Biblical Interpretation*.

Castelli, Elizabeth A., Stephen D. Moore, Gary A. Phillips, and Regina M. Schwartz, ed. *The Postmodern Bible*. New Haven: Yale Univ. Press, 1995.

Childs, Brevard S. "The *Sensus Literalis* of Scripture: An Ancient and Modern Problem." Pp. 80–93 in H. Donner et. al., ed. *Beiträge zur alttestamentlichen Theologie* (Göttingen: Vandenhoeck and Ruprecht, 1977.

_____. *Introduction to the Old Testament As Scripture*. Philadelphia: Fortress, 1979.

_____. *Biblical Theology of the Old and New Testaments*. London: SCM, 1992.

Clark, S. H. *Paul Ricoeur*. London: Routledge, 1990.

Clayton, Philip. *God and Contemporary Science*. Grand Rapids: Eerdmans and Edinburgh: Edinburgh Univ. Press, 1998.

Clifford, W. K. *Lectures and Essays*. London: Macmillan, 1886.

Clines, David J. A., Stephen Fowl, and Stanley E. Porter, ed. *The Bible in Three Dimensions: Essays in Celebration of Forty Years of Biblical Studies in the Univ. of Sheffield*. Sheffield: Sheffield Academic Press (JSOT Supple. Ser. 87), 1990.

Clines, David J. A. "Deconstructing the Book of Job." Pp. 65–80 in Warner, ed., *The Bible As Rhetoric*.

_____. "Possibilities and Priorities of Biblical Interpretation in an International Perspective." *Biblical Interpretation* 1 (1993): 67–87.

Coady, C. A. J. *Testimony: A Philosophical Study*. Oxford: Clarendon, 1992.

Coggins, R. J. "A Future for the Commentary?" Pp. 163–75 in Watson, ed., *The Open Text*.

Coggins, R. J., and J. L. Houlden, ed. *A Dictionary of Biblical Interpretation*. London: SCM and Philadelphia: Trinity Press International, 1990.

Cooper, John W. "Reformed Apologetics and the Challenge of a Post-Modern Relativism." *Calvin Theological Journal* 28 (1993): 108–20.

Cotterell, Peter, and Max Turner. *Linguistics and Biblical Interpretation*. London: S.P.C.K., 1989.

Crews, Frederick C. *The Pooh Perplex: A Student Casebook*. London: Robin Clark, 1979.

Critchley, Simon. *The Ethics of Deconstruction: Derrida and Lévinas*. Oxford: Blackwell, 1992.

Croatto, J. Severino. *Biblical Hermeneutics: Toward a Theory of Reading As the Production of Meaning*. Tr. Robert R. Barr. Maryknoll, N.Y.: Orbis, 1987.

Culler, Jonathan. *Structuralist Poetics: Structuralism, Linguistics and the Study of Literature*. London: Routledge, 1975.

Cupitt, Don. *The Long-Legged Fly: A Theology of Language and Desire*. London: SCM, 1987.

_____. *The Last Philosophy*. London: SCM, 1995.

Currie, Gregory. "Text Without Context: Some Errors of Stanley Fish." *Philosophy and Literature* 15 (1991): 212–28.

Darr, John A. *On Character Building: The Reader and the Rhetoric of Characterization in Luke-Acts*. Louisville: Westminster/John Knox, 1992.

Dasenbrock, Reed Way, ed. *Literary Theory After Davidson*. University Park, Pa: Pennsylvania State Univ. Press, 1993.

Davies, Margaret. "Exegesis." Pp. 220–22 in Coggins, ed., *A Dictionary of Biblical Interpretation*.
_____. *Rhetoric and Reference in the Fourth Gospel*. Sheffield: JSOT Press, 1992.
Davis, Ellen F. "Holy Preaching: Ethical Interpretation and the Practical Imagination." Pp. 197–224 in Ephraim Radner and George R. Sumners, ed., *Reclaiming Faith: Essays on Orthodoxy in the Episcopal Church and the Baltimore Declaration*. Grand Rapids: Eerdmans, 1993.
Dawsey, James. *The Lukan Voice: Confusion and Irony in the Gospel of Luke*. Macon, Ga: Mercer Univ. Press, 1986.
Dawson, David. *Literary Theory*. Guides to Theological Inquiry. Minneapolis: Fortress Press, 1995.
De Bruyn, Frans. "Genre Criticism." Pp. 79–85 in Makaryk, ed., *Encyclopedia of Contemporary Literary Theory*.
De Man, Paul. *Allegories of Reading: Figural Language in Rousseau, Nietzsche, Rilke, and Proust*. New Haven: Yale Univ. Press, 1979.
_____. *Blindness and Insight: Essays in the Rhetoric of Contemporary Criticism*. 2d ed. London: Methuen, 1983.
_____. *The Resistance to Theory*. Minneapolis: Univ. of Minnesota Press, 1989.
Derrida, Jacques. "Structure, Sign and Play in the Discourse of the Human Sciences." Pp. 247–65 in Richard Macksey and Eugene Donato, ed., *The Languages of Criticism and the Sciences of Man*. Baltimore: Johns Hopkins Univ. Press, 1970.
_____. *La Dissémination*. Paris: Seuil, 1972.
_____. "Violence and Metaphysics: An Essay on the Thought of Emmanuel Lévinas." Pp. 79–153 in *Writing and Difference*. Tr. Alan Bass. London: Routledge and Kegan Paul, 1978.
_____. "White Mythology: Metaphor in the Text of Philosophy." *New Literary History* 5 (1974): 5–74.
_____. *Of Grammatology*. Tr. Gayatri Chakravorty Spivak. Baltimore and London: Johns Hopkins Univ. Press, 1976.
_____. "Signature Event Context." *Glyph* 1 (1977): 172–97.
_____. "Limited Inc abc." *Glyph* 2 (1977): 162–254.
_____. *Dissemination*. Tr. Barbara Johnson. London: Athlone, 1981.
_____. *Positions*. Tr. Alan Bass. Chicago: Univ. of Chicago Press, 1981.
_____. *Margins of Philosophy*. Tr. Alan Bass. Chicago: Univ. of Chicago Press, 1982.
_____. "The Principle of Reason: The University in the Eyes of Its Pupils." *Diacritics* 29 (1983): 3–20.
_____. *The Ear of the Other: Otobiography, Transference, Translation*. Ed. Christie McDonald. Tr. Peggy Kamuf. Lincoln and London: Univ. of Nebraska Press, 1988.
_____. "Afterword: Toward an Ethic of Discussion." Pp. 111–54 in *Limited Inc*. Evanston, Ill.: Northwestern Univ. Press, 1988.
_____. "How to Avoid Speaking: Denials." In Harold Coward and Toby Foshay, ed., *Derrida and Negative Theology*. Albany, NY: SUNY Press, 1992.
_____. *Acts of Literature*. Ed. Derek Attridge. New York and London: Routledge, 1992.
_____. "Remarks on Deconstruction and Pragmatism." Pp. 77–88 in Mouffe, ed., *Deconstruction and Pragmatism*.
Detweiler, Robert, ed. *Derrida and Biblical Studies: Semeia* 23 (1982).
Duff, R. A. *Intention, Agency and Criminal Liability: Philosophy of Action and the Criminal Law*. Oxford: Basil Blackwell, 1990.
Dunn, James D. G. *The Living Word*. Philadelphia: Fortress, 1988.
Eagleton, Terry. *Literary Theory: An Introduction*. Minneapolis: Univ. of Minnesota Press and Oxford: Blackwell, 1983.
_____. *Against the Grain: Essays 1975–85*. London: Verso, 1986.

_____. *Ideology: An Introduction*. London: Verso, 1991.

Eco, Umberto. *The Limits of Interpretation*. Bloomington: Indiana Univ. Press, 1990.

_____. *Foucault's Pendulum*. London: Picador, 1990.

Eco, Umberto, with Richard Rorty, Jonathan Culler, and Christine Brooke-Rose. Ed. Stefan Collini. *Interpretation and Overinterpretation*. Cambridge: Cambridge Univ. Press, 1992.

Edwards, Bruce, and Branson Woodward. "Wise As Serpents, Harmless As Doves: Christians and Contemporary Critical Theory." *Christianity and Literature* 39 (1990): 303–15.

Edwards, Michael. *Towards a Christian Poetics*. Grand Rapids: Eerdmans, 1984.

Eliot, T. S. "The Function of Criticism." In *Selected Essays*. London: Faber and Faber, 1932.

_____. "The Frontiers of Criticism." Pp. 103–18 in *On Poetry and Poets*. London: Faber and Faber, 1957.

Ellis, John. *Against Deconstruction*. Princeton: Princeton Univ. Press, 1989.

Ellul, Jacques. *The Humiliation of the Word*. Grand Rapids: Eerdmans, 1985.

Evans, G. R. *The Language and Logic of the Bible: The Earlier Middle Ages*. Cambridge: Cambridge Univ. Press, 1984.

_____. *The Language and Logic of the Bible: The Road to Reformation*. Cambridge: Cambridge Univ. Press, 1985.

_____. *Problems of Authority in the Reformation Debates*. Cambridge: Cambridge Univ. Press, 1992.

Farrar, Frederic W. *History of Interpretation*. Grand Rapids: Baker, 1961.

Farrell, Frank B. *Subjectivity, Realism, and Postmodernism: The Recovery of the World*. Cambridge: Cambridge Univ. Press, 1994.

Felder, Cain Hope, ed. *Stony the Road We Trod: African-American Biblical Interpretation*. Minneapolis: Fortress, 1991.

Felerpin, Howard. *Beyond Deconstruction: The Uses and Abuses of Literary Theory*. Oxford: Clarendon, 1985.

Feuerbach, Ludwig. *The Essence of Christianity*. Tr. George Eliot. Buffalo: New York: Prometheus Books, 1989.

Feyerabend, Paul. *Against Method: Outline of an Anarchistic Theory of Knowledge*. London: New Left Books, 1975.

Fiorenza, Elisabeth Schüssler. *In Memory of Her: A Feminist Theological Reconstruction of Christian Origins*. New York: Crossroad, 1983.

_____. *Bread Not Stone: The Challenge of Feminist Biblical Interpretation*. Boston: Beacon, 1984.

_____. "The Ethics of Interpretation: Decentering Biblical Scholarship." *Journal of Biblical Literature* 107 (1988): 101–15.

Fish, Stanley. *Is There a Text in This Class? The Authority of Interpretive Communities*. London and Cambridge, Mass: Harvard Univ. Press, 1980.

_____. *Surprised by Sin: The Reader in Paradise Lost*. New York: Macmillan, 1987.

_____. *Doing What Comes Naturally: Change, Rhetoric, and the Practice of Theory in Literary and Legal Studies*. Oxford: Clarendon, 1989.

Fiske, John. *Introduction to Communication Studies*. 2d ed. London: Routledge, 1990.

Florovsky, Georges. *Bible, Church, Tradition: An Eastern Orthodox View*. Belmont, Mass.: Nordland, 1972.

Foucault, Michel. "What is an Author?" Pp. 141–60 in Josué V. Harari, *Textual Strategies*. London: Methuen, 1979.

Fowl, Stephen. "The Ethics of Interpretation or What's Left Over After the Elimination of Meaning." Pp. 69–81 in *SBL 1988 Seminar Papers* (Atlanta: Scholars, 1990).

_____. "How the Spirit Reads and How to Read the Spirit." Pp. 348–63 in John Rogerson, et al., ed., *The Bible in Ethics*.

Fowl, Stephen E., and Gregory Jones. *Reading in Communion: Scripture and Ethics in Christian Life*. Grand Rapids: Eerdmans, 1991.

Fowler, Alistair. *Kinds of Literature: An Introduction to the Theory of Genres and Modes*. Oxford: Clarendon, 1982.

Fowler, Robert M. *Let the Reader Understand: Reader-Response Criticism and the Gospel of Mark*. Minneapolis: Fortress, 1991.

Fox, Michael V. "The Uses of Indeterminacy." *Semeia* 71 (1995): 173–92.

Freadman, Richard, and Seumas Miller. *Re-thinking Theory: A Critique of Contemporary Literary Theory and an Alternative Account*. Cambridge: Cambridge Univ. Press, 1992.

Freeman, Curtis. "Towards a *Sensus Fidelium* for an Evangelical Church: Postconservatives and Postliberals on Reading Scripture." Pp. 162–79 in Timothy Phillips and D. Ockholm, ed. *The Nature of Confession: Evangelicals and Postliberals in Dialogue*. Downers Grove, Ill.: InterVarsity, 1996.

Frei, Hans. *The Eclipse of Biblical Narrative. A Study in Eighteenth and Nineteenth Century Hermeneutics*. New Haven: Yale Univ. Press, 1974.

_____. "The 'Literal Reading' of Biblical Narrative in the Christian Tradition: Does It Stretch or Will It Break?" Pp. 36–77 in Frank McConnell, ed. *The Bible and the Narrative Tradition*. New York: Oxford Univ. Press, 1986.

_____. *Types of Christian Theology*. Ed. George W. Hunsinger and William C. Placher. London and New Haven: Yale Univ. Press, 1992.

Frye, Northrop. *Anatomy of Criticism*: Four Essays. Princeton: Princeton Univ. Press, 1957.

_____. *The Great Code: The Bible and Literature*. London: Routledge and Kegan Paul, 1982.

_____. *Words with Power, Being a Second Study of the Bible and Literature*. New York: Harcourt Brace Jovanovich, 1990.

Gabel, John B. and Wheeler, Charles B. *The Bible As Literature: An Introduction*. New York and Oxford: Oxford Univ. Press, 1986.

Gadamer, Hans-Georg. *Truth and Method*. New York: Seabury, 1975.

Gaipa, Mark, and Robert Scholes. "On the Very Idea of a Literal Meaning." Pp. 160–79 in Dasenbrock, ed., *Literary Theory After Davidson*.

Gamble, Richard C. "*Brevitas et facilitas*: Toward an Understanding of Calvin's Hermeneutic." *Westminster Theological Journal* 47 (1985): 1–17.

Garcia, Jorge J. E. "Can There Be Texts Without Historical Authors?" *American Philosophical Quarterly* 31 (1994): 245–53.

Gasché, Rodolphe. *The Tain of the Mirror: Derrida and the Philosophy of Reflection*. Cambridge, Mass: Harvard Univ. Press, 1986.

Gass, William. *Habitations of the Word*. New York: Simon and Schuster, 1985.

Geddert, Timothy J. *Watchwords: Mark 13 in Markan Eschatology*. JSNT Suppl. Series 26. Sheffield: Sheffield Academic Press, 1989.

Geertz, Clifford. *The Interpretation of Cultures: Selected Essays*. London: Fontana, 1993.

Gill, Jerry. *Mediated Transcendence. A Postmodern Reflection*. Macon, Ga.: Mercer Univ. Press, 1989.

Gloversmith, Frank. ed. *The Theory of Reading*. Sussex: Harvester, 1984.

Goodman, Nelson. *Ways of Worldmaking*. Indianapolis: Hackett, 1978.

Graham, Susan Lochrie. "On Scripture and Authorial Intent: A Narratological Proposal." *Anglican Theological Journal* 77 (1995): 307–20.

Grant, Robert, and David Tracy. *A Short History of Biblical Interpretation*. 2d ed. Philadelphia: Fortress, 1984.

Green, Joel (ed.). *Hearing the New Testament: Strategies for Interpretation*. Grand Rapids: Eerdmans, 1995.

Grice, H. P. "Meaning." *Philosophical Review* 66 (1957): 377–88.

_____. "Utterer's Meaning and Intentions." *Philosophical Review* 78 (1969): 147–77.

Groden, Michael, and Martin Kreiswirth, ed. *The Johns Hopkins Guide to Literary Theory and Criticism.* Baltimore: Johns Hopkins Univ. Press, 1994.

Gundry, R. H. *Soma in Biblical Theology, With Emphasis on Pauline Anthropology.* Cambridge: Cambridge Univ. Press, 1976.

_____. *Matthew: A Commentary on His Literary and Theological Art.* Grand Rapids: Eerdmans, 1982.

_____. *Mark: A Commentary on His Apology for the Cross.* Grand Rapids: Eerdmans, 1993.

Gunton, Colin. *The One, the Three and the Many: God, Creation and the Culture of Modernity.* Cambridge: Cambridge Univ. Press, 1993.

_____. *A Brief Theology of Revelation.* Edinburgh: T. & T. Clark, 1995.

Habermas, Jürgen. "Philosophy As Stand-In and Interpreter." Pp. 296–313 in Baynes, ed., *After Philosophy.*

_____. "What is Universal Pragmatics?" Pp. 1–68 in *Communication and the Evolution of Society.* Tr. Thomas McCarthy. London: Heinemann, 1979.

_____. *The Theory of Communicative Action. Vol. I. Reason and the Rationalization of Society.* Tr. Thomas McCarthy. Boston: Beacon, 1984.

_____. *Philosophical Discourses of Modernity.* Tr. Frederick G. Lawrence. Cambridge: Polity, 1987.

_____. *Justification and Application: Remarks on Discourse Ethics.* Cambridge, Mass: MIT Press, 1993.

Hagen, Kenneth. *Luther's Approach to Scripture As Seen in His "Commentaries" on Galatians 1519–1538.* Tübingen: J. C. B. Mohr, 1993.

Hall, Ronald L. *Word and Spirit: A Kierkegaardian Critique of the Modern Age.* Bloomington: Indiana Univ. Press, 1993.

Handelmann, Susan. *The Slayers of Moses: The Emergence of Rabbinic Interpretation in Modern Literary Theory.* Albany: SUNY Press, 1982.

Harris, Wendell V. *Interpretive Acts: In Search of Meaning.* Oxford: Clarendon, 1988.

_____. *Literary Meaning: Reclaiming the Study of Literature.* London: Macmillan, 1996.

Hart, Kevin. *The Trespass of the Sign: Deconstruction, Theology and Philosophy.* Cambridge: Cambridge Univ. Press, 1989.

_____. "The Poetics of the Negative." Pp. 281–340 in Prickett, ed., *Reading the Text: Biblical Criticism and Literary Theory.*

Hartman, Geoffrey H. *The Fate of Reading and Other Essays.* Chicago: Univ. of Chicago Press, 1975.

Harvey, Van. *The Historian and the Believer: The Morality of Historical Knowledge and Christian Belief.* New York: Macmillan, 1966.

Hauerwas, Stanley. *Unleashing the Scripture: Freeing the Bible from Captivity to America.* Nashville, Tenn.: Abingdon, 1993.

Hays, Richard. *The Faith of Jesus Christ: An Investigation of the Narrative Substructure of Paul's Theology in Galatians 3:1–4:11.* SBL Dissertation Series 56. Chico, Calif.: Scholars, 1983.

_____. *Echoes of Scripture in the Letters of Paul.* New Haven: Yale Univ. Press, 1989.

Heidegger, Martin. *Poetry, Language, Thought.* Tr. Albert Hofstadter. New York: Harper and Row, 1971.

Heil, John Paul. *Paul's Letter to the Romans: A Reader-Response Commentary.* New York: Paulist, 1987.

Hesse, Mary. *Models and Analogies in Science.* Notre Dame: Univ. of Notre Dame Press, 1966.

Hirsch, E. D., Jr. *Validity in Interpretation.* New Haven: Yale Univ. Press, 1967.

_____. *The Aims of Interpretation.* Chicago: Univ. of Chicago Press, 1976.

_____. "The Politics of Theories of Interpretation." In W. J. T. Mitchell, ed. *The Politics of Interpretation.* Chicago: Univ. of Chicago Press, 1983.

_____. "Meaning and Significance Reinterpreted." *Critical Inquiry* 11 (1984): 202–24.

_____. "Transhistorical Intentions and the Persistence of Allegory." *New Literary History* 25 (1994): 549–67.

Hix, H. L. *Morte d'Author: An Autopsy* Philadelphia: Temple Univ. Press, 1990.

Holub, Robert C. *Reception Theory: A Critical Introduction.* London: Methuen, 1984.

Honderich, Ted. ed. *The Oxford Companion to Philosophy.* Oxford: Oxford Univ. Press, 1994.

Houlden, J. H., ed. *The Interpretation of the Bible in the Church.* London: SCM, 1995.

Hoy, David, and Thomas McCarthy. *Critical Theory.* Great Debates in Philosophy. Oxford: Blackwell, 1994.

Hoy, David. *The Critical Circle: Literature, History and Philosophical Hermeneutics.* Berkeley: Univ. of California Press, 1978.

_____. "Must We Mean What We Say? The Grammatological Critique of Hermeneutics." Pp. 397–415 in Brice R. Wachterhauser, ed. *Hermeneutics and Modern Philosophy.* Albany: SUNY Press, 1986.

Ingraffia, Brian. *Postmodern Theory and Biblical Theology.* Cambridge: Cambridge Univ. Press, 1995.

Iser, Wolfgang. *The Implied Reader: Patterns of Communication in Prose Fiction from Bunyan to Beckett.* Baltimore: Johns Hopkins Univ. Press, 1974.

Jacobsen, Douglas. "The Calvinist-Arminian Dialectic in Evangelical Hermeneutics." *Christian Scholar's Review* 23 (1993): 72–89.

Jakobson, Roman. "Linguistics and Poetics." Pp. 350–77 in T. A. Sebeok, ed. *Style in Language.* Cambridge, Mass: MIT Press, 1960.

Jauss, Hans Robert. *Towards an Aesthetic of Reception Theory.* Minneapolis: Univ. of Minnesota Press, 1982.

Jeanrond, Werner G. *Text and Interpretation As Categories of Theological Thinking.* New York: Crossroad, 1988.

_____. "Karl Barth's Hermeneutics." Pp. 80–97 in Nigel Biggar, ed. *Reckoning with Barth: Essays in Commemoration of the Centenary of Karl Barth's Birth.* London: Mowbray, 1988.

_____. *Theological Hermeneutics: Development and Significance.* London: Macmillan, 1991.

Jeffrey, David Lyle. "*Caveat Lector:* Structuralism, Deconstruction, and Ideology." *Christian Scholar's Review* 17 (1988): 436–48.

Jobling, David. "Writing the Wrongs of the World: The Deconstruction of the Biblical Text in the Context of Liberation Theologies." *Semeia* 51 (1990): 81–118.

Jowett, Benjamin. *The Interpretation of Scripture and Other Essays.* London: George Routledge and Sons, n.d.

Juhl, P. D. *Interpretation: An Essay in the Philosophy of Literary Criticism.* Princeton: Princeton Univ. Press, 1980.

Jüngel, Eberhard. *Karl Barth: A Theological Legacy.* Tr. Garrett E. Paul. Philadelphia: Westminster, 1986.

Kant, Immanuel. *Religion Within the Limits of Reason Alone.* Tr. T. N. Greene and H. H. Hudson. New York: Harper and Row, 1960.

Kent, Thomas. "Interpretation and Triangulation: A Davidsonian Critique of Reader-Oriented Literary Theory." Pp. 37–58 in Dasenbrock, ed., *Literary Theory after Davidson.*

Kermode, Frank. *The Genesis of Secrecy: On the Interpretation of Narrative.* Cambridge, Mass: Harvard Univ. Press, 1979.

Kerr, Fergus. *Theology After Wittgenstein.* Oxford: Basil Blackwell, 1986.

Kierkegaard, Søren. *For Self-Examination: Recommended for the Times.* Tr. Edna and Howard Hong. Minneapolis: Augsburg, 1940.

Kirkpatrick, Frank G. *Together Bound: God, History and the Religious Community*. Oxford: Oxford Univ. Press, 1994.

Knapp, Steven, and Walter Benn Michaels. "Against Theory." Pp. 11a–30 in Mitchell, ed., *Against Theory*.

———. "Reply to Rorty." Pp. 139–46 in Mitchell, ed., *Against Theory*.

———. "Against Theory 2: Hermeneutics and Deconstruction." *Critical Inquiry* 14 (1987/88): 49–68.

———. "Reply to John Searle." *New Literary History* 25 (1994): 669–75.

Knapp, Steven. *Literary Interest: The Limits of Anti-Formalism*. Cambridge, Mass. and London: Harvard Univ. Press, 1993.

Kristeva, Julia. *Desire in Language: A Semiotic Approach to Literature and Art*. New York: Columbia Univ. Press, 1980.

Kurz, William S. *Reading Luke-Acts: Dynamics of Biblical Narrative*. Louisville: Westminster/John Knox, 1993.

LaFargue, Michael. "Are Texts Determinate? Derrida, Barth, and the Role of the Biblical Scholar." *Harvard Theological Review* 81 (1988): 341–57.

Lanser, Susan Snaider. *The Narrative Act: Point of View in Prose Fiction*. Princeton: Princeton Univ. Press, 1981.

Lategan, Bernard C. "Introduction: Coming to Grips with the Reader." *Semeia* 48 (1989): 3–17.

Lawlor, Leonard. "Dialectic and Iterability: The Confrontation between Paul Ricoeur and Jacques Derrida." *Philosophy Today* 32 (1988): 181–94.

Lehrer, Keith. *Thomas Reid*. The Arguments of the Philosophers. London and New York: Routledge, 1989.

Leitch, Vincent B. *Deconstructive Criticism: An Advanced Introduction*. London: Hutchinson, 1983.

Lentricchia, Frank. *After the New Criticism*. London: Methuen and Chicago: Univ. of Chicago Press, 1980.

Lévinas, Emmanuel. *Ethics and Infinity*. Tr. R. A. Cohen. Pittsburgh: Duquesne Univ. Press, 1985.

Lewis, C. S., and E. M. W. Tillyard. *The Personal Heresy: A Controversy*. Oxford: Oxford Univ. Press, 1939.

Lewis, C. S. *A Preface to Paradise Lost*. Oxford: Oxford Univ. Press, 1942.

———. *Reflections on the Psalms*. London: Geoffrey Bles, 1958.

———. *An Experiment in Criticism*. Cambridge: Cambridge Univ. Press, 1961.

———. "Myth Became Fact." Pp. 63–67 in *God in the Dock: Essays on Theology and Ethics*. Ed. Walter Hooper. Grand Rapids: Eerdmans, 1970.

Lindbeck, George A. *The Nature of Doctrine: Religion and Theology in a Postliberal Age*. Philadelphia: Westminster, 1984.

———. "Scripture, Consensus, and Community." Pp. 74–101 in Richard John Neuhaus, ed. *Biblical Interpretation in Crisis: The Ratzinger Conference on Bible and Church*. Encounter Series. Grand Rapids: Eerdmans, 1989.

Lipton, Peter. *Inference to the Best Explanation*. London: Routledge, 1991.

Livingstone, Paisley. *Literary Knowledge: Humanistic Inquiry and the Philosophy of Science*. Ithaca: Cornell Univ. Press, 1988.

———. *Literature and Rationality: Ideas of Agency in Theory and Fiction*. Cambridge: Cambridge Univ. Press, 1991.

Longman, Tremper III. *Literary Approaches to Biblical Interpretation*. Foundations of Contemporary Interpretation. Grand Rapids: Zondervan, 1987.

Lundin, Roger, Anthony Thiselton, and Clare Walhout. *The Responsibility of Hermeneutics*. Grand Rapids: Eerdmans and Exeter: Paternoster, 1985.

Lyotard, François. *The Postmodern Condition: A Report on Knowledge*. Minneapolis: Univ. of Minnesota Press, 1984.

Mackey, Louis. "Slouching Towards Bethlehem: Deconstructive Strategies in Theology." *Anglican Theological Review* 65 (1983): 255–72.

Macmurray, John. *The Self As Agent*. London: Faber and Faber, 1957.

Madison, G. B. *The Hermeneutics of Postmodernity: Figures and Themes*. Studies in Phenomenology and Existential Philosophy. Bloomington: Indiana Univ. Press, 1988.

Mailloux, Stephen. "Rhetorical Hermeneutics." *Critical Inquiry* 11 (1985): 620–41.

Makaryk, Irena R., ed. *Encyclopedia of Contemporary Literary Theory: Approaches, Scholar, Terms*. Toronto: Univ. of Toronto Press, 1993.

Malbon, Elizabeth Struthers, and Edgar V. McKnight, ed. *The New Literary Criticism and the New Testament*. Sheffield: Sheffield Univ. Press, 1994.

Margolis, Joseph. *Interpretation Radical but Not Unruly: The New Puzzle of the Arts and History*. Berkeley: Univ. of California Press, 1995.

Marion, Jean-Luc. *God Without Being: Hors-Texte*. Tr. Thomas A. Carlson. Chicago: Univ. of Chicago Press, 1991.

Marshall, Bruce D. "Meaning and Truth in Narrative Interpretation: A Reply to George Schner." *Modern Theology* 8 (1992): 173–79.

Martindale, Charles. *Redeeming the Text: Latin Poetry and the Hermeneutics of Reception*. Cambridge: Cambridge Univ. Press, 1993.

Mayes, A. D. H. "Deuteronomistic History." Pp. 174–76 in Coggins and Houlden, ed., *A Dictionary of Biblical Interpretation*.

McFague, Sallie. *Models of God: Theology for an Ecological, Nuclear Age*. Philadelphia: Fortress, 1987.

McKeever, Kerry. "How to Avoid Speaking about God: Poststructuralist Philosophers and Biblical Hermeneutics." *Journal of Literature and Theology* 6 (1992): 228–38.

McKnight, Edgar V. *The Bible and the Reader: An Introduction to Literary Criticism*. Philadelphia: Fortress, 1985.

_____. *Post-Modern Use of the Bible: The Emergence of Reader-Oriented Criticism*. Nashville, Tenn.: Abingdon, 1988.

Metzger, Bruce M., and Michael D. Coogan. *The Oxford Companion to the Bible*. Oxford: Oxford Univ. Press, 1993.

Mey, Jacob L. *Pragmatics: An Introduction*. Oxford: Blackwell, 1993.

Meyer, Ben F. *Critical Realism and the New Testament*. Allison Park, Pa.: Pickwick, 1989.

_____. "The Challenges of Text and Reader to the Historical-Critical Method." Pp. 3–12 in Wim Beuken, Sean Freyne, and Anton Weiler, eds. *The Bible and Its Readers. Concilium* 1991/1. London: SCM, 1991.

Milbank, John. *Theology and Social Theory: Beyond Secular Reason*. Oxford: Blackwell, 1990.

Mitchell, W. J. T. ed., *Against Theory: Literary Studies and the New Pragmatism*. Chicago: Univ. of Chicago Press, 1985.

Moi, Toril. *Sexual/Textual Politics: Feminist Literary Theory*. London: Methuen, 1985.

Molina, David Newton-de. *On Literary Intention*. Edinburgh: Edinburgh Univ. Press, 1976.

Montefiore, Alan. "Philosophy, Literature and the Restatement of a Few Banalities." *Monist* 69 (1986): 56–67.

Moore, Stephen D. *Literary Criticism and the Gospels: The Theoretical Challenge*. New Haven: Yale Univ. Press, 1989.

_____. *Poststructuralism and the New Testament: Derrida and Foucault at the Foot of the Cross*. Minneapolis: Fortress, 1994.

Morgan, Robert, with John Barton. *Biblical Interpretation*. Oxford Bible Series. Oxford: Oxford Univ. Press, 1988.

Morson, Gary Saul, and Caryl Emerson, eds. *Mikhail Bakhtin: Creation of a Prosaics*. Palo Alto, Calif: Stanford Univ. Press, 1990.

Mouffe, Chantal, ed. *Deconstruction and Pragmatism*. London: Routledge, 1996.

Muecke, D. C. *The Compass of Irony*. London: Methuen, 1969.

Murphy, Nancey. *Beyond Liberalism and Fundamentalism: How Modern and Postmodern Philosophy Set the Theological Agenda*. Valley Forge, Pa.: Trinity Press International, 1996.

_____. *Anglo-American Postmodernity: Philosophical Perspectives on Science, Religion, and Ethics*. Boulder, Colo: Westview, 1997.

Nehemas, Alexander. "The Postulated Author: Critical Monism As a Regulative Ideal." *Critical Inquiry* 8 (1981): 133–49.

_____. "What an Author Is." *Journal of Philosophy* 83 (1986): 685–91.

_____. "Writer, Text, Work, Author." Pp. 265–91 in Anthony J. Cascardi, ed. *Literature and the Question of Philosophy*. Baltimore: Johns Hopkins Univ. Press, 1987.

Neufeld, Dietmar. *Reconceiving Texts As Speech Acts: An Analysis of 1 John*. Leiden: E. J. Brill, 1994.

Neusner, Jacob. *What is Midrash?* Philadelphia: Fortress, 1987.

Nida, Eugene A. *Toward a Science of Translating*. Leiden: E. J. Brill, 1964.

Nida, Eugene A., and Charles R. Taber. *The Theory and Practice of Translation*. Leiden: E. J. Brill, 1974.

Niebuhr, H. Richard. "The Meaning of Responsibility." Pp. 19–38 in James M. Gustafson and James T. Laney, ed. *On Being Responsible: Issues in Personal Ethics*. London: SCM, 1969.

Nietzsche, Friedrich. *The Will to Power*. Tr. Walter Kaufmann. New York: Vintage, 1967.

Noble, Paul R. "The *Sensus Literalis*: Jowett, Childs, and Barr." *Journal of Theological Studies* 54 (1993): 1–23.

_____. "Hermeneutics and Post-Modernism: Can We Have a Radical Reader-Response Theory? Part I." *Religious Studies* 30 (1994): 419–36.

_____. "Hermeneutics and Post-Modernism: Can We Have a Radical Reader-Response Theory? Part II." *Religious Studies* 31 (1995): 1–22.

_____. *The Canonical Approach: A Critical Reconstruction of the Hermeneutics of Brevard S. Childs*. Leiden: E. J. Brill, 1995.

Noll, Stephen. "Reading the Bible As the Word of God." *Churchman* 107 (1993): 227–53.

Norris, Christopher. *Deconstruction: Theory and Practice*. London: Methuen, 1982.

_____. *Contest of the Faculties: Philosophy and Theory after Deconstruction*. London: Methuen, 1985.

_____. *Derrida*. Fontana Modern Masters. London: Fontana, 1987.

_____. *What's Wrong with Postmodernism? Critical Theory and the Ends of Philosophy*. London: Harvester Wheatsheaf, 1990.

Novitz, David. "The Rage for Deconstruction." *Monist* 69 (1986): 39–55.

Nuttall, A. D. *A New Mimesis: Shakespeare and the Representation of Reality*. London: Methuen, 1983.

Ogden, C. K., and I. A. Richards. *The Meaning of Meaning: A Study of the Influence of Language Upon Thought and of the Science of Symbolism*. New York and London: Harcourt Brace Jovanovich, 1989.

Ohmann, Richard. "Speech Acts and the Definition of Literature." *Philosophy and Rhetoric* 4 (1971): 1–19.

_____. "Literature As Act." Pp. 81–107 in Seymour Chatman, ed. *Approaches to Poetics*. New York: Columbia Univ. Press, 1973.

Olsen, Stein Haugom. *The End of Literary Theory*. Cambridge: Cambridge Univ. Press, 1987.

Osborne, Grant R. *The Hermeneutical Spiral: A Comprehensive Introduction to Biblical Interpretation*. Downers Grove, Ill.: InterVarsity, 1991.

Packer, J. I. "In Quest of Canonical Interpretation." Pp. 35–55 in Robert K. Johnston, ed. *The Use of the Bible in Theology: Evangelical Options*. Atlanta: John Knox, 1985.

Patte, Daniel. "Speech Act Theory and Biblical Exegesis." *Semeia* 41 (1988): 85–102.

Peacocke, Arthur. *Theology for a Scientific Age*. Rev. ed. London: SCM, 1993.

Pepper, Stephen. *World Hypotheses: A Study in Evidence*. Los Angeles: Univ. of California Press, 1970.

Petersen, Norman R. *Literary Criticism for New Testament Critics*. Philadelphia: Fortress, 1978.

Petrey, Sandy. *Speech Acts and Literary Theory*. London: Routledge, 1990.

Peukert, Helmut. *Science, Action and Fundamental Theology: Towards a Theory of Communicative Action*. Cambridge, Mass: MIT Press, 1984.

Phillips, Gary A. "Exegesis As Critical Practice: Reclaiming History and Text from a Postmodern Perspective." *Semeia* 51 (1990): 7–49.

_____. "The Ethics of Reading Deconstructively, or Speaking Face-to-Face: The Samaritan Woman Meets Derrida at the Well." Pp. 283–325 in Elizabeth Struthers Malbon and Edgar McKnight, *The New Literary Criticism and the New Testament*.

_____. "'You Are Either Here, Here, Here, or Here': Deconstruction's Troublesome Interplay." *Semeia* 71 (1995): 193–211.

Pinker, Stephen. *The Language Instinct: How the Mind Creates Language*. New York: William Morrow, 1994.

Pinnock, Clark H. *The Scripture Principle*. San Francisco: Harper and Row, 1984.

Plantinga, Alvin. "Advice to Christian Philosophers," an inaugural lecture to the John A. O'Brien Professor of Philosophy at the Univ. of Notre Dame (Nov. 4, 1983). Published in *Faith and Philosophy* 1 (1984): 253–71.

_____. "Augustinian Christian Philosophy." *Monist* 75 (1992): 291–320.

_____. *Warrant and Proper Function*. New York and Oxford: Oxford Univ. Press, 1993.

Plato. *The Dialogues of Plato*. Tr. Benjamin Jowett. Oxford: Clarendon, 1892.

Polanyi, Michael. *Personal Knowledge: Towards a Post-Critical Philosophy*. Chicago: Univ. of Chicago Press, 1962.

Pols, Edward. *Meditations on a Prisoner: Towards Understanding Action and Mind*. Edwardsville: Southern Illinois Univ. Press, 1975.

Polzin, Robert. *Moses and the Deuteronomist: A Literary Study of the Deuteronomic History*. New York: Seabury, 1980.

_____. "Deuteronomy." Pp. 92–101 in Alter, ed., *The Literary Guide to the Bible*.

Poythress, Vern S. *Science and Hermeneutics*. Foundations of Contemporary Interpretation. Grand Rapids: Zondervan, 1988.

_____. "Christ the Only Savior of Interpretation." *Westminster Theological Journal* 50 (1988): 305–21.

Pratt, Mary Louise. *Towards a Speech Act Theory of Literary Discourse*. Bloomington: Indiana Univ. Press, 1977.

Prickett, Stephen. *Words and the Word: Language, Poetics and Biblical Interpretation*. Cambridge: Cambridge Univ. Press, 1986.

_____, ed. *Reading the Text: Biblical Criticism and Literary Theory*. Oxford: Blackwell, 1991.

Provan, Iain. *1 and 2 Kings*. Sheffield: Sheffield Academic Press, 1997.

Putnam, Hilary. *Reason, Truth, and History*. Cambridge: Cambridge Univ. Press, 1981.

_____. *Realism with a Human Face*. Cambridge, Mass: Harvard Univ. Press, 1990.

Ramm, Bernard. *The Pattern of Religious Authority*. Grand Rapids: Eerdmans, 1957.

_____. *The Witness of the Spirit: An Essay on the Contemporary Relevance of the Internal Witness of the Holy Spirit*. Grand Rapids: Eerdmans, 1959.

_____. *Protestant Biblical Interpretation: A Textbook of Hermeneutics*. 3d ed. Grand Rapids: Baker, 1970.

_____. *The Evangelical Heritage: A Study in Historical Theology*. Grand Rapids: Baker, 1981.

Raschke, Carl A. "The Deconstruction of God." Pp. 1–33 in Thomas Altizer, et al., ed. *Deconstruction and Theology*. New York: Crossroad, 1982.

Rasmussen, David M. *Reading Habermas*. Oxford: Basil Blackwell, 1990.

Reed, Walter L. *Dialogues of the Word: The Bible As Literature According to Bakhtin*. Oxford: Oxford Univ. Press, 1993.

Ricoeur, Paul. *Freud and Philosophy: An Essay on Interpretation*. New Haven: Yale Univ. Press, 1970.

_____. *The Conflict of Interpretations: Essays in Hermeneutics*. Evanston: Northwestern Univ. Press, 1974.

_____. *Interpretation Theory: Discourse and the Surplus of Meaning*. Fort Worth, Tex.: Texas Christian Univ. Press, 1976.

_____. *The Rule of Metaphor: Multi-Disciplinary Studies of the Creation of Meaning in Language*. Trs. R. Czerny, K. McLaughlin, and J. Costello. London: Routledge and Kegan Paul, 1978.

_____. "Creativity in Language: Word, Polysemy, Metaphor." Pp. 120–33 in *The Philosophy of Paul Ricoeur*.

_____. *The Philosophy of Paul Ricoeur: An Anthology of His Work*. Eds. Charles E. Reagan and David Stewart. Boston: Beacon, 1978.

_____. "Myth As the Bearer of Possible Worlds." Pp. 36–45 in Richard Kearney, ed. *Dialogues with Contemporary Continental Thinkers*. Manchester: Manchester Univ. Press, 1984.

_____. *Hermeneutics and the Human Sciences: Essays on Language, Action and Interpretation*. Ed. John B. Thompson. Cambridge: Cambridge Univ. Press, 1985.

_____. *Time and Narrative*. 3 vols. Chicago: Univ. of Chicago Press, 1984–88.

_____. *A Ricoeur Reader: Reflection and Imagination*. Ed. Mario J. Valdés. New York and London: Harvester Wheatsheaf, 1991.

_____. *Oneself As Another*. Tr. Kathleen Blamey. Chicago: Univ. of Chicago Press, 1992.

_____. *Figuring the Sacred: Religion, Narrative and Imagination*. Ed. Mark I. Wallace. Minneapolis: Fortress, 1995.

Robbins, J. Wesley. "'You Will Be Like God': Richard Rorty and Mark C. Taylor on the Theological Significance of Human Language Use." *Journal of Religion* 72 (1992): 389–402.

Rogers, Eugene F. Jr. "How the Virtues of an Interpreter Presuppose and Perfect Hermeneutics: The Case of Thomas Aquinas." *Journal of Religion* 76 (1996): 64–81.

Rogerson, John W., Margaret Davies, and M. Daniel Carroll, ed. *The Bible in Ethics*. JSOT Suppl. Series 207. Sheffield: Sheffield Academic Press, 1995.

Rorty, Richard. *The Linguistic Turn*. Chicago: Univ. of Chicago Press, 1967.

_____. *Philosophy and the Mirror of Nature*. Princeton: Princeton Univ. Press, 1979.

_____. *Consequences of Pragmatism*. Minneapolis: Univ. of Minnesota Press, 1982.

_____. "Texts and Lumps." *New Literary History* 17 (1985): 1–15.

_____. "Pragmatism and Philosophy." Pp. 26–66 in Baynes, ed., *After Philosophy*.

_____. *Contingency, Irony, and Solidarity*. Cambridge: Cambridge Univ. Press, 1989.

_____. *Objectivity, Relativism, and Truth. Philosophical Papers*. Vol. 1. Cambridge: Cambridge Univ. Press, 1991.

_____. "Philosophy without Principles." Pp. 132–38 in Mitchell, ed., *Against Theory*.

_____. "Remarks on Deconstruction and Pragmatism." Pp. 13–18 in Mouffe, ed., *Deconstruction and Pragmatism*.

Rowland, Christopher. "Materialist Interpretation." Pp. 430–32 in Coggins, ed., *A Dictionary of Biblical Interpretation*.

Rutledge, David. *Reading Marginally: Feminism, Deconstruction and the Bible*. Biblical Interpretation 21. Leiden: E. J. Brill, 1996.

482 **Is There a Meaning in This Text?**

Saussure, Ferdinand de. *Course in General Linguistics*. New York: McGraw-Hill, 1959.

Saye, Scott C. "The Wild and Crooked Tree: Barth, Fish, and Interpretive Communities." *Modern Theology* 12 (1996): 435–58.

Schildgen, Brenda Deen. "Augustine's Answer to Jacques Derrida in the *de Doctrina Christiana*." *New Literary History* 25 (1994): 383–97.

Schneiders, Sandra M. *The Revelatory Text: Interpreting the New Testament As Sacred Scripture*. San Francisco: Harper, 1991.

Scholes, Robert. *Protocols of Reading*. New Haven: Yale Univ. Press, 1989.

Schwartz, Regina, ed. *The Book and the Text: The Bible and Literary Theory*. Oxford: Basil Blackwell, 1990.

Scott, Nathan A. Jr. "The New *Trahison des Clercs*: Reflections on the Present Crisis in Humanistic Studies." *The Virginia Quarterly Review* 62 (1986): 402–21.

Scott, Nathan A., and Ronald A. Sharp, ed. *Reading George Steiner*. London and Baltimore: The Johns Hopkins Univ. Press, 1994.

Searle, John R. *Speech Acts: An Essay in the Philosophy of Language*. Cambridge: Cambridge Univ. Press, 1969.

_____. "The Logical Status of Fictional Discourse." *New Literary History* 6 (1975): 319–32.

_____. "Reiterating the Differences." *Glyph* 1 (1977): 198–208.

_____. *Expression and Meaning: Studies in the Theory of Speech Acts*. Cambridge: Cambridge Univ. Press, 1979.

_____. "The World Turned Upside Down," review of Jonathan Culler's *On Deconstruction*. Pp. 74–79 in *New York Times Review of Books* (Oct. 27, 1983).

_____. *Intentionality: An Essay in the Philosophy of Mind*. Cambridge: Cambridge Univ. Press, 1983.

_____. "Literary Theory and Its Discontents." *New Literary History* 25 (1994): 637–67.

_____. "Structure and Intention in Language: A Reply to Knapp and Michaels." *New Literary History* 25 (1994): 677–81.

Seely, David. *Deconstructing the New Testament*. Biblical Interpretation Series. Leiden: E. J. Brill, 1994.

_____. *The Construction of Social Reality*. London: Penguin, 1995.

Segovia, Fernando F. "The Text As Other: Towards a Hispanic American Hermeneutic." Pp. 277–85 in Daniel Smith-Christopher, ed., *Text and Experience*.

Selden, Raman. *A Reader's Guide to Contemporary Literary Theory*. 2d ed. New York and London: Harvester Wheatsheaf, 1989.

Sheriff, John K. *The Fate of Meaning: Charles Peirce, Structuralism, and Literature*. Princeton: Princeton Univ. Press, 1989.

Silva, Moises. *Biblical Words and Their Meaning: An Introduction to Lexical Semantics*. Grand Rapids: Zondervan, 1983.

_____. *Has the Church Misread the Bible? The History of Interpretation in the Light of Current Issues*. Foundations of Contemporary Interpretation;. Grand Rapids: Zondervan, 1987.

Smalley, Beryl. *The Study of the Bible in the Middles Ages*. 3d ed. Oxford: Basil Blackwell, 1983.

Smith-Christopher, Daniel, ed. *Text and Experience: Towards a Cultural Exegesis of the Bible*. Sheffield: Sheffield Academic Press, 1995.

Soskice, Janet Martin. *Metaphor and Religious Language*. Oxford: Clarendon, 1985.

Staten, Henry. *Wittgenstein and Derrida*. Lincoln: Univ. of Nebraska Press, 1984.

Steiner, George. *After Babel: Aspects of Language and Translation*. London and New York: Oxford Univ. Press, 1975.

_____. *On Difficulty and Other Essays*. Oxford: Oxford Univ. Press, 1978.

_____. "'Critic'/'Reader.'" *New Literary History* 10 (1979): 423–52.

_____. "Narcissus and Echo: A Note on Current Arts of Reading." *American Journal of Semiotics* 1 (1981): 1–12.

_____. *Real Presences*. Chicago: Univ. of Chicago Press, 1989.

Sternberg, Meir. *The Poetics of Biblical Narrative: Ideological Literature and the Drama of Reading.* Bloomington: Indiana Univ. Press, 1985.

_____. "Biblical Poetics and Sexual Politics: From Reading to Counterreading." *Journal of Biblical Literature* 111 (1992): 463–88.

Stiver, Dan. *The Philosophy of Religious Language: Sign, Symbol, and Story.* Cambridge: Cambridge Univ. Press, 1996.

Stout, Jeffrey. "The Relativity of Interpretation." *Monist* 69 (1986): 103–18.

_____. "What Is the Meaning of a Text?" *New Literary History* 14 (1982): 1–12.

Strawson, P. F. *Individuals: An Essay in Descriptive Metaphysics.* London: Methuen, 1957.

_____. *Logico-Linguistic Papers.* London: Methuen, 1971.

Sugirtharajah, R. S., ed. *Voices from the Margin: Interpreting the Bible in the Third World.* Maryknoll, N.Y.: Orbis, 1991.

Swartley, Willard M. ed. *Essays on Biblical Interpretation: Anabaptist-Mennonite Perspectives.* Elkhart, Ind.: Institute of Mennonite Studies, 1984.

Taylor, Charles. *Human Agency and Language: Philosophical Papers 1.* Cambridge: Cambridge Univ. Press, 1985.

Taylor, Mark C. "Text As Victim." Pp. 58–78 in Thomas Altizer, et al., ed. *Deconstruction and Theology.* New York: Crossroad, 1982.

_____. *Deconstructing Theology.* AAR Studies in Religion 28. Chico, Calif.: Scholars, 1982.

_____. *Erring: A Postmodern A/theology.* Chicago: Univ. of Chicago Press, 1984.

Thiel, John E. *Imagination and Authority: Theological Authorship in the Modern Tradition.* Minneapolis: Fortress, 1991.

Thiselton, Anthony C. *The Two Horizons: New Testament Hermeneutics and Philosophical Description.* Grand Rapids: Eerdmans, 1980.

_____. "On Models and Methods: A Conversation with Robert Morgan." Pp. 337–567 in David J. A. Clines, ed., *The Bible in Three Dimensions.*

_____. *New Horizons in Hermeneutics: The Theory and Practice of Transforming Biblical Reading.* Grand Rapids: Zondervan, 1992.

_____. *Interpreting God and the Postmodern Self: On Meaning, Manipulation and Promise.* Scottish Journal of Theology: Current Issues in Theology. Edinburgh: T. & T. Clark, 1995.

Thomassen, Niels. *Communicative Ethics in Theory and Practice.* Tr. John Irons. London: Macmillan, 1992.

Thompson, John B. *Studies in the Theory of Ideology.* Cambridge: Polity, 1984.

_____. *Ideology and Modern Culture: Critical Social Theory in the Era of Mass Communication.* Palo Alto, Calif.: Stanford Univ. Press, 1990.

Tomkins, Jane P., ed. *Reader-Response Criticism: From Formalism to Post-Structuralism.* Baltimore: Johns Hopkins Univ. Press, 1980.

Tracy, David. *Blessed Rage for Order: The New Pluralism in Theology.* Minneapolis: Winston Seabury, 1975.

_____. *Plurality and Ambiguity: Hermeneutics, Religion, Hope.* San Francisco: Harper and Row, 1987.

Tuckett, Christopher. *Reading the New Testament: Methods of Interpretation.* Philadelphia: Fortress, 1987.

Vanderveken, Daniel. *Meaning and Speech Acts*; vol. 1. *Principles of Language Use.* Cambridge: Cambridge Univ. Press, 1990.

Vanhoozer, Kevin J. "The Semantics of Biblical Literature: Truth and Scripture's Diverse Literary Forms." Pp. 49–104 in D. A. Carson and John D. Woodbridge, ed. *Hermeneutics, Authority, and Canon*. Grand Rapids: Zondervan, 1986.

_____. "A Lamp in the Labyrinth: The Hermeneutics of 'Aesthetic' Theology." *Trinity Journal* 8 (1987): 25–56.

_____. *Biblical Narrative in the Philosophy of Paul Ricoeur: A Study in Hermeneutics and Theology*. Cambridge: Cambridge Univ. Press, 1990.

_____. "The World Well Staged? Theology, Culture, and Hermeneutics." Pp. 1–30 in D. A. Carson and John Woodbridge, ed. *God and Culture*. Grand Rapids: Eerdmans, 1993.

_____. "The Hermeneutics of I-Witness Testimony: John 21:20–24 and the 'Death' of the 'Author.'" Pp. 366–78 in A. Graeme Auld, ed. *Understanding Poets and Prophets*. Sheffield: JSOT Press, 1993.

_____. "God's Mighty Speech Acts: The Doctrine of Scripture Today." Pp. 143–81 in Philip E. Sattherwaite and David F. Wright, eds. *A Pathway into the Holy Scripture*. Grand Rapids: Eerdmans, 1994.

_____. "The Reader in NT Study." Pp. 301–28 in Joel Green, ed. *Hearing the New Testament: Strategies for Interpretation*. Grand Rapids: Eerdmans, 1995.

_____. "The Bible—Its Relevance Today." Pp. 9–30 in David W. Torrance, ed. *God, Family and Sexuality*. Carberry, Scotland: Handsel, 1997.

_____. "Human Being, Individual and Social." Pp. 158–88 in Colin Gunton, ed. *The Cambridge Companion to Christian Doctrine*. Cambridge: Cambridge Univ. Press, 1997.

_____. "The Spirit of Understanding: Special Revelation and General Hermeneutics." Pp. 131–65 in Roger Lundin, ed. *Disciplining Hermeneutics: Interpretation in Christian Perspective*. Grand Rapids: Eerdmans, 1997.

_____. "The Trials of Truth: Mission, Martyrdom, and the Epistemology of the Cross." In Andrew Kirk and Kevin Vanhoozer, ed. *To Stake a Claim: Christian Mission in Epistemological Crisis*. Maryknoll, N.Y.: Orbis, 1998.

Vickers, Brian. *Appropriating Shakespeare*. New Haven: Yale Univ. Press, 1993.

Walhout, Clarence. and Leland Ryken, Leland, eds. *Contemporary Literary Theory: A Christian Appraisal*. Grand Rapids: Eerdmans, 1991.

Ward, Graham. *Barth, Derrida and the Language of Theology*. Cambridge: Cambridge Univ. Press, 1995.

Ward, Patricia. "'An Affair of the Heart': Ethics, Criticism, and the Teaching of Literature." *Christianity and Literature* 39 (1990): 181–91.

Warner, Martin, ed. *The Bible As Rhetoric: Studies in Biblical Persuasion and Credibility*. Warwick Studies in Philosophy and Literature. London: Routledge, 1990.

Warrior, Robert Allen. "A Native American Perspective: Canaanites, Cowboys, and Indians." Pp. 287–95 in Sugirtharajah, *Voices from the Margin*.

Watson, Francis. *Text, Church and World: Biblical Interpretation in Theological Perspective*. Grand Rapids: Eerdmans, 1994.

Watson, Francis, ed. *The Open Text: New Directions for Biblical Studies?* London: SCM, 1993.

White, Hugh C. "Introduction: Speech Act Theory and Literary Criticism." *Semeia* 41 (1988): 1–24.

Williams, Rowan. "The Literal Sense of Scripture." *Modern Theology* 7 (1990): 121–34.

_____. "Between Politics and Metaphysics." *Modern Theology* 11 (1995): 3–22.

Williams, Timothy. "Realism and Anti-Realism." Pp. 746–48 in Honderich, ed., *The Oxford Companion to Philosophy*.

Wimsatt, W. K. and Beardsley, Monroe. "The Intentional Fallacy." Pp. 3–18 in Wimsatt, *The Verbal Icon*.

_____. *The Verbal Icon: Studies in the Meaning of Poetry*. Lexington: Univ. of Kentucky Press, 1954.

_____. "Genesis: A Fallacy Revisited." Pp. 116–38 in Molina, ed., *On Literary Intention*.

Wittgenstein, Ludwig. *Tractatus Logico-Philosophicus*. London: Routledge and Kegan Paul, 1961.

_____. *Philosophical Investigations*. 3d ed. Tr. G. E. M. Anscombe. Oxford: Blackwell, 1958.

Wollheim, Richard. *Painting As an Art*. Princeton: Princeton Univ. Press, 1987.

Wolterstorff, Nicholas. *Works and Worlds of Art*. Oxford: Clarendon, 1980.

_____. *Divine Discourse: Philosophical Reflections on the Claim That God Speaks*. Cambridge: Cambridge Univ. Press, 1995.

_____. "Between the Pincers of Increased Diversity and Supposed Irrationality." Pp. 13–20 in William J. Wainwright, ed. *God, Philosophy and Academic Culture: A Discussion Between Scholars in the AAR an the APA*. Atlanta: Scholars, 1996.

Wondra, Ellen K. "By Whose Authority? The Status of Scripture in Contemporary Feminist Theologies." *Anglican Theological Journal* 75 (1993): 83–101.

Wood, Charles M. *The Formation of Christian Understanding: An Essay in Theological Hermeneutics*. Philadelphia: Westminster, 1981.

_____. *An Invitation to Theological Study*. Valley Forge, Pa.: Trinity Press International, 1994.

Wright, N. T. *The New Testament and the People of God*. London: S.P.C.K., 1992.

Yoder, John Howard. "The Hermeneutics of the Anabaptists." Pp. 11–28 in Swartley, ed., *Essays on Biblical Interpretation: Anabaptist-Mennonite Perspectives*.

Young, Frances. *The Art of Performance: Towards a Theology of Holy Scripture*. London: Darton, Longman and Todd, 1990.

_____. "Alexandrian Interpretation." Pp. 10–12 in Coggins and Houlden, ed., *A Dictionary of Biblical Interpretation*.

_____. "The Pastoral Epistles and the Ethics of Reading." *Journal for the Study of the New Testament* 45 (1992): 105–20.

_____. *The Theology of the Pastoral Epistles*. Cambridge: Cambridge Univ. Press, 1994.

_____. "Interpretative Genres and the Inevitability of Pluralism." *Journal for the Study of the New Testament* 59 (1995): 93–110.

Zagzebski, Linda Trinkhaus. *Virtues of the Mind: An Inquiry into the Nature of Virtue and the Ethical Foundations of Knowledge*. Cambridge: Cambridge Univ. Press, 1996.

Zuck, Roy B. "The Role of the Holy Spirit in Hermeneutics." *Bibiotheca Sacra* 141 (1984): 120–30.

NAME INDEX

SUBJECT INDEX